Finding The Right Pitch
II

A Guide To The Study Of Basic Harmony

David Nivans

California State University Dominguez Hills

World Bet Books

Copyright © 2012 David Nivans

All rights reserved. No part of this publication may be reproduced, transmitted, stored in a retrieval system or a database in any form or by any means, be it graphic, electronic, or mechanical, including but not limited to photocopying, recording, scanning, digitizing, or otherwise, without prior written permission of the publisher.

World Bet Books
www.worldbetbooks.com
worldbetbooks@gmail.com

ISBN 978-1-937214-01-2

Library of Congress Control Number: 2012938251

This book is printed on acid-free paper.

To the Memory of

Wally Bower

1929–2008

About the Author

David Nivans holds a Ph.D. in historical musicology from University of California Los Angeles. He has taught courses in music fundamentals, harmony, counterpoint, musicianship, world music, music appreciation, music and art appreciation, music history, and surveys of popular music, jazz, rock, and film music. Dr. Nivans is also the author of *Introduction To Music Fundamentals And Lead-Sheet Terminology* and *Finding The Right Pitch: A Guide To The Study Of Music Fundamentals*.

TABLE OF CONTENTS

Preface xi

Chapter 1 A Review of Fundamentals 1

    Ties and Dots 3

    Meter and Beat 3

    Divisions of Beats 4

    Time Signatures 5

    Counting Note Values 6

    Rhythm 8

    Syncopation 8

    Simple and Compound Meter Exchange 9

    Triplets 9

    Duplets 9

    Asymmetrical Meter 10

    Pitch 11

    Accidentals and Enharmonic Equivalency 12

    The Great Staff and Clefs 14

    Octave Registers 15

    The Major Scale 17

    Moving the Major Scale to Octaves Other Than C with the Addition of Sharps 19

    Moving the Major Scale to Octaves Other Than C with the Addition of Flats 21

    Major Key Signatures 23

    The Circle of 5ths 24

    Identifying Major Key Signatures 26

    Diatonicism, Chromaticism, and Tonality 26

    Intervals 27

    The Essential Diatonic Intervals of Major 28

    Two Principles for Recognizing and Constructing the Qualities of Intervals 29

The Principle of Like Inflection	30
Compound Intervals	31
Interval Inversion	31
Consonance and Dissonance	32
The Minor Mode	33
The Natural Minor Mode	34
The Relative Minor	34
The Parallel Minor and the Parallel Major	35
The Relative Major	36
The Circle of 5ths for Minor	36
The Harmonic Minor Mode	38
The Melodic Minor Mode	38
The Ascending Form of the Melodic Minor	38
The Descending Form of the Melodic Minor	40
Finding the Variable Scale Degrees in the Minor Mode	41
Triads	41
Triad Quality	43
Triad Qualities in Major	44
Inverting Major, Minor, Diminished, and Augmented Triads	44
Applying the Principle of Like Inflection to Triads	47
Triad Qualities in Minor	47
Roman Numeral Chord Symbols	48
Four-Part Texture	50
Triad Voicing	50
Vocal Range	51
Close and Open Structure	52
Spacing Between Adjacent Voices	52
Stem Direction	53
The Doubling of Chord Tones in Four-Voice Texture	53
Tonality	55
The Harmonic Series	56
Omitting the Fifth in Four-Voice Texture	57

Chapter 2 The Church Modes 59

    Major and Minor Prototypes 61

    Relating the Church Modes to the Major Mode 63

    Mode Transposition 63

    Given the Key and Mode, Find the Right Key Signature 67

    Given the Key and Key Signature, Find the Right Mode 73

    Triad Formation within the Seven Church Modes 75

    Triad Formation and Mode Transposition 79

    Triad Inversion 82

    Singing the Major, Chromatic, and Minor Scales 86

    Singing the Church Modes 88

Chapter 3 Voice Leading 91

    Types of Motion Between Any Two Voices 91

    Parallel Motion 91

    Similar Motion 94

    Direct Motion: Incorrect Similar Motion 94

    Contrary Motion 96

    Consecutive Motion: Incorrect Contrary Motion 97

    Oblique Motion 97

    General Principles 98

    Motion in Any Single Voice Between Unlike Chords 98

    Motion in Any Two Voices Between Unlike Chords 101

    Motion in All Four Voices Between Unlike Chords 101

    The Chordal Skip 102

    Using the Chordal Skip to Correct Faulty Motion 102

    Creating Incorrect Motion with the Chordal Skip 104

Chapter 4 The Six-Four Chord 105

    The Origins of the Cadential $^6_4$ 105

    The Cadential $^6_4$ 107

The Passing $^6_4$ 108

The Pedal Embellishing $^6_4$ 108

The Arpeggiated $^6_4$ 110

The Neighboring $^6_4$ 111

The Appoggiatura $^6_4$ 112

Chapter 5 The Chord Seventh 113

Adding the Seventh to the Triad 113

The Origin of the Seventh Chord 114

The Suspended Seventh 114

The Freestanding Seventh Chord 115

The Real Seventh Chord 115

The Four Principal Types of "White-Key" Seventh Chords 116

The Dominant Seventh Chord 116

Inversions of the Dominant Seventh Chord 117

Adding the Chord Seventh to the Cadential $^6_4$ 118

Chapter 6 The Cadence 121

The Dominant Family of Chords: the Tonal Harmonic Dominant
and the Tonal Melodic Dominant 121

Tonic-oriented Cadences: the Authentic Cadence 121

Tonic-oriented Cadences: the Harmonic Perfect Authentic Cadence 122

Tonic-oriented Cadences: the Harmonic Imperfect Authentic Cadence 122

Tonic-oriented Cadences: the Contrapuntal Perfect Authentic Cadence 123

Tonic-oriented Cadences: the Contrapuntal Imperfect Authentic Cadence 124

Tonic-oriented Cadences: the Deceptive Cadence 125

Tonic-oriented Cadences: Perfect and Imperfect Plagal Cadences 126

Non-Tonic-oriented Cadences: Harmonic and Contrapuntal Half Cadences 127

Non-Tonic-oriented Cadences: the Phrygian Half Cadence on V 130

Chapter 7　The Chord Progression 133
 The Basic Harmonic Progression 133
 The Basic Contrapuntal Progression 135
 The Secondary Harmonic Progression 137
 The Secondary Contrapuntal Progression 139

Chapter 8　The Chord Seventh Revisited 141
 The Formation of Seventh Chords in the Church Mode System 141
 The Formation of Seventh Chords in the Major Mode 145
 The Seventh Chords of the Subdominant and Dominant in the Major Mode 146
 The Seventh Chord of the Leading Tone in the Major Mode 147
 The Formation of Seventh Chords in the Minor Mode 148
 The Seventh Chords of the Dominant in the Minor Mode 150
 The Seventh Chords of the Leading Tone in the Minor Mode 150
 The Sound and Applications of the Fully Diminished Seventh Chord in the Minor Mode 151
 The Seventh Chords of the Subtonic 153
 The Applications of the Subtonic Chord 153
 Notation for Inversions of Tonic and Subtonic Sevenths 155
 More About Real and Apparent Seventh Chords 156
 Real and Apparent Seventh Chords in Harmonic and Contrapuntal Progressions 157
 The Seventh Chord of the Mediant and Its Triads 161
 The Passing Chord Between the Mediant and the Dominant 164
 Interlocking Root-Position Chords of the Seventh (Harmonic Bass) 165
 The Sequence 165
 The Modal Dominant 166
 Interlocking Inverted Chords of the Seventh (Contrapuntal Bass) 167
 The Two-Progression Framework 169
 Singing the Seven Seventh-Chord Qualities in All Positions 173
 The Added 6th 178

Chapter 9   Nonharmonic Tones **181**

    Non-Appoggiaturas 182

    The Passing Tone 182

    The Complete Neighbor Tone 182

    The Complete and Incomplete Changing-Note Group (Double Neighbor) 183

    Special Uses of the Incomplete Neighbor Tone: the Cambiata and the Échappée 184

    Other Incomplete Neighbor Tones 185

    The Anticipation Tone 185

    Appoggiaturas 186

    The Accented Passing Tone 186

    The Accented Complete Neighbor Tone 186

    The Appoggiatura Itself (the Incomplete Neighbor Tone) 187

    The Suspension 188

    Using Appoggiatura Tones without a Change of Harmony 190

    Accented Correctives to Faulty Motion: the Suspension, Incomplete Neighbor,
        and Passing Tone 191

    Unaccented Correctives to Faulty Motion: the Anticipation and the Exceptional
        Use of the Cambiata 192

    Unaccented Nonharmonic Tones that Fail to Correct Faulty Parallel Motion 194

    Unaccented Dissonant Nonharmonic Tones Causing Acceptable Parallel 5ths 194

    Nonharmonic Tones in Combination 195

    Avoid Conflicts Between the Resolution of the Suspension and Other
        Nonharmonic Tones 196

Appendix A   Keyboard Harmony **197**

Appendix B   CLT Chords **223**

Index **227**

Worksheets **235**

Preface

Finding The Right Pitch II: A Guide To The Study Of Basic Harmony focuses on voice leading, a process that controls the linear succession of tones in each voice (i.e., melodic line), optimizing how each voice moves through time in relation to the rest of the musical texture. The text begins with an extensive review of music fundamentals, drawn from my book *Finding The Right Pitch: A Guide To The Study Of Music Fundamentals*.

Finding The Right Pitch II covers a range of topics, including the formation and construction of triads within the church mode system; singing, transposing, and identifying the church modes; the different types of six-four chords; cadences; harmonic and contrapuntal progressions; the properties of seventh chords; the formation of seventh chords within the church modes and the major-minor tonal system; using the interval of the 7th to improve voice leading; real and apparent seventh chords; interlocking seventh chords; harmonic and contrapuntal sequences; the two-progression framework; singing seventh chords in all positions from a common bass pitch; the utility of nonharmonic tones for correcting faulty motion between chords; and the application of voice-leading principles and chord progression to the piano keyboard. For more information about my theory books, go to www.worldbetbooks.com.

The Worksheets

The worksheets, which follow the index, may serve as either practice exercises, homework assignments, or test materials. Since metric and rhythmic skills are acquired over time through a continuous study of music's temporal framework, exercises for meter and rhythm accompany each chapter of worksheets. Thus, the student learns about the basic principles of harmony while also exploring the properties of meter and rhythm.

To The Instructor

Instructors will notice that some of the concepts put forward in this text are based on the analytic tradition of Heinrich Schenker and those who have since promoted his theories, particularly William J. Mitchell, Felix Salzer, and Carl Schachter. The writings of Mitchell, Salzer, and Schachter have had an immeasurable impact on my understanding of music.

I believe that a case can be made for exposing students to Schenkerian principles early in their music education; however, some instructors may consider basic harmony to be an inappropriate starting point for the introduction of these ideas. Accordingly, I focus on some of the more accessible insights put forward by Schenker and his disciples but without subjecting the reader to a catalog of challenging expressions and graphic symbols.

Finding The Right Pitch II references a few exceptional terms used by Salzer and Schachter. The sources for these expressions are Salzer's *Structural Hearing: Tonal Coherence In Music* (first published in 1952 by Charles Boni) and Salzer and Schachter's *Counterpoint In Composition* (first published in 1969 by McGraw-Hill).

The "fundamental harmonic progression" and "two harmonic progressions in succession," discussed by Salzer in *Structural Hearing*, are presented in *Finding The Right Pitch II* as the "basic harmonic progression" and the "two-progression framework." My treatment of the "secondary harmonic progression" differs from that of Salzer, but the term is his. For Salzer, the secondary harmonic progression is one in which the chord of the submediant serves as an intermediary harmony between the initial tonic and final dominant. Salzer places the other intermediary harmonies of the supertonic, mediant, and subdominant into a separate category as "elaborations" of the fundamental progression (*Structural Hearing*, p. 90).

Finding The Right Pitch II incorporates the various elaborations of the fundamental progression into the secondary harmonic progression. That is to say, the chords of the supertonic, mediant, subdominant, *and* submediant may each occupy the intermediary position as a member of the secondary harmonic progression.

The concepts of the "contrapuntal progression" and the "contrapuntal leading-tone chord" were first introduced in *Structural Hearing* and *Counterpoint In Composition* respectively. Chapters 7 and 8 of *Finding The Right Pitch II* illustrate contrapuntal progressions, while Chapters 6, 7, and 8 demonstrate the application of the contrapuntal leading-tone chord. Appendix B provides further analysis of this chord, referred to there as the CLT chord.

All of the terms cited in this preface are reinterpreted and adapted to the pedagogy offered herein. *Finding The Right Pitch II* simplifies Salzer's taxonomy by conflating the elaborations of the fundamental progression with the secondary harmonic progression. *Finding The Right Pitch II* supplements Salzer's two categories of harmonic progression by classifying contrapuntal progressions as either basic or secondary (see Chapter 7).

In *Counterpoint In Composition*, Salzer and Schachter identify contrapuntal leading-tone chords within a chromatic context as "contrapuntal equivalents of the applied dominant" (pp. 210–211). *Finding The Right Pitch II* broadens the definition of the chord's operation to include any diatonic framework in which a dominant-family chord approaches the tonic chord by step.

Acknowledgments

I extend my lasting gratitude to the following people for giving generously of their time to review portions of the manuscript: Marius Sapkus; Tommy Harrison, Jacksonville University; Alyson McLamore, Cal Poly San Luis Obispo; Tom Owens, El Camino College; Ted Stern, Glendale College; and David Bradfield, California State University Dominguez Hills.

Wally Bower

Finally, as with my previous books, *Introduction To Music Fundamentals And Lead-Sheet Terminology* and *Finding The Right Pitch: A Guide To The Study Of Music Fundamentals,* this volume honors the memory of my teacher, the late Wallace Henry Bower, Jr., professor of music theory at El Camino College in Torrance, California. The study of harmony was but one of his many lifelong interests. Wally's fluency in German, French, Italian, Spanish, modern Greek, and Portugese as well as his longstanding inability to resist the temptation of a good crossword puzzle underscored his love for languages.

David Nivans

Chapter 1 A Review of Fundamentals

This chapter summarizes the most important principles of music fundamentals as presented in *Finding The Right Pitch: A Guide To The Study Of Music Fundamentals*.

The creation of music involves the organization of two complementary elements: sound and silence. An aural art that depends on the unfolding of time for its performance and appreciation, music is produced from fixed units of duration called notes and rests. Notes represent musical sound while rests represent musical silence. Musical sound and silence are signified in written form by the shapes of the notes and rests that exist on a set of five parallel lines and four spaces called a staff.

Example 1–1 illustrates the differences in the shapes of the various musical sounds on the staff. Both whole notes and half notes appear as oval hollowed-out structures. This structure is called the note head. Quarter notes, eighth notes, sixteenth notes, thirty-second notes, and sixty-fourth notes all have filled-in note heads.

All notes smaller than the whole note contain a stem (1–1). Eighth notes, sixteenth notes, thirty-second notes, and sixty-fourth notes also carry a flag, an additional component that is always attached to the right side of the stem. Eighth notes have one flag, sixteenth notes two, thirty-second notes three, and sixty-fourth notes four. As we shall soon see, any two notes with flags may be joined together with a thick horizontal line called a beam. Since half notes and quarter notes do not have flags, neither can they have beams.

Example 1–1: note values on the staff

Another significant aspect of a note's musical shape involves its location on the staff and the position of its stem (1–1). If a stemmed note in a single vocal or instrumental part occurs above the center line, then the stem proceeds downwards from the left side of the note head. If a stemmed note in a single vocal or instrumental part occurs below the center line, then the stem proceeds upwards from the right of the note head. If a stemmed note is located on the center line, then the stem may point in either direction according to the musical context. In most cases, however, the stem of a note on the center line points down.

The staff is also the means by which pitches can be distinguished from one another in written form. The relative highness or lowness of any pitch corresponds to the highness or lowness of the line or space of the staff on which the pitch is located. In 1–1 above, the notes with downward stems are higher in pitch than those with upward stems. (Although the highness or lowness of a pitch is best represented with a staff, musical durations can be indicated without a staff.) Example 1–2 displays the shapes of the corresponding rests for each of the notes discussed above. Unlike the notes on the staff, which can appear on any space or line, the rests are always located in the same position.

Example 1–2: rest values on the staff

As indicated in example 1–3, half notes, quarter notes, eighth notes, sixteenth notes, thirty-second notes, and sixty-fourth notes have a mathematical relationship to each other and to the whole note. Assuming that the duration of the whole note carries a relative value of "one," two halves, four quarters, eight eighths, sixteen sixteenths, thirty-two thirty-seconds, and sixty-four sixty-fourths will all fill the span of a single whole note.

Further, two quarters fill the duration of a single half note, two eighths equal a single quarter, two sixteenths equal a single eighth, two thirty-seconds equal a single sixteenth, and two sixty-fourths equal a single thirty-second. Thus, smaller note divisions in relation to the whole note exhibit the following equivalent durations:

Example 1–3: mathematical relationships between note values

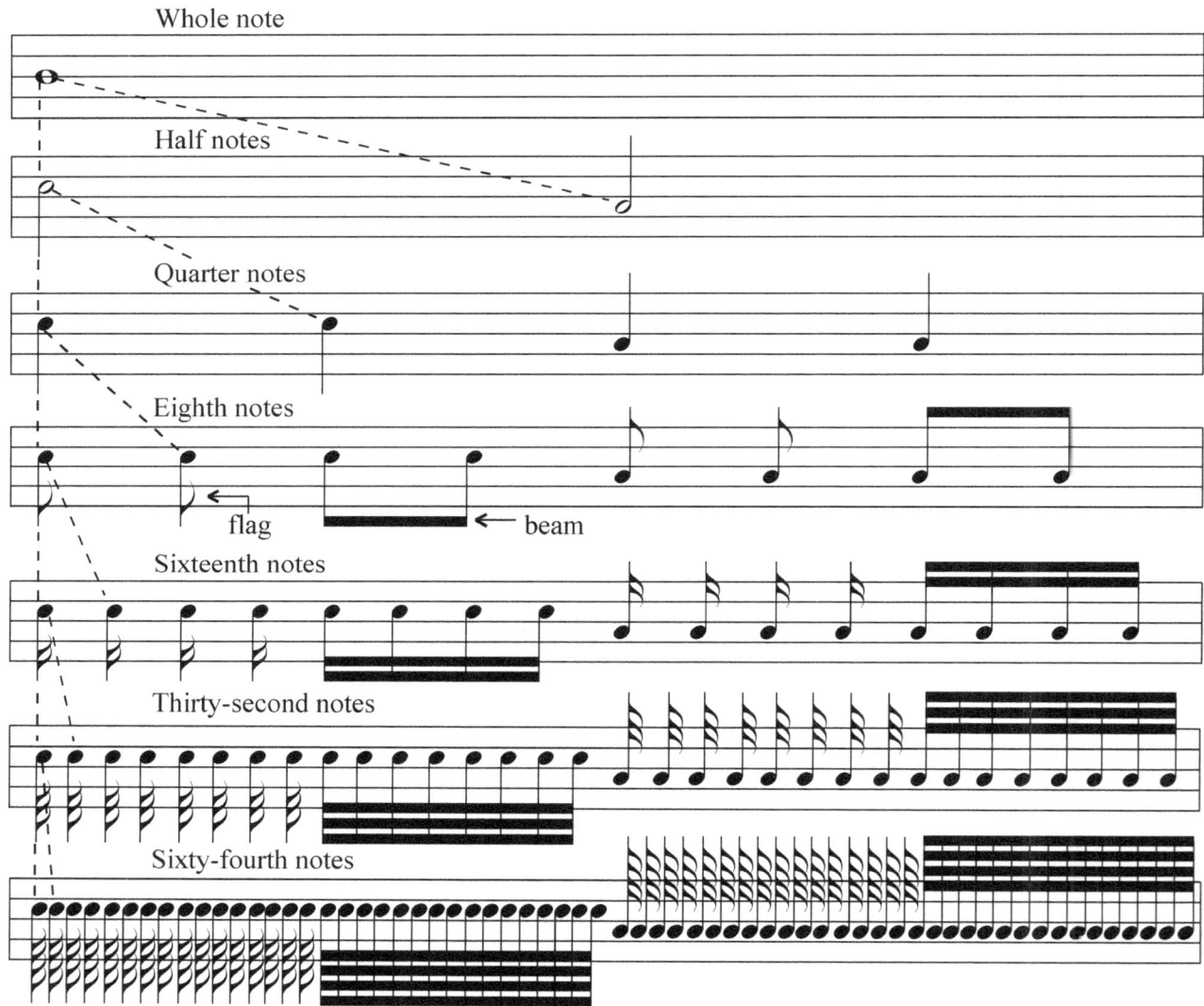

Ties and Dots

There are two different ways to extend the duration of any note: with a tie or a dot. A tie, as shown in example 1–4, is a curved line that connects two or more notes together; however, only the first note of any tied pair or group of notes is articulated. The second note of the tied pair (or group of notes) is sustained for the duration of the note values presented. Tied notes are particularly useful for extending the duration of a note across the bar line (we shall discuss the bar line in the next section).

The second way to extend the duration of a note is to add a dot to it, as shown in example 1–5. The addition of a dot extends the duration of a note (or rest) by *one half its original value*. The tied notes in 1–4 correspond to the dotted note and rest values in 1–5. Thus, the whole note tied to the half note on the center line of 1–4 corresponds to the dotted whole note on the center line of 1–5. The same holds true for the other tied and dotted values on each of the lines and spaces in both examples.

Adding a second dot extends the duration of a note (or rest) by *one half the value of the first dot*. Therefore, if a single dot extends the duration of a quarter note by one eighth, then a second dot extends the duration by one sixteenth. If a single dot extends the duration of a half note by one quarter note, then a second dot extends the duration by one eighth.

Example 1–4

Example 1–5

Meter and Beat

In music, notes and rests are organized into a series of pulses, or beats. Some of these beats are theoretically stronger and receive more emphasis than others. The stronger beats, or stressed beats, are called primary accents. Indicated in example 1–6 with the uppercase letter P, they are the first accents we perceive when hearing a stream of accents unfold in time as a piece of music is being performed. The weaker beats, or unstressed beats, are called secondary accents, indicated in 1–6 with the letter s.

Usually, the notes and rests that signify both the primary and secondary accents of a musical composition are arranged in various configurations that produce a larger temporal framework called meter. As demonstrated in 1–6, it is the distance between primary accents that determines the meter (see the brackets in the example), a distance measured by the number of intervening secondary accents that both precede and follow the primary accents.

4 Chapter 1 A Review of Fundamentals

At least two basic types of meter, namely, duple and triple, arise from the distances that span any two primary accents. Duple meter (1–6a) has one intervening secondary accent between primary accents: P s P s. Quadruple meter (1–6b), a subcategory of duple meter, has three intervening secondary accents: P s S s P s S s, the second of which receives more stress than the first or third (notice the uppercase S). The other main type of meter, triple meter (1–6c), has two intervening secondary accents: P s s P s s. Duple, quadruple, and triple meters are all considered to be symmetrical meters because they can be divided evenly by either 2 or 3.

The distance between two primary accents, in addition to producing meter, constitutes a unit of measured musical space. And each unit so measured is marked off by vertical lines called bar lines, or measure lines. The spaces these lines enclose are called measures, or bars.

The value of the beat for the measures of duple, quadruple, and triple meters displayed in 1–6 is the quarter note. To count primary and secondary accents within duple, quadruple, and triple meters, we use the numbers: 1-2, 1-2-3-4, and 1-2-3 respectively.

Example 1–6: the distance between primary accents in duple, quadruple, and triple meters

a. duple meter (two beats per measure, one secondary accent between primary accents)

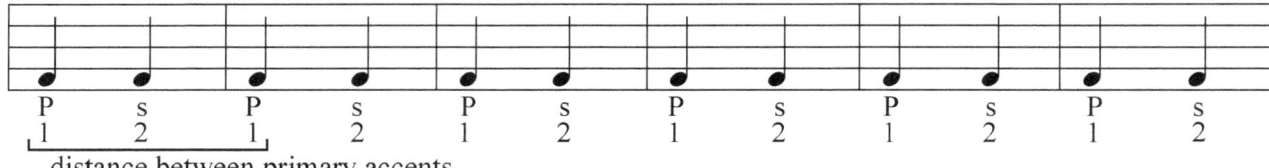

b. quadruple meter (four beats per measure, three secondary accents between primary accents)

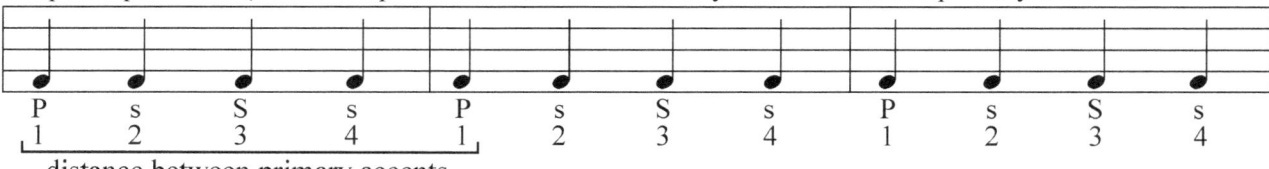

c. triple meter (three beats per measure, two secondary accents between primary accents)

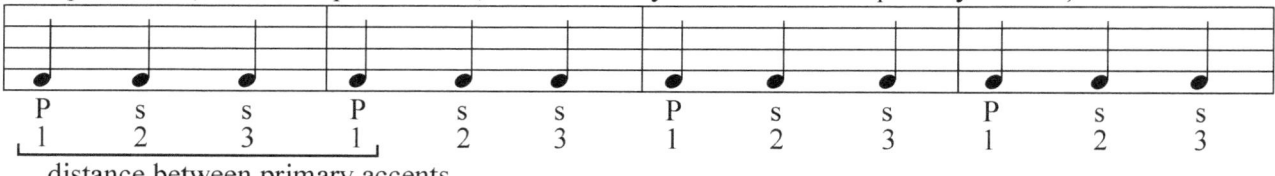

Divisions of Beats

There are two basic ways to divide the beat of any meter. If each of the beats is divided into two equal parts (or multiples of two), then the meter is classified as simple. If, however, each of the beats is divided into three equal parts (or multiples of three), then the meter is classified as compound. Therefore, any duple, quadruple, or triple meter may have either a simple division or compound division of the beat.

As shown in example 1–7, the first simple division of the quarter-note beat is the eighth note while the second division is the sixteenth note (on beat 2 of the first measure, a quarter rest is used instead of a quarter note). *A plus sign indicates the location of where the second half of each quarter-note beat falls.*

Example 1–7: simple duple meter

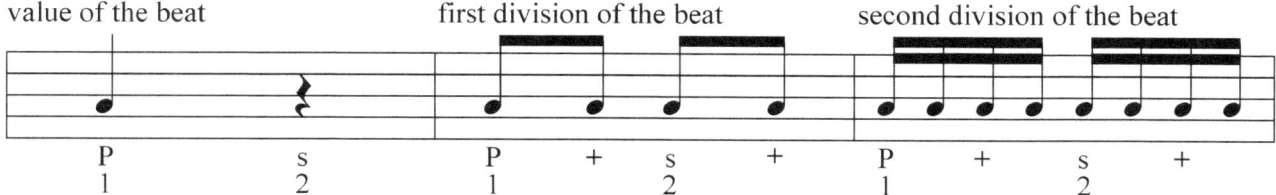

The next example illustrates the difference between a duple meter with a *simple* division of the beat and a duple meter with a *compound* division of the beat. In the latter (example 1–8b), the value of the beat is a dotted quarter note (on beat 2 of the first measure, a dotted quarter rest is used instead of a dotted quarter note). As we have said, the beat of a compound meter is divided into three equal parts or multiples of three. A dotted quarter can be divided into either three eighth notes (the first compound division) or six sixteenth notes (the second division).

Example 1–8: simple and compound duple meter

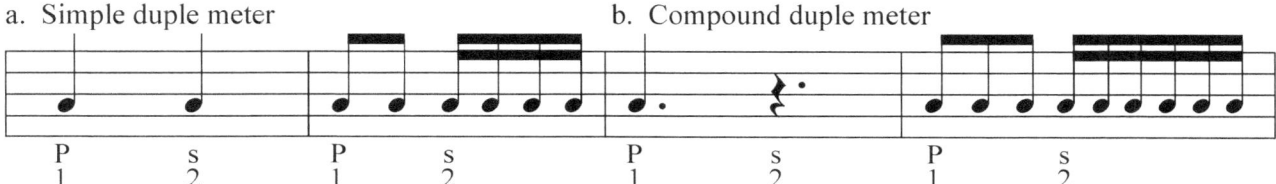

Time Signatures

Examples 1–8 and 9 demonstrate how some of the most basic configurations of notes and rests may occur within simple and compound meters. It is not difficult to see where these configurations of notes and rests coincide with the primary and secondary accents because they are clearly marked. Since the primary and secondary accents are not so identified in actual music, it would be helpful to have a sign or symbol that could tell us the value of the beat and how many beats are distributed across each measure.

The time signature, or meter signature, provides this valuable information. Consisting of two components, the time signature appears as a pair of Arabic numbers, one located directly above the other. If the meter is simple, then the top number designates the number of beats per measure and the bottom number reveals the value of each beat. All simple meters are read in this way.

If, therefore, the bottom number is 4 in a simple meter, then the value of the beat is the quarter note. There are two quarter-note beats per measure in example 1–9a, four quarter-note beats per measure in 1–9b, and three quarter-note beats per measure in 1–9c. Had the bottom number in examples 1–9a, 9b, and 9c been 16, the value of the beat would have been a sixteenth note.

Example 1–9: simple meters

The reading of compound time signatures is somewhat more complicated. If we attempt to read the meters represented in example 1–10 according to the method for reading simple meters described above, then 1–10a would have six eighth-note beats per measure, 1–10b would have twelve eighth-note beats per measure, and 1–10c would have nine eighth-note beats per measure. But as we shall see presently, this is usually not the way to interpret compound signatures, unless the meter is performed very slowly.

In order to identify, read, and classify compound meters accurately, it is necessary to perform a basic arithmetic operation. If dividing the number 3 into the top number of the time signature results in a quotient is 2, 3, or 4, then the number of beats per measure is 2, 3, or 4. To determine the value of the beat, take the note value that the bottom number represents, proceed to the note value that is one denomination higher, and add a dot to that note value.

If the bottom number is 8, which signifies an eighth note, then proceed to the quarter note and add a dot; therefore, the value of the beat is a dotted quarter. In examples 1–10a, 10b, and 10c, the value of the beat is the dotted quarter note with two, four, and three beats distributed across each respective measure. Had the bottom number in examples 1–10a, 10b, and 10c been 16, the value of the beat would have been a dotted eighth.

Example 1–10: compound meters

a. compound duple meter
(two beats per measure)

b. compound quadruple meter
(four beats per measure)

c. compound triple meter
(three beats per measure)

Counting Note Values

When performing or reading note values such as those put forward in example 1–7 above, musicians vocalize or internalize the numbers and plus signs. Usually, musicians counting aloud replace the plus sign with the word "and." Accordingly, both the beat and the first division of the beat in example 1–11 below would be expressed as: "one and two and." If we include the second and third divisions of the beat, then additional syllables may be used.

With the quarter note as the value of the beat, the second division brings us to the level of the sixteenth note—four sixteenth notes fill the duration of one quarter (1–11, measure 3). For each group of four sixteenths, the syllables "e" (pronounced ee) and "a" (pronounced uh or ah) are applied to the second and fourth sixteenth notes respectively. Counting at the level of the third division requires no other syllables beyond those already employed for the second division (the "in 2" designation in the example means that there are two beats to each measure).

Example 1–11: counting the first, second, and third divisions of the beat in simple duple meter (in 2)

We avoid adding syllables below the second division of the beat in simple meter because vocalizing or internalizing syllables and words becomes unwieldy if the note values are performed at a very quick pace. In any event, it can be seen that the note values in example 1–11 all have a mathematical relationship to each other: a single quarter note can be divided into two eighths, four sixteenths, or eight thirty-seconds.

Earlier, we said that the reading of time signatures for compound meter is more complicated than reading those for simple meter. Two different methods for counting aid the performance and reading of note values in compound meter. Example 1–12 illustrates the first method. The value of the beat is the dotted quarter note. The first division of the beat would be counted as: 1 + a 2 + a ("one and uh two and uh").

Notice that for the second division of the beat, every other sixteenth note does not receive a syllable. For the third division of the beat, only six of twenty-four thirty-second notes are counted. As in example 1–11, the note values in 1–12 all have a mathematical relationship to each other: a dotted quarter note can be divided into three eighths, six sixteenths, or twelve thirty-seconds.

Example 1–12: counting the first, second, and third divisions of the beat in compound duple meter (in 2)

in 2:   1   2   1 + a 2 + a   1 + a 2 + a   1   +   a   2   +   a

The second method for performing and reading compound meter appears to contradict the process of classifying time signatures by dividing three into the top number and by adding a dot to the note value that is one denomination higher than the bottom number (see above, p. 6). That compound meters are sometimes performed very slowly accounts for the apparent contradiction. When a compound meter such as $\frac{6}{8}$ is performed slowly, we hear the first division rather than the dotted quarter note as the value of the beat. Thus, the meter in 1–12 above would be interpreted as having not *two* beats per measure but *six* and the value of the beat would be the eighth note, not the dotted quarter.

Example 1–13 demonstrates how the preceding example would be counted if the notes were played slowly. When interpreting the first division of a compound meter as the value of the beat, the note values are counted with the syllables used in simple meter. According to this method, the second division of compound meter is counted as if it were in simple meter with every note receiving a syllable (1 + 2 + 3 + 4 + 5 + 6 +).

Example 1–13: counting compound duple meter with six beats to the measure

in 6: 1 2 3 4 5 6   1 2 3 4 5 6   1 + 2 + 3 + 4 + 5 + 6 +   1 e + a 2 e + a 3 e + a 4 e + a 5 e + a 6 e + a

Rhythm

If meter is the distance between two primary accents, then rhythm is the measurement of both the primary and secondary accents within that meter. Rhythm involves how the accents are organized, or configured. It would be instructive to tap out the rhythm to the song "Jingle Bells" to see if your friends can identify the music without actually hearing the words or the tune. Not surprisingly, most listeners recognize the music from hearing only the rhythm. To be sure, the song has a very distinctive rhythmic profile. But in any case, we can take from this exercise the following lesson: *rhythm is that particular arrangement of notes and rests within each measure that ultimately helps to inform the individuality of a musical composition.*

Syncopation

Under normal musical conditions, we expect notes of longer duration to fall on primary accents and those of shorter duration to occur on secondary accents. When divisions of beats are emphasized and/or when the strongest part of the primary accent is left either unarticulated or weakened in some way, it disrupts the regular distribution of note values and creates an effect known as syncopation. *Syncopation makes strong that which is otherwise weak.*

Musicians produce syncopations by using ties, rests, or shorter notes followed by longer ones. The syncopated figure in example 1–14a shifts the focus to the first division of the quarter-note beat by introducing an eighth note on the strongest part of the primary accent and following it with a quarter, a note value that is twice as long as the preceding eighth.

Example 1–14: two types of syncopation

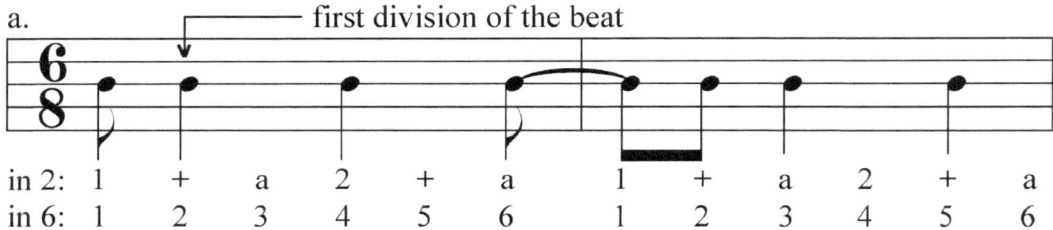

Example 1–14b shows syncopation within the second division of the beat at the level of the sixteenth note. The rhythmic syllables in parentheses indicate that their inclusion here adds nothing to the basic count and that their absence would not obscure the recognition of any of the beats or first divisions of beats.

Simple and Compound Meter Exchange

In music, it is possible and often desirable to place either a simple division of the beat into a compound meter or a compound division of the beat into a simple meter. A simple (two-part) division of the beat occurring in a compound meter is referred to as the duplet. A compound (three-part) division of the beat used in a simple meter is called the triplet.

Triplets

To understand the triplet, let us compare two duple meters: $\frac{2}{4}$ and $\frac{6}{8}$. In $\frac{2}{4}$ time (example 1–15a), the value of the beat occurs at the level of the quarter note; in $\frac{6}{8}$ time (1–15b), however, the value of the beat is the dotted quarter note. The first division of the beat for both meters is the eighth note. Because both $\frac{2}{4}$ and $\frac{6}{8}$ are duple meters and have beat values of the same note denomination (i.e., the quarter note and the dotted quarter note), we refer to these meters as "parallel duple meters."

Example 1–15: parallel duple meters

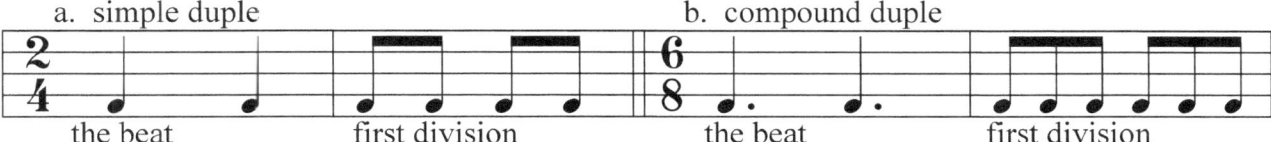

When a simple meter borrows the first division of the beat from a compound meter, the first division carries the number 3 above the note group and is referred to generally as the triplet; in this text, the triplet of the first division is termed "the small triplet." Examples 1–16a and 16b show how the triplet appears in $\frac{2}{4}$, first with all three notes beamed together (1–16a) and then expressed as a quarter note and eighth (1–16b). The method for counting the triplet is taken from compound meter (1 + a 2 + a).

If the triplet is not beamed (1–16b), then the figure adds a bracket to the number 3 in order to show the correct grouping of the notes. In example 1–16b, the first two eighth notes of the triplet are replaced by a quarter note, thereby modifying the triplet's basic three-note framework.

Example 1–16: the small triplet

Duplets

A simple (two-part) division of the beat occurring in a compound meter is referred to as a duplet. When a compound meter borrows the first division of the beat from a simple meter, the first division carries the number 2 above the note group and is identified as a duplet. Example 1–17 shows how the duplet appears in the compound duple meter of $\frac{6}{8}$; the origin of the eighth-note duplet in $\frac{6}{8}$ can be traced to the first division of the beat in $\frac{2}{4}$ (the parallel duple meter of $\frac{6}{8}$). The example below displays two methods for counting the duplet in compound duple meter, in 2 and in 6.

Example 1–17: the duplet and its origin

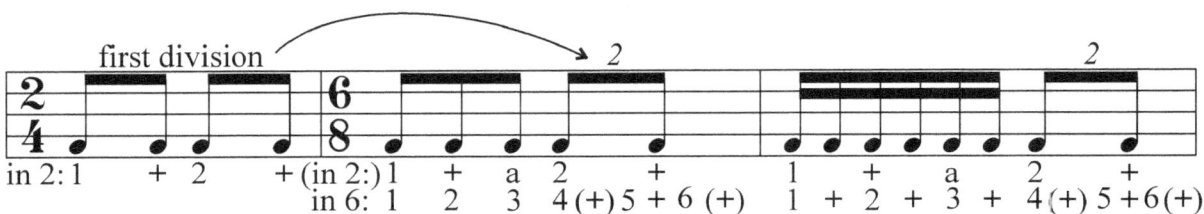

Asymmetrical Meter

We know that duple, triple, and quadruple meters are all considered to be symmetrical meters because they are divisible by either 2 or 3. Most of the time, a single, symmetrical meter will be used *consistently* throughout a piece of music. In other words, compositions that begin in, say, duple meter, usually remain in duple meter until the end. Sometimes, however, a piece of music might begin in one meter but subsequently change to another meter or a series of meters before the conclusion. Further, it is possible to have a meter with an odd number of beats per measure, a meter that is not divisible by either 2 or 3. Such meters are usually referred to as either asymmetrical meters or odd meters.

Let us consider a meter with five beats per measure. A meter "in 5" results when duple and triple meters are combined. There are a few ways in which to indicate a meter in 5. One method involves using two different time signatures in succession, such as the combination of $\frac{2}{4}$ and $\frac{3}{4}$ shown in example 1–18a. An alternative approach would be to place the two time signatures at the beginning of the composition and separate them with a plus sign, that is: $\frac{2}{4} + \frac{3}{4}$. If the bottom number for both time signatures represents the same note value, then the following option is available: $\frac{2+3}{4}$. In either instance, the person reading the music would understand that each pair of measures alternates between the two time signatures until the end or until a change in the metric structure occurs. This method avoids having to notate each measure of $\frac{2}{4}$ and $\frac{3}{4}$ throughout the entire composition.

The most common way to express a meter in 5, however, would be to simply consolidate $\frac{2}{4}$ and $\frac{3}{4}$ into $\frac{5}{4}$ time, as displayed in 1–18b. We classify $\frac{5}{4}$ time as a *simple* asymmetrical meter because dividing the number 3 into the top number of the time signature does not produce a whole number quotient greater than 4 (such as 5 or 7). Accordingly, the meter is simple rather than compound. The dotted line in example 1–18b indicates what would otherwise be a measure of $\frac{2}{4}$ and a measure of $\frac{3}{4}$.

Again, combining duple and triple meters produces a meter in 5: either a measure of duple meter is followed by measure of triple meter ("two plus three") or a measure of triple meter is followed by a measure of duple meter ("three plus two"). Thus, a meter with five beats per measure can be subdivided and counted as either 1-2 1-2-3 (two plus three) or 1-2-3 1-2 (three plus two).

Example 1–18

a. expressing a meter in 5 with two time signatures in succession

b. expressing a meter in 5 with one time signature (two plus three)

Pitch

An object moved by force produces vibrations that in turn create displacements throughout the surrounding area. The displaced area, which can be a liquid, a solid, or a gas, serves as a medium of transmission that carries the vibrations to the human ear. Functioning as a receptor, the ear perceives the vibrations as sound. The number of sound vibrations completed in one second of time is called frequency.

If the vibrating object produces a regular number of frequencies at a steady rate, then the sound will be heard as a musical tone. Such tones are referred to as pitches. The relative lowness or highness of any pitch corresponds to the rate of the vibrating frequency of the sound-producing object. Slower vibrating frequencies result in lower pitches, while faster vibrating frequencies produce higher pitches.

An inspection of the piano keyboard demonstrates the difference between lower and higher pitches. The standard 88-key piano, as represented in example 1–19, has 52 white keys and 36 black keys. Moving from the extreme left to the extreme right of the keyboard, each key produces a pitch that is incrementally higher and its equivalent frequency faster. From the lowest to the highest pitch, the frequencies range from 27.5 to 4186 vibrations per second. All of the pitches on the keyboard have names that correspond to the first seven letters of the alphabet, letters A through G. Every eighth pitch and letter repeats the first; this repetition is called an octave. Any two pitches of the same letter name that are one octave apart have a frequency ratio of 2:1.

Musicians interpret the numerical relationship between pitches in spatial terms, using the word interval to describe the distance from one pitch to any other pitch. On the keyboard, the distance between any two immediately adjacent piano keys constitutes an increment in pitch called a half step. There are twelve half steps within any single octave.

Example 1–19: the standard 88-key piano

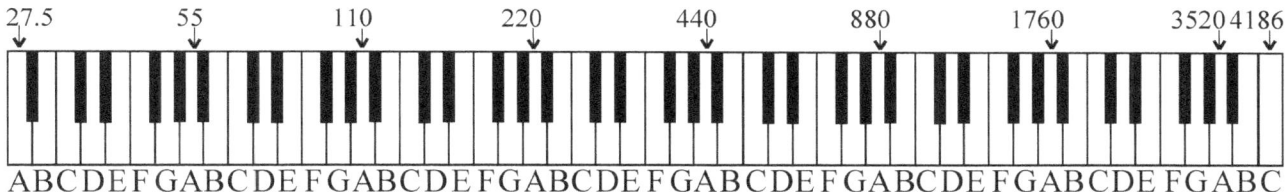

Study example 1–20 and notice the intervallic distances between both the white and black keys of the piano keyboard. The black keys are arranged in alternating groups of two and three with one intervening black key between each white key except in two places: from E to F and from B to C. Since the distance between any two immediately adjacent piano keys is a half step, E to F and B to C constitute the only two places within the octave where there are half steps between two adjacent white keys.

Example 1–20

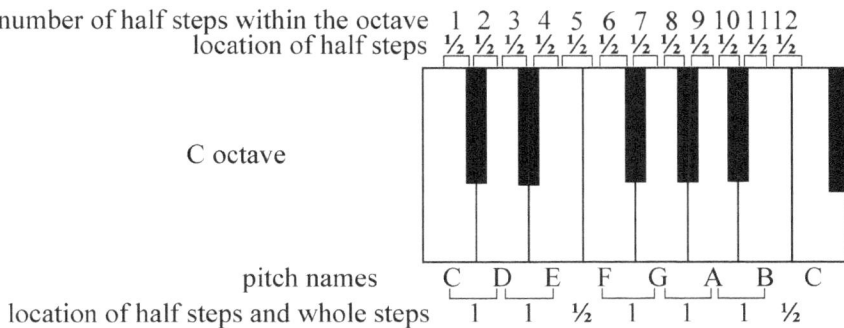

12   Chapter 1 A Review of Fundamentals

In all other places, two adjacent white keys produce two half steps because a black key separates each pair. Two consecutive half steps between any two piano keys comprise the interval of a whole step (sometimes referred to as a "step"). Thus, with the exception of E to F and B to C, the distance between white keys is always a whole step. With respect to the alternating groups of two and three black keys that extend across the piano keyboard, three half steps separate each group while the distance between black keys within each group is a whole step (example 1–21).

Example 1–21

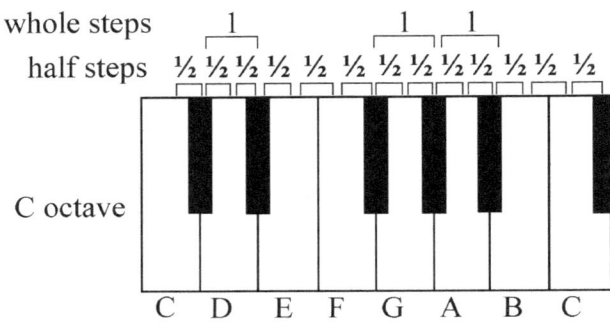

Accidentals and Enharmonic Equivalency

A conflict arises from the fact that twelve half steps fill the span of any octave but only seven alphabet letters are available to designate pitches. The conflict is more apparent than real because each of the seven pitch names can have more than one spelling of itself; that is to say, the seven pitch names can be modified with additional symbols called accidentals.

Accidentals raise or lower any of the seven pitch names. The names and the shapes of the accidentals are as follows: sharp (♯), flat (♭), double flat (♭♭), double sharp (×), and natural (♮). The natural sign cancels any accidental used to raise or lower a pitch. Each pitch and its associated name can be raised one half step with the addition of a sharp or lowered one half step with the addition of a flat. In music notation, the accidental immediately *precedes* the pitch to which it applies. When speaking or writing about an accidental that is attached to a pitch, however, the symbol or the word for the accidental *follows* the pitch name, as for example: C♯ or C sharp.

Example 1–22 shows how the pitch C can be raised one half step on the piano keyboard with the addition of a sharp to become C♯ (pronounced C sharp). The pitch B can be lowered one half step with the addition of a flat to become B♭ (pronounced B flat). Raising the pitch from C to C♯ requires a move from the left to the right of the keyboard, whereas lowering the pitch from B to B♭ necessitates a move from right to left. In both cases, the move to C♯ and B♭ ends on one of the black keys.

Example 1–22

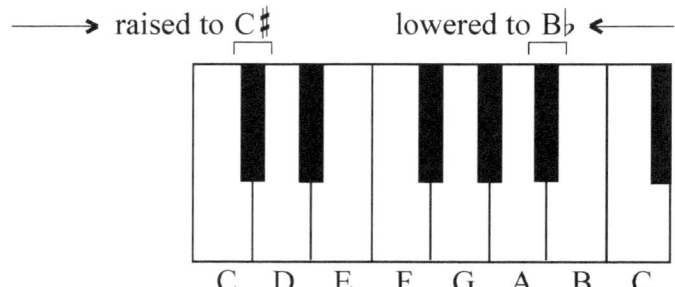

It is also possible to raise a pitch (and its name) two half steps with the addition of a double sharp and to lower it two half steps with the addition of a double flat. As illustrated in example 1–23, a move from C to C𝗫 (pronounced C double sharp) can be accomplished by raising the pitch from C to C♯ and then from C♯ to C𝗫 (example 1–23). Similarly, the move to B♭♭ (pronounced B double flat) can be made by lowering the pitch from B to B♭ and then from B♭ to B♭♭.

Raising C to C𝗫 takes us to the equivalent white key and pitch of D. If we lower B two half steps, the operation changes the white key and pitch of A into B♭♭. By using sharps, flats, double sharps, and double flats, at least two different letter names may be assigned to any single pitch. In fact, every pitch can have three different letter names except for G♯ and A♭ (see example 1–24 below). When we apply different letter names to the same pitch, the names are called enharmonic equivalents.

Example 1–23

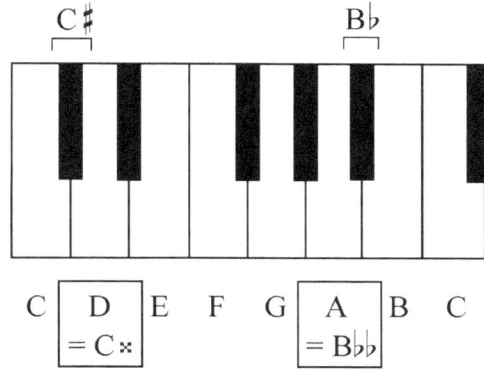

Example 1–24 locates all of the possible enharmonic equivalents within the C octave; the names of these pitches remain the same regardless of the octave in which they occur. Again, every pitch can have at least three different letter names except for G♯ and A♭.

Example 1–24

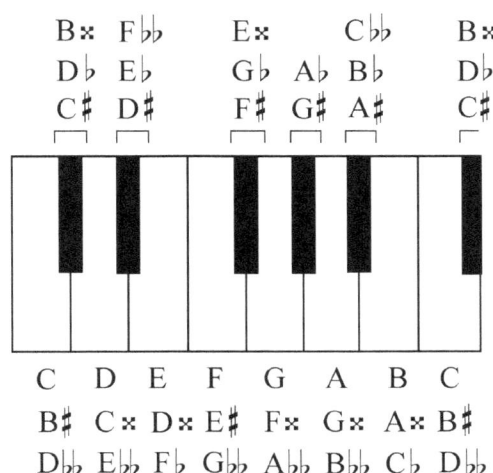

The Great Staff and Clefs

As mentioned in earlier, the staff consists of five lines and four spaces and is an integral component of most music notation. Example 1–25 displays two staffs, or staves (an alternate plural for staff), joined together by a bracket in the left margin known as a brace. This apparent two-staff ten-line configuration is referred to variously as the great staff, the grand staff, or the piano staff. The staff alone cannot represent pitches, however. Any set or range of pitches requires the use of a symbol called a clef sign. The two most common clefs are the F clef and the G clef.

Example 1–25 shows the location and appearance of both the F clef and the G clef on the great staff. The F clef is so named because the sign's two dots surround the line on which the pitch F is fixed. Another name for the F clef is the bass clef. The G clef takes its name from the swirl around the second line from the bottom, the line on which the pitch G is designated. Another name for the G clef is the treble clef. With F and G located on the staff by their respective clefs, it is possible to find the other pitches on the lines and spaces according to the letters of the alphabet (1–25).

Between the two staves of the great staff is an additional line called a ledger line. Here, the line designates a pitch called "middle C." Musicians use ledger lines to retain within a single clef pitches that exceed the limits of any single staff (see example 1–28 below).

Example 1–25

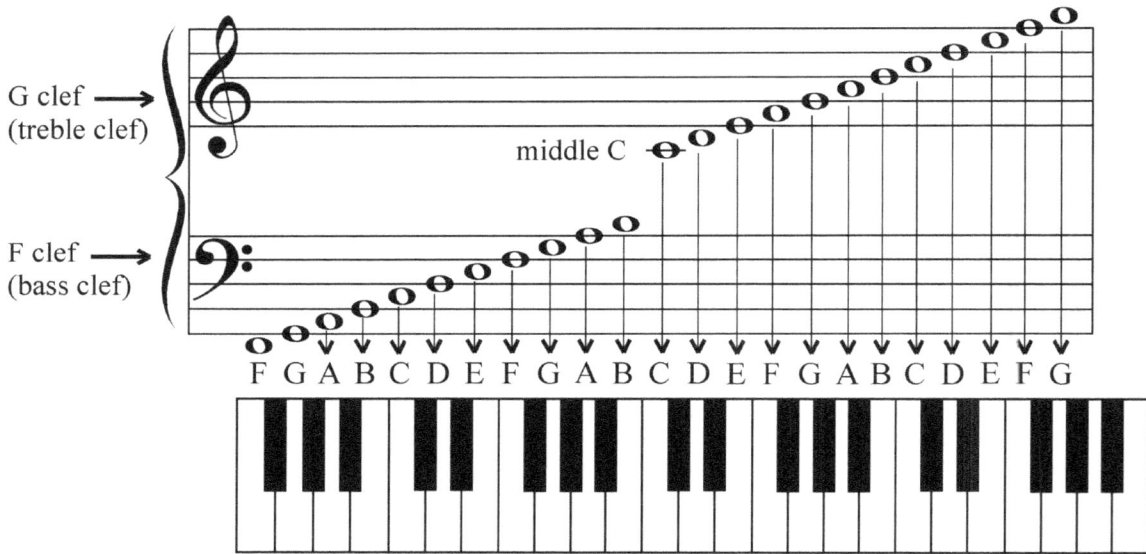

Other clefs use middle C to fix the location of the seven pitch names. Such clefs are called C clefs because they locate middle C with a design that encircles the line on which middle C is to be read. C clefs can be placed on any of the five lines of the staff and therefore are considered to be movable clefs. More than two hundred years ago, C clefs were widely used; however, today, only two C clefs are commonly found, namely, the alto and tenor clefs. The alto clef is used for the viola and the alto trombone and the tenor clef often serves the upper register of the trombone, bassoon, and cello.

Example 1–26 presents all five C clefs on each of the five lines of the staff along with their respective names. As with the F and G clefs, the other pitches of the C clef precede and follow middle C according to the order of the alphabet.

Example 1–26

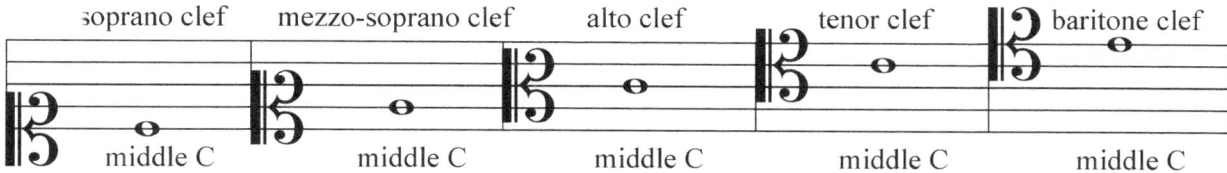

Octave registers

In the previous sections of this chapter, we located the seven basic pitch names on the standard 88-key piano, introduced the five types of accidental signs, explained the concept of enharmonic equivalency, explored the range of the great staff within the general context of the F and G clefs, and discussed the principal characteristics of the various C clefs.

Initially, we used uppercase letters to represent the seven pitch names that span the seven octaves of the keyboard. Middle C, which is expressed on the great staff with the use of a single ledger line, is the fourth C from the extreme left of the keyboard. If we are referring to pitches in general terms, then there is no need to identify any given pitch within a specific octave register. But if we want to identify a pitch that occurs within a particular octave, then the problem of precise pitch location, or pitch register, arises—a problem for which a couple of different solutions have been put forward.

One solution for identifying a pitch within a specific octave register, shown in examples 1–27 and 28, divides the keyboard into seven segments of pitches with each segment beginning on C and ending on B. The first of the seven segments is preceded by the pitches A and B while the seventh segment is followed by the seventh repetition of C. All of the segments as well as the additional pitches at both extremes of the keyboard are given names to identify the exact register of any given pitch.

The designations for the various registers (and segments) are sub-contra, contra, great, small, one-line or prime, two-line or double prime, three-line or triple prime, four-line or quadruple prime, and five-line or quintuple prime. Pitches occurring in the prime registers use lowercase letters and carry either superscripts or vertical slashes. For example, middle C appears as either c^1 or c'. In the double prime register, C is written as either c^2 or c". (Example 1–28 shows all of the pitches on the great staff in relation to their location on the keyboard.)

Both the sub-contra and contra registers take uppercase letters and use subscript numbers. A_2 and B_2 of the sub-contra register are pronounced as "double A" and "double B." In the great and small registers, pitches are represented with uppercase and lowercase lettering respectively. The alternative to describing the sub-contra and contra registers with uppercase letters followed by subscripts is to use three uppercase letters for the sub-contra register and two uppercase letters for the contra register (1–28).

Example 1–27

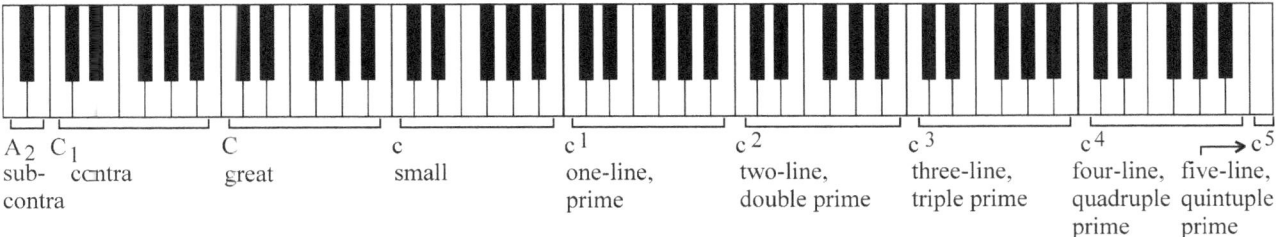

16 Chapter 1 A Review of Fundamentals

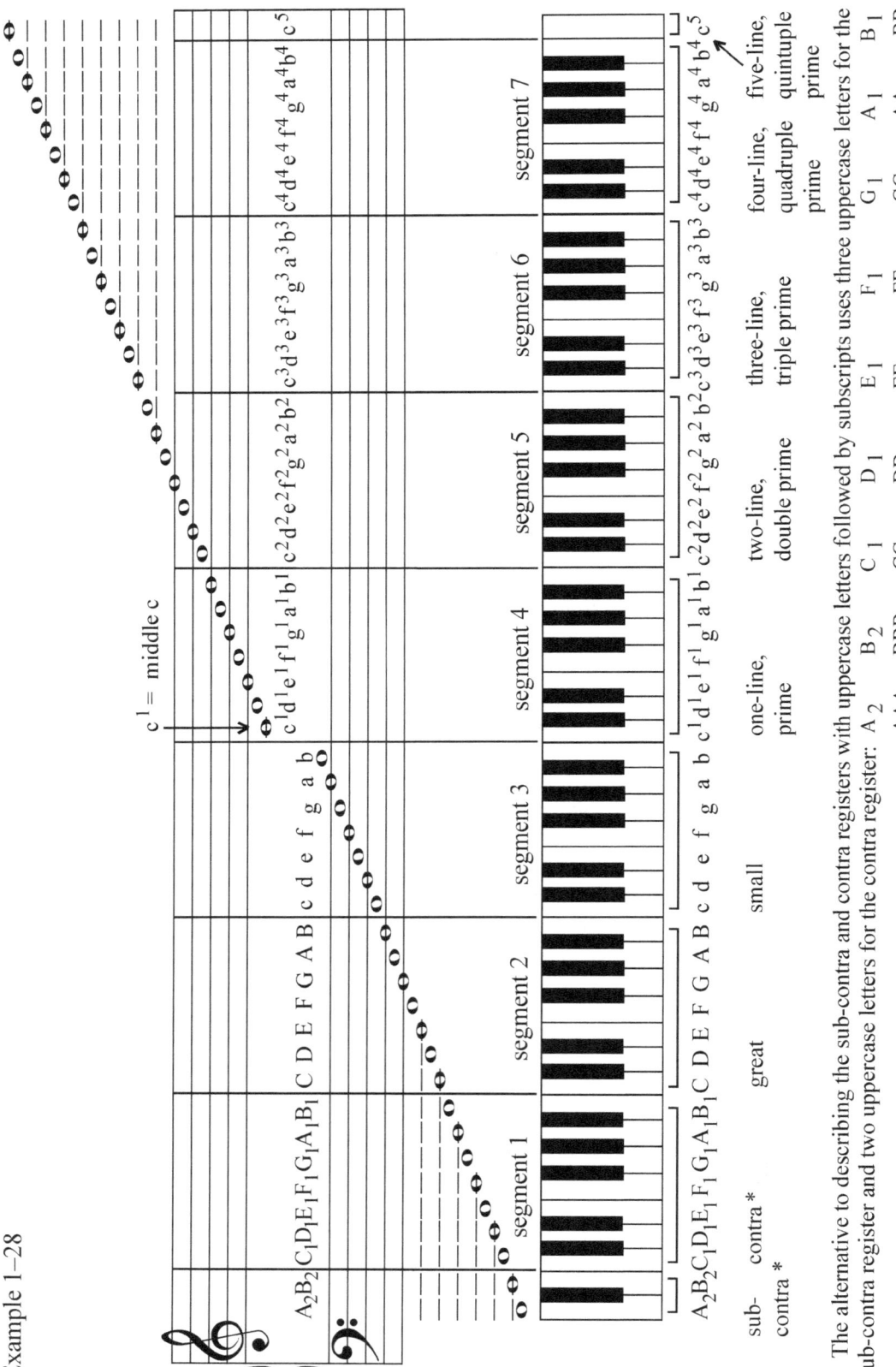

Example 1-28

The Major Scale

Earlier in this chapter, we saw an octave span on and C in which eight pitches were arranged alphabetically in an ascending stepwise pattern (example 1–20). This octave configuration bring us to the concept of scale. The term scale derives from the Italian word *scala*, which means ladder. A scale is a ladder of tones: a representation of stepwise pitches running upwards or downwards. The tones of the scale are identified by the letter names of the alphabet.

The chromatic scale, as presented in example 1–29, divides the octave into twelve half steps. Sharps are generally used when the scale is notated in its ascending form, flats in its descending form. The chromatic scale contains pairs of pitches that involve two different versions of the same letter name, that is, chromatic half steps: in the ascending form, C–C♯, D–D♯, F–F♯, G–G♯, and A–A♯ (1–29a); and in the descending form, B–B♭, A–A♭, G–G♭, E–E♭, and D–D♭ (1–29b).

Two exceptional areas of the chromatic scale have diatonic half steps, that is, two consecutive pitches with different letter names: E to F and B to C. In the examples below, the tones of the chromatic scale occur within the span of a single octave; however, the chromatic scale may be expressed in any register, starting on any of the seven alphabet names.

Example 1–29: the chromatic scale on C

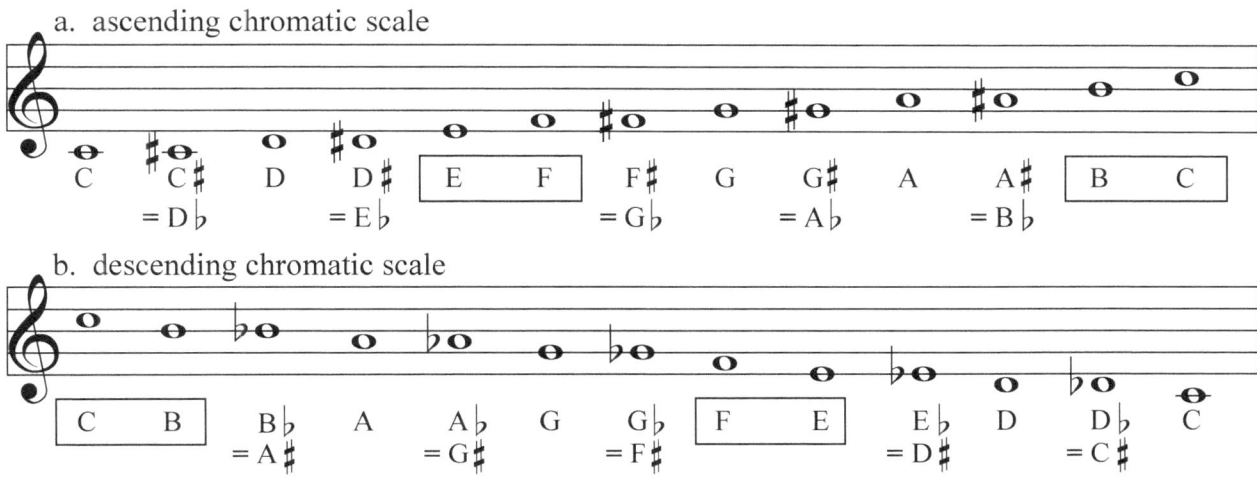

A scale having only one letter name for each of its seven pitches, spanning a single octave, and comprising five whole steps and two half steps is called a diatonic scale. The distribution of whole steps and half steps across the seven pitches of a diatonic scale can be found by examining the white keys of the piano within any octave of the keyboard. Example 1–30 shows a diatonic scale within the C octave.

Example 1–30

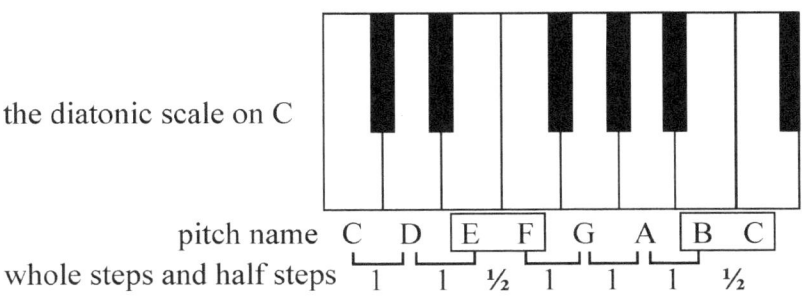

Each of the seven pitches of the diatonic scale is called a scale degree and assigned a number according to its relationship to the first pitch of the scale. Example 1–31 identifies C as scale degree 1 and D, E, F, G, A, and B as scale degrees 2, 3, 4, 5, 6, and 7 respectively. The octave duplication of C is 8, which is equivalent to scale degree 1. All diatonic scales can be divided into two four-note segments: from scale degrees 1 to 4 and 5 to 8. These segments are called tetrachords; they are usually separated by a whole step between scale degrees 4 and 5 (example 1–31).

The major scale on C occurs naturally on the white keys of the piano. The combined distribution of whole steps and half steps across the C-major octave creates, in this case, two matching tetrachords (whole step, whole step, half step from scale degrees 1 to 4 and whole step, whole step, half step from scale degrees 5 to 8). The *profile* of the complete scale consists of half steps between scale degrees 3 and 4 and scale degrees 7 and 8, with all other adjacent notes being whole steps.

Example 1–31

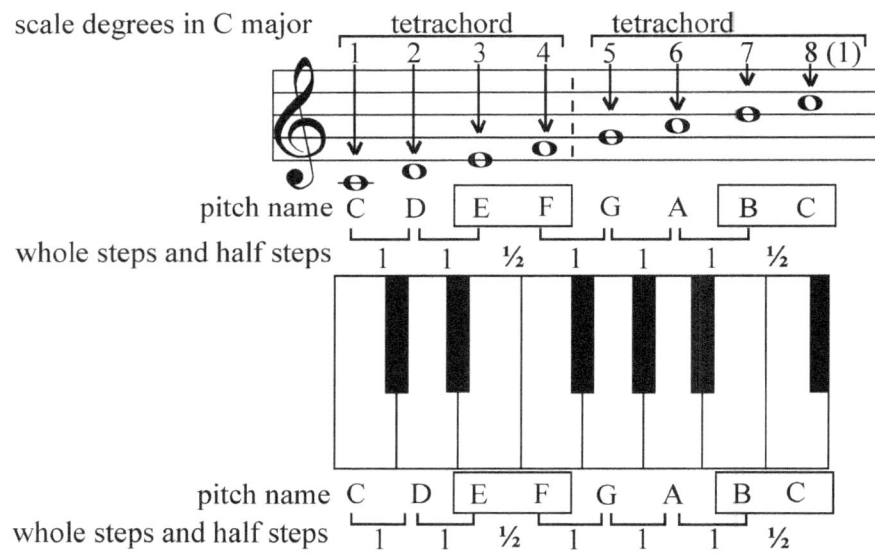

The pattern of half steps and whole steps in the major scale reflects two things, namely, key and mode. Key, which is also known variously as the keynote or tonal center, is that pitch to which all other pitches are related and toward which they ultimately move. If we play every pitch of the C-major scale in the numerical order of its scale degrees, starting with C as scale degree 1, the arrival of scale degree 7 confirms the strength of the key; for here, there is a compelling drive to complete the upward succession of pitches by ending on scale degree 8.

In addition to having an assigned number, each scale degree has a name. Scale degree 1 (or 8) is called the tonic, scale degree 2 the supertonic, 3 the mediant, 4 the subdominant, 5 the dominant, 6 the submediant, and 7 the leading tone.

The mode of a composition has a more direct relationship to the actual music than does the concept of scale, which is merely an alphabetical inventory of pitches derived from the music. Expressing certain characteristic patterns and configurations of pitches, the mode confirms and establishes the key of a musical work. Among the most important characteristic patterns of any mode is the arrangement of linear half steps and whole steps such as the one shown above in 1–31, which illustrates the C-major scale and mode. Indeed, its profile of half steps between scale degrees 3 and 4 and scale degrees 7 and 8 distinguishes the major mode from the profiles of other diatonic modes.

Moving the Major Scale to Octaves Other than C with the Addition of Sharps

Since there are twelve half steps and pitches within any octave, each pitch may have its own major mode and scale. It is therefore possible to move the C-major scale to any of the remaining eleven pitches within the octave. However, when moving the major scale to octaves other than C, its profile of half steps can be maintained only with the inclusion of one or more black keys of the piano.

Let us begin with the G octave. The first step is to start on C, scale degree 1 of C major, and go up to G, scale degree 5 of C major (example 1–32). Note carefully that the distance from C to G is 3½ steps (3½ steps is an abbreviation for three whole steps and one half step). Later in this chapter, we shall refer to this distance as a perfect 5th.

Example 1–32

Once the G octave has been identified, C major's profile of half steps and whole steps must be preserved in G major. In order for the half steps to remain between scale degrees 3 and 4 and scale degrees 7 and 8, the tetrachord structure of the major mode has to be maintained (each tetrachord contains within its four-note span the following pattern: whole step, whole step, half step).

In example 1–33, we can see that the lower tetrachord, scale degrees 1 to 4, does not require the addition of black keys to preserve the four-note pattern of whole steps and half steps; however, the *upper tetrachord*, scale degrees 5 to 8, does. In order to establish a half step between scale degrees 7 and 8 and to maintain the tetrachord structure, it is necessary to raise the F one half step to F♯.

Example 1–33

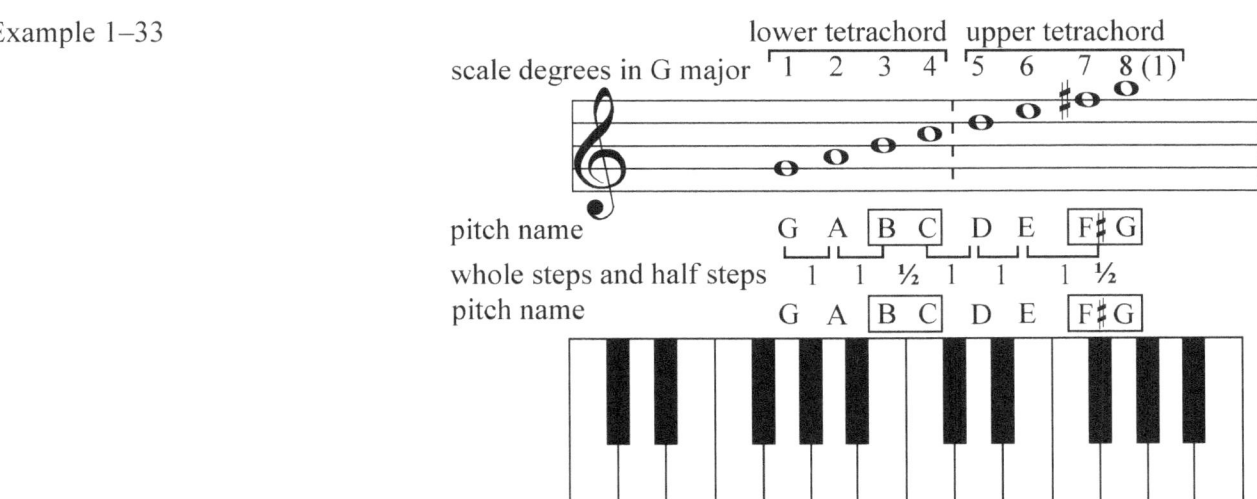

20   Chapter 1   A Review of Fundamentals

Moving upwards in 3½-step increments from C takes us through what is called the sharp side of major. The starting notes for the seven major scales on the sharp side consist of G, D, A, E, B, F♯, and C♯. *As long as the starting note of each scale is 3½ steps above the one that preceded it, all of the sharps added previously for each scale will be used in subsequent formations; and, each new scale will add one sharp to those that have been retained from previous formations.* As indicated in example 1–34, the additional sharp creates scale degree 7 within the upper tetrachord of each new scale (see the circled notes). (Notice that the starting notes D, E, B, and C♯ appear below rather than above the starting note of the previous scale. After counting upwards in 3½-step increments to find these notes in a higher register, transferring each of them down into a lower octave minimizes the use of ledger lines.)

Example 1–34: the sharp side of major

G major (3½ steps above C)

D major (3½ steps above G)

A major (3½ steps above D)

E major (3½ steps above A)

B major (3½ steps above E)

F♯ major (3½ steps above B)

C♯ major (3½ steps above F♯)

Moving the Major Scale to Octaves Other Than C with the Addition of Flats

To locate the first octave in which to construct a major scale with flats, count downwards 3½ steps from C to F (example 1–35). As we shall see, moving downwards in 3½-step increments from C takes us through the following octaves: F, B♭, E♭, A♭, D♭, G♭, and C♭. In order to best illustrate each of these octaves and their respective scale constructions, it will be easier to move upwards in 2½-step increments. Later in this chapter, we shall refer to this distance as a perfect 4th.

    Looking at example 1–35, notice that if we start on c prime (c^1) and continue upwards 2½ steps, our destination will be f prime (f^1). Proceeding downwards 3½ steps from c prime leads to small f. Therefore, the same pitch letter can be reached by moving either up 2½ steps (a perfect 4th) or down 3½ steps (a perfect 5th) from any given pitch (in this instance, c prime); however, each pitch of the same letter will be in a different octave register.

    In any case, having located the F octave, let us build the F major scale. In order to preserve the half step between scale degrees 3 and 4, a B♭ must be added to the *lower tetrachord* (example 1–36). The upper tetrachord requires no changes, as a half step already exists between E and F, scale degrees 7 and 8.

Example 1–35

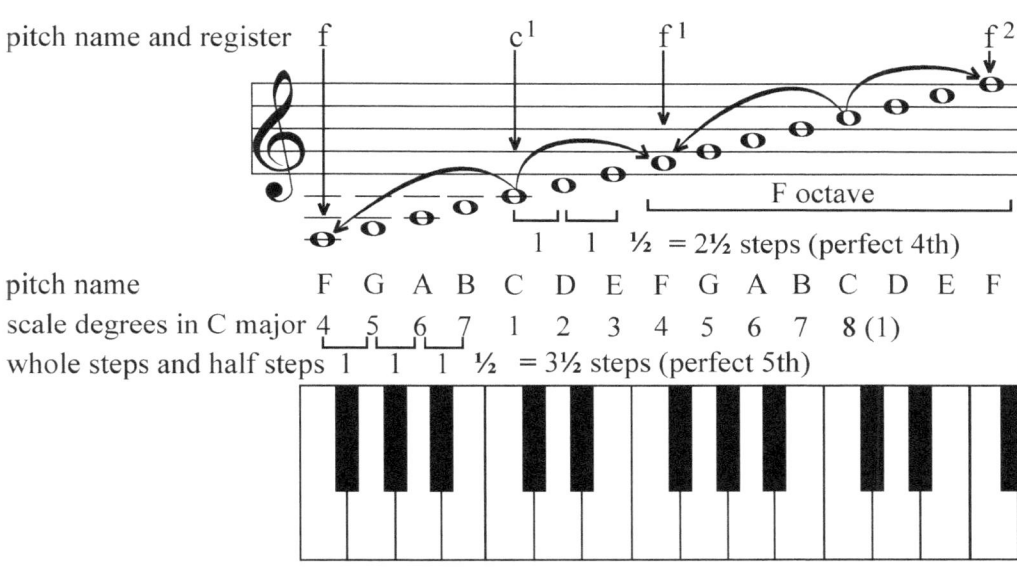

Example 1–36

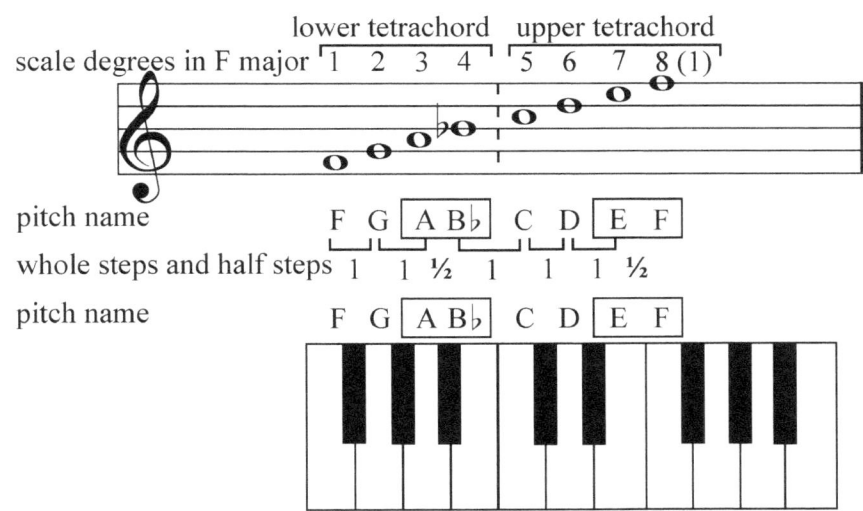

During our construction of the sharp side of major, we said that as long as the starting note of each scale is 3½ steps above the one that preceded it, all of the sharps added previously for each scale will be used in subsequent formations; and, each new scale will add one sharp to those that have been retained from previous formations. With respect to the construction of major scales with flats, the addition of each new flat will occur within the *lower tetrachord*, as long as the starting note of each scale is 2½ steps above the one that preceded it (or 3½ steps below the one that preceded it). As shown in example 1–37, for the flat side of major, the addition of a flat in the lower tetrachord occurs on scale degree 4 (see the circled notes).

Example 1–37: the flat side of major

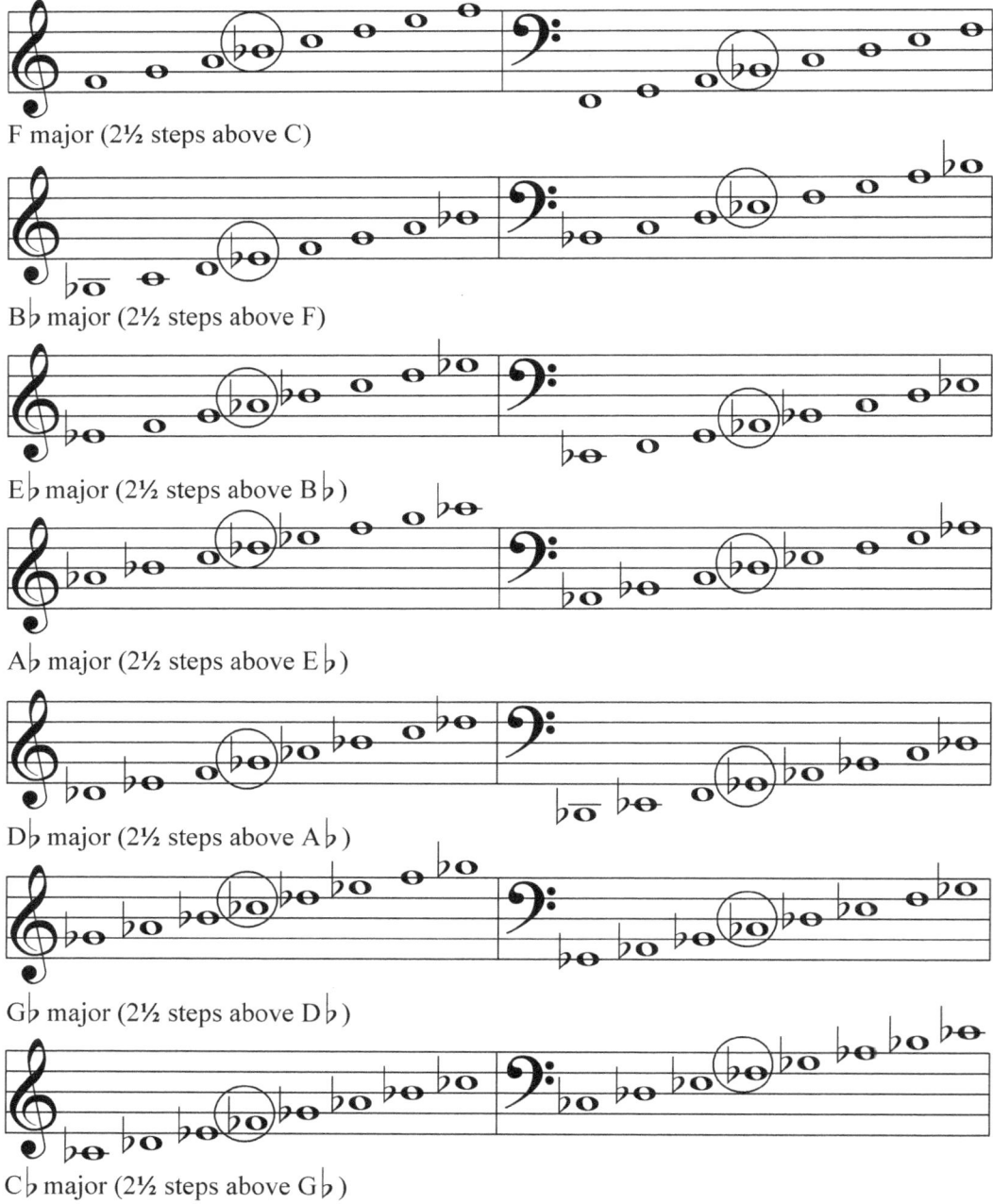

F major (2½ steps above C)

B♭ major (2½ steps above F)

E♭ major (2½ steps above B♭)

A♭ major (2½ steps above E♭)

D♭ major (2½ steps above A♭)

G♭ major (2½ steps above D♭)

C♭ major (2½ steps above G♭)

Major Key Signatures

In the previous section, we learned that when moving the major scale to octaves other than C, the half steps between scale degrees 3 and 4 and scale degrees 7 and 8 can be maintained only with the inclusion of one or more black notes of the piano. It is, however, unwieldy to place all of the sharps or flats of the mode throughout the notated score of a music composition. Accordingly, the accidentals (sharps or flats) of any mode appear in a type of shorthand notation known as a key signature.

The key signature identifies the specific notes that are appropriate to the mode of a musical work. There are two sides to the major mode: a flat side and a sharp side. We shall find a the connection between these two side in the next section, The Circle of 5ths.

Look at the configurations of the key signatures for C♯ major and C♭ major as they appear on both the G clef (treble clef) and the F clef (bass clef). Examples 1–38a and 38b present the key signature as a collection of accidentals that appears between the clef sign and the time signature. The key signature forms a pattern that is logically designed to keep all of the accidentals within the limits of the staff and to facilitate reading.

The pattern for both sharp and flat keys is consistently maintained except in one place. Starting with F♯, the pattern for sharp keys is down a 4th and up a 5th, except for the A♯, which continues down another 4th before the pattern resumes. Determine the intervals of a 4th and 5th by counting each line and space on the staff. The key signature pattern for flat keys contains no irregularities: up a 4th and down a 5th.

Example 1–38

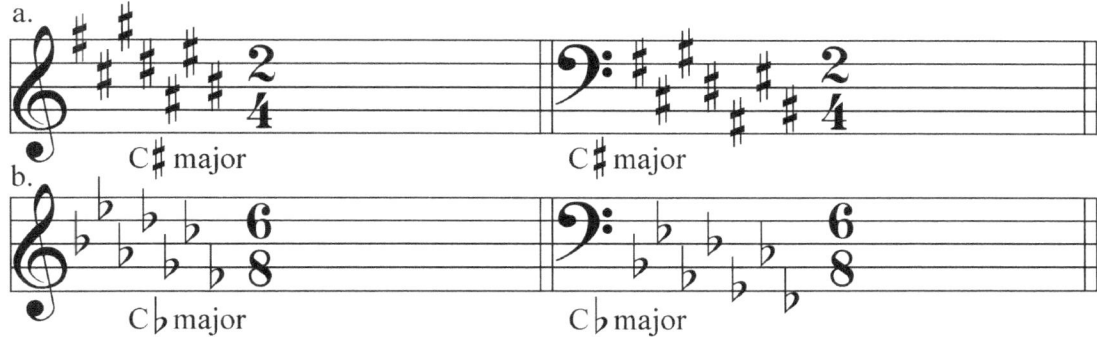

Consider what would have happened to the A♯ if the pattern of descending 4ths and ascending 5ths had been consistently observed. Both the A♯ and the B♯ would have required ledger lines and thereby exceeded the limits of the staff (example 1–39).

Example 1–39

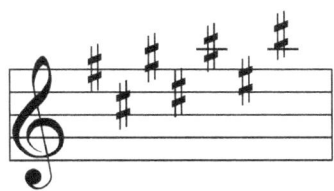

The Circle of 5ths

The circle of 5ths uses C major as a starting point and ascends in perfect-5th intervals through G, D, A, E, B, F♯, and C♯, increasing by one the number of sharps for each successive key (example 1–40). The other side of the circle descends from C in perfect-5th intervals through F, B♭, E♭, A♭, D♭, G♭, and C♭, increasing by one the number of flats for each successive key. Out of these formations, fifteen major keys emerge, seven with sharps, seven with flats, and C major, which has neither sharps nor flats.

As shown in example 1–40, the procession of ascending perfect 5ths on the sharp side of major and descending perfect 5ths on the flat side of major forms a circle, a circle of 5ths. Notice the three pairs of keys located on the lower portion of the circle, namely, D♭ and C♯, G♭ and F♯, and C♭ and B. Play the scales for these three pairs of keys on the piano and you will find that each pair sounds the same; they are enharmonic keys. The enharmonic keys close the circle of 5ths by bringing the sharp and flat sides of major together.

Example 1–40: the sharp and flat sides of major in the circle of 5ths

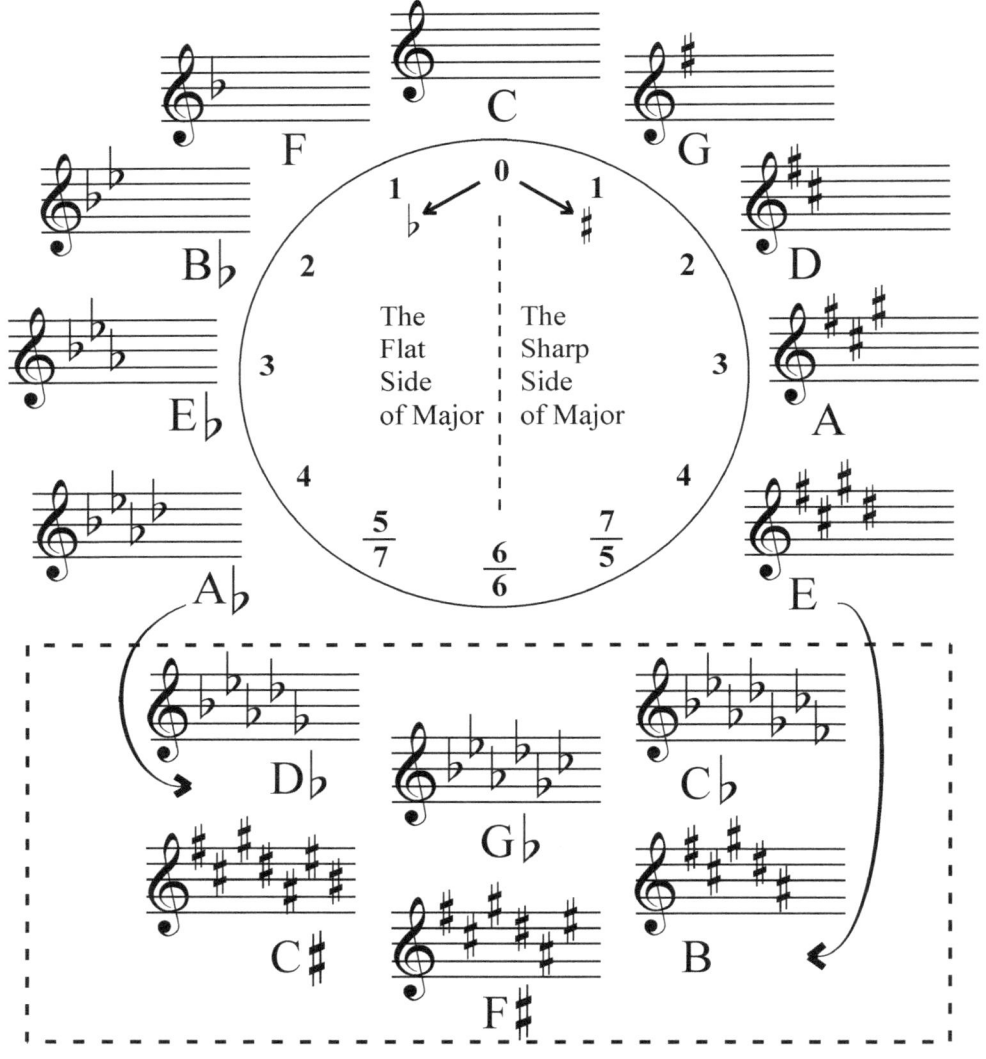

Examples 1–41a, 41b, 41c, and 41d show both the sharp and flat key signatures in their respective treble and bass clefs. As stated above, the arrangement for sharps is down a 4th and up a 5th, except for the A♯, which continues down another 4th before the initial pattern is resumed. For the flat keys, the pattern reverses the configuration of the sharp keys: up a 4th and down a 5th, with no irregularities.

A useful way to remember the order of sharps as they appear on the staff is to associate them respectively with the first letter of each word of the sentence "friends can go dancing at Ernie's bar." For flats, remember that the first four flats spell the word BEAD, followed by the letters GCF, which we could read as an abbreviation for "good cars fast."

Example 1–41

Example 1–42 illustrates some of the common mistakes that music students make when writing key signatures.

Example 1–42

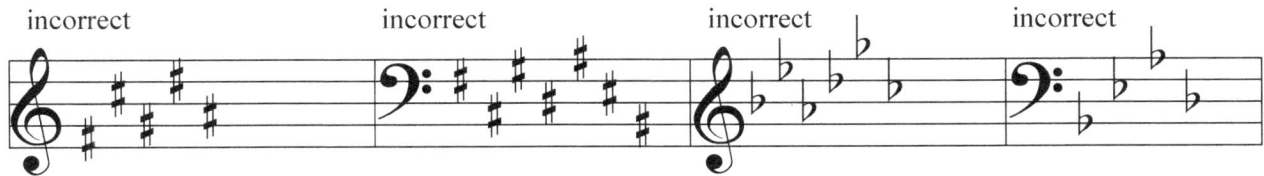

Identifying Major Key Signatures

There is a paradox in the relationship between key signatures and the scales and modes they signify. The paradox involves the difference in the order of accidentals that appear in the construction of a scale versus the order of accidentals as they appear in that scale's key signature. Consider the scale construction for C♯ major (example 1–43a); here, the order of sharps is C♯, D♯, E♯, F♯, G♯, A♯, and B♯. Compare the sequence of sharps in the construction of the C♯-major scale to the order of sharps in the key signature (1–43b): F♯, C♯, G♯, D♯, A♯, E♯, and B♯.

The only common factor of significance between the order of accidentals in the construction of a scale with sharps and the order of accidentals in the scale's key signature is as follows: the last sharp added to the scale (not including scale degree 8, which is a duplication of scale degree 1) is scale degree 7, the leading tone; the last sharp of the key signature is also scale degree 7. In the case of C♯ major, scale degree 7 is B♯.

The fact that the last pitch of the key signature is scale degree 7 helps us to identify the keynote of any sharp key, as the note following scale degree 7 is scale degree 8, the keynote (see the upward arrow pointing to C♯ in 1–43b). And so, for all of the sharp key signatures, look at the last sharp and realize that the keynote is one half step above that last sharp.

Example 1–43: C♯ major

For flat keys, we find the same paradox in the relationship between key signatures and the scales and modes they signify (examples 1–44a and 44b); however, the last flat of the signature cannot help us identify the keynote. Rather, a different principle must be applied to acquire this information. If the flat key has two or more flats in its key signature, then the next-to-the-last flat will be the keynote. The key with one flat is F major and you will simply have to memorize this fact.

Example 1–44: C♭ major

Diatonicism, Chromaticism, and Tonality

We know that the pattern of half steps and whole steps in the major scale reflects two things, namely, key and mode. The mode of a composition expresses certain characteristic designs that confirm and establish the key. The key is that pitch to which all other pitches are related and toward which they ultimately move. The key represents the tonality of the mode.

Tonality in music is analogous to the gravitational force exerted by the Sun upon any object that comes within its field of attraction. Tonality is a system of pitch organization that establishes its own field of attraction around one central tone. All of the other tones of the mode seek to revolve around and gravitate toward this central tone in a hierarchical order.

The tonic, as the principal tone of this hierarchy, exerts its gravitational force upon all of the other tones of the mode, each of which assumes a position of relative strength and stability within the tonic's field of attraction. In other words, within the framework of the key and mode, some tones have a stronger relationship to the tonic than others.

In broad terms, the concepts of key, mode, and tonality bring us to a consideration of the principles of diatonicism and chromaticism. The study of music fundamentals deals largely with diatonic usages in music. Perhaps the best way to understand diatonicism is to recognize that every mode (including those that we have yet to examine) has certain tones that represent its unique profile of half steps and whole steps. The tones that are specific and appropriate to the mode are diatonic elements; these tones are part of the key's orbital system.

In most cases, the diatonic elements will be reflected in the key signature. However, the key signature may not represent all of the pitch content of a music composition. The tones that are neither native to the mode nor reflected in the key signature are referred to as chromatic pitches. Chromaticism, if used extensively in a musical work, can not only undermine both the key and mode, it can eliminate them altogether.

Intervals

The term interval describes the distance from one pitch to any other pitch. It is possible to measure the numerical distance between two pitches by counting the letter names from the lower pitch to the higher pitch or from the higher pitch to the lower pitch. For example, C to D, is called a 2nd, C to E a 3rd, C to F a 4th, C to G a 5th, C to A a 6th, and C to B a 7th (example 5–1a). When speaking of the numerical distance from C to C (the second C is a duplication of the first in a higher register), we use the term octave rather than the number 8. The abbreviation for octave is 8ve.

When two or more musicians perform the same pitch in the same register, the terms unison or prime are used to designate the interval. If two pitches occur simultaneously, then the interval is called a harmonic interval. Example 1–45a illustrates some of the harmonic intervals that may exist within the range of a single C octave; intervals no larger than an octave are called simple intervals.

Example 1–45b demonstrates what happens if the upper pitch of each pair of simple intervals is moved into the next higher octave; this action produces what are referred to as compound intervals, intervals exceeding the span of an octave. To determine the numerical designation for a compound interval, add the number 7 to its simple intervallic counterpart: 2+7 becomes a 9th, 3+7 a 10th, 4+7 an 11th, 5+7 a 12th, 6+7 a 13th, 7+7 a 14th, and 8+7 a 15th. Since the top pitch of the octave duplicates the bottom pitch, we add 7 rather than 8 to the simple interval in order to avoid counting the same pitch twice.

Example 1–45: harmonic intervals

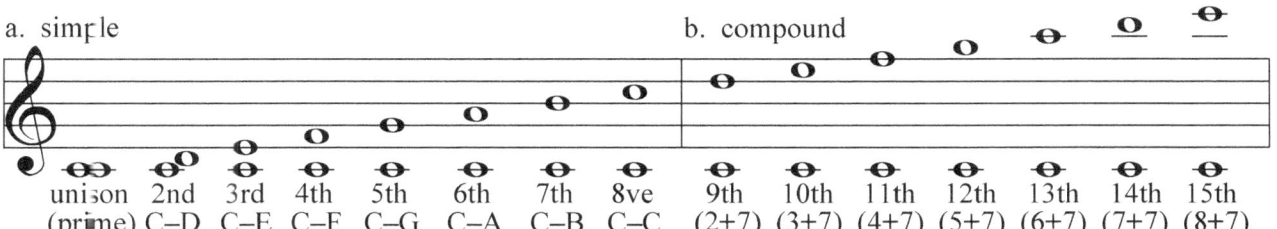

If two pitches occur in succession, then the interval is called a melodic interval. Example 1–46 demonstrates two different types of melodic succession between adjacent pitches, namely, conjunct motion and disjunct motion. Conjunct motion involves movement between pitches that are either a half step or whole step apart, whereas disjunct motion occurs when movement between pitches is greater than a whole step. Another term for conjunct motion is melodic motion. In Example 1–46, the distance between the bottom C and the upper pitches of each melodic interval becomes increasingly larger until the octave is reached.

Example 1–46: melodic intervals

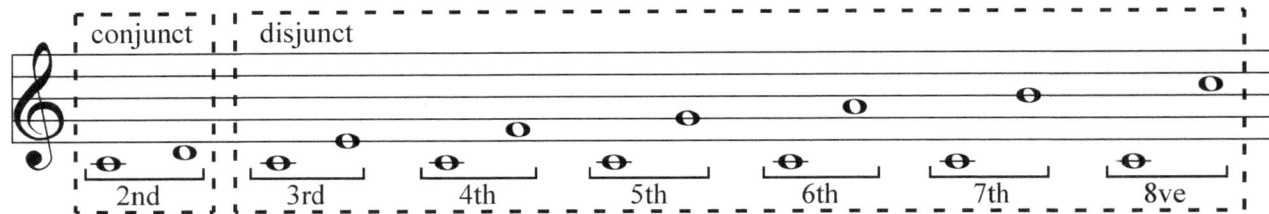

The Essential Diatonic Intervals of Major

In order to recognize and calculate the exact distance between two pitches, you must understand the intervallic relationships between scale degree 1 and all of the other scale degrees of the major mode. As stated above, the numerical size of an interval in major can be determined by counting the pitch names between the bottom note and each note above it.

Intervals can be measured not only in terms of their numerical value but also according to their quality. "Perfect," "major," "minor," "diminished," "doubly diminished," "augmented," and "doubly augmented" are all qualitative descriptions applied to the distance between two pitches. Doubly diminished and doubly augmented intervals are far less common than the other five varieties; however, you will encounter them if your study of music theory continues beyond the purview of music fundamentals and basic harmony.

In C major, the intervals formed between scale degree 1 and the diatonic scale degrees that occur above scale degree 1 are described as either major or perfect. Major and perfect intervals are the two categories of "essential diatonic intervals" from which all invervallic relationships are determined; and when we move these intervals to keys other than C major, such as G major, the same numerical and qualitative relationships are preserved.

If, as shown in example 1–47, the interval's numerical distance from scale degree 1 is a 2nd, 3rd, 6th, or 7th, *and* if the top note of the interval is part of the scale (and therefore part of its key signature), then the quality of the interval is always major in a major mode. Moreover, the term major can be applied only to 2nds, 3rds, 6ths, and 7ths.

If the interval's numerical distance from scale degree 1 is a 4th, 5th, octave, or even a unison, *and* if the top note of the interval is part of the scale, then the quality of the interval is always perfect in a major mode (a perfect unison, however, does not have a top note since both pitches of the interval are identical). The term perfect can be applied only to 4ths, 5ths, octaves, and unisons.

Example 1–47: the essential diatonic intervals in C major

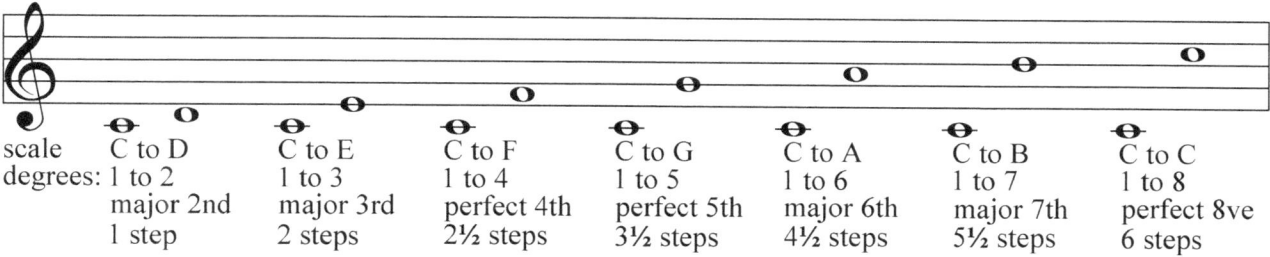

```
scale      C to D     C to E     C to F     C to G     C to A     C to B     C to C
degrees:   1 to 2     1 to 3     1 to 4     1 to 5     1 to 6     1 to 7     1 to 8
           major 2nd  major 3rd  perfect 4th perfect 5th major 6th major 7th perfect 8ve
           1 step     2 steps    2½ steps   3½ steps   4½ steps   5½ steps   6 steps
```

Two Principles for Recognizing and Constructing the Qualities of Intervals

In the foregoing section, we stated that if the bottom note of an interval is scale degree 1 of a major scale and if the top note of the interval coincides with a diatonic scale degree of the scale, then the quality of the interval is either major or perfect. The coincidence of the top note of the interval with a diatonic scale degree is the *first principle* for recognizing and constructing the qualities of intervals.

The *second principle*, referred to here as the re-sizing principle, is applied when the top note does not appear as a diatonic scale degree above scale degree 1. As demonstrated in example 1–48 below, the re-sizing principle uses the following qualitative terms: minor, diminished, doubly diminished, augmented, and doubly augmented. Accordingly,

(1) decreasing the size of a perfect interval by one half step produces a diminished interval (1–48a);
(2) reducing the size of diminished interval by one half step gives us a doubly diminished interval;
(3) a perfect interval increased in size by one half step becomes an augmented interval;
(4) expanding the size of any augmented interval by one half step results in a doubly augmented interval;
(5) decreasing the size of a major interval by one half step yields a minor interval (1–48b);
(6) reducing the size of a minor interval by one half step creates a diminished interval; and,
(7) a major interval increased in size by one half step becomes an augmented interval.

Example 1–48: the re-sizing principle

   a. re-sizing perfect intervals (principle two)

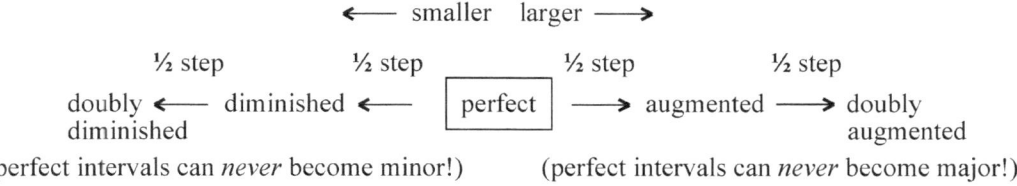

   b. re-sizing major intervals (principle two)

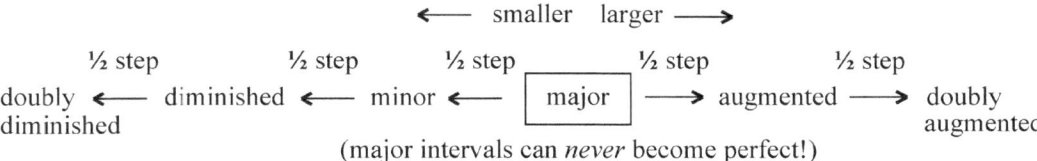

30   Chapter 1   A Review of Fundamentals

And so, to calculate the quality of an interval, evaluate the lower note as scale degree 1 of a major mode, if the top note coincides with a diatonic scale degree of that mode (based upon the mode's half-step profile and key signature), then according to principle one, the quality is either major or perfect. If, however; the top note does not constitute a diatonic scale degree of a major mode, then determine the quality according to the re-sizing principle as put forward in 1–48 above.

Let us consider some of the intervals that may occur when the diatonic pitches above scale degree 1 are either raised or lowered by one half step with the addition of either a sharp or flat. You will notice that these alterations produce minor, diminished, and augmented qualities (example 1–49).

All qualitative descriptions of intervals take the following abbreviations: major as M, minor as m, diminished as d, and augmented as A. Uppercase and lowercase letters are used to distinguish between intervallic qualities. The filled-in note heads without stems in the example do not represent specific durational values.

Example 1–49: producing minor, diminished, and augmented intervals above C

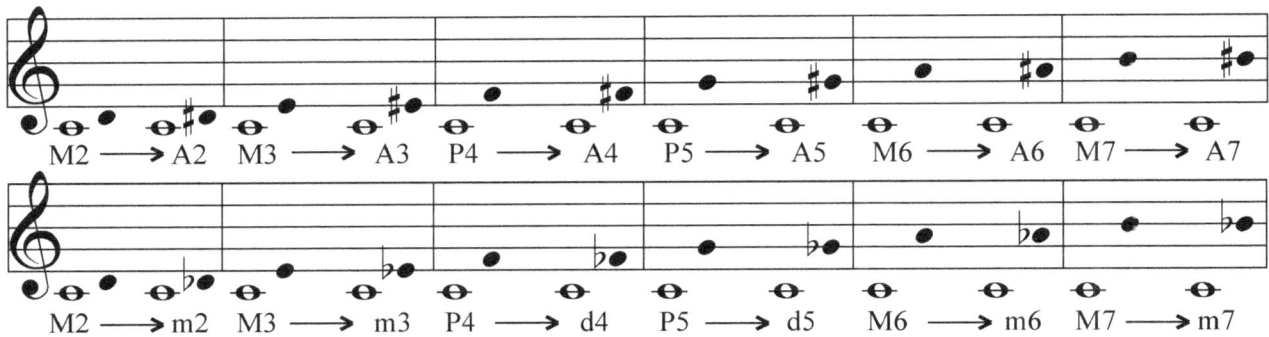

The Principle of Like Inflection

An inflection is a note that has been altered with the addition of an accidental. If both pitches of an interval are inflected equally in the same direction, upwards or downwards, then the quality of the interval does not change. This phenomenon may be referred to as "the principle of like inflection." The only aspect of the interval that does change is that it occurs at a higher or lower pitch level depending on whether sharps or flats are used. Example 1–50 illustrates this fact.

Example 1–50: the principle of like inflection

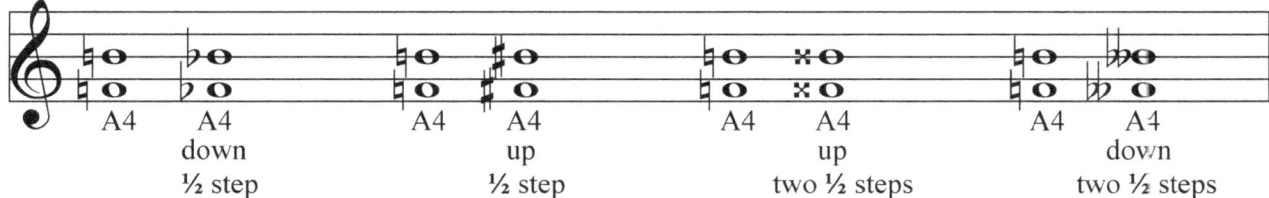

Compound Intervals

Earlier in this chapter, we learned that intervals may exceed the span of an octave. As shown in example 1–51b, the numerical designation for a compound interval is determined by adding the number 7 to its simple intervallic counterpart. Although the numerical designation of a compound interval changes, its qualitative description does not. All minor intervals remain minor in their compound forms, major intervals remain major, perfect intervals remain perfect, diminished intervals remain diminished, and augmented intervals remain augmented. Thus, a major 2nd becomes a major 9th, a major 3rd becomes a major 10th, a perfect 4th becomes a perfect 11th, a perfect 5th becomes a perfect 12th, a major 6th becomes a major 13th, a major 7th becomes a major 14th, and a perfect octave becomes a perfect 15th.

Example 1–51

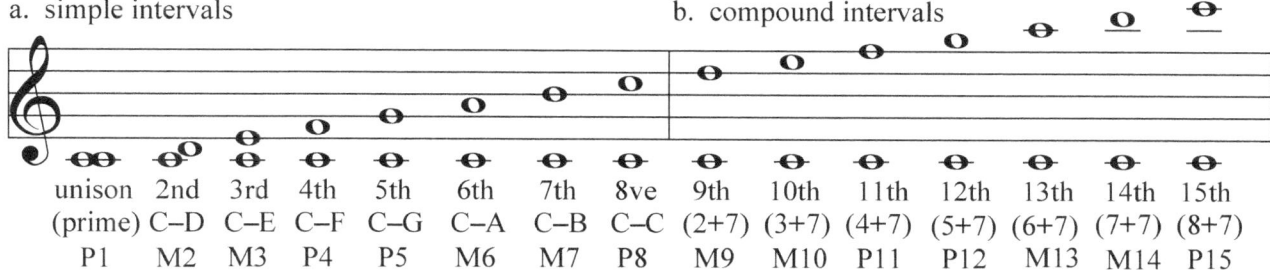

Interval Inversion

What happens to the numerical distance and quality of a simple interval when its two pitches are turned upside down or flipped, that is, when either the bottom note of the simple interval is placed one octave higher to become the top note or the top note is moved one octave lower to become the bottom note? Intervals that undergo this type of alteration are said to be inverted.

Using C major as our reference key and mode, let us consider the inversions of intervals in example 1–52a. Notice that when c^1 is moved one octave higher into the c^2 register, the unison (or prime) becomes an octave, the 2nd a 7th, the 3rd a 6th, the 4th a 5th, the 5th a 4th, the 6th a 3rd, the 7th a 2nd, and the octave a unison. If you add the pair of numbers that the interval and its inversion represent, the sum is always nine: 1+8=9, 2+7=9, 3+6=9, 4+5=9, 5+4=9, 6+3=9, 7+2=9, and 8+1=9. As indicated in 1–52b, perfect intervals (P) remain perfect upon inversion, whereas major intervals (M) become minor (m).

Example 1–52

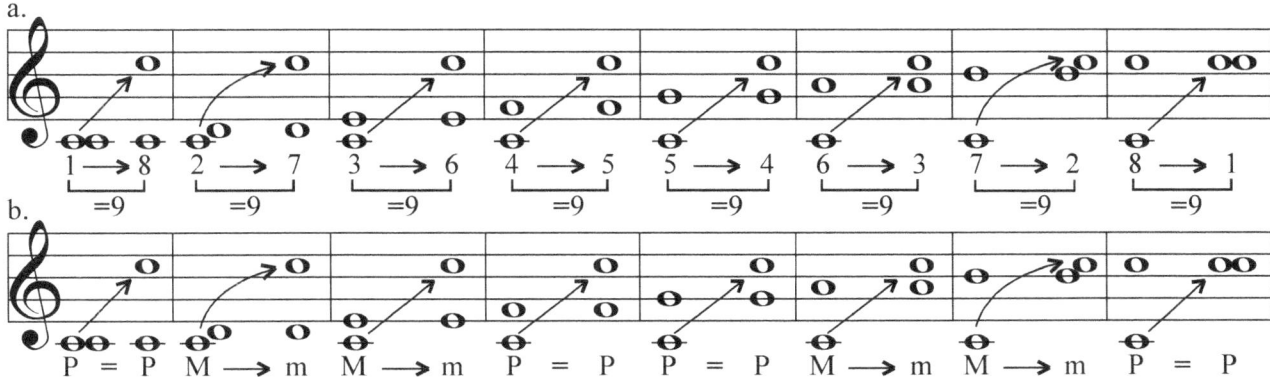

Example 1–53 summarizes the numerical and qualitative changes that occur when an interval is inverted. Note carefully that upon inversion, diminished intervals become augmented and augmented intervals become diminished.

Example 1–53

Upon inversion:

the unison (prime) becomes an octave	1 → 8 (= 9)	
the 2nd becomes a 7th	2 → 7 (= 9)	Therefore,
the 3rd becomes a 6th	3 → 6 (= 9)	upon inversion:
the 4th becomes a 5th	4 → 5 (= 9)	
the 5th becomes a 4th	5 → 4 (= 9)	P1 → P8 → P1
the 6th becomes a 3rd	6 → 3 (= 9)	M2 → m7 → M2
the 7th becomes a 2nd	7 → 2 (= 9)	M3 → m6 → M3
the octave becomes a unison	8 → 1 (= 9)	P4 → P5 → P4
		P5 → P4 → P5
Upon inversion:		M6 → m3 → M6
		M7 → m2 → M7
perfect intervals remain perfect	P = P	P8 → P1 → P8
major intervals become minor	M → m	
minor intervals become major	m → M	A4 → d5 → A4
diminished intervals become augmented	d → A	d5 → A4 → d5
augmented intervals become diminished	A → d	

Consonance and Dissonance

The distinction between consonance and dissonance in music is a means by which intervals are classified according to whether they are perceived by listeners as either stable or unstable. Consonant intervals exhibit a feeling of rest while dissonant intervals exude a sense of tension. Dissonant intervals usually seek to form connections to consonant intervals in a process known as resolution. Traditionally, dissonances resolve to consonances. When a dissonant interval is resolved to a consonance, a feeling of relaxation is produced. Resolutions of dissonance endow most of the tonal music of the Western tradition with a sense of forward motion, as the alternation between tension and relaxation propels the music ever forward.

There are two classes of consonant intervals, perfect consonances and imperfect consonances. The perfect consonances are the unison, the perfect octave, the perfect 5th, and *sometimes the perfect 4th*. The imperfect consonances consist of both major and minor 3rds and 6ths. The dissonant intervals include 2nds, 7ths, the augmented 4th, diminished 5th, and *sometimes the perfect 4th*.

The diminished 5th and the augmented 4th are notable for their sound and construction. Both intervals are often referred to as the tritone because each of its forms consists of three whole tones (i.e., three whole steps). The tritone stands exactly in the middle of the octave, dividing it in half. The sound of the tritone remains the same when it inverts because it always consists of three whole tones. The only change that occurs with the inversion of the tritone is within the context its numerical size: 4ths always invert to become 5ths and *vice versa*.

Of all the consonant and dissonant intervals, the status of the perfect 4th, depends on its position within the musical texture. If the perfect 4th occurs between the lowest note of the musical texture, called the bass (pronounced bās), and an upper note, then the interval is treated as a dissonance (example 1–54a). If, however, the perfect 4th does not occur between the bass and an upper note, then the interval is consonant (1–54b).

Therefore, the consonant perfect 4th is a 4th that occurs between two pitches above the bass; neither of the two upper pitches form the interval of a 4th with the bass. Example 1–54 illustrates the difference between the consonant and dissonant 4th. The brackets show the two pitches that form the interval of the perfect 4th. Notice that both the consonant and the dissonant 4th can appear as either a simple or compound interval (a perfect 11th).

Example 1–54

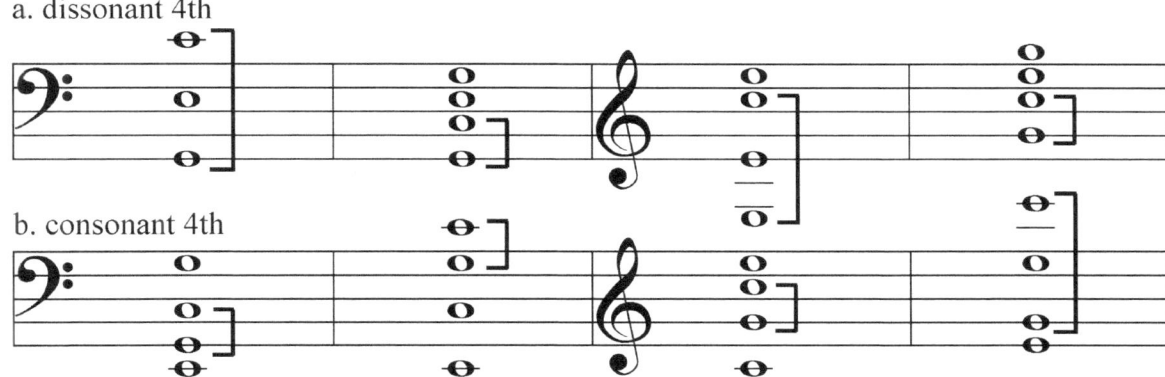

The Minor Mode

The major mode is not the only mode in music that has a tonal center; however, its profile of half steps and whole steps distinguishes major from the profiles of other diatonic modes.

In major, certain scale degrees are relatively stable while other scale degrees are relatively unstable. That is to say, some scale degrees seek to move to other scale degrees while some scale degrees have less of a tendency to move. Scale degrees 1, 3, 5, and 8 are comparatively stable and can be referred to as rest tones. The scale degrees between the rest tones, scale degrees 2, 4, 6, and 7, are unstable; the unstable scale degrees seek to move to one of the more stable rest tones. The unstable scale degrees shall be called active tones.

Scale degree 2 usually moves to either scale degrees 1 or 3, scale degree 4 to either 3 or 5, and scale degree 6 to either 5 or 7. If scale degree 6 proceeds to 7, the leading tone, then the motion frequently continues upwards to the tonic note (8). It is important to understand the relatively unstable nature of active tones because their tendency to attach themselves to the more stable rest tones accounts for some of the melodic patterns that occur in both the major and minor modes. In this text, we refer to the major and minor modes collectively as the major-minor tonal system.

The Natural Minor Mode

The minor mode has three forms, the harmonic minor, the melodic minor, and the natural minor, which is also known as the pure minor and the Aeolian mode (for a discussion of the Aeolian mode and the other modes that have Greek names, see Chapter 2). The natural minor can be located on the piano keyboard by finding the A octave in any register. As shown in example 1–55, the natural minor in the A octave consists of white keys only; no black keys are involved and no pitches inflected. Since the pitches E to F and B to C constitute the only two places within the octave where there are half steps between two adjacent white keys, the combined distribution of whole steps and half steps across the A octave produces a profile of half steps between scale degrees 2 and 3 and scale degrees 5 and 6.

Example 1–55

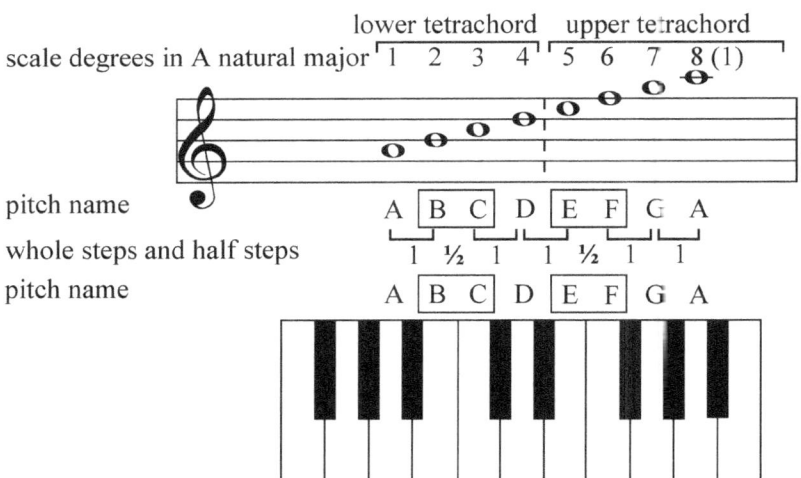

The natural minor takes from the major mode the names of the tonic, supertonic, mediant, subdominant, dominant, and submediant to designate scale degrees 1, 2, 3, 4, 5, and 6 respectively. Scale degree 7, however, is a special case. Unlike the major mode, the natural minor contains a whole step rather than a half step between scale degrees 7 and 8. Scale degree 7 of the natural minor is called the subtonic in order to distinguish it from the leading tone of the major mode. The natural minor does not share the major mode's compelling drive to move upwards by half step from scale degree 7 to scale degree 8. It is therefore more difficult to define and hear the tonic of the natural minor. The presence of the subtonic note may well be the natural minor's most distinctive feature. (In Chapter 2, however, we shall encounter other modes that also have the subtonic scale degree.)

Following the method introduced earlier for describing major and minor intervals, we use lowercase letters when referring to the tonic of any minor mode. Therefore, the minor mode in the A octave will be written as "a minor" rather than as "A minor" (and pronounced as ā minor, not ă minor). On the other hand, major keys such as C major, F♯ major, and D♭ major use uppercase letters.

The Relative Minor

Since no black keys are involved in the construction of a minor, its key signature is identical to that of C major. Having neither sharps nor flats, both modes possess exactly the same pitch content and therefore *share the same key signature* (example 1–56). The principal differences between C major and a minor are their tonics and ranges. C major's scale degree 1 is C; its range extends across the C octave. Scale degree 1 of a minor is A; its range falls within the A octave.

Despite these differences, the common pitch content between C major and a minor constitutes an important *relationship* between the two modes. Indeed, within the context of C major, a minor is described as the relative minor key area of C major. The relative minor key area always occurs on scale degree 6 of the corresponding major mode.

Example 1–56

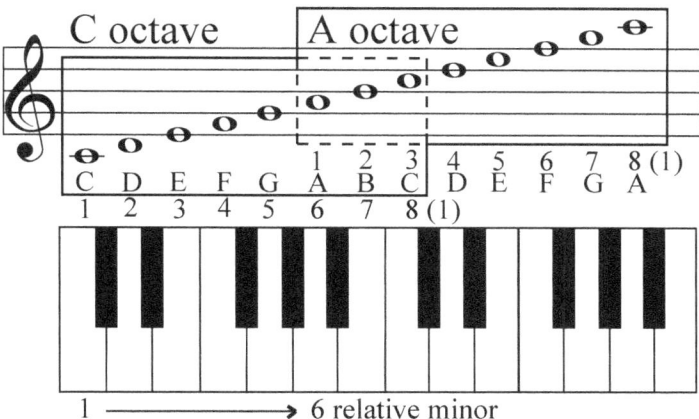

Each of the fourteen transpositions of C major has a relative minor. To find the relative minor of any transposed major mode, transpose the relationship between C major and a minor. In other words, locate scale degree 6 of any transposed major mode and that pitch will be the relative minor key area. For example, what is the relative minor key of G major? Scale degree 6 of G major is E. Therefore, e minor is the relative minor of G major; and both modes have one sharp (F♯) in their key signatures.

Another way to find the relative minor of any transposed major mode is to recognize that scale degree 6 is always a major 6th above the tonic note. Also, remember that the inversion of a major 6th is a minor 3rd (see example 1–53 above); accordingly, we can find the relative minor of any major mode by proceeding either up a major 6th *or* down a minor 3rd from the tonic note. Either direction from scale degree 1 leads to scale degree 6.

The Parallel Minor and the Parallel Major

In the foregoing paragraphs, we saw how major and minor modes standing in a relative relationship to one another share the same key signature (and therefore the same pitch content) but always have different tonics and different ranges. Another type of modal relationship involves two modes that have different key signatures but share the same tonic and the same range.

Because both modes have the same tonic note, they are considered to be *parallel* to one another. Every major mode has a parallel minor mode, every minor mode a parallel major. Using C as scale degree 1, examples 1–57a and 57b illustrate the differences and the similarities between two parallel modes.

Example 1–57

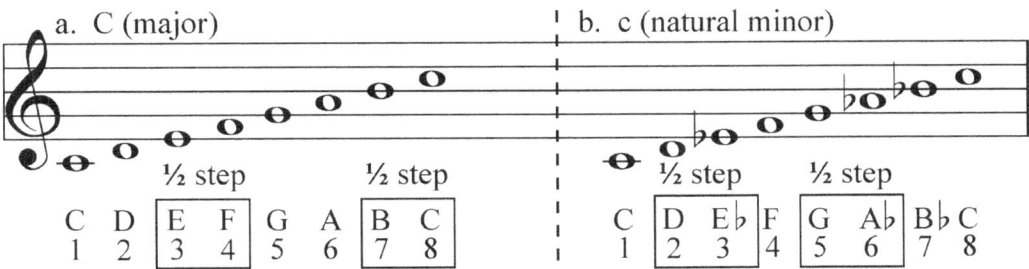

Example 1–57b above presents the scale formation for the natural minor within the C octave. Since C is the tonic, the mode must include an E♭, A♭, and B♭ (scale degrees 3, 6, and 7) in order to preserve the profile of half steps between scale degrees 2 and 3 and scale degrees 5 and 6. On the other hand, C major maintains its profile of half steps with E♮, A♮, and B♮.

The Relative Major

Although it is possible to construct the scale for the natural minor on any pitch and add the appropriate accidentals to preserve its half-step profile, there is a faster and easier way to find the accidentals that comprise the key signature for the minor mode. In the preceding section, we noted that every major mode has a parallel minor and every minor a parallel major. And just as every major mode has a relative minor, every minor mode has a relative major.

To find the relative major, proceed to scale degree 3 of the minor mode by counting up a minor 3rd from the minor mode's tonic pitch. Once you have located the relative major, its key signature will provide the pitch content and the key signature for the natural minor (see example 1–58b, A up to C is a minor 3rd).

Examples 1–58a and 58b show the various options for finding relative major and minor key areas. We know that the relative minor of a major mode can be found by counting either up a major 6th or down a minor 3rd from the major mode's tonic pitch (1–58a). Similarly, it is possible to locate the relative major key area of any minor mode by counting either down a major 6th *or* up a minor 3rd from the minor mode's tonic pitch (1–58b).

Example 1–58

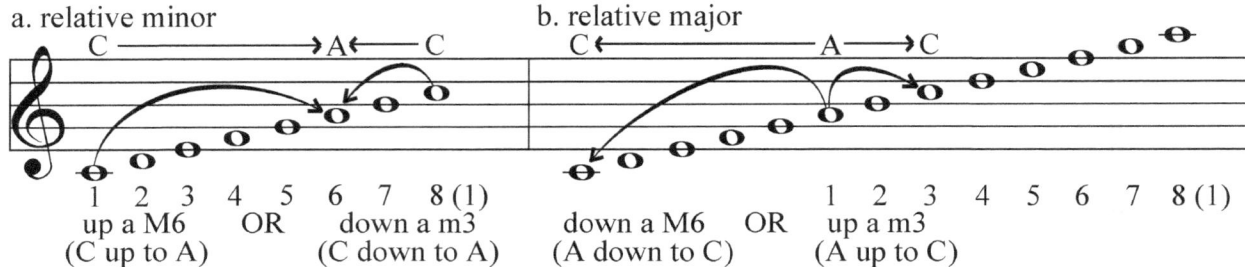

To summarize parallel and relative modal relationships: any two modes that stand in a parallel relationship to one another will share the same tonic pitch and range but have different key signatures. Any two modes that stand in a relative relationship to one another will share the same key signature but have different tonics and different ranges. Scale degree 6 of the major mode is the relative minor key area. Scale degree 3 of the natural minor is the relative major key area.

The Circle of 5ths for Minor

Earlier in this chapter, we assembled a group of ascending and descending perfect 5ths to form a circle of 5ths for the major mode (see example 1–40 above), a circle that has a sharp side of ascending perfect 5ths and a flat side of descending perfect 5ths. Three of the keys located in the lower portion of the circle (D♭ and C♯, G♭ and F♯, and C♭ and B) constitute enharmonic keys that close the circle of 5ths and bring the sharp and flat sides of major together.

The minor mode also has a circle of 5ths (example 1–59) and it is organized in exactly the same way as the circle of 5ths for the major mode. As with the major mode, the minor mode has fifteen key and scale formations, seven with sharps, seven with flats, and the key of a minor, which has neither sharps nor flats.

On the sharp side of minor, the circle begins with a minor and ascends in perfect 5ths through the keys of e, b, f♯, c♯, g♯, d♯, and a♯, increasing by one the number of sharps for each successive key. Similarly, on the flat side of minor, the circle begins on a minor and descends in perfect 5ths through d, g, c, f, b♭, e♭, and a♭. Three pairs of enharmonic keys located in the lower position of the circle, namely, b♭ and a♯, e♭ and d♯, and a♭ and g♯, close the circle of 5ths and bring the sharp and the flat sides of minor together.

Example 1–59: the sharp and flat sides of minor in the circle of 5ths

The Harmonic Minor Mode

The harmonic minor and the natural minor are almost identical—except for one *very* important difference. The natural minor employs the subtonic, which is one whole step below the tonic. The harmonic minor, on the other hand, borrows the leading tone from the parallel major; which in effect raises the subtonic by one half step and produces a half step between scale degrees 7 and 8 (examples 1–60a and 60b).

The harmonic minor's use of the leading tone (instead of the natural minor's subtonic scale degree) intensifies the melodic motion upwards to the tonic note. Moreover, the drive upwards by half step from scale degree 7 to scale degree 8 helps to firmly establish the key center. Conversely, the subtonic scale degree lacks the leading tone's compelling drive to move upwards by half step to the tonic; thus, as we have said, the key center is more clearly defined in those modes that employ the leading tone and more difficult to hear in modes that have subtonics, such as the natural minor.

Example 1–60: the harmonic minor and its parallel major

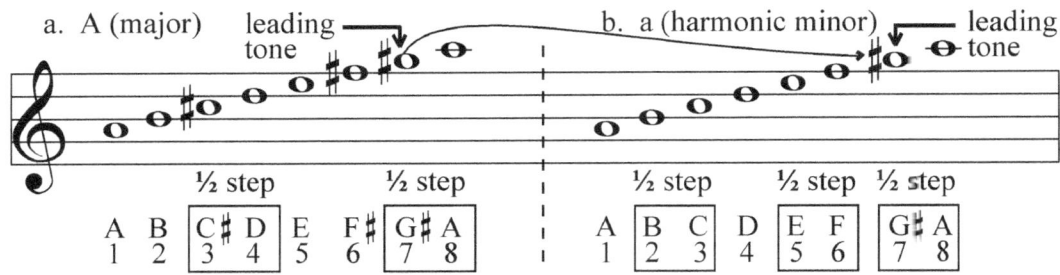

The harmonic minor retains all of the pitch content of the natural minor *except* for the incorporation of the major mode's leading tone. This one difference, however, produces a very unusual mode and scale. First, the harmonic minor has half steps between scale degrees 2 and 3, scale degrees 5 and 6, and scale degrees 7 and 8—a mode and scale with three pairs of half steps. Secondly, by raising the subtonic one half step to produce a half step approach to scale degree 8, an augmented 2nd (1½ steps) is created between scale degrees 6 and 7 (see example 1–61a below). The augmented 2nd is far more difficult to sing than either the major or minor 2nd.

Finally, the leading tone of the harmonic minor is never indicated in the key signature for the minor mode. Notably, both the harmonic minor and the melodic minor base their key signatures on the pitch content of the natural minor, despite the fact that both modes have tones that do not occur in the natural minor.

The Melodic Minor Mode

The melodic minor contains elements of the major mode and the natural minor. The melodic minor arises from two important factors:
(1) the inherent tendency of active tones to move to more stable rest tones; and,
(2) the preference of composers to create conjunct (i.e., stepwise) melodic structures that avoid awkward intervals such as the augmented 2nd.

The Ascending Form of the Melodic Minor

When a melody in the harmonic minor moves upwards towards scale degree 8, composers usually raise scale degree 6 by one half step in order to eliminate the augmented 2nd that would otherwise occur between scale degrees 6 and 7 (example 1–61).

Example 1–61

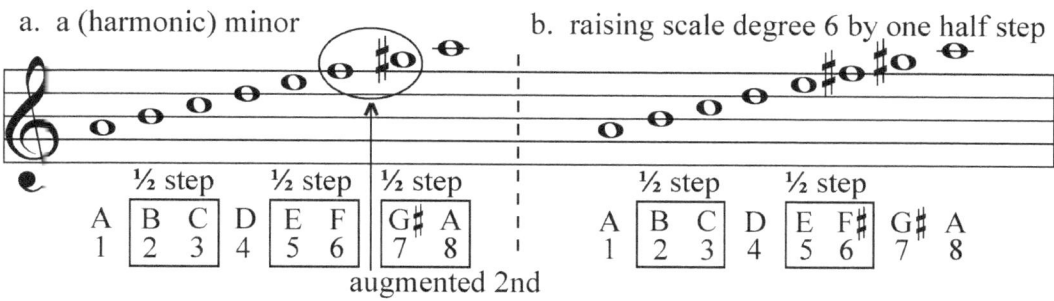

Raising scale degree 6 by one half step to avoid the augmented 2nd of the harmonic minor results in an upper tetrachord with a profile of half steps and whole steps that is identical to the upper tetrachord of the major mode, that is: whole step, whole step, half step (example 1–62). Borrowing the upper tetrachord of the major mode produces what is referred to as the "ascending" form of the melodic minor. Whenever the melodic activity of a composition written in the minor mode moves upwards in the direction of scale degree 8, the ascending form of the melodic minor is usually preferred.

Notice that the key signature for c minor in the second measure of example 1–62 has three flats but that an A♮ (rather than an A♭) is used to avoid the augmented 2nd that would occur in the harmonic minor between scale degrees 6 and 7 (A♭ to B♮). Henceforth, we refer to scale degrees 6 and 7 as "raised 6" and "raised 7" when the ascending melodic minor is used. The symbols for raised 6 and raised 7 are ♯6 and ♯7.

Example 1–62: borrowing the upper tetrachord of major to produce the ascending melodic minor

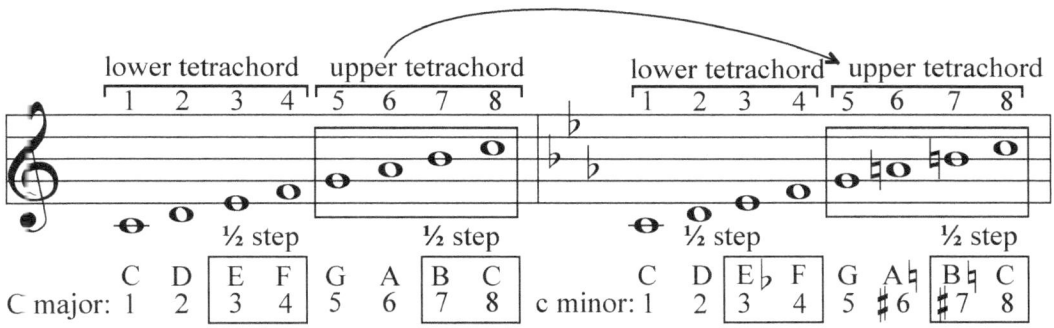

The use of the sharp (♯) in front of the number does not necessarily mean that the pitch itself carries a sharp. Indeed, in 1–62 above, the pitches for ♯6 and ♯7 are A♮ and B♮. It is central to our understanding of the minor mode to recognize that scale degrees ♯6 and ♯7 are not reflected in the minor key signature. If, therefore, a composition is written in a key such as c minor, which has three flats in its key signature (B♭, E♭, and A♭), the music will probably also include an A♮ and/or a B♮, particularly when the melody moves upwards towards scale degree 8. And so, when reading music in the minor mode, it would be well to expect that tones representing scale degrees ♯6 and ♯7 are likely to appear and that their presence will contradict the implied pitch content of the key signature.

The Descending Form of the Melodic Minor

If the minor mode descends towards scale degree 5, scale degrees 6 and 7 are each lowered by one half step from their raised counterparts, scale degrees ♯6 and ♯7. Lowering scale degrees 6 and 7 produces what is called the "descending" melodic minor (example 1–63). We call the lowered forms of scale degrees 6 and 7 "lowered 6" and "lowered 7" to distinguish them from their raised counterparts, scale degrees ♯6 and ♯7. The symbols for lowered 6 and lowered 7 are ♭6 and ♭7. Notably, the pitch content of the descending form of the melodic minor is identical to that of the natural minor.

Let us consider the key of c minor in example 1–63 to see how the process of lowering scale degrees 6 and 7 works. The ascending form of the melodic minor in the key of c minor shows A♮ and B♮ as scale degrees ♯6 and ♯7. But when the c-minor scale moves down in the direction of scale degree 5 (G) in the descending form of the melodic minor, both the A♮ and B♮ are lowered by one half step to A♭ and B♭.

Example 1–63: the ascending and descending forms of the melodic minor

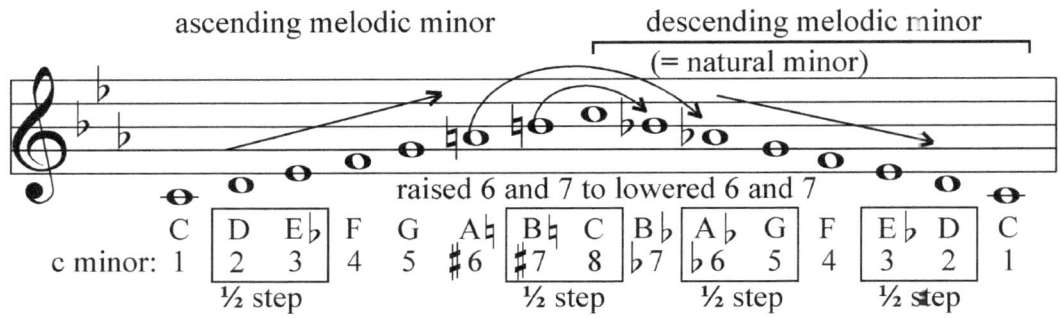

The use of scale degrees ♭6 and ♭7 intensifies the melodic motion downwards to scale degree 5 by creating a half-step approach from scale degree ♭6 to scale degree 5. We term scale degrees 6 and 7 raised or lowered and apply symbols to them (either ♯ or ♭) because on each of these scale degrees, the melodic minor has two different versions of the same letter name. For example, in c minor, scale degrees 6 and 7 may be either A♮ or A♭ and B♮ or B♭, according to whether the tones are either raised or lowered. The sharp or flat in front of the number merely indicates that there are two pitches with the same letter name and that one pitch is either raised or lowered *in relation to the other pitch*.

Having two versions of the same letter name, scale degrees 6 and 7 are *variable* tones in the melodic minor; we therefore refer to scale degrees 6 and 7 as "variable scale degree 6" and "variable scale degree 7." A more complete and specific verbal description of the variable scale degrees in the melodic minor would be as follows: "variable scale degree raised 6," "variable scale degree raised 7," "variable scale degree lowered 6," and "variable scale degree lowered 7."

It is important to understand that the flat (♭) in front of the number 6 and 7 does not necessarily mean that the pitch itself carries a flat. For example, compare the keys of c minor and a minor. In c minor (1–63 above), the lowered variables happen to take flats (A♭ and B♭), whereas in the key of a minor (example 1–64), the lowered variables do not carry flats (F♮ and G♮).

Example 1–64

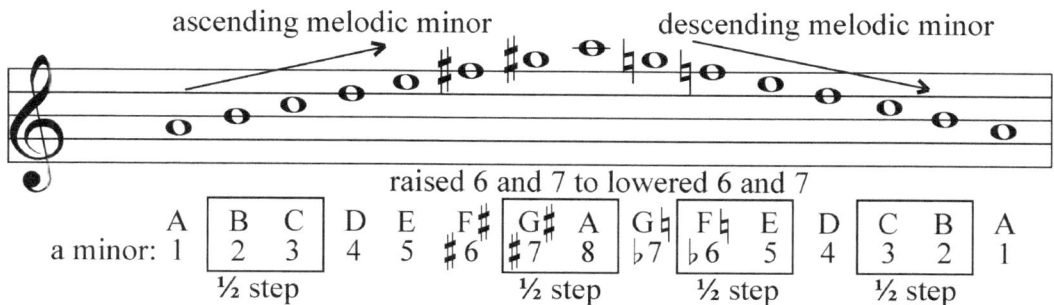

Finding the Variable Scale Degrees of the Melodic Minor

Variables ♯6, ♯7, ♭6, and ♭7 may be located in any key according to the following guidelines:
(1) ♭6 is one half step above scale degree 5 (and a minor 6th above scale degree 1).
(2) ♭7 is one whole step below scale degree 1 (and a minor 7th above scale degree 1).
(3) ♯6 is one whole step above scale degree 5 (and a major 6th above scale degree 1).
(4) ♯7 is one half step below scale degree 1 (and a major 7th above scale degree 1).
(5) ♭6 and ♭7 are one half step lower than ♯6 and ♯7.
(6) ♯6 and ♯7 are one half step higher than ♭6 and ♭7.
(7) ♯6 and ♯7 are *never* included in the key signature of the minor mode.
(8) ♭6 and ♭7 are *always* included in the key signature of the minor mode.
(9) ♯6 and ♯7 correspond to scale degrees 6 and 7 of the parallel major mode.
(10) The pitch content of the descending melodic minor is exactly the same as the natural minor.
(11) Since ♯6 and ♯7 of the melodic minor correspond to scale degrees 6 and 7 of the parallel major mode, ♯6 and ♯7 can be found easily if you know the key signature of that minor key's parallel major mode. For example: what are variables ♯6 and ♯7 in the key and mode of a minor?
   (a) The parallel major of a minor is A major, which has three sharps (F♯, C♯, and G♯).
   (b) Scale degrees 6 and 7 in A major are F♯ and G♯.
   (c) Therefore, variables ♯6 and ♯7 in the key and mode of a minor are also F♯ and G♯.

Triads

Since the ninth century of the Common Era in Western Europe, music makers have combined two or more musical tones together, creating sounds that are either pleasing or displeasing to the ear. The perception of what constitutes a good or bad combination of musical tones at any point in history changes over time. Moreover, the many diverse cultures of the world do not necessarily share the same musical values and therefore may have different opinions and beliefs regarding the qualities of musical sounds.

For example, someone accustomed to listening to the music of the Western European tradition might have difficulty appreciating the performance of *ganga* songs found in the mountainous regions of Bosnia and Herzegovina, which exhibit close combinations of tones, particularly the interval of the 2nd. The performers of *ganga* songs consider the sounds of 2nds to be pleasing to the ear; conversely, we in the West are more accustomed to the perceived richness of 3rds.

Earlier in this chapter, we learned that when two pitches occur simultaneously, the resulting sound is a harmonic interval. Any time two or more pitches occur simultaneously, it produces an effect known as harmony. When three or more *different* pitches sound simultaneously, the resulting harmony is called a chord.

Examples 1–65a, 65b, and 65c demonstrate three forms of harmony that assume chord status; in each instance, the chord has five different pitches and at least four intervals. The first type of chord, shown in 1–65a, is secundal; a secundal chord results from a combination of major and/or minor 2nds. (Although secundal harmonies must contain major and/or minor 2nds, they may also have 3rds.) Example 1–65b illustrates quartal harmony, a chord formation consisting of 4th intervals.

The most common harmonic construction to appear in the music of the Western European tradition and the one with which we are concerned here is tertian harmony. As illustrated in 1–65c, tertian chords have two or more superimposed 3rds. When notated on the staff, secundal and quartal harmonies involve a combination of spaces and lines. On the other hand, tertian harmonies (when positioned in a close structure on a single staff) are placed on either spaces or lines, rather than a combination of both.

The tertian harmony in 1–65c displays intervals of the 3rd, 5th, 7th, and 9th above the lowest pitch of the chord; so constructed, we have a chord of the ninth, or ninth chord (C E G B D). Removing the ninth produces a chord of the seventh, or seventh chord (C E G B).

Example 1–65

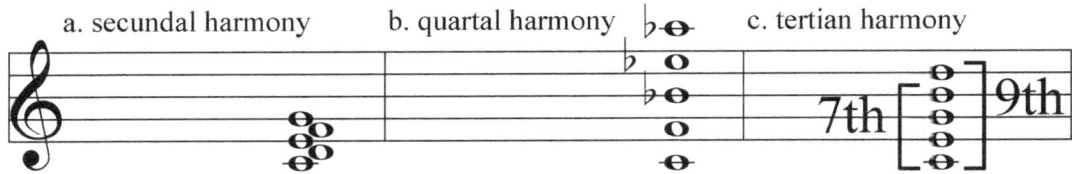

Tertian harmony has been an important component of Western music for more than five hundred years. As early as the fifteenth century, people in Western Europe began to have a decided preference for the interval of the 3rd and its inversion, the 6th. Today, chords built from the interval of the 3rd are still favored in nearly every style of music in the Western world.

When a tertian harmony contains three different pitches and two intervals of the 3rd, the chord is referred to as a triad. The triad in example 1–66 contains the pitches C, E, and G and has two 3rds formed above C, the lowest pitch of the musical texture and the foundation of the chord.

Example 1–66: the triad

The lowest pitch upon which the other two pitches of the triad are built is called the root. In example 1–67, C is identified as the root of the triad (R). The remaining tones of the triad, E and G, are known as the third (3) and the fifth (5) because they are located at the intervals of a 3rd and a 5th above the root. The triad in 1–67 is said to be in root position because the root is positioned as the lowest pitch of the musical texture.

Example 1–67: the components of the triad

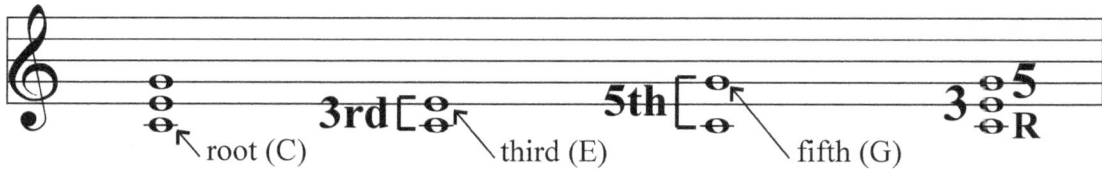

The triad derives its name from the root. For example, if the triad is built on the subdominant scale degree of the major mode (scale degree 4), then the chord would be termed the subdominant triad. Since there are seven tones in a major key and scale, it is possible to build a triad on each of these seven tones (see example 1–69 below).

Triad Quality

Triads, like intervals, may be classified according to their quality. There are four types of triad qualities: the major triad (MT), the minor triad (mt), the diminished triad (d°t), and the augmented triad (A+T). The quality of a triad is based upon the intervallic distance between the root and the third, the third and the fifth, and the root and the fifth.

Example 1–68 illustrates the configuration of intervals for the four triad qualities, all of which share the common tone C as the root. R – 3 represents the distance from the root to the third, 3 – 5 the distance from the third to the fifth, and R – 5 the distance from the root to the fifth. The superscript circle in the chord symbol d°t is a conventional sign for indicating diminished quality; it can be used with diminished chords and with diminished intervals (e.g., 5° or °5 = diminished 5th). The plus sign in the A+T chord symbol is the traditional designation for showing augmented quality; it appears in connection with augmented chords and with augmented intervals (e.g., 5+ or +5 = augmented 5th).

Example 1–68: the configuration of intervals for the four triad qualities rooted on C

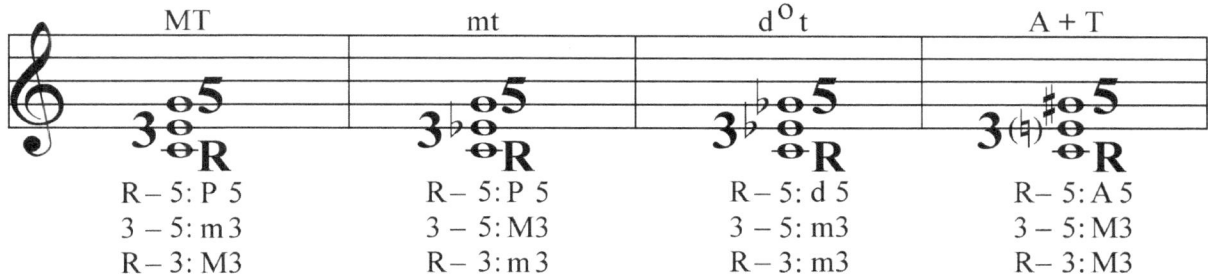

The major triad in example 1–68 contains a major 3rd from the root to the third (C to E) and a minor 3rd from the third to the fifth (E to G). Additionally, the chord has a perfect 5th from the root to the fifth (C to G). The minor triad has a minor 3rd from the root to the third (C to E♭), a major 3rd from the third to the fifth (E♭ to G), and a perfect 5th from the root to the fifth (C to G).

Although both major and minor triads are made up of a combination of major 3rds and minor 3rds, the internal configuration of 3rds in the minor triad is the reverse of that of the major triad. The ordering of thirds up from the root of the major triad is: M3/m3. The ordering of thirds up from the root of the minor triad is: m3/M3.

The diminished triad bears a similarity to the minor triad in that it has a minor 3rd from the root to the third (C to E♭). Instead of having a perfect 5th from the root to the fifth, however, the diminished triad has a diminished 5th from the root to the fifth (C to G♭). From the third to the fifth, the diminished triad has a minor 3rd (E♭ to G♭). Thus, the ordering of thirds up from the root of the diminished triad is: m3/m3.

The augmented triad, like the major triad, has a major 3rd from the root to the third (C to E). The distance from the root to the fifth of the augmented triad, however, is an augmented 5th (C to G♯), exceeding by one half step the perfect 5ths of the major and minor triads. From the third to the fifth, the augmented triad has a major third (E to G♯). The ordering of the thirds up from the root of the augmented triad is: M3/M3.

Triad Qualities in Major

In example 1–69, we return to the root-position triads constructed above each of the seven scale degrees of C major and identify the combinations of intervals in each chord. In C major, the major triad appears on the tonic (C E G), the subdominant (F A C), and the dominant (G B D), whereas the minor triad resides in the supertonic (D F A), the mediant (E G B), and the submediant (A C E). The diminished triad occurs in the scale degree area of the leading tone (B D F).

Notice that the diatonic pitch content of C major cannot support the formation of the augmented triad; therefore, the augmented triad cannot exist in any transposition of C major. Later in this chapter, however, we shall see that the augmented triad can be formed in the minor mode.

Example 1–69: triad qualities in C major

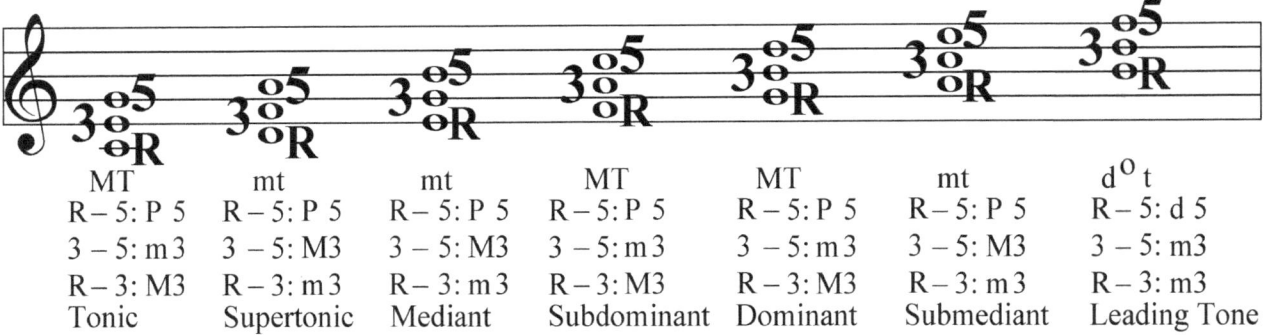

MT	mt	mt	MT	MT	mt	d°t
R–5: P 5	R–5: P 5	R–5: P 5	R–5: P 5	R–5: P 5	R–5: P 5	R–5: d 5
3–5: m3	3–5: M3	3–5: M3	3–5: m3	3–5: m3	3–5: M3	3–5: m3
R–3: M3	R–3: m3	R–3: m3	R–3: M3	R–3: M3	R–3: m3	R–3: m3
Tonic	Supertonic	Mediant	Subdominant	Dominant	Submediant	Leading Tone

Inverting Major, Minor, Diminished, and Augmented Triads

Triads are created from combinations of intervals, intervals of the 3rd in particular. The 3rd can be transformed into the interval of the 6th by placing the bottom note of the 3rd one octave higher (example 1–70a) or by moving the top note of the 3rd one octave lower to become the bottom note (1–70b).

Example 1–70: inverting the interval of the 3rd

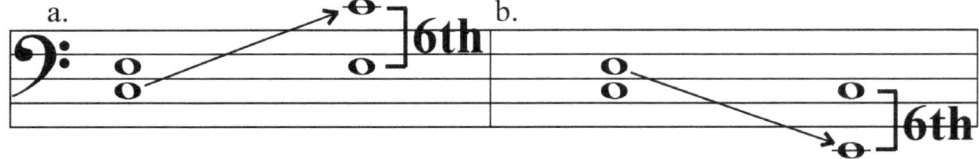

Example 1–71 shows how interval inversion changes the structure of the major triad in root position. Again, the two elements of the triad standing above the root are referred to respectively as the third and the fifth because they are located at the intervals of a 3rd and a 5th above the root. The three elements of the major triad in root position appear in the following order from the lowest to the highest pitch: root, third, and fifth.

Example 1–71a presents an alternative description for the intervallic structure of the root-position triad, designating the chord in "$^5_3$ position." The Arabic numbers indicate the placement of certain intervals and pitches (in this case, E and G) above the lowest note of the musical texture (C); the numbers are referred to as figured bass ("figuring" means counting the intervals and pitches up from the bass note).

In 1–71b, the first inversion of the major triad is displayed. Shifting the root of the major triad into the next higher octave leaves the third of the chord (E) as the bass pitch. The figured bass for the first inversion of the triad is $^6_3$, which means that the intervals of a 3rd (E to G) and a 6th (E to C) occur above the lowest note (E). The three elements of the major triad in first inversion appear in the following order from the lowest to the highest pitch: third, fifth, and root.

Example 1–71c illustrates the second inversion of the major triad. Moving the third component of the first-inversion triad up one octave leaves the fifth of the chord (G) in the bass. The figured bass for the second inversion of the triad is $^6_4$, which means that the intervals of a 4th (G to C) and a 6th (G to E) occur above the lowest note (G). The three elements of the major triad in second inversion appear in the following order from the lowest to the highest pitch: fifth, root, and third.

Example 1–71: the major triad in root position, first inversion, and second inversion

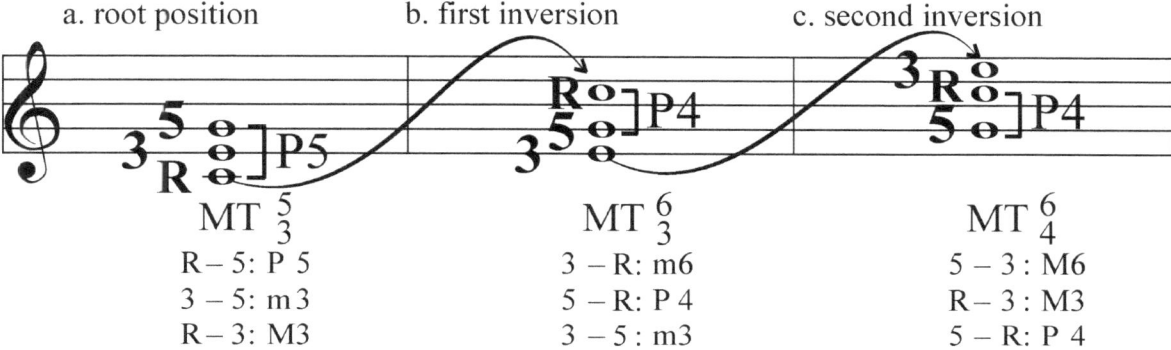

Example 1–72: the minor triad in root position, first inversion, and second inversion

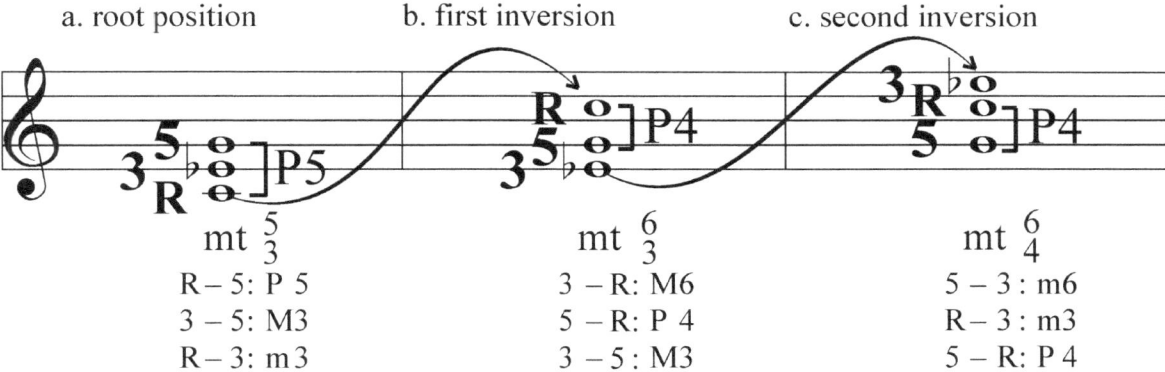

Remember that the only difference between a major triad and a minor triad with the same root is the middle component of each respective chord, the third. In the minor triad, the third is one half step lower than the corresponding third of the major triad. Raising the third of the minor triad by one half step produces a major triad.

The diminished triad (example 1–73a) has a diminished 5th between the root and the fifth (C to G♭). When the diminished triad inverts (examples 1–73b and 73c), the diminished 5th becomes an augmented 4th, as the root is placed above the fifth (G♭ to C). Two minor 3rds comprise the structure of the chord in root position. A minor 3rd occurs between the root and the third (C to E♭) and between the third and the fifth (E♭ to G♭).

Example 1–73: the diminished triad in root position, first inversion, and second inversion

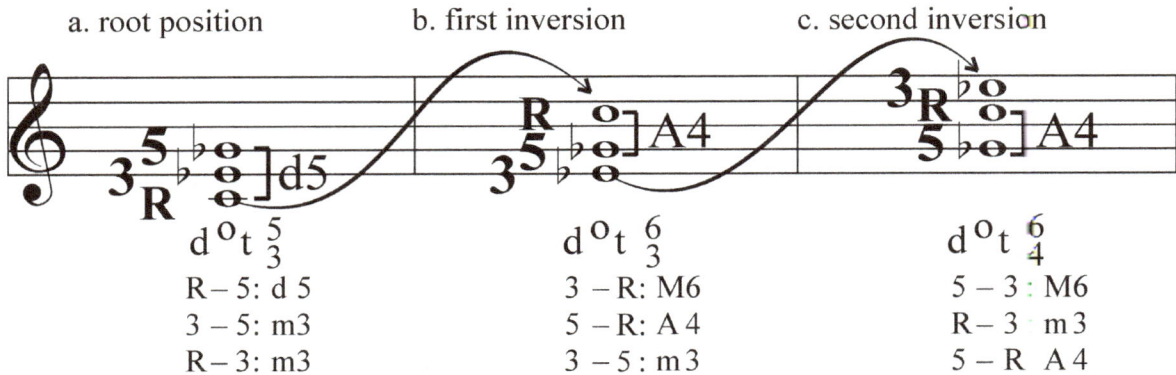

We know that the intervallic structures of the diminished triad and the minor triad are the same except for the distances between their respective roots and fifths. The minor triad has a perfect 5th from the root to the fifth, whereas the diminished triad has a diminished 5th from the root to the fifth.

There are also certain similarities between the intervallic structures of the augmented triad and the major triad. Both the augmented triad and the major triad are the same except for the distances between their respective roots and fifths. As we have seen, the distance from the root to the fifth of the major triad is a perfect 5th, whereas the distance from the root to the fifth of the augmented triad is an augmented 5th.

Example 1–74 shows the augmented triad in root position, first inversion, and second inversion. In 1–74a, which illustrates the root position of the chord, we have two major 3rds, one between the root and the third (C to E) and the other between the third and the fifth (E to G♯). When the augmented triad inverts, as demonstrated in examples 1–74b and 74c, the root is placed above the fifth, changing the augmented 5th between the root and the fifth (C to G♯) into a diminished 4th (G♯ to C).

Example 1–74: the augmented triad in root position, first inversion, and second inversion

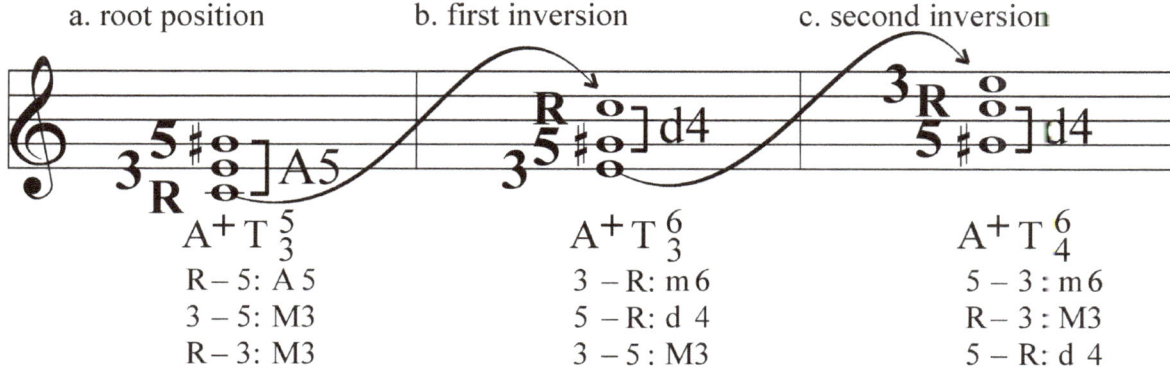

It should be understood that the diminished 4th between the fifth and the root of the augmented triad exists only within the *written context* of the chord because the *sound* of the diminished 4th is identical to that of another interval, the major 3rd. Therefore, the diminished 4th should be referred to properly as a contextual interval.

Although the diminished 4th and the major 3rd are both identifiable within the written context, the major 3rd may also be classified as an acoustic interval because it has only one aural interpretation—the major 3rd cannot be heard as a diminished 4th. The acoustical major 3rd from the fifth up to the root gives the augmented triad a neutral-sounding profile that precludes hearing the chord as an inverted structure. Regardless of its written position, the augmented triad sounds like two superimposed major 3rds. The augmented 5th (the inversion of the diminished 4th) is also a contextual interval because the *sound* of the augmented 5th is identical to that of another interval, the minor 6th.

Applying the Principle of Like Inflection to Triads

The principle of like inflection may be applied to any combination of intervals that produces triads and other chords. Thus, if C E G is a major triad, assigning a sharp or a flat to each pitch does not change the quality of the chord. In example 1–75, each pitch of the major triad on C is inflected equally, upwards (sharps) or downwards (flats).

Example 1–75

Triad Qualities in Minor

As we have said, the augmented triad cannot be formed in the major mode, nor can it appear in the natural minor. All four qualities of the triad do occur, however, in the other two forms of minor: the harmonic minor and the melodic minor. Since the melodic minor contains the most complete inventory of pitches of all three forms of minor, we shall use the melodic minor to demonstrate the formation of triads in the minor mode.

Example 1–76 shows the triads that occur in the ascending melodic minor. With the exception of the tonic triad (C E♭ G), all of the triads in the ascending melodic minor contain either variable ♯6 or variable ♯7 within their respective chord structures. The filled-in note heads in examples 1–76 and 77 designate the variable scale degrees as the root, third, or fifth of the triad.

Using ♯6 (A) as the fifth of the chord, a minor triad (D F A) is formed in the supertonic area. An augmented triad (E♭ G B) occurs in the mediant, with ♯7 (B) as the fifth of the chord. Variables ♯6 and ♯7 appear as third components of two major triads: the subdominant (F A C) and the dominant (G B D). Variables ♯6 and ♯7 constitute the roots of two diminished triads: the submediant (A C E♭) and the leading tone (B D F).

Example 1–76: ascending melodic minor

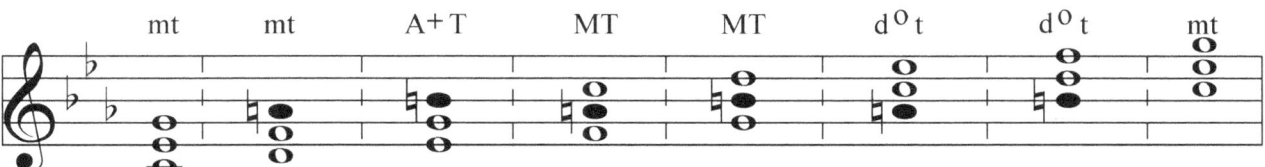

On the descending side of the melodic minor, as displayed in example 1–77, variable ♭7 (B♭) serves as the root of the major triad in the subtonic (B♭ D F) and as the fifth of the major triad in the mediant (E♭ G B♭); variable ♭6 (A♭) forms the root of the major triad in the submediant (A♭ C E♭). Excluding the tonic triad (C E♭ G), the descending melodic minor has two other minor triads, both of which contain a variable scale degree as an element of their chord structures. Variable ♭7 appears as the third of the minor dominant triad (G B♭ D); variable ♭6 constitutes the third of the minor subdominant triad (F A♭ C). Finally, variable ♭6 occurs as the fifth of the diminished supertonic triad (D F A♭).

Example 1–77: descending melodic minor

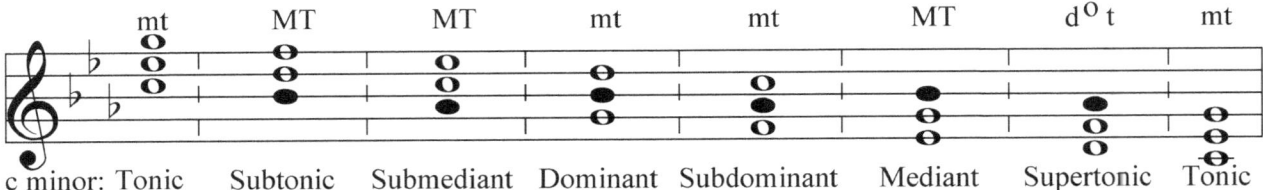

Example 1–78 incorporates elements of both the ascending and descending forms of the melodic minor into a single ascending scale that projects various chord qualities in each of its seven scale degree areas for a total of thirteen triads.

Example 1–78: the thirteen triads of the melodic minor

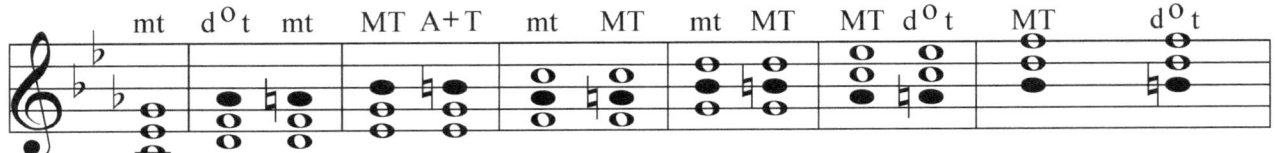

Roman Numeral Chord Symbols

We know that each note of the scale and mode can be referred to as a scale degree and assigned a number according to its position within the scale in relation to the tonic pitch, with the tonic identified as scale degree 1. Additionally, each scale degree has one of the following names: tonic, supertonic, mediant, subdominant, dominant, submediant, and leading tone. When scale degree 7 is located one whole step below the tonic note, as in the natural minor, we use the term subtonic to distinguish it from the leading tone of the major mode, the harmonic minor, and the ascending form of the melodic minor.

Ultimately, the numbers and names that represent the scale degrees of the mode constitute an important means for providing information about music; as such, the numbers and names are referential, serving as symbols for communication between those who create music and those who listen to and/or study it. Another method for providing information about music designates Roman numerals for the chords that can be formed on each scale degree of the mode; in other words, it is possible to represent each chord, or triad, with a Roman numeral according to the scale degree on which its root occurs. A longstanding convention of Roman numeral chord symbols maintains the following two practices:

(1) if the chord, or triad, has a major 3rd between the root and its third, then the Roman numeral is expressed in uppercase (e.g., major and augmented triads);

(2) if the chord, or triad, has a minor 3rd between the root and its third, then the Roman numeral is expressed in lowercase (e.g., minor and diminished triads).

In addition to using uppercase and lowercase Roman numerals to distinguish major and augmented triads from minor and diminished triads, augmented triads are further identified with a plus sign (+), diminished triads with a superscript circle ($^\circ$). As stated earlier, the plus sign is the traditional designation for showing augmented quality, while the superscript circle is a conventional sign for indicating diminished quality.

Example 1–79 presents the Roman numeral chord symbols for the triads that occur in the major mode. The three major triads are indicated as I, IV, and V, the minor triads as ii, iii, and vi, and the diminished triad as vii$^\circ$. When triads in both the major and minor modes invert, chord symbols and figured bass are combined. It is not necessary to attach figured bass to the chord symbol of a root-position triad. For a triad in $^6_3$ position, the 3 under the 6 is omitted. With the $^6_4$ position, however, the 4 below the 6 cannot be removed because the absence of the 4 would render the figured bass for the first and second inversions indistinguishable (examples of Roman numerals with figured bass in major are: vii$^{\circ 6}$, V$^6_4$, I^6, IV$^6_4$).

Example 1–79

C major: I   ii   iii   IV   V   vi   vii$^\circ$

Mastering the triadic content of the melodic minor constitutes a formidable challenge, as it has a much richer vocabulary of chords than either the major mode, the natural minor, or the harmonic minor. Example 1–80 revisits the thirteen triads that are formable above each scale degree of the melodic minor. The increased number of triads in the melodic minor is attributed to the presence of variable scale degrees 6 and 7 as either the root, third, or fifth elements of each chord (again, the filled-in note heads designate the variable scale degrees).

Except for the tonic triad, the basic quality for triads in the melodic minor is determined by the presence of a variable scale degree and identified with uppercase and lowercase Roman numerals and the addition of either the plus sign for the augmented triad or the superscript circle for the diminished triad. If the root of the triad is a variable scale degree, then the Roman numeral is preceded by either a flat or a sharp (1–80), just as the individual pitches for the variable scale degrees of the melodic minor are indicated as either ♯6 and ♯7 or ♭6 and ♭7.

As we have said, the use of a sharp or a flat in front of the variable scale degree does not necessarily mean that the pitch carries either a sharp or a flat; rather, the sharp or flat indicates that the pitch is either raised or lowered (see above, pp. 39–40). We apply the same principle to the flat or sharp in front of the Roman numeral. Thus, the major triads of the melodic minor are represented as III, IV, V, ♭VI, and ♭VII, the minor triads as i, ii, iv, and v, the diminished triads as ii$^\circ$, ♯vi$^\circ$, and ♯vii$^\circ$, and the augmented triad as III+ (examples of Roman numerals with figured bass in minor are: ♭VII$^6_4$, ii^6, ♯vi$^{\circ 6}$, i$^6_4$, V^6).

Example 1–80

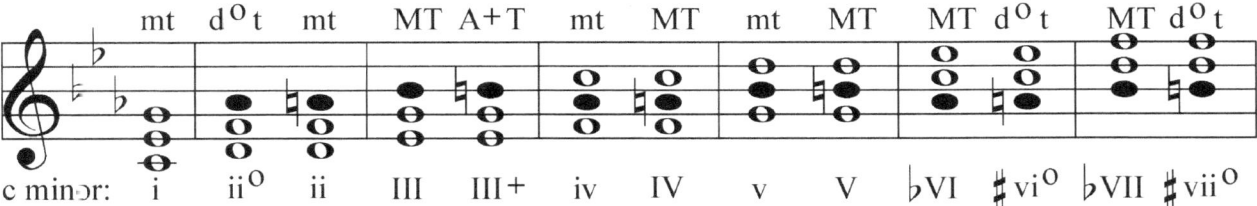

c minor: i   ii$^\circ$ ii   III   III+   iv   IV   v   V   ♭VI   ♯vi$^\circ$ ♭VII   ♯vii$^\circ$

Four-Part Texture

Most of the vocal and instrumental music written during the eighteenth and nineteenth centuries either implies four parts or is reducible to four parts. Frequently, we may add a fourth part to music with three parts without disturbing the harmonic framework of the original setting. Conversely, a composition whose texture seems to exhibit a high level of density is often the result of part doubling; once we remove the doublings, a chord structure in four parts emerges.

When expressing a triad in four parts, at least one of the three elements of the chord must be doubled to produce the fourth part; however, as suggested here, additional duplications of chord tones may result in textures that are more apparent than real. (The doubling of chord tones is a separate and complex issue that will be addressed later in this chapter.)

Regardless of how we configure the triad, any combination of instruments and/or human voices may perform each of the various elements of the chord. Notably, we refer to chord tones as voices even if instruments constitute the only medium of performance. Moreover, if an instrument performs any of the chord's voices, then that instrument will probably exhibit the same simplicity of design and lyrical quality that would inform a vocal setting.

The complexity of expression found in instrumental writing is generally absent in four-part textures. To be sure, performance media such as the string quartet often contain technical challenges that are impossible to duplicate with the human voice; but even in these instances, a simpler four-part texture usually underlies the musical surface.

Triad Voicing

Not only does voice refer to musical sounds produced by vocal cords and/or instruments, we also use the term voice to describe how the tones of the triad are configured on the staff, in other words, how the elements of the chord are spaced or distributed. In the previous examples of this chapter, we spaced the root, third, and fifth of the triad as closely together as possible within the confines of the octave.

This type of triad structure is known as close voicing, close structure, or close position. When limiting the expression of the triad to one octave, a single staff is sufficient for representing a close arrangement of tones. It is possible, however, to voice the triad with a close structure on more than one staff, especially if we double one of the chord tones to produce four parts. When the triad in close structure has four parts and is written on two staves, the upper three parts will fit into a single octave (see example 1–81c below).

When the three elements of the triad extend across more than one octave and are *not* voiced as closely together as possible, the configuration of tones is referred to as open voicing, open structure, or open position. Although we may express an open disposition of the triad on one staff, the great staff is usually preferred when the voicing of the chord exceeds the span of a single octave.

Example 1–81 illustrates the following possible configurations for the triad: close structure on one staff (1–81a), open structure on one staff (1–81b), close structure on two staves (1–81c), and open structure on two staves (1–81d). The differences between close and open triad structures are discussed later in this chapter; for now, notice how the open structure appears in relation to the close structure (and how the two structures sound if you have access to a music keyboard).

Example 1–81

[musical example showing close and open structures labeled a, b, c, d on grand staff]

Vocal Range

A basic four-part texture consists of the following designated voices: soprano, alto, tenor, and bass, often abbreviated as SATB. Remember that it is possible to perform each of these parts with any combination of instruments and/or human voices. The guiding principle for SATB texture is that the voices maintain a simplicity of design and lyrical quality comparable to that found in a vocal composition.

The ranges for the soprano, alto, tenor, and bass voices are given in example 1–82. The high and low extremes of each voice might be extended or contracted by one pitch depending on the actual performance situation; for example, some alto singers might struggle to produce the high D in the double prime register, while some bass singers could possibly manage a low E in the great register (the filled-in note head in the example). Hence, the ranges provided in this book assume that the vocalists possess neither exceptional nor professional capabilities.

Example 1–82

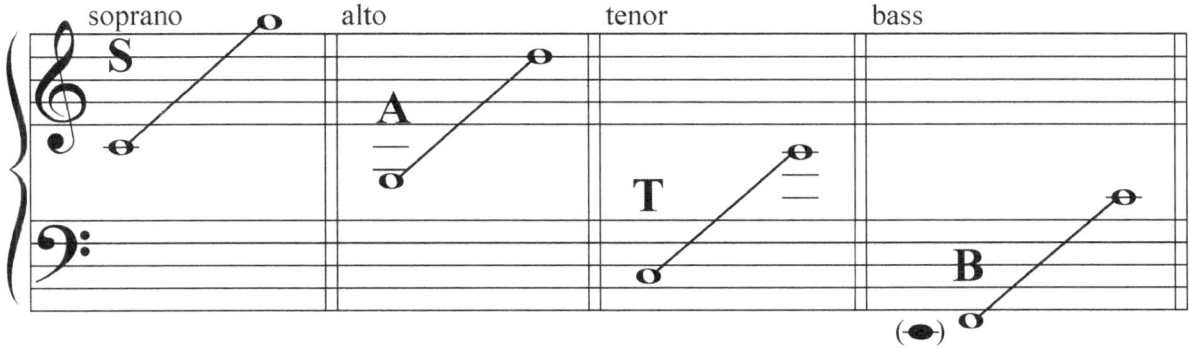

Close and Open Structure

Throughout this chapter, we have seen that spacing the elements of the triad as closely together as possible results in what is referred to as close voicing, close structure, or close position. Further, when a triad in close structure appears on two staves, the upper three parts fit into the span of a single octave. *Voicing a triad in open structure requires at least one octave between the soprano and tenor voices.*

Using the C-major triad in root position, example 1–83 exhibits various dispositions of close and open structure. When two staves are used, the soprano and alto voices are written in the treble clef, whereas the tenor and bass voices are in the bass clef.

Example 1–83

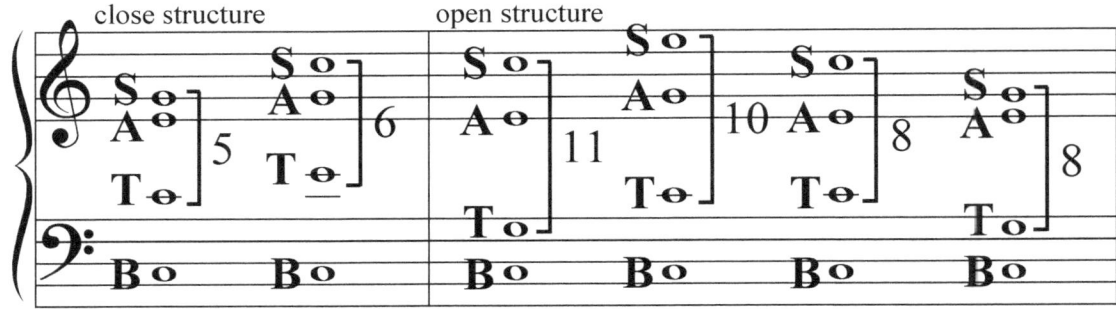

As demonstrated in example 1–84, *open chord structures allow for at least one potential chord tone to be placed between the soprano and alto voices, alto and tenor voices, or between both pairs of voices* (the filled-in note heads represent potential chord tones).

Example 1–84

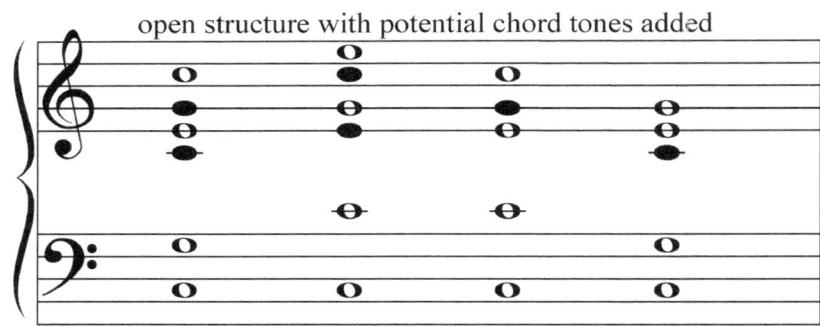

Spacing Between Adjacent Voices

There should be no more than one octave between adjacent voices except between the tenor and bass voices. If more than one octave occurs between the soprano, alto, and tenor voices, then the chord will likely sound thin and imbalanced.

Although a close positioning between the tenor and bass voices of the chord is acceptable, an arrangement between the lower voices that is too close sounds dark and perhaps even muddy. A wider spacing of intervals at the bottom of the chord usually produces more desirable results. Example 1–85 illustrates a few acceptable and unacceptable spacings for the C-major triad in root position.

Example 1–85

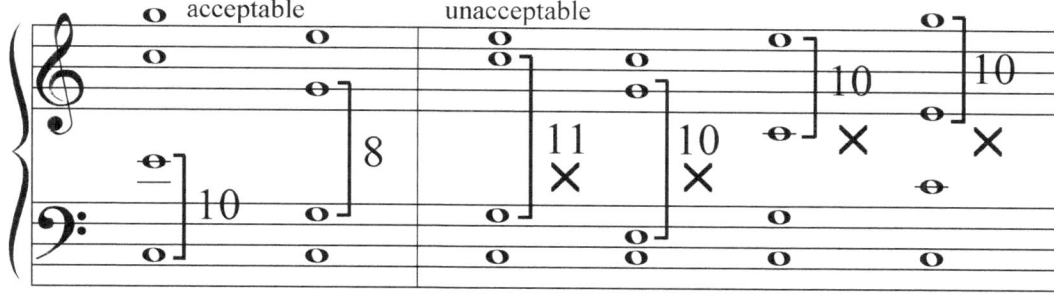

Stem Direction

Heretofore, all of the triads shown in both close and open structure have used whole-note values. Obviously, actual music is expressed with a variety of note values, most of which include stems. As demonstrated in example 1–86, when two voices are written on one staff, the soprano and tenor voices have upward stems, whereas the alto and bass voices have downward stems.

Example 1–86: stem direction in four-voice texture

The Doubling of Chord Tones in Four-Voice Texture

The doubling of chord tones in four-voice texture is a complex issue that involves two important considerations:
  (1) The goal of good four-voice writing is to assure the individuality of each melodic line while at the same time blending the parts together to produce a harmonious vertical sound.
  (2) The conventional expression of tonality in music conveys a sense of forward motion, best effected in chordal textures by successions between unlike chords, that is, chords whose roots are different. A sense of motion in tonal music is less evident when melodic activity does not produce a chord change. In order to create a feeling of movement in chordal music, careful attention must be given as to how the voices of one chord connect to those of the next chord. (In Chapter 3, we will learn to form strong connections between chords by optimizing how each voice moves through time in relation to the rest of the musical texture, a process known as voice leading.)

Improper doubling of chord tones usually produces a poor connection between chords, a loss of melodic integrity, and vertical structures that sound imbalanced. Example 1–87 illustrates some general guidelines for doubling the chord tones of triads. The triads in the example are related to each other as a unit of musical expression called a "chord progression." The progression is in the key and mode of f minor.

54   Chapter 1   A Review of Fundamentals

The principles cited below are keyed to the progression in 1–87. These principles are general recommendations; the actual context of any given music composition may demand doublings that contradict some of the guidelines presented here.

(1) When triads are used in a four-voice texture, the preference—subject to exceptions—is to double scale degrees 1, 4, and 5 of the tonic key (examples 1–87a, 87e, 87f, 87g, 87h, 87i, and 87j).

(2) Avoid doubling the variable scale degrees of the minor mode. (Examples 87b, 87c, 87d, 87e, and 87f show the correct usage for variables ♭6, ♭7, and ♯7. Example 1–87i demonstrates an exceptional treatment of the leading tone in the alto voice, which moves to scale degree 5 in 87j instead of the tonic.)

(3) For major and minor triads in $^5_3$ position, double the root (examples 87f, 87i, and 87j), the fifth, or third—usually in that order. However, doubling the third of the tonic chord is always a good secondary choice.

(4) For major and minor triads in $^6_3$ position, double whatever chord tone appears in the soprano voice; alternatively, double the root (1–87a), fifth, and third—in that order.

(5) For triads in $^6_4$ position, double the fifth, that is, the bass voice (examples 87b and 87h).

(6) Avoid doubling the leading tone; therefore,
   (a) do not double the root of the vii° chord,
   (b) do not double the third of the V chord.

(7) The diminished triad is best limited to $^6_3$ position; in this context, double the third (1–87e) or the fifth.

Example 1–87

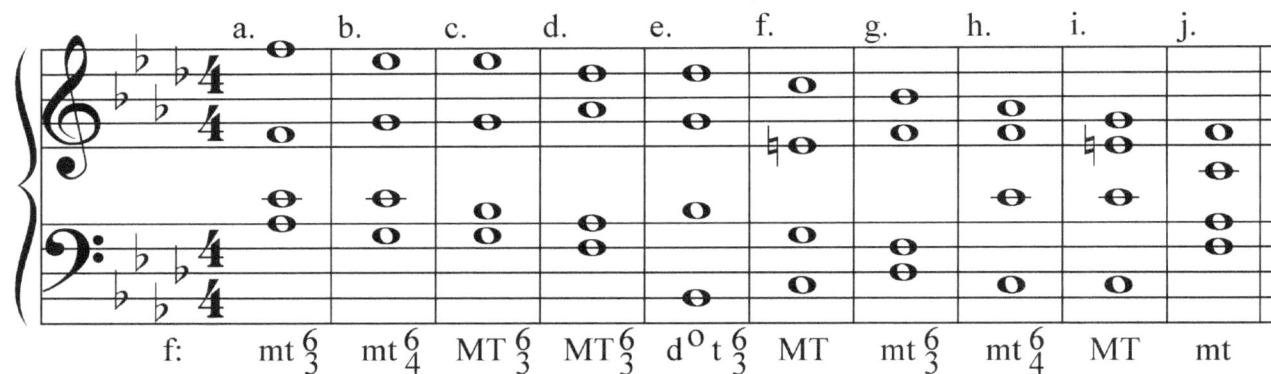

As shown in example 1–88, the $^5_3$ and $^6_4$ positions of the diminished triad are usually avoided because of the tritone (augmented 4th or diminished 5th) interval between the lowest voice of the texture and one of the upper voices. In $^6_3$ position, the tritone in the diminished triad is somewhat hidden because it occurs between two upper voices—in other words, the lowest voice is not one of the components of the tritone interval. For this reason, the diminished triad is usually expressed in $^6_3$ position.

Example 1–88

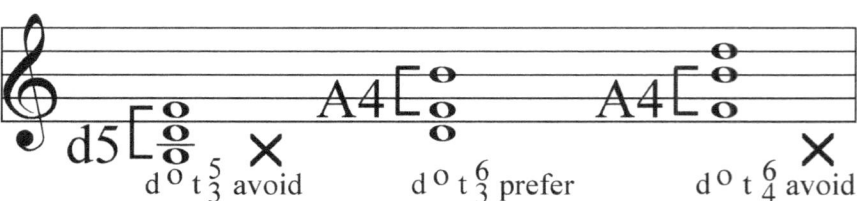

Tonality

We have discovered that the major mode is not the only mode in music that has a tonal center, that the numbers 1 through 7 can be used to represent each of the scale degrees of the mode, and that each of the scale degrees of the mode has one of the following names: tonic, supertonic, mediant, subdominant, dominant, submediant, and leading tone. When scale degree 7 is located one whole step below the tonic note, the term subtonic is used to distinguish it from the leading tone, as the subtonic lacks the compelling drive of the leading tone to *lead* upwards by half step to the tonic.

Tonality in music is analogous to the gravitational force exerted by the Sun upon any object that comes within its field of attraction. Tonality is a system of pitch organization that establishes its own field of attraction around one central tone. All the other tones of the key and mode seek to revolve around and gravitate toward this central tone in a hierarchical order.

The tonic, as the principal tone of this hierarchy, exerts its gravitational force upon all of the other tones, each of which holds a position of relative strength and stability within the tonic's field of attraction. Since the pitch content of the key and mode provides the material from which chords may be formed on each of the seven scale degrees, the chords also assume a hierarchical position within the tonal framework. Thus, some tones and chords have a stronger relationship to the tonic than others.

Standing at the interval of the perfect 5th above the tonic and serving as the primary definer of a composition's tonality, the dominant scale degree forms the strongest relationship with the tonic. The perfect 5th, which has its origin in a natural phenomenon known as the harmonic series (see below, pp. 56–57), constitutes the closest intervallic relationship between two unlike pitches. The field of attraction between the dominant and the tonic is based upon the prominence of the perfect 5th within the harmonic series.

In example 1–89, we have the triad of the dominant addressing the tonic in a falling perfect 5th and rising perfect 4th root and bass relationship. Movement in the bass of either the perfect or tritone 5th and 4th is called harmonic motion. The falling perfect 5th (and its inversion, the rising perfect 4th) presents the strongest expression of harmonic motion in tonal music.

When the dominant triad is major, it contains as its chord third the second most important scale degree within the tonal hierarchy, namely, the leading tone. Therefore, as shown in 1–89, the movement between the dominant and tonic chords produces two optimal conditions for affirming the tonality of a musical work: the compelling melodic drive upwards from the leading tone to the tonic and the strong harmonic motion of a falling perfect 5th or a rising perfect 4th in the bass.

Example 1–89: the harmonic root and bass relationship between the dominant and tonic triads

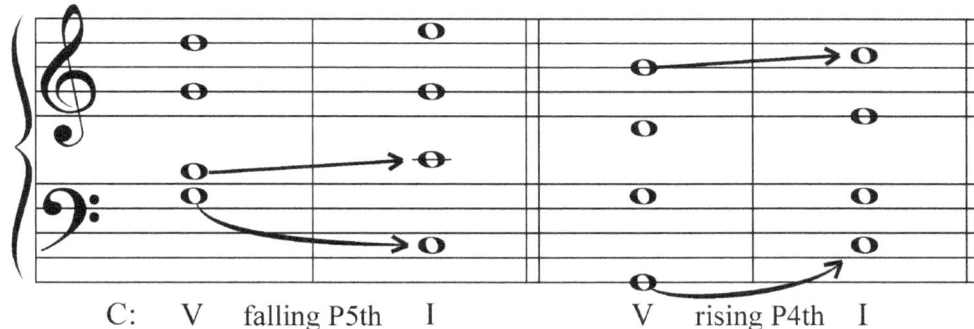

The next chord within the tonal hierarchy is the triad of the leading tone, which shares two pitches in common with the triad of the dominant. The root and the third of the leading-tone triad are the same pitches as the third and the fifth of the corresponding dominant triad. Example 1–90 demonstrates the common pitch content of the two chords in the key and mode of C major.

For the purpose of comparison in the example, the leading-tone triad is expressed in $\frac{5}{3}$ position; however, it should be remembered that limiting the diminished triad to its $\frac{6}{3}$ position (first inversion) avoids the dissonant tritone between the bass and one of the upper voices. The remaining areas of the supertonic, mediant, subdominant, and submediant assume subordinate status within the key and mode.

Example 1–90: common pitch content between the leading-tone and dominant triads

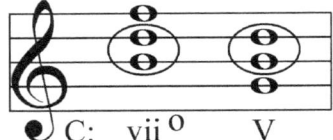

C: vii°   V

The Harmonic Series

In the foregoing section, we stated that the interval of the perfect 5th is of central importance to the definition of a music composition's tonality. Additionally, it spans the distance from the root to the fifth of the major and minor triad. Both major and minor triads are relatively stable chords, while diminished and augmented triads are relatively unstable. The diminished triad has a diminished 5th from its root to fifth. The augmented triad has a contextual 5th from its root to fifth but not an acoustical 5th (see above, p. 47). As we shall see, the major triad is the most stable of all four chord qualities.

The stability of the major triad and the role of the dominant as the chief definer of the tonality is associated with the harmonic series. A portion of the harmonic series with a starting pitch of C is shown below in example 1–91 (the series can begin on any pitch). Before we consider how this series works and how it relates to the strength of the dominant and the stability of the major triad, it would be well to review briefly the nature of musical tones and how they are created.

We know that an object moved by force produces vibrations that are carried through a medium of transmission to the human ear. A sound that generates a regular number of frequencies at a steady rate is perceived as a musical tone. The relative lowness or highness of any pitch corresponds to the rate of the vibrating frequency of the sound-producing object. Slower vibrating frequencies result in lower pitches, while faster vibrating frequencies produce higher pitches. The rate of vibration generating the pitch is called the fundamental frequency, also known as the first partial or first harmonic.

A musical tone is a combination of two components: the fundamental pitch and a spectrum of higher frequencies called overtones. Projecting varying degrees of intensity (volume) from within the harmonic series, overtones are usually not loud enough to be heard as pitches in their own right. Rather, the fundamental frequency and its overtones are blended together into a single composite sound. This composite sound is referred to variously as tone quality, tone color, or timbre (pronounced *tam*ber).

Although the individual overtones cannot be heard as distinct pitches, they do *color* the fundamental frequency and collectively generate the timbre of a musical instrument—overtones enable us to identify the source of the musical sound. On any given instrument, some overtones are relatively stronger than others. The reason two different instruments sound differently is due to the fact that each makes its own unique selection of overtones from a much larger inventory of weaker overtones. For example, we can distinguish the sound of the clarinet and the violin even when both instruments are playing the exact same pitch because each instrument projects its own unique profile of overtones, its own sonic fingerprint.

The fundamental frequency and its overtones together produce the harmonic series, which is why the harmonic series is also called the overtone series. The number of overtones that are generated above the fundamental pitch is potentially infinite; however, in order to maintain a reasonable degree of simplicity, discussions of the harmonic series in publications are usually limited to the first sixteen pitches.

Example 1–91 restricts our view of the harmonic series to the first five pitches, starting with the fundamental on great C. These five pitches reveal two important bits of information:

(1) the first tone that is *not* a duplication of the fundamental is a compound perfect 5th (circled G) and
(2) the first five tones of the harmonic series produce the major triad (measure 2).

Example 1–91: the first five pitches of the harmonic series

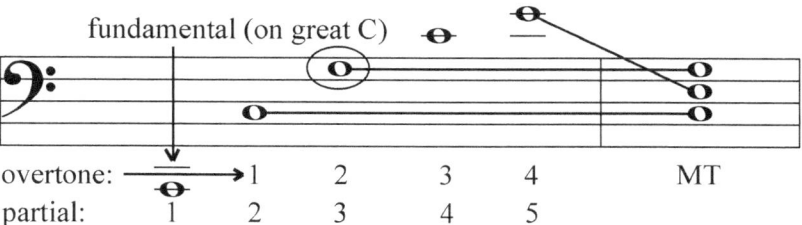

As noted earlier, the fundamental is also called the first partial or first harmonic. When discussing the harmonic series, a distinction should be made between the fundamental and the overtones that occur above it. Although the fundamental is the first partial (or first harmonic), it is *not* the first overtone. Examples 1–91 above and 92 below indicate that the first overtone is actually the second partial (or second harmonic), the second overtone is the third partial (or third harmonic), and so on. Therefore, we never refer to the fundamental frequency as the first overtone.

Example 1–92: the first five pitches of the harmonic series on great C

	Overtone Series		Harmonic Series
great C :	fundamental		fundamental (first partial or first harmonic)
small c :	first overtone	=	second partial (second harmonic)
small g :	second overtone	=	third partial (third harmonic)
c^1	: third overtone	=	fourth partial (fourth harmonic)
e^1	: fourth overtone	=	fifth partial (fifth harmonic)

Omitting the Fifth in Four-Voice Texture

The strength of the perfect 5th within the harmonic series makes it possible in four-voice textures to omit the fifth of major and minor triads in root position, using an additional root or third as the fourth part. In this instance, the missing fifth is understood to be generated by the harmonic series.

It is also possible to omit the 5th with root-position seventh chords in a four-voice texture if the underlying triad is either a major or minor triad. The omission produces a seventh chord with a doubled root, a third, and a seventh.

Chapter 2   The Church Modes

Mode, or modality, is a collection of pitch relationships exhibiting certain characteristic melodic and chordal configurations that confirm and establish the key of a musical work. Our present-day concept of mode is the result of centuries of evolution and practice. Out of this evolution, the major-minor tonal system emerged as the most widely used system of pitch organization in the Western world. But long before the development of this system in the late-seventeenth century, other modes existed.

Known as the church modes, or ecclesiastical modes, they were used for hundreds of years, through the Middle Ages and the Renaissance. Thereafter, the church modes receded from view for about two hundred years but then recaptured the imagination of composers during the second half of the nineteenth century. Before we consider the modal system in its current state, let us take a brief excursion into the early history of this system.

The church modes were developed during the eighth and ninth centuries of the Common Era as a means for analyzing and classifying the monophonic music of the Roman Catholic Church. Monophony is a type of musical texture that consists of a single melodic line. The music of the Roman Church is referred to generally as plainchant (*cantus planus*) and more specifically as Gregorian chant. The latter reference is an attribution to the charismatic pope St. Gregory I (540?–604), who traditionally receives credit for composing the chant for the services of the Roman Church during his papacy. St. Gregory is a central figure in the history of the Roman Church, one of the four Doctors (teachers) of the Church, along with St. Ambrose (340?–397), St. Augustine (354–430), and St. Jerome (340?–420?).

Although St. Gregory may have helped to bring the chant repertory of the Roman Church together through his extraordinary service as an administrator, it is unlikely that he composed any of the music himself. Still, given the magnitude of St. Gregory's role in establishing both the papacy as a world power and the independence of the Western Church, it is understandable that the surviving corpus of Western chant would bear his name.

The first discussions of the church modes began to appear in the treatises of the ninth century. Based upon certain references to the scale system of the ancient Greeks found in a sixth-century treatise called *De institutione musica* (The Fundamentals of Music), some writers concluded that the modes were of Greek origin. The treatise was written by the Roman statesman Boethius (ca. 480–ca. 524), the most widely read authority on the music theory of antiquity.

Misinterpreting Boethius's account of the Greek scales, medieval theoreticians improperly assigned the Greek names associated with these scales to the modes of the Roman Church. Although the musical scales of ancient Greece had nothing in common with the modal system of the Middle Ages, the church modes as we understand them today retain their Hellenistic names.

The history of the church modes is one in which the usage differs from one era to another, from the Middle Ages through the second half of the nineteenth century. The treatment of the church modes during the last hundred and fifty years or so, however, constitutes a relatively consistent practice. Focusing on the characteristics of the modes as they occur in the music literature of the recent past will deepen our understanding of the concepts that concern beginning music students, especially pitch, key, scale, mode, key signature, interval, and harmony.

Example 2–1 below illustrates the seven church modes with their Greek names, tonic triads, and half-step profiles. All of the modes shown in the example appear as diatonic scales, each with five whole steps and two half steps. The placement of the half steps, however, is different for each of the seven modes. Two modes should be recognized immediately, the Ionian mode and the Aeolian mode. The half-step profile of the Ionian mode is identical to that of the major mode, whereas the half-step profile of the Aeolian mode is identical to that of the natural minor.

Example 2–1: the seven church modes with their Greek names, tonic triads, and half-step profiles

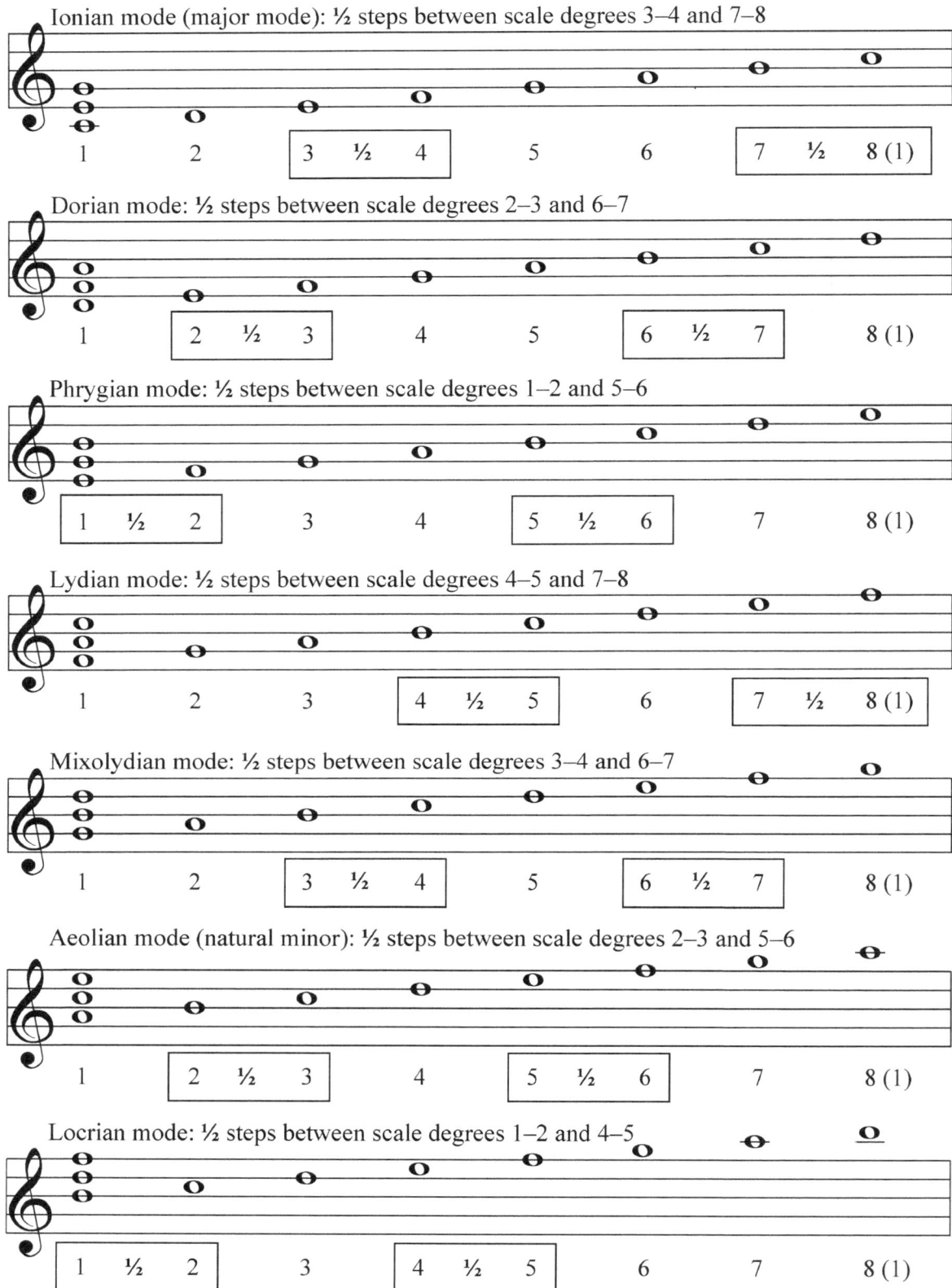

The white keys of the piano keyboard contain all of the pitch content for each of the seven modes in their *untransposed* forms. As displayed in example 2–1 above, the untransposed Ionian mode (or major mode) spans the white keys of the C octave, the Dorian mode the D octave, the Phrygian mode the E octave, the Lydian mode the F octave, the Mixolydian mode the G octave, the Aeolian mode the A octave, and the Locrian mode the B octave. In the next section, we shall place the seven untransposed modes into two separate categories according to the quality of their respective tonic triads and the intervallic relationship between their tonic and mediant scale degrees.

Major and Minor Prototypes

The Lydian and Mixolydian modes are "major prototypes" because they have both a major triad on the tonic and a major 3rd between their tonic and mediant scale degrees (example 2–2).

Compare the untransposed mode of F Lydian to its parallel major, F major. Notice that there are similarities between the two modes, except that F Lydian's scale degree 4 is raised one half step in relation to the F-major scale. F Lydian contains a B natural, F major a B♭ (examples 2–2a and 2b). The untransposed Mixolydian mode on G is similar to its parallel major, G major, except that G Mixolydian's scale degree 7 is lowered one half step in relation to the G-major scale. G Mixolydian contains an F natural, G major an F♯ (examples 2–2c and 2d).

Example 2–2: major prototype modes

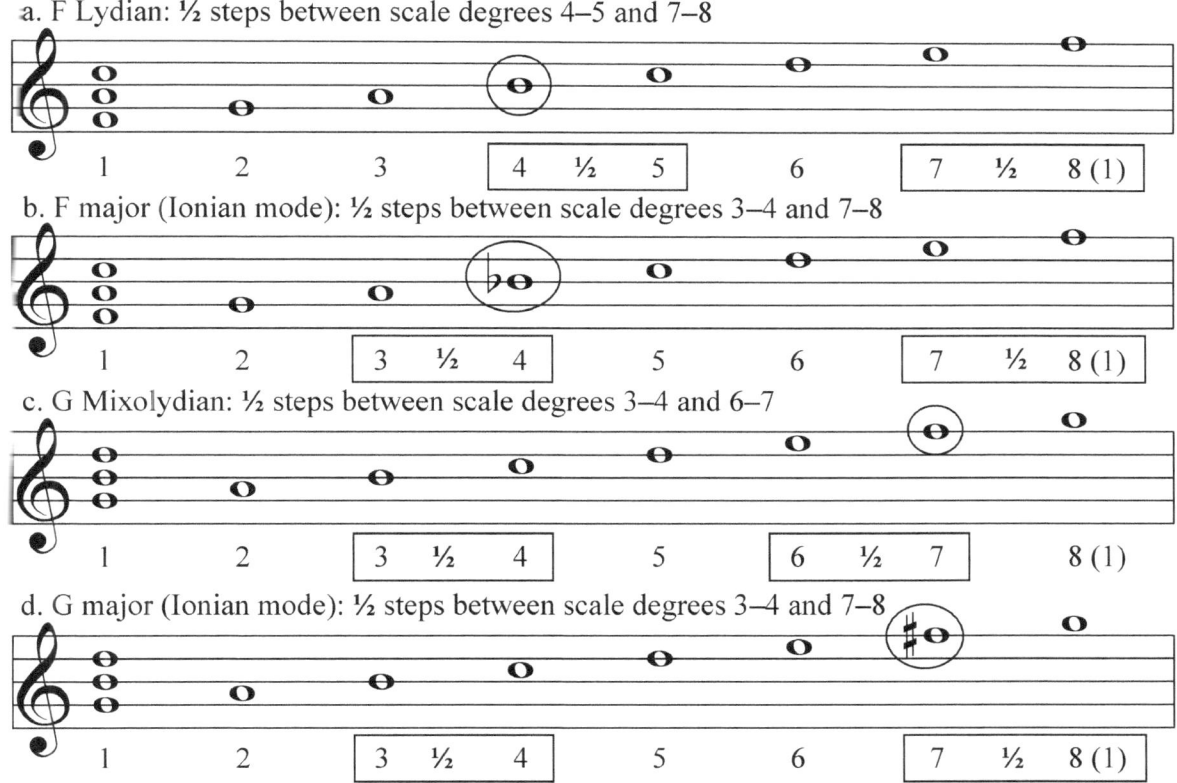

The Dorian and Phrygian modes, on the other hand, are "minor prototypes" because they have both a minor triad on the tonic and a minor 3rd between their tonic and mediant scale degrees (example 2–3). The untransposed Dorian mode on D resembles the parallel natural minor on D, except that D Dorian's scale

62   Chapter 2 The Church Modes

degree 6 is raised one half step in relation to the d-minor scale. D Dorian contains a B natural, d minor a B♭ (examples 2–3a and 3b). The untransposed Phrygian mode on E is similar to its parallel natural minor, e minor, except that E Phrygian's scale degree 2 is lowered one half step in relation to the e-minor scale. E Phrygian contains an F natural, e minor an F♯ (examples 2–3c and 3d).

Example 2–3: minor prototype modes

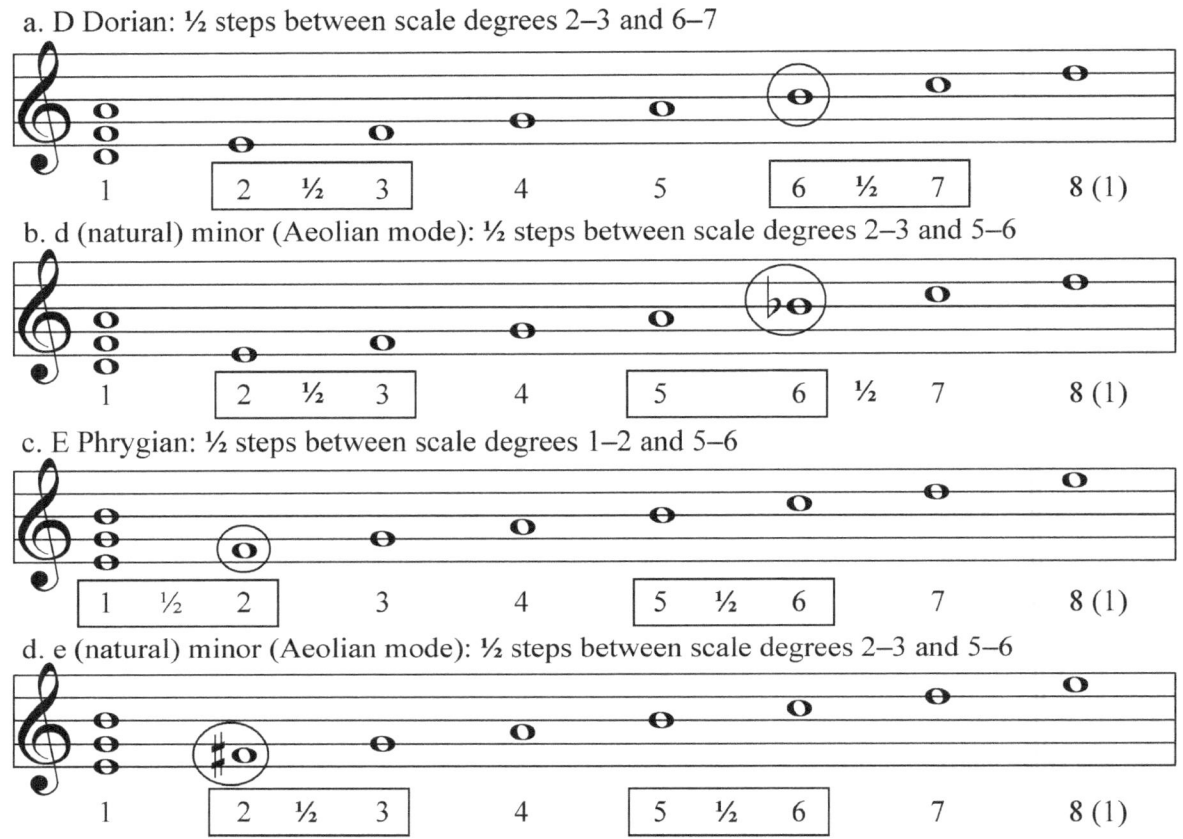

Example 2–4: the exceptional Locrian mode

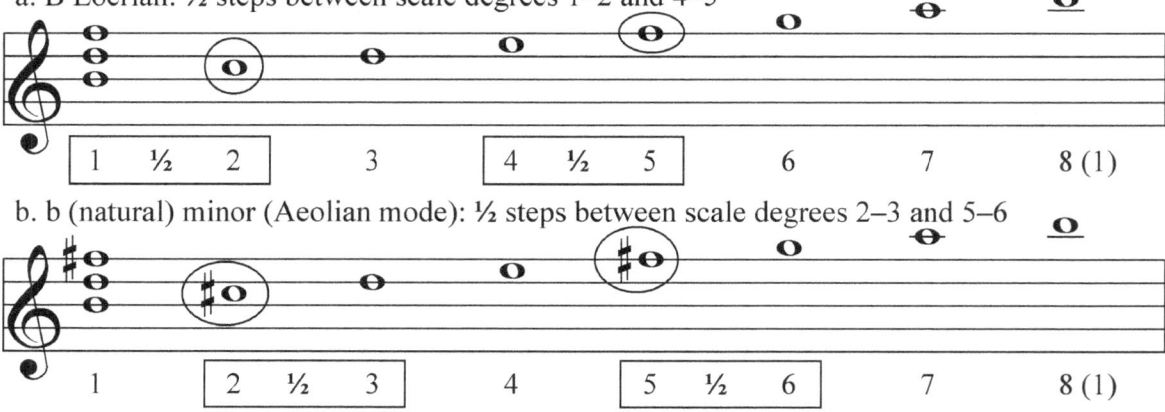

The Locrian mode, as illustrated in 2–4 above, is an exceptional case for two reasons: the mode has two scale degrees that differ from the natural minor and its tonic triad is diminished and therefore inherently unstable. B Locrian's scale degrees 2 and 5 are each lowered one half step in relation to its parallel natural minor, b minor. The untransposed Locrian mode on B contains a C natural and an F natural, whereas b minor has both a C♯ and an F♯. Still, because the Locrian mode has a minor 3rd between its tonic and mediant scale degrees (as does the Dorian and Phrygian modes), we classify Locrian as a minor prototype, albeit an unusual one.

Relating the Church Modes to the Major Mode

Earlier in this chapter, we noted that the white keys of the piano keyboard contain all of the pitch content for the seven modes in their untransposed forms. As demonstrated in example 2–5, the first note of each mode may be placed within the context of the C-major scale. Accordingly, we assign the names of the seven church modes to each of the seven scale degrees of C major, starting with the untransposed Ionian mode.

Thus, the keynote of the Ionian mode begins on C, the keynote of the Dorian mode on D, the keynote of the Phrygian mode on E, the keynote of the Lydian mode on F, the keynote of the Mixolydian mode on G, the keynote of the Aeolian mode on A, and the keynote of the Locrian mode on B.

Example 2–5: the church mode areas within the context of the C-major scale

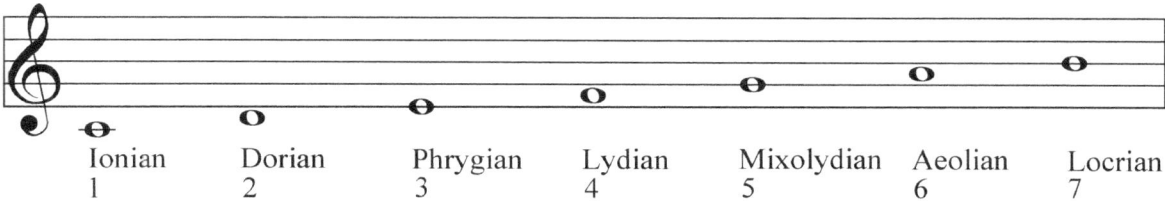

Mode Transposition

Since all seven church modes in their untransposed forms use only the white keys of the piano keyboard and appear within the context of the C-major scale, the respective key signatures and pitch content of D Dorian, E Phrygian, F Lydian, G Mixolydian, A Aeolian, and B Locrian are all *related* to the key signature and pitch content of C major (or C Ionian).

As we observed in Chapter 1, any two modes standing in a relative relationship to one another will share the same key signature and the same pitch content but have different tonics and different octave ranges. For example, any major mode, transposed or untransposed, has a relative minor key area with which it shares the same key signature and pitch content.

Presently, we shall apply the concept of relative relationships between major and minor modes to all of the church modes, designating scale degree 2 of C major as its relative Dorian area, scale degree 3 as its relative Phrygian area, scale degree 4 as its relative Lydian area, scale degree 5 as its relative Mixolydian area, scale degree 6 as its relative Aeolian area, and scale degree 7 as its relative Locrian area (see 2–5 above).

As we explore the characteristics of the church modes, our reference point will be the untransposed key and mode of C major. Let us begin with the relationship between the untransposed mode of C major and its relative Dorian, D Dorian, as shown in example 2–6 below. Notice that both modes share the same pitch content but have different tonics and different ranges.

64   Chapter 2 The Church Modes

Example 2–6: D, the relative Dorian of C major (scale degree 2 of C Major)

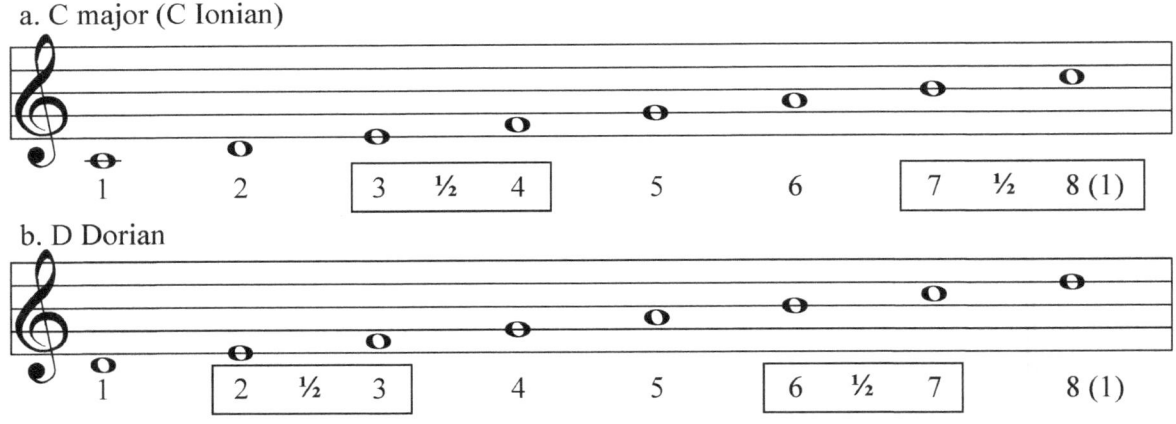

The names of the seven church modes remain unchanged when transposing the C major to another key (example 2–7).

Example 2–7: the church mode areas of B♭ major

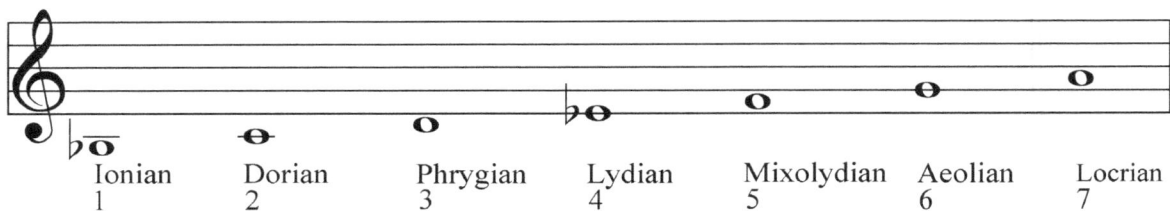

Example 2–8 moves the relationship between C major and D Dorian down one whole step, to B♭ major and C Dorian; both modes share the same pitch content, including a B♭ and an E♭, but have different tonics and different ranges.

Example 2–8: C, the relative Dorian of B♭ major (scale degree 2 of B♭ major)

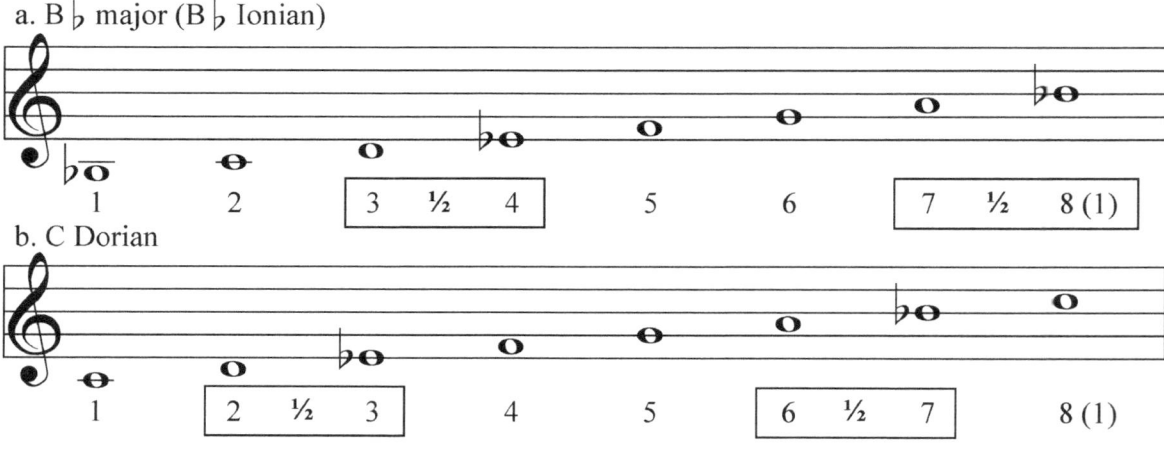

Let us stay with B♭ major for a few more examples. If C Dorian has the same pitch content as B♭ major, then any of the other relative modes of B♭ major will also have seven tones in common. In example 2–9, we have B♭ major and its relative Phrygian, D Phrygian. Both C Dorian (example 2–8b) and D Phrygian (2–9b) have the same key signature as B♭ major: two flats, B♭ and E♭. All three modes (B♭ major, C Dorian, and D Phrygian), however, have different tonics and different ranges.

Example 2–9: D, the relative Phrygian of B♭ major (scale degree 3 of B♭ major)

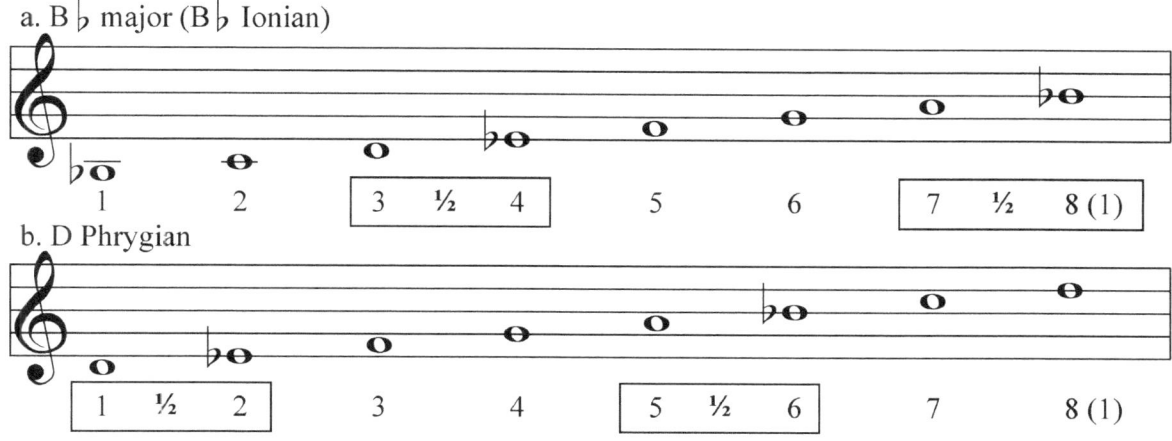

Example 2–10 compares B♭ major to its relative Lydian, E♭ Lydian; again, the pitch content is the same for both modes but their respective tonics and ranges are different.

Example 2–10: E♭, the relative Lydian of B♭ major (scale degree 4 of B♭ major)

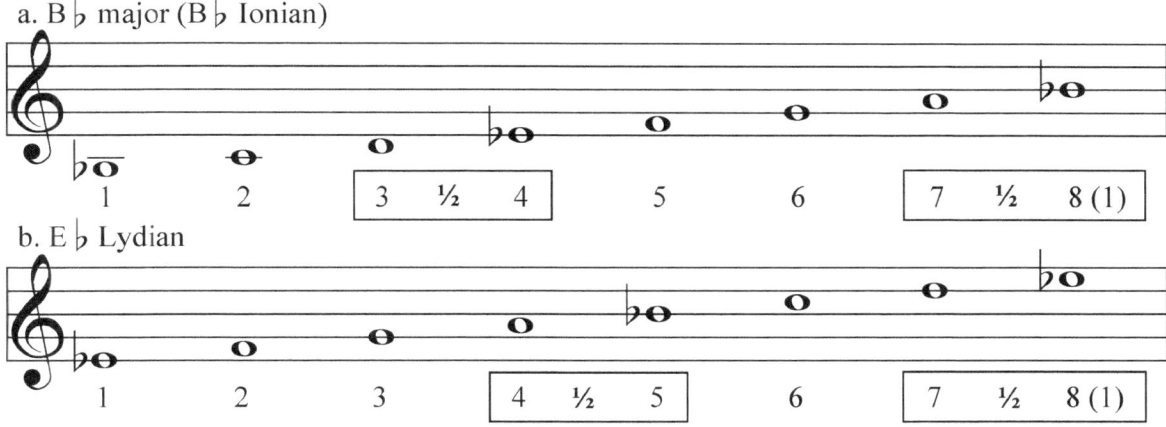

As shown in example 2–11, the relative Mixolydian of B♭ major is F Mixolydian. Both modes have the same pitch content but different tonics and different ranges.

Example 2–11: F, the relative Mixolydian of B♭ major (scale degree 5 of B♭ major)

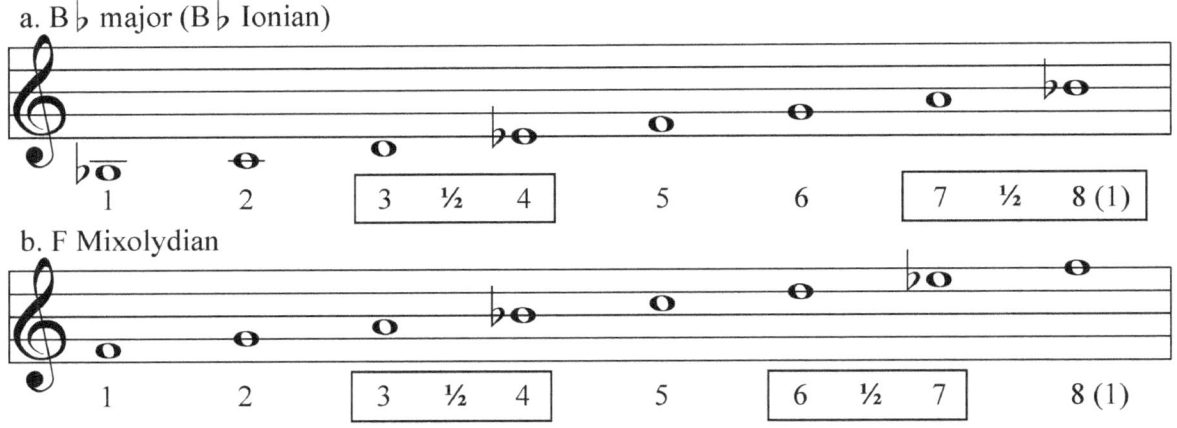

Example 2–12 illustrates the relative Aeolian of B♭ major, G Aeolian. As we have observed, the Aeolian mode is identical to that of the natural minor; therefore, the relationship between the two modes shown below is the same as the relationship between B♭ major and its relative minor.

Example 2–12: G, the relative Aeolian of B♭ major (scale degree 6 of B♭ major)

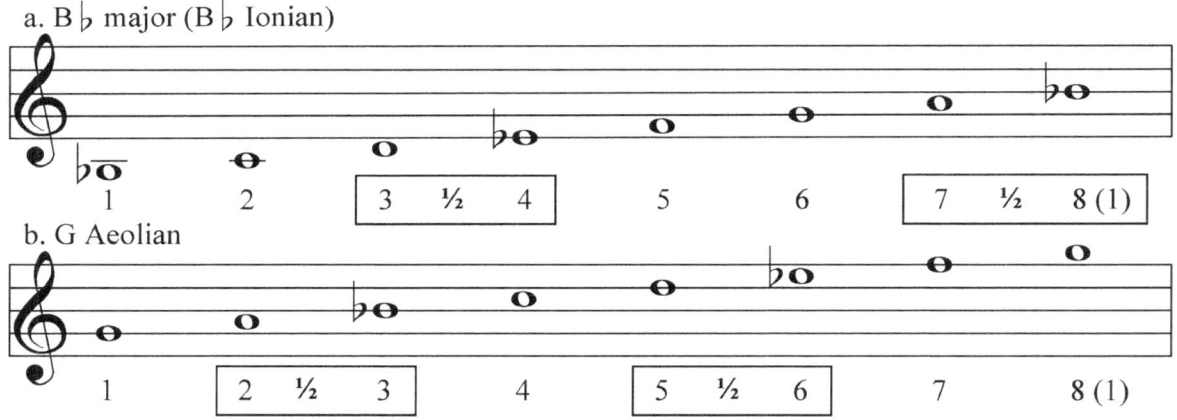

Finally, example 2–13 presents the relative Locrian of B♭ major, A Locrian. We know that the Locrian mode's tonic scale degree projects a diminished triad. The Locrian mode is the only church mode that has a diminished 5th between its scale degrees 1 and 5. The unstable properties of the Locrian mode has tended to discourage its use throughout most periods of music history; indeed, the tritone relationship between its tonic and dominant as well as the lack of a stable tonic triad make it difficult to establish a strong tonal center.

Example 2–13: A, the relative Locrian of B♭ major (scale degree 7 of B♭ major)

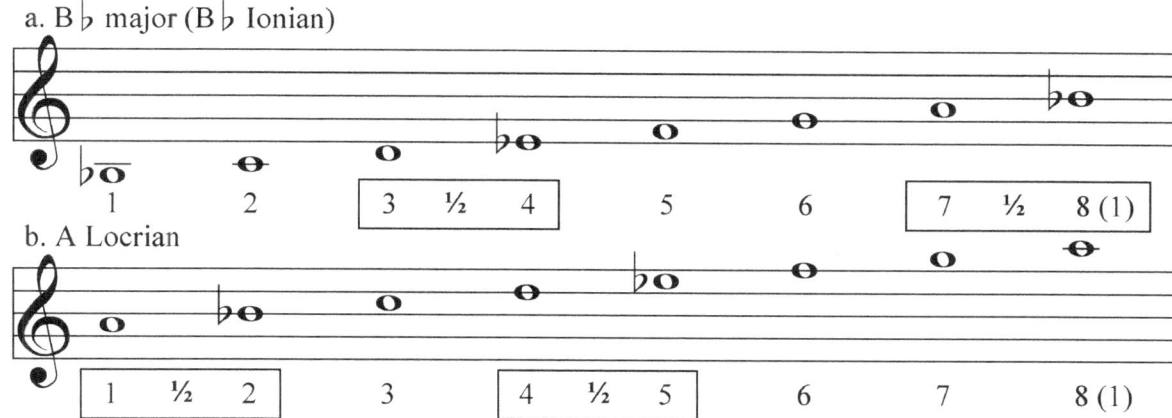

Given the Key and Mode, Find the Right Key Signature

In the foregoing discussion, we learned that if the relative modal key areas of C major share the same pitch content and key signature as C major, then the relative modal key areas of B♭ major share the same pitch content and key signature as B♭ major. Finding the relative modal key area of any transposed major mode is one way of understanding the principle of mode transposition. There are, however, other ways to approach this inquiry.

Drawing upon the information gleaned from the modal relationships considered in examples 2–8 through 13, we shall now arrange two pairs of conditions into the following proposition in order to find the relationship between them: *untransposed major is to untransposed mode as transposed major is to transposed mode.*

As presented in example 2–14, the first pair of conditions contains two known values and is therefore complete; the second pair, however, contains one unknown value and is therefore incomplete: C major is to D Dorian as the unknown value (X) is to C Dorian. Finding the correct value will tell us the keynote of the transposed major and provide the answer to the following question:

(1) What is the key signature for the transposed mode of C Dorian (2–14)?
(2) D Dorian is the untransposed mode and scale degree 2 of the untransposed major, C major.
(3) C Dorian occurs on scale degree 2 of what transposed major (X)?
(4) C major is to D Dorian (a major 2nd) as X major is to C Dorian; what is a major 2nd *below* C?
(5) If you cannot find a major 2nd below C, find a minor 7th above C (the inversion of a major 2nd). B♭ is a minor 7th above C and therefore a major 2nd below C.
(6) C major is to D Dorian as B♭ major (X) is to C Dorian.
(7) B♭ major has two flats (B♭ and E♭) and so does C Dorian.

Example 2–14: the key signature of C Dorian

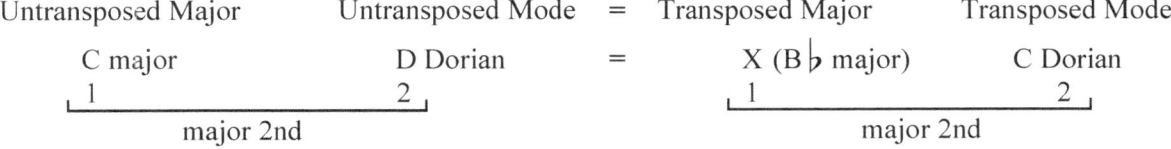

68   Chapter 2 The Church Modes

Two skills are absolutely necessary at this point in your study. You must know the major key signatures *and* be able to calculate easily the intervals of the major 2nd, major 3rd, perfect 4th, perfect 5th, major 6th, and major 7th *below* any given tone. In this exercise, the given tone represents the transposed mode; X represents the key signature of that transposed mode.

(1) What is the key signature for the transposed mode of D Phrygian (example 2–15)?
(2) E Phrygian is the untransposed mode and scale degree 3 of the untransposed major, C major.
(3) D Phrygian occurs on scale degree 3 of what transposed major (X)?
(4) C major is to E Phrygian (a major 3rd) as X major is to D Phrygian; what is a major 3rd *below* D?
(5) If you cannot find a major 3rd below D, then find a minor 6th above D (the inversion of a major 3rd). B♭ is a minor 6th above D and therefore a major 3rd below D.
(6) C major is to E Phrygian as B♭ major (X) is to D Phrygian.
(7) B♭ major has two flats (B♭ and E♭) and so does D Phrygian.

Example 2–15: the key signature of D Phrygian

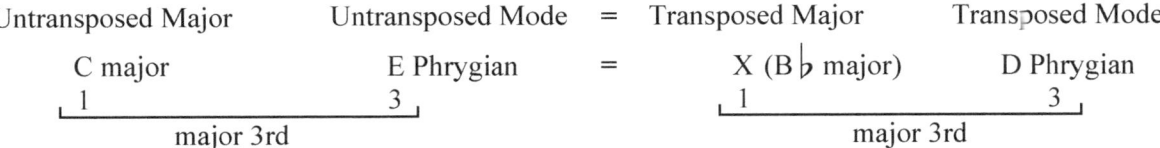

(1) What is the key signature for the transposed mode of E♭ Lydian (example 2–16)?
(2) F Lydian is the untransposed mode and scale degree 4 of the untransposed major, C major.
(3) E♭ Lydian occurs on scale degree 4 of what transposed major (X)?
(4) C major is to F Lydian (a perfect 4th) as X major is to E♭ Lydian; what is a perfect 4th *below* E♭?
(5) If you cannot find a perfect 4th below E♭, then find a perfect 5th above E♭ (the inversion of a perfect 4th). B♭ is a perfect 5th above E♭ and therefore a perfect 4th below E♭.
(6) C major is to F Lydian as B♭ major (X) is to E♭ Lydian.
(7) B♭ major has two flats (B♭ and E♭) and so does E♭ Lydian.

Example 2–16: the key signature of E♭ Lydian

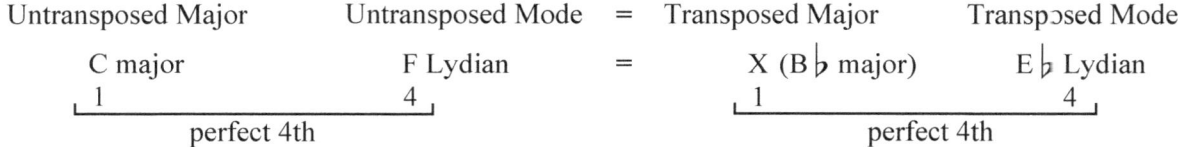

(1) What is the key signature for the transposed mode of F Mixolydian (example 2–17)?
(2) G Mixolydian is the untransposed mode and scale degree 5 of the untransposed major, C major.
(3) F Mixolydian occurs on scale degree 5 of what transposed major (X)?
(4) C major is to G Mixolydian (a perfect 5th) as X major is to F Mixolydian; what is a perfect 5th *below* F?
(5) If you cannot find a perfect 5th below F, then find a perfect 4th above F (the inversion of a perfect 5th). B♭ is a perfect 4th above F and therefore a perfect 5th below F.
(6) C major is to G Mixolydian as B♭ major (X) is to F Mixolydian.
(7) B♭ major has two flats (B♭ and E♭) and so does F Mixolydian.

Example 2–17: the key signature of F Mixolydian

Untransposed Major	Untransposed Mode	=	Transposed Major	Transposed Mode
C major	G Mixolydian	=	X (B♭ major)	F Mixolydian
1	5		1	5
perfect 5th			perfect 5th	

(1) What is the key signature for the transposed mode of G Aeolian (example 2–18)?
(2) A Aeolian is the untransposed mode and scale degree 6 of the untransposed major, C major.
(3) G Aeolian occurs on scale degree 6 of what transposed major (X)?
(4) C major is to A Aeolian (a major 6th) as X major is to G Aeolian; what is a major 6th *below* G?
(5) If you cannot find a major 6th below G, then find a minor 3rd above G (the inversion of a major 6th). B♭ is a minor 3rd above G and therefore a major 6th below G.
(6) C major is to A Aeolian as B♭ major (X) is to G Aeolian.
(7) B♭ major has two flats (B♭ and E♭) and so does G Aeolian.

Example 2–18: the key signature of G Aeolian

Untransposed Major	Untransposed Mode	=	Transposed Major	Transposed Mode
C major	A Aeolian	=	X (B♭ major)	G Aeolian
1	6		1	6
major 6th			major 6th	

(1) What is the key signature for the transposed mode of A Locrian (example 2–19)?
(2) B Locrian is the untransposed mode and scale degree 7 of the untransposed major, C major.
(3) A Locrian occurs on scale degree 7 of what transposed major (X)?
(4) C major is to B Locrian (a major 7th) as X major is to A Locrian; what is a major 7th *below* A?
(5) If you cannot find a major 7th below A, then find a minor 2nd above A (the inversion of a major 7th). B♭ is a minor 2nd above A and therefore a major 7th below A.
(6) C major is to B Locrian as B♭ major (X) is to A Locrian.
(7) B♭ major has two flats (B♭ and E♭) and so does A Locrian.

Example 2–19: the key signature of A Locrian

Untransposed Major	Untransposed Mode	=	Transposed Major	Transposed Mode
C major	B Locrian	=	X (B♭ major)	A Locrian
1	7		1	7
major 7th			major 7th	

Up to this point in our study of mode transposition, we have systematically explored the possibilities of modes with two flats from two different but related perspectives. First, we ascended through the modal key areas of B♭ major one scale degree at a time (pp. 64–67). Second, armed with the knowledge of the first perspective, or approach, we held the key signature of B♭ major in the background as an unknown quantity (X) and then endeavored to find the key signatures for the transposed modes of C Dorian, D Phrygian, E♭ Lydian, F Mixolydian, G Aeolian, and A Locrian (pp. 67–69).

Of course, we already knew that all six transposed modes of examples 2–14 through 19 would have two flats in their respective key signatures, as that fact was determined from our prior consideration of examples 2–8 through 13. For the next several examples, however, let us practice finding the key signatures of transposed modes *without the benefit of knowing from previous exercises* what key would be entered into the unknown quantity of X.

(1) What is the key signature for the transposed mode of F Dorian (example 2–20)?
(2) D Dorian is the untransposed mode and scale degree 2 of the untransposed major, C major.
(3) F Dorian occurs on scale degree 2 of what transposed major (X)?
(4) C major is to D Dorian (a major 2nd) as X major is to F Dorian; what is a major 2nd *below* F?
(5) If you cannot find a major 2nd below F, then find a minor 7th above F (the inversion of a major 2nd). E♭ is a minor 7th above F and therefore a major 2nd below F.
(6) C major is to D Dorian as E♭ major (X) is to F Dorian.
(7) E♭ major has three flats (B♭, E♭, and A♭) and so does F Dorian.

Example 2–20: the key signature of F Dorian

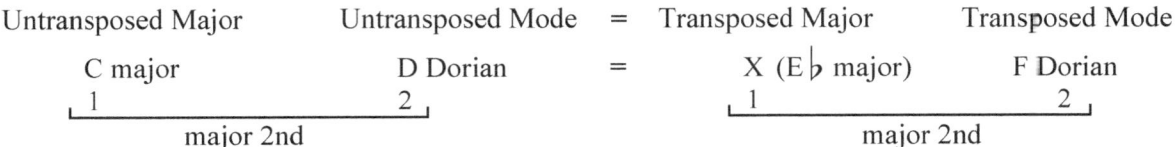

(1) What is the key signature for the transposed mode of C Lydian (example 2–21)?
(2) F Lydian is the untransposed mode and scale degree 4 of the untransposed major, C major.
(3) C Lydian occurs on scale degree 4 of what transposed major (X)?
(4) C major is to F Lydian (a perfect 4th) as X major is to C Lydian; what is a perfect 4th *below* C?
(5) If you cannot find a perfect 4th below C, then find a perfect 5th above C (the inversion of a perfect 4th). G is a perfect 5th above C and therefore a perfect 4th below C.
(6) C major is to F Lydian as G major (X) is to C Lydian.
(7) G major has one sharp (F♯) and so does C Lydian.

Example 2–21: the key signature of C Lydian

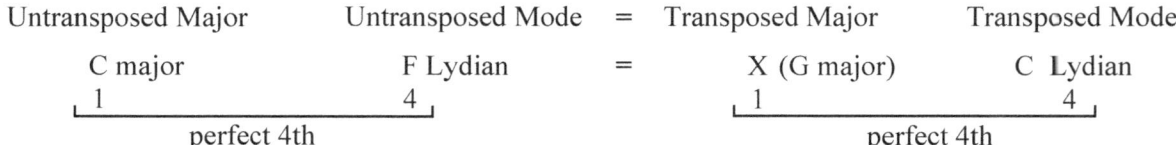

(1) What is the key signature for the transposed mode of F♯ Aeolian (example 2–22)?
(2) A Aeolian is the untransposed mode and scale degree 6 of the untransposed major, C major.
(3) F♯ Aeolian occurs on scale degree 6 of what transposed major (X)?
(4) C major is to A Aeolian (a major 6th) as X major is to F♯ Aeolian; what is a major 6th *below* F♯?
(5) If you cannot find a major 6th below F♯, then find a minor 3rd above F♯ (the inversion of a major 6th). A is a minor 3rd above F♯ and therefore a major 6th below F♯.
(6) C major is to A Aeolian as A major (X) is to F♯ Aeolian.
(7) A major has three sharps (F♯, C♯, and G♯) and so does F♯ Aeolian.

Example 2–22: the key signature of F♯ Aeolian

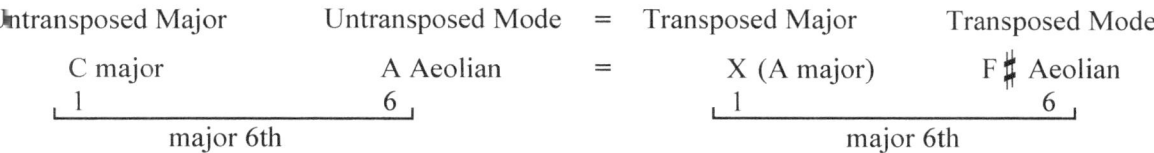

Again, a reminder: with respect to the key signature, the relative Aeolian and the relative minor are equivalent terms. The relative minor of A major is F♯ minor; both modes have three sharps.

(1) What is the key signature for the transposed mode of F Phrygian (example 2–23)?
(2) E Phrygian is the untransposed mode and scale degree 3 of the untransposed major, C major.
(3) F Phrygian occurs on scale degree 3 of what transposed major (X)?
(4) C major is to E Phrygian (a major 3rd) as X major is to F Phrygian; what is a major 3rd *below* F?
(5) If you cannot find a major 3rd below F, then find a minor 6th above F (the inversion of a major 3rd). D♭ is a minor 6th above F and therefore a major 3rd below F.
(6) C major is to E Phrygian as D♭ major (X) is to F Phrygian.
(7) D♭ major has five flats (B♭, E♭, A♭, D♭, and G♭) and so does F Phrygian.

Example 2–23: the key signature of F Phrygian

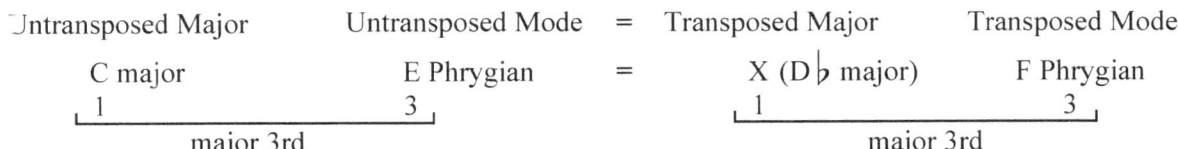

(1) What is the key signature for the transposed mode of D♯ Locrian (example 2–24)?
(2) B Locrian is the untransposed mode and scale degree 7 of the untransposed major, C major.
(3) D♯ Locrian occurs on scale degree 7 of what transposed major (X)?
(4) C major is to B Locrian (a major 7th) as X major is to D♯ Locrian; what is a major 7th *below* D♯?
(5) If you cannot find a major 7th below D♯, then find a minor 2nd above D♯ (the inversion of a major 7th). E is a minor 2nd above D♯ and therefore a major 7th below D♯.
(6) C major is to B Locrian as E major (X) is to D♯ Locrian.
(7) E major has four sharps (F♯, C♯, G♯, and D♯) and so does D♯ Locrian.

Example 2–24: the key signature of D♯ Locrian

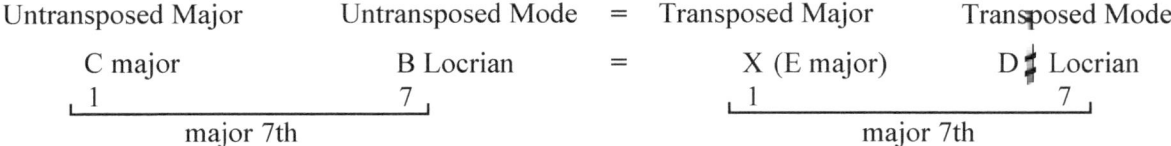

(1) What is the key signature for the transposed mode of D♭ Mixolydian (example 2–25)?
(2) G Mixolydian is the untransposed mode and scale degree 5 of the untransposed major, C major.
(3) D♭ Mixolydian occurs on scale degree 5 of what transposed major (X)?
(4) C major is to G Mixolydian (a perfect 5th) as X major is to D♭ Mixolydian; what is a perfect 5th *below* D♭?
(5) If you cannot find a perfect 5th below D♭, then find a perfect 4th above D♭ (the inversion of a perfect 5th). G♭ is a perfect 4th above D♭ and therefore a perfect 5th below D♭.
(6) C major is to G Mixolydian as G♭ major (X) is to D♭ Mixolydian.
(7) G♭ major has six flats (B♭, E♭, A♭, D♭, G♭ and C♭) and so does D♭ Mixolydian.

Example 2–25: the key signature of D♭ Mixolydian

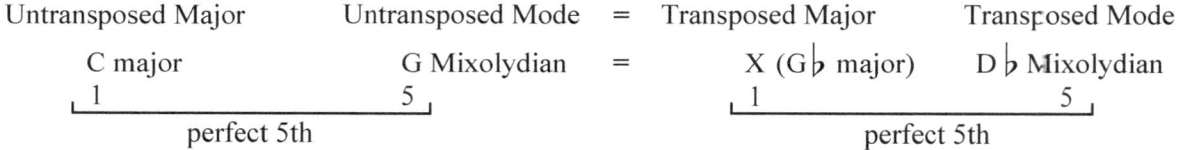

Given the Key and Key Signature, Find the Right Mode

The exercises introduced in the foregoing examples will help you to play (or sing) scales and/or melodies in any key using any of the various diatonic modes discussed in this chapter. Once you have found the key signature of a specified key center and mode, it is a relatively simple task to run through the tones of the mode, assuming that you have some degree of facility with an instrument (or voice).

In examples 2–14 through 25, we found the relationship between two pairs of conditions by placing an unknown value (X) into the second pair. In examples 2–26 through 31, we find the relationship between two pairs of conditions by moving the unknown value to the first pair, from the transposed major to the untransposed mode. With the first pair of conditions now containing the unknown value, the object of the inquiry becomes the identity of the transposed mode rather than its key signature. Accordingly, given both the key center (transposed mode) and the key signature (transposed major), what is the *mode* of the music?

(1) Given the tonic key of E♭ and a key signature with four flats, what is the name of the transposed mode (example 2–26)?
(2) The key signature of four flats represents the transposed major key of A♭ major.
(3) E♭ is scale degree 5 of the transposed major, A♭ major; A♭ is a perfect 5th *below* E♭.
(4) The perfect 5th between A♭ and E♭ must be duplicated between C major and the untransposed mode X. A perfect 5th above C is G. G represents the untransposed Mixolydian mode.
(5) C major is to G Mixolydian as A♭ major is to E♭ Mixolydian
(6) Therefore, the transposed mode is E♭ Mixolydian.
(7) A♭ major has four flats (B♭, E♭, A♭, and D♭) and so does E♭ Mixolydian.

Example 2–26: What mode on E♭ has four flats?

Untransposed Major	Untransposed Mode	=	Transposed Major	Transposed Mode
C major	X (G Mixolydian)	=	A♭ major (4 Flats)	E♭
1	5		1	5
perfect 5th			perfect 5th	

(1) Given the tonic key of F♯ and a key signature with four sharps, what is the name of the transposed mode (example 2–27)?
(2) The key signature of four sharps represents the transposed major key of E major.
(3) F♯ is scale degree 2 of the transposed major, E major; E is a major 2nd *below* F♯.
(4) The major 2nd between E and F♯ must be duplicated between C major and the untransposed mode X. A major 2nd above C is D. D represents the untransposed Dorian mode.
(5) C major is to D Dorian as E major is to F♯ Dorian.
(6) Therefore, the transposed mode is F♯ Dorian.
(7) E major has four sharps (F♯, C♯, G♯, and D♯) and so does F♯ Dorian.

Example 2–27: What mode on F♯ has four sharps?

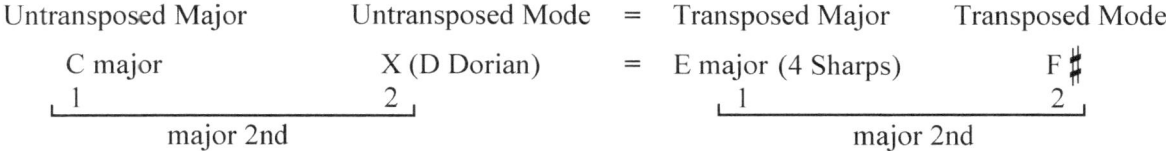

(1) Given the tonic key of B♭ and a key signature with seven flats, what is the name of the transposed mode (example 2–28)?
(2) The key signature of seven flats represents the transposed major key of C♭ major.
(3) B♭ is scale degree 7 of the transposed major, C♭ major; C♭ is a major 7th *below* B♭.
(4) The major 7th between C♭ and B♭ must be duplicated between C major and the untransposed mode X. A major 7th above C is B. B represents the untransposed Locrian mode.
(5) C major is to B Locrian as C♭ major is to B♭ Locrian.
(6) Therefore, the transposed mode is B♭ Locrian.
(7) C♭ major has seven flats (B♭, E♭, A♭, D♭, G♭, C♭, and F♭) and so does B♭ Locrian.

Example 2–28: What mode on B♭ has seven flats?

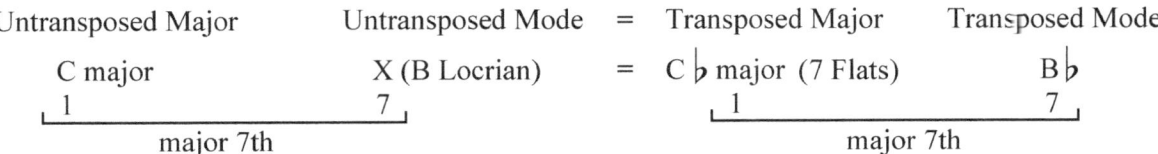

(1) Given the tonic key of B and a key signature with one sharp, what is the name of the transposed mode (example 2–29)?
(2) The key signature of one sharp represents the transposed major key of G major.
(3) B is scale degree 3 of the transposed major, G major; G is a major 3rd *below* B.
(4) The major 3rd between G and B must be duplicated between C major and the untransposed mode X. A major 3rd above C is E. E represents the untransposed Phrygian mode.
(5) C major is to E Phrygian as G major is to B Phrygian.
(6) Therefore, the transposed mode is B Phrygian.
(7) G major has one sharp (F♯) and so does B Phrygian.

Example 2–29: What mode on B has one sharp?

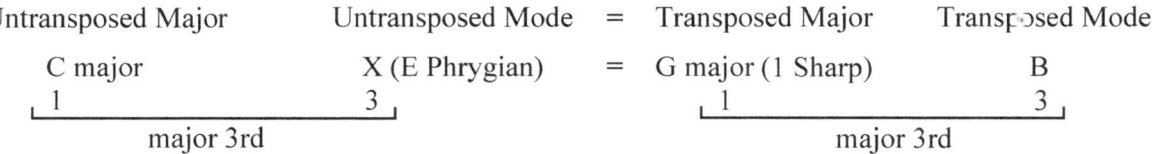

(1) Given the tonic key of E♭ and a key signature with six flats, what is the name of the transposed mode (example 2–30)?
(2) The key signature of six flats represents the transposed major key of G♭ major.
(3) E♭ is scale degree 6 of the transposed major, G♭ major; G♭ is a major 6th *below* E♭.
(4) The major 6th between G♭ and E♭ must be duplicated between C major and the untransposed mode X. A major 6th above C is A. A represents the untransposed Aeolian mode.
(5) C major is to A Aeolian as G♭ major is to E♭ Aeolian.
(6) Therefore, the transposed mode is E♭ Aeolian.
(7) G♭ major has six flats (B♭, E♭, A♭, D♭, G♭, and C♭) and so does E♭ Aeolian.

Example 2–30: What mode on E♭ has six flats?

Untransposed Major	Untransposed Mode	=	Transposed Major	Transposed Mode
C major	X (A Aeolian)	=	G♭ major (6 Flats)	E♭
1 — major 6th — 6			1 — major 6th — 6	

(1) Given the tonic key of G and a key signature with two sharps, what is the name of the transposed mode (example 2–31)?
(2) The key signature of two sharps represents the transposed major key of D major.
(3) G is scale degree 4 of the transposed major, D major; D is a perfect 4th *below* G.
(4) The perfect 4th between D and G must be duplicated between C major and the untransposed mode X. A perfect 4th above C is F. F represents the untransposed Lydian mode.
(5) C major is to F Lydian as D major is to G Lydian.
(6) Therefore, the transposed mode is G Lydian.
(7) D major has two sharps (F♯ and C♯) and so does G Lydian.

Example 2–31: What mode on G has two sharps?

Untransposed Major	Untransposed Mode	=	Transposed Major	Transposed Mode
C major	X (F Lydian)	=	D major (2 Sharps)	G
1 — perfect 4th — 4			1 — perfect 4th — 4	

Examples 2–26 through 31 have demonstrated how to identify the mode of a music composition, *if we know both its key center and pitch content* (as represented in the key signature). We must add one caveat to the process of mode identification, however. The melody of the composition may contain tones that are not appropriate to the mode—chromatic notes (see above, p. 27). Upon mastering the fundamentals of music and basic harmony, you will have the requisite knowledge to ferret out these "inappropriate" tones and recognize those components of the music that are native (that is, diatonic) to the mode and those that are not.

Triad Formation within the Seven Church Modes

Now that we have addressed the challenges of mode transposition and identification, let us consider the formation of triads in each of the seven church modes, starting the mode with which we are most familiar, the Ionian mode, or major mode. Memorize the qualities of the triads as they occur on the white keys of the piano keyboard within the C-major octave. This knowledge will make it much easier to determine the triadic content for each of the remaining church modes in both their untransposed and transposed forms. After considering the triad qualities in each of the seven untransposed modes, we shall learn how to recognize and create triads in any transposed mode.

In examples 2–14 through 31, we referenced the names and octave ranges of the church modes from the perspective of the C-major scale in order to either identify the transposed mode or find its key signature. It should be remembered, however, that each scale degree of any diatonic mode may also have one of the following names: tonic, supertonic, mediant, subdominant, dominant, submediant, and leading tone or subtonic (we use the term leading tone if the distance from scale degree 7 to 8 is a half step and subtonic if the distance from scale degree 7 to 8 is a whole step).

Example 2–32 presents these names within the familiar context of C major and shows all of the triad possibilities for the mode: major triads occur in the tonic, subdominant, and dominant areas. Minor triads appear in the supertonic, mediant, and submediant areas. The leading-tone area of the major mode projects a diminished triad.

Example 2–32: scale-degree names and triad qualities in C Major

MT	mt	mt	MT	MT	mt	d°t
1	2	3	4	5	6	7
Tonic	Supertonic	Mediant	Subdominant	Dominant	Submediant	Leading Tone

In D Dorian (example 2–33), major triads occur in the mediant, subdominant, and subtonic areas. Minor triads appear in the tonic, supertonic, and dominant areas. The submediant area of the Dorian mode projects a diminished triad.

Example 2–33: scale-degree names and triad qualities in D Dorian

mt	mt	MT	MT	mt	d°t	MT
1	2	3	4	5	6	7
Tonic	Supertonic	Mediant	Subdominant	Dominant	Submediant	Subtonic

In E Phrygian (example 2–34), major triads occur in the supertonic, mediant, and submediant areas. Minor triads appear in the tonic, subdominant, and subtonic areas. The dominant area of the Phrygian mode projects a diminished triad.

Example 2–34: scale-degree names and triad qualities in E Phrygian

mt	MT	MT	mt	d°t	MT	mt
1	2	3	4	5	6	7
Tonic	Supertonic	Mediant	Subdominant	Dominant	Submediant	Subtonic

In F Lydian (example 2–35), major triads occur in the tonic, supertonic, and dominant areas. Minor triads appear in the mediant, submediant, and leading-tone areas. The subdominant area of the Lydian mode projects a diminished triad.

Example 2–35: scale-degree names and triad qualities in F Lydian

[musical notation: F Lydian scale with triads labeled MT, MT, mt, d°t, MT, mt, mt on scale degrees 1–7: Tonic, Supertonic, Mediant, Subdominant, Dominant, Submediant, Leading tone]

In G Mixolydian (example 2–36), major triads occur in the tonic, sudominant, and subtonic areas. Minor triads appear in the supertonic, dominant, and submediant areas. The mediant area of the Mixolydian mode projects a diminished triad.

Example 2–36: scale-degree names and triad qualities in G Mixolydian

[musical notation: G Mixolydian scale with triads labeled MT, mt, d°t, MT, mt, mt, MT on scale degrees 1–7: Tonic, Supertonic, Mediant, Subdominant, Dominant, Submediant, Subtonic]

In A Aeolian (example 2–37), major triads occur in the mediant, submediant, and subtonic areas. Minor triads appear in the tonic, subdominant, and dominant areas. The supertonic area of the Aeolian mode projects a diminished triad. (In order to keep as many triads as possible within the limits of the staff, the range of the Aeolian mode in 2–37 begins one octave register lower in relation to the range of the Mixolydian mode in example 2–36 above.)

Example 2–37: scale-degree names and triad qualities in A Aeolian

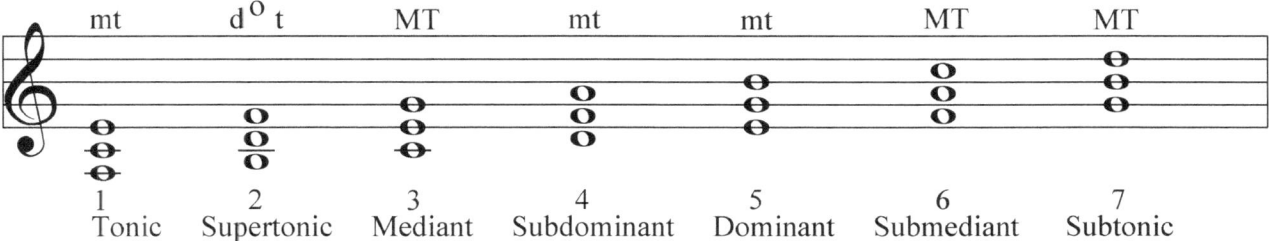

[musical notation: A Aeolian scale with triads labeled mt, d°t, MT, mt, mt, MT, MT on scale degrees 1–7: Tonic, Supertonic, Mediant, Subdominant, Dominant, Submediant, Subtonic]

In B Locrian (example 2–38), major triads occur in the supertonic, dominant, and submediant areas. Minor triads appear in the mediant, subdominant, and subtonic areas. The tonic area of the Locrian mode projects a diminished triad. (In order to keep as many triads as possible within the limits of the staff, the range of the Locrian mode in 2–38 begins one octave register lower in relation to the range of the Mixolydian mode in example 2–36 above.)

Example 2–38: scale-degree names and triad qualities in B Locrian

	1	2	3	4	5	6	7
	d° t	MT	mt	mt	MT	MT	mt
	Tonic	Supertonic	Mediant	Subdominant	Dominant	Submediant	Subtonic

The seven church modes exhibit certain similarities and differences among their half-step profiles and triad formations. Example 2–39 shows the correspondences and differences between the seven modes by identifying the locations of major and minor triads in the respective scale degree areas of each mode. We omit the diminished triad, as it occurs on a different scale degree in each of the seven modes. In order to the maintain a consistent terminology, the major mode is referred to here as the Ionian mode.

The circled Roman numerals in the example constitute a *generalized* type of chord symbol that, without describing the specific chord quality, nonetheless indicates the exact scale degree of the mode upon which a triad may be formed. Since this generalized type of chord symbol makes no distinction between triad qualities, the Roman numerals are all expressed in uppercase. Therefore, in addition to knowing how to transpose and identify the modes, we must commit the properties of the modes to memory, including their half-step profiles and triadic contents.

Example 2–39: major and minor triad formations on each scale degree of the seven church modes

scale degree	major triad	minor triad
I	Ionian, Lydian, Mixolydian	Dorian, Phrygian, Aeolian
II	Phrygian, Lydian, Locrian	Ionian, Dorian, Mixolydian
III	Dorian, Phrygian, Aeolian	Ionian, Lydian, Locrian
IV	Ionian, Dorian, Mixolydian	Phrygian, Aeolian, Locrian
V	Ionian, Lydian, Locrian	Dorian, Mixolydian, Aeolian
VI	Phrygian, Aeolian, Locrian	Ionian, Lydian, Mixolydian
VII	Dorian, Mixolydian, Aeolian	Phrygian, Locrian, Lydian

As we have observed, the Ionian, Lydian, and Mixolydian modes have major tonic triads and fall into the category of major prototypes, while the Dorian, Phrygian, and Aeolian modes have minor tonic triads and are consequently minor prototypes. The Locrian mode occupies an exceptional position as a minor prototype because it has a diminished tonic triad.

Example 2–39 indicates that within the category of major prototypes, the Ionian and Mixolydian modes have major subdominants and minor supertonics. The Ionian and Lydian modes have major dominants and minor mediants. The Ionian, Lydian, and Mixolydian modes have minor submediants.

Within the category of minor prototypes, both the Phrygian and Locrian modes have major supertonics. The Dorian, Phrygian, and Aeolian modes have major mediants. The Phrygian, Aeolian, and Locrian modes have major submediants and minor subdominants. The Dorian and Aeolian modes have major subtonics and minor dominants. The Phrygian and Locrian modes have minor subtonics.

Triad Formation and Mode Transposition

In this section, we are provided with three bits of information for meeting the following challenge: given the key, the mode, and generalized chord symbol in the examples below, find the appropriate triad, spell it with three voices in close structure, and then supply a four-part voicing in open structure.

Once we have located the correct scale degree upon which to construct the triad using the generalized chord symbol, our knowledge of the key and mode will enable us to determine the key signature and thus the root, third, and fifth elements of the chord. Remember that the specific quality of the triad as either major, minor, or diminished is a function of the given mode's pitch content, derived from the key signature (augmented triads are not diatonically formable within the modal system).

In this exercise, we use whole-notes for the close structures and half notes for the open structures; moreover, since the four-part textures contain half notes, careful observance of the correct stem direction is required.

The abbreviations for the six modes referenced in the present exercise are D (Dorian), P (Phrygian), Ly (Lydian), M (Mixolydian), A (Aeolian), and L (Locrian). The absence of figured bass in the circled chord symbol indicates root position.

(1) In A Dorian, spell the supertonic triad in close structure and then in open structure (example 2–40).
(2) What is the key signature of the transposed mode of A Dorian?
(3) The interval of a major 2nd spans the distance between the untransposed modes of C major and D Dorian. C major is to D Dorian as X is to A Dorian. A major 2nd *below* A is G.
(4) Therefore, X is G. G major has one sharp (F♯) and so does A Dorian.
(5) The supertonic scale degree of A Dorian is B.
(6) Using the pitch content of A Dorian, build the triad that occurs on the supertonic of A Dorian (B).
(7) The chord tones for the supertonic of A Dorian are B D F♯, a minor triad in $\frac{5}{3}$ position. The open structure of 2–40 has a doubled third.

Example 2–40: the supertonic triad of A Dorian

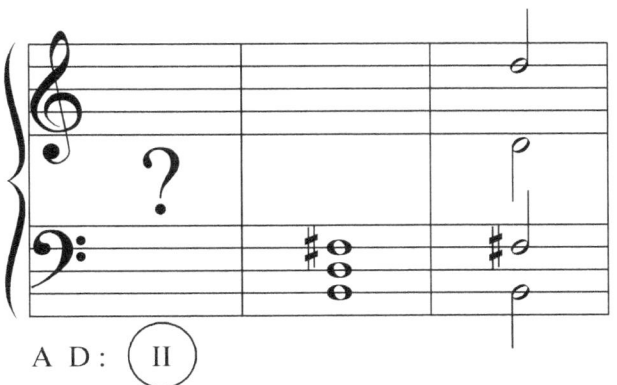

80   Chapter 2   The Church Modes

(1) In G Phrygian, spell the mediant triad in close structure and then in open structure (example 2–41).
(2) What is the key signature of the transposed mode of G Phrygian?
(3) The interval of a major 3rd spans the distance between the untransposed modes of C major and E Phrygian. C major is to E Phrygian as X is to G Phrygian. A major 3rd *below* G is E♭.
(4) Therefore, X is E♭. E♭ major has three flats (B♭, E♭, and A♭) and so does G Phrygian.
(5) The mediant scale degree of G Phrygian is B♭.
(6) Using the pitch content of G Phrygian, build the triad that occurs on the mediant of G Phrygian (B♭).
(7) The chord tones for the mediant of G Phrygian are B♭ D F, a major triad in $^5_3$ position. The open structure of 2–41 has a doubled root.

Example 2–41: the mediant triad of G Phrygian

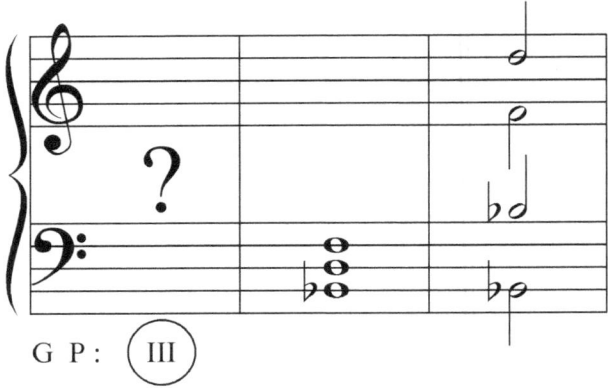

(1) In D♯ Locrian, spell the dominant triad in close structure and then in open structure (example 2–42).
(2) What is the key signature of the transposed mode of D♯ Locrian?
(3) The interval of a major 7th spans the distance between the untransposed modes of C major and B Locrian. C major is to B Locrian as X is to D♯ Locrian. A major 7th *below* D♯ is E.
(4) Therefore, X is E. E major has four sharps (F♯, C♯, G♯, and D♯) and so does D♯ Locrian.
(5) The dominant scale degree of D♯ Locrian is A.
(6) Using the pitch content of D♯ Locrian, build the triad that occurs on the dominant of D♯ Locrian (A).
(7) The chord tones for the dominant of D♯ Locrian are A C♯ E, a major triad in $^5_3$ position. The open structure of 2–42 has a doubled root.

Example 2–42: the dominant triad of D♯ Locrian

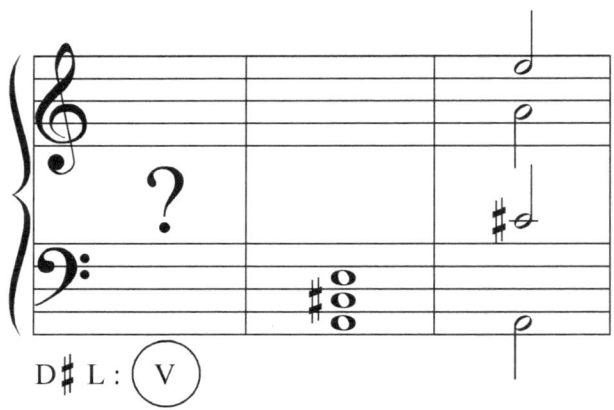

(1) In F Aeolian, spell the subtonic triad in close structure and then in open structure (example 2–43).
(2) What is the key signature of the transposed mode of F Aeolian?
(3) The interval of a major 6th spans the distance between the untransposed modes of C major and A Aeolian. C major is to A Aeolian as X is to F Aeolian. A major 6th *below* F is A♭.
(4) Therefore, X is A♭. A♭ has four flats (B♭, E♭, A♭, and D♭) and so does F Aeolian.
(5) The subtonic scale degree of F Aeolian is E♭.
(6) Using the pitch content of F Aeolian, build the triad that occurs on the subtonic of F Aeolian (E♭).
(7) The chord tones for the subtonic of F Aeolian are E♭ G B♭, a major triad in $\frac{5}{3}$ position. The open structure of 2–43 has a doubled fifth.

Example 2–43: the subtonic triad of F Aeolian

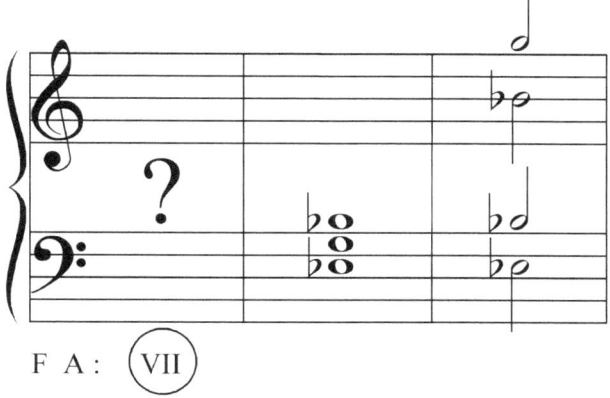

F A: VII

(1) In F♯ Lydian, spell the submediant triad in close structure and then in open structure (example 2–44).
(2) What is the key signature of the transposed mode of F♯ Lydian?
(3) The interval of a perfect 4th spans the distance between the untransposed modes of C major and F Lydian. C major is to F Lydian as X is to F♯ Lydian. A perfect 4th *below* F♯ is C♯.
(4) Therefore, X is C♯. C♯ major has seven sharps (F♯, C♯, G♯, D♯, A♯, E♯, and B♯) and so does F♯ Lydian.
(5) The submediant scale degree of F♯ Lydian is D♯.
(6) Using the pitch content of F♯ Lydian, build the triad that occurs on the submediant of F♯ Lydian (D♯).
(7) The chord tones for the submediant of F♯ Lydian are D♯ F♯ A♯, a minor triad in $\frac{5}{3}$ position. The open structure of 2–44 has a doubled third.

Example 2–44: the submediant triad of F♯ Lydian

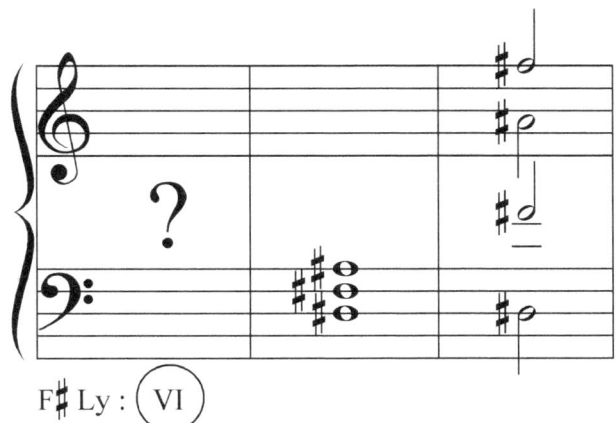

F♯ Ly: VI

82   Chapter 2 The Church Modes

(1) In G♭ Mixolydian, spell the subdominant triad in close structure and then in open structure (example 2–45).
(2) What is the key signature of the transposed mode of G♭ Mixolydian?
(3) The interval of a perfect 5th spans the distance between the untransposed modes of C major and G Mixolydian. C major is to G Mixolydian as X is to G♭ Mixolydian. A perfect 5th *below* G♭ is C♭.
(4) Therefore, X is C♭. C♭ has seven flats (B♭, E♭, A♭, D♭, G♭, C♭, and F♭) and so does G♭ Mixolydian.
(5) The subdominant scale degree of G♭ Mixolydian is C♭.
(6) Using the pitch content of G♭ Mixolydian, build the triad that occurs on the subdominant of G♭ Mixolydian (C♭).
(7) The chord tones for the subdominant of G♭ Mixolydian are C♭ E♭ G♭, a major triad in $^5_3$ position. The open structure of 2–45 has a doubled fifth.

Example 2–45: the subdominant triad of G♭ Mixolydian

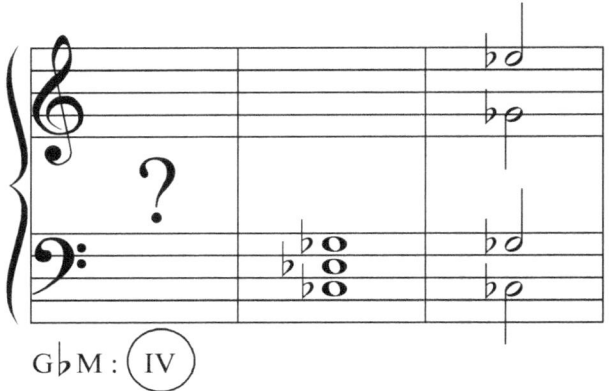

Triad Inversion

The following exercises contain one additional step in that all of the triads are inverted. Observe the doubling principles for triads carefully. In particular, double the third of the diminished triad in $^6_3$ position and the fifth of all triads in $^6_4$ position. (Remember, both the $^5_3$ and $^6_4$ positions of the diminished triad are usually avoided because of the tritone interval that occurs between the lowest voice of the texture and one of the upper voices.)

(1) In G Dorian, spell the submediant triad in close structure, place it in $^6_3$ position, and then voice the chord in open structure (example 2–46).
(2) What is the key signature of the transposed mode of G Dorian?
(3) The interval of a major 2nd spans the distance between the untransposed modes of C major and D Dorian. C major is to D Dorian as X is to G Dorian. A major 2nd *below* G is F.
(4) Therefore, X is F. F major has one flat (B♭) and so does G Dorian.
(5) The submediant scale degree of G Dorian is E.
(6) Using the pitch content of G Dorian, build the triad that occurs on the submediant of G Dorian (E).
(7) The chord tones for the submediant of G Dorian are E G B♭, a diminished triad.
(8) Once the E-diminished triad has been constructed in $^5_3$ position, move the root of the chord up one octave (into the prime register) so that the third of the chord is exposed as the lowest note of the musical texture. With the third in the bass (G), the chord is now in $^6_3$ position, first inversion. In open structure, the E-diminished triad has a doubled third.

Example 2–46: the submediant triad of G Dorian

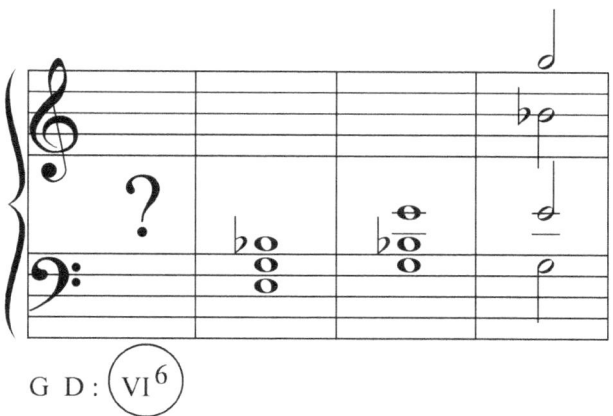

G D: VI^6

(1) In D Lydian, spell the leading-tone triad in close structure, place it in $^6_4$ position, and then voice the chord in open structure (example 2–47).
(2) What is the key signature of the transposed mode of D Lydian?
(3) The interval of a perfect 4th spans the distance between the untransposed modes of C major and F Lydian. C major is to F Lydian as X is to D Lydian. A perfect 4th *below* D is A.
(4) Therefore, X is A. A major has three sharps (F♯, C♯, and G♯) and so does D Lydian.
(5) The leading-tone scale degree of D Lydian is C♯.
(6) Using the pitch content of D Lydian, build the triad that occurs on the leading tone of D Lydian (C♯).
(7) The chord tones for the leading tone of D Lydian are C♯ E G♯, a minor triad.
(8) Once the C♯-minor triad has been constructed in $^5_3$ position, move the fifth of the chord down one octave (into the great register) so that the fifth of the chord becomes the lowest note of the musical texture. With the fifth in the bass (G♯), the chord is now in $^6_4$ position, second inversion. In open structure, the C♯-minor triad has a doubled fifth.

Example 2–47: the leading-tone triad of D Lydian

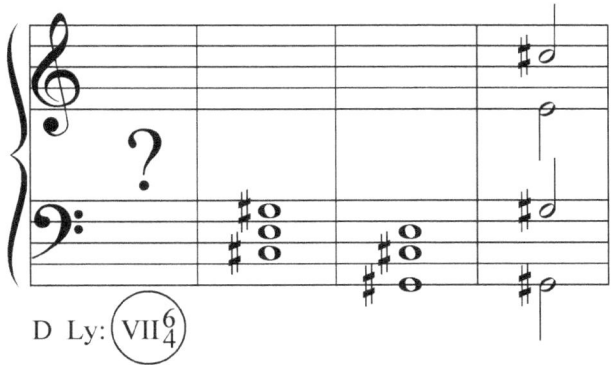

D Ly: VII$^6_4$

84   Chapter 2 The Church Modes

(1) In A Phrygian, spell the supertonic triad in close structure, place it in $^6_3$ position, and then voice the chord in open structure (example 2–48).
(2) What is the key signature of the transposed mode of A Phrygian?
(3) The interval of a major 3rd spans the distance between the untransposed modes of C major and E Phrygian. C major is to E Phrygian as X is to A Phrygian. A major 3rd *below* A is F.
(4) Therefore, X is F. F major has one flat (B♭) and so does A Phrygian.
(5) The supertonic scale degree of A Phrygian is B♭.
(6) Using the pitch content of A Phrygian, build the triad that occurs on the supertonic of A Phrygian (B♭).
(7) The chord tones for the supertonic of A Phrygian are B♭ D F, a major triad.
(8) Once the B♭-major triad has been constructed in $^5_3$ position, move the root of the chord up one octave (into the small register) so that the third of the chord is exposed as the lowest note of the musical texture. With the third in the bass (D), the chord is now in $^6_3$ position, first inversion. In open structure, the B♭-major triad has a doubled third.

Example 2–48: the supertonic triad of A Phrygian

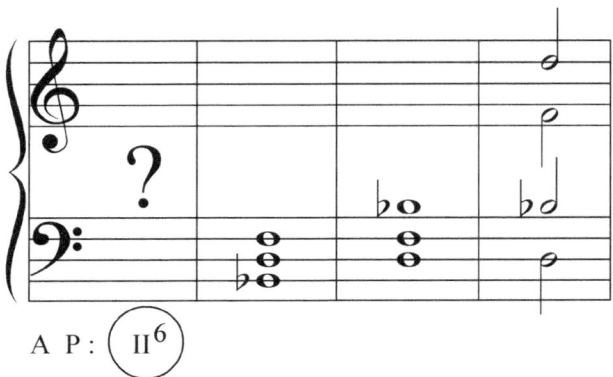

A P: II⁶

(1) In B Mixolydian, spell the dominant triad in close structure, place it in $^6_4$ position, and then voice the chord in open structure (example 2–49).
(2) What is the key signature of the transposed mode of B Mixolydian?
(3) The interval of a perfect 5th spans the distance between the untransposed modes of C major and G Mixolydian. C major is to G Mixolydian as X is to B Mixolydian. A perfect 5th *below* B is E.
(4) Therefore, X is E. E major has four sharps (F♯, C♯, G♯, and D♯) and so does B Mixolydian.
(5) The dominant scale degree of B Mixolydian is F♯.
(6) Using the pitch content of B Mixolydian, build the triad that occurs on the dominant of B Mixolydian (F♯).
(7) The chord tones for the dominant of B Mixolydian are F♯ A C♯, a minor triad.
(8) Once the F♯-minor triad has been constructed in $^5_3$ position, move the fifth of the chord down one octave (into the small register) so that the fifth of the chord becomes the lowest note of the musical texture. With the fifth in the bass (C♯), the chord is now in $^6_4$ position, second inversion. In open structure, the F♯-minor triad has a doubled fifth.

Example 2–49: the dominant triad of B Mixolydian

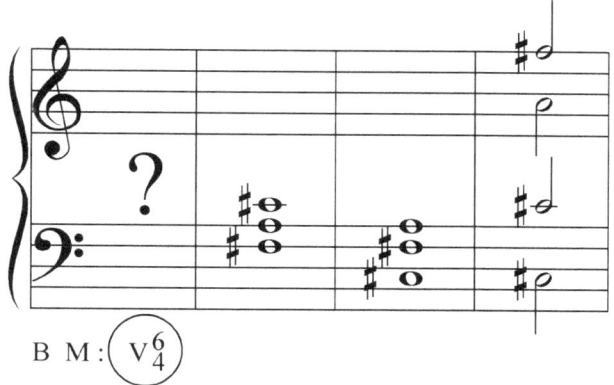

(1) In C Locrian, spell the subdominant triad in close structure, place it in $^6_4$ position, and then voice the chord in open structure (example 2–50).
(2) What is the key signature of the transposed mode of C Locrian?
(3) The interval of a major 7th spans the distance between the untransposed modes of C major and B Locrian. C major is to B Locrian as X is to C Locrian. A major 7th *below* C is D♭.
(4) Therefore, X is D♭. D♭ major has five flats (B♭, E♭, A♭, D♭, and G♭) and so does C Locrian.
(5) The subdominant scale degree of C Locrian is F.
(6) Using the pitch content of C Locrian, build the triad that occurs on the subdominant of C Locrian (F).
(7) The chord tones for the subdominant of C Locrian are F A♭ C, a minor triad.
(8) Once the F-minor triad has been constructed in $^5_3$ position, move the fifth of the chord down one octave (into the small register) so that the fifth of the chord becomes the lowest note of the musical texture. With the fifth in the bass (C), the chord is now in $^6_4$ position, second inversion. In open structure, the F-minor triad has a doubled fifth.

Example 2–50: the subdominant triad of C Locrian

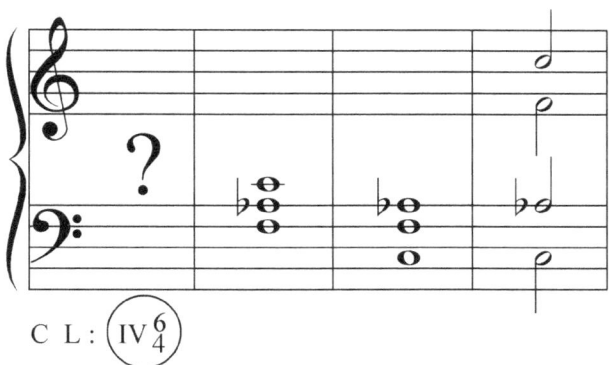

(1) In D♯ Aeolian, spell the mediant triad in close structure, place it in $^6_3$ position, and then voice the chord in open structure (example 2–51).
(2) What is the key signature of the transposed mode of D♯ Aeolian?
(3) The interval of a major 6th spans the distance between the untransposed modes of C major and A Aeolian. C major is to A Aeolian as X is to D♯ Aeolian. A major 6th *below* D♯ is F♯.
(4) Therefore, X is F♯. F♯ major has six sharps (F♯, C♯, G♯, D♯, A♯, and E♯) and so does D♯ Aeolian.
(5) The mediant scale degree of D♯ Aeolian is F♯.
(6) Using the pitch content of D♯ Aeolian, build the triad that occurs on the mediant of D♯ Aeolian (F♯).
(7) The chord tones for the mediant of D♯ Aeolian are F♯ A♯ C♯, a major triad.
(8) Once the F♯-major triad has been constructed in $^5_3$ position, move the root of the chord up one octave (into the small register) so that the third of the chord is exposed as the lowest note of the musical texture. With the third in the bass (A♯), the chord is now in $^6_3$ position, first inversion. In open structure, the F♯-major triad has a doubled third.

Example 2–51: the mediant triad of D♯ Aeolian

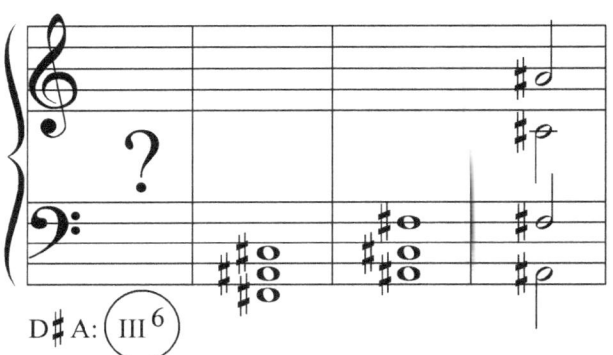

Singing the Major, Chromatic, and Minor Scales

In Chapter 1, we said that a scale was an alphabetical inventory of pitches abstracted from the music. The scale has two practical purposes: first of all, the scale shows the pitch content for the key and mode in which the music is written; and secondly, a scale is a succession of pitches that musicians practice on their respective instruments, usually as a "warm up" exercise before playing or singing actual music. One of the ways to sing a major scale is to assign syllables to each scale degree. This approach is generally referred to as "solmization."

The most common method for singing the major scale assigns the syllables *do, re, mi, fa, sol, la, ti,* and *do* (pronounced doe, ray, mee, fah, soh or soul, lah, tee, and doe) to scale degrees 1, 2, 3, 4, 5, 6, 7, and 8 respectively. As shown in example 2–52, when the scale is moved from the C octave to any other octave, such as F, the syllables remain attached to the scale degrees rather than to the pitches. Thus, scale degrees 1, 2, 3, 4, 5, 6, 7, and 8 in both C major and F major carry the syllables *do, re, mi, fa, sol, la, ti,* and *do*.

Example 2–52: the major scale

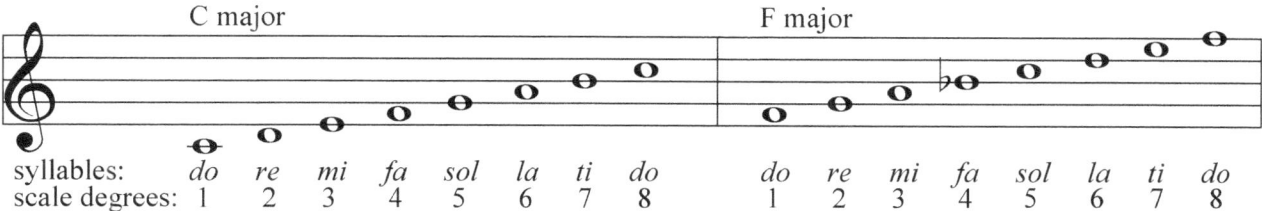

To learn how to sing these syllables and pitches, you should first play the pitches on the piano (if one is available) and then try to match the pitches with your voice. Since the C octave already projects a major scale without incorporating any black keys, first try to play the pitches of C major on the piano, starting in either the small or prime register; secondly, try matching the pitches with your voice using the syllables.

If the range of the C octave is not suitable, you may have to play the scale in a different octave and thereby use some of the black keys. In any case, once you have found a suitable register and octave range, sing the major scale in its ascending and descending form, using the syllables *do, re, mi, fa, sol, la, ti, do* when singing upwards and then *do, ti, la, sol, fa, mi, re, do* when singing downwards (see examples 2–53a and 53b).

Example 2–53

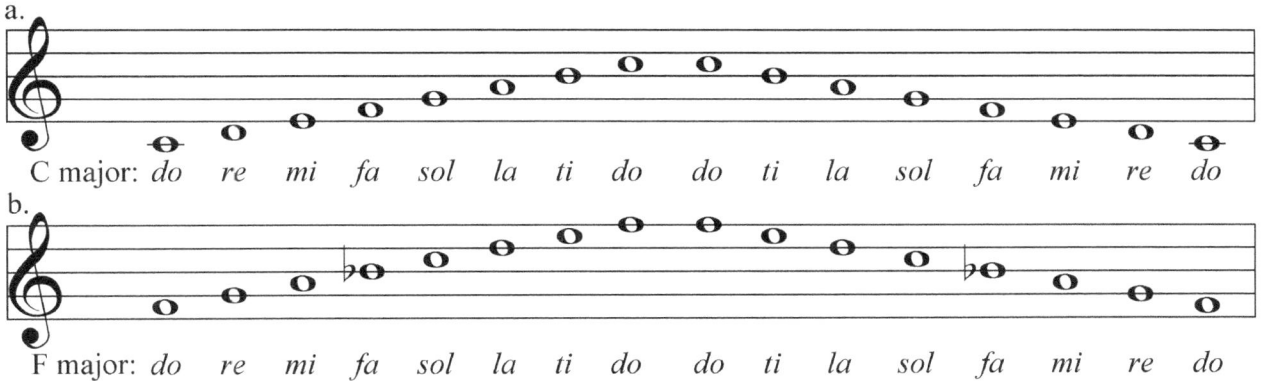

It is also possible to attach syllables to the pitches of the twelve-tone chromatic scale in both its ascending and descending forms (see example 2–54 below). Since the chromatic scale consists primarily of pairs of pitches that involve two different versions of the same letter name, the syllables must change as each pitch moves from one version of itself to the other. We call this type of change syllable inflection.

Just as the pitch names change depending upon the upward or downward direction of the scale, some of the syllable inflections in the ascending chromatic scale are not the same as those of the descending form (*re-ra, mi-me, si-se, li-le*). (Notice that *di* occurs only in the ascending form while *te* appears only in the descending form.)

Example 2–54: the chromatic scale

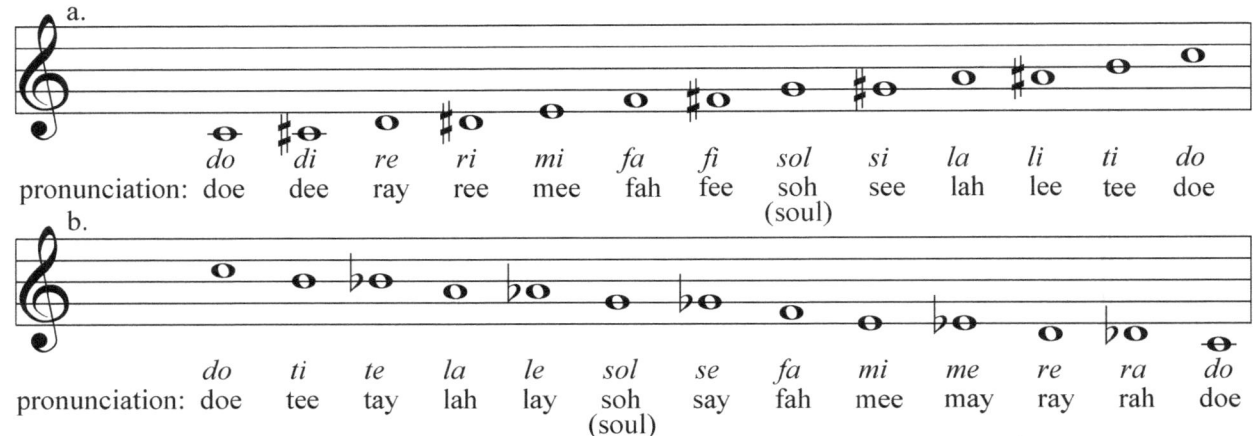

Example 2–55 presents the three forms of minor with the appropriate syllables for singing each scale pattern. When singing the natural minor, scale degrees 3, 6, and 7 carry the syllables *me*, *le*, and *te* respectively, instead of *mi*, *la*, and *ti*. The harmonic minor uses *me* and *le* (scale degrees 3 and 6) instead of *mi* and *la*; however, *ti* is used instead of *te* because it constitutes the leading tone. The melodic minor employs *la* and *ti* (scale degrees ♯6 and ♯7) in its ascending form and *le* and *te* (scale degrees ♭6 and ♭7) in its descending form; *me* is retained in both forms.

Example 2–55

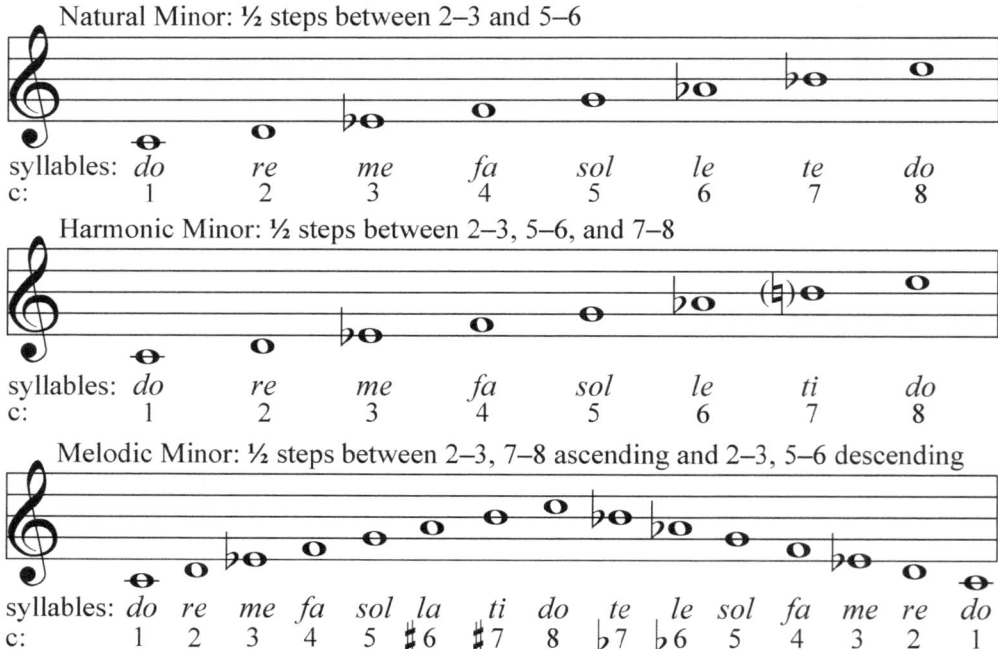

Singing the Church Modes

In example 2–56 below, the techniques of solmization and syllable inflection are demonstrated with all seven church modes, including the Ionian and Aeolian modes.

Example 2–56

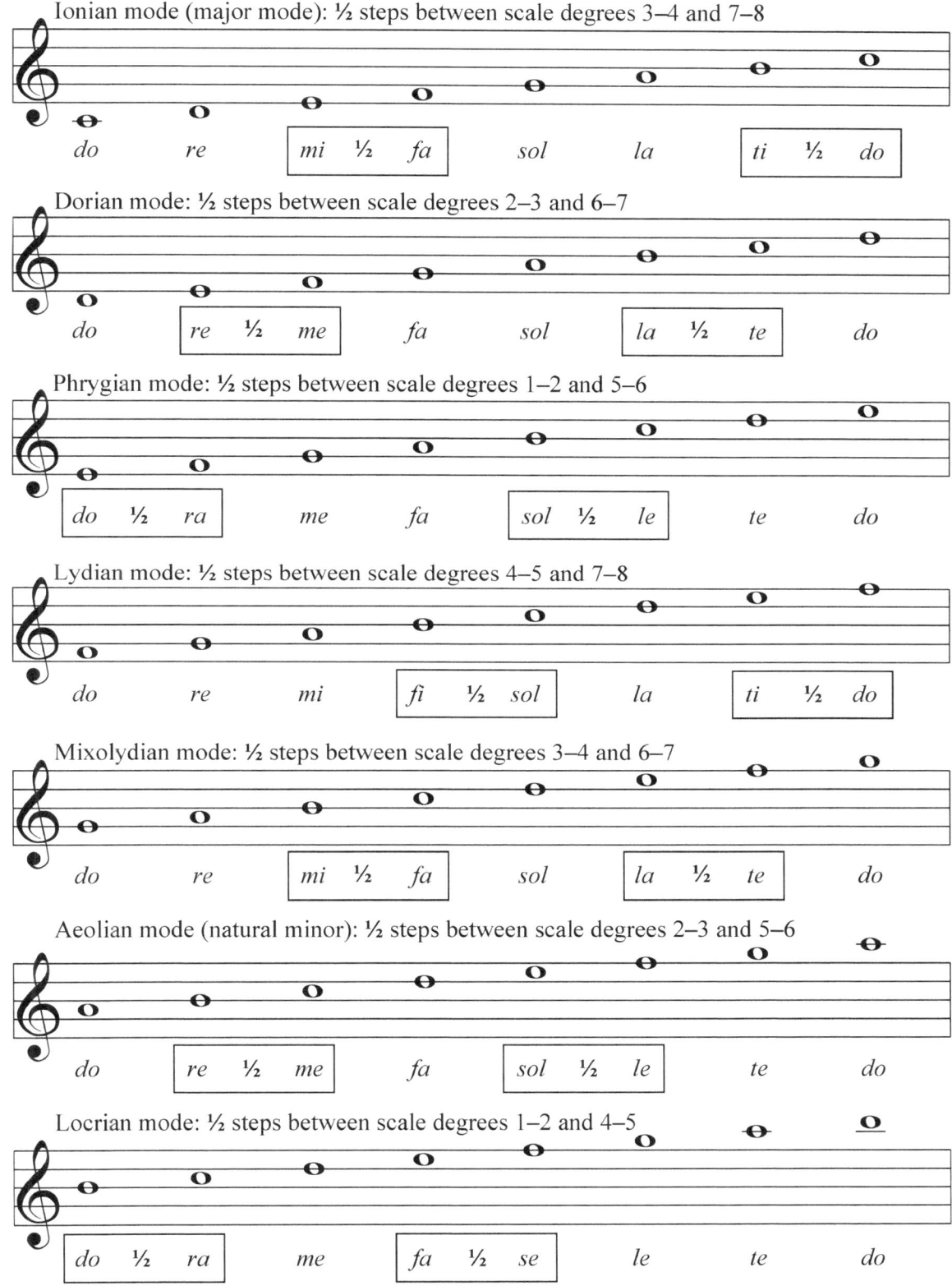

Chapter 3 Voice Leading

The term voice has several different applications. We can use voice, as presented in Chapter 1, to describe the construction and positioning of triads within a four-voice texture. This texture may involve either a close or wide spacing of pitches, sometimes referred to respectively as "close voicing" or "open voicing." A voice may also constitute a melody performed by either vocal cords or an instrument. We may even use voice as part of a verbal phrase describing the technique for "voicing" a chord, observing carefully the appropriate guidelines for the spacing and range of the parts.

Another reference for the term is voice leading. Voice leading takes place during music composition as a process that governs the linear succession of tones in each voice, optimizing how each voice *moves* through time in relation to the rest of the musical texture. In other words, voice leading determines how two or more voices of one chord proceed to those of the next chord. Good voice leading counts among the factors that create a sense of forward motion in music, more evident when the melodic activity of the composition results in connections between unlike chords (that is, chords whose roots are different) than when chord changes do not occur. This chapter is concerned with chord changes and the connections between them that the principles of voice leading regulate.

The principles of voice leading presented in this chapter are based on the music of the "common practice period," the art music that flourished in Western Europe from about 1600 to 1900 C. E. The dates are not precise; however, what emerged during some three hundred years of music composition was the major-minor tonal system, a system with which we are concerned here.

Types of Motion Between Any Two Voices

As stated in Chapter 1 (see p. 53), the goal of good four-voice writing is to maintain the individuality of each melodic line while blending the parts together to produce a harmonious vertical sound. We begin our study of voice leading with the four basic types of motion between any single pair of voices proceeding from one chord to the next: parallel motion, similar motion, contrary motion, and oblique motion.

Parallel Motion

Parallel motion is movement in the same direction, upwards or downwards, between *like* numerical intervals. Generally, there is no problem with parallel motion unless perfect 5ths, perfect octaves, or perfect unisons are involved.

Example 3–1 illustrates some acceptable forms of parallel motion between two voices; throughout these presentations, notice that the voices are indicated by the clef to which they are attached and the direction of their stems. There are never any objections to parallel 3rds or 6ths; 3–1a has parallel 6ths between the tenor and alto voices, 3–1b shows parallel 3rds (10ths) between the tenor and soprano voices.

Example 3–1: acceptable parallel motion

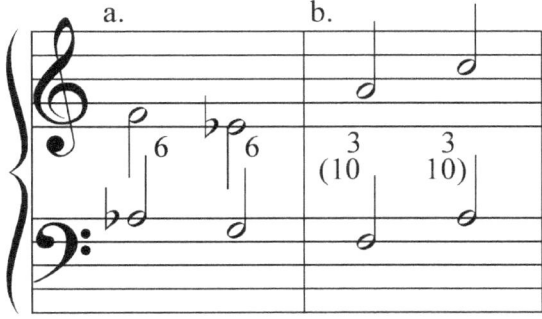

When 4ths are involved in parallel motion, both voices must be above the bass; that is to say, the lower component of the 4th cannot involve the bass voice. Example 3–2a demonstrates acceptable parallel 4ths between the tenor and soprano voices; 3–2b, however, exhibits unacceptable parallel 4ths between the bass and tenor. *Parallel 4ths must not occur between the bass and any upper voice.*

Example 3–2: acceptable and unacceptable parallel 4ths

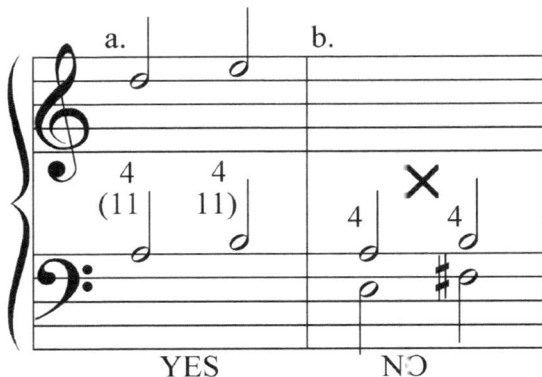

Under no circumstances should we ever have parallel 7ths or 2nds; these are dissonant intervals that must not be used in succession (example 3–3). Each dissonant 7th or 2nd needs to resolve to a consonance.

Example 3–3: unacceptable parallel 7ths and 2nds

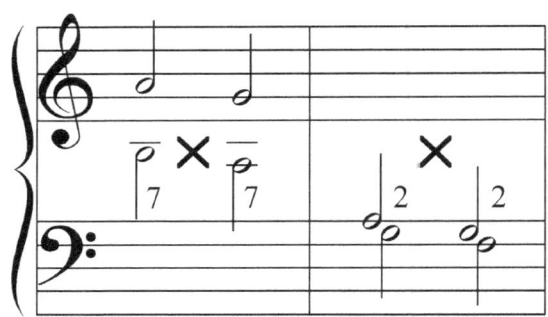

Parallel perfect 5ths, perfect octaves, and perfect unisons should never occur in traditional four-voice textures (example 3–4).

Example 3–4: unacceptable parallel perfect 5ths, perfect octaves, and perfect unisons

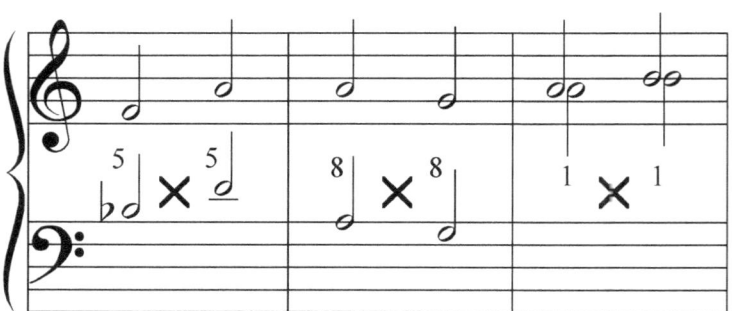

Parallel 5ths are permitted if one of the 5ths is diminished, a succession of intervals sometimes referred to as "unequal 5ths." However, some theoreticians maintain that if the order of succession is the diminished 5th to the perfect 5th, then the dissonant diminished 5th cannot resolve properly. The diminished 5th normally contracts to the interval of the 3rd, which cannot happen if the second 5th is perfect. Still, we will allow parallel successions of 5ths, but only according to the following guidelines:

(1) One of the 5ths must be diminished.
(2) Avoid such movement between the outer voices (that is, the bass and the soprano), especially when the succession is diminished 5th to perfect 5th. The best way to connect the diminished 5th to the perfect 5th is to place the diminished 5th within the triad of the leading tone in first-inversion and the perfect 5th within the tonic triad in first inversion (see below, p. 124, examples 6–4e and 4j).
(3) In both voices, each 5th must move by step.

Example 3–5 demonstrates the license for certain types of parallel movement between 5ths; again, however, parallel perfect 5ths, perfect octaves, and perfect unisons are strictly prohibited. (In 3–5, the diminished 5th is designated with the superscript circle.)

Example 3–5: acceptable parallel 5ths

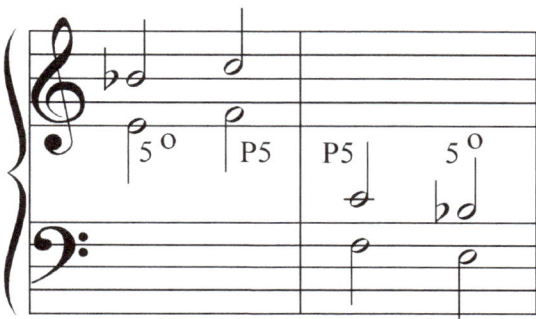

Finally, realize that *the immediate repetition of the same perfect interval between any single pair of voices does not constitute incorrect use of parallel motion* because motion has not actually taken place between those voices (examples 3–6a and 6c). Additionally, the immediate repetition of the same perfect interval between *different pairs of voices* does not constitute incorrect use of parallel motion because the motion is not between the same pair of voices (examples 3–6b and 6d). In both of the cases cited above, the immediate repetition of the same perfect interval may occur between unlike chords (example 3–6a and 6b) or within the same chord (examples 3–6c and 6d).

Example 3–6: acceptable voice leading involving non-parallel perfect octaves

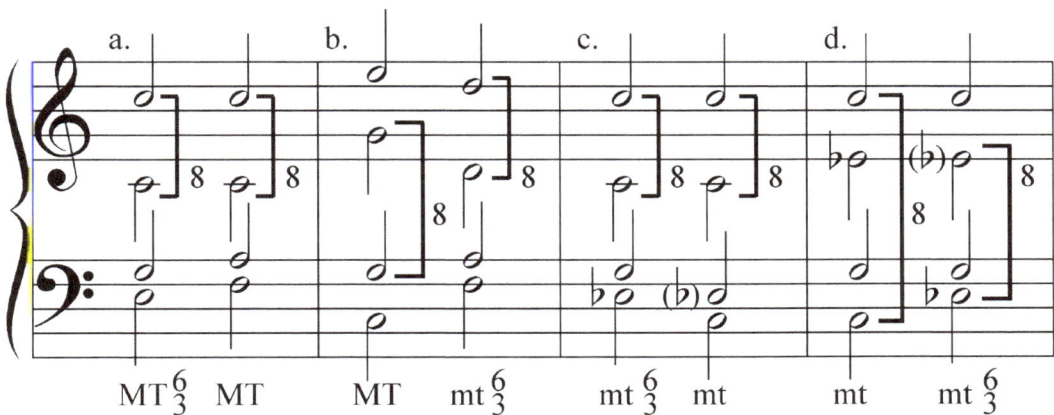

Similar Motion

Similar motion is movement in the same direction, upwards or downwards, between *unlike* numerical intervals. First and foremost, there is never a problem moving in the same direction between unlike intervals unless the second of the two intervals is a perfect 5th, diminished 5th, perfect octave, or perfect unison. In example 3–7, we have acceptable similar motion into a 6th (3–7a) and into a 3rd (3–7b).

Example 3–7: acceptable similar motion into the 6th and the 3rd

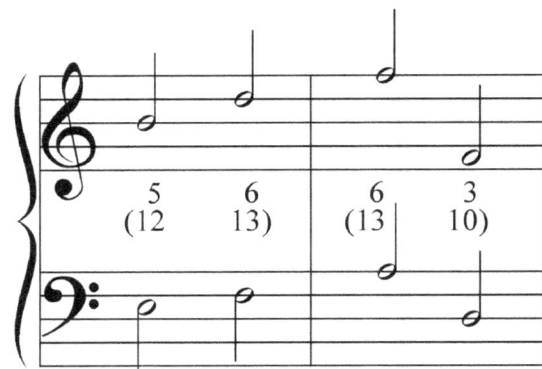

Similar motion into either a *downward or upward* 5th is always correct provided the upper or lower voice moves by a whole step or half step as the opposite voice leaps a 4th or more (examples 3–8a and 8b). Similar motion into a *downward* perfect octave is also correct as long as the upper or lower voice moves by a whole step or half step and the opposite voice leaps a 4th or more (examples 3–8c and 8d).

Example 3–8: acceptable similar motion into the perfect 5th and the downward perfect octave

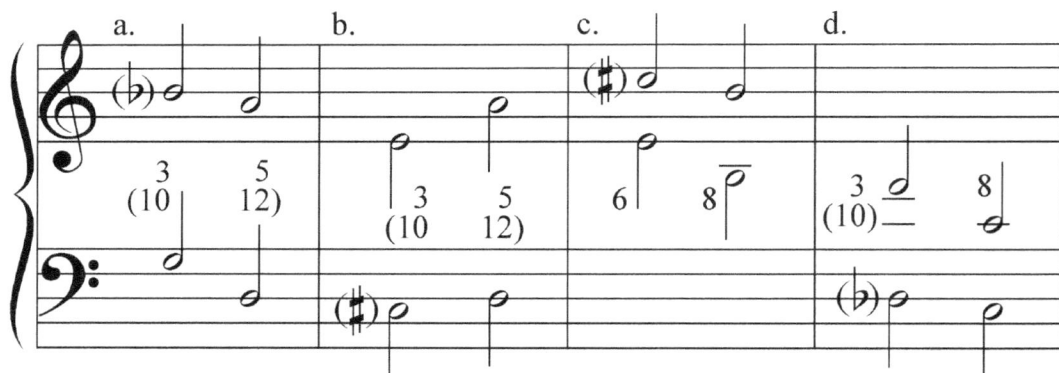

Direct Motion: Incorrect Similar Motion

For *upward* motion into the perfect octave, the upper voice must move by one half step as the lower voice leaps a 4th or more. Example 3–9a illustrates the correct approach into the perfect octave from below by one half step (E to F, alto voice). Examples 3–9b and 9c show incorrect approaches into the perfect octave from below; here, the upper voice moves into the perfect octave at an interval greater than the half step (D to E and E to A respectively). Incorrect similar motion is called direct motion; examples 3–9b and 9c exhibit two instances of what would be called the "direct octave."

Example 3–9: the difference between acceptable and unacceptable upward motion into the perfect octave

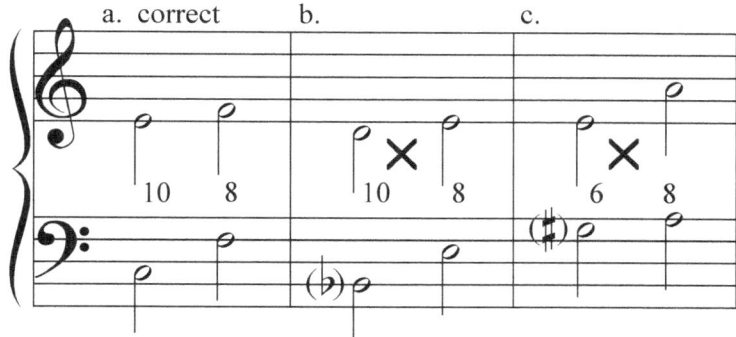

The upward approach to the perfect octave by half step is preferable because it either mimics the upward half-step motion of the leading tone to the tonic or is the leading tone proceeding to the tonic. Without the half-step approach of the upper voice into the octave, the focus shifts to the leaping voice and the ear attempts to supply the intervening pitches of the larger interval, resulting in what is often referred to as "hidden octaves."

As demonstrated in example 3–10, the last "supplied" pitch approaching the actual perfect octave would be *another* perfect octave (see the filled-in note heads and vertical brackets). Thus, example 3–10a gives us hidden perfect octaves on G and A, while 3–10b presents another view of hidden perfect octaves on G (or possibly G♯) and A—both are instances of incorrect similar motion, that is, direct motion.

Example 3–10: direct motion into the octave (incorrect similar motion)

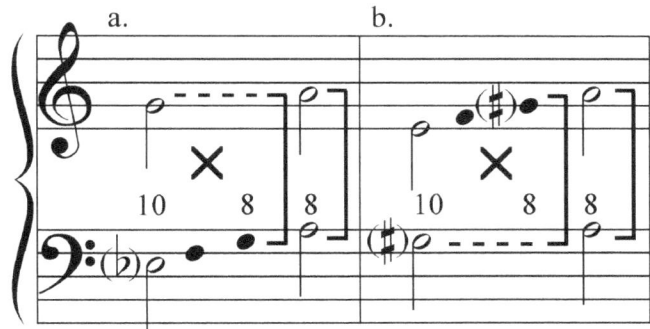

Remember, similar motion into a downward 5th, an upward 5th, or a downward perfect octave is never a problem as long as the upper or lower voice moves by either a whole step or a half step while the opposite voice leaps by a 4th or more. The next few examples will display some of the actions that produce direct motion, which in all cases are instances of wrong similar motion.

96   Chapter 3   Voice Leading

In example 3–11 below, both voices approach the intervals of the 5th and perfect octave disjunctly, that is, by leap, resulting in direct 5ths and direct octaves.

Example 3–11: direct motion into the 5th and the octave (incorrect similar motion)

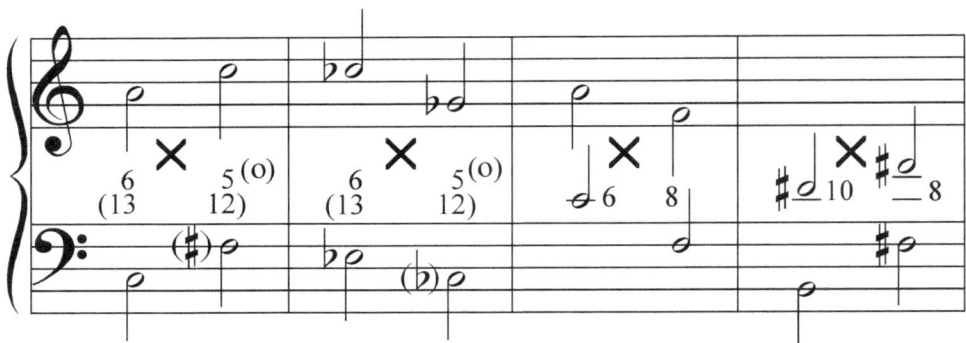

Even if one voice connects to the 5th or perfect octave by a whole step or half step, a leap of only a 3rd in the opposite voice will also result in direct motion, albeit direct motion of a less objectionable variety. Still, avoid such motion between the bass and the soprano, particularly when the downward perfect octave is involved. In all cases, the ear will attempt to fill in the 3rd with an intervening tone, thereby producing the hidden 5th or octave (example 3–12).

Example 3–12: direct motion into the 5th and the octave (incorrect similar motion)

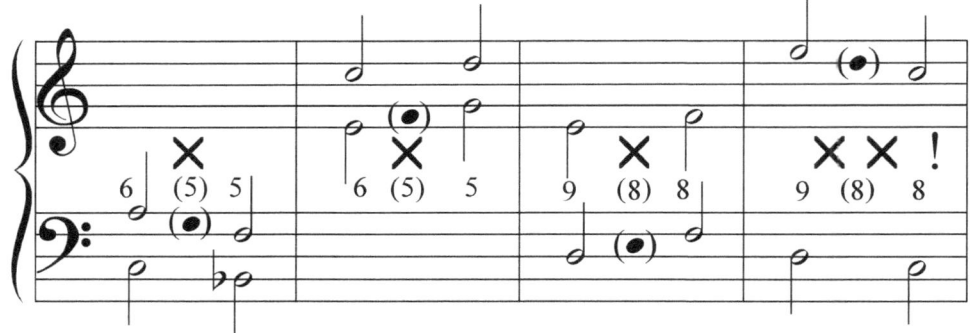

Contrary Motion

Contrary motion is movement in which the voices proceed in opposite directions. Example 3–13 shows the proper employment of contrary motion. The two voices move either towards or away from each other. There is no problem with *unlike* intervals moving in opposite directions.

Example 3–13: acceptable contrary motion

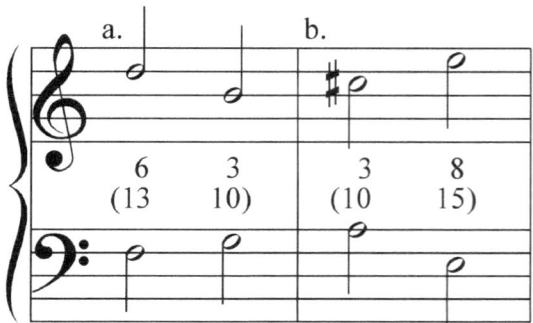

Consecutive Motion: Incorrect Contrary Motion

Let us revisit the problem of parallel motion. With parallel motion, the danger is in the treatment of perfect 5ths, perfect octaves, and perfect unisons. These intervals are just as problematic when using contrary motion; for wrong parallel motion cannot be corrected by shifting the register of one voice to change its direction, as demonstrated in example 3–14. If the motion is incorrect when intervals are moving parallel to each other, then the motion is still incorrect when those same intervals are moving in opposite directions. Wrong contrary motion is called consecutive motion or anti-parallel motion.

Example 3–14: consecutive or anti-parallel perfect 5ths, octaves, and unisons

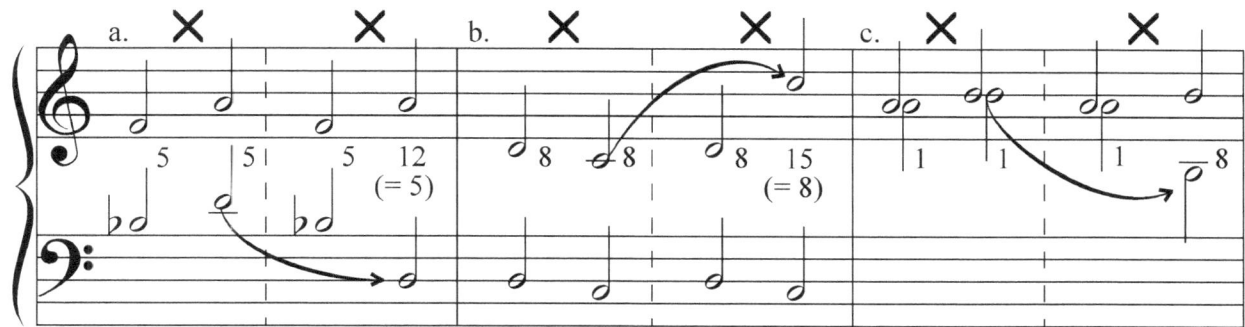

Again, there is no problem with *unlike* intervals moving in opposite directions. The difficulties arise when attempting to move certain *like* intervals in opposite directions: perfect 5ths, perfect octaves, and perfect unisons.

Oblique Motion

Oblique motion, which is always correct motion, involves one stationary voice and an opposing voice that moves. Example 3–15 shows two instances of oblique motion, one in which the lower voice is stationary against a moving upper voice and the other in which the upper voice is stationary against a moving lower voice. There are three basic ways to express the stationary voice: with a note value that is
  (1) longer in duration than that of the opposing voice,
  (2) a tied note, or,
  (3) a re-articulated tone (that is, repeated).

Example 3–15: oblique motion

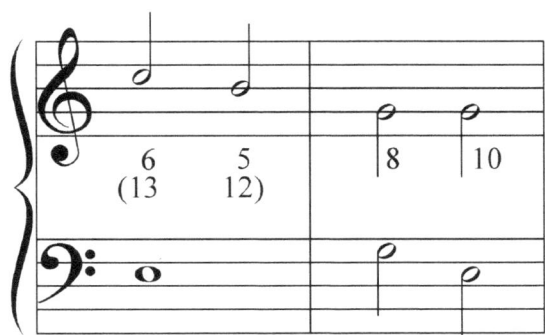

Let us summarize the basic principles of motion between two voices from one chord to an unlike chord:
(1) Oblique motion is always correct.
(2) Parallel motion is correct unless it involves more than one perfect 5th, perfect octave, or perfect unison in immediate succession.
(3) Similar motion is not a problem unless the second of the two intervals is a perfect 5th, diminished 5th, perfect octave, or perfect unison. *Incorrect similar motion is called direct motion.*
(4) Contrary motion presents no difficulties unless two perfect 5ths, two perfect octaves, or any combination of perfect octaves and unisons proceed in opposite directions. Wrong parallel motion between perfect consonances cannot be fixed by shifting the register of one voice to change its direction. *Incorrect contrary motion is called consecutive motion, or anti-parallel motion.*

General Principles

The next three sections list and examine some of the general guidelines that govern melodic and/or harmonic motion in
(1) any single voice between unlike chords,
(2) any two voices between unlike chords, and,
(3) all four voices between unlike chords.

Motion in Any Single Voice Between Unlike Chords

(1) Observe the recommended ranges for soprano, alto, tenor and bass voices (see example 1–82 above, p. 51).
(2) Maintain common tones *in the same voice* between unlike chords in the soprano, alto, or tenor voices. Common tones are pitches of the same alphabet letter name. Repeating a common tone in the same voice between unlike chords often prevents the kind of motion problems discussed earlier.
(3) Avoid melodic leaps of the tritone (diminished 5th or augmented 4th) in the soprano, alto, or tenor voices. The tritone leap in the bass voice is acceptable. In all voices, avoid the augmented 2nd, the 6th, the 7th, and any compound intervals. An octave leap, however, is acceptable and often desirable.
(4) Avoid doubling tones that have a tendency to move (that is, active tones); particularly, the variable scale degrees of minor (see above, p. 54). Ignoring the linear sensitivity of active tones will likely result in numerous voice-leading difficulties, a few of which are illustrated below.
  (a) Example 3–16a, in C major, has the leading tone doubled (the third of dominant triad), which produces parallel octaves between the soprano and bass.
  (b) Examples 3–16b, 16c, and 16d, all in c minor, demonstrate some of the hazards of doubling variable scale degrees. Example 3–16b shows a doubling of variable ♭6, which creates parallel octaves between the soprano and bass and also a direct 5th between the bass and tenor. Example 3–16c doubles variables ♯6 and ♯7, which gives us parallel octaves between the bass and soprano. Finally, doubling variable ♭6 in 3–16d produces parallel octaves between the tenor and alto and results in a dominant "chord" with a missing third. In turn, the missing third gives rise to parallel octaves between the bass and the tenor.

Example 3–16: some of the dangers of doubling active tones

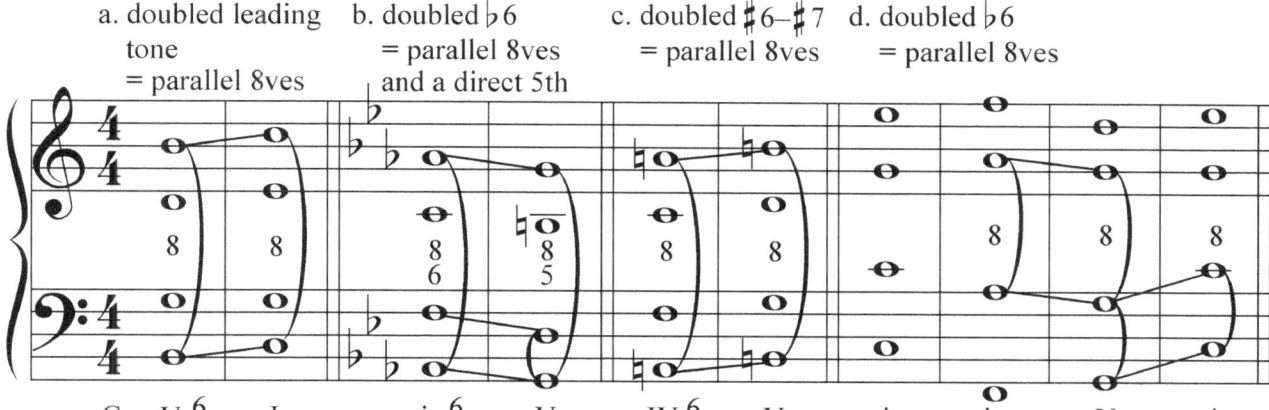

(5) Avoid doubling any chromatically altered pitches that might arise. As stated in Chapter 1, some of the pitches that occur in music compositions are not indicated in the key signature (see p. 27); tones that are neither native to the mode nor reflected in the key signature are referred to as chromatic pitches. One could argue that the raised variables ($\sharp 6$ and $\sharp 7$) of the melodic minor constitute a form of chromaticism since these tones are not reflected in the minor key signature.

(6) In those voices that do not have common tones, move as conjunctly as possible (that is, by step), upwards or downwards.

(7) In those voices that do not have common tones, an occasional upward or downward leap of a 3rd or 4th is acceptable. However, both the integrity and independence of any single voice part are best preserved by reversing the direction of the line before and after the leap, *whenever possible*. Thus, immediately before and after a leap that *ascends*, the melodic line should employ descending conjunct motion (note the direction of the arrows in example 3–17a). Conversely, immediately before and after a leap that *descends*, the melodic line should employ ascending conjunct motion (note the direction of the arrows in 3–17b).

Example 3–17: recommended motion between unlike tones in any single voice part

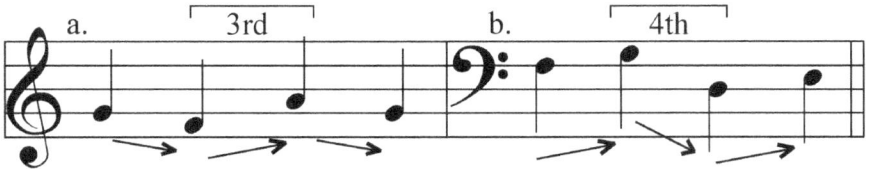

(8) When the leading tone (in either the major or minor mode) is in the soprano voice, it must proceed upwards to the tonic pitch when the chord involves either the dominant triad or the leading-tone triad moving to the tonic chord, as shown in examples 3–18a and 18c. If, however, the leading tone appears in either the alto or tenor voice, then it may fall back to scale degree 5, as displayed in examples 3–18b and 18d. This license is most effective when the bass voice moves in contrary motion to the voice that carries the leading tone.

Example 3–18: options for the leading tone

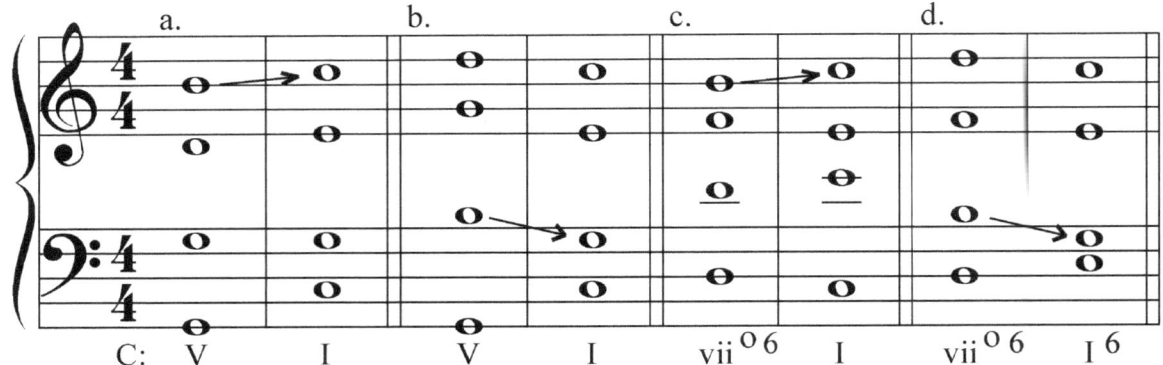

The upward resolution of the leading tone in the soprano voice does not apply to the leading tone when it is the fifth component of the minor mediant triad in the major mode, nor to variable ♭7 when it is the fifth of the major mediant triad in the minor mode. In major, the fifth of the mediant typically moves down to scale degree 6; in minor, ♭7 as the fifth of the mediant moves down to variable ♭6.

In 3–18d above, the tonic appears in $^6_3$ position. Notice that expressing the tonic in root position, as shown in example 3–19 below, would have created a direct or hidden 5th between the tenor and the bass (B in the tenor leaping down a 3rd to G gives us a potential A intervening to produce D/A and C/G). Hence, moving the bass in the opposite direction of the voice that carries the leading tone promises a better result. Moreover, placing the bass in contrary motion to the tenor (as shown above in 3–18d) prevents all of the voices from moving in the same direction (downwards). Generally, having all of the voices move in the same direction undermines the melodic independence of the four parts.

We could also retain the C in the bass and still avoid the direct 5th by simply moving the tenor voice up from B to C (3–19, C in parentheses); however, the final disposition of the C-major triad would be incomplete: a tripled root, third, and no fifth (G). As stated in Chapter 1 (p. 57), there is no problem with omitting the fifth because of its prominent position within the harmonic series as the third partial.

Example 3–19: direct 5th between the tenor and the bass

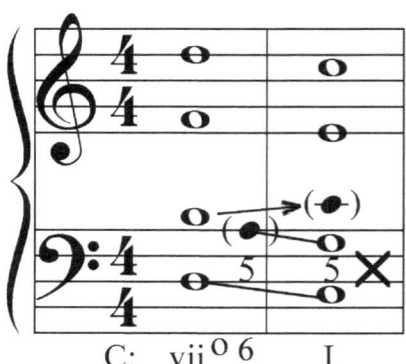

Motion in Any Two Voices Between Unlike Chords

(1) With the exception of the tenor and bass, allow no more than one octave between adjacent voices.
(2) Prefer contrary motion or oblique motion between the outer voices, that is, the bass and the soprano.
(3) Do not bypass or cross adjacent voices, especially between the tenor and the bass. In example 3–20a, the alto voice (B♭, second half note) bypasses the previous soprano (A). In 3–20b, the tenor voice (C♯, second half note) bypasses the preceding bass (D). When one voice crosses another, as in examples 3–20c and 20d, both voices exchange positions. In 3–20c, the soprano moves below the alto (A to E) while the alto proceeds upwards (F to G). In 3–20d, the bass leaps above the tenor (C to F) while the tenor continues downwards (E to D).

Example 3–20: bypassing and crossing adjacent voices

(4) Always avoid incorrect motion: wrong parallel motion, consecutive motion, and direct motion.
(5) When moving from a triad in $^6_4$ position, the upper dissonant interval of the 4th above the bass should resolve downwards by step in the same voice whenever possible.
(6) Generally, any other dissonant intervals formed above the bass should also resolve downwards by step in the same voice whenever possible.
(7) Avoid the cross relation, also known as the false relation, by maintaining chromatically altered versions of the same tone in the same voice whenever possible. Example 3–21a shows the cross relation B♭ and B♮ between the soprano and bass voices, while 3–21b illustrates the correct placement of chromatically altered tones in the bass voice (see the circled B♭ and B♮).

Example 3–21: the cross relation

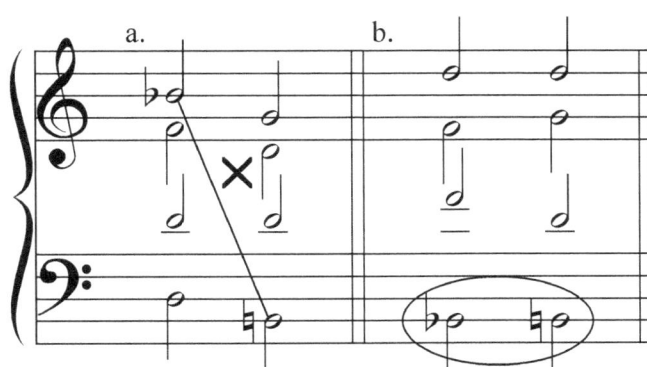

Motion in All Four Voices Between Unlike Chords

(1) Avoid moving all four voices in the same direction (between unlike chords).
(2) You may omit the fifth of any major or minor triad in $^5_3$ position, tripling the root or third.
(3) It is permissible to move from one element of the chord to another within the same chord if the operation improves the connection between chords. In the final section of this chapter, we shall explore the advantages of using this technique to avoid potential problems in the voice leading.

The Chordal Skip

The chordal skip, which is also known as the consonant skip, usually involves a single leap to either the root, third, or fifth of the chord. Moving between two elements of a chord, that is, "re-voicing the chord," may occur in one voice or in two or more voices (as in example 3–23b). Re-voicing the bass, however, is restricted to upward or downward leaps of an octave in order to maintain the chord's position. Chordal skips can

  (1) change the doublings of a chord correctly arrived at (or correct faulty doublings) to facilitate a smoother movement to the next chord (3–23a);
  (2) create a more animated line (example 3–22);
  (3) bring a voice up or down to effect more favorable registers, especially useful in the soprano and bass (3–23b);
  (4) serve as a corrective to faulty motion between chords (3–23);
  (5) occasionally arpeggiate a triad with consecutive leaps involving either two 3rds or a 4th and a 3rd. If used sparingly, re-voicing the chord with consecutive leaps prevents a melodic line from becoming excessively conjunct, adding variety and interest to the texture (3–23).

Given the broad range of applications for re-voicing chords, we are limited to a few illustrations. Let us focus on the tenor voice of example 3–22. On beat 2, the tone C moves down a 3rd to A with the arrival of the IV chord. Although it would have been acceptable to hold on to the common tone C when the chord changed (to IV), moving to A creates a more active tenor line.

Having approached the IV chord correctly, we can re-voice the tenor back up to C in order to provide a smoother connection to the next chord on beat 3, the I$^6_4$. To be sure, we could have moved to the I$^6_4$ without re-voicing the A up to C (in the tenor), leaving the IV with a doubled third and omitted fifth. Still, re-voicing to the C gives us the fifth of the chord, which was missing in the initial disposition of the IV.

Example 3–22: re-voicing with the chordal skip

C: I   IV   I$^6_4$ V I

Using the Chordal Skip to Correct Faulty Motion

The voice leading in example 3–23a resembles that of 3–22 but with some significant differences. On beat 3 (3–23a), a root-position V with a doubled third (B, alto and tenor) follows the IV. As suggested above (p. 98), doubling a tone that has a tendency to move, such as the leading tone, usually results in faulty voice leading. The connection to and from a dominant chord with a doubled third is fraught with danger because its third is the leading tone. With the thirds of both the IV and V doubled, we have the potential for parallel octaves between the alto and tenor voices (see the dotted lines in 3–23a).

One way to eliminate the parallel octaves in 3–23a to re-voice the IV *using the chordal skip*. As in 3–22, the A in the tenor moves up to C on the second half of beat 2; now there is a 6th between the tenor and the alto, which breaks up the two octaves (8 6 8). Although we have prevented the first set of parallel octaves, the doubled leading tone within the dominant remains. If the V is not re-voiced, then the leading tone in both the tenor and alto will continue upwards to scale degree 1, producing another instance of parallel octaves.

Notice that the alto voice takes two downward leaps of a 3rd: B moves down to G (beat 3) and then continues down to E with the arrival of the I chord (beat 4). Although too many consecutive leaps in a simple four-part texture threaten to undermine the vocal quality of the melodic lines, an occasional arpeggiation of a triad with either two 3rds or a combination of the 4th and the 3rd can provide welcome variety to a melodic line that might otherwise exhibit too much stepwise motion.

Example 3–23b presents two reasons for using the chordal skip to re-voice the chord, one of which we observed in 23a, namely, the correction of wrong parallel motion as a result of voice leading from the previous chord. On beats 1 and 2 between the tenor and bass, parallel 5ths would have been produced were it not for the chordal skip from the fifth of the C-major triad to its third, from G up to E. Once the E is reached on the second half of beat 1 in the tenor, an intervening 10th (5 10 5) breaks up the parallel 5ths.

On beats 3 and 4, the tenor and the soprano voices would have given us parallel octaves on B and C were it not for the tenor moving away from the chord third to the chord fifth, from B up to D. The D creates an intervening 6th that breaks up the parallel octaves (8 6 8). Additionally, re-voicing to the D removes the doubled third of the V (B) and produces a doubled fifth (D) at the unison.

The other reason for re-voicing in example 3–23b is to bring the soprano, alto, and tenor voices up into a more favorable register in order to better connect to the higher disposition of the IV on beat 2. Although it may seem that the upward leaps of a 5th (alto) and 6th (soprano and tenor) contradict the allowance for an occasional upward or downward leap of a 3rd or 4th, these motions are within the same chord, not between unlike chords. Hence, leaps such as these are perfectly acceptable *if* they occur within the same chord.

Example 3–23: correcting faulty motion with the chordal skip

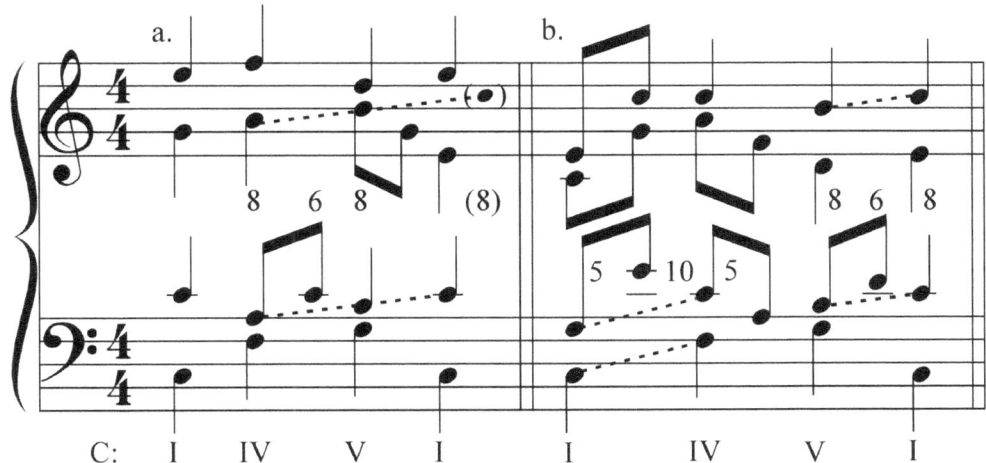

Creating Incorrect Motion with the Chordal Skip

Finally, when re-voicing a chord, be very careful not to create incorrect motion with the chordal skip. Example 3–24 illustrates but one of the potential hazards resulting from the improper use of the chordal skip; here, faulty re-voicing between the alto and tenor (beats 1 and 2) and between the alto and bass (beats 2 and 3) produce two instances of parallel octaves.

Example 3–24: creating incorrect motion with the chordal skip

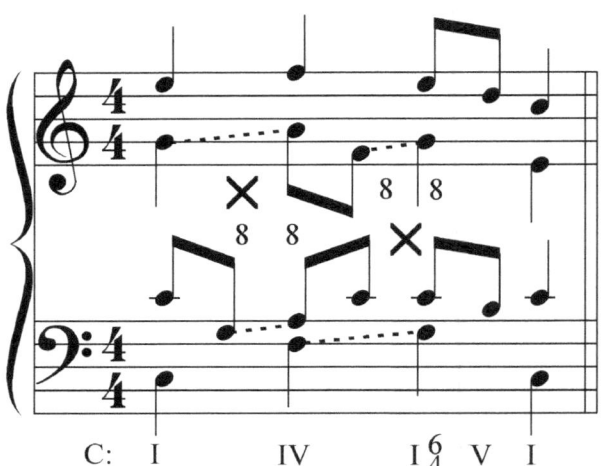

Chapter 4 The Six-Four Chord

In Chapter 1, we noted that if the interval of the perfect 4th occurs between the bass and an upper note, then the interval is treated as a dissonance (see above, p. 33). If, however, the perfect 4th does not occur between an upper note and the bass, then the interval is consonant. The first inversion of the triad has the consonant 4th; the second inversion, however, places the 4th in the dissonant position.

In this chapter, we shall explore the various usages of the $^6_4$ chord, starting with the origins of the cadential $^6_4$, a linear and harmonic formation that often appears at the end of a segment of music known as the phrase. The phrase is the smallest element of musical form in which a combination of melodic, rhythmic, and chordal components together comprise the beginning, middle, and end of a musical thought.

The Origins of the Cadential $^6_4$

One of the origins of the cadential $^6_4$ is the passing tone. Either dissonant or consonant with another voice, the passing tone usually connects two harmonic consonances; it is approached and left by step and may occur on either a strong or weak beat. The passing tone also appears on either a strong or weak portion of a beat.

In example 4–1a, the soprano voice moves down a minor 3rd from D to B; the tone C (P) fills in the distance between the two pitches on beat 1 of measure 2. Forming a *dissonant* passing 4th with the bass, C connects two harmonic consonances, a major 6th and a major 3rd (compound intervals in the example are identified in their simple forms). A combination of figured-bass numbers and a dash between them (4—3) indicates the downward movement of the 4th (G/C) to the 3rd (G/B) over a stationary bass. Despite the limitations of the two-voice texture shown in 4–1a, the arrival of the major 3rd on beat 3 of measure 2 implies a G-major triad, the dominant of C major (the chord symbols in parentheses indicate the implied chords).

Example 4–1b places the passing 4th (P) within the framework of four parts with the addition of the alto and tenor voices. The combination of four voices gives us the tones G G D C on beat 1 of measure 2. The C in the soprano is not an inherent component of the chord and therefore counts among the various techniques falling within the category of the nonharmonic tone, or nonchord tone (nonharmonic tones are discussed in Chapter 9). The nonharmonic passing 4th *delays* the complete formation of the G dominant. However, with the arrival of B on beat 3 of the second measure, we have the third of the chord and therefore all three components of the G-major triad. These intervals are counted above the bass pitch. Since the 4th occurs on a strong beat, we should refer to it more precisely as an "*accented* passing tone."

Finally, there is one problem with the voice leading in 4–1b: the direct 5th between the alto and tenor voices in measure 2. We shall soon see how the employment of the cadential $^6_4$ corrects the direct 5th.

Example 4–1: the dissonant passing 4th

The cadential $^6_4$ grew out of the desire to rhythmically *delay* the formation of the dominant chord at the end of a musical phrase in a two-chord pattern known as the cadence (see Chapter 6). The accented passing tone constitutes one means for delaying the appearance of the dominant chord.

Examples 4–2a and 2b below demonstrate another technique for delaying certain elements of the dominant chord. As with the dissonant passing tone, the second measure of examples 4–2a and 2b contains a dissonant 4th on the first beat of the measure, which once again shifts the third of the G chord to beat 3. However, in this instance, the third of the dominant is delayed by a type of nonharmonic tone known as the suspension. As shown in 4–2a, the suspension has three parts:

(1) the suspension is *prepared* ("prep"), usually as a consonance (but sometimes as a dissonance); then,
(2) the preparation is held, or *suspended* ("susp"), as the opposing voice (usually the bass) moves to form a dissonance with the suspended voice (though a consonant suspension is also possible); and finally,
(3) the suspended voice moves down by step to *resolve* to a consonance ("res"). In measure 2 of both examples 4–2a and 2b, the interval of the 4th (susp) moves down by step to form a consonant 3rd on the second half note (res). We call the suspended 4th the "4—3 suspension."

An essential feature of the suspension is the degree of metric stress each part of the operation receives. First and foremost, the resolution (res) should be metrically weaker than the suspension itself (susp). The initial preparation, however, can be made from either a strong or weak position. In the preparation of 4–2a, notice that the second half note of measure 1 is tied into the first half note of measure 2. The result of this tie lengthens the duration of the second half note.

Although the tie is the most common means for executing the suspension, 4–2b shows how an actual tie between two note values is not required to employ this technique, as a repeated pitch also lengthens the duration of the second half note (in measure 1). Normally, without either tying or repeating the pitch, the second half note of measure 1 would be weaker than the first half note. However, by increasing its duration, the second half note becomes stronger than the first half note, resulting in syncopation.

Example 4–2: the 4—3 suspension

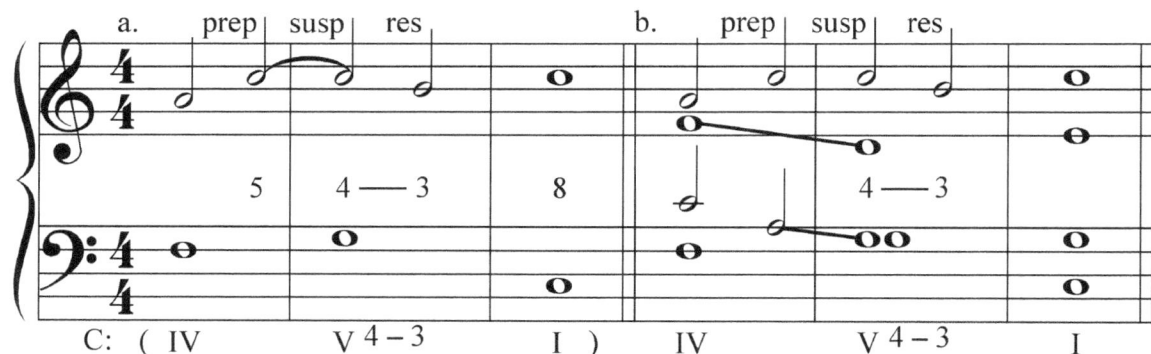

Example 4–2b places the suspended 4th within the framework of four parts with the addition of the alto and tenor voices. The complete formation of the dominant triad (G B D) does not occur until the suspended 4th between the bass and soprano voices moves down by step to form a consonant 3rd on beat 3 of the second measure (4—3). The soprano voice in measure 1 prepares the 4th by moving upwards to the subdominant's fifth (C) as the tenor proceeds to its third (A). The alto remains on F, the root of the IV.

When the soprano voice in 4–2b prepares the 4th (prep) by moving upwards to the fifth of the chord in measure 1 (A up to C), it removes the third of the IV chord from the texture. The tenor reinstates the third by reversing the motion (C down to A). In so doing, however, the two voices duplicate the direct 5th shown earlier in 4–1b above (A/F to G/D). We shall find a solution to this problem in the next section.

The Cadential $^6_4$

The cadential $^6_4$ is also known as the "accented $^6_4$" because it is rhythmically strong, usually falling on the strongest beat of the measure (or, in triple meter, occasionally falling on beat 2 and resolving on beat 3). The cadential $^6_4$ occurs at the conclusion of a musical phrase and is approached either by step (with chords such as the IV or the ii^6), by a supertonic chord in root position, by a tonic chord in root position, or by a tonic chord in first inversion.

In example 4–3a, the suspended 4th is first prepared in the soprano as a consonance and then held as the bass moves up to G to create the dissonance. The soprano moves down by step to a consonant 3rd on the second half note of measure 2 while the consonant E in the alto continues down to D. The downward motion of both the soprano and alto voices over the stationary bass is represented by a combination of figured-bass numbers and dashes between them: $^6_4 - ^5_3$.

The figured bass in example 4–3 indicates what appears to be a succession of two distinct chords: a C-major triad in $^6_4$ position moving to a G-major triad in $^5_3$ position. However, the C and E in the soprano and alto voices are not native to the chord. In other words, what we have here is not a C-major triad in $^6_4$ position, but rather the arrival of the dominant pitch in the bass (G), over which two nonharmonic tones on the strongest beat of the measure occur. The E in both examples 4–3a and 3b is a consonant accented passing tone (the 6th above G), while the C in 4–3a is part of the dissonant suspension (the 4th above G).

In 4–3b, the dissonant 4th is not prepared as a suspension; instead, we have a stepwise approach to both the dissonant 4th and the consonant the 6th of the cadential $^6_4$. The circle around the figured-bass $^5_3$ attached to the chord symbol V $^6_4 - ^5_3$ indicates that the real chord, the dominant (G B D), is formed on beat 3 of the second measure when all three elements of the chord are present.

The example shows the solution for correcting the direct 5th mentioned above (see the dotted lines). The correction of the direct 5th occurs in the alto voice with the creation of a 6th above the bass in measure 2 (G/E). The direct 5th is eliminated because faulty direct motion has been transformed into acceptable oblique motion (G/E to G/D). At the same time, the soprano moves down from the dissonant 4th to the consonant 3rd.

Example 4–3: the cadential $^6_4$

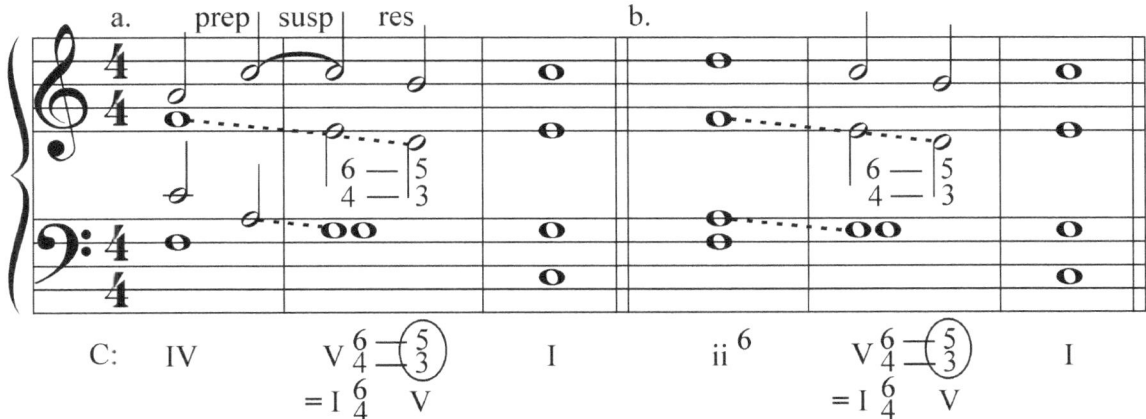

It is instructive to interpret the nonharmonic activity occurring above the stationary root of the dominant chord as an *elaboration* of that chord; as such, we can describe the cadential $^6_4$ as "the elaborated dominant." Indeed, the use of the Roman numeral V in front of the figured-bass 4—3 is justified because even though a literal tonic $^6_4$ chord is formed on the first half note of the measure, the tonic is *not a real chord*, but rather, an apparent chord. Hence, the cadential $^6_4$ has two parts: the apparent $^6_4$ chord and the real chord, the dominant in $^5_3$ position (E and C move to D and B respectively).

The Passing $^6_4$

The passing $^6_4$ chord fills in the interval between two chords. The bass moves by step, upwards or downwards, and usually involves the span of a 3rd. The passing $^6_4$ chord occurs on a rhythmically weak beat or weak portion of the beat. Virtually any chord may serve as a passing $^6_4$. Looking at example 4–4 below, notice that the interval of the 4th is not treated as a dissonance and does not move down, as the $^6_4$ chord typically shares a common tone with the chords that precede and follow it. Instead, the bass moves *through* the dissonant 4th. The passing $^6_4$ chord is approached and left conjunctly.

In example 4–4a, the passing $^6_4$ connects a root-position tonic to a first-inversion tonic; in 4–4b, it connects a first-inversion subdominant to a root-position subdominant. In each example, the passing $^6_4$ connects two different positions of the same chord. However, the passing $^6_4$ may also connect two unlike chords, as shown in 4–4c. (The three naturals in the key signature area of the staff indicate that the previous key signature is no longer in effect. Here, the key and mode of C major is re-established.)

Example 4–4: the passing $^6_4$

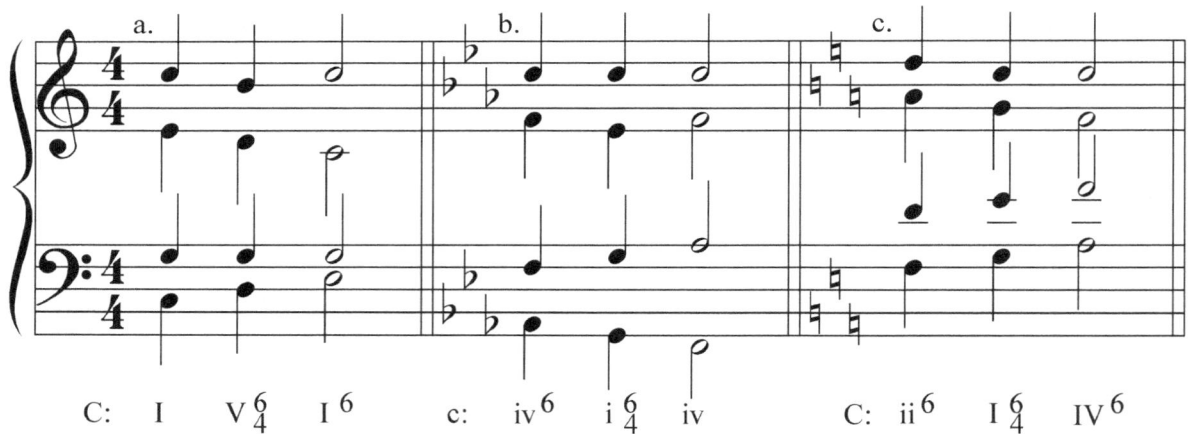

The Pedal Embellishing $^6_4$

The pedal embellishing $^6_4$ is also called the "neighboring $^6_4$" and the "auxiliary $^6_4$." Forming intervals of the 6th and the 4th over a stationary bass, the pedal embellishing $^6_4$ is usually placed on a weak beat or weak portion of the beat.

Example 4–5 demonstrates two ways to describe the linear events that occur over the stationary bass of the pedal embellishing $^6_4$. The first method starts from the premise that the intervals of the 6th and the 4th above the bass are nonharmonic tones forming apparent chords. We identify the real chords by circling the figured bass for the $^5_3$ position. (The second method is discussed later in this section.)

Thus, in 4–5a, the tonic chord appears on beat 1 ($^5_3$ circled), followed by an apparent $^6_4$ chord on beat 2, returning to the real chord on beat 3. The notation for 4–5b has one complication: the flat in front of the figured-bass 6 indicates that the A♭ in the alto voice is variable ♭6, *occurring at the interval of a 6th above the bass*. This generic use of a flat in front of the figured bass tells us that the tone in question is lowered within the context of the key and mode. After reaching the apparent chord on beat 2, the bass moves to B♮ to support the dominant triad in first inversion.

Example 4–5c begins with an F-minor triad, the subdominant of c minor. An apparent $^6_4$ chord is heard on beat 2 followed by a return to the subdominant. The flat in front of the figured-bass 4 indicates that variable ♭7 (B♭) is *occurring at the interval of a 4th above the bass*.

Example 4–5: the pedal embellishing $^6_4$

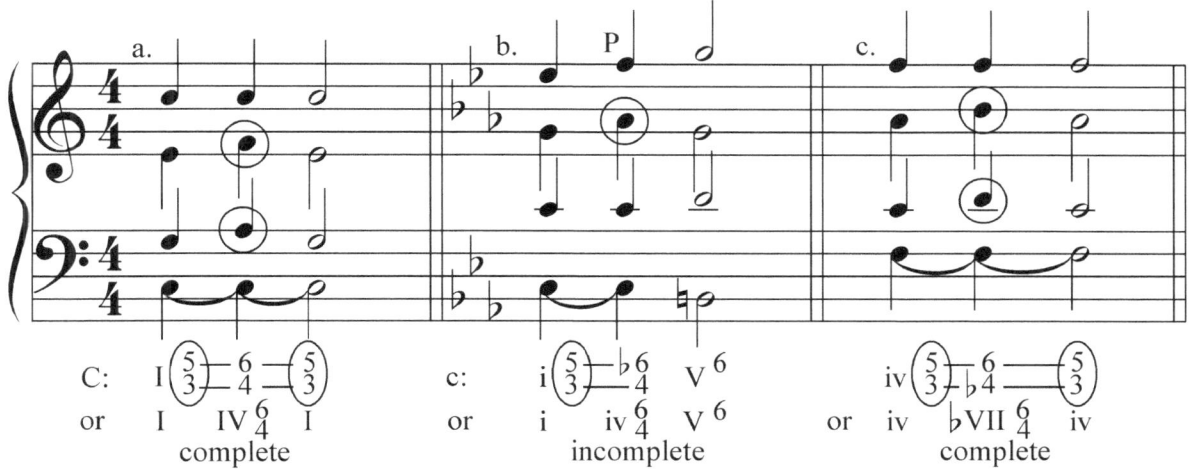

The activity of the voices above the stationary bass approaching and leaving the pedal embellishing $^6_4$ exhibit either passing (P in 4–5b) or neighboring motions (circled pitches). A neighbor tone moves upwards or downwards by step to and/or from another tone, referred to here as the principal tone. Neighbor tones may be either consonant or dissonant with the bass.

If the principal tone both precedes and follows the neighbor tone, then we term the neighbor complete. A neighbor tone that stands above the principal tone is described as an upper neighbor, whereas a neighbor located below the principal tone is called a lower neighbor.

The E♭ in the alto voice on beat 2 of example 4–4b (F–E♭–F) is a complete lower neighbor, as it leaves and returns by step to the principal tone, F. It is also a *consonant* complete lower neighbor (the E♭ occurs above the G). The F in the alto voice on beat 2 of 4–5a (E–F–E) is a complete upper neighbor, as it leaves and returns by step to the principal tone, E. It is also a *dissonant* complete upper neighbor (the F occurs above C). The A in the tenor voice on beat 2 of 4–5a (G–A–G) is a consonant complete upper neighbor, as it leaves and returns by step to the principal tone, G.

If the neighbor tone does not proceed from and return to the principal tone, then we call the neighbor incomplete. In effect, the neighbor tone, be it complete and incomplete, "decorates" the tone that it leaves and/or approaches. (Chapter 9 contains numerous examples of incomplete neighbors.)

Similar to the neighbor tone in its operation, the pedal embellishing $^6_4$ is considered complete if it returns to the chord that preceded it. In example 4–5a, the $^6_4$ chord follows and precedes a tonic chord. Beat 2 of 4–5b has an the incomplete pedal embellishing $^6_4$. Notice that the bass of the $^6_4$ chord does not return to the preceding chord; rather, the chord changes and the bass moves down to a B♮, the third of the dominant.

The alternative method for describing the linear activity of the pedal embellishing $^6_4$ simply provides a literal account of what tertian structures are formed above the stationary bass. According to this approach, 4–5a presents a tonic, subdominant $^6_4$, and tonic; 4–5b displays a tonic, subdominant $^6_4$, and dominant $^6_3$. Example 4–5c has a subdominant, subtonic $^6_4$, and subdominant. One disadvantage of the second method is that it fails to distinguish between real and apparent chords.

Finally, the use of the word pedal in association with the term embellishing $^6_4$ derives from the practice of playing an organ with both hands while using the feet to sustain a single tone with one of the instrument's pedal keys, a technique known as organ point or pedal point. Typically, several chords are played over a single pedal tone; but regardless of what harmonic formations unfold over the bass, the pedal tone almost invariably emphasizes the root of the main chord, which frequently turns out to be either the tonic or the dominant.

The Arpeggiated $^6_4$

The arpeggiated $^6_4$, also referred to as the "accompanying $^6_4$" and the "stable $^6_4$," may be either rhythmically strong or weak. The arpeggiated $^6_4$ is an arpeggiation of a chord's root, third, and/or fifth, expressing the $^6_4$ position and at least one other position, either $^5_3$ and/or $^6_3$. Although the arpeggiated $^6_4$ is not commonly found in four-part vocal textures, we include its main features here in order to provide a comprehensive account of $^6_4$- chord usage.

In example 4–6a, we have a complete statement of the arpeggiated $^6_4$ in which all three triad positions are present. Within this elaborated expression of the chord (4–6a), the traditional principles of voice leading need not apply; for the unfolding of tones from within the arpeggiated $^6_4$ constitutes a succession of chordal skips. In other words, once the arpeggiated $^6_4$ has been approached correctly from an unlike chord, it is possible to leap in and out of any voice and triad position without worrying about such faulty types of motion as parallel octaves or the direct 5th.

And so, we are not concerned with the voice leading between the different positions of the same chord. However, when the arpeggiated $^6_4$ proceeds to the next chord, it must connect into that chord observing the voice-leading principles outlined previously in Chapter 3.

Examples 4–6b, 6c, and 6d all demonstrate incomplete expressions of the arpeggiated $^6_4$ with only two rather than three positions of the chord. Example 4–6d requires further explanation; for here we have an initial statement of the $^6_4$ position *before* the $^5_3$ position has been heard.

If the $^5_3$ position is articulated first, the subsequent performance of the $^6_4$ is perceived as a consonant rather than dissonant chord. However, when the $^6_4$ position is articulated first, the effect is quite different and yet the result is still the same. Although we are surprised to hear what seems at first to be a dissonant $^6_4$ position, our ears attempt to stabilize the chord by anticipating the $^5_3$ position to come as an expression of a delayed root. Retroactively, then, the articulation of the root makes the preceding $^6_4$ chord acceptable.

Example 4–6: the arpeggiated $^6_4$

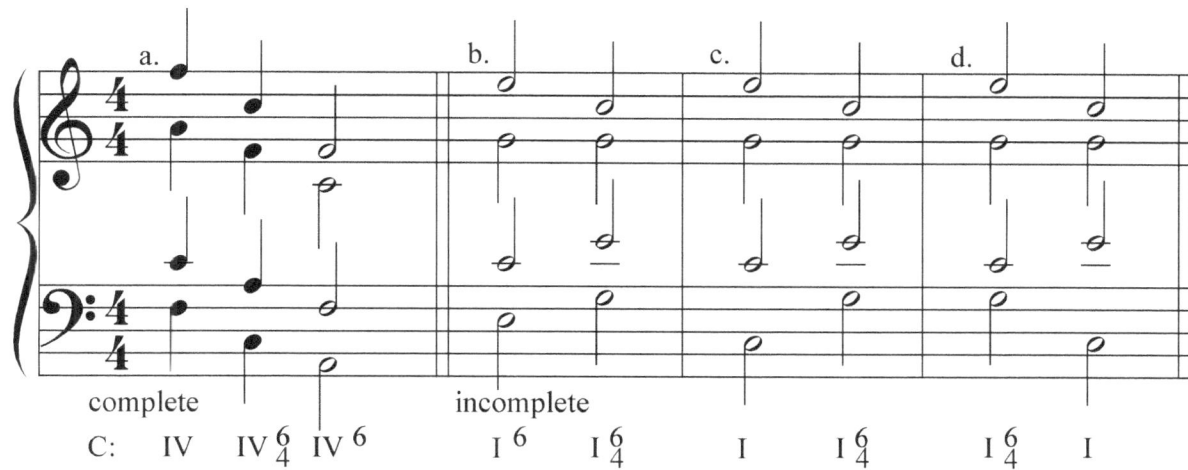

The Neighboring $^6_4$

The neighboring $^6_4$ occupies a central position above or below the bass of a stable chord, functioning as either an upper or lower neighbor to that chord. As with the passing $^6_4$, the neighboring $^6_4$ is rhythmically weak and shares a common tone with the stable chord. Thus, its 4th is not treated as a dissonance and does not need to move down. Rather, the bottom note of the 4th moves in and out of the dissonance while the top note of the interval remains stationary as a common tone. Examples 4–7a and 7b illustrate the upper and lower neighbor $^6_4$. As both examples confirm, the chord that the neighboring $^6_4$ addresses may be expressed in either root position or first inversion.

Example 4–7: the neighboring $^6_4$

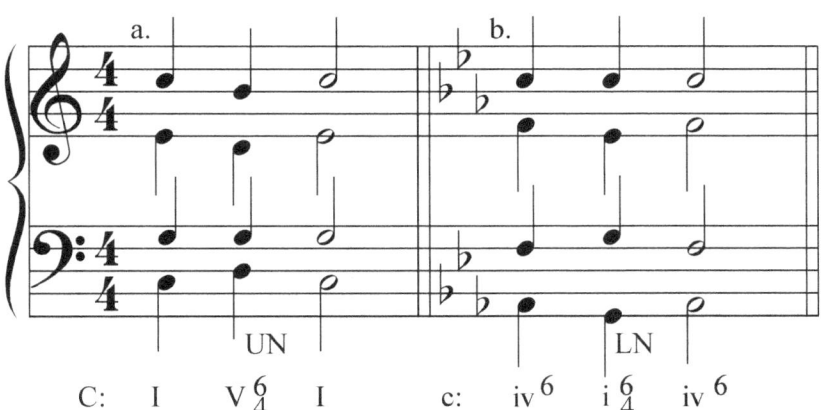

The Appoggiatura $^6_4$

The appoggiatura $^6_4$, like the cadential $^6_4$, is also called the "accented $^6_4$" because it is rhythmically strong. Since both chords are referred to as accented and occur on strong beats, let us distinguish between them with the stipulation that there are two similar types, namely, the accented cadential $^6_4$ and the accented noncadential $^6_4$.

The Italian term appoggiatura is derived from the verb *appoggiare*, one meaning of which is to lean. Within a musical context, the appoggiatura refers to an accented dissonance that resolves by step to a consonance (that is, the accented dissonance "leans" into the consonance). The appoggiatura may resolve upwards or downwards but a downward resolution is more common. Since the cadential $^6_4$ is like an appoggiatura, we could refer to it as the appoggiatura cadential $^6_4$. Therefore, the $^6_4$ under consideration presently would be called the appoggiatura noncadential $^6_4$, or simply, the appoggiatura $^6_4$.

As with the cadential $^6_4$, the appoggiatura $^6_4$ involves linear motion above a stationary bass and thus contains nonharmonic tones as one of its components. Unlike the cadential $^6_4$, however, the appoggiatura $^6_4$ is usually associated with chords other than the dominant. It occurs internally within a phrase, at the beginning of a phrase, or within the tonic chord as part of a cadence (example 4–8c).

For the appoggiatura $^6_4$, we have two options for describing its operation. In example 4–8a, the conventional approach interprets the D-minor triad on beat 1 of the second measure as a real chord, as a ii $^6_4$ proceeding to vi on beat 2. An alternative interpretation recognizes that the D and F in the soprano and alto voices on beat 1 are nonharmonic tones that seek resolution to C and E on beat 2. The ii $^6_4$ is an apparent chord, whereas the vi is real. In other words, the submediant scale degree is reached in the bass on beat 1, but the rest of the vi chord is delayed ($^5_3$ circled) until beat 2.

In 4–8b, the conventional interpretation finds the ii $^6_4$ on beat 1 of the second measure to be real. Alternatively, the subdominant scale degree is reached in the bass on beat 1 over which an apparent ii $^6_4$ delays the arrival of the real IV ^{6} ($^6_3$ circled) until beat 2. In 4–8c, the tonic scale degree is reached in the bass on beat 1 of the second measure over which an apparent iv $^6_4$ delays the arrival of the real tonic chord ($^5_3$ circled) until beat 2. Since variable ♭6 (A♭) is *occurring at the interval of a 6th above the bass* on beat 1 in the tenor voice, the figured-bass 6 takes a flat to indicate the presence of a lowered variable.

Example 4–8: the appoggiatura $^6_4$

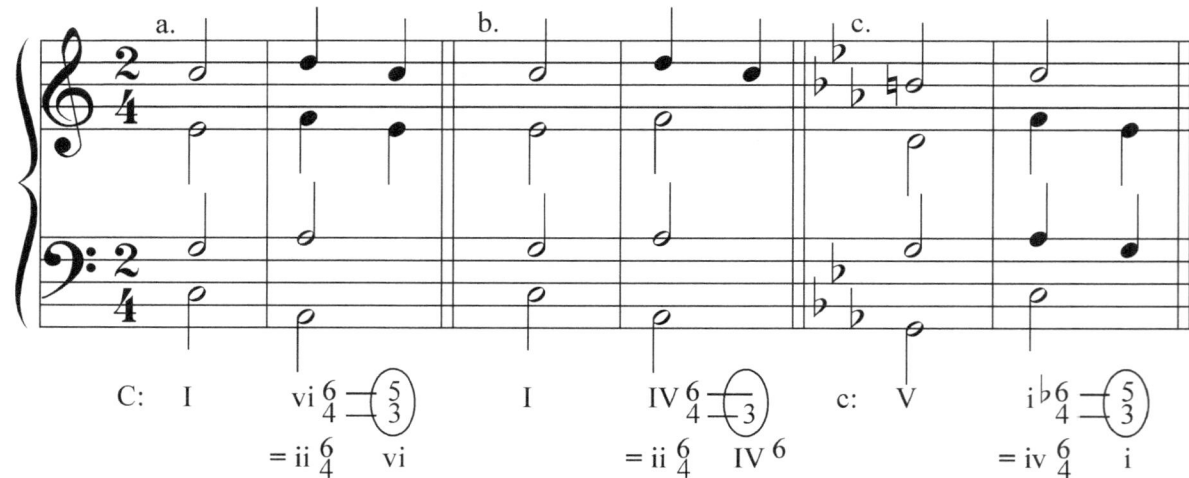

Chapter 5   The Chord Seventh

The seventh chord is a tertian harmony consisting of four chord tones: a root, third, fifth, and seventh. As shown in example 5–1, the seventh chord is produced by adding the interval of the 3rd above the fifth of the triad. The additional 3rd produces a *dissonant* 7th between the root and the seventh of the chord.

Example 5–1

Adding the Seventh to the Triad

The creation of the chord seventh involves the addition of either a major or minor 3rd above the fifth of the triad; seventh chords are never produced by adding either augmented or diminished 3rds. Therefore, if we add a 3rd above the fifth of a C-major triad, as in example 5–2 below, the tone is either B♮ (a major 3rd above G) or B♭ (a minor 3rd above G); neither B♯ (an augmented 3rd above G) nor B♭♭ (a diminished 3rd above G) can be used as the seventh of the chord.

Placing a B♯ above the fifth of the C-major triad produces a tone that is enharmonic with the root, resulting in a doubled root (one of which is misspelled as B♯) and no seventh. The addition of a B♭♭ above the fifth creates a chord that contains an enharmonic and acoustical interval of a 6th above the root (C up to A) but no chord seventh. Although it is possible to hear the B♭♭ as the misspelled root (A) of a seventh chord with its third in the bass (C E G A), our concern in this section is with seventh chords in *root position*.

Example 5–2

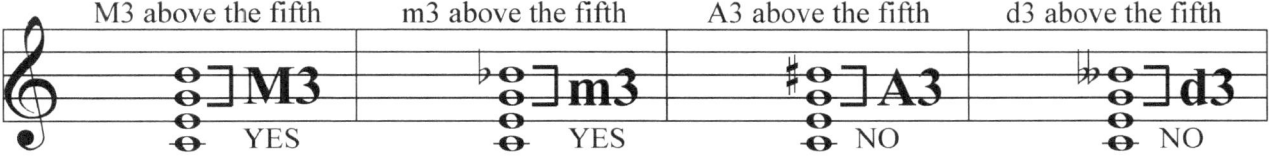

Example 5–3 demonstrates the formation of tertian harmonies with vertical structures containing more than four chord tones: the ninth chord has five tones (5–3a), the eleventh chord six (5–3b), and the thirteenth chord seven (5–3c). Chords of the seventh, ninth, eleventh, and thirteenth exist as extensions of the triad and arise from considerations of voice leading, particularly passing activity and the suspension. Moreover, these extensions do not alter the status or function of the triad within the key and mode in which it occurs.

Example 5–3: chords of the ninth, eleventh, and thirteenth

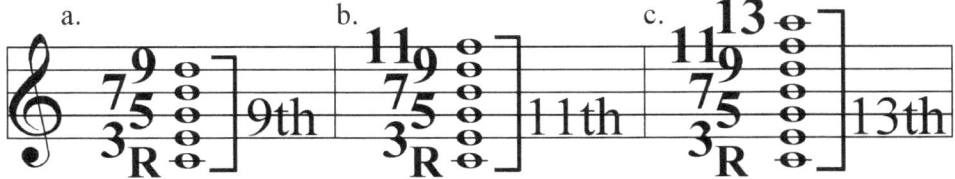

113

The Origin of the Seventh Chord

The principal origin of the seventh chord is the descending passing tone. Either dissonant or consonant with another pitch, the passing tone usually connects two harmonic consonances; it is approached and left by step and may occur on either a strong or weak beat. The passing tone also appears on either a strong or weak portion of a beat.

In example 5–4a, the tone F (P) fills in the interval of a 3rd between G and E. A dissonant passing 7th occurs on beat 3 of the first measure between the bass and the top melodic line (in half notes). The passing 7th connects two harmonic consonances, a perfect octave and a major 3rd (the compound intervals in the example are identified in their simple forms). Despite the limitations of the two-line texture shown in the example, the arrival of the major 3rd (C/E) in the second measure implies a C-major triad. The figure 8—7 indicates the downward movement of the octave to the 7th over a stationary bass (G).

Example 5–4b places the passing 7th (P) more clearly within a chordal framework. On beat 3 of the first measure, we have the tones G B D F, the four elements of the most common type of seventh chord, the dominant seventh. The dominant seventh will be discussed later in this chapter; for now, suffice it to say that the chord has a major triad and a minor 7th from the root to its seventh. As in 5–4a, the passing 7th in 5–4b moves down by step to form a consonant 3rd in the second measure (C/E).

Example 5–4: the passing 7th

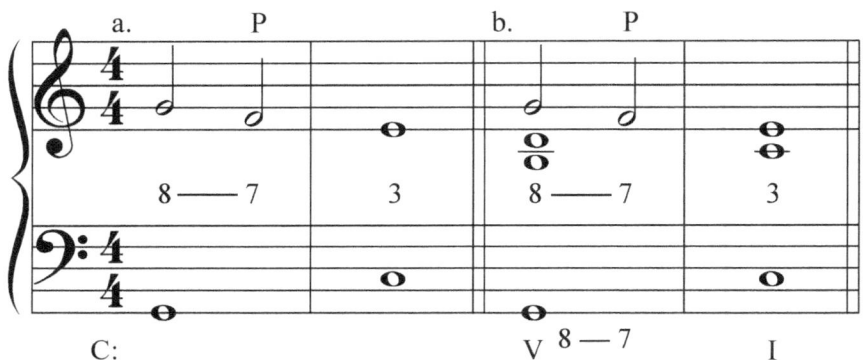

The Suspended Seventh

In examples 5–5a, 5b, and 5c below, the technique of suspension is used to *delay* the appearance of the dissonant 7th so that it falls on the first beat of the measure. As with the dissonant passing tone shown above, the 7th in examples 5–5b and 5c fills in the melodic interval of a descending 3rd between G and E. In each instance, the 7th is both preceded and followed by a harmonic consonance. Let us review the three parts of the suspension presented earlier in Chapter 4:
  (1) the suspension is *prepared* ("prep"), usually as a consonance (but sometimes as a dissonance); then,
  (2) the preparation is held, or suspended ("susp"), as the opposing voice (usually the bass) moves to form a dissonance with the suspended voice (though a consonant suspension is also possible); and finally,
  (3) the suspended voice moves down by step to *resolve* to a consonance ("res").
The actual suspension (part 2) should be metrically stronger than the resolution (part 3). The initial preparation (part 1), however, can be made from either a strong or weak position.

In measure 2 of examples 5–5a, 5b, and 5c, the interval of the 7th moves down by step in the same voice to form a consonance on the second half note. The 7th in 5–5a resolves over a *stationary* bass (7—6) to form a consonant 6th (G/E); we call the suspended 7th and its subsequent resolution the "7—6 suspension." In examples 5–5b and 5c, the bass moves simultaneously with the dissonant 7th to form a consonant 3rd (C/E), a "7 3 suspension." (Since the voice opposing the 7 3 suspension does not remain stationary during the resolution, the dash is not applied to the figured bass.)

Example 5–5: the 7—6 and 7 3 suspensions

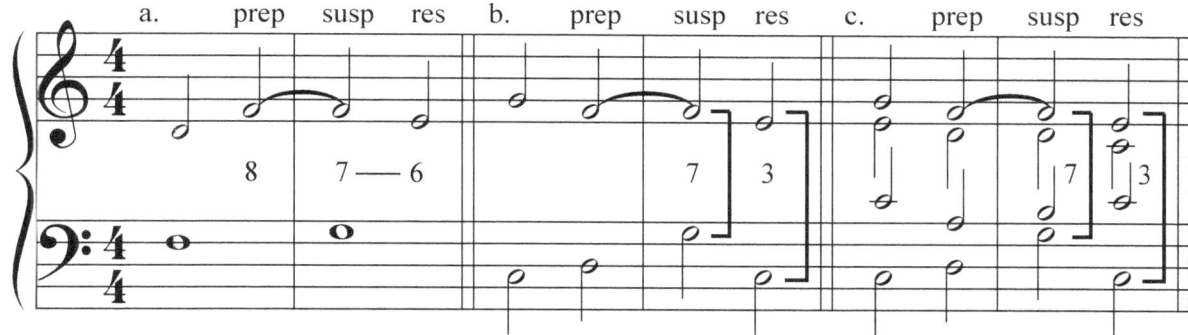

Example 5–5c places the suspended 7th within the framework of four-parts with the addition of the alto and tenor voices. As in the first measure of example 5–4b above, 5–5c illustrates the formation of the dominant seventh chord (G B D F); this time, however, it occurs on the first half note of the second measure. Once again, the chord of resolution is a C-major triad with an omitted fifth and a tripled root.

The Freestanding Seventh Chord

In example 5–6, we abandon the technique of suspension altogether and move directly into the dissonant 7th as part of a *freestanding* seventh chord (again, the fifth is omitted from the C-major triad on the second half note of measure 2). Here, the seventh chord as a standalone entity is derived from the passing 7th. (Indeed, we could have placed 5–6 after examples 5–4a and 4b and labeled it "example 5–4c.")

Example 5–6

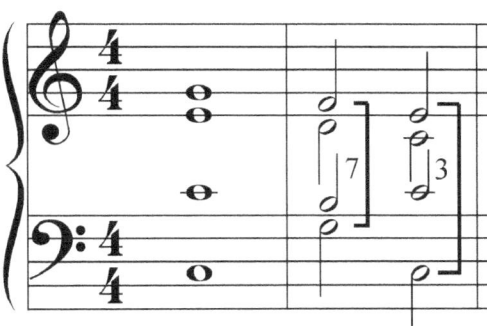

The Real Seventh Chord

In the course of our studies, we shall find that the seventh component of a *real* seventh chord always seeks to move down by step to form a consonance within the next chord—*if there is a tone of resolution available in the next chord*. This downward resolution to a consonance is central to the authenticity of the seventh chord because it replicates the operation of its progenitor, the descending dissonant passing tone.

A second requirement for a real seventh involves the root relationship it shares with the chord of resolution. In the traditional study of harmony, one of the following conditions must be met to have a real seventh chord:
(1) either the seventh chord stands in a rising 2nd root relationship to the chord it addresses; or,
(2) the seventh chord stands in either a falling 5th or rising 4th root relationship to the chord it addresses.
If the conditions cited above are not met, then we are not dealing with a real seventh chord. Some other explanation accounts for the presence of the seventh in the chord.

The Four Principal Types of "White-Key" Seventh Chords

This section focuses primarily on the white keys of the piano keyboard and examines the four types of seventh chords that emerge therefrom. Later, in Chapter 8, we shall encounter three other types of seventh chords that can be created from a combination of both the white and black keys of the piano keyboard, seventh chords that arise (though not exclusively) from the properties of the melodic minor.

As we have indicated, converting a triad into a seventh chord, regardless of the triad's quality, does not alter the status or function of the chord within the key and mode in which it occurs. The seventh element of the chord is simply an extension of the basic triad, just as ninth, eleventh, and thirteenth elements are all extensions of the underlying seventh chord.

All four triad qualities may have a seventh component added to their respective structures. However, remember that the diatonic pitch content of the major mode (as well as that of the church modes) cannot support the formation of the augmented triad. The augmented triad usually shows up in music that involves either the harmonic minor, the melodic minor, or some degree of mixture between the major mode and the minor mode. Modal mixtures are common in music literature; however, the study of this practice is best reserved for those who first develop a thorough understanding of music fundamentals and basic harmony.

Example 5–7 displays the four types of seventh chords formable on the white keys of the piano keyboard, namely, the major seventh (M7), the minor seventh (m7), the dominant seventh (D7), and the half-diminished seventh ($\emptyset$ 7). The major seventh has a major triad and a major 7th from the root to the seventh (MT / M7), the minor seventh has a minor triad and a minor 7th (mt / m7), the dominant seventh has a major triad and a minor 7th (MT / m7), and the half-diminished seventh has a diminished triad and a minor 7th (d°t / m7). The chord symbol for the half-diminished seventh includes a superscript circle with a diagonal slash.

There are three areas in which major triads appear on the white keys of the piano keyboard: C, F, and G. Both the C-major triad and the F-major triad may form major seventh chords (5–7). The major triad on G can have the dominant seventh. There are three areas where minor triads occur: D, E, and A, all of which may have minor seventh chords. Finally, on B, there is the one diminished triad available and therefore one half-diminished seventh chord. (Although 5–7 features the C octave, the four qualities of white-key seventh chords may be constructed on any white key in any octave register.)

Example 5–7

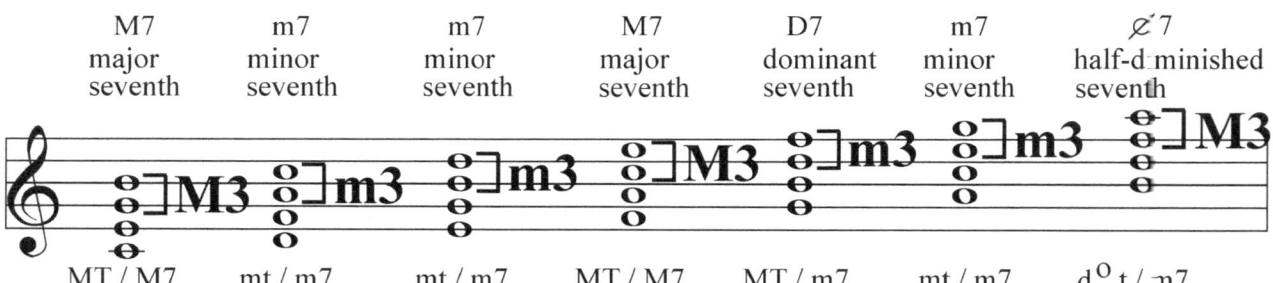

The Dominant Seventh Chord

The dominant seventh is the most important seventh chord for the major-minor tonal system. Both the dominant seventh and the dominant triad are so-named because their root is the dominant scale degree of the major, harmonic, and melodic minor modes. A dominant seventh chord in root position occurring on the dominant scale degree takes the chord symbol V^7.

As demonstrated in example 5–8, when the dominant seventh is in root position and addresses the tonic chord, it stands in a falling perfect 5th and rising perfect 4th root *and* bass relationship to the tonic chord. The falling perfect 5th (and its inversion, the rising perfect 4th) presents the strongest expression of harmonic motion in tonal music (see above, p. 55). In both major and minor modes, the dominant seventh contains the leading tone as its chord third. Therefore, the movement between the dominant and tonic chords produces the most effective melodic motion and the most effective harmonic motion for affirming the tonality of a musical work.

Example 5–8 illustrates an important principle in the treatment of the dissonant interval of the 7th (G/F): *if a seventh chord stands in a falling 5th or rising 4th root relationship to another chord, then the seventh of the first chord will move down by step in the same voice to become the third of the second chord.* Thus, the seventh of the dominant chord (F) moves down by step in the alto voice to become the third of the tonic triad (E).

Example 5–8: the dominant seventh chord

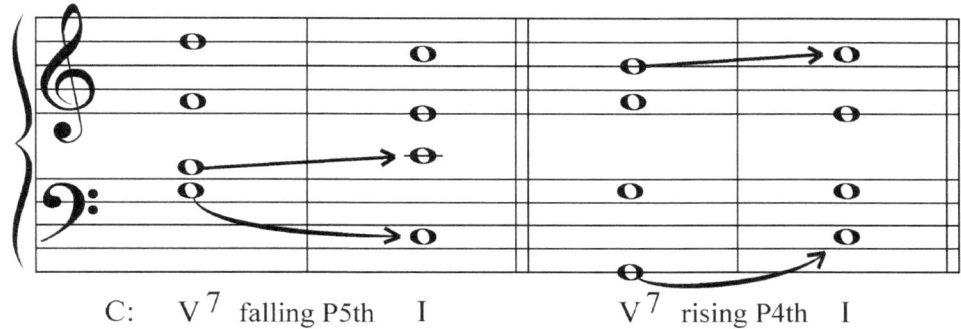

Inversions of the Dominant Seventh Chord

Since the dominant seventh chord consists of four tones, it has four chord positions: root position, first inversion, second inversion, and third inversion. In first inversion, the third is the bass pitch, in second inversion the fifth, and in third inversion the seventh. Example 5–9 shows all four positions of the dominant seventh in C major. If the seventh chord is in root position, then *the bottom note of the interval of the 7th indicates the location of the root* (see the bracketed arrow).

The *complete* figured-bass description for the intervals above the lowest tone of the dominant seventh in root position is signified with the Arabic numbers $^7_5{}_3$. The numbers designate the intervals of the 3rd, 5th, and 7th above the root of the chord. When either an alphabet letter or a Roman numeral precedes the figured bass of the seventh chord in root position, we omit the Arabic numbers 5 and 3 and retain the 7. The term dominant seventh is abbreviated as D^7 (example 5–9a).

The first inversion of the seventh chord (5–9b) has the third in the bass. Upon inversion, the interval of the 7th above the root (G/F) becomes the interval of the 2nd (F/G). If the bottom note of the 7th indicates the location of the root, then *the upper note of the 2nd identifies the root of the seventh chord in all three of its inverted positions* (see the bracketed arrows in examples 5–9b, 9c, and 9d).

The *complete* figured-bass description for the intervals above the third of the seventh chord in first inversion is signified with the Arabic numbers $\begin{smallmatrix}6\\5\\3\end{smallmatrix}$. The numbers represent the intervals of the 3rd, 5th, and 6th above the third of the chord (B D F G). When either an alphabet letter or a Roman numeral precedes the figured bass of the seventh chord in first inversion, we omit the Arabic number 3 and retain the 6 and the 5 (see 5–9b).

Example 5–9: inversions of the dominant seventh chord

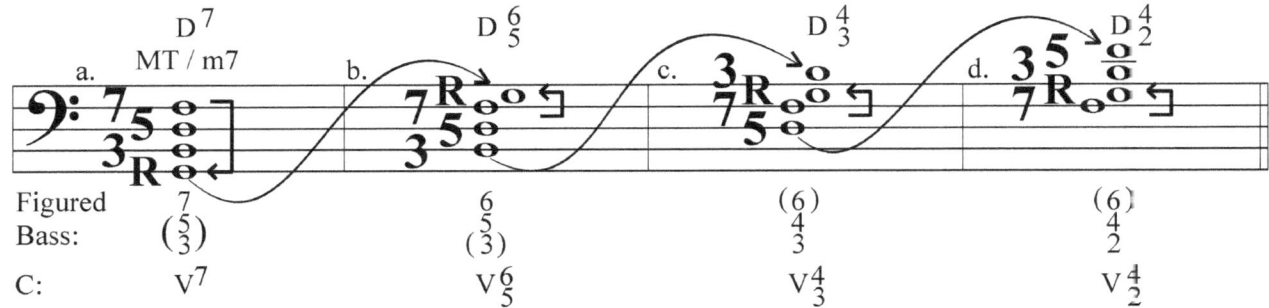

The second inversion of the seventh chord (5–9c) has the fifth in the bass. Again, upon inversion, the upper note of the 2nd identifies the root of the seventh chord. The *complete* figured-bass description for the intervals above the fifth of the seventh chord in second inversion is signified with the Arabic numbers $\begin{smallmatrix}6\\4\\3\end{smallmatrix}$. The numbers denote the intervals of the 3rd, 4th, and 6th above the fifth of the chord (D F G B). When either an alphabet letter or a Roman numeral precedes the figured bass of the seventh chord in second inversion, we omit the Arabic number 6 and retain the 4 and the 3 (5–9c).

The third inversion of the seventh chord (5–9d) has the seventh in the bass. As in examples 5–9b and 4c, the upper note of the 2nd identifies the root of the seventh chord. The *complete* figured-bass description for the intervals above the seventh of the seventh chord in third inversion is signified with the Arabic numbers $\begin{smallmatrix}6\\4\\2\end{smallmatrix}$. The numbers indicate the intervals of the 2nd, 4th, and 6th above the seventh of the chord (F G B D). When either an alphabet letter or a Roman numeral precedes the figured bass of the seventh chord in third inversion, we omit the Arabic number 6 and retain the 4 and the 2 (5–9d). In sum, the four positions of the seventh chord are abbreviated as: 7, $\begin{smallmatrix}6\\5\end{smallmatrix}$, $\begin{smallmatrix}4\\3\end{smallmatrix}$, and $\begin{smallmatrix}4\\2\end{smallmatrix}$.

Adding the Chord Seventh to the Cadential $\begin{smallmatrix}6\\4\end{smallmatrix}$

Examples 5–10 and 11 illustrate some of the ways to use the chord seventh with the elaborated dominant, the cadential $\begin{smallmatrix}6\\4\end{smallmatrix}$. In examples 5–10a and 11a, the chord seventh is part of a downward passing motion over a stationary bass (8—7) that resolves into the third of the tonic (with a tripled root in 10a and a doubled third in 11a).

Examples 5–10b and 11b present an alternative voice leading for the cadential $^6_4$. Since the interval of the 6th in the alto voice of measure 1 (G/E or G/E♭) is not a dissonance, it is free to move up to form the seventh component of the dominant on beat 3 (6—7). The 6th is doubled in the soprano voice, which proceeds downwards to form a 5th above the bass (6—5).

In examples 11a and 11b, the leading tone in the tenor voice drops back to the fifth of the tonic chord while the bass moves in contrary motion. This special license for the leading tone, mentioned earlier in Chapter 1 (p. 54), can be used only in the alto or tenor voices. When the leading tone appears in the soprano voice, it must move to the tonic, as in 5–11c.

Examples 10c and 11c take the consonant 6th (G/E or G/E♭) up to the dissonant 7th (G/F). In both examples, however, we have a stationary octave on G (8—), which leaves no place for the fifth of the dominant chord (see the dotted diagonal line from 6 to 7 and the crossed-out 5).

Example 5–10: adding the chord seventh to the cadential $^6_4$ in major

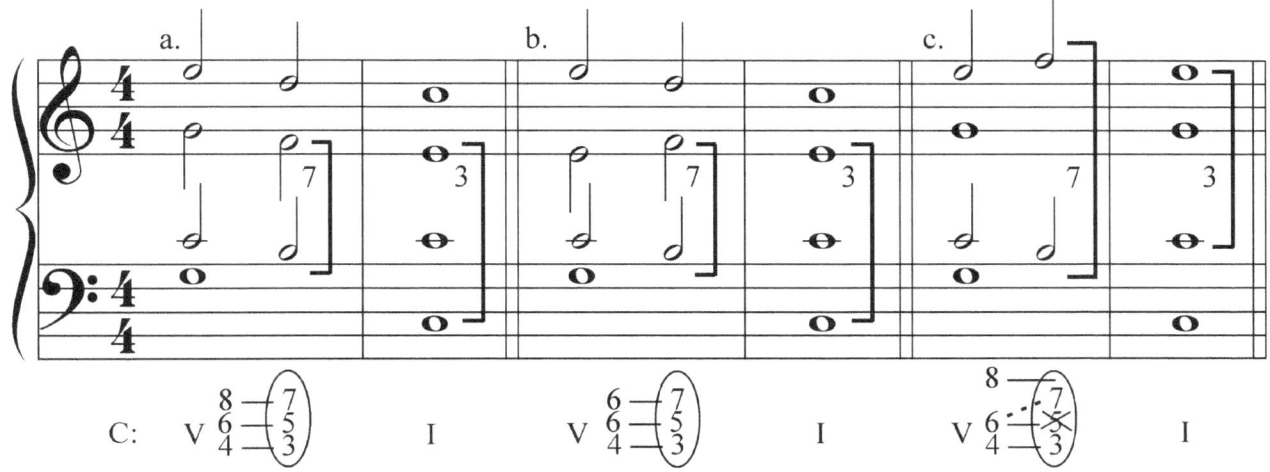

Example 5–11: adding the chord seventh to the cadential $^6_4$ in minor

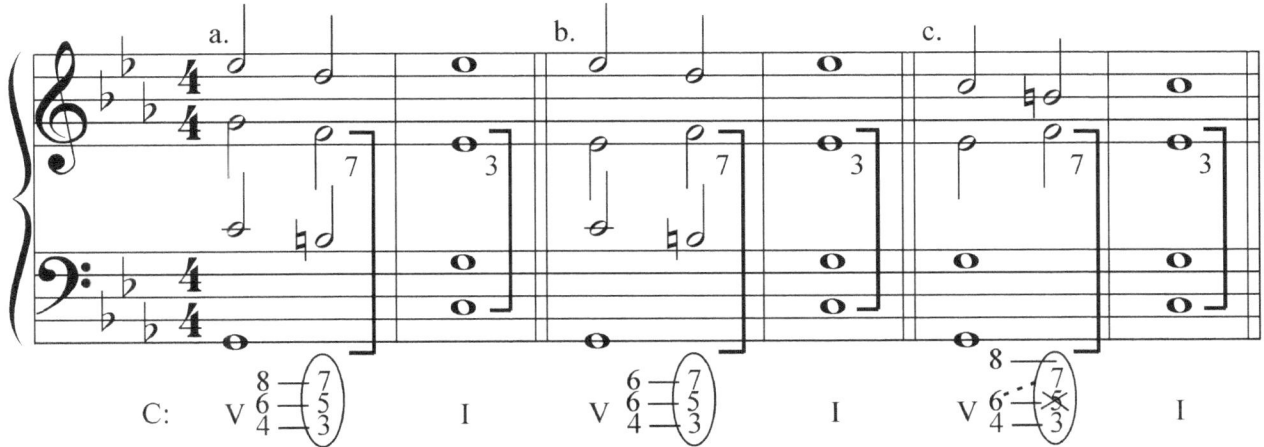

Chapter 6   The Cadence

The cadence is a two-chord pattern that forms the end of a musical phrase. As stated in Chapter 4, the phrase is the smallest element of musical form in which a combination of melodic, rhythmic, and chordal components together comprise the beginning, middle, and end of a musical thought. The ending may be permanent or temporary, whether or not the activity within the phrase is continuous or segmented into smaller units known as sub-phrases. These sub-phrases, if present, may also contain endings marked off by cadences.

The first part of the two-chord pattern is called the *approach chord* because it addresses the second chord, known as the *cadential chord*. The approach chord may include dissonant upper extensions beyond the root, third, and fifth of the basic triad, such as the seventh and the ninth. (Some of the approach chords shown in the examples of this chapter include the seventh, while others are expressed as triads.) Since the cadential chord constitutes either a permanent or temporary ending, avoid dissonant chords here because consonant chords more effectively convey a state of rest. There are two basic types of cadences, each defined according to how the approach chord addresses the cadential chord:

(1) If the approach to the cadential chord in the bass involves either a falling 5th or rising 4th motion (or a falling 4th or rising 5th motion), then we describe the cadence as a harmonic cadence.
(2) If the approach to the cadential chord in the bass involves the melodic interval of a major or minor 2nd, then we describe the cadence as a contrapuntal cadence.

The Dominant Family of Chords: the Tonal Harmonic Dominant and the Tonal Melodic Dominant

When the major triad of the dominant is in root position and addresses the tonic chord, it produces two optimal conditions for affirming the tonality of a music composition: the compelling melodic drive upwards from the leading tone to the tonic and the strong harmonic motion of a falling perfect 5th or a rising perfect 4th in the bass. Because of its function as the chief definer of the tonality, the dominant chord is termed here the "tonal harmonic dominant."

The second most important triad for defining the tonality of a music composition occurs in the area of the leading tone, which shares two pitches in common with the dominant triad and stands in a rising minor 2nd root relationship to the tonic. The root and the third of the leading-tone triad are the same pitches as the third and the fifth of the corresponding dominant triad (see above, p. 56).

Because of its key-defining function and common pitch content with the dominant, the leading-tone triad functions in most cases as a dominant chord. As such, all of the chords built on the leading tone belong to the "dominant family" of chords. To be sure, there are circumstances in which the chord of the leading tone may not be functioning as a dominant but rather serving some other purpose within a particular musical context. However, in most cases, the leading-tone triad is appropriately recognized as a chord of the dominant family; accordingly, we further describe it as the "tonal melodic dominant."

Tonic-oriented Cadences: the Authentic Cadence

The authentic cadence is part of a large category of tonic-oriented cadences. The approach chord of the authentic cadence is a dominant-family chord. The cadential chord is the tonic chord. There are two general classes of authentic cadences, each defined according to how the approach chord addresses the cadential chord: harmonic authentic cadences and contrapuntal authentic cadences. Additionally, within the general category of the authentic cadence, there are two subclasses, each grouped according to what scale degrees appear in the bass and soprano voices: the perfect authentic cadence and the imperfect authentic cadence. The most permanent-sounding close to a musical phrase is produced by the authentic cadence, particularly, the perfect authentic cadence.

The following four sections examine each variety of authentic cadence: the harmonic perfect authentic cadence, the harmonic imperfect authentic cadence, the contrapuntal perfect authentic cadence, and the contrapuntal imperfect authentic cadence. Subsequently, we shall consider two other tonic-oriented cadences: the deceptive cadence and the plagal cadence. Finally, our study of cadences concludes with the non-tonic-oriented cadence known as the half cadence.

Tonic-oriented Cadences: the Harmonic Perfect Authentic Cadence

Unlike all of the other types of cadences, the harmonic perfect authentic cadence is described generally as a "closed cadence," or "full cadence" (example 6–1). Having either a falling 5th or rising 4th root and bass relationship between its approach chord and cadential chord, the harmonic perfect authentic cadence produces a sense of finality not present in other cadences because it has scale degree 1 in both outer voices (that is, the bass and soprano voices) of the tonic chord.

Notice the exceptional treatment of the leading tone (B♮) in the tenor voice of examples 6–1c and 1d, which drops back to the fifth of the tonic chord (G). As demonstrated in examples 6–1b and 1d, the approach chord for the harmonic perfect authentic cadence may also involve the cadential $^6_4$. The tonal harmonic dominant, as either a standalone chord (6–1a and 1c) or as the second part of the cadential $^6_4$ (6–1b and 1d), becomes more effective in its approach to the tonic with the addition of the dissonant 7th.

Example 6–1: the harmonic perfect authentic cadence

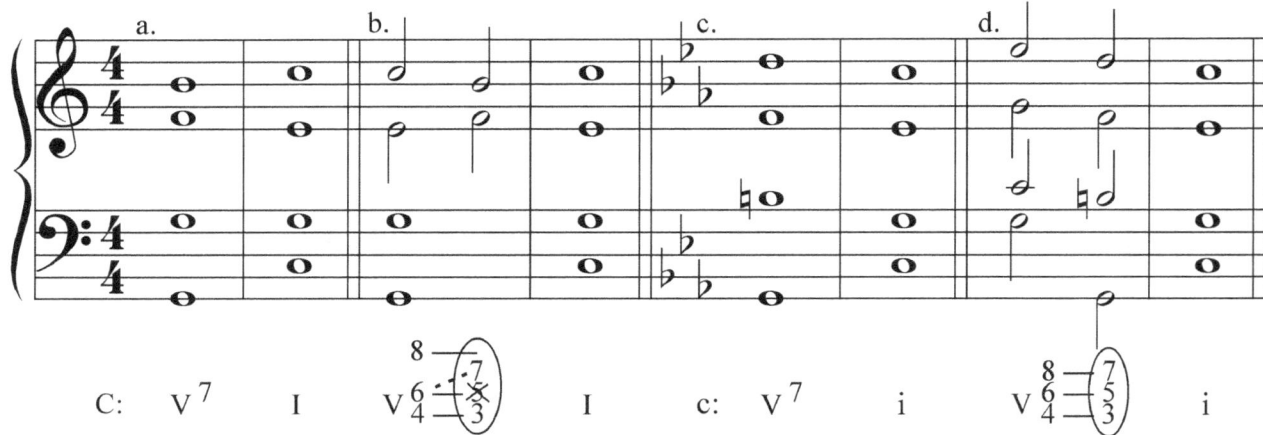

Tonic-oriented Cadences: the Harmonic Imperfect Authentic Cadence

Example 6–2 shows various dispositions of the harmonic imperfect authentic cadence, a subclass of the authentic cadence. The chief characteristic of the harmonic imperfect authentic cadence is the appearance of either scale degree 3 or 5 in the soprano voice of the tonic chord (see the circled pitches). Since the harmonic imperfect authentic cadence must have a falling 5th or rising 4th root and bass relationship between its approach chord and cadential chord, the tonic chord maintains scale degree 1 in the bass.

The cadential $^6_4$ may serve as the approach chord for the harmonic imperfect authentic cadence (examples 6–2e, 2f, 2g, and 2h). As with every type of cadence other than the harmonic perfect authentic cadence, the imperfect authentic cadence is one of the many types of "open cadences" because scale degree 1 does not appear in both outer voices of the cadential chord. (In the tenor voice of examples 6–2a, 2b, 2d and 2g, the leading tone drops back to the fifth of the tonic chord.)

Example 6–2: the harmonic imperfect authentic cadence

Tonic-oriented Cadences: the Contrapuntal Perfect Authentic Cadence

The contrapuntal perfect authentic cadence has scale degree 1 in both outer voices and a stepwise approach in the bass to the cadential tonic. In example 6–3, we have two of the most common approach chords for this cadence: V^6 in major and minor, vii○^{6} in major, and ♯vii○^{6} in minor.

In their approach to the cadential tonic, these dominant-family chords (which can also be expressed as sevenths) share important features that ultimately confer upon them a functional description beyond their respective chord symbols. Since both chords contain the leading tone and define the tonic chord while approaching it by step, we shall further call them "contrapuntal leading-tone chords," a term put forward by Felix Salzer and Carl Schachter in *Counterpoint In Composition* (New York: McGraw-Hill, 1969).

Example 6–3: the contrapuntal perfect authentic cadence

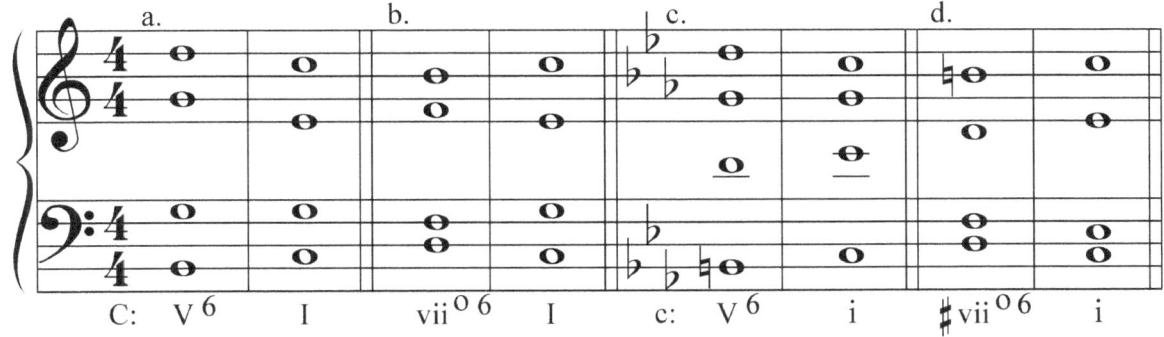

Tonic-oriented Cadences: the Contrapuntal Imperfect Authentic Cadence

In the contrapuntal imperfect authentic cadence, the cadential chord has a scale degree other than the tonic in at least one of its outer voices. Example 6–4 demonstrates some of the more common possibilities in both major and minor, all of which employ first-inversion chords of the dominant family that approach the cadential tonic by step as contrapuntal leading-tone chords.

Example 6–4 the contrapuntal imperfect authentic cadence

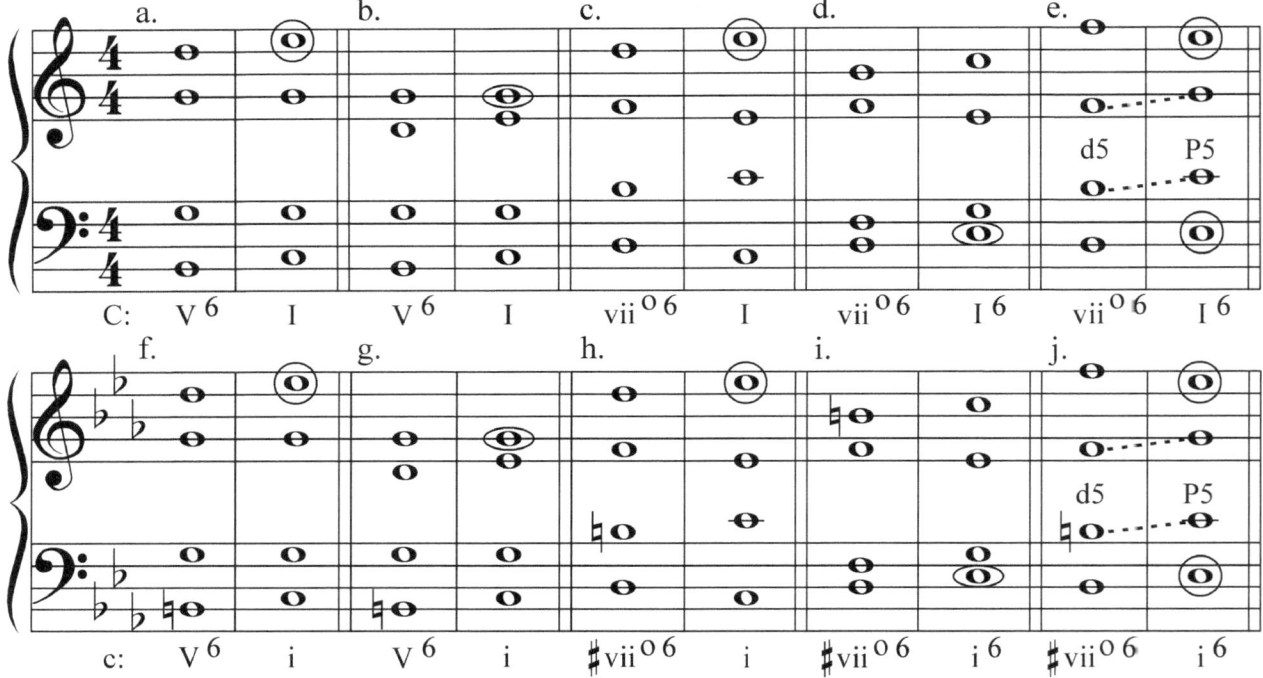

As indicated in example 6–4 above, the cadential chord can be in either $\frac{5}{3}$ or in $\frac{6}{3}$ position but not in $\frac{6}{4}$ position. Examples 6–4a, 4b, 4c, 4f, 4g, and 4h all have scale degree 1 in the bass of the cadential chord. Scale degree 3 occurs in the soprano of examples 6–4a, 4c, 4e, 4f, 4h, and 4j. In examples 6–4d, 4e, 4i, and 4j, we have scale degree 3 in the bass. Examples 6–4b and 4g both present scale degree 5 in the soprano.

Before we proceed with a few more varieties of tonic-oriented cadences, let us consider briefly the voice leading for examples 6–4e and 4j. Here, in the tenor and alto, we have the diminished 5th in the approach chord proceeding to a perfect 5th in the cadential chord. In Chapter 3, we stated that some theoreticians prohibit this particular succession of unequal parallel 5ths (see p. 93). According to this view, if the order of succession is the diminished 5th to the perfect 5th, then the dissonant diminished 5th cannot resolve properly (the diminished 5th normally contracts to the interval of the 3rd). Indeed, it would be well to observe caution with this succession of intervals.

In the example, we have placed the two 5ths in the inner voices, the tenor and alto, covering them sufficiently to allow, *if used sparingly*. Notice that the bass, tenor, and alto voices all move in the same direction (upwards). Although we want to avoid moving too many voices in the same direction, examples 6–4e and 4j show the soprano moving down to provide good contrary motion between the outer voices. This disposition of the two chords would be one of the preferred ways to voice lead the succession from the parallel diminished 5th to the perfect 5th.

Tonic-oriented Cadences: the Deceptive Cadence

The deceptive cadence falls within the category of tonic-oriented cadences because the cadential chord contains scale degree 1 and is approached by the dominant chord. However, even though the leading tone proceeds to scale degree 1 in the cadential chord, the tonic chord itself is usually replaced with either the subdominant or the submediant. Example 6–5 exhibits some common dispositions of the deceptive cadence in major and minor, using the submediant as the cadential chord.

With the deceptive cadence, the *only* tone of choice for doubling is the tonic pitch, which is the third of the submediant. Supporting scale degree 1 with the chord of the submediant rather than the tonic produces a state of suspense by delaying the sense of closure, leaving the listener to anticipate the arrival of the tonic chord.

Example 6–5: the deceptive cadence with the submediant as the cadential chord

Example 6–6 illustrates a less common deceptive cadence involving the subdominant, which appears in $^6_3$ position as the cadential chord (F A C or F A♭ C); its fifth is scale degree 1 of the key. When following the dominant with the subdominant, however, be very careful not to produce parallel 5ths above and between the respective roots of the approach chord and the cadential chord.

In examples 6–6a, 6c, and 6d, parallel 5ths would occur (see the dotted lines) were it not for the action of an inner voice, which proceeds down to F on the second half note of measure 1 (the alto in 6a and 6d, the tenor in 6c). Forming the dissonant interval of a 7th with the G bass, the F actually belongs to the following chord, the cadential subdominant. In other words, the F *anticipates* the arrival of the subdominant's root. This usage is commonly referred to as a dissonant anticipation tone.

Example 6–6: the deceptive cadence with the subdominant as the cadential chord

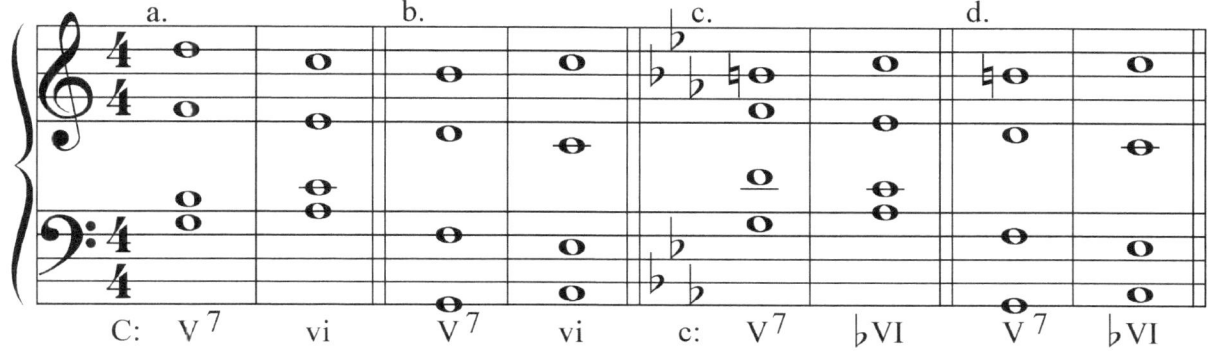

Within the context of the dominant triad (G B D), the anticipation (F) in example 6–6 above is a nonharmonic tone. The anticipation breaks up the parallel 5ths by transforming the approach to the second 5th from a parallel to an oblique motion: G/D to F/C becomes G/D to F/D to F/C (5 6 5). The anticipation tone occurs most frequently in the soprano voice; however, it can certainly be employed in any upper voice to correct the parallel 5ths between the dominant and subdominant chords. As we shall discover in Chapter 9, nonharmonic tones such as the anticipation can be used as correctives to faulty motion.

Another way to fix parallel 5ths is to simply flip them over and convert them into 4ths, as illustrated in 6–6b. The soprano voice of 6–6a becomes the alto voice in 6–6b. In all of the above examples featuring the deceptive cadence, scale degree 1 of the key is doubled as either the third or the fifth of the cadential chord. Thus, 6–6 shows the leading tone resolving to the tonic; however, the chord within which scale degree 1 occurs is the subdominant in $^6_3$ position.

Tonic-oriented Cadences: Perfect and Imperfect Plagal Cadences

The plagal cadence often occurs after the actual cadence as a kind of post-cadential extension. The cadential chord (the tonic portion of the plagal cadence) is approached harmonically by a non-dominant chord above scale degree 4 in the bass. Most listeners recognize the plagal cadence as the famous "Amen" closing for many religious forms of music such as the hymn.

Two dispositions of the plagal cadence are possible: the perfect plagal cadence and the imperfect plagal cadence, shown in examples 6–7 and 8 respectively. The first disposition, the perfect plagal cadence, has scale degree 1 in both the soprano and bass. Since scale degree 4 is the root of the subdominant triad (examples 6–7a and 7c) and the third of the supertonic triad (examples 6–7b and 7d), either chord may approach the cadential tonic of the plagal cadence.

Example 6–7: the perfect plagal cadence

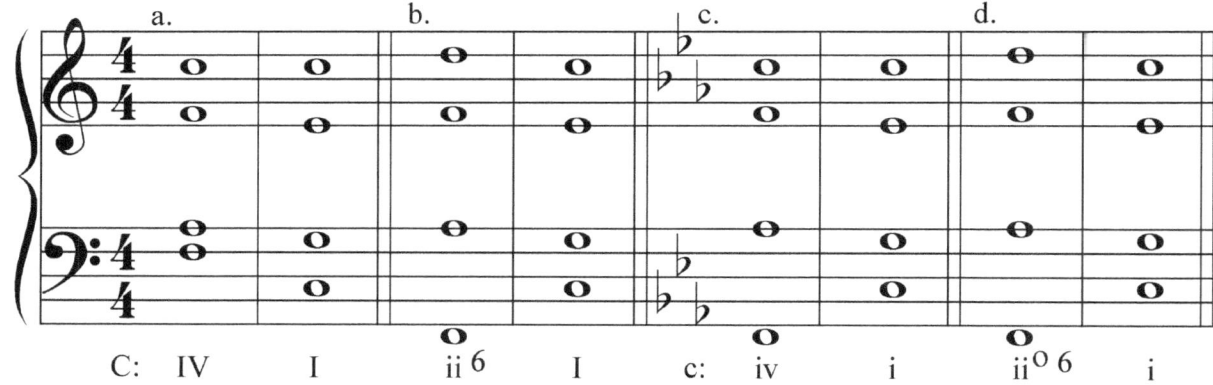

Compare the actions of the tenor and bass voices in example 6–7. In 6–7a, the perfect 5th between the tenor and bass of the cadential tonic is approached with acceptable similar motion. Examples 6–7b, 7c, and 7d take the bass voice down one octave in the approach chord so that contrary motion effects the connection to the perfect 5th between the tenor and the bass in the cadential tonic.

The imperfect plagal cadence has scale degree 3 or 5 in the soprano voice. Various voicings of the approach and cadential chords are given in example 6–8. In order to avoid parallel 5ths in 6–8d between the soprano and alto voices, we double the third of the cadential tonic rather than its root, as a C in the alto of the tonic chord would have produced parallel 5ths (D/A and C/G). Example 6–8h shows the corresponding relationship in minor with voicing identical to that of 6–8d. However, we could have taken the alto down to C in the cadential chord of 6–8h because the 5th in the approach chord is diminished, giving us unequal parallel 5ths (potentially, D/A♭ and C/G). Still, the voice leading we have in 6–8h gives us more instances of contrary motion between the four voices—almost always preferable.

Example 6–8: the imperfect plagal cadence

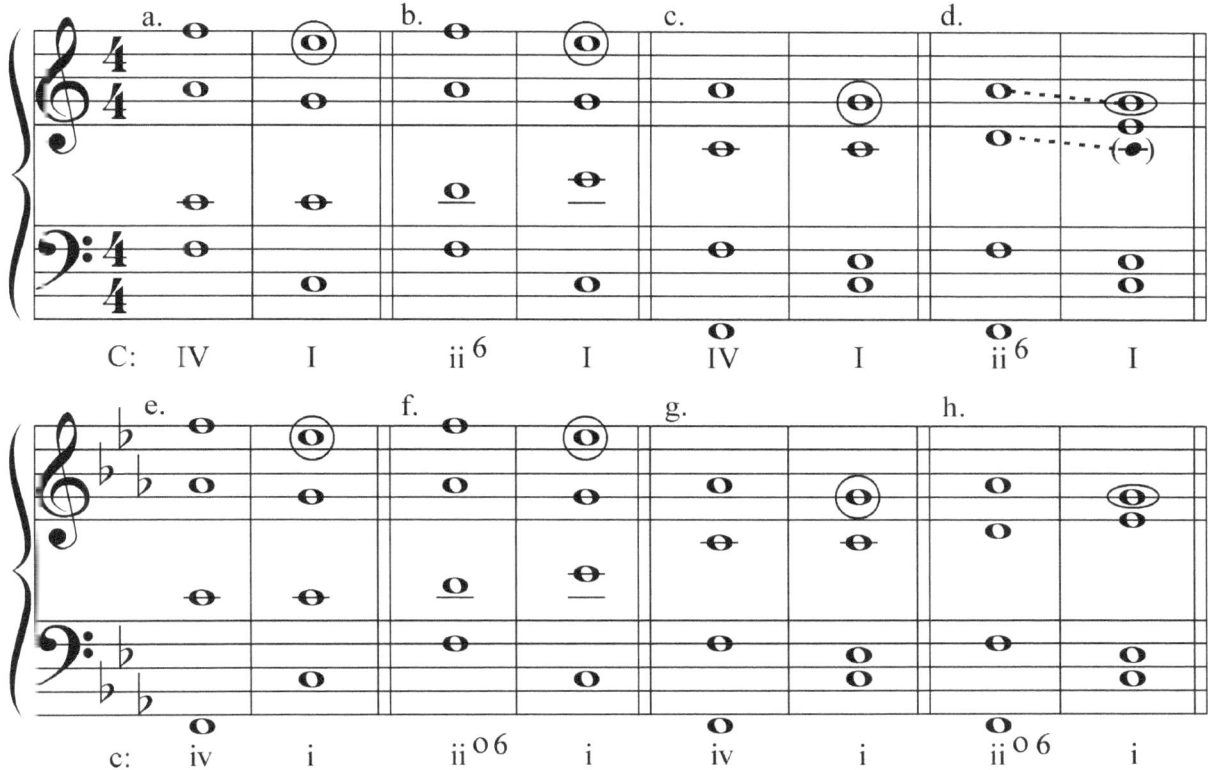

Non-Tonic-oriented Cadences: Harmonic and Contrapuntal Half Cadences

The half cadence, also known as the semicadence, consists of a non-dominant approach chord and a cadential chord other than the tonic; it is often analogized to a comma in speech, a stopping point that nonetheless seeks continuation to complete the musical thought. The half cadence exhibits either a harmonic or contrapuntal bass relationship between its two chords.

For the harmonic half cadence in major, illustrated in examples 6–9a through 9d, the tonic or the supertonic constitute the most common approaches to the cadential chord. The dominant triad or the cadential $^6_4$ are the most frequently used cadential chords. When either the dominant or the cadential $^6_4$ appears as the cadential chord, a triad rather than a seventh chord is preferred because a consonant chord establishes a feeling of repose more successfully than a dissonant one. Three of the harmonic half cadences in 6–9 should be avoided: 9g, 9h, and 9i.

In minor, the tonic often serves as the approach chord of choice (examples 6–9e and 9f). The diminished supertonic can be used as an approach chord but not in root position, as the diminished 5th formed above its root is too dissonant (examples 6–9g and 9h). When, however, a 3rd is added above the fifth, transforming the diminished triad into a half-diminished seventh chord, the harshness of the diminished 5th above the root is mitigated.

Shown below in examples 6–9i and 9j, the half-diminished seventh takes a superscript circle with a diagonal slash. As a half-diminished seventh chord, the root-position supertonic makes a better connection to the dominant.

Examples 6–9g and 9i demonstrate one of the hazards of connecting the diminished supertonic in root position to the dominant triad: a probable direct 5th, shown here between the soprano and alto (see the dotted lines). Ultimately, the best way to avert the direct 5th in this instance is to use the cadential $^6_4$, as shown in 6–9j.

Example 6–9: the harmonic half cadence

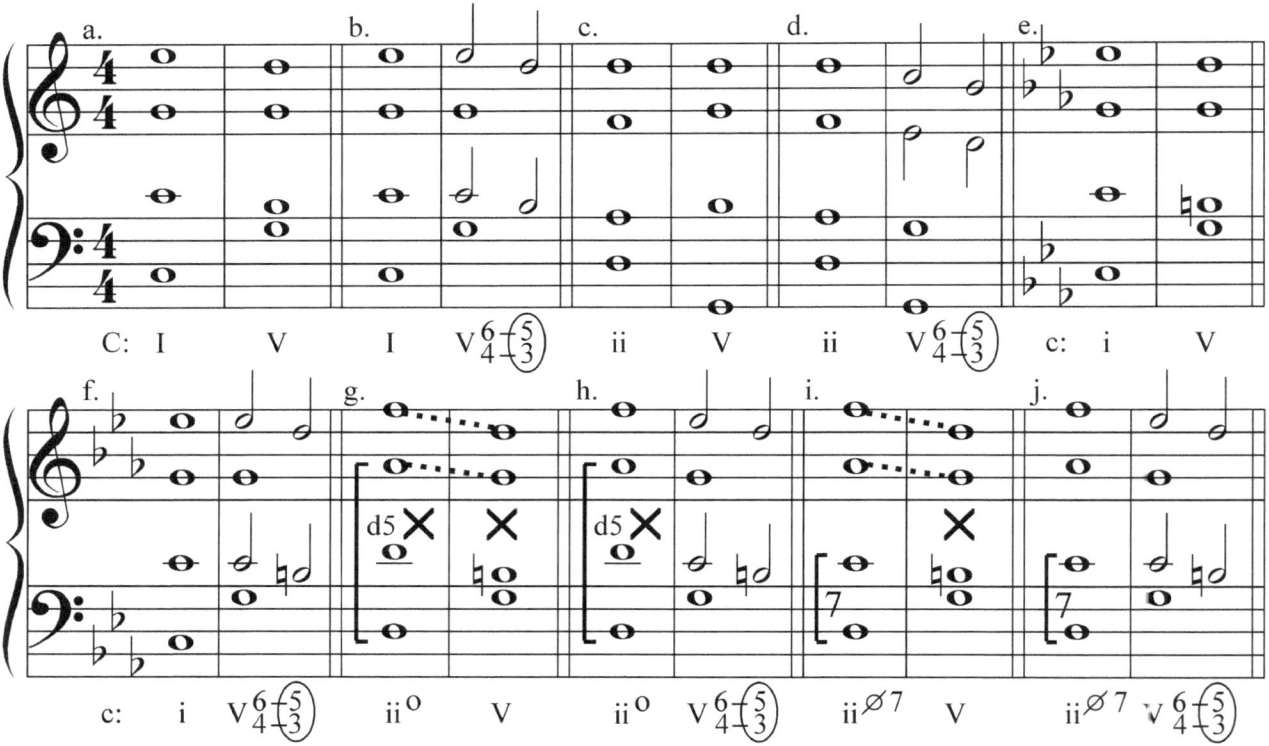

The minor supertonic triad is less likely to occur as an approach chord in minor than in major because its fifth is variable ♯6 rather than ♭6; hence, the option to move down to scale degree 5 is not available (example 6–10).

Example 6–10: the harmonic half cadence

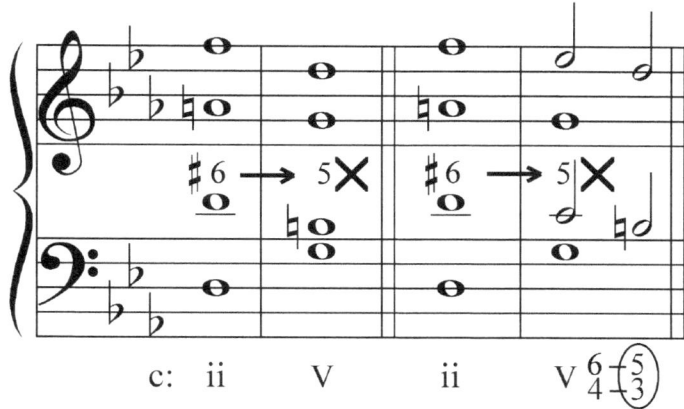

c: ii   V   ii   V $^6_4$–$^5_3$

The contrapuntal half cadence presents more varied possibilities for the approach chord, while the cadential chord is expressed in either root position, first inversion, or as a cadential $^6_4$. The approach to the cadential chord is usually made from above or below by step. Although the limitations of space preclude a complete listing of all the available approach chords for the contrapuntal half cadence, example 6–11 demonstrates a few of the simplest ways to address the cadential chord.

Example 6–11: the contrapuntal half cadence

a.   b.   c.   d.
C: IV   V   vi   V   ii^6 V   I   V^6

e.   f.   g.   h.
c: iv   V   ♭VI   V   ii°^{6} V   i   V^6

Examples 6–12a, 12b, 12c, and 12d use chords of the subdominant, minor supertonic, submediant, and diminished supertonic to demonstrate the stepwise approach to the cadential $^6_4$. In 6–12c, notice how the cadential $^6_4$ breaks up potential parallel 5ths between the bass and tenor voices (A♭/E♭ to G/D) *by disrupting the vertical alignment of the second 5th*, transforming faulty parallel motion into oblique (G/E♭ to G/D). Remember that in the first part of the cadential $^6_4$, we have the arrival of the dominant pitch in the bass over which two nonharmonic tones on the strongest beat of the measure occur. Here, the nonharmonic tones constitute a double suspension: a dissonant 4th (G/C) and a consonant 6th (G/E♭).

Example 6–12: the contrapuntal half cadence

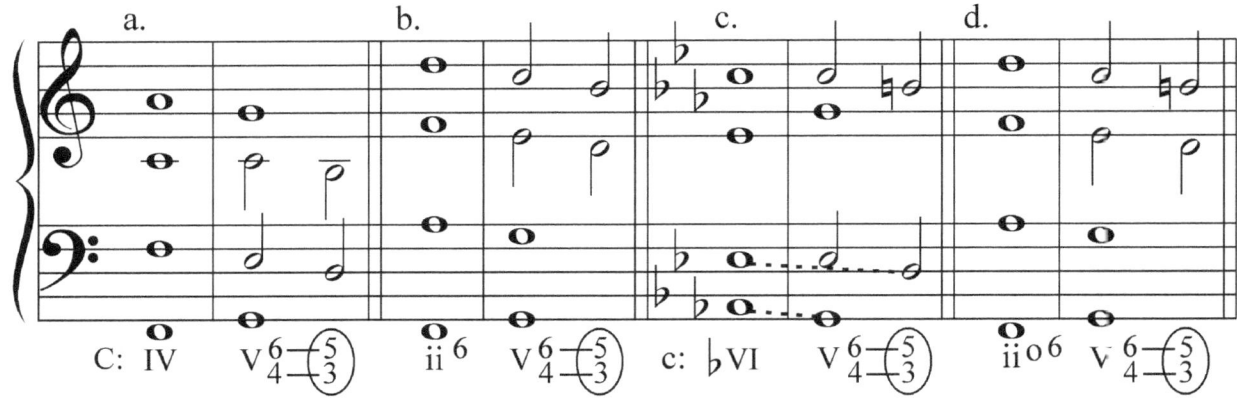

Non-Tonic-oriented Cadences: the Phrygian Half Cadence on V

The final contrapuntal half cadence to consider is the Phrygian cadence. A brief review of the properties of the Phrygian mode will shed some light on why we refer to this cadence as Phrygian.

Earlier, we classified the Phrygian mode a minor prototype mode because its tonic triad is minor. The untransposed Phrygian mode on E is similar to its parallel natural minor, e minor, except that E Phrygian's scale degree 2 is lowered one half step in relation to the e-minor scale. E Phrygian contains an F natural, e minor an F♯ (see Chapter 2, examples 2–3c and 3d).

Frequently, the final tonic of a segment of music written in the Phrygian mode will take a major triad rather than a minor triad. Despite the apparent contradiction in classifying the Phrygian mode as a minor prototype, ending a composition or segment of a composition that is otherwise written in minor with a major tonic triad is based upon a very old tradition.

Around the beginning of the sixteenth century, composers began to show a preference for ending minor compositions with a major triad on the tonic. This practice continued for about two hundred years of music composition. The assignment of the major tonic triad in a composition written in the minor mode was later referred to in French as the *tierce de Picardie*, in English, the picardy third. Within the context of the minor mode, the tonic triad is viewed as having a raised 3rd, raised one half step from the characteristic minor 3rd between the root and third of the chord.

The Phrygian cadence occurs in the minor mode and involves a iv ^{6} approach to a cadential V chord (Example 6–13). With the subdominant's third in the bass, the root of the V chord is approached from above by half step. This approach resembles the Phrygian mode's half-step descent from scale degrees 2 down to 1. The half-step relationship between the Phrygian mode's supertonic and tonic scale degrees is sometimes referred to as the "upper leading tone."

Example 6–13a demonstrates the contrapuntal Phrygian half cadence in the key and mode of c minor. The best doubling for the subdominant in first inversion is the fifth. In minor, any chord with variable ♭6 as one of its components followed by a chord with variable ♯7 can potentially produce a melodic augmented 2nd between variables ♭6 and ♯7, an awkward interval to sing that should be avoided whenever possible (see the alto voice of 6–13b).

Comparing examples 6–13a and 13c, we can see the relationship between the two chords of the Phrygian cadence in both c minor and G Phrygian (G P). In G Phrygian, which has the same key signature as c minor, the relationship becomes that of a first-inversion subtonic proceeding to the tonic G. Note carefully, however, that the tonic triad is major, as it contains the picardy third (the P in parentheses below the chord symbol in uppercase denotes the picardy third).

Example 6–13: the Phrygian half cadence on V

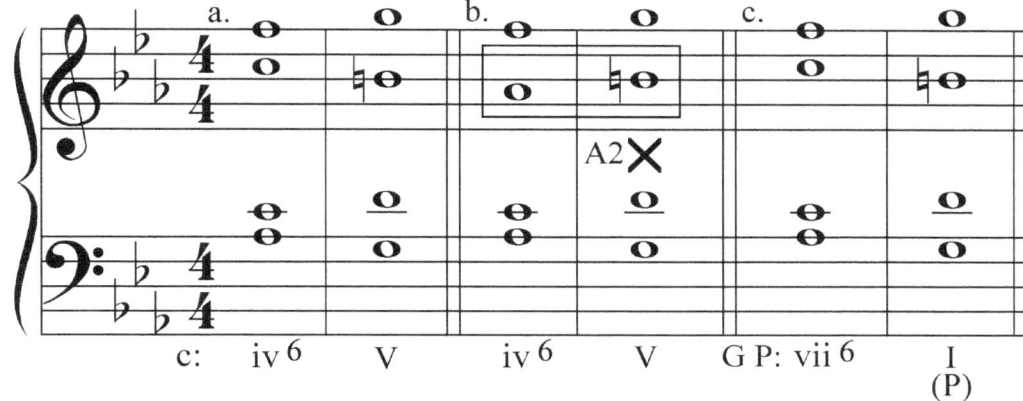

Chapter 7 The Chord Progression

Our objective in the foregoing pages has been to discover the best ways to optimize the connections between unlike chords within the context of four voices and create a sense of forward motion in music. This momentum is enhanced by the proper treatment of consonance and dissonance within the tonal framework.

Defining the tonic with a chord of the dominant family also produces the effect of movement, of progression from one chord to the next. The strongest chord progression comes from the authentic cadence, which always contains an approach chord of the dominant family.

The authentic cadence produces either a harmonic or contrapuntal approach to the tonic, using either a tonal harmonic dominant in root position or a contrapuntal leading-tone chord such as the V^6 in major and minor, the $vii^{\circ 6}$ in major, or the $\sharp vii^{\circ 6}$ in minor. Any series of chords lacking an approach chord of the dominant family constitutes a *succession* of chords rather than a *progression* of chords. Moreover, the dominant-family chord occupies the penultimate position in the progression, that is, the next-to-the-last chord immediately preceding the final tonic. This chapter surveys four types of chord progressions, all of which have a chord of the dominant family in the penultimate position:

(1) the basic harmonic progression;
(2) the basic contrapuntal progression;
(3) the secondary harmonic progression; and,
(4) the secondary contrapuntal progression.

These progressions, as represented in the following examples, exhibit stepwise melodic descents in the soprano voice, conjunct motions that are, to a considerable extent, the skeletal frameworks of far more elaborate melodies. Indeed, if melodies were limited to the scale-like formations that we are about to inspect, they would fail to hold the attention of their listeners.

An actual melody usually contains both conjunct and disjunct motions with leaps that are likely (though not always) followed by a reversal of direction. Actual melodies rise and fall at the will of the composer, typically exhibiting more rhythmic variety than those illustrated in this chapter. Such devices as nonharmonic tones and chordal skips are also common.

The use of conjunct and disjunct motion, varied rhythmic patterns, and nonharmonic tones all count among the elements that make up the outer skin or flesh surrounding the bare bones of a musical work. Indeed, the details that constitute the musical surface of a composition help to establish its individuality; moreover, the details of a musical work bring the composition to life so that it can engage the listener.

The harmonic and contrapuntal progressions that accompany melodies are seldom limited to three or four chords. Still, the study of music fundamentals and basic harmony must begin with the simplest of melodic and harmonic constructions. To be sure, a much wider variety of chord progressions occur in music than those put forward here; however, the four types of progressions cited above form the underlying harmonic and contrapuntal frameworks for many of these more varied progressions.

The Basic Harmonic Progression

We begin our study of chord progression with the understanding that some of the triads shown in the following examples may carry tertian elements of higher extension, producing chords of the seventh, ninth, eleventh, and/or thirteenth. These upper extensions, however, do not alter the function of the triads that occur within the types of progressions cited in this chapter. (Some of the chords in the examples of this chapter include the seventh, while others are expressed as triads.)

The authentic cadence (V – I or V – i) comprises two-thirds of the basic harmonic progression; the remaining third consists of an initial tonic. Together, the three chords produce the following progression: I – V – I in major or i – V – i in minor. This is the minimal number of chords for a *complete* basic harmonic progression. In fact, the authentic cadence constitutes an *incomplete* basic harmonic progression.

Example 7–1 demonstrates the basic harmonic progression with a stepwise melodic descent in the soprano voice from scale degrees 3 down to 1. Here, in examples 7–1a and 1b, the tonal harmonic dominant (beat 3, measure 1) supports scale degree 2 (D), which fills in the descending 3rd. In effect, scale degree 2 constitutes a consonant passing tone supported by the dominant chord in root position.

Example 7–1: the basic harmonic progression using V^7, from scale degree 3

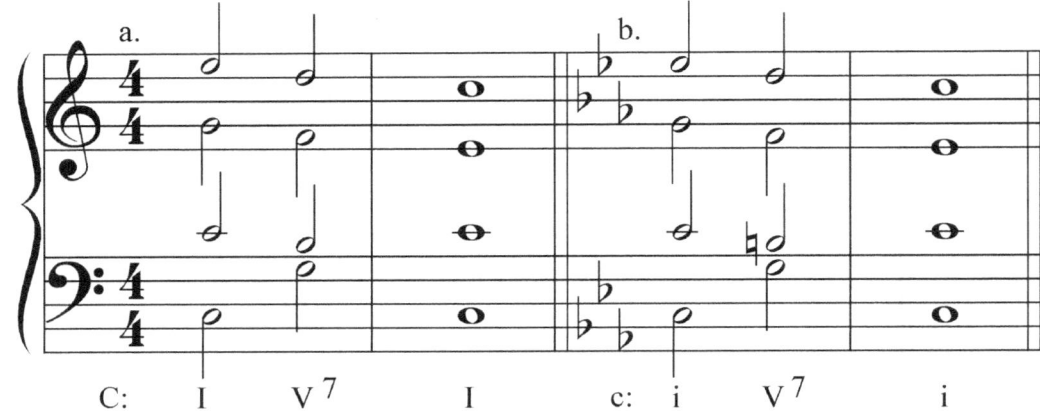

Example 7–2 displays the basic harmonic progression with a melodic descent in the soprano voice from scale degrees 5 to 1. Notice how the subdominant chord on beat 2 of examples 7–2a and 2b supports scale degree 4 (F) in the soprano voice. The subdominant decorates, or embellishes, the tonic chord on beats 1 and 3. Since the bass relationship between the subdominant and the tonic is that of a 4th—a harmonic relationship (see above, p. 55)—we can say that the subdominant is functioning as a harmonic embellishing chord to the tonic.

In any case, the motion from the tonic to the subdominant and back to the tonic does not constitute a progression because there is no dominant-family chord preceding the tonic on beat 3. Thus, we do not know that a progression is taking place until the arrival of the tonal harmonic dominant on beat 4, the penultimate chord.

Example 7–2: the basic harmonic progression using V^7, from scale degree 5

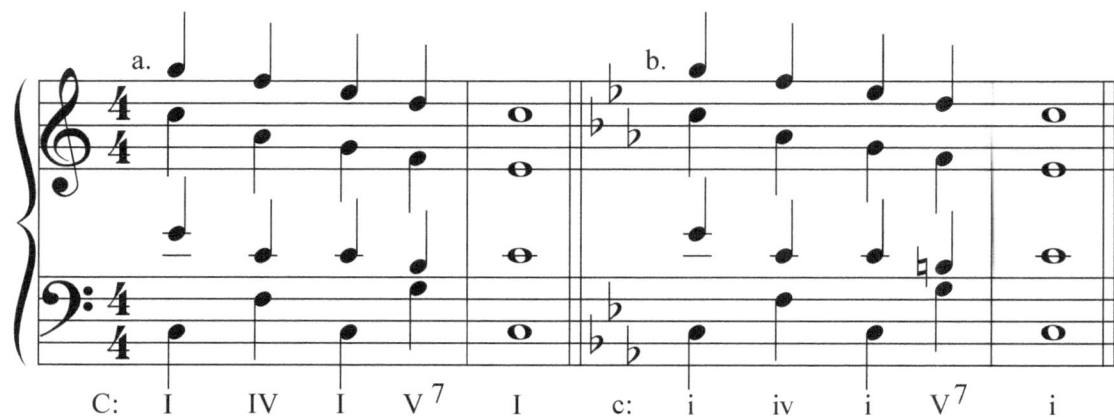

The Basic Contrapuntal Progression

The basic contrapuntal progression is like the basic harmonic progression except that the approach to the final tonic is accomplished by stepwise motion using a contrapuntal leading-tone chord, such as the V^6 in major and minor, the vii^{o6} in major, or the $\sharp vii^{o6}$ in minor. In example 7–3, we have a melodic descent in the soprano from scale degrees 3 to 1 with V^6 supporting scale degree 2 (in the soprano).

Example 7–3: the basic contrapuntal progression using V^6, from scale degree 3

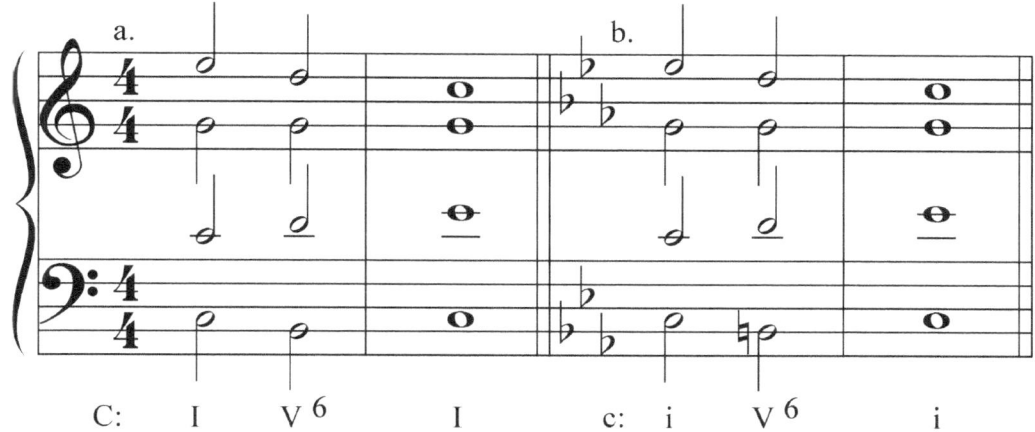

Example 7–4 shows the basic contrapuntal progression with the leading-tone triad in first inversion as the penultimate chord. The final tonic is also in first inversion to avoid the parallel octaves that would otherwise occur between the bass and the soprano voices if the D in the bass had descended to C (see the dotted lines and the C in parentheses). The first-inversion tonic produces a transfer between the outer voices in which the E (or E♭) soprano and C bass in measure 1 exchange positions in measure 2—the C appears in the soprano, the E (or E♭) in the bass.

The succession of unequal parallel 5ths involving one diminished 5th (C/G to B/F to C/G), placed in the inner voices of the alto and tenor, is covered by the voice exchange between the soprano and bass.

Example 7–4: the basic contrapuntal progression using vii^{o6} or $\sharp vii^{o6}$, from scale degree 3

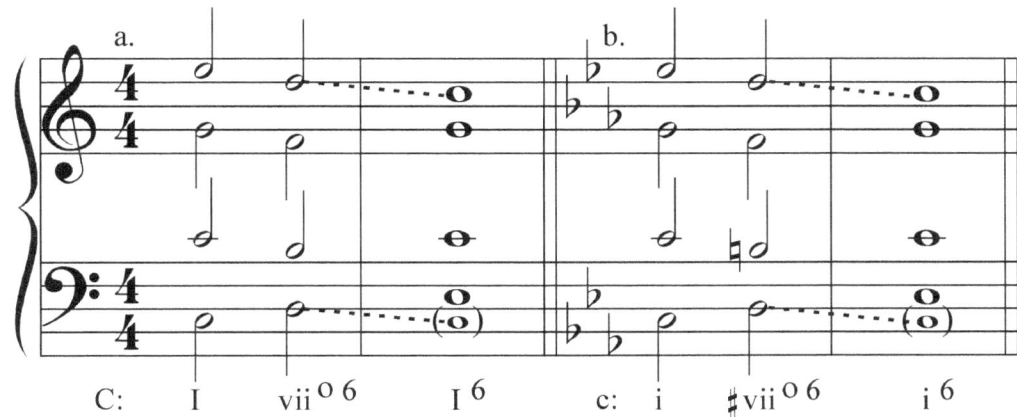

In example 7–5, the top voice descends from scale degrees 5 to 1. The penultimate V^6_5 chord supports scale degree 2. As with example 7–2, a harmonic embellishing chord supports scale degree 4; however, in this instance, the chord is the supertonic in first inversion rather than the subdominant.

Example 7–5: the basic contrapuntal progression using V^6_5, from scale degree 5

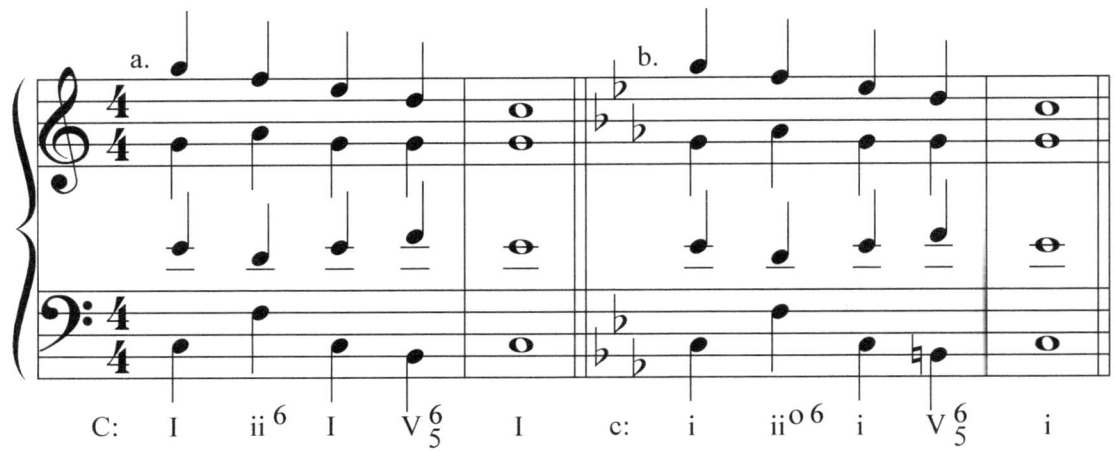

Example 7–6 employs the leading-tone triad in first inversion as the approach chord to the final tonic. As in example 7–4 above, the final tonic is placed in first inversion to avoid the potential parallel octaves that would otherwise occur between the outer voices if the D in the bass descended to C. The unequal parallel 5ths in the alto and tenor voices (measures 1–2 of examples 7–6a and 6b) are covered by the voice exchange between the bass and soprano.

Example 7–6: the basic contrapuntal progression using vii°⁶ or ♯vii°⁶, from scale degree 5

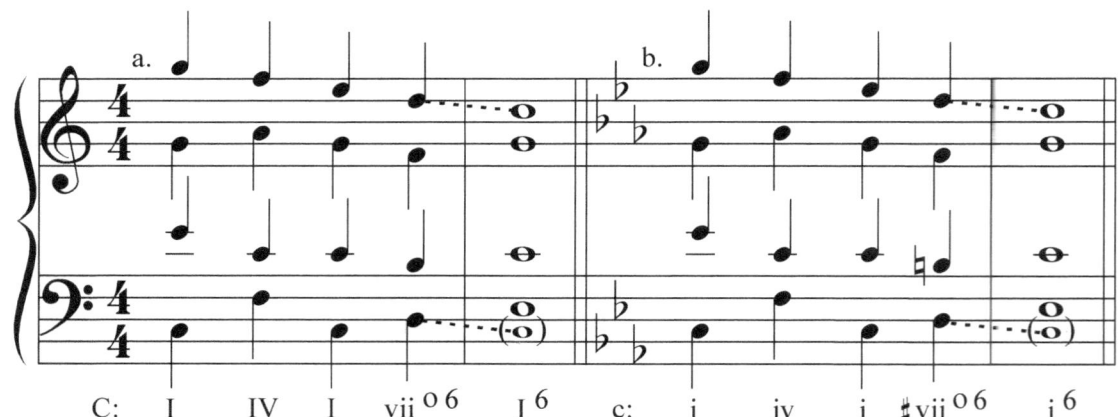

Chapter 7 The Chord Progression

The Secondary Harmonic Progression

Secondary progressions have an additional chord that occupies an intermediary position between the initial tonic and the penultimate chord of the dominant family. This chord is used to support the melodic activities of the top voice, the soprano. Composers draw upon the areas of the supertonic, mediant, subdominant, and submediant for these intermediary chords, each of which constitutes an interchangeable value within the framework of either the secondary harmonic progression or the secondary contrapuntal progression.

Since the value of the intermediary chord varies from one secondary progression to the next, it assumes the status of what in mathematics would be called X, "the unknown quantity." As such, the supertonic, mediant, subdominant, and submediant chords all become X-chord values of the secondary harmonic progression: I – X – V – I or i – X – V – i. (We shall consider the utility of the mediant as an X-chord later in Chapter 8.)

In example 7–7, we have the supertonic in first inversion as the X-chord, supporting scale degree 2 in the top voice. The melodic descent is from scale degrees 3 to 1. The first appearance of the tonic pitch in the soprano (C) occurs within the first part of the cadential $^6_4$ as a nonharmonic tone on beat 1 of the second measure. With the arrival of the dominant in $^5_3$ position on beat 3, the leading tone in the soprano moves to scale degree 1 to complete the melodic descent in the third measure.

Example 7–7: the secondary harmonic progression using the cadential $^6_4$, from scale degree 3

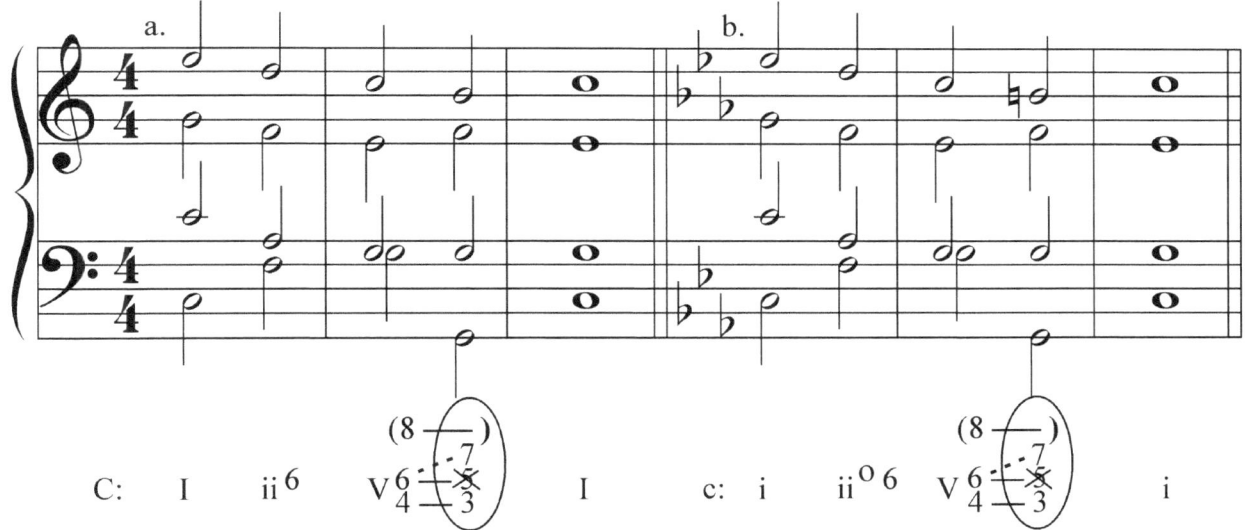

138   Chapter 7   The Chord Progression

Example 7–8 presents the subdominant as a root-position X-chord, supporting scale degree 4 in the soprano. In the role of X-chord, the subdominant becomes an active member of the progression rather than a harmonic embellishment of the tonic chord (as previously seen in examples 7–2 and 7–6).

The cadential $^6_4$ in the second measure carries both scale degree 1 and the leading tone; however, unlike example 7–7 above, the first part of the cadential $^6_4$ provides consonant support for scale degree 3 in the soprano on the first beat of the second measure (G/E in 7–8a and G/E♭ in 7–8b).

Example 7–8: the secondary harmonic progression using the cadential $^6_4$, from scale degree 5

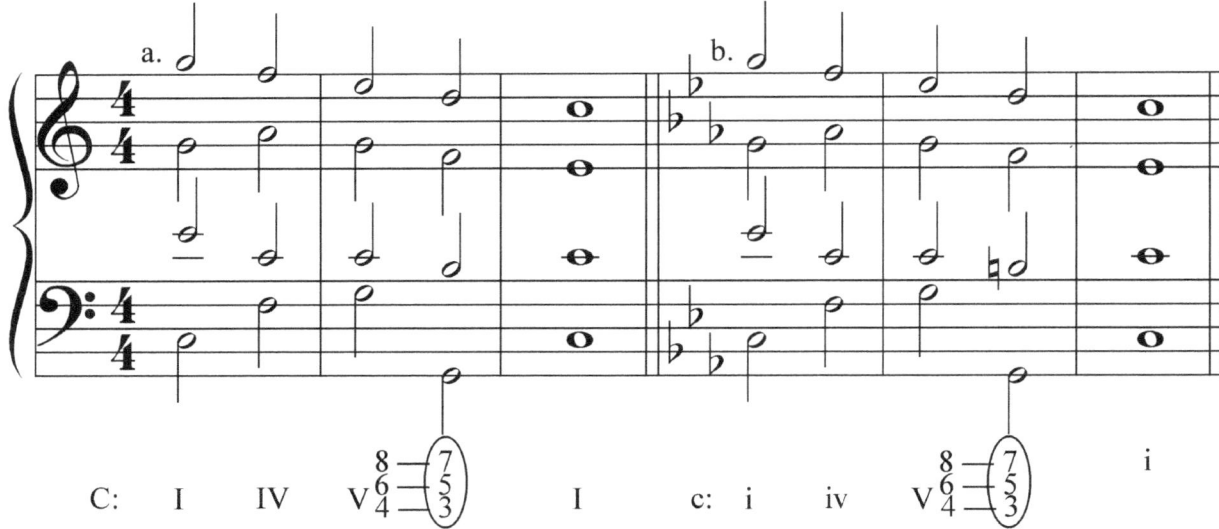

In Chapter 6, we learned that when the chord of the submediant approaches the root-position dominant from above, the voice leading between the two chords may well yield parallel 5ths. Example 6–12c offered the cadential $^6_4$ as a corrective for the faulty motion. The problem of chord connection between the submediant and the dominant limits the former's utility as an X-chord. A successful connection to the dominant is far easier to achieve with an X-chord of either the supertonic or the subdominant, particularly if the progression supports a melodic descent.

Example 7–9: the secondary harmonic progression using the cadential $^6_4$, from scale degree 3

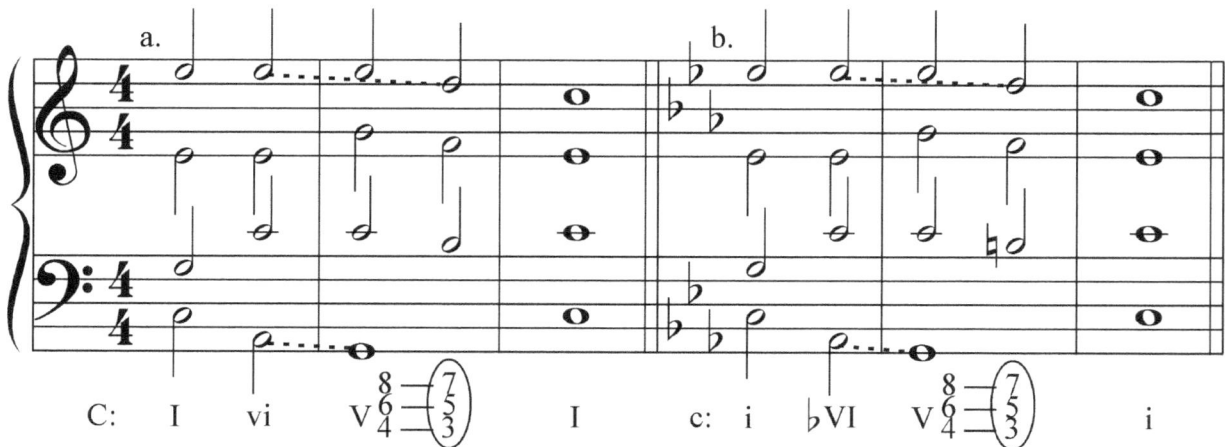

Example 7–9 above underscores the potential hazard of using the submediant as an X-chord with a descending melodic line. In this instance, the cadential $^6_4$ offers the best solution for breaking up the parallel 5ths. The submediant supports the second appearance of scale degree 3 in the soprano. Notice that the tenor voice leaps upwards a perfect 4th but then balances the leap with a reversal of direction as the cadential $^6_4$ resolves to the $^5_3$ position on beat 3.

There are a couple of circumstances in which the submediant may serve as an X-chord supporting an ascending melody. In examples 7–10a and 10b, the soprano moves upwards from scale degrees 1 to 3; here, the submediant is used successfully as an X-chord in both major and minor. A dissonant anticipation tone on the second eighth note of beat 3 (G, measure 1) avoids a direct 5th between the alto and soprano on beat 4 (G/D). (Using the anticipation tone to correct faulty motion was discussed earlier, pp. 125–126.)

Another possibility, shown in 7–10c, works in major but not in minor. The melodic line in this example has an ascent from scale degrees 5 to 1. In major, the submediant is a minor triad and presents no difficulties. However, in the minor mode, the root of the submediant is either variable ♭6 or ♯6; therefore, the quality of chord depends upon which variable is used. Given the ascent of the melody from scale degrees 5 to 1, variable ♯6 is the only option in the soprano; but it cannot be used to approach scale degree 5 in the bass.

Variable ♯6 projects a diminished triad in c minor (A C E♭). Since diminished triads in root position are generally undesirable, supporting a melodic ascent from 5 to 1 in minor with the raised submediant is unacceptable. Moreover, the lowered submediant is impractical because of the melodic augmented 2nd that occurs between variable ♭6 and ♯7 when the chord moves to the dominant.

Example 7–10: the secondary harmonic progression with an ascending soprano voice

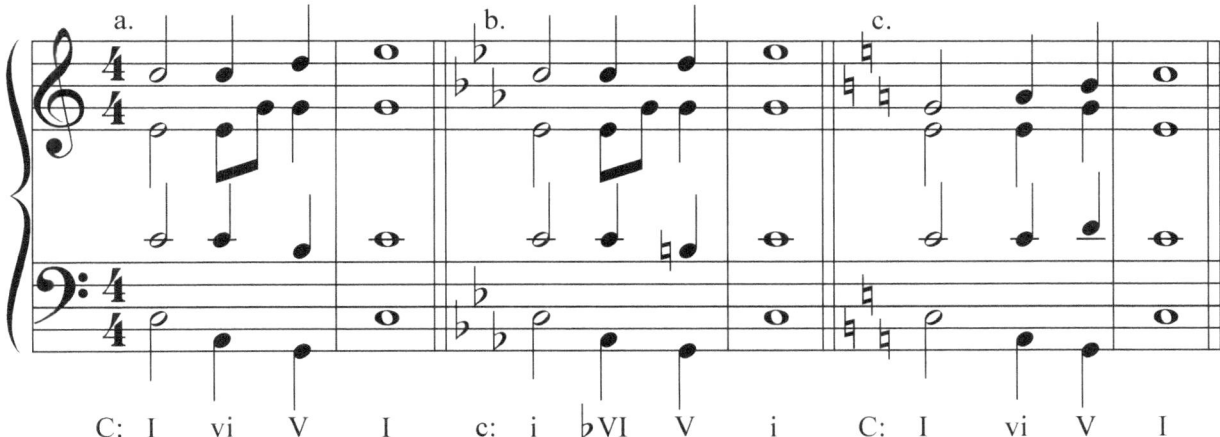

The Secondary Contrapuntal Progression

The secondary contrapuntal progression usually assumes one of the following combinations of chords:

(1) in major: I – X – V^6 – I
(2) in major: I – X – vii°^{6} – I
(3) in minor: i – X – V^6 – i
(4) in minor: i – X – ♯vii°^{6} – i

The two central features of the secondary contrapuntal progression are the inclusion of the X-chord and a contrapuntal (stepwise) approach to the final tonic using a contrapuntal leading-tone triad or seventh chord in the penultimate position.

140   Chapter 7 The Chord Progression

In example 7–11, notice the leap of the tritone in the bass on beats 3 and 4. As stated earlier (see above, p. 98), such motion, if confined to the bass voice, is perfectly acceptable.

Example 7–11: the secondary contrapuntal progression using V^6, from scale degree 3

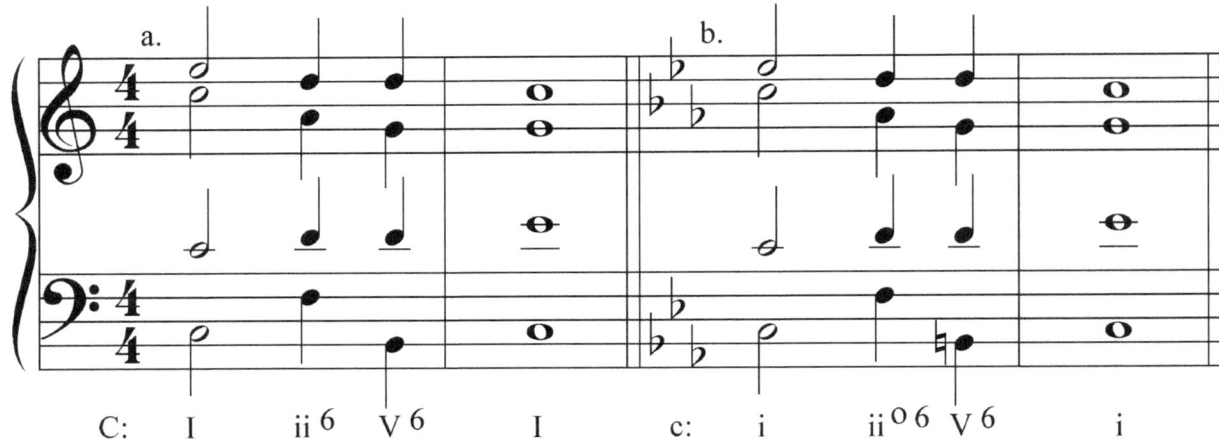

Example 7–12, which has a descent from scale degrees 5 to 1, shows the subdominant as the harmonic embellishing chord supporting scale degree 4, the supertonic X-chord in first inversion, the tritone leap in the bass, and a contrapuntal approach to the final tonic.

Example 7–12: the secondary contrapuntal progression using V^6, from scale degree 5

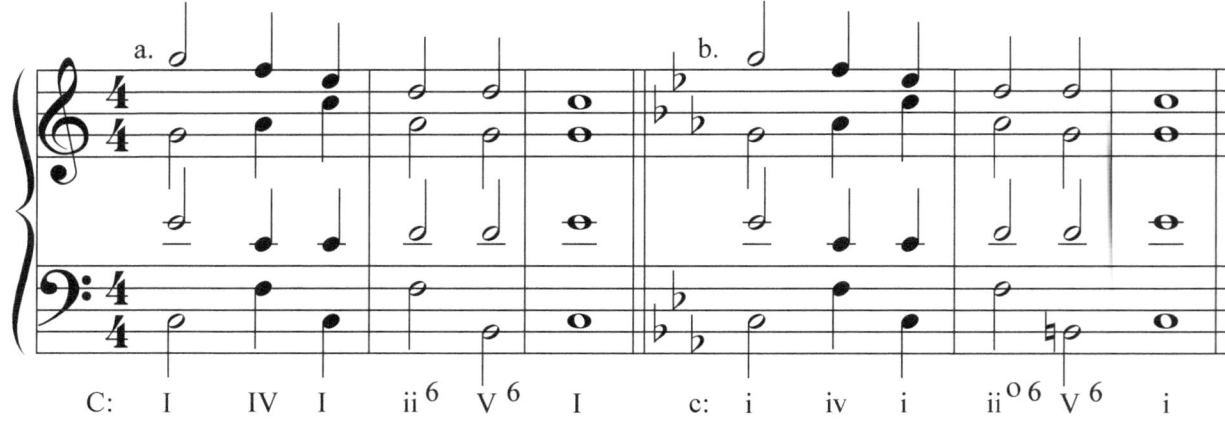

Chapter 8 The Chord Seventh Revisited

This chapter is divided into seven areas of inquiry, dealing with
(1) the formation of seventh chords within the context of the church mode system (pp. 141–145);
(2) the formation and treatment of seventh chords in the major mode, with an emphasis on the chords of the subdominant, dominant and leading tone (pp. 145–148);
(3) the formation and treatment of seventh chords in the minor mode, including a discussion of real and apparent sevenths (pp. 148–164);
(4) interlocking (and sequential) seventh chords with harmonic and contrapuntal basses (165–168);
(5) several different types of chord progressions that fall into the category of what shall be called the "two-progression framework" (pp. 169–173);
(6) the technique of singing seventh chords above a common-tone bass (pp. 173–178); and finally,
(7) the "added-6th chord" embedded within the first inversion of the half-diminished seventh and the minor seventh (pp. 178–179).

The Formation of Seventh Chords in the Church Mode System

In example 8–1, we consider the white-key seventh chords from the perspective of the church modes, starting once again with the C octave, but referred to here as the Ionian mode rather than as the major mode. As explained in Chapter 2 (see above, p. 78), the circled Roman numerals constitute a generalized type of chord symbol that, without describing the specific chord quality, nonetheless indicates the exact scale degree of the mode upon which a triad or seventh may be formed.

Since this generalized type of chord symbol makes no distinction between triad or seventh chord qualities, the Roman numerals are all expressed in uppercase. The Arabic number 7 attached to each Roman numeral indicates the presence of the seventh element for each root-position seventh chord.

Example 8–1: seventh chords in the Ionian mode

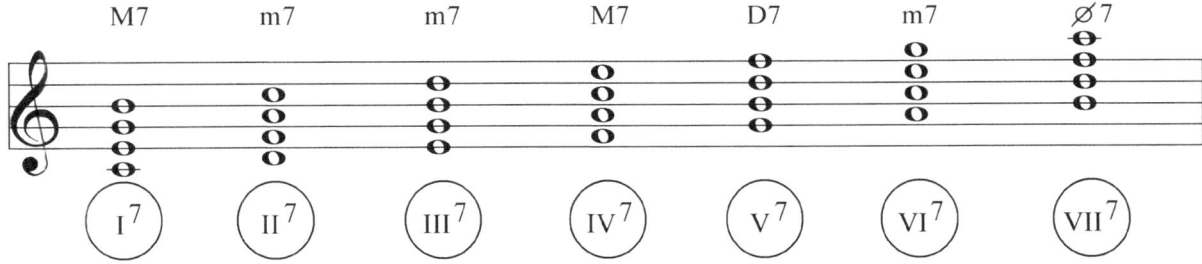

The Ionian mode supports the major seventh on the tonic and subdominant, the minor seventh on the supertonic, mediant, and submediant, the dominant seventh on the dominant, and the half-diminished seventh on the leading tone. The dominant seventh is the most important seventh chord for the major-minor tonal system. As mentioned in Chapter 5, the chord is called the dominant seventh because it is usually associated with the dominant scale degree of the major (and the equivalent Ionian), harmonic, and melodic minor modes.

However, the dominant seventh also occurs in areas other than the dominant scale degree in six of the seven church modes: it appears on the subdominant of the Dorian mode, the mediant of the Phrygian mode, the supertonic of the Lydian mode, the tonic of the Mixolydian mode, the subtonic of the Aeolian mode, and the submediant of the Locrian mode. The dominant seventh also exists on the subdominant, dominant, and subtonic scale degrees of the melodic minor. Thus, the chord can be used on various scale degrees within the context of several different modes, not just those that comprise the major-minor tonal system.

If the dominant seventh exists within a diverse range of modal contexts, then the same degree of applicability holds true for the other white-key seventh chords (that is, the major seventh, minor seventh, and half-diminished seventh). The following examples demonstrate the variety of seventh-chord vocabularies for the Dorian, Phrygian, Lydian, Mixolydian, Aeolian, and Locrian modes. But regardless of the mode, understand that of the four types of white-key seventh chords, there are three minor sevenths, two major sevenths, one dominant seventh, and one half-diminished seventh in each mode.

Example 8–2 displays the seventh chords in the Dorian mode. The tonic, supertonic, and dominant scale degrees support the minor seventh. The Dorian mediant and subtonic take the major seventh. As mentioned above, the dominant seventh occurs on the subdominant while the half-diminished seventh falls on the submediant.

It would behoove us to *memorize* the seventh-chord qualities that occur on the white keys of the piano keyboard and then consider them within the various contexts of the seven church modes. Naming and then spelling a particular seventh chord of any transposed mode becomes a relatively simple task if we know how to use the white-note modes as referential scales. In fact, it is not even necessary to know the key signature of a given transposed mode, if we know the seventh-chord vocabulary of its untransposed counterpart.

Example 8–2: seventh chords in the Dorian mode

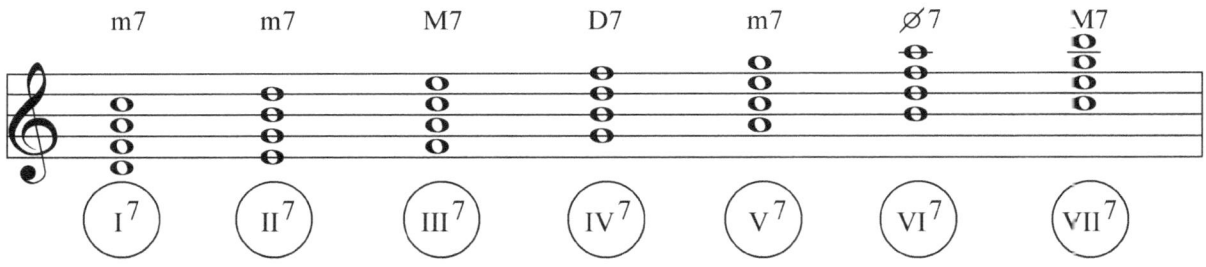

For instance, to build the seventh chord on scale degree 5 of B♭ Dorian, proceed to the untransposed D Dorian. Recall that scale degree 5 of D Dorian is a perfect 5th above the tonic and that the pitch content of the mode supports a minor seventh chord. A perfect 5th above B♭ is F; a minor seventh chord on F is spelled F A♭ C E♭. It is that easy (or that difficult). To be sure, we can always find the key signature first (which would be four flats: B♭, E♭, A♭, D♭); however, at this point in our study of basic harmony, we should be able to draw easily upon the seventh-chord content (as well as the triadic content) of the untransposed modes.

The seventh-chord content of the Phrygian mode is shown in example 8–3. The Phrygian mode has a subtonic scale degree and therefore a whole-step approach to its tonic. The subtonic lacks the compelling drive of the leading tone to *lead* upwards by half step to the tonic. Accordingly, the key center is less clear in those modes that have subtonics than in those employing leading tones.

The Phrygian mode has a half step between its supertonic and tonic scale degrees. In Chapter 6, we noted that the term upper leading tone is sometimes used to describe this intervallic relationship. (The Locrian mode also has a half step between its supertonic and tonic scale degrees.) Apart from the upper leading tone, the Phrygian mode's most notable characteristic is the diminished triad and half-diminished seventh chord that stand on its dominant scale degree. The inherent instability of both the half-diminished seventh and its underlying triad weakens the *harmonic root relationship* between the Phrygian's dominant and tonic chords (see above, p. 55).

The dominant seventh of the Phrygian mode occurs on its mediant. The tonic, subdominant, and subtonic scale degrees project the minor seventh chord. The supertonic and submediant support the major seventh.

Example 8–3: seventh chords in the Phrygian mode

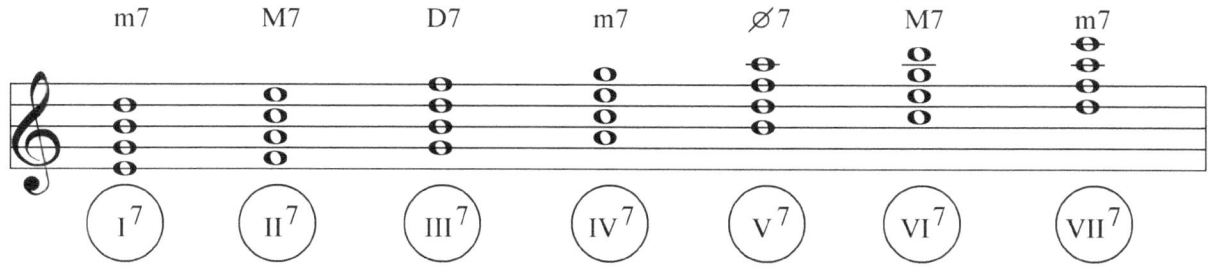

The properties of the Lydian mode are similar to those of the Ionian mode. Both modes have a leading tone; however, there are some differences. The Lydian mode has an augmented 4th between its tonic and subdominant scale degrees. Conversely, the distance between the tonic and subdominant scale degrees of the remaining six church modes, including the Ionian, is a perfect 4th. Other differences between the Ionian and Lydian modes are found in the projection of seventh chords above their respective scale degrees.

Example 8–4 presents the vocabulary of seventh chords for the Lydian mode. Both the Lydian tonic and dominant have the major seventh. The supertonic supports the dominant seventh. The mediant, submediant, and leading-tone scale degrees of the Lydian mode all project the minor seventh. The Lydian subdominant is the half-diminished seventh.

Example 8–4: seventh chords in the Lydian mode

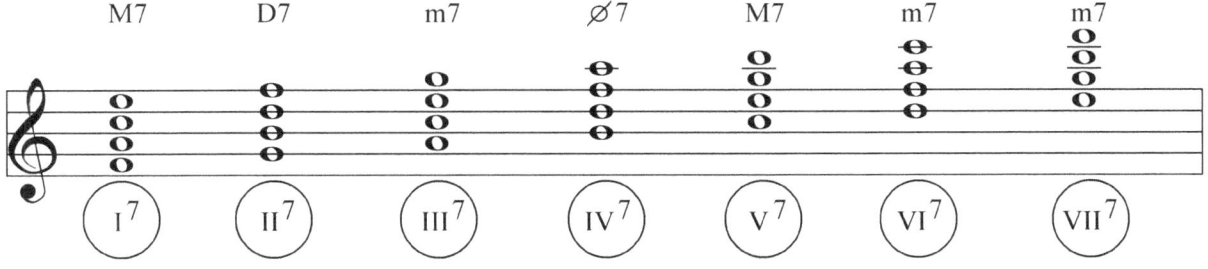

Example 8–5 displays an arrangement of the four white-key seventh chords within the Mixolydian mode. The tonic seventh of the Mixolydian mode is the dominant seventh. The mediant supports the half-diminished seventh. The supertonic, dominant, and submediant scale degrees project the minor seventh, while the subdominant and subtonic carry the major seventh. (The range of the Mixoydian mode in 8–5 begins one octave register lower in relation to the range of the Lydian mode in example 8–4 above.)

Example 8–5: seventh chords in the Mixolydian mode

Example 8–6 illustrates the formation of seventh chords for the Aeolian mode, which may be more familiar to us as the natural minor. As with the Dorian and Phrygian modes, the tonic seventh of the Aeolian mode is the minor seventh; the remaining two minor sevenths are on the mode's subdominant and dominant. Both the Aeolian mediant and submediant scale degrees support the major seventh. The Aeolian mode has a half-diminished supertonic and a dominant-seventh subtonic.

Example 8–6: seventh chords in the Aeolian mode

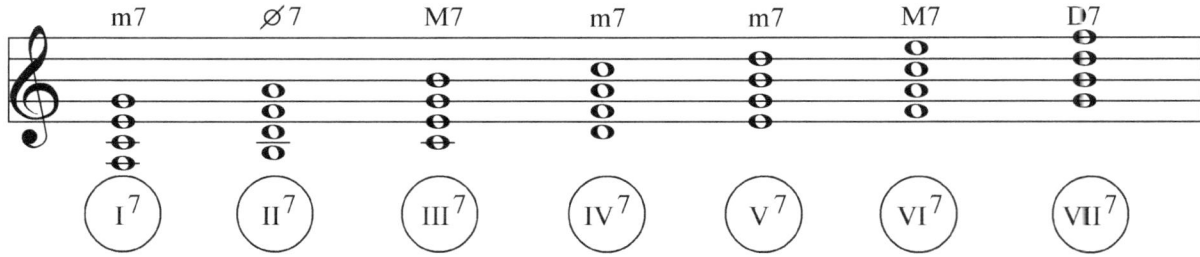

The addition of chord sevenths to the triads of the Locrian mode is shown in example 8–7. The Locrian mediant, subdominant, and subtonic all carry the minor seventh, while the submediant projects the dominant seventh. Both the supertonic and the dominant take major sevenths. These additions present no difficulties for those who would use the Locrian mode in music composition. However, as we observed in Chapter 2 (p. 63), there are certain problems associated with the Locrian mode, despite the fact that the sevenths do enrich the mode's chordal vocabulary.

The unstable diminished triad of the tonic becomes, with the addition of the seventh, an unstable half-diminished seventh chord. Further, the harmonic root relationship between the tonic and dominant chords of the Locrian mode is weak; for the distance between the scale degrees upon which they stand remains a diminished 5th (B to F) rather than a perfect 5th (B to F♯).

Example 8–7: seventh chords in the Locrian mode

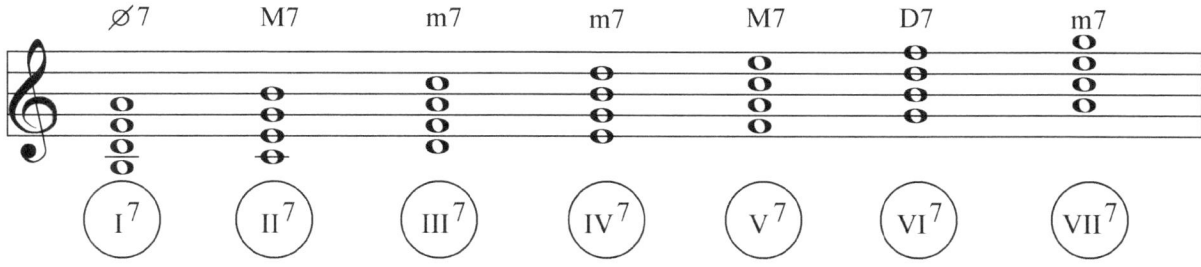

At this point in our study of the seventh chord, it would be instructive to attempt some of the worksheets at the end of the book that deal with the four white-key seventh chords both as standalone harmonic structures and as diatonic components of the Dorian, Phrygian, Lydian, Mixolydian, Aeolian, and Locrian modes.

The Formation of Seventh Chords in the Major Mode

Before studying the basic voice leading of the seventh chord, let us review the formation of the four types of white-key seventh chords and describe them within the context of the major mode. As with the diatonic church modes, the seventh chord content for major has two major sevenths, three minor sevenths, one dominant seventh, and one half-diminished seventh (example 8–8).

The method for describing the location of the roots and qualities of the sevenths that occur in the major mode is identical to the approach implemented for the signification of triads. If the basic triad has a major 3rd between the root and its third, then the Roman numeral of the seventh chord is expressed in uppercase. If the basic triad has a minor 3rd between the root and its third, then the Roman numeral of the seventh chord is expressed in lowercase.

Both the half-diminished seventh and the fully diminished seventh (to be discussed later) take a superscript circle because the underlying triad is diminished. A superscript circle with a diagonal slash ($\emptyset^7$) represents the half-diminished seventh (8–8); a circle without a slash (o^7) represents the fully diminished seventh (example 8–13). In our examination of the minor mode, we shall see that if the basic triad is augmented, then the seventh chord will incorporate a plus sign (+) into its Roman numeral description.

Example 8–8: the seventh-chord content for the major mode

The Seventh Chords of the Subdominant and Dominant in the Major Mode

This section examines the addition of the chord seventh to the subdominant and dominant triads within the framework of the secondary harmonic progression and demonstrates the proper treatment of the seventh and how it can be used to avoid potential voice-leading problems. However, the seventh not only constitutes a powerful corrective agent but also connective one; for when the chord in which it occurs stands in either a falling 5th or rising 4th or rising 2nd root relationship to another chord, the resolution of its dissonance intensifies the motion between the two chords.

In 8–9a, the subdominant triad proceeds to the dominant chord, which in turn resolves to the tonic. Notice that the root of the subdominant (F) in the soprano prepares the seventh of the dominant as a suspension (although the F is repeated rather than tied, it is still a suspension). *If a seventh chord stands in a falling 5th or rising 4th root relationship to another chord, then the seventh of the first chord will move down by step in the same voice to become the third of the second chord.* This is the relationship between the dominant seventh and the tonic, as shown in 8–9. Here, the seventh is handled correctly, as the suspended seventh of the dominant in the soprano moves down by step in the same voice to become the third of the tonic (measures 3 and 4 of examples 8–9a and 9b).

There is one problem, however. Parallel perfect 5ths between the bass and the tenor afflict measures 2 and 3 of example 8–9a. Example 8–9b offers a simple solution that eliminates the parallel 5ths: substitute the supertonic in first inversion for the subdominant by changing the C in the tenor to a D, the root of the supertonic. Additionally, the D connects more smoothly into the fifth of the dominant as a common tone.

Example 8–9: voice leading the V^7

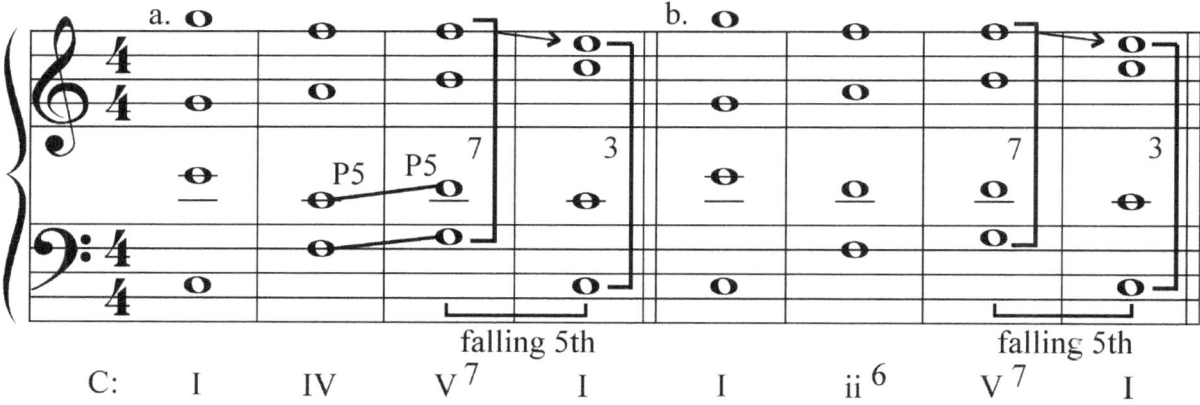

Example 8–10a avoids the parallel 5ths by transforming the subdominant triad into a seventh chord with the addition of E in the tenor (measure 2). The third of the tonic in the tenor of measure 1 prepares the seventh of the subdominant as a suspension. *If a seventh chord stands in a rising 2nd root relationship to another chord, then the seventh of the first chord will move down by step in the same voice to become the fifth of the second chord.* After the seventh becomes the fifth of the second chord in the tenor voice (E to D, measures 2–3), a suspended seventh in the soprano voice moves down by step in the same voice to become the third of the tonic chord (F to E, measures 3–4).

Example 8–10b averts the parallel 5ths by retaining the subdominant as a triad and using the cadential $^6_4$ to maintain the common-tone C in the tenor (measures 1–2). The C as the fifth of the subdominant prepares the suspended 4th of the cadential $^6_4$. The upper note of the G octave between the bass and the alto moves down to form the seventh component of the dominant (G to F, measure 2). The seventh in the alto then proceeds downwards by step in the same voice to become the third of the tonic chord (F to E, measures 2–3).

Example 8–10: voice leading the IV^7 and the V^7

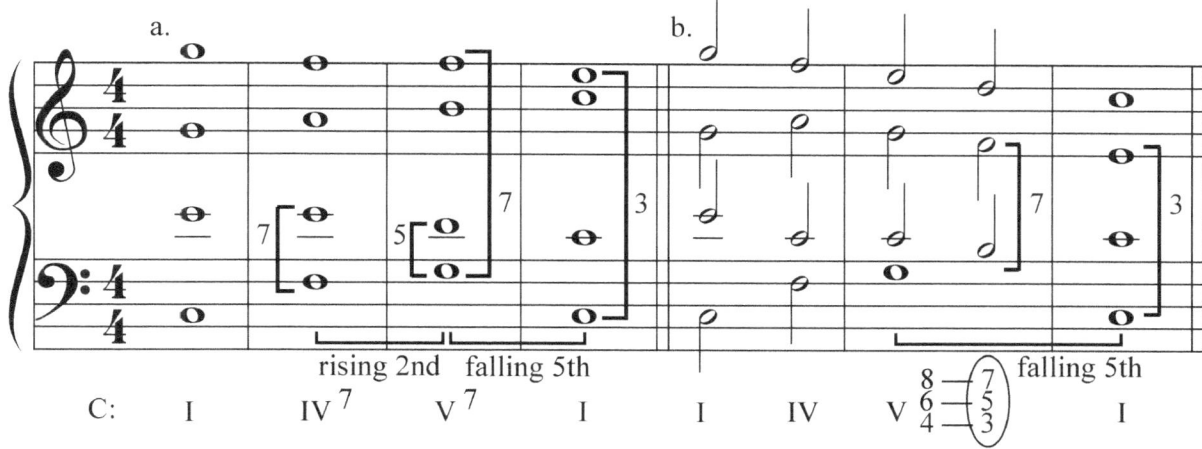

The Seventh Chord of the Leading Tone in the Major Mode

We know that the leading-tone triad and the major triad of the dominant share two tones in common; that is to say, the root and the third of the leading-tone triad are the same pitches as the third and the fifth of the corresponding dominant triad. This common-tone relationship was illustrated in example 1–90 of Chapter 1 (see p. 56).

Adding a chord seventh to the major triad of the dominant brings the relationship between the two chords even closer together, as example 8–11 demonstrates. With the addition of the seventh to the G-major triad in 8–11, the resulting dominant seventh of C major contains all of the components of the leading-tone triad, its root, third, and fifth (B D F).

Sharing three of the dominant seventh's four chord tones, the leading-tone triad is sometimes considered to be a dominant seventh chord with a missing root (B D F minus the G). This interpretation recognizes that the leading-tone triad functions in most circumstances as a dominant chord. As observed in Chapter 6, chords built on the leading tone are usually found within the dominant family of chords.

Example 8–11: common tones between the leading-tone triad and the dominant seventh chord

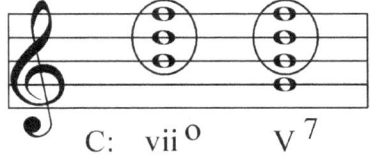

The half-diminished seventh chord of the leading tone, which stands in a rising 2nd root relationship to the tonic and occurs in all chord positions, is often used as a dominant chord. Since the leading-tone chord, either with or without its seventh element, commonly defines the tonality of the mode, we describe it as the tonal melodic dominant when the chord is functioning as a dominant (see above, p. 121). Notice that the seventh of the leading-tone seventh (A) in example 8–12 moves down by step in the same voice to become the fifth (G) of the tonic chord.

Example 8–12: voice leading the tonal melodic dominant in the major mode

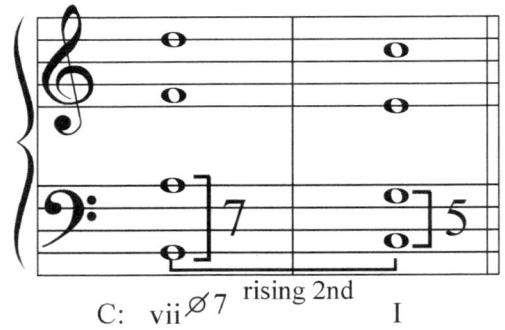

The Formation of Seventh Chords in the Minor Mode

The pitch content of the major mode yields a formation of seven seventh chords, one for each of its diatonic scale degrees. Presently, we shall focus our attention on the richest form of minor in terms of pitch content, the melodic minor; for here, we have a greater number of potential seventh chords than those found in any of the seven-tone diatonic scales.

In Chapter 1, we learned that a sharp in front of a number designating a variable scale degree does not necessarily mean that the pitch itself carries a sharp, nor does a flat in front of a number necessarily mean that the pitch itself carries a flat. Rather, the accidental merely indicates that there are two pitches with the same letter name and that one pitch is either raised or lowered in relation to the other one. For example, if c minor has both an A♮ and an A♭, then A♮ is raised in relation to A♭ and A♭ is lowered in relation to A♮. Thus, A♮ is raised 6 (♯6) and A♭ is lowered 6 (♭6).

Similarly, if the root of a triad in the melodic minor is a variable scale degree, then the Roman numeral chord symbol is preceded by either a flat or a sharp, just as individual pitches for the variable scale degrees are indicated as either ♯6 and ♯7 or ♭6 and ♭7. The principles cited here are applicable to the formation of seventh chords in the melodic minor.

The pitch content of the melodic minor produces a vocabulary of thirteen triads, more chords than either the major mode, the natural minor, or the harmonic minor. The addition of the chord seventh to the triads of the melodic minor increases the number of chords to sixteen. In actual practice, however, the melodic minor's capacity for seventh chords falls somewhat short of its potential, as two of these sixteen seventh chords cannot be used and another two rarely occur in music literature.

Still, how does a mode with nine pitches give rise to sixteen potential seventh chords? Example 8–13 demonstrates how the addition of the chord seventh increases the number of chords on three scale degrees: the tonic, subtonic, and leading-tone. Variables ♭7 and ♯7 become seventh components of two tonic chords (i♭7 and i♯7). Variables ♭6 and ♯6 form sevenths for two subtonic chords (♭VII♭7 and ♭VII♯7) and for two on the leading tone (♯vii°7 and ♯viiø7)—six chords.

In four of the six chords cited above, when a variable comprises the seventh, we need to account for the additional element in the chord symbol. On the tonic and subtonic, the chord symbols carry either a flat or a sharp in front of the figured-bass 7: i$^{\flat 7}$, i$^{\sharp 7}$, $\flat$VII$^{\flat 7}$, and $\flat$VII$^{\sharp 7}$. We will consider these four chords and their symbolic representation in more detail later; for the present, know that the flat or sharp in front of the 7 indicates that the seventh element of the chord is either a lowered or raised variable and is occurring at the interval of a 7th above the bass (and root).

Despite the presence of a variable as the seventh element of the leading-tone chords, no additional descriptive terminology is needed beyond the inclusion of the superscript circle mentioned earlier. As we have said, the superscript circle with the diagonal slash ($\varnothing$ 7) represents the half-diminished seventh; the circle without the slash represents the fully diminished seventh (o 7). We shall discuss the structural difference between the two chords later.

Upon close inspection of examples 8–13 and 8–14, we find that the addition of variable $\sharp$6 above the respective fifths of the leading-tone triad and the subtonic triad renders impractical the use of both resulting seventh chords, the $\sharp$vii $\varnothing$ 7 and the $\flat$VII $^{\sharp 7}$ (marked "not used"). Further, the viability of two other seventh chords is also questionable (marked "very rare"): the tonic seventh chord with variable $\sharp$7 as its seventh component (m-M7) and the augmented-mediant seventh chord with $\sharp$7 as its fifth component (A-M7) are rarely used.

The reasons for the exclusion of two and perhaps even four of the sixteen seventh chords in the melodic minor will be discussed as we examine the chords that may be formed above scale degrees 1, 3, $\flat$7, and $\sharp$7. The filled-in note heads in 8–13 identify the variable scale degrees that constitute the root, third, fifth, or seventh of each chord.

Example 8–13: the seventh-chord content of the melodic minor

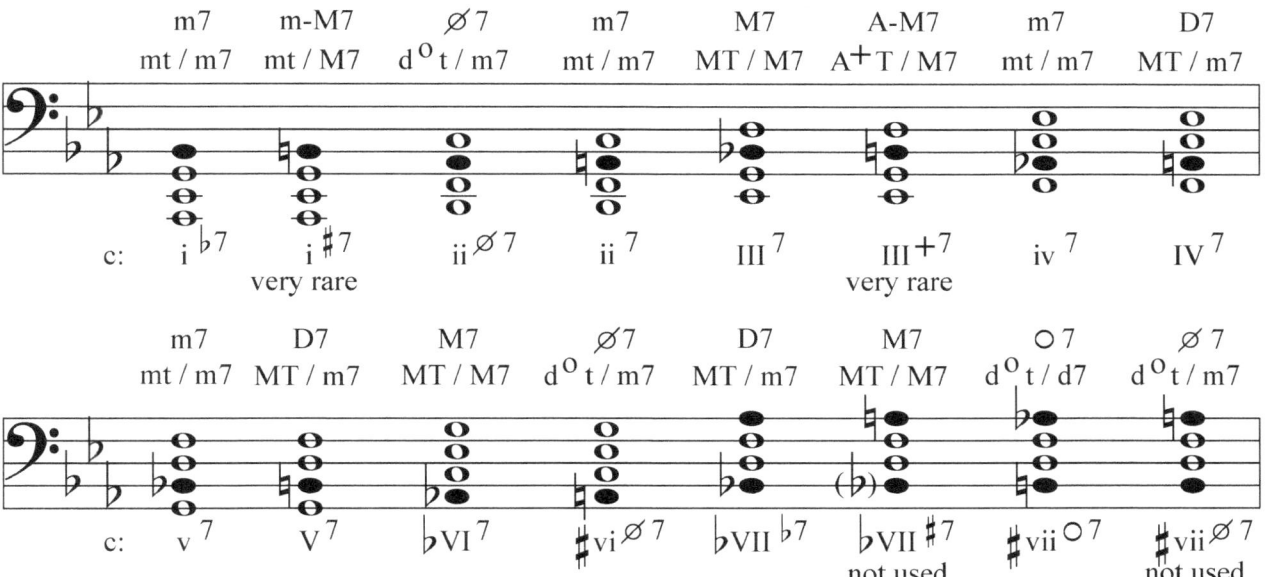

The Seventh Chords of the Dominant in the Minor Mode

The first seventh chords we consider are formed above scale degrees 5 and ♯7, as these areas typically define the tonality of the mode. In the dominant area of the melodic minor, the use of variables ♭7 and ♯7 produces two different seventh-chord possibilities, a minor seventh and a dominant seventh (8-13). The minor seventh chord has ♭7 as its third element, which gives rise to a minor triad. Because the underlying triad is minor, the Roman numeral chord symbol is expressed in lowercase with an Arabic number 7 attached to indicate that the chord has a seventh component. Since the third of the v^7 chord lacks the leading tone, it cannot be the tonal harmonic dominant. (Example 8-22 below demonstrates one of the common uses for the minor dominant in which it serves as a passing chord.)

The other seventh chord that occurs above scale degree 5 is the dominant seventh (8-13). This seventh chord is expressed in uppercase because the underlying triad is major. Confirming its status as the tonal harmonic dominant, the V^7 chord has both the leading tone as its chord third and a strong harmonic bass in relation to the tonic chord (that is, a falling 5th or a rising 4th root relationship with the tonic chord).

The V^7 chord of the melodic minor corresponds to the V^7 chord of the parallel major. There are two other seventh chords common to the melodic minor and its parallel major mode:

(1) the minor seventh chord of the supertonic area (the ii^7 in major and the ii^7 in minor); and,
(2) the half-diminished seventh found in the leading-tone area (the vii^{ø7} in major and the ♯vii^{ø7} in minor). In the next section, we find out why the ♯vii^{ø7} in minor is not used.

The Seventh Chords of the Leading Tone in the Minor Mode

As shown in example 8-14a, variable ♭6 is used as the seventh component for one of the seventh chords of the leading tone; ♭6 produces a fully diminished seventh, a chord with a diminished triad and a diminished 7th from the root to the seventh. Following the descending form of the melodic minor, ♭6 moves down one half step to scale degree 5 in the next chord if that pitch is available.

We describe the ♯vii^{o7} chord ("raised seven fully diminished seventh") as the tonal melodic dominant because of its viability within the melodic minor and its usual function as a dominant chord resolving into the tonic. This is the seventh chord of the leading tone that shows up in music literature.

Example 8-14b illustrates the difficulty in using the half-diminished seventh chord of the leading tone, a chord that carries variable ♯6 as its seventh. The ♯vii^{ø7} chord ("raised seven half-diminished seventh") is afflicted with two mutually exclusive problems involving the presence of ♯6 as the seventh of the chord. Variable ♯6 should move upwards to variable ♯7; however, the dissonant 7th above the bass demands a downward resolution.

The linear demands of ♯6 and the harmonic tendency of the dissonant 7th to resolve downwards operate at cross-purposes, resulting in motion to a tonic seventh chord that contains a minor triad and a major 7th from the root to the seventh (8-14b). Instead of resolving downwards, however, notice that the chord seventh of the ♯vii^{ø7} as well as all the other tones of the chord slide upwards into a tonic seventh chord, the i$^{♯7}$. (In example 8-20 below, we shall see why this tonic seventh is rarely used. The sharp preceding the figured-bass 7 of the chord indicates that the seventh element is a raised variable; in this case, variable ♯7 is the seventh of the tonic chord, occurring at the interval of a 7th above the bass.)

Example 8–14: a comparison of the leading-tone seventh chords

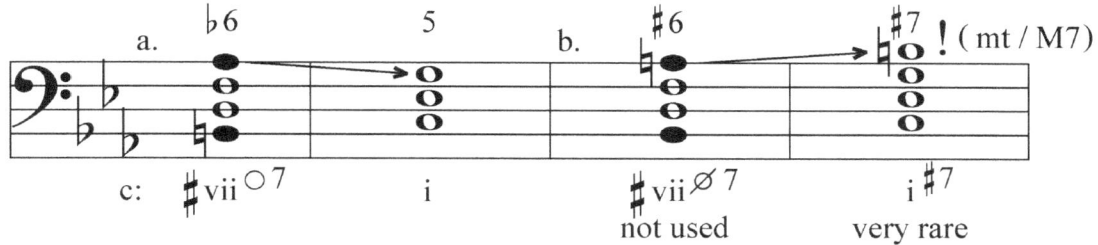

Although avoiding downward resolutions of dissonant intervals can certainly be found in commercial music and jazz, having all of the voices moving in the same direction will undermine the individuality of each melodic line. In Chapter 3, we referred to this kind of movement between voices as parallel motion, a technique that can be an effective expressive device within certain musical contexts but which nonetheless tends to produce musical textures that have less independent melodic activity—the focus shifts from the horizontal dimension of music to the vertical, from melody to harmony.

The Sound and Applications of the Fully Diminished Seventh Chord in the Minor Mode

Let us take a closer look at the fully diminished seventh chord of the leading tone in terms of its sound and structure. From the root to the seventh of the ♯vii°7 chord in example 8–14a above, we have a diminished 7th, B to A♭, which sounds exactly like a major 6th, B to G♯. Although both the diminished 7th and the major 6th are enharmonically equivalent, all diminished and augmented intervals are heard as dissonances and treated accordingly. Moreover, the seventh of the ♯vii°7 chord is variable ♭6, a tone that usually moves down to scale degree 5 in the next chord, if that pitch is available.

Acoustically, though not contextually, the fully diminished seventh presents certain challenges when determining the position of the chord. Remember, there are two general guidelines for locating the root of the seventh chord and consequently for identifying its position:

(1) if the chord is in root position, the bottom note of the 7th indicates the location of the root; or,
(2) if the chord is inverted, the upper note of the 2nd indicates the root.

Using these guidelines to identify by ear the position of the fully diminished seventh is problematic. Indeed, as we have said, the fully diminished seventh has a diminished 7th rather than an acoustical 7th.

When the chord inverts, as illustrated in example 8–15, the diminished 7th from the root to the seventh becomes an augmented 2nd from the seventh to the root (examples 8–15b, 15c, and 15d). The problem for identifying the fully diminished seventh is that we always hear the augmented 2nd as a minor 3rd; the augmented 2nd is a contextual interval, the minor 3rd an acoustical one.

Example 8–15: inversions of the fully diminished seventh chord

And so, the fully diminished seventh does not have a 2nd that actually sounds like a 2nd. In fact, the fully diminished seventh is similar to the augmented triad in that there is no differentiation in its profile of intervals; the structure of the fully diminished seventh is completely symmetrical, consisting of minor 3rds from root to third, third to fifth, and fifth to seventh.

It is therefore impossible to determine by ear the position of the fully diminished seventh when played in isolation, in other words, outside of any musical context. We must know what chord the fully diminished seventh addresses before assessing its position. There are at least two reasons for caution when attempting to identify the root and position of the chord:

(1) the fully diminished seventh's symmetrical structure yields numerous different spellings of itself; and,

(2) the fully diminished seventh has several different applications and possible functions, one of which is to serve as the tonal melodic dominant.

A complete study of all of the applications and functions of the fully diminished seventh chord is beyond the scope of basic harmony; however, it would be instructive to see how this chord's symmetrical structure and consequent flexibility enables it to resolve to more than one key and triad.

Based upon the three inverted positions of the fully diminished seventh chord presented in example 8–15 above, example 8–16 demonstrates how we can reinterpret each of these inversions as a sounding fully diminished seventh chord in *root position*. These "new" fully diminished seventh chords in turn serve as tonal melodic dominants resolving to "new" tonic triads.

In other words, reinterpreting the bass pitch of each inverted position as the root of a fully diminished seventh and then in some cases respelling other components of the chord results in resolutions to e♭ minor (8–16a), f♯ minor (8–16b), and a minor (8–16c). Since each of the "new" keys represented in example 8–16 would have a different key signature, the three flats used previously to designate c minor are omitted here. Notice also that the dotted curved lines in the example show the enharmonic connections between the old and new versions of the pitches.

Example 8–16: reinterpreting the fully diminished seventh chord

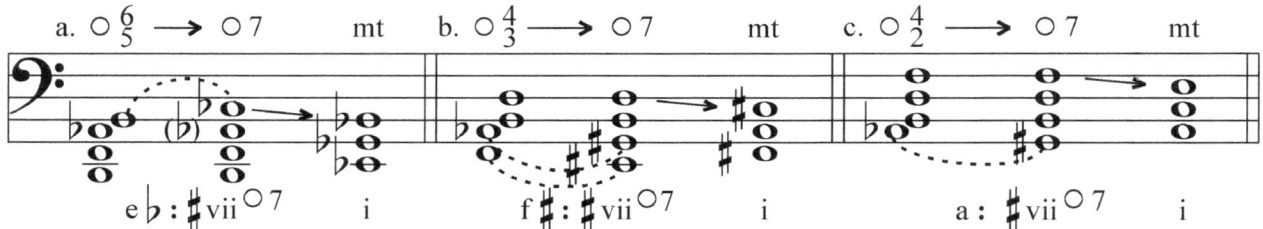

Because of the inherent ambiguity of the fully diminished seventh and its numerous applications, be wary when assessing the root and function of the chord. Do not to rush to judgement until you understand the context in which the fully diminished seventh chord occurs.

The Seventh Chords of the Subtonic

The subtonic area of the melodic minor projects two qualities of seventh chords: the dominant seventh and the major seventh. The dominant seventh that occurs on the subtonic is one of three dominant sevenths found in the melodic minor, the other two dominant seventh chords being formed on the subdominant and dominant scale degrees. As shown in example 8–17, the chord symbol for the dominant-seventh subtonic is ♭VII ♭7 ("subtonic lowered seventh"); the chord symbol for the major-seventh subtonic is ♭VII ♯7 ("subtonic raised seventh").

The dominant-seventh subtonic has variable ♭6 as its seventh component; the flat in front of the figured-bass 7 for the ♭VII ♭7 chord indicates that variable ♭6 is occurring at the interval of a 7th above the bass (and root). The major-seventh subtonic has variable ♯6 as its seventh; the sharp in front of the 7 for the ♭VII ♯7 chord indicates that ♯6 is occurring at the interval of a 7th above the bass (and root).

As we have said, ♭6 proceeds down to scale degree 5 and variable ♯6 should move upwards to variable ♯7. Usually, the variables ♭6 and ♯6 present no difficulties in their employment; however, when a variable is also the seventh component of the chord, the linear demands of the variable on the one hand may conflict with the harmonic tendency of the dissonant 7th to resolve downwards on the other. Indeed, we encountered this problem in our examination of the ♯vii ø7 chord.

The seventh of the ♭VII ♭7 chord (8–17a), variable ♭6, moves down to scale degree 5 in the next chord, if that pitch is available. Additionally, the seventh of the chord seeks a downward resolution to a harmonic consonance. Hence, both the melodic and harmonic demands of the ♭VII ♭7 chord are met. However, the conflict between the melodic tendency of variable ♯6 to move up to variable ♯7 and the demand for the dissonant 7th to resolve downwards afflicts the major-seventh chord of the subtonic, the ♭VII ♯7 (8–17b). This chord is not used.

Example 8–17: a comparison of the subtonic seventh chords

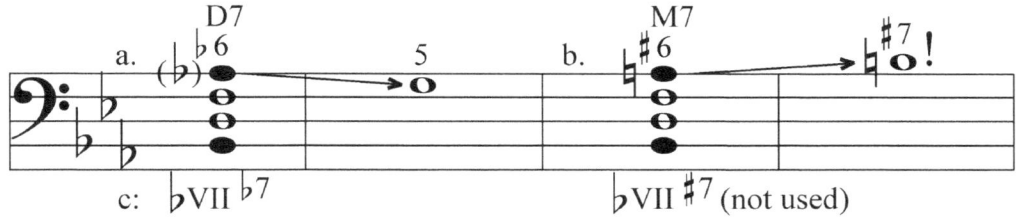

The Applications of the Subtonic Chord

The two most common applications for the subtonic chord, either with or without its seventh element, are:
(1) to address the chord of the mediant (example 8–18); and,
(2) to facilitate passing motion between other chords (example 8–19).

Earlier in this chapter, we stated that composers rarely use the mediant seventh chord that contains variable ♯7 as its fifth component. Frequently referred to as the "augmented-major seventh," this chord has an augmented triad and a major 7th from the root to the seventh; its chord symbol is III+7.

The other mediant contains variable ♭7 as its fifth component. Expressed as III 7, this is the mediant that shows up in music literature; it has a major triad and a major seventh from the root to the seventh. The III chord, either with or without its seventh element, often occurs in connection with the subtonic.

Example 8–18 illustrates the ♭VII ♭7 chord addressing the III 7. The subtonic presents the first in a series of seventh-chord resolutions. Arrows indicate the downward resolution of the seventh into the consonance of the following chord. Each seventh moves down to either the third or fifth of the next chord, depending on the root relationship between the approach chord and the chord that carries the resolution.

154   Chapter 8 The Chord Seventh Revisited

One of the arrows is more elongated than the others; it leads away from the iv⁷ chord (measure 4, alto), extends through the first part of the cadential $^6_4$ (measure 5), and points ultimately to the completion of the V⁷ chord (measure 6). The extension of the arrow indicates that the seventh of the iv⁷ chord, E♭, cannot resolve downwards until the fifth of the V⁷ chord, D, becomes available.

The first part of the $^6_4$ chord forms an octave between the bass and the tenor (G/G, measure 5). Subsequently (measure 6), the octave moves down to become the chord seventh of the completed dominant (indicated as 8—7 in the example). Resolving downwards in the tenor, the seventh of the V⁷ (F) becomes the chord third of the C-minor tonic (E♭). The progression ends with a harmonic perfect authentic cadence.

Example 8–18: the subtonic addressing the mediant in a series of downward seventh-chord resolutions

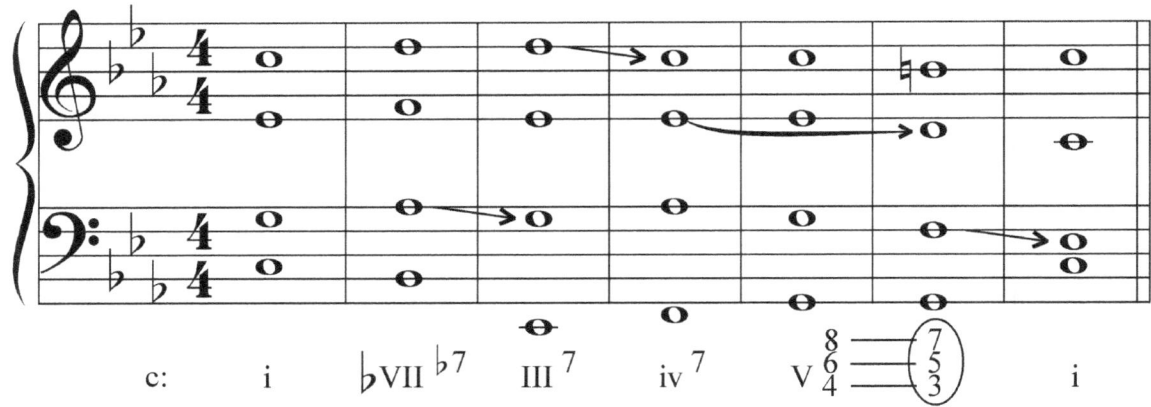

c: i   ♭VII ♭⁷   III⁷   iv⁷   V $^{8\,6}_{\,\,4}$ — $\left(^7_5_3\right)$ i

The other most common application of the subtonic, either with or without its seventh element, is to place the chord within the context of a stepwise passing motion in the bass, such as that displayed in example 8–19. Projecting five chords, the bass line descends through scale degrees 3–2–1–♯7 and ends with a contrapuntal imperfect authentic cadence (scale degree 5 in the top voice). The soprano voice descends through the following scale degrees: 8–♭7–♭6–5.

The first four chords are all in first inversion, the last of which, the V$^6_5$, presents a contrapuntal approach to the final tonic. Even though the dominant is inverted, the seventh component of the chord, F, still has a downward resolution to the third of the tonic chord, E♭ (tenor).

Example 8–19: the subtonic triad as a passing chord

c: i⁶   ♭VII⁶   ♭VI⁶   V$^6_5$ i

Notation for Inversions of Tonic and Subtonic Sevenths

As shown in example 8–13 above, the minor triad in the tonic area of the melodic minor can form a seventh chord with either variable ♭7 or ♯7. The tonic seventh found most commonly in music literature has variable ♭7 as its chord seventh and is written as i ♭7. Since the triad has a minor 7th above the root, the chord is called a minor seventh.

The other tonic seventh does not have a universally accepted name; however, it is usually called the "minor-major seventh." Indicated here as i ♯7 to account for variable ♯7 as its seventh component, the chord has a minor triad and a major 7th above its root, and, most notably, no practical application.

Example 8–20 illustrates why the minor-major seventh of the tonic is not a viable seventh chord: variable ♯7 moves upwards to the tonic, resulting in a tonic chord with a doubled root and no seventh. As we have observed with the chords of the ♯vii ⌀7 and the ♭VII ♯7, using a raised variable to form the seventh of a chord produces a conflict between the tendencies of the raised variable to move upwards and the dissonant interval of the 7th to move downwards. *A true seventh seeks to move down by step to become either the third or fifth of the chord it addresses, if there is a tone of resolution available.*

Example 8–20: the minor-major seventh of the tonic

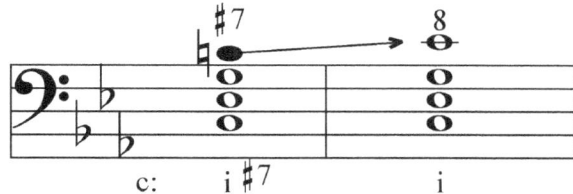

The chord symbol for the tonic minor seventh is i ♭7. The flat in front of the figured-bass 7 for the chord indicates that variable ♭7 is occurring at the interval of a 7th above the bass (and root). When the i ♭7 inverts, the description becomes somewhat more complicated because we want to account for the variable scale degree that forms the seventh component of the chord. The same problem confronts the inversions of the i ♯7, ♭VII ♭7, and ♭VII ♯7.

Example 8–21 demonstrates how we shall indicate the presence of the variable when either the tonic or subtonic seventh chords invert. These are the only two areas of the melodic minor in which the chord symbol requires a sharp or flat in front of the figured-bass 7. Since the ♭VII ♯7 is not used and the status of the i ♯7 as a viable seventh chord questionable, we shall focus on the descriptions for the inversions of the i ♭7 and the ♭VII ♭7. (In the example below, filled-in note heads designate variable scale degrees.)

Example 8–21: inversions of the i ♭7 and the ♭VII ♭7

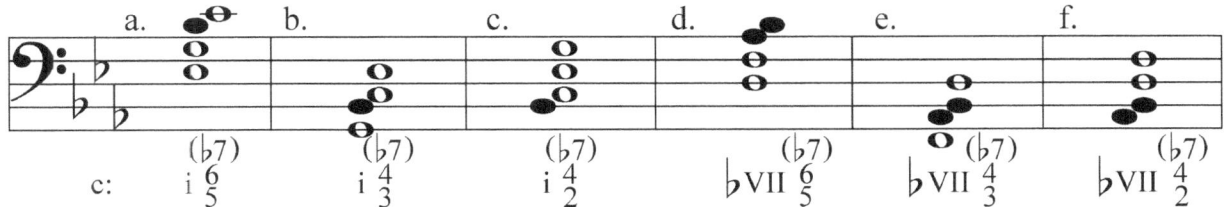

When either the i ♭7 or the ♭VII ♭7 inverts (8–21), we indicate the quality of the seventh by placing the symbol for lowered 7 in parentheses (♭7) above the traditional figured bass, identifying the position of the chord and designating it to be of the "lowered variety." Theoretically, we could indicate the inversions of the i ♯7 or the ♭VII ♯7 with the symbol for raised 7 in parentheses (♯7) above the standard figured bass, identifying both chords as being of the "raised variety." However, since neither chord is likely to appear in music literature, our concern is with the tonic and subtonic sevenths that are found in common practice, the i♭7 and the ♭VII♭7.

As illustrated in example 8–21, we identify the variety of the seventh above the traditional figured bass with the symbol (♭7), indicating the chord quality regardless of chord position. The C-minor tonic seventh in 8–21a would read as follows: the "tonic six-five lowered seventh variety." We read the seventh chord of the subtonic in examples 8–21d, 21e, and 21f as the "subtonic six-five lowered seventh variety," "subtonic four-three lowered seventh variety," and "subtonic four-two lowered seventh variety" respectively.

More About Real and Apparent Seventh Chords

In Chapter 5, we observed that the interval of the 7th seeks to move down by step, *if there is a tone of resolution available in the next chord*. But what if a downward resolution for the 7th is not possible? Indeed, it is reasonable to question the status of any tertian harmony as a *real* seventh chord if the seventh element of that chord *does not seek a downward resolution*. As we have said, a real seventh chord either stands in a rising 2nd, a falling 5th, or rising 4th root relationship to the chord it addresses.

Example 8–22 presents six chords in the key and mode of f minor. As in example 8–19 above, there is a stepwise descent in the bass; however, in this instance, the bass line descends through scale degrees 8–♭7–♭6–5, ending with a harmonic imperfect authentic cadence (scale degree 3 in the soprano).

In measures 4 and 5, the interval of the 6th in the cadential $^6_4$ moves up to form the seventh component of the dominant in measure 5 (see the dotted diagonal line from 6 to 7 in the example). The formation of the dominant seventh chord in measure 5 exhibits an omitted fifth and a doubled root—a perfectly acceptable voicing. The seventh (B♭) moves down by step to become the third (A♭) of the tonic chord in measure 6; hence, there is no question that the V^7 is a real seventh chord.

But is the minor dominant in the second measure of the example a real seventh chord? Certainly, regardless of its status as a seventh chord, we can say that the minor dominant functions as a passing chord that helps to produce the descending bass line mentioned above. It appears to be a seventh chord in first inversion with the third in the bass, variable ♭7 (E♭). Notice that the seventh of the chord, B♭, does not have a downward resolution; rather, the B♭ is repeated in the next chord, the iv^6. Indeed, the B♭ in the minor dominant *anticipates* the root of the subdominant (the dotted curved line in the tenor voice of the example indicates the B♭ common to both chords).

Although the B♭ in measure 2 is technically the chord seventh, it is actually an apparent seventh, part of an ascending-3rd motion in the tenor voice: A♭–B♭–C. As such, the B♭ is a consonant passing tone, rather than a real chord seventh of the minor dominant.

Example 8–22: the passing minor dominant

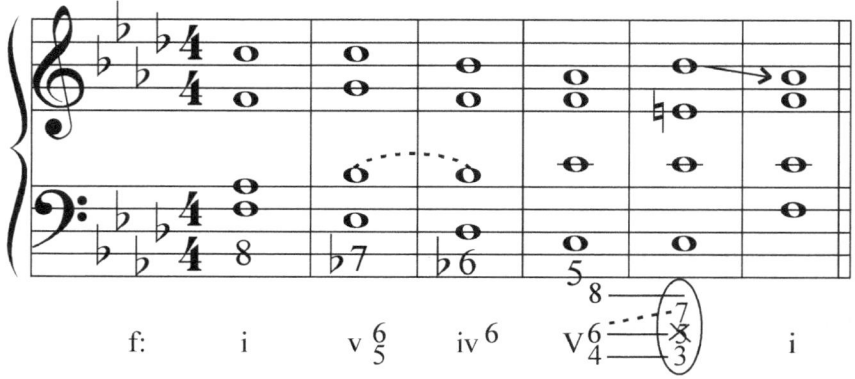

Real and Apparent Seventh Chords in Harmonic and Contrapuntal Progressions

Example 8–23 illustrates the secondary harmonic progression in g minor, which concludes with a harmonic perfect authentic cadence. The i♭7 in third inversion serves as a passing chord (beat 3, measure 1) addressing the subdominant in first inversion (beat 1, measure 2), a chord with which the tonic shares a falling 5th or rising 4th root relationship. The first-inversion subdominant is also a passing chord and part of a descending motion in the bass. (Usually, $\frac{4}{2}$ chords resolve to either $\frac{6}{3}$ or $\frac{6}{5}$ chords.)

The bass uses the lowered variables to descend by step from scale degrees 8 down to 4 (8–♭7–♭6–5–4), which then reverses direction and moves upwards to the penultimate chord, the tonal harmonic dominant (beat 3, measure 3). A second appearance of the subdominant (as an X-chord, beat 1, measure 3) supports an ascending soprano line in which the raised variables are used to approach the final tonic (5–♯6–♯7–8).

Example 8–23: the tonic $\frac{4}{2}$ lowered variety as a passing chord

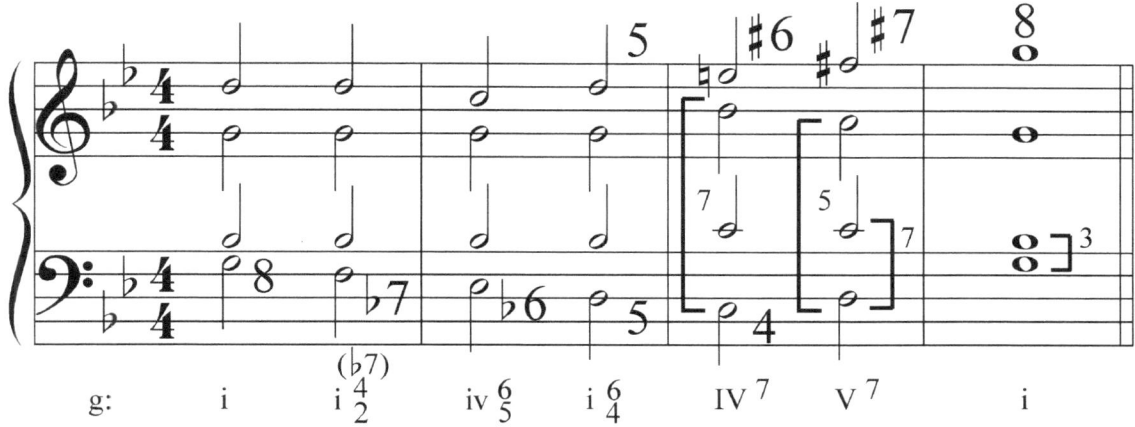

The linear demands of the lowered and raised variables determine the qualities of the chords that contain them. Variable ♭7 (F) forms the minor seventh of the tonic (beat 3, measure 1), which *moves down* by step in the bass to become the third (E♭) of the next chord, the C-minor subdominant in first inversion (beat 1, measure 2). Therefore, the seventh component in the tonic chord is *real*.

In the subdominant's first appearance, the basic triad is minor because its third is ♭6 (E♭). But is the seventh element of the subdominant, B♭, a real seventh? This B♭ is also the third of the chord that both precedes and follows it, the G-minor tonic. As a common tone, the B♭ may form the seventh of the minor subdominant, but the pitch does not move down, instead it is repeated for two measures within the tenor voice as part of both the tonic and the subdominant—this seventh is *apparent*. The B♭ of the subdominant holds on and becomes the third of a tonic $\frac{6}{4}$ chord, a passing $\frac{6}{4}$ (beat 3, measure 2).

158   Chapter 8 The Chord Seventh Revisited

Example 8–24 below restates the principal elements of the secondary harmonic progression shown above in example 8–23, omitting the stepwise descending bass and the passing chords that arise therefrom. We are left with the initial tonic, the subdominant X-chord, dominant, and tonic.

The soprano voice ascends from scale degrees 5 to 8. The subdominant chord supports variable ♯6 (E♮) in the soprano line (beat 1, measure 2). Since the soprano moves upwards, we use the raised variable rather than the lowered variable (E♭). The use of variable ♯6 produces a C-major triad (with an omitted fifth), which also carries a minor 7th from the root to its seventh (B♭) and thus presents a dominant seventh quality *on the subdominant*. We need not account for the presence of the raised variable beyond expressing the subdominant chord in uppercase, indicating that the quality of the underlying triad for this seventh chord is major. The seventh element is reflected in the attached figured-bass 7.

The use of variable ♯7 (F♯) in the soprano produces a D-major triad of the dominant (beat 3, measure 2), which also has a minor 7th from the root to its seventh (C). The uppercase chord symbol and attached figured-bass 7 indicate the quality of the chord as a dominant seventh. With the subdominant and dominant chords, then, there are two consecutive dominant sevenths, one on C, the other on D. Remember that connecting two triads whose roots are a 2nd apart can lead to wrong parallel motion. Adding sevenths to the texture avoids these potential hazards. Thus, the seventh of the subdominant moves down by step in the alto to become the fifth of the dominant (B♭ resolves to A, beats 1 and 3, measure 2).

The dominant has its seventh in the tenor voice (beat 3, measure 2); the seventh (C) is prepared from the root of the previous subdominant. As the dominant proceeds to the final tonic, its seventh moves down by step in the tenor to become the third of the G-minor chord (C resolves to B♭ in measure 3).

Example 8–24: the secondary harmonic progression in g minor

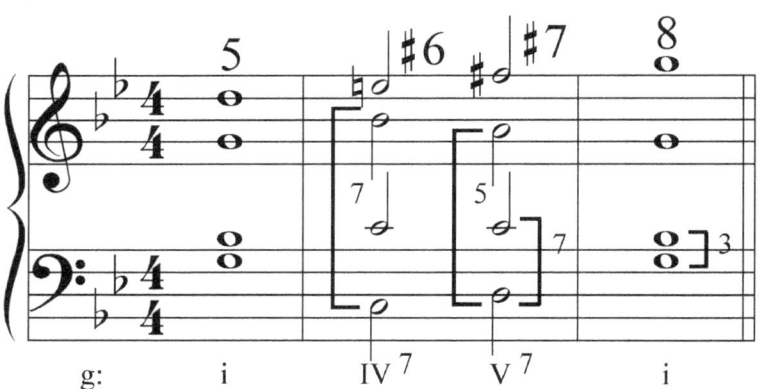

Example 8–25 uses virtually the same chords as 8–24 but places variables ♯6 and ♯7 in the bass, resulting in a secondary contrapuntal progression in g minor with an imperfect authentic cadence. Both the C-subdominant and D-dominant chords are in first inversion (measure 2).

Most of the soprano lines in the previous examples move upwards or downwards. The melody in example 8–25, however, is somewhat stationary; it moves away from B♭ only once, down to A and then back up to B♭. Hence, the tone A decorates the B♭ as a consonant complete lower neighbor. Notably, the static quality of the soprano line is partially responsible for the formation of a dominant *triad* instead of a seventh chord in measure 2 (beat 3).

Indeed, given both the voicing of the initial G-minor tonic (with its third in the soprano) and the contrapuntal bass line of the progression, placing the seventh component of the dominant in the alto voice would transform the D-dominant into a leading-tone triad in root position (F♯ A C) and produce an undesirable tritone (F♯/C) between the bass and alto (note the C in parentheses in measure 2, beat 3).

On the other hand, adding the seventh component (B♭) to the preceding subdominant triad provides a smoother connection into the dominant chord. Located in the soprano voice, the seventh of the subdominant resolves downwards by step to the chord fifth of the dominant triad (A). The bass line of the progression involves a downward skip of a 3rd and a reversal of direction leading back up to the tonic using the raised variables (8–♯6–♯7–8). With its third in the bass, the dominant functions as a contrapuntal leading-tone chord, presenting a stepwise approach to the tonic.

Example 8–25: the secondary contrapuntal progression in g minor, raised variables in the bass

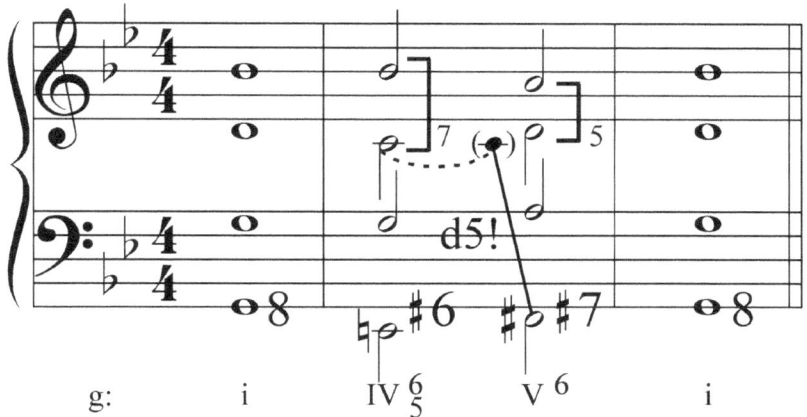

What happens to the treatment of the sevenths when we change the voicing of the initial tonic triad from that shown above in 8–25? In example 8–26, placing the third (B♭) in the tenor, the fifth (D) in soprano, and the root (G) in the alto affords a different set of voice-leading options. Though the bass remains the same as that of 8–25, the soprano descends from scale degrees 5 to 3.

The seventh-chord resolutions in 8–26 occur between the three upper voices, the tenor, alto, and soprano. The tones comprising the 7th interval in the subdominant chord in 8–25 have been inverted in 8–26 to produce a compound 2nd. In other words, instead of C up to B♭ between the alto and soprano, we have B♭ up to C between the tenor and the soprano. Since the B♭ is the seventh element of the chord, which now appears at the interval of a 2nd (or 9th) between the tenor and the soprano, it must move down by step to form a consonance in the next chord. The nearest consonance to which the 2nd can resolve by step is the interval of the 3rd (or 10th): B♭/C moves to A/C.

Example 8–26: the secondary contrapuntal progression, alternative voicing

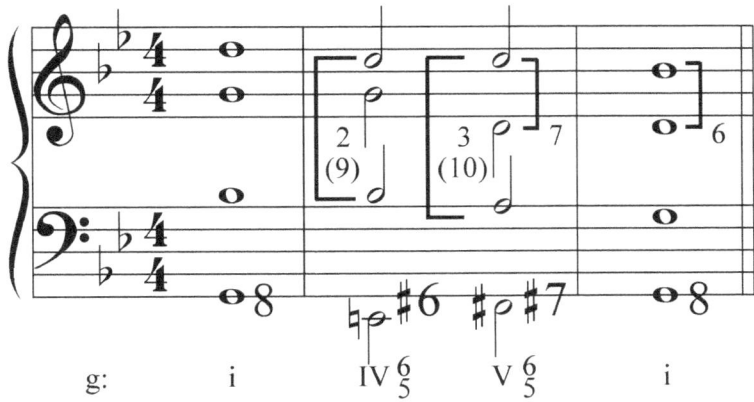

Had the dissonant 2nd and its resolution to the consonant 3rd been placed between the bass and one of the upper voices, the operation would have been known as the "2—3 suspension." In Chapter 5, we examined the 7—6 and 7 3 suspensions (pp. 114–115).

Example 8–27 shows the derivation of the 2—3 suspension from the 7—6 suspension and demonstrates the resolution of the dissonant 2nd (or 9th) into the consonant 3rd (or 10th). The 7—6 suspension of 8–27a inverts to become the 2—3 suspension of 8–27b. In 8–27c, the 2—3 suspension assumes its compound form: 9—10.

Example 8–27: how the 2—3 suspension works and its derivation from the 7—6 suspension

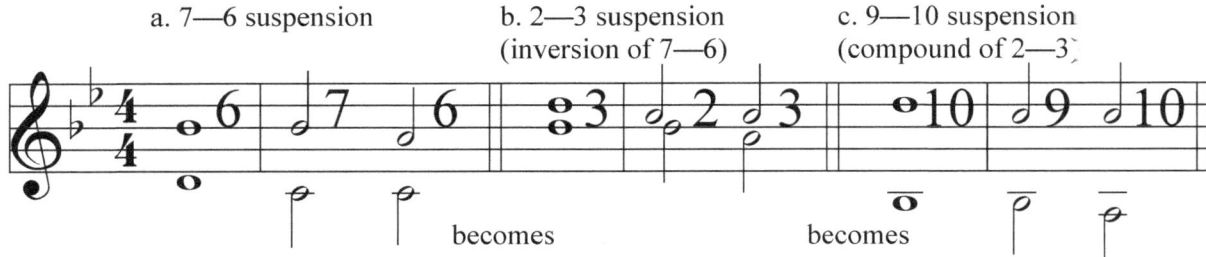

Example 8–28 limits our view to the first-inversion subdominant and dominant chords of example 8–26 so that we can focus on the treatment of the 2—3 motion as it appears between the tenor and soprano voices. On beat 3, B♭ resolves to A in the tenor, forming the interval of the 3rd (or 10th), A/C. Notice that A is the fifth of the dominant chord, the tone to which the seventh of a real seventh chord typically moves *when there is a rising 2nd root relationship between the two chords.*

Example 8–28: the 2—3 motion between the tenor and soprano voices

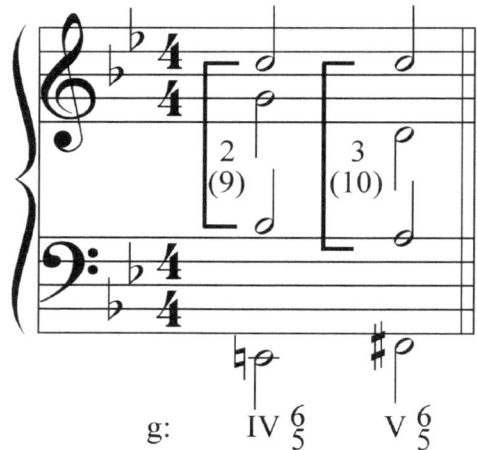

Remember that a real seventh replicates the operation of the descending dissonant passing tone by taking a downward resolution to a consonance. There are only two root relationships between chords that support the real seventh; the two chords must stand in either

(1) a rising 2nd root relationship to each other (as in 8–28); or,
(2) a falling 5th or rising 4th root relationship to each other.

In example 8–29, a real seventh occurs as the first part of a contrapuntal imperfect authentic cadence: the dominant in first-inversion proceeds to the tonic in root position. The interval of the 7th is occurring in the upper voices; the alto voice carries a stationary D between the D-dominant seventh and G-tonic triad (see the dotted box). Over the stationary alto, the seventh of the dominant (C) moves down by step to become the third of the tonic (B♭).

Above the repeated D, the 7th proceeds to a 6th; accordingly, we have a 7—6 motion between the soprano and alto voices. Additionally, the dissonant tritone between the soprano and bass (F♯/C) contracts to a consonant 3rd (G/B♭). (Notice that in this instance, the tritone involves the third and seventh of an inverted dominant seventh rather than the root and fifth of a root-position leading-tone triad.)

Example 8–29: 2—3 and 7—6 motions between upper voices

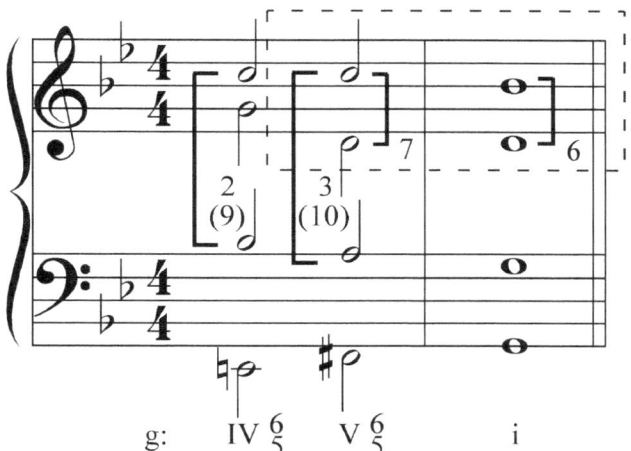

The Seventh Chord of the Mediant and Its Triads

The mediant scale degree and pitch content of the melodic minor projects a major triad and an augmented triad, each of which may contain a seventh component. We begin this section with a look at the augmented triad of the mediant and its seventh.

Although there is no universally accepted name for the augmented-mediant seventh chord, it is usually called the "augmented-major seventh" (of the mediant) because the basic triad is augmented and the interval from the root to the seventh is a major 7th. The augmented triad in general and the augmented mediant in particular usually grows out of some kind of linear motion and/or chromatic activity. The augmented mediant rarely stands on its own. With or without its seventh, the augmented mediant is almost invariably associated with either tonic or dominant chords.

162   Chapter 8 The Chord Seventh Revisited

Example 8–30 exhibits some of the more likely (but by no means the only) linear configurations that bind the augmented mediant to another chord. The circled figured bass in the example identifies the real chord to which the augmented mediant, with or without its seventh, is attached.

In 8–30a, the sharp in front of the 5 indicates that variable ♯7 (B♮) occurs at the interval of a 5th above the bass (E♭). A combination of figured-bass numbers and a dash between them (♯5—6) represents the upward movement of the interval of the 5th to the 6th over a stationary bass (E♭). Variable ♯7, as expected, moves up to scale degree 8 (B♮ to C) and forms consequently the tonic triad in first inversion. Therefore, the augmented triad (E♭ G B) on beat 1 is apparent, the C-minor triad (E♭ G C) on beat 3 real.

Example 8–30b has the same augmented triad as 8–30a (E♭ G B) but adds what appears to be a seventh component (D) to the chord, producing an augmented-major seventh. Above the bass, we have the downward movement of the 7th to the 6th and the upward movement of the 5th to the 6th over the bass ($\substack{7 \\ \sharp 5} - \substack{6 \\ 6}$). In this instance, variable ♯7 moves up to scale degree 8 (B♮ to C) and scale degree 2 resolves down to scale degree 1 (D to C), resulting in the tonic triad in first inversion.

Examples 8–30c and 30d show how altering one pitch of the augmented mediant can also change the chord into either the dominant triad or the dominant seventh with its fifth omitted. Variable ♯7 (B♮), which is a major 3rd above the root of the chord, does not require a sharp in front of the figured bass because the uppercase Roman numeral V already tells us that we have a major 3rd above the root. Hence, the number 3 followed by a long dash (3——) indicates that the variable ♯7 remains stationary while a tone in another voice (the alto) moves.

In 8–30c, a 6th above the bass proceeds downwards to a 5th (6—5, E♭ to D). The real chord is a dominant triad in root position, formed with the second half note. As 8–30d demonstrates, moving the interval of a 6th up to a 7th above the bass (6—7, E♭ to F) produces a dominant seventh chord with a doubled root and an omitted fifth.

Example 8–30: apparent augmented mediants in minor

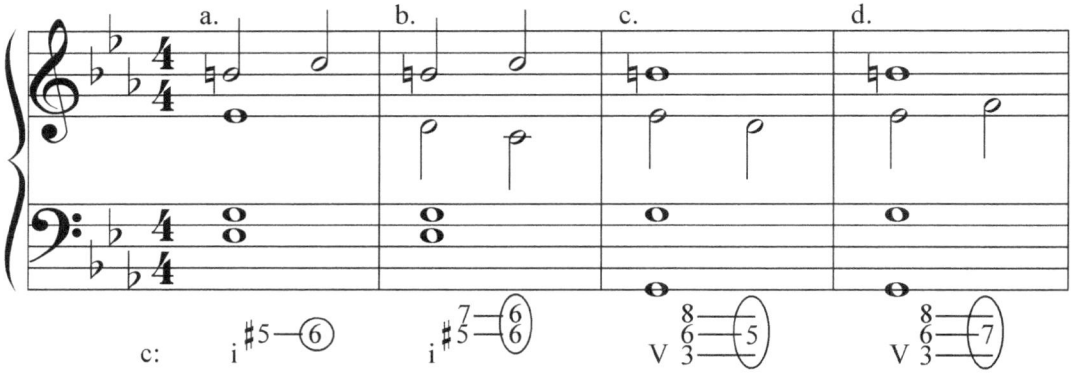

As shown in example 8–31, the problem with both the augmented mediant in minor (31a) and the minor mediant in major (31b) is that they each have two tones in common with their respective tonic and dominant triads: the third and fifth of the tonic and the root and third of the dominant. (The filled-in note heads in the example indicate the pitch content that the tonic and dominant triads share with the mediant.)

Therefore, in most circumstances, the utility of the augmented mediant in minor is somewhat limited because it does not produce a convincing change of chord. The minor mediant in major suffers from the same problem as that of the augmented mediant (in minor); for when it follows the major tonic in a chord progression, the mediant is usually heard as some kind of elaboration of the preceding tonic. Accordingly, the mediant occurs infrequently as an X-chord in major.

Example 8–31: common pitch content for the mediant triads in both minor and major

c: i   III+   V   C: I   iii   V

With respect to the minor mode, a comparison between the augmented and major triads of the mediant within the context of a chord progression underscores the limitations of the former and the potential of the latter. Example 8–32 illustrates how unproductive the augmented mediant becomes as an X-chord of the secondary harmonic progression. Anticipating the leading tone (B♮) within the mediant chord (measure 2) weakens the impact of its appearance within the tonal harmonic dominant (measure 3).

Example 8–32: the secondary harmonic progression with the augmented mediant as the X-chord

c: i   III+   V⁷   i

Example 8–33 offers some improvement with the introduction of the major triad of the mediant, which has ♭7 (B♭) rather than ♯7 (B♮) as its fifth. As a result of scale degree ♭7 moving up by half step to scale degree ♯7 (B♭ up to B♮) in the tenor, we have a clearer sense that a chord change has taken place between the mediant and the dominant. In minor, the major mediant, with or without its seventh, is the chord of the mediant that usually appears in music literature.

Example 8–33 the secondary harmonic progression with the major mediant as the X-chord

c: i   III   V⁷   i

The Passing Chord Between the Mediant and the Dominant

Inserting an additional chord between the mediant and the dominant in minor generally improves the voice leading to the dominant. Example 8–34 adds the ii○6 as a passing chord between the III and the V⁷, a chord that contains variable ♭6 as its fifth (A♭). The passing ii○6 enables us to move ♭7 (E♭) down to ♭6 in the tenor voice (8–♭7–♭6–5) in accordance with the descending form of the melodic minor. Moreover, the ii○6 breaks up the half-step motion from ♭7 up to ♯7 in the tenor and consequently forces ♯7 into another voice (the soprano). Both the mediant X-chord and the dominant have been strengthened and a clear sense of chord change established.

Example 8–34: the secondary harmonic progression with the ii○6 between the III and the V⁷

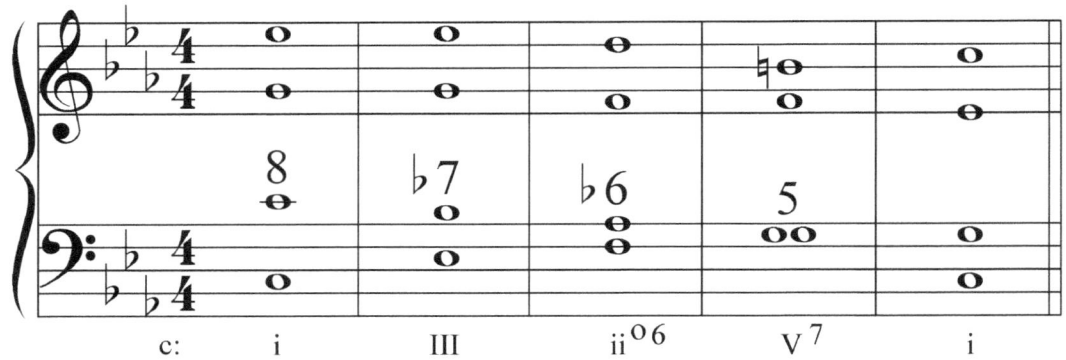

Example 8–35 places the descending form of the melodic minor in the alto and supports this motion with a seventh chord of the mediant and a minor triad of the subdominant as a passing chord. The mediant contains ♭7 (B♭), whereas the subdominant supports ♭6 (A♭). A rising 2nd root relationship between the III⁷ and the iv provides the seventh of the mediant with a tone of resolution; the seventh of the mediant moves down by step to become the fifth of the subdominant. In turn, the fifth of the subdominant (C) prepares the suspended 4th of the elaborated dominant, the cadential $^6_4$.

Example 8–35: 7 5 motion between the mediant as a real seventh addressing the subdominant

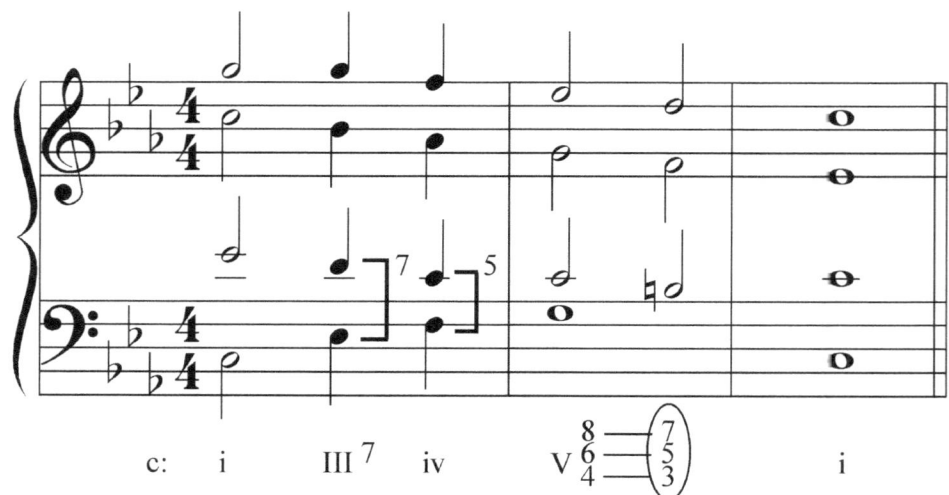

Interlocking Root-Position Chords of the Seventh (Harmonic Bass)

When two seventh chords stand in a falling 5th or rising 4th root relationship to each other, it is possible to form a two-chord pattern of overlapping resolutions in which the seventh of the first chord moves to the third of the second chord while the third of the first chord becomes the seventh of the second chord. This operation is called interlocking seventh chords. When the chords are in root position, the pattern forms a descending harmonic bass line that is subsequently repeated at different pitch levels. Example 8–36 demonstrates interlocking seventh chords in the key and mode of a minor:

(1) The seventh of chord 1 moves down by step in the same voice to become the third of chord 2 (C down to B, measures 2–3, tenor) as the third of chord 1 (F, alto) prepares the seventh of chord 2 (see the dotted curved line in measures 2–3, alto).

(2) This two-chord pattern expands into a *series* of interlocking sevenths as the third of chord 2 (B, tenor) prepares the seventh of the next chord (measures 3–4, tenor). In effect, chord 2 initiates another pair of interlocking sevenths.

Thus, while chord 2 *completes* a 7 3 motion in one voice (C down to B, measures 2–3, tenor), it is also *initiating* a 7 3 motion with the next chord in a different voice (F down to E, measures 3–4, alto). In four voices, this two-chord pattern is maintained with root-position sevenths by alternating a complete seventh chord with an incomplete seventh chord (or an incomplete seventh chord alternating with a complete seventh chord). A complete seventh chord has all chord tones present; an incomplete seventh omits the fifth and doubles the root.

Example 8–36: interlocking series of root-position seventh chords in a minor

The Sequence

Interlocking seventh chords demonstrate one application of a procedure known as the sequence, which includes a variety of techniques. Some sequences are melodic, chordal, or both. A sequence consists of a pattern that is repeated at different pitch levels in order to shift all of the voices upwards or downwards. The original pattern and its duplications exhibit consistent intervallic relationships in all or most of the voices above the bass.

In 8–36 above, we have a chain of *root-position* seventh chords in which the bass moves through seven diatonic scale degrees in a falling 5th and rising 4th motion (A–D–G–C–F–B–E–A). To be sure, it is possible to deploy fewer (or more) than seven scale degrees in this series of interlocking sevenths; however, we must have at least one repetition of the two-chord pattern to shift all of the voices to a different pitch level. The chain begins in the key and mode of a minor with the tonic chord and passes through the following sequence of seventh chords: iv^7, ♭VII$^{♭7}$, III^7, ♭VI^7, ii^{ø7}, and V^7. Once the dominant seventh is reached in 8–36, the progression ends with a harmonic perfect authentic cadence.

166   Chapter 8 The Chord Seventh Revisited

This particular sequential pattern is sometimes referred to as a descending 5th sequence because all of the voices proceed downwards through a falling 5th and rising 4th (or rising 4th and falling 5th) root movement between chords. Since the mode is minor and the voices are moving downwards, the lower variables are used. Although the ii ⌀7 in measure 6 (8–36) does not have its fifth component included in the texture, the *descending* motion of the voices tells us that the missing fifth of the chord is F (♭6) rather than F♯ (♯6) and that the overall quality is that of a half-diminished seventh (B D F A).

Notice that the approach interval to the supertonic in 8–36 above is a falling tritone 5th (a diminished 5th). All diatonic modes have a tritone interval somewhere within their respective scale structures. In the minor mode, the tritone is located between scale degrees 2 and ♭6.

Example 8–37 presents a descending 5th series of interlocking sevenths in the key and mode of C major. Here, we find the tritone (augmented 4th) between scale degrees 4 and 7 (measures 2–3).

Example 8–37: interlocking series of root-position seventh chords in C major

The Modal Dominant

This section compares the chords of the descending 5th sequence in the major-minor tonal system to the tonic and dominant relationship within the church modes; for every pair of chords in the descending 5th sequence that shares a falling 5th or rising 4th root relationship also exists as a dominant and tonic in one of the corresponding church modes.

For instance, reviewing the seventh-chord content for the untransposed Locrian mode presented in example 8–7 (see above, p. 145) reminds us that the quality of the dominant chord in B Locrian is that of a *major seventh* on F. The Locrian tonic is a *half-diminished* seventh on B. The major seventh on F stands in a rising tritone 4th or falling tritone 5th root relationship to the half-diminished seventh on B (Although we usually avoid the diminished triad in root-position because of the tritone formed between the bass and an upper voice, adding a major 3rd above the fifth of the chord to create a half-diminished seventh "softens" the harsh quality of the tritone and makes the underlying diminished triad in root position acceptable.)

The interlocking sevenths in 8–37 above begin in C major with the IV⁷ addressing the vii⌀7, a *major seventh* on F resolving to a *half-diminished* seventh on B. The IV⁷ stands in a rising tritone 4th (or falling tritone 5th) root relationship to the vii ⌀7. This harmonic (tritone) relationship between the seventh chords of the subdominant and the leading tone corresponds to the relationship in B Locrian between its major-seventh dominant and half-diminished tonic.

Therefore, if we take the idea of a modal dominant relationship in B Locrian between the major seventh on F and the half-diminished seventh on B and transfer it to C major, then the IV⁷ in C major can be described as the modal dominant of vii ⌀ 7. The pattern of interlocking sevenths presented earlier, in both major and minor, demonstrate a *chain* of modal dominants, each seventh chord constituting a modal dominant to the next in the series (by virtue of the falling 5th or rising 4th root relationship between them).

The modal dominant, then, is *any chord within a diatonic mode having either a perfect or tritone falling 5th or rising 4th root relationship to the following chord other than the tonal harmonic dominant to the tonic.* A few more examples will help to clarify this concept.

In example 8–38 below, the bottom staff shows the relationship between dominant and tonic chords in the untransposed modes of B Locrian, E Phrygian, F Lydian, and D Dorian. Equivalent modal dominant relationships in major and minor are presented on the top staff. In 8–38a, the dominant and tonic of B Locrian are thus isolated, displayed in close structure, and placed below the IV^7 and the vii$\emptyset^7$ of C major. We may assume the following analogical relationship between the two pairs of chords within the contexts of C major and B Locrian: the IV^7 is to the vii$\emptyset^7$ in C major as the dominant is to the tonic in B Locrian. (As explained earlier, the circled Roman numerals, displayed in the example, constitute a generalized type of chord symbol that signifies only the exact scale degree of the mode upon which a seventh chord may be formed, making no distinction between triad or seventh chord qualities. Therefore, the Roman numerals are all expressed in uppercase.)

Examples 8–38b, 38c, and 38d show how the modal dominant relationship may occur in both major and minor. In the key and mode of E Phrygian, shown in 8–38b, the half-diminished seventh of the dominant on B addresses the minor seventh of the tonic. Within the tonal context of C major, vii$\emptyset^7$ is the modal dominant of iii^7 (top staff).

Turning to the key and mode of a minor, 8–38c has III^7 as the modal dominant of ♭VI^7 (top staff), which in F Lydian is a dominant to tonic relationship—both chords are major sevenths. In 8–38d, we have two minor seventh chords. The tonic minor seventh, i$^{♭7}$, is the modal dominant of the iv^7. Once again, the modal dominant relationship between these two chords is analogous to D Dorian's dominant to tonic relationship. (Understand that the modal dominant relationship between any two chords of an untransposed mode, such as that between the IV^7 and the vii$\emptyset^7$ in C major, may be transposed to any other key.)

Example 8–38: a comparison of modal dominants within untransposed modes

Interlocking Inverted Chords of the Seventh (Contrapuntal Bass)

Examples 8–36 and 37 above demonstrate how a series of *root-position* seventh chords can be interlocked to produce a descending 5th sequence of modal-dominant seventh chords, chords that stand in a falling 5th or rising 4th root *and* bass relationship to each other and display consequently a harmonic bass line. As defined above, the modal dominant is any chord within a diatonic mode having either a perfect or tritone falling 5th or rising 4th root relationship to the following chord other than the tonal harmonic dominant to the tonic.

Example 8–39 inverts every other seventh chord in the descending 5th sequence of interlocking sevenths to produce a contrapuntal bass in the key and mode of a minor. It should be noted that when either one or both chords of a two-chord pattern of interlocking sevenths is inverted, both chords will be complete, voiced with all chord tones present.

In 8–39, the two-chord pattern alternates between second-inversion and root-position sevenths. The interval of the tritone, present within the scale structure of all diatonic modes, occurs between scale degrees 2 and ♭6 in a minor (see the straight dotted line between the bass and soprano). Inverting one or both of the two sevenths of the two-chord pattern produces an unavoidable "cross-relation tritone."

Example 8–39: interlocking series of inverted seventh chords in a minor ($\begin{smallmatrix} 6 & 7 \\ 4 & 5 \\ 3 & 3 \end{smallmatrix}$)

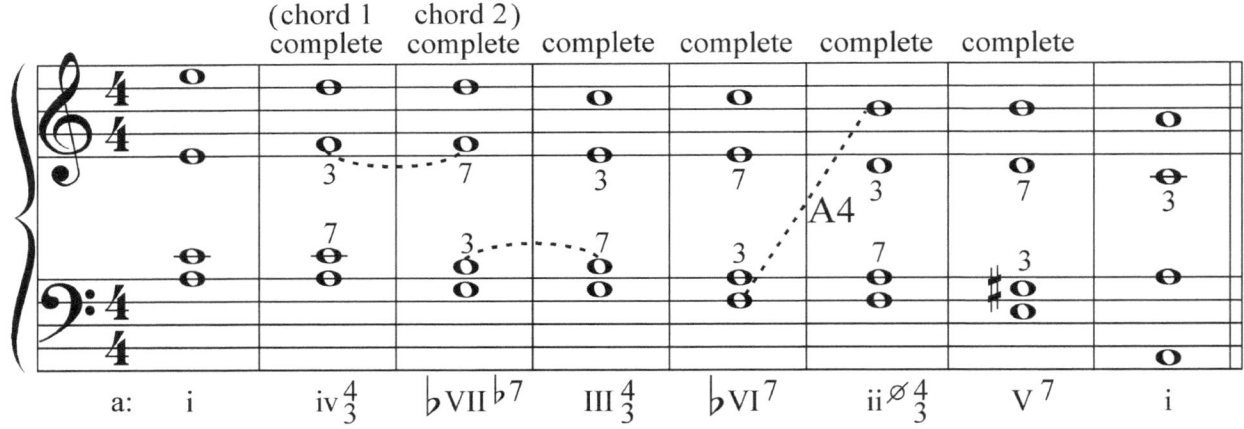

Example 8–40 illustrates the interlocking pattern between second-inversion and root-position seventh chords in the key and mode of C major. The cross-relation tritone occurs between scale degrees 4 and 7.

Example 8–40: interlocking series of inverted seventh chords in C major ($\begin{smallmatrix} 6 & 7 \\ 4 & 5 \\ 3 & 3 \end{smallmatrix}$)

The Two-Progression Framework

Our previous studies have shown how a single progression, harmonic or contrapuntal, may support melodic descents from scale degrees 5 or 3. The two-progression framework is particularly effective in supporting descents from scale degree 5, as it provides more options for supporting the top melodic voice. Example 8–41 cites *some* of these options. The abbreviations for 8–41 are: BHP (basic harmonic progression), SHP (secondary harmonic progression), BCP (basic contrapuntal progression), and SCP (secondary contrapuntal progression). The first four progressions listed in 8–41 represent completely harmonic frameworks (1–4); the second four indicate combined contrapuntal and harmonic frameworks (5–8).

Example 8–41: combinations of harmonic and contrapuntal progressions, from scale degree 5

	1	2			1	2
1	BHP	BHP		5	BCP	BHP
2	BHP	SHP		6	BCP	SHP
3	SHP	BHP		7	SCP	BHP
4	SHP	SHP		8	SCP	SHP

Example 8–42 illustrates a two-progression framework consisting of two basic harmonic progressions. The last tonic chord of progression 1 (the progressions are numbered under the brackets in the example) is also the first chord of progression 2, supporting scale degree 3 in the soprano. The seventh element of the dominant appears in the top voice as scale degree 4 (F, beat 3, measure 1), initiating the melodic descent from scale degrees 5 to 1.

The second appearance of the dominant chord carries scale degree 2 in the soprano (D, beat 3, measure 2). An upward leap of a 3rd in the tenor (beats 3 and 4, measure 2) replaces one of the doubled fifths of the dominant with its chord seventh, which then resolves by step in the same voice to the third of the tonic chord (E or E♭). The seventh serves as a dissonant incomplete upper neighbor to the tonic's chord third.

As stated in Chapter 4 (see above, pp. 109–110), a neighbor tone usually moves by step, upwards or downwards, from a preceding tone; in this instance, however, the neighbor is reached by an upward leap. Since the dissonance is not preceded by the tone that it decorates (which would have given us E–F–E in major or E♭–F–E♭ in minor), the neighbor is incomplete (that is: F–E in major and F–E♭ in minor).

Example 8–42: two-progression framework, BHP–BHP

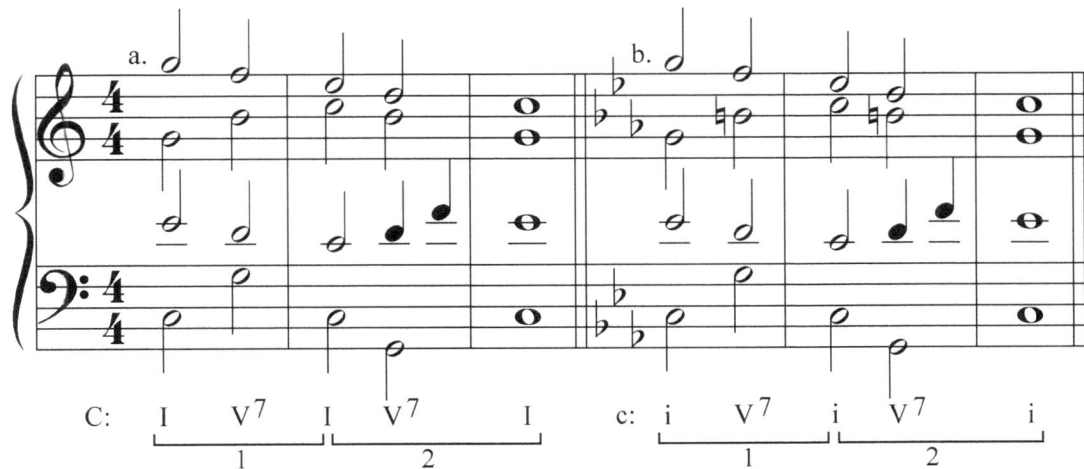

Progression 1 of example 8–43 corresponds to progression 1 of example 8–42 above. Progression 2, however, is a secondary harmonic progression with an X-chord of the supertonic in first inversion supporting the first appearance of scale degree 2 in the soprano (beat 3, measure 2). The inner-voice alto of the tonic chord (beat 1, measure 2) re-voices into the fifth (G) to connect more smoothly into the X-chord. The dominant in progression 2 has an 8—7 motion over the stationary bass.

Example 8–43: two-progression framework, BHP–SHP

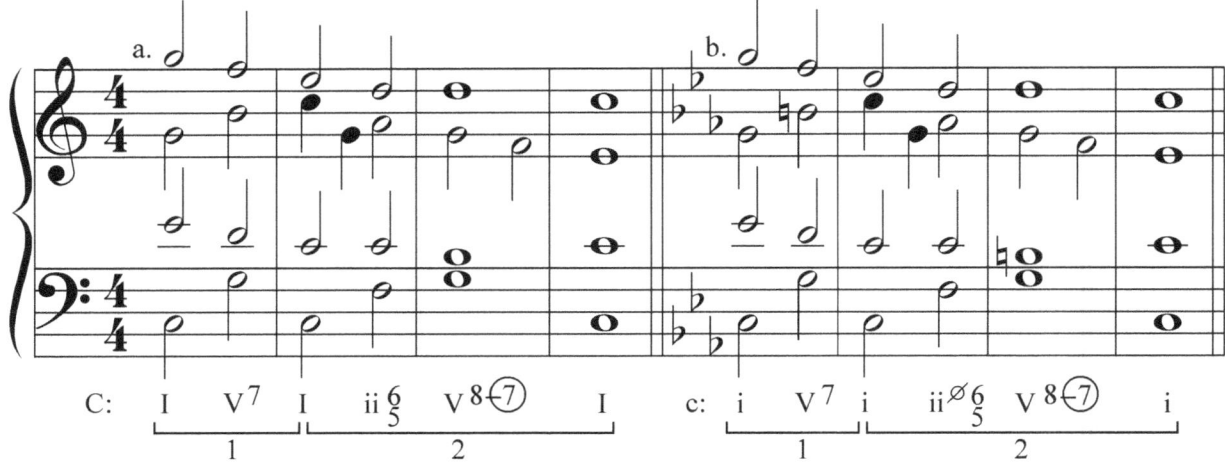

Example 8–44 reverses the order of the two progressions from that displayed in example 8–43 so that progression 1 is a secondary harmonic progression, progression 2 a basic harmonic progression. The X-chord of progression 1, a supertonic seventh in root position, supports the first appearance of scale degree 4 in the soprano. Additionally, the supertonic X-chord stands in a modal dominant relationship to the dominant (that is, a rising 4th root relationship). The disposition of the two chords is that of an incomplete seventh with an omitted fifth to a complete seventh with all chord tones present.

In the minor mode (8–44b), we interpret the missing fifth of the supertonic as A♭: D–F–A♭–C. The correct selection of variable ♭6 (A♭) would determine the quality of the chord as the half-diminished seventh, ii$^{\emptyset 7}$.

Example 8–44: two-progression framework, SHP–BHP

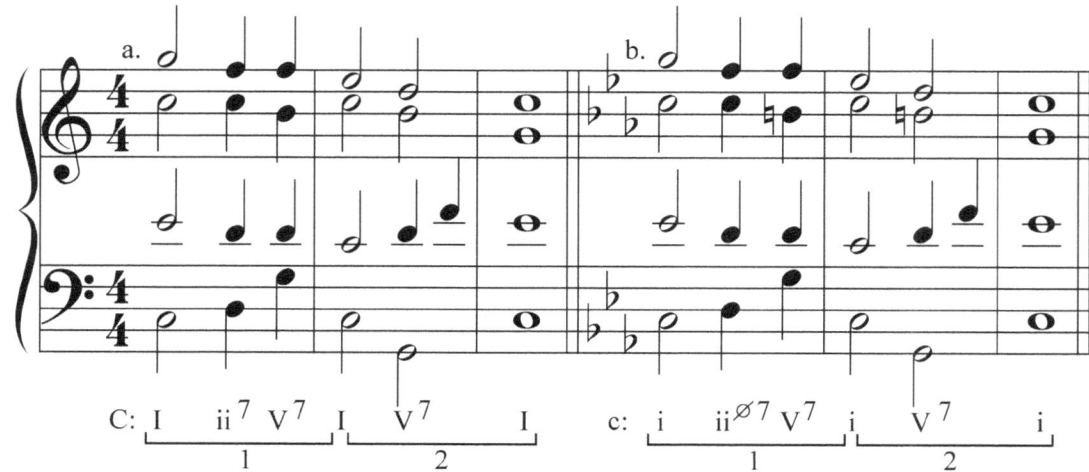

Example 8–45 contains two secondary harmonic progressions, the first of which has an X-chord of the subdominant supporting scale degree 4 in the top voice (beat 3, measure 1). The second appearance of scale degree 3 in the soprano is supported by an X-chord of the mediant in progression 2 (beat 3, measure 2).

A supertonic triad in first inversion (beat 2, measure 3) passes between the X-chord and the tonal harmonic dominant. The passing supertonic carries scale degree 2 in the top voice. The dominant seventh is incomplete, containing a doubled root but lacking the fifth. In the soprano voice, the leading-tone serves as a substitute for scale degree 2 (D), the missing fifth of the dominant. The inclusion of scale degree 2 as the fifth of the dominant chord would have produced the following melodic descent from scale degree 5 (the omitted fifth is italicized): G–F–F–E–E–*D*–D–C (or G–F–F–E♭–E♭–*D*–D–C in minor).

Example 8–45b illustrates the consecutive use of both the ascending and descending melodic minor in two different voices. The ascending form occurs in progression 1 (G–A♮–B♮–C, measures 1 and 2, alto voice), the descending form in progression 2 (C–B♭–A♭–G, measures 2 and 3, tenor voice).

Example 8–45: two-progression framework, SHP–SHP

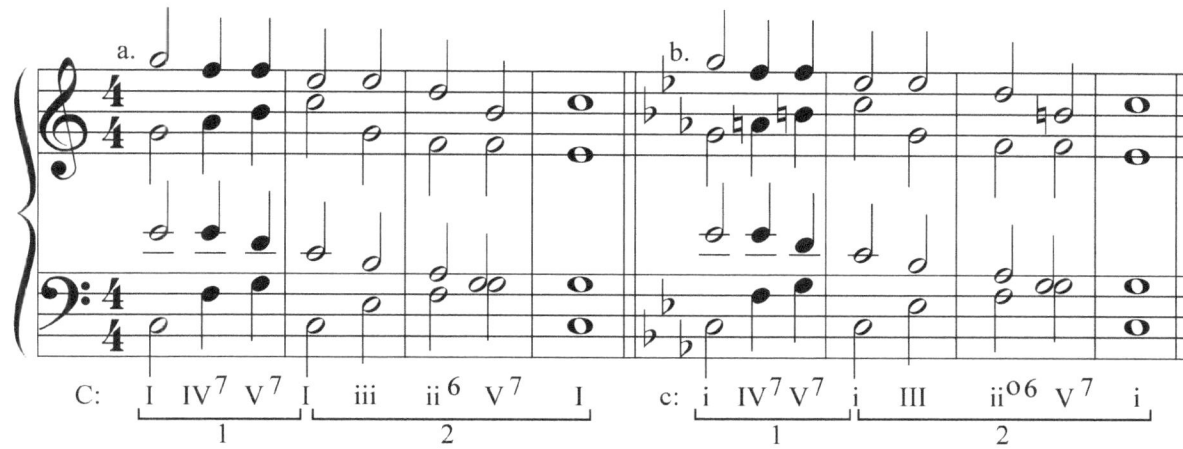

Progression 1 of example 8–46 contains a contrapuntal leading-tone chord, the V^4_3, which supports scale degree 4 in the soprano and appears as a complete upper neighbor to the tonic in the bass. Progression 2 shows a harmonic approach to the final tonic with the dominant in root position.

Example 8–46: two-progression framework, BCP–BHP

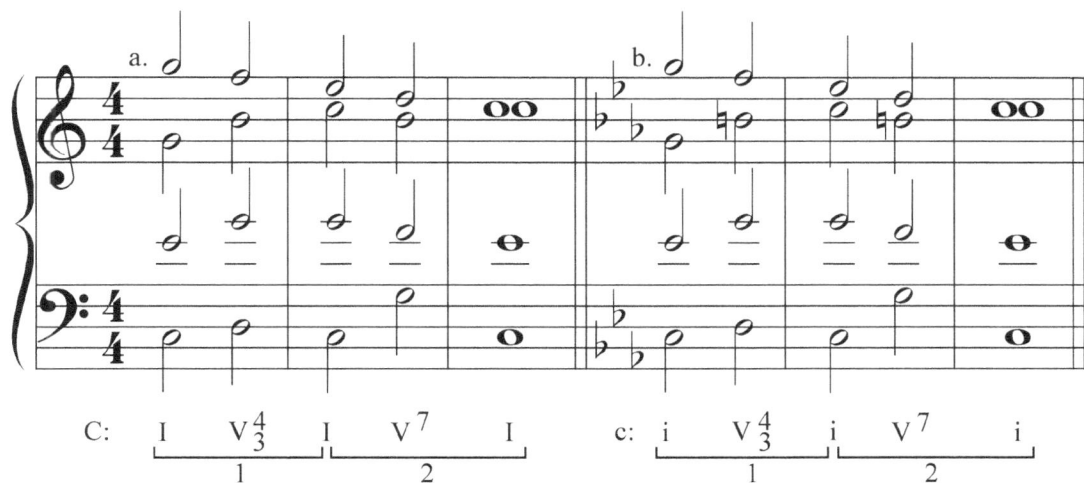

Example 8–47 combines the basic contrapuntal progression of example 8–46 with the secondary harmonic progression introduced earlier in Chapter 7, example 7–7. Progression 2 of 8–47 expands the basic harmonic progression with both the addition of an X-chord of the supertonic and the cadential $^6_4$. The elaboration of the dominant forms a complete seventh chord in root position, including its fifth (beat 3, measure 3). Although scale degree 1 is reached in the soprano with the onset of the cadential $^6_4$ (8–47, beat 1, measure 3), it occurs within the context of an apparent chord and therefore constitutes a nonharmonic tone. The true arrival of scale degree 1 takes place with the appearance of the final tonic chord (measure 4).

Example 8–47: two-progression framework, BCP–SHP

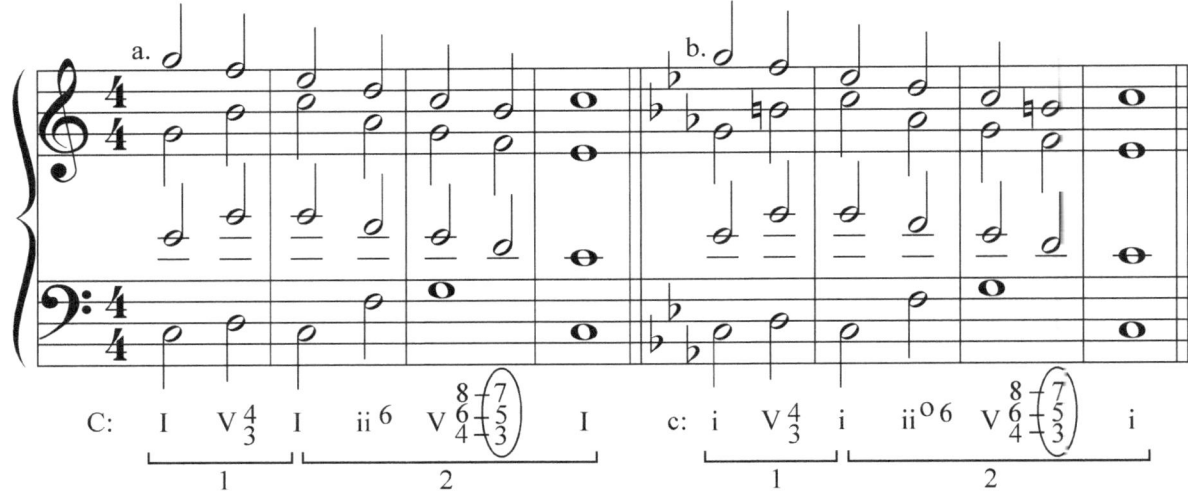

A secondary contrapuntal progression and a basic harmonic progression support the melodic descent from scale degrees 5 to 1 in example 8–48. Scale degree 4 is harmonized twice, first with an X-chord of the supertonic in first inversion (beat 3, measure 1, soprano voice) and secondly with a contrapuntal leading-tone chord, the V$^6_5$ (beat 4). Remember that we allow the dissonant melodic leap of the tritone only when it occurs in the bass voice, as between the supertonic and dominant chords of progression 1 (beats 3 and 4, measure 1).

Example 8–48: two-progression framework, SCP–BHP

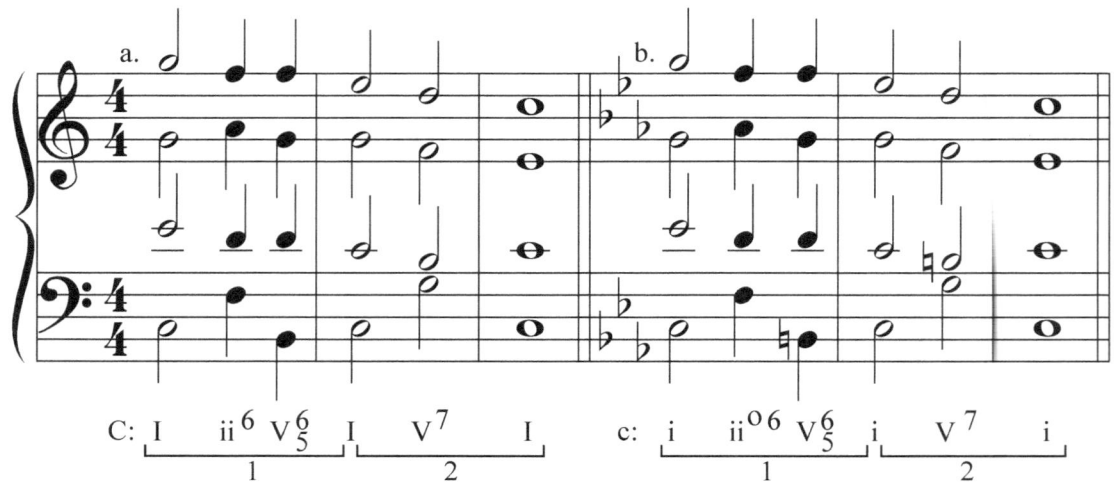

Example 8–49 supports the melodic descent from scale degrees 5 to 1 with a secondary contrapuntal progression and a secondary harmonic progression. The first progression corresponds to progression 1 of example 8–48. Progression 2 is similar to the second progression of example 8–45 except that here the cadential $^6_4$ is used instead of the unelaborated dominant.

The first part of the cadential $^6_4$ (8–49, beat 1, measure 3) takes the alternative voice leading for the interval of the 6th (see above, p. 119). Since the 6th is not a dissonance (G/E or G/E♭), it is free to move up to form the seventh component of the dominant chord (see the dotted line from 6 to 7 in the example). Thus, the formation of the dominant seventh (beat 3, measure 3) is necessarily incomplete, the fifth omitted, the root doubled.

As in example 8–47, scale degree 1 (8–49) is reached in the soprano with the commencement of the cadential $^6_4$; however, it occurs within the disposition of an apparent chord and therefore functions as a nonharmonic tone. The completion of the descent from scale degree 5 and the true arrival of scale degree 1 takes place with the appearance of the final tonic chord (measure 4).

As in example 8–45, we may interpret the leading tone in the soprano of 8–49 as a substitute for scale degree 2 (D), the missing fifth of the dominant chord (beat 3, measure 3). Indeed, including the seventh component within the four-voice disposition of the dominant forces the omission of the fifth from the texture.

Example 8–49: two-progression framework, SCP–SHP

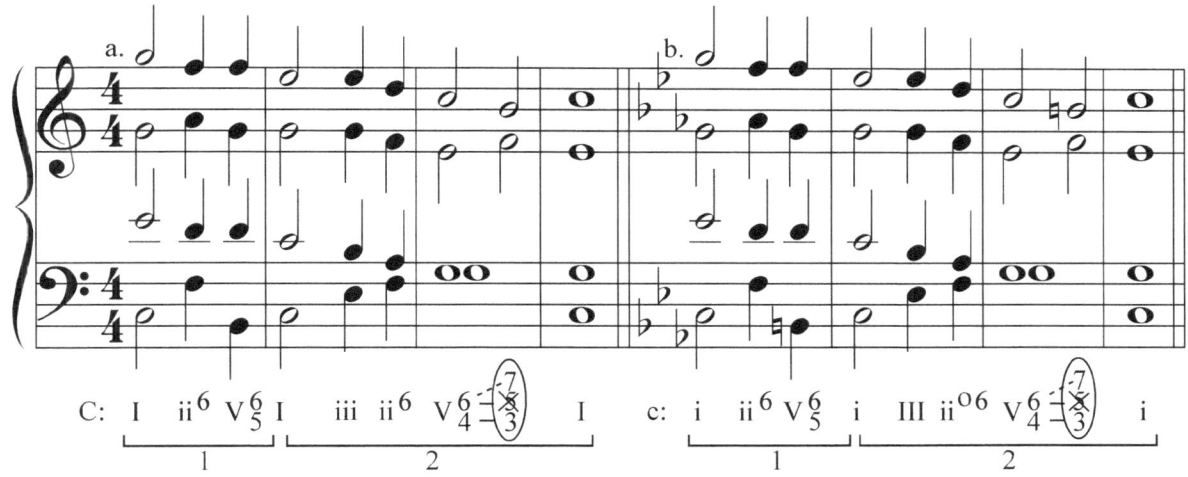

Singing the Seven Seventh-Chord Qualities in All Positions

In this section, we will learn how to sing the seven qualities of seventh chords in all four positions above a common-tone C in the bass. When ascending and descending through each of the four positions, the notes above the common tone must be adjusted to preserve the quality of the seventh chord while retaining the C-octave between the outside pitches (the bass tone is duplicated at the octave above).

The challenge is preserving the outside octave while adjusting the internal intervals to maintain the correct chord quality and position. The numbers 1, 3, 5, and 7 designate the root, third, fifth, and seventh of the chord respectively (1-3-5-7-1-7-5-3-1). Both the intervals and the numbers change as the C becomes the third (3-5-7-1-3-1-7-5-3), fifth (5-7-1-3-5-3-1-7-5), and seventh (7-1-3-5-7-5-3-1-7) of the chord. Singing the numbers 7-1 ascending or 1-7 descending produces either a major or minor 2nd (except for the fully diminished seventh).

In all positions, the upper note of the interval of the 2nd (the inversion of the 7th) denotes the written and sounding root of the chord. As you proceed through the various seventh chords and positions, notice whether the interval of the 2nd between the seventh and the root is either major or minor.

The seventh chords with the major 2nd from the seventh up to root are the dominant seventh, minor seventh, and half-diminished seventh. The seventh chords with the minor 2nd from the seventh up to the root are the major seventh, minor-major seventh, and the augmented-major seventh. Since the fully diminished seventh has neither a major nor minor 2nd from the seventh up to the root, we shall address its structure and arpeggiation separately in example 8–56.

Every seventh chord in root position has two components: the basic triad (root, third, and fifth) and the interval of the 7th above the root, forming the seventh element. We refer to the basic triad of the seventh chord as the "root triad," which is heard immediately upon arpeggiating the complete chord upwards (see the solid brackets in example 8–50a). The root triad also appears in both the second and third inversions above the common-tone bass but not as part of the seventh chord's lowest component (see the brackets in examples 8–50c and 50d). Put differently, the root triad occurs when 1-3-5 is sung in the upward arpeggiation of the root-position, second inversion, and third inversion of the seventh chord. The root triad also appears in the downward arpeggiation when singing 5-3-1.

The first inversion, on the other hand, projects a "false triad" upwards from its bass, consisting of the seventh chord's third, fifth, and seventh elements. The false triad occurs in the upward arpeggiation when 3-5-7 is sung (see the dotted brackets in 8–50b). The false triad also appears in the downward arpeggiation when 7-5-3 is sung. This false triad has a different quality than that of the actual root triad for each seventh chord (except for the fully diminished seventh). Immediately following the false triad (3-5-7) is the actual root of the seventh chord (7-1).

Example 8–50: the major seventh chord

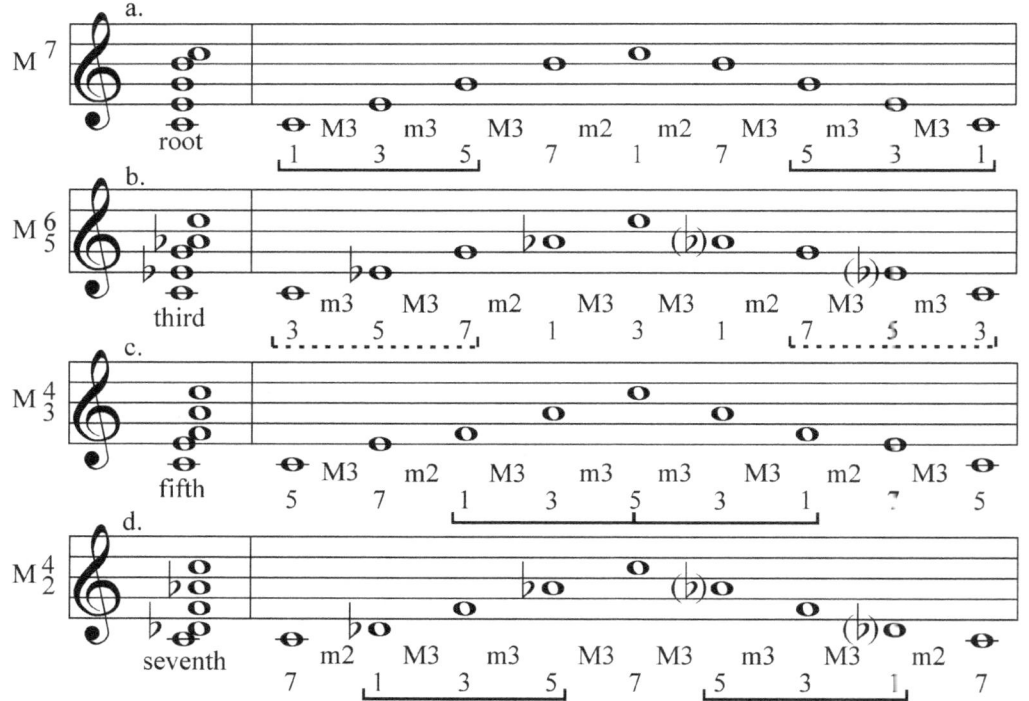

Chapter 8 The Chord Seventh Revisited 175

Example 8–51: the dominant seventh chord

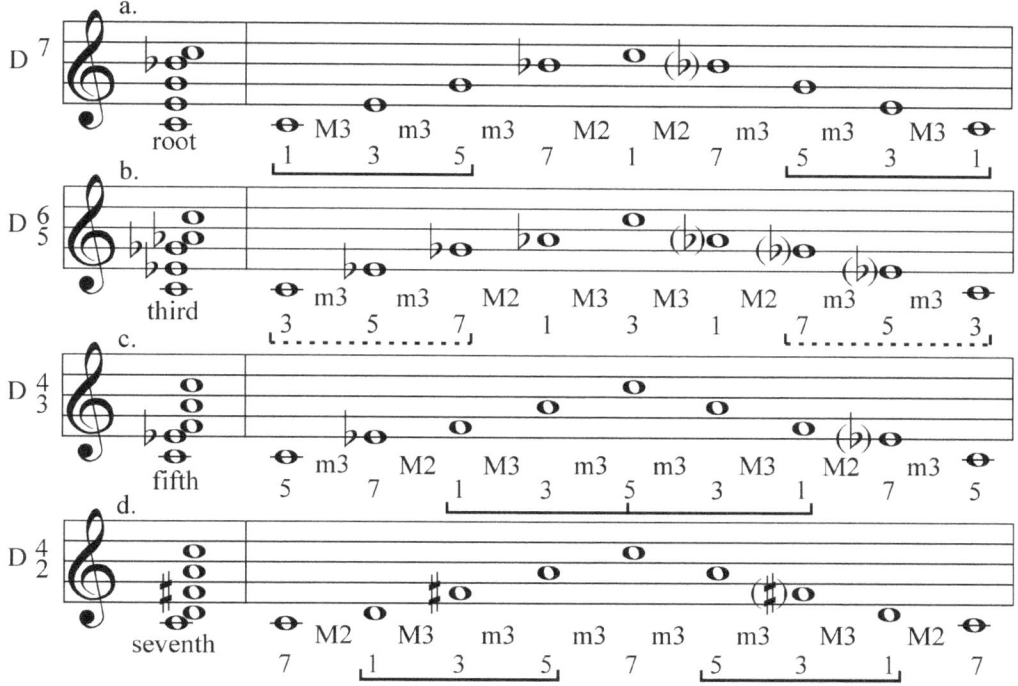

Example 8–52: the minor seventh chord

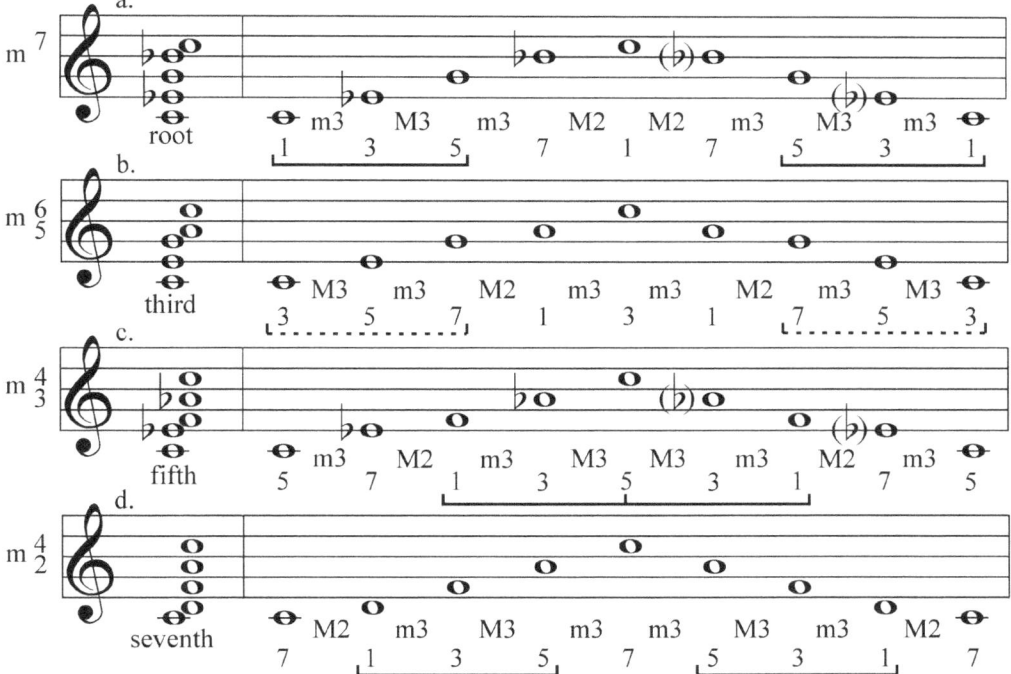

176   Chapter 8 The Chord Seventh Revisited

Example 8–53: the half-diminished seventh chord

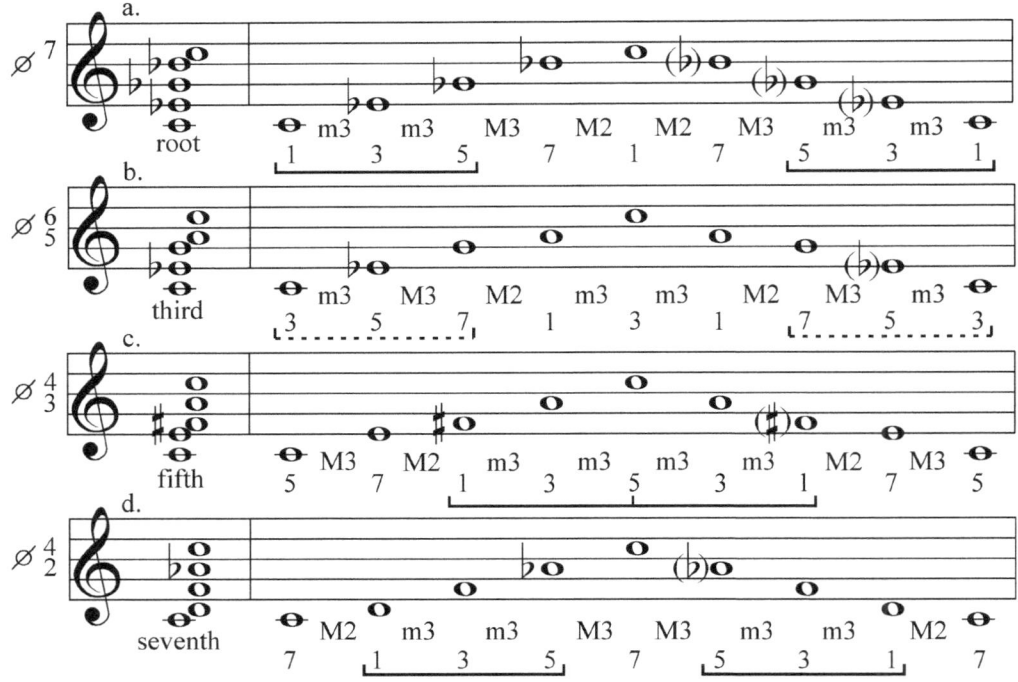

Example 8–54: the minor-major seventh chord

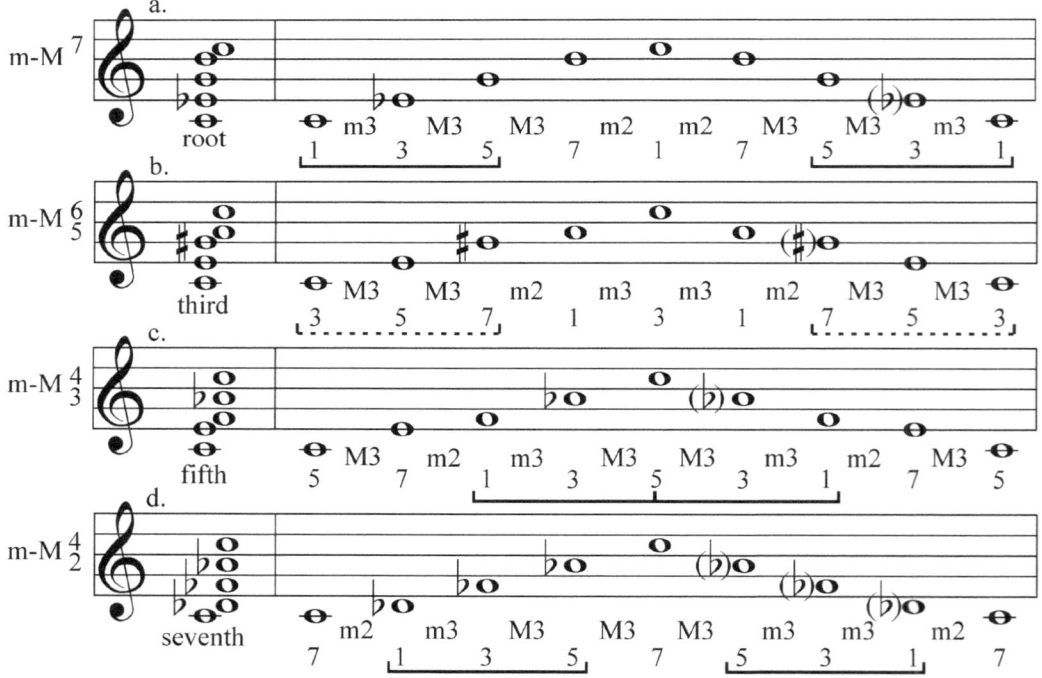

Example 8–55: the augmented-major seventh chord

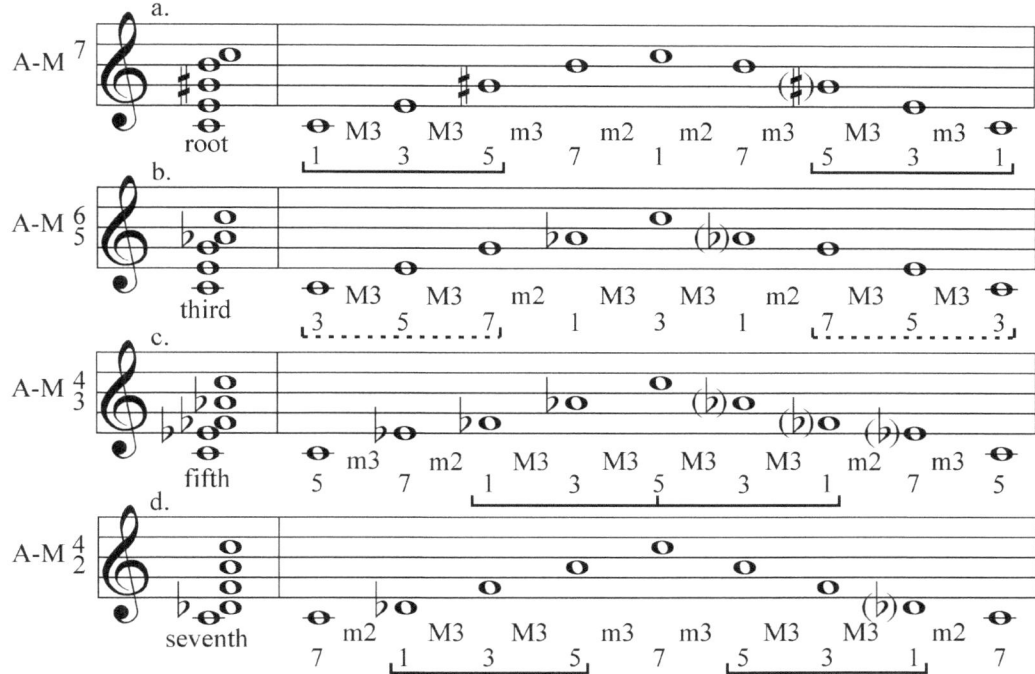

The fully diminished seventh (example 8–56) has an augmented 2nd from the seventh up to the root rather than an acoustical 2nd. As we have observed, the augmented 2nd is a contextual interval equivalent to that of an acoustical minor 3rd. Therefore, we cannot determine the sounding position of the fully diminished seventh because it projects a neutral-sounding profile of acoustical minor 3rds regardless of how it is notated (see examples 8–15 and 16 above).

Singing the fully diminished seventh using the common-tone method results in performing the same acoustical pitches four times as you proceed through all four chord positions; however, each time, the numbers assigned to those same pitches will change. With the fully diminished seventh, the pitches remain unchanged for each chord position but the numbers assigned to those pitches require four different sequences of numbers, the same numerical assignments applied to the other six common-tone sevenths:

(1) root position   1-3-5-7-1-7-5-3-1
(2) first inversion   3-5-7-1-3-1-7-5-3
(3) second inversion   5-7-1-3-5-3-1-7-5
(4) third inversion   7-1-3-5-7-5-3-1-7

Example 8–56: the fully diminished seventh chord

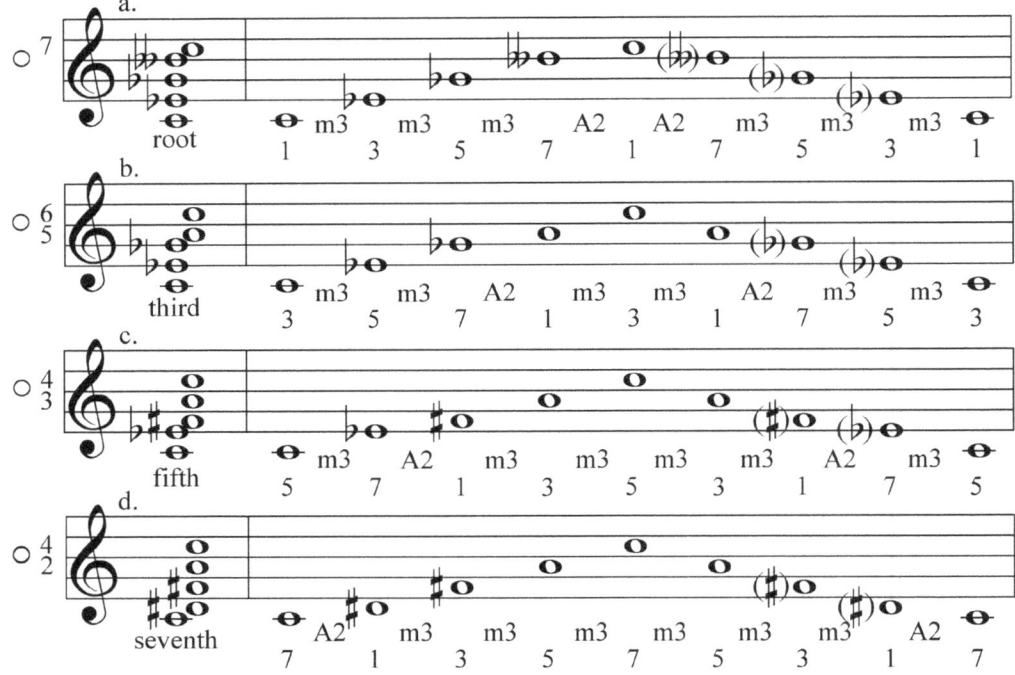

The Added 6th

In examples 8–50 through 55, we identified a false triad consisting of the third, fifth, and seventh elements of the seventh chord in first inversion (see the dotted brackets). As shown in example 8–57, what would be interpreted as the false "root" of the false triad is the actual third of the seventh chord. (The neutral-sounding profile of the fully diminished seventh precludes listing it below.)

Example 8–57: the false triads of the first-inversion seventh chords

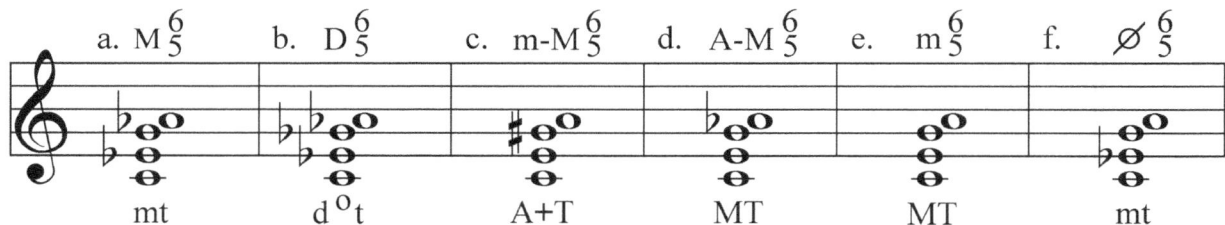

The two most important false triads for our purposes are shown in examples 8–58 and 59 below (note the key signatures). The examples illustrate the first inversions for the minor seventh chord and the half-diminished seventh chord. The third, fifth, and seventh of the minor seventh chord (8–58) projects a false major triad ("C E G") with a major 2nd above its false fifth ("G" up to A) or a major 6th above its false root ("C" up to A). The third, fifth, and seventh of the half-diminished seventh chord (8–59) projects a false minor triad ("C E♭ G") with a major 2nd above its false fifth ("G" up to A) or a major 6th above its false root ("C" up to A).

Both false triads have a major 6th above their respective false roots ("C" up to A). In each chord, the 6th also constitutes a major 2nd above the false fifth ("G" up to A). In certain circumstances, the major 2nd above the chord fifth is viewed as an addition to the basic triad, an "added 6th." It is possible to add tones to the triad, tones positioned most frequently at the intervals of the 4th, 6th, and 9th above the root. In this section, our concern is confined to the addition of the 6th to the false triads contained within the first inversion of the minor seventh and the half-diminished seventh.

Is the 6th in examples 8–58 and 59 simply an addition to the basic triad or the root of a seventh chord in first inversion? Although the limits of space prevent a complete answer to this question, suffice it to say that a real seventh chord should have its seventh component function as a dissonance in relation to the root of the chord. A real seventh component should resolve down by step into the next chord, if there is a tone of resolution available in that chord. If the two chords share a falling 5th or rising 4th or rising 2nd root relationship, then we probably have a first-inversion seventh chord.

Still, in some cases, the tone may not be a seventh but rather an addition to the basic triad, the added 6th. If the triad has an added 6th, then our chord symbol would be a plus sign attached to the *right* of the number 6. (Remember that the plus sign positioned to the *left* of the figured bass designates an augmented triad.) In 8–58, there is not enough musical context to determine if the chord is either a IV $^{6\,+}$ or a ii $^{6}_{5}$ in the key and mode of G major. However, most of the time, it is a chord of the seventh in first inversion.

Example 8–58: major triad with an added 6th or minor seventh in first inversion?

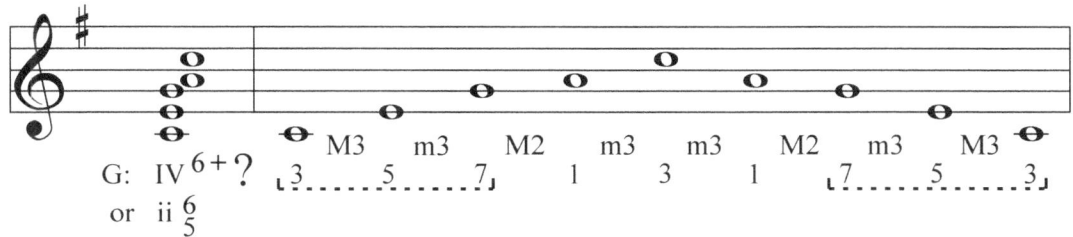

Example 8–59: minor triad with an added 6th or half-diminished seventh in first inversion?

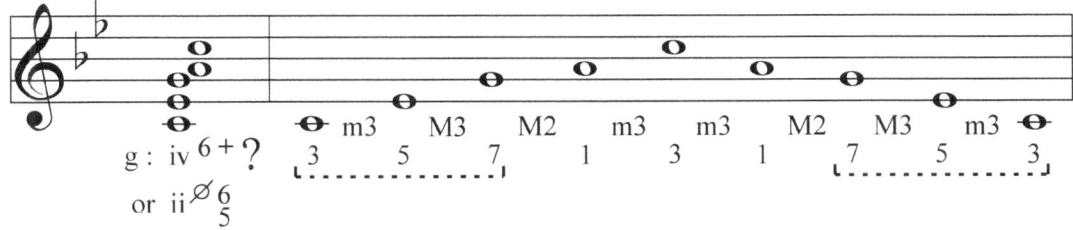

In commercial music and jazz, the default interpretation always favors the added 6th; there is no indication that the tone in question is the root of either the minor seventh chord or the half-diminished seventh chord. In 8–59, the chord is either a iv $^{6\,+}$ or a ii $\varnothing\,^{6}_{5}$ in the key and mode of g minor; however, our default position recognizes a chord of the seventh in first inversion.

Finally, let us conclude with two stipulations that effectively eliminate the first inversion of the major seventh, dominant seventh, minor-major seventh, and augmented-major seventh as added-6th chords: the added 6th should not involve a minor 6th above the root of the basic major or minor triad, nor should an added 6th appear above the root of the diminished triad or the augmented triad.

Chapter 9 Nonharmonic Tones

When is the existence of a chord more apparent than real? In our study of the cadential $^6_4$ (Chapter 4), we discovered that while certain combinations of tones may be recognized as intervals forming tertian harmonies and placed consequently within the context of a given key and mode, their status as real chords is questionable. The cadential $^6_4$ is ultimately an elaboration of the dominant chord with two pitches that are not inherent components of that chord—they are nonharmonic tones.

There are two classes of nonharmonic tones: appoggiaturas and non-appoggiaturas. Appoggiaturas are rhythmically stressed, non-appoggiaturas unstressed. The following outline presents a brief overview of these two categories:

(1) Non-Appoggiaturas: rhythmically *unaccented* nonharmonic tones
  (a) the passing tone
  (b) the complete and incomplete neighbor tone
  (c) the anticipation tone
(2) Appoggiaturas: rhythmically *accented* nonharmonic tones
  (a) the passing tone
  (b) the complete and incomplete neighbor tone (the "appoggiatura itself")
  (c) the suspension

We base our classification of nonharmonic tones on the understanding that rhythmically unstressed tones are those occurring on weak beats in relation to stronger beats or those falling on weak divisions of beats. What we are recognizing here differs somewhat from the distinction made between primary and secondary accents in Chapter 1. That distinction enables us to define the meter by measuring the distance between two primary accents, a distance marked by the number of intervening secondary accents. In order to define nonharmonic tones, however, secondary accents may be considered strong beats, particularly in relation to their divisions.

In example 9–1a, which has the half note as the value of the beat in $^2_2$ time, the second and fourth quarter notes are divisions of the beat and therefore weaker in relation to the first and third quarter notes. Using the same note durations in $^4_4$ time, 9–1b conveys a feeling of two beats per measure rather than four—despite the fact that now the quarter note rather than the half note represents the value of the beat. Thus, simulating duple meter within the framework of quadruple meter renders the quarters on the second and fourth beats weak in relation to the quarters on the first and third beats, just as they were in 9–1a.

If, however, the quadruple meter exhibits a clear expression of four beats, as proposed in the expression of $^4_4$ time in 9–1c, and if our intention is to define or use a nonharmonic tone, then we may want to recognize that *all four beats* would be strong in relation to their respective divisions.

To a great extent, then, the strength or weakness of a beat depends on how the meter is expressed and what questions we are asking. Moreover, such factors as syncopation further complicate the task of determining whether the nonharmonic tone is rhythmically stressed or unstressed. We will, for the most part, avoid rhythmic procedures that would impede our study of nonharmonic tones within their most natural and demonstrable settings.

Example 9–1: simple duple meter ($^2_2$ time) versus simple quadruple meter ($^4_4$ time)

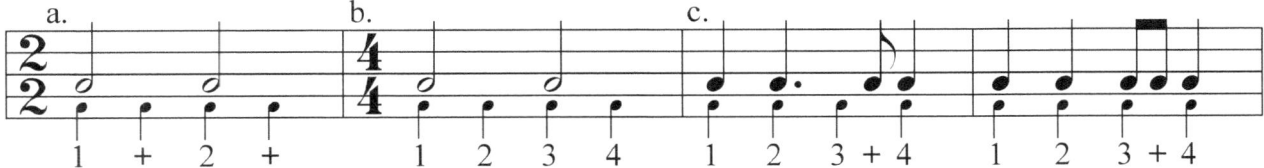

Non-Appoggiaturas

There are three types of non-appoggiaturas: the passing tone, the neighbor tone, and the anticipation tone. In general, all non-appoggiatura types constitute unaccented nonharmonic motions that usually precede and/or follow the inherent components of the chord. Although there are a few exceptions, nonharmonic tones generally resolve either by whole step or by half step. Examples 9–4b and 4c, 6, and 7 illustrate nonharmonic tones that lack stepwise resolutions. In this chapter, a plus sign attached to a note indicates a tone with an unaccented nonharmonic function.

The Passing Tone

The passing tone is approached and left by step and occurs on either a strong or weak beat; it also appears on either a strong or weak portion of a beat. Hence, the passing tone belongs to both classes of nonharmonic tones: appoggiaturas and non-appoggiaturas.

Example 9–2 shows the unaccented variety of passing tone, ascending (9–2a) and descending (examples 9–2b and 2c). Passing tones are either consonant or dissonant with another voice and may occur within one chord (9–2a) or between different chords (9–2b). Typically, a single passing tone fills in the interval of a 3rd, connecting one chord tone to another; however, more than one passing tone may lead in direct succession to another. Further, the passing tone may serve a *harmonic* function as a component of the chord. For example, the second passing tone in 9–2c (E, second eighth note, alto voice) is the chord third of the C-major triad.

Example 9–2: the passing tone

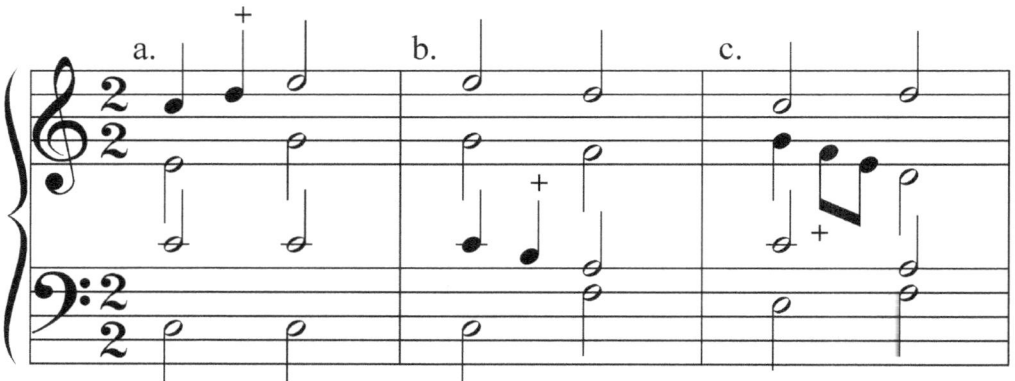

The Complete Neighbor Tone

A neighbor tone usually moves by step, upwards or downwards, from a preceding tone and may be either consonant or dissonant with the bass. Neighbor tones, which are also known as auxiliary tones, occur within the same chord or between different chords. As demonstrated in example 9–3, a neighbor tone that returns to the tone to which it has left is described as complete. (We shall encounter the incomplete neighbor in subsequent examples.)

Example 9–3a (alto voice) shows a neighbor tone moving upwards from the tone that preceded it, a complete upper neighbor. Example 9–3b (tenor voice) demonstrates a neighbor tone moving downwards from the tone that introduced it, a complete lower neighbor. The sharp in parentheses indicates that we have an F♯ as an option for the neighbor. In this instance, we prefer the F♯ because the lower neighbor usually stands a minor 2nd rather than a major 2nd below the tone it decorates.

Example 9–3: the complete neighbor tone

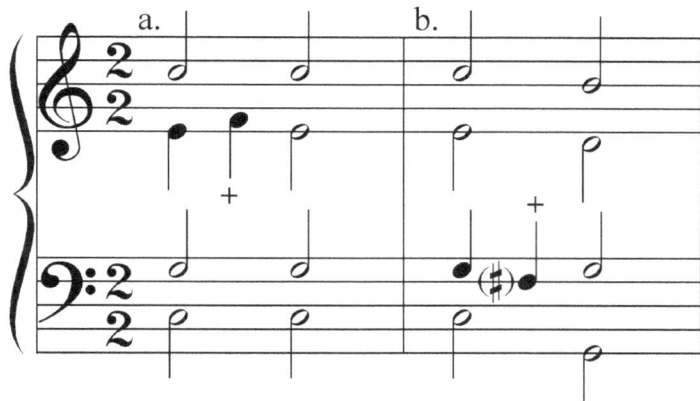

The Complete and Incomplete Changing-Note Group (Double Neighbor)

The changing-note group, which is also called the double neighbor, has *two* unaccented neighbors occurring in either direct or indirect succession. Example 9–4a shows an indirect succession of neighbors in which a chord tone appears between them, whereas examples 9–4b and 4c display a direct succession of neighbors without an intervening chord tone. Thus, we apply the term changing-note group to any figure that has two unaccented neighbors (that is, double neighbors) in either direct or indirect succession.

Example 9–4 exhibits both complete and incomplete changing-note groups:
(1) if the first of the two neighbors returns to the tone that it has left, that is, the principal tone, then the changing-note group is complete and presents an indirect succession (9–4a: the complete changing-note group);
(2) if the first neighbor proceeds to the second neighbor without returning to the principal tone first, then the group is incomplete and presents a direct succession (examples 9–4b and 4c: the incomplete changing-note group).

Ultimately, the second neighbor of the changing-note group (in both its complete and incomplete forms) *resolves by whole step or by half step into the principal tone of the figure* (in this case, E).

If the principal tone does not appear immediately before *and* after the neighbor tone, then the neighbor is referred to as incomplete. The alto F in 9–4b is an incomplete upper neighbor to the preceding E; the alto D is an incomplete lower neighbor to the following E. The alto D in 9–4c is an incomplete lower neighbor to the preceding E; the alto F is an incomplete upper neighbor to the following E.

Example 9–4: complete and incomplete changing-note group

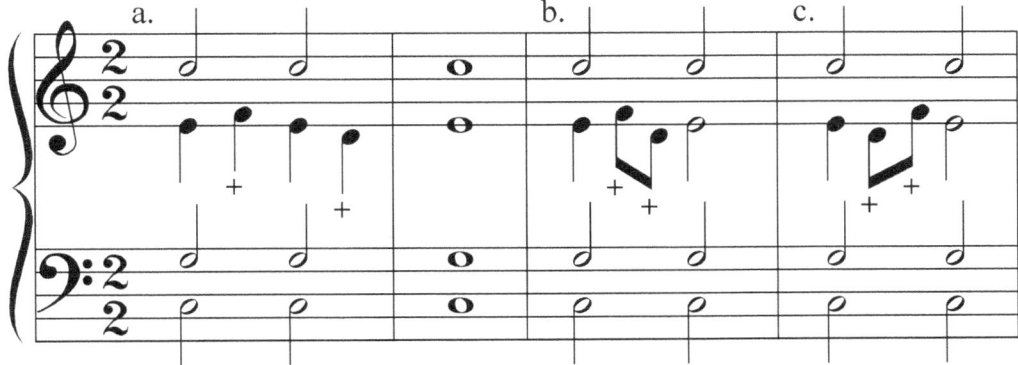

Special Uses of the Incomplete Neighbor Tone: the Cambiata and the Échappée

The cambiata (pronounced cam-bee-yah-tah) *begins with a leap and ends with a stepwise resolution*, becoming an incomplete neighbor to the chord tone it addresses. The arrows in example 9–5 demonstrate the operation of the cambiata figure, which leaps one pitch beyond the tone of resolution, overreaching the harmonic component of the next chord before resolving into it. In 9–5a, the cambiata figure reaches upwards (in the tenor) from G to B before reversing direction and settling on A; and in 9–5b, it moves downwards (in the soprano) from D to B before reversing direction and resolving to C.

Example 9–5: the cambiata

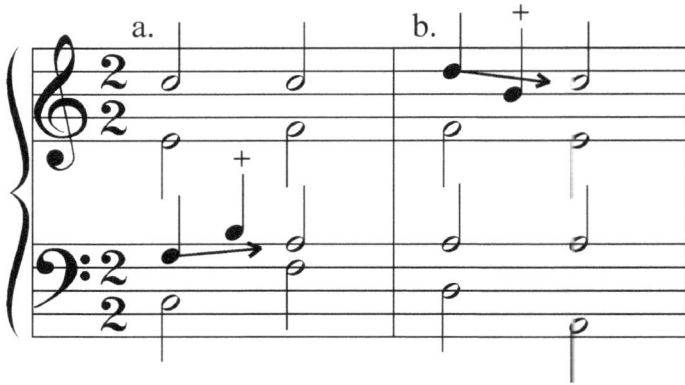

The échappée (pronounced ā-shah-pay), or escape tone, *begins with stepwise motion and ends with a leap into the tone of resolution*, becoming an incomplete neighbor to the chord tone it leaves. If the tone of resolution is part of a descending line, as in example 9–6a (E down to D, soprano), then the échappée (F) moves upwards in the opposite direction. If the tone of resolution is part of an ascending line, as in 9–6b (E up to F, alto), then the échappée (D) proceeds downwards in the opposite direction.

Example 9–6: the échappée

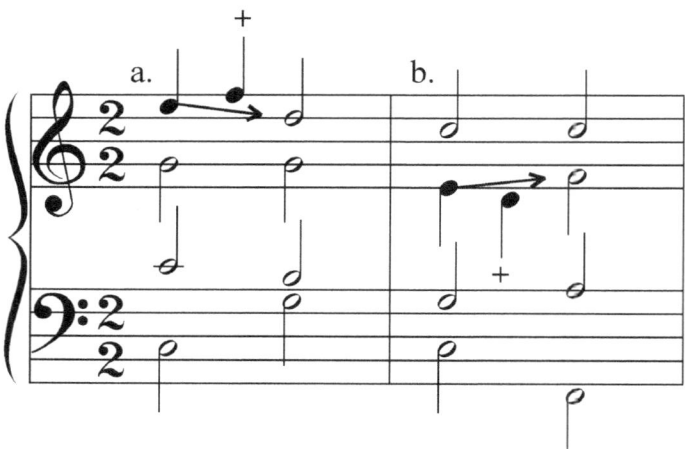

And so, while both the cambiata and the échappée fall within the category of non-appoggiaturas, they present entirely different linear operations:
(1) the cambiata figure leaps to a nonharmonic tone and then moves by whole step or by half step to a chord tone (9–5); whereas,
(2) the échappée figure moves by whole step or by half step to a nonharmonic tone and then leaps to a chord tone (9–6).

Other Incomplete Neighbor Tones

Examples 9–7a and 7b present an incomplete neighbor that neither overreaches the harmonic component of the next chord (as in the cambiata) nor moves against the prevailing direction of the line (as in the échappée). However, the respective operations of the incomplete neighbor shown below and the échappée are basically the same: both are approached by stepwise motion and left by leap.

In 9–7, the incomplete neighbor reduces the size of the leap into the chord tone on beat 2 from a 5th to a 4th: G up to D becomes A up to D (9–7a) and E down to A becomes D down to A (9–7b). (On beat 2 of 9–7a, the inclusion of the F in the alto voice produces a chord consisting of the tones G B D F, a dominant seventh with its third, B, in the bass.)

Example 9–7: other incomplete neighbors

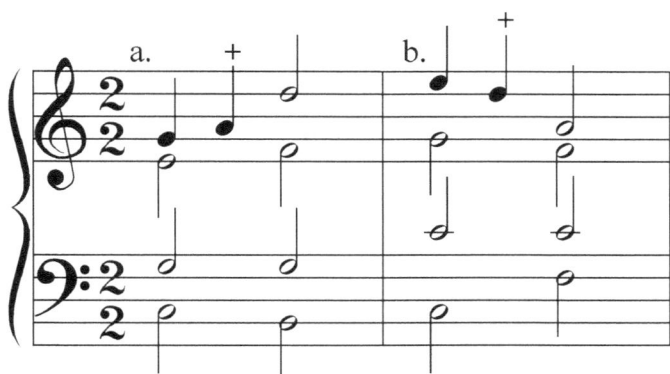

The Anticipation Tone

The anticipation tone previews one of the harmonic components of the following chord, bringing that component forward in time. Since the pitch remains the same when it occurs subsequently within the chord to which it belongs, the previewed tone has no actual resolution and may be either dissonant or consonant with the bass. As example 9–8 confirms, the preview (see the plus sign) assumes the status of a chord tone either in the voice of its initial appearance or in another voice.

In examples 9–8a and 8b, the preview remains in the same voice as the tone it anticipates. Examples 9–8c and 8d exhibit a less typical use of the anticipation in which the preview tone is transferred into another voice when the chord changes (see the dotted line). Ultimately, placing the anticipation tone in another voice produces an incomplete neighbor and transforms the anticipation figure into an échappée (as in examples 9–8c and 8d). (Note the dominant seventh with the omitted fifth on beat 1 of 9–8a and the complete dominant seventh on beat 1 of 8b.)

Example 9–8: the anticipation tone

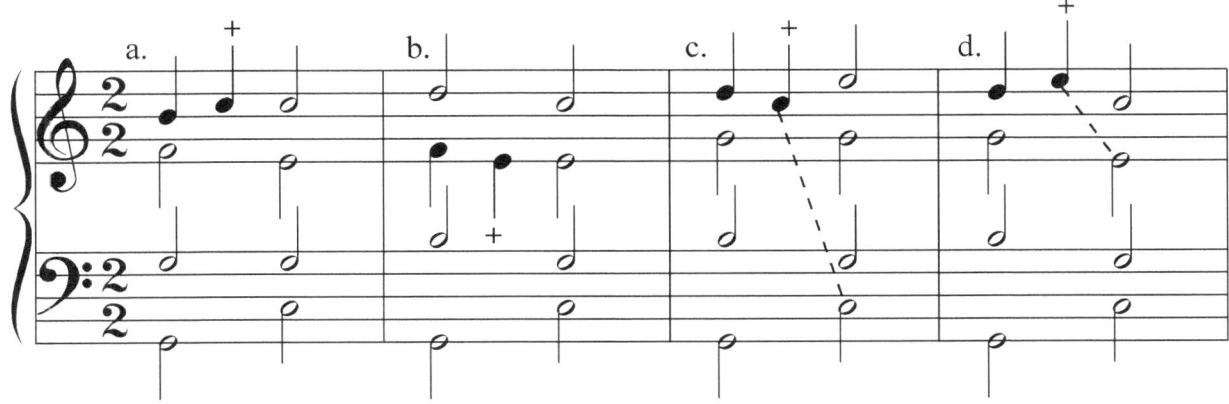

Appoggiaturas

There are four types of appoggiaturas: the passing tone, the complete neighbor tone, the suspension, and finally, the incomplete neighbor, termed here the appoggiatura itself. In general, all appoggiatura types constitute accented nonharmonic motions that usually precede and/or follow inherent components of the chord. As with most of the other nonharmonic tones, appoggiaturas have stepwise resolutions. In this text, a circled plus sign identifies the nonharmonic element as an appoggiatura type, as a rhythmically stressed tone.

The Accented Passing Tone

The accented passing tone is virtually the same as the unaccented passing tone except that the former has been shifted to a strong beat or strong portion of a beat. As we have said, the passing tone is approached and left by step. Example 9–9 presents the accented passing tone in its ascending (9–9a) and descending (9–9b) forms.

Appoggiaturas in general are usually found with a change of harmony. Later in this chapter, however, we shall find a few instances in which the nonharmonic tone appears within the framework of a single chord but nonetheless qualifies as an appoggiatura type.

Example 9–9: the accented passing tone

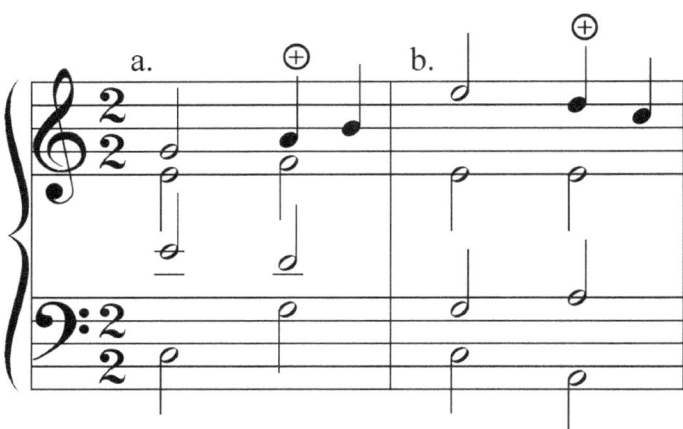

The Accented Complete Neighbor Tone

The accented complete neighbor, like the accented passing tone, is approached and left by stepwise motion (example 9–10). In example 9–10b, the accented lower neighbor appears as a rhythmically stressed tone resolving upwards by half step to the chord third.

Example 9–10b is but one illustration of the upward resolution of a rhythmically stressed tone; we shall also encounter this operation in examples 9–11b and 9–14. It should be noted that the accented lower neighbor frequently lies one half step below the tone of resolution in order to draw a closer connection between the nonharmonic tone and the pitch to which it proceeds.

Example 9–10: the accented neighbor tone

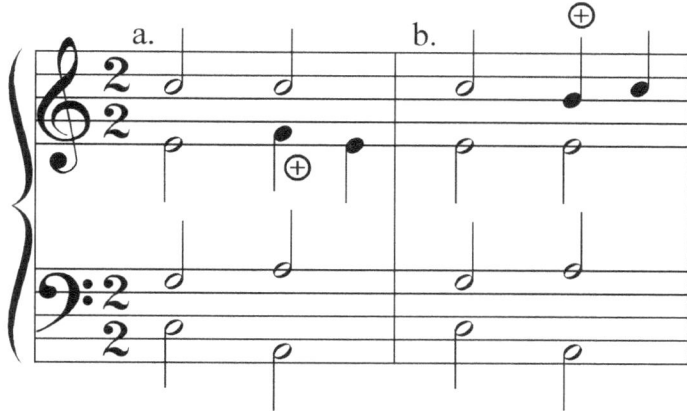

The Appoggiatura Itself (the Incomplete Neighbor Tone)

At the end of Chapter 4, we observed that the Italian term appoggiatura comes from the verb *appoggiare*, one meaning of which is to lean. In musical terms, the appoggiatura refers to an accented dissonance that resolves by step to a consonance (that is, the accented dissonance "leans" into the consonance).

This chapter presents the appoggiatura as a general category within which various subtypes of accented nonharmonic tones are evident. One subtype, which operates as either an accented upper or lower neighbor, is the appoggiatura itself. In order to assume the form of an incomplete neighbor, the appoggiatura itself must be introduced by leap.

The appoggiatura in example 9–11a has an upward leap into a major 9th which then resolves downwards to the root of a C-major triad; the nonharmonic tone (D) constitutes an accented incomplete upper neighbor to the tone of resolution (C). In 9–11b, an augmented 4th resolves upwards to the chord fifth of an F-major triad; the nonharmonic tone (B) becomes an accented incomplete lower neighbor to the tone of resolution (C).

Example 9–11: the appoggiatura itself

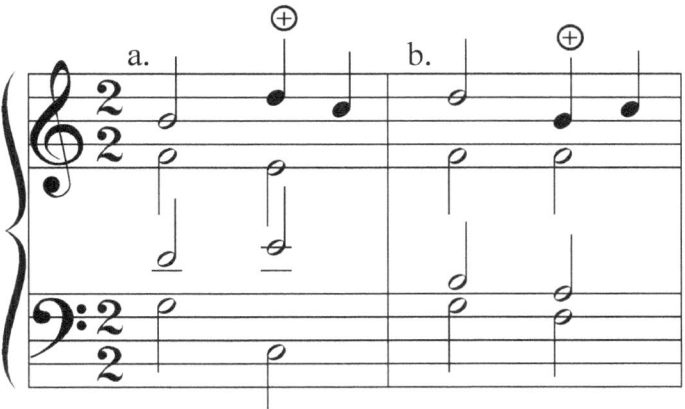

The Suspension

In Chapter 4, we found that the operation of the suspension was one of the central factors in the development of the cadential $^6_4$. The suspension has three parts:

(1) the suspension is *prepared*, usually as a consonance (but not always, see example 9–12d below);
(2) the preparation is held, or *suspended*, as the opposing voice (usually the bass) moves to form a dissonance with the suspended voice (though a consonant suspension is also possible); and finally,
(3) the suspended voice moves down by step to *resolve* to a consonance. (Example 9–14 shows the suspension with an exceptional upward resolution.)

As we have stipulated, the actual suspension (part 2) is metrically stronger than the resolution (part 3). The initial preparation (part 1), however, can be made from either a strong or weak position.

Example 9–12a demonstrates a suspended 7th in the soprano voice, producing a 7—6 suspension. Over the stationary bass, the 7th resolves to a consonant 6th on the weak portion of the beat.

In 9–12b, the resolution of the dissonant 7th in the soprano from D to C receives a "decoration" in the form of a chromatic passing tone, D♭; this process is referred to properly as a "decorated resolution." It is also possible to use other nonharmonic figures such as the anticipation tone, the cambiata, and the échappée to decorate the resolution. Notice that the tone of resolution falls in the same place within the measure as it would have without the decoration.

Example 9–12c is not a suspension. Instead, we have shortened the process introduced in 9–12b by leaving out the suspended tone (D) and proceeding directly to the chromatic passing tone (D♭). In so doing, however, we lose the suspension and gain an accented chromatic passing tone.

Example 9–12d illustrates a *dissonant* preparation of the suspension in the alto voice. The dissonant 7th of the dominant chord on G is suspended into the tonic chord on C to produce a dissonant 4th, which then resolves to the chord third on the weak portion of the beat (4—3).

Example 9–12: the suspension (downward)

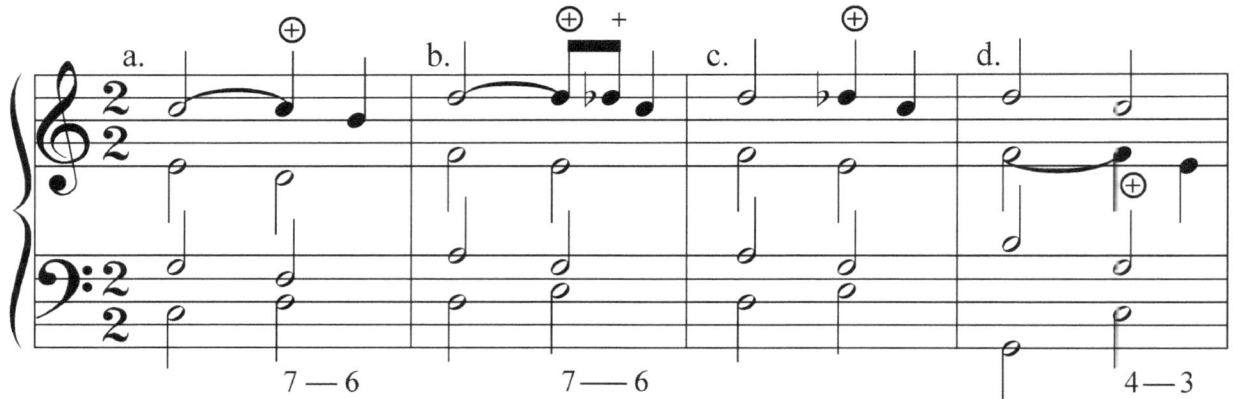

When writing for soprano, alto, tenor, and bass, it is best to withhold the tone of a downward resolution from all of the upper parts except for the suspended voice. In other words, you should not "preview" the tone of resolution in any upper voice other than the suspended voice because it spoils the expected resolution.

Examples 9–13a and 13b present two different dispositions of the 7—6 suspension between the bass and the soprano. Play both examples on the piano. You will discover that the suspension in 9–13a is more successful than that of 13b because the resolution of the dissonant C is confined to the suspended voice; no other voice above the bass carries B, the tone of resolution. Example 9–13b, on the other hand, previews the B in the tenor voice, undermining the strength of the resolution.

Example 9–13c illustrates the only exception to our recommendation for avoiding a preview of the resolution. If the suspension involves the interval of the 9th moving to an octave, a 9—8 suspension, then the bottom note of the 9th and the tone of resolution are one and the same. In a four-voice texture, the best position for the bottom note of the 9th is the bass voice.

Therefore, the tone of resolution for the 9—8 suspension typically appears in the bass. Previewing the tone of resolution in the bass for the 9—8 suspension is acceptable because the bottom note of the 9th is likely to be the root, which finds its most natural position to be the generating voice for the chord, the bass.

Example 9–13: previewing the tone of resolution

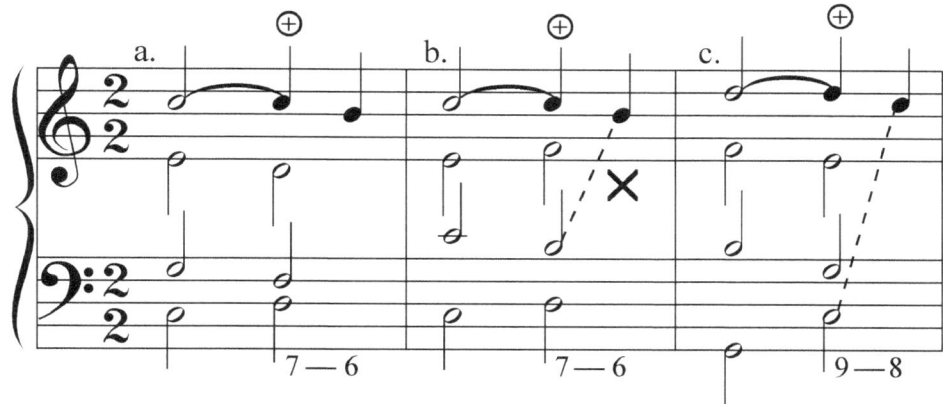

Most suspensions take downward resolutions; however, some suspensions have upward resolutions. Example 9–14a demonstrates the most common upward resolution of the suspension. As an upper voice of a dominant-family chord, the leading tone (B) is suspended into the tonic chord. The resolution of the dissonant 7th proceeds upwards to the tonic scale degree, producing a 7—8 motion over the stationary bass (C). The upward resolution of a suspension is sometimes referred to as a retardation, a term traditionally reserved for the suspension. However, in a more general sense, retardation may describe any upward resolution of an accented nonharmonic tone.

It is also possible to suspend two or more voices simultaneously, one of which might involve retardation. Example 9–14b shows how to suspend the third, fifth, and seventh components of the dominant seventh into the tonic triad, producing multiple 9—8, 7—8, and 4—3 motions over the bass. As with the cadential $^6_4$ chord (see Chapter 4), the circle around the figured bass attached to the chord symbol indicates that the real chord is formed on the second half of beat 2.

Example 9–14: the suspension (upward)

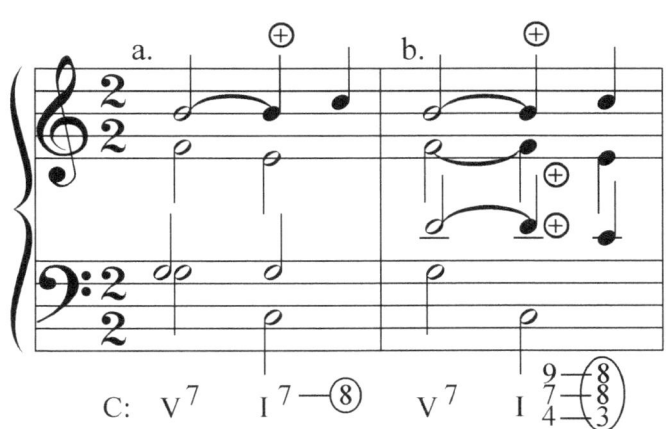

190   Chapter 9 Nonharmonic Tones

Using Appoggiatura Tones without a Change of Harmony

As we have said, *accented* nonharmonic tones are usually found with a change of harmony. Indeed, motion between unlike chords strengthens the effect of the nonharmonic tone. However, under certain circumstances, the nonharmonic tone may appear within the framework of a single chord and still constitute an appoggiatura type. As demonstrated in examples 9–15 and 16 (see the circled plus signs), a nonharmonic tone that occurs within a single chord is an appoggiatura type if it

(1) falls on beat 1 (9–15a, measure 2);
(2) is syncopated (9–15b, soprano) or otherwise stressed (9–15b, beat 2, tenor);
(3) is an incomplete neighbor on any beat, especially a *chromatic* incomplete lower neighbor (9–15c);

Example 9–15: appoggiaturas within the same chord

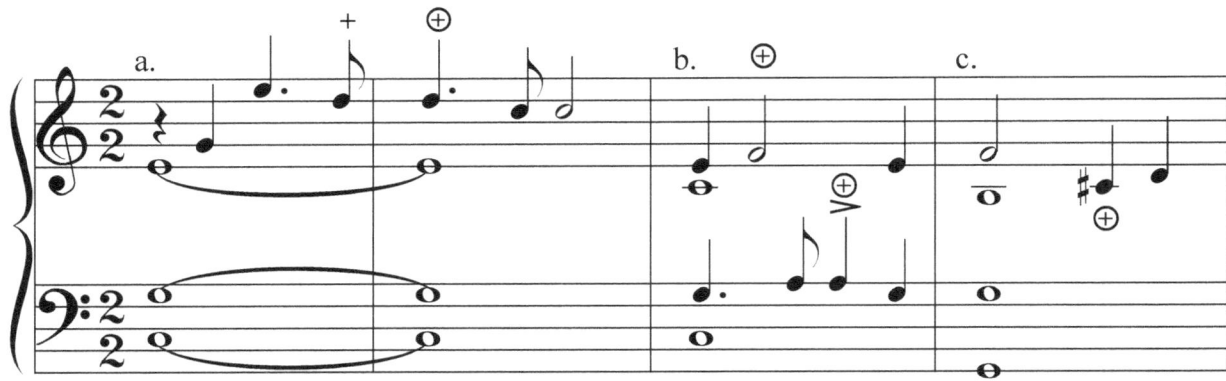

(4) is a complete neighbor or passing tone that resolves to a chord tone within the same beat (9–16a);
(5) is a passing tone that continues to another passing tone within the same beat (9–16b);
(6) is the first component of an incomplete changing-note group (double neighbor) within the same beat (9–16c).

Example 9–16: appoggiaturas within the same chord

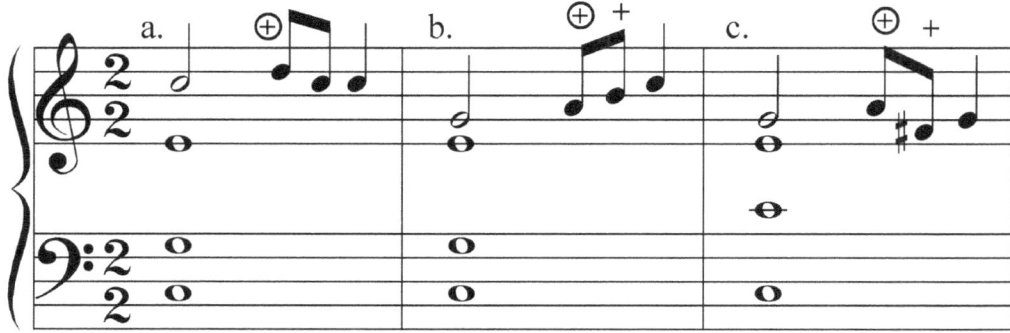

Accented Correctives to Faulty Motion: the Suspension, Incomplete Neighbor, and Passing Tone

This section examines how to solve voice-leading problems with nonharmonic tones; additionally, we shall come to understand that using nonharmonic tones as correctives to faulty motion is not without its limitations.

Example 9–17 demonstrates the suspension as a corrective to parallel 5ths and octaves. In each instance, one of the two components of the second 5th (or octave) is shifted out of alignment so that the two pitches of the offending interval sound separately rather than together (we first encountered this operation in example 6–6, pp. 125–126). (In 9–17, S, A, T, and B are abbreviations for soprano, alto, tenor, and bass respectively. The curved lines located between the numeric figures indicate the placement of the suspension. Dotted lines represent the parallel 5ths or octaves that would result without the corrective application of the suspension.)

The suspension transforms the motion to the second interval from a parallel to an oblique disposition. In the soprano and bass of 9–17a, the parallel 5ths from G/D to F/C become G/D to F/D to F/C. The tone of resolution, C, occurs on the second half of beat 2. Both the D and the C in the soprano voice (beat 2) present oblique motion against the F in the bass. The 6—5 motion disrupts the vertical alignment of the second 5th, breaking up the parallel 5ths and preserving the independence of the two lines. The suspension in example 9–17b breaks up the parallel 5ths by displacing one of the two pitches of the second 5th, initiating a 4—5 move between the soprano and alto.

In example 3–23 (Chapter 3), we introduced the chordal skip as an effective *harmonic* agent for breaking up parallel octaves. Some theorists maintain that only the chordal skip (also known as the consonant skip) is capable of breaking up parallel octaves. Consisting of the fundamental pitch and its first overtone, the octave is inherently more stable than intervals containing two different pitches. Although this stability makes the octave (or the unison) an effective closing device at the end of a music composition, the sense of stasis it conveys can also impede the forward motion of the voice leading and undermine the independence of the voices if used improperly.

The 9—8 suspension, as presented in 9–17c, constitutes the sole *nonharmonic* corrective to parallel octaves. The suspension of the 9th (E), which is dissonant with both the root and the bass of a D-minor seventh chord, shifts one of the two pitches of the second octave out of alignment (producing oblique motion), providing a sense of motion to an otherwise immobile interval.

Example 9–17: the suspension as a corrective to parallel 5ths and octaves

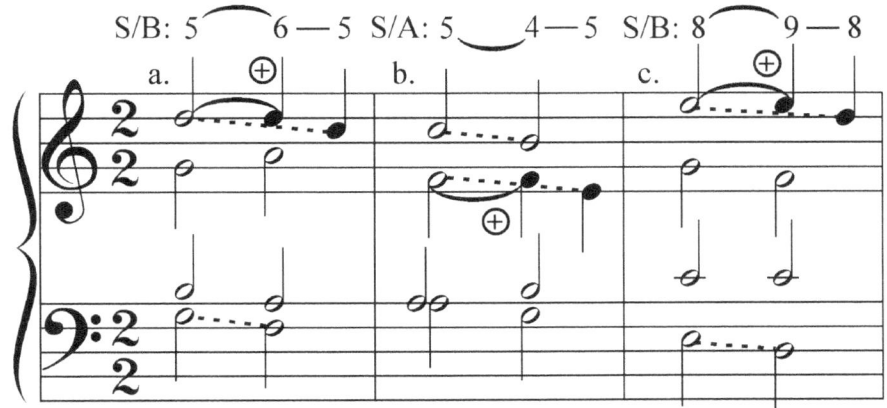

Example 9–18 outlines two additional ways to avert parallel 5ths with accented nonharmonic tones: the appoggiatura itself, or more specifically, the accented incomplete upper neighbor (examples 9–18a and 18c) and the accented incomplete lower neighbor (9–18b); and secondly, the accented passing tone (9–18d).

Examples 9–18a and 18c have downward resolutions, whereas examples 9–18b and 18d illustrate upward resolutions (retardations). Both of the upward nonharmonic tones are dissonant with the bass. It should be emphasized, however, that either dissonant or consonant expressions of the nonharmonic tone will correct parallel 5ths *as long as the two pitches of the second 5th are prevented from occurring simultaneously.*

Example 9–18: the accented incomplete neighbor and passing tone as correctives to parallel 5ths

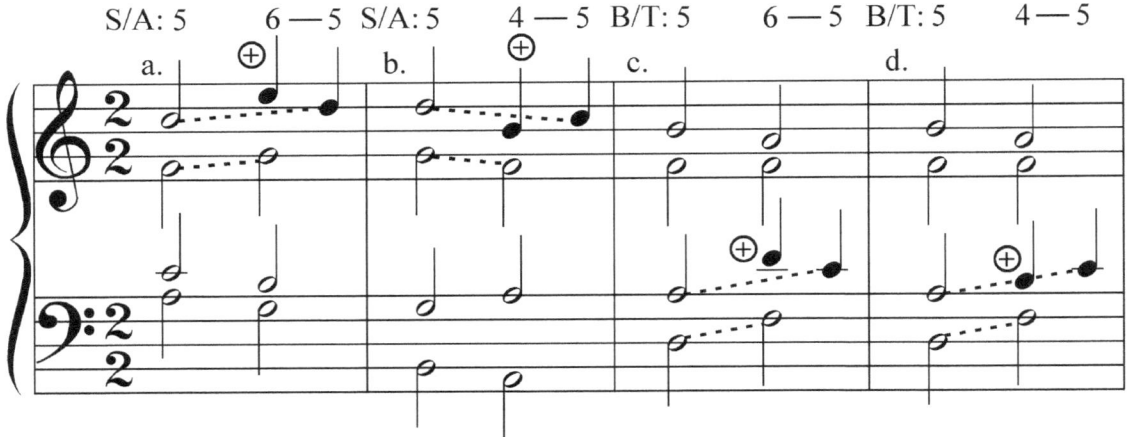

Unaccented Correctives to Faulty Motion: the Anticipation and the Exceptional Use of the Cambiata

In the foregoing section, we learned that the suspension, accented incomplete neighbor, and accented passing tone are all successful voice-leading correctives because they transform faulty parallel motion into oblique by *delaying* one of the two components of the second problematic interval. The rhythmic stress that each operation receives prevents both pitches of the second interval from sounding simultaneously.

The anticipation, shown in example 9–19 on the second half of beat 1, also shifts the two pitches of the second interval out of alignment; however, as an *unaccented* nonharmonic tone, it produces the opposite effect of the accented nonharmonic figures cited above. Instead of delaying one of the two components of the second interval, the anticipation brings one of them *forward* in time, in advance of the chord change.

In 9–19a, the soprano voice previews the fifth of the D-minor seventh. The root of an F-major triad (in first inversion) is anticipated in the alto of 9–19b, while the fifth of a G-major triad appears in the soprano before the chord change in 9–19c. Although the anticipation effectively breaks up parallel 5ths, it cannot overcome the tonal stability of the octave (or the unison).

Example 9–19: the anticipation as a corrective to parallel 5ths (but not parallel octaves)

In its role as an unaccented incomplete upper neighbor, the cambiata constitutes an interesting adaptation of, or perhaps substitute for, the chordal skip. The exceptional use of the cambiata, as demonstrated in example 9–20c, corrects the voice-leading difficulties that arise between two chords whose roots are a 2nd apart, a root relationship fraught with the danger of parallel 5ths and octaves.

Example 9–20a illustrates one disposition of the problem: parallel 5ths between the bass and alto voices. Example 9–20b eliminates the faulty motion between the two chords with the addition of a seventh to the first chord. The seventh provides a smoother connection to the second chord and results in a 7 5 motion in the alto voice (F to E). (Recall that if there is a rising 2nd root relationship between two chords, the seventh of the first chord will move down by step to become the fifth of the second chord.)

Example 9–20c shows the chord fifth leaping into the seventh on the second half of beat 1 (D to F). The downward resolution of the dissonant seventh within the second chord completes the cambiata figure and successfully breaks up the parallel 5ths. Since the motion between the two chord tones produces a harmonic dissonance rather than a consonance, the leap should not be referred to as a chordal skip. At best, we might call the move from the fifth to the seventh an *apparent* chordal skip.

Example 9–20: the unaccented incomplete upper neighbor as a dissonant corrective to parallel 5ths

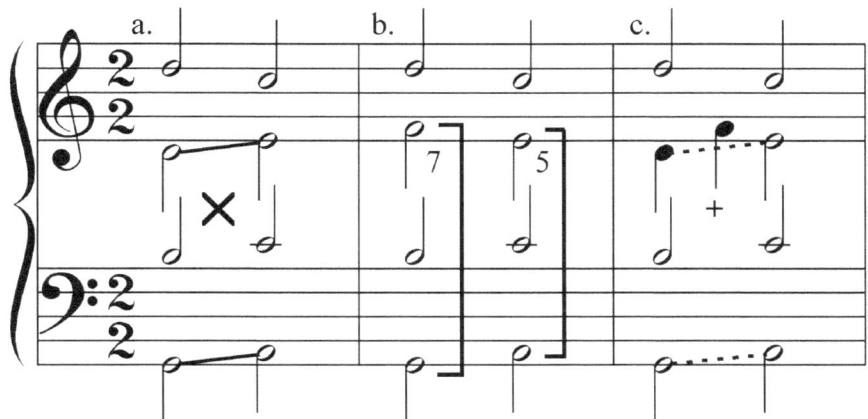

Unaccented Nonharmonic Tones that Fail to Correct Faulty Parallel Motion

As we observed in the previous section, there are only two circumstances in which unaccented nonharmonic tones avert faulty parallel 5ths:

(1) the anticipation tone, and,
(2) the cambiata as an unaccented incomplete upper neighbor, *when the relationship between the two chords produces a motion involving the seventh of one chord resolving into the fifth of the next chord.*

Example 9–21a illustrates the unsuccessful use of the cambiata. Here, the cambiata tone (E) is *consonant* with the bass. The components of each perfect 5th occur simultaneously on each beat. To be sure, we might interpret the E as the seventh component of an F-major chord in first inversion; however, placing the root in the alto voice instead of in the bass undermines the strength of what would otherwise be a 7 5 motion (F/E to G/D). Notice that the cambiata tone in 9–21a also creates parallel 5ths between the bass and the soprano (A/E to G/D). (In the next section, we shall find a more acceptable disposition of parallel 5ths in which one of the offending intervals constitutes a nonessential 5th, that is, a 5th containing a nonharmonic tone.)

The unaccented passing tone in 9–21b is too insignificant an event to overcome the simultaneous sounding of perfect 5ths on each beat. The échappée in 9–21c is no more effective in correcting parallel 5ths than either the consonant cambiata or the passing tone; the parallel 5ths on each beat remain undisturbed. Although the anticipation offered in 9–21d transforms parallel motion into oblique, it is not strong enough to surmount the inherent stability of the octave.

Example 9–21: unaccented nonharmonic tones that cannot correct faulty motion

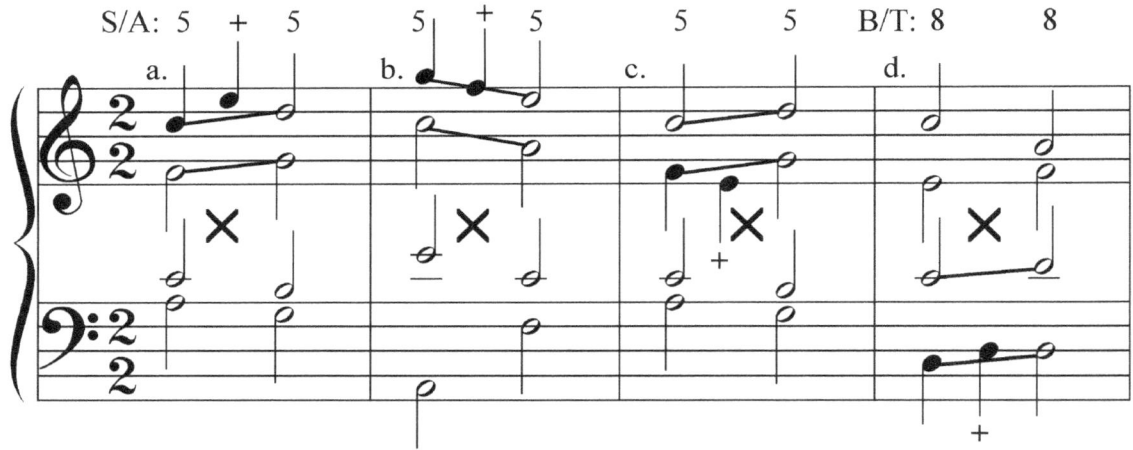

Unaccented Dissonant Nonharmonic Tones Causing Acceptable Parallel 5ths

In some cases, when a *dissonant* nonharmonic tone *creates* parallel 5ths, we allow its use because the tone does not constitute part of a chordal 5th. That is to say, the nonharmonic tone produces a 5th in which only one of its two components is related to the chord. Such 5ths are superficial and incapable of compromising the individuality of each melodic line. Example 9–22 presents the conditions under which dissonant neighbor, passing, and anticipation tones produce acceptable parallel 5ths.

In example 9–22a, a complete upper neighbor in the soprano produces a 5th with the alto; however, since it forms a dissonant 7th with the bass, the neighbor belongs to neither chord. Forming a dissonant 9th with the bass, the passing tone in 9–22b creates a nonessential 5th between the soprano and alto.

In the soprano of 9–22c, a dissonant anticipation tone (C) previews the root of the second chord, whereas the alto contains a passing 7th related to the first chord but dissonant with both. A nonessential 5th results from the combination; therefore, the basic connections between the two chords, a G-major triad and C-major triad, remain undisturbed.

Example 9–22: the dissonant neighbor, passing tone, and anticipation causing acceptable parallel 5ths

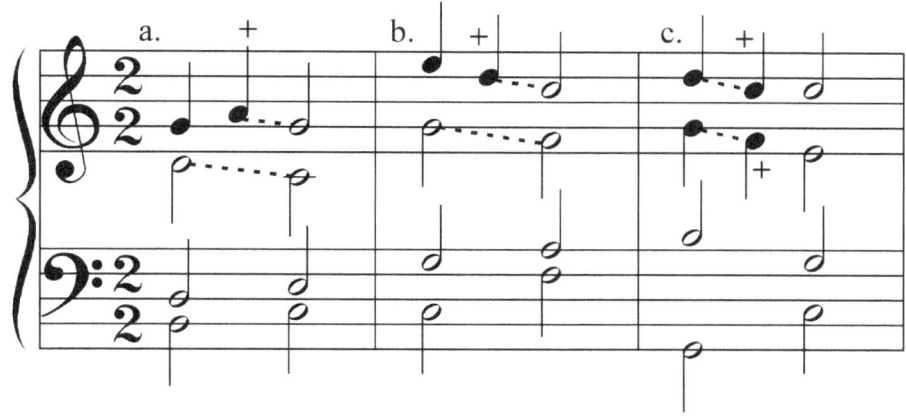

Nonharmonic Tones in Combination

Example 9–22c above raised the possibility of using more than one nonharmonic tone simultaneously. The first guiding principle for this operation is that each nonharmonic tone must be handled correctly in its own part. Assuming that we have met this requirement and avoided all types of faulty motion, it is permissible to use nonharmonic tones consonant with each other in any combination and resolution.

In example 9–23, we have various treatments of nonharmonic tones in consonant combinations. Four of these combinations involve chord changes (examples 9–23a, 23b, 23d, and 23e); four are unaccented (examples 9–23a, 23b, 23c, and 23e) and one accented (9–23d).

Of the unaccented types, 9–23a combines the passing tone (alto) and complete upper neighbor (tenor), 23b the complete upper neighbor (alto) and incomplete lower neighbor (tenor), 23c the complete upper neighbor (soprano and alto), and 23e the échappée (alto) and cambiata (tenor).

The accented combination of nonharmonic tones in 9–23d consists of the complete upper neighbor (soprano) and appoggiatura itself (tenor, also described as an incomplete lower neighbor).

Example 9–23: nonharmonic tones in consonant combinations

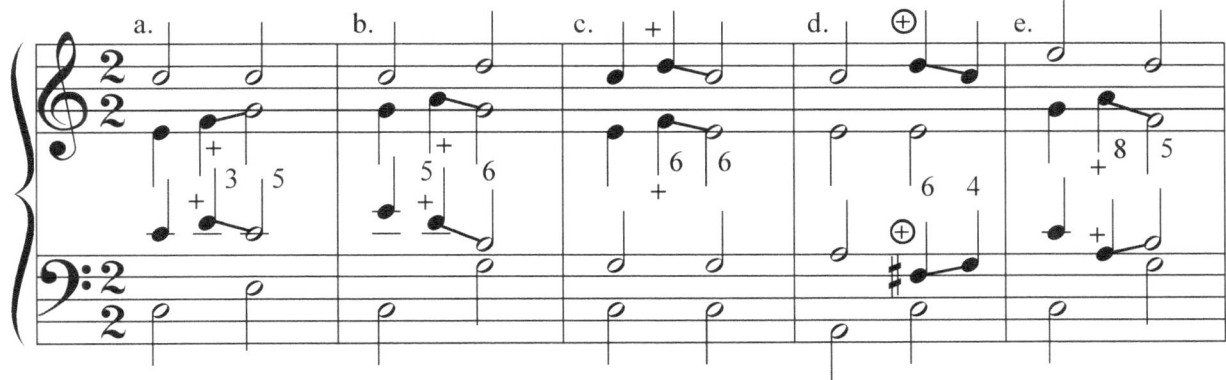

196 Chapter 9 Nonharmonic Tones

Avoid Conflicts Between the Resolution of the Suspension and Other Nonharmonic Tones

Finally, study example 9–24. Notice that a dissonant unaccented upper neighbor in the tenor voice of 9–24b occurs simultaneously with the resolution of the suspension in the soprano voice. This is a poor result, as it prevents a complete disposition of the G-major triad from being heard clearly. Therefore, avoid using an unaccented nonharmonic tone in one voice at the same time that another voice resolves any appoggiatura type.

Example 9–24c solves the problem by simply lengthening the note value in the tenor, thus delaying the entry of the upper neighbor until *after* the resolution of the suspension has taken place.

Example 9–24: avoid interfering with the resolution of an accented nonharmonic tone

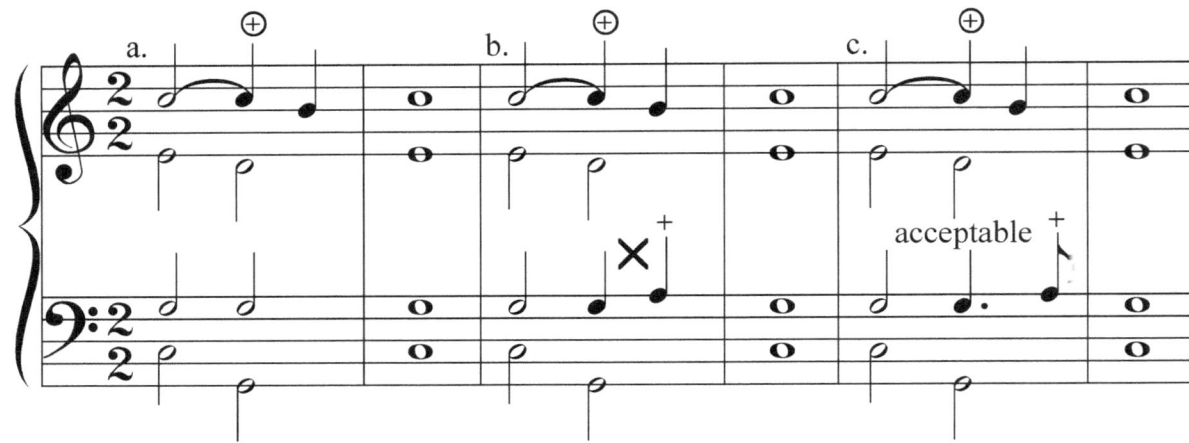

Appendix A Keyboard Harmony

This appendix presents chord progressions in keyboard style, a style that assigns the bass line to the left hand (F clef) and some or all of the chord tones to the right hand (G clef). The pitches played by the right hand remain within the range of a single octave to facilitate performance, as the reach of most hands is usually limited to an octave. The range restrictions of vocal writing, however, are not applied to the keyboard style.

The stem direction of the notes is determined by the principles put forward in Chapter 1. If the stemmed note occurs above the center line, then the stem points downwards. If the stemmed note occurs below the center line, then the stem points upwards. Stemmed notes located on the center line point in either direction according to the musical context. If most of the notes in a chord (in the right hand) take upward stems, then all of the notes are stemmed above the center line. If, however, most of the notes in a chord take downward stems, then all of the notes are stemmed below the center line. Occasionally, we may contradict the principle of stem direction if it improves the notation of the progression. (An alternative keyboard style for the right hand assigns an upward stem to the soprano line and a downward stem to the other tones of the chord.)

Whenever possible, the keyboard style should adhere to the principles of voice leading outlined in Chapter 3. Hence, the exercises in this appendix avoid incorrect motion, especially between the outer voices; resolve sensitive intervals such as 4ths and 7ths; move variable scale degrees correctly; and, observe the optimal doubling of chord tones.

Any two pitches preceded by dotted lines provide the reader with the option of moving to either note of the pair (as in the left hand of exercise 1, either great G or small g). These exercises should be practiced as written in C major and C minor before transposing them to any of the sharp or flat keys. Later in this appendix, the following abbreviations are used: BCP (basic contrapuntal progression); SHP (secondary harmonic progression; and, SCP (secondary contrapuntal progression).

Exercise A–1: secondary harmonic progression, the X-chord with scale degree 2 in the bass

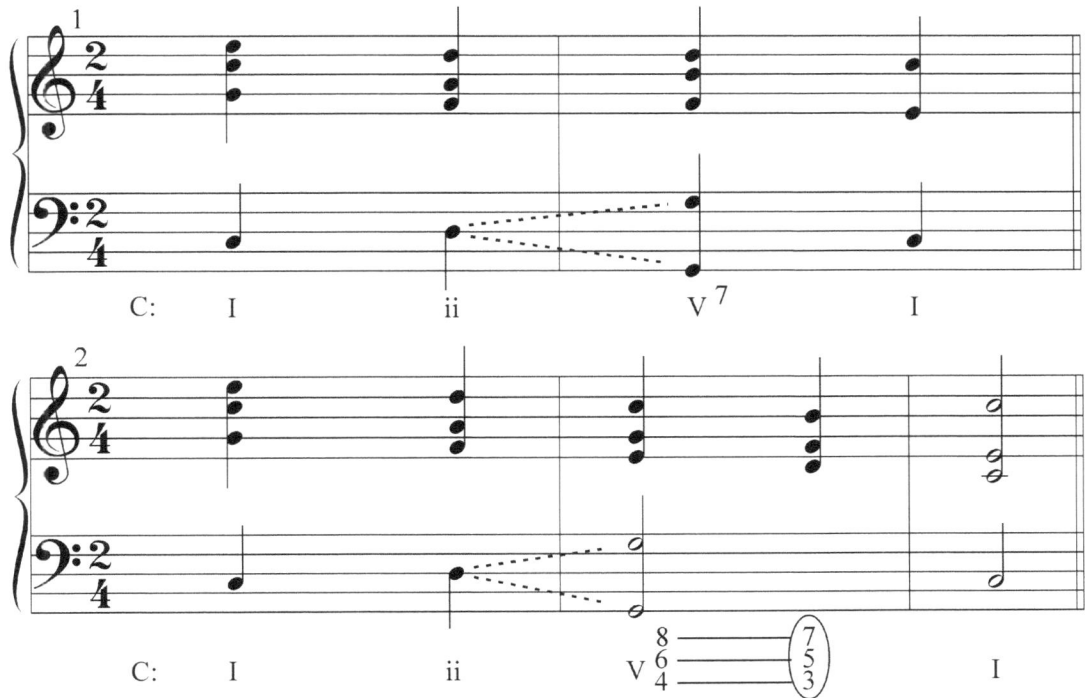

Exercise A–2: secondary harmonic progression, the X-chord with scale degree 2 in the bass

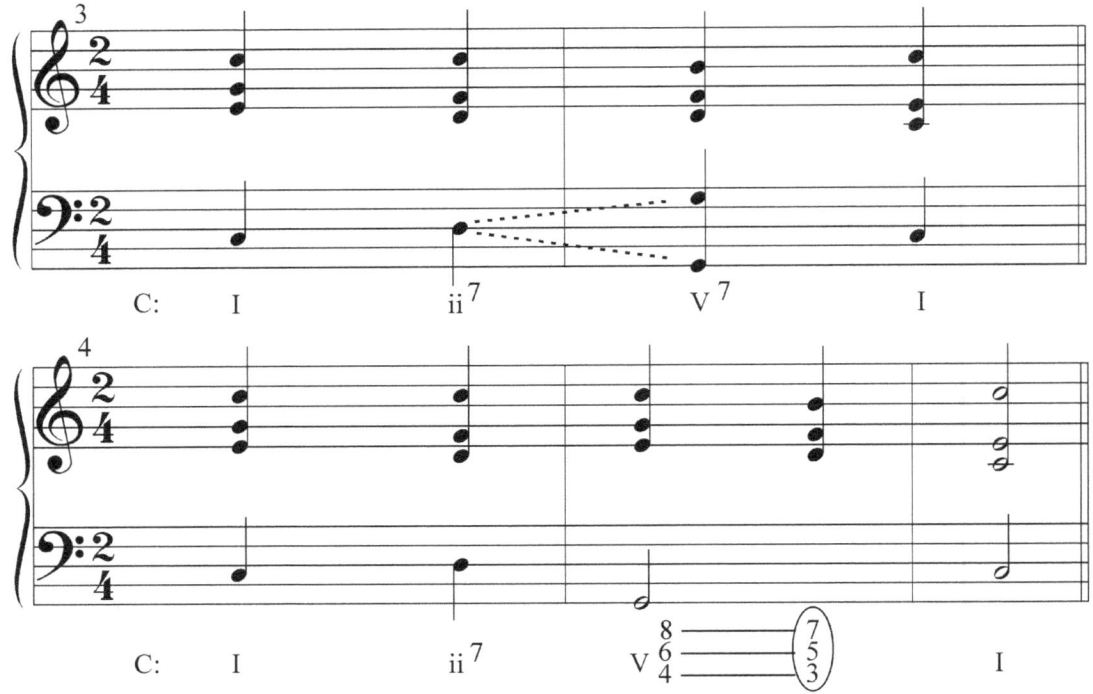

Exercise A–3: secondary harmonic progression, the X-chord with scale degree 2 in the bass

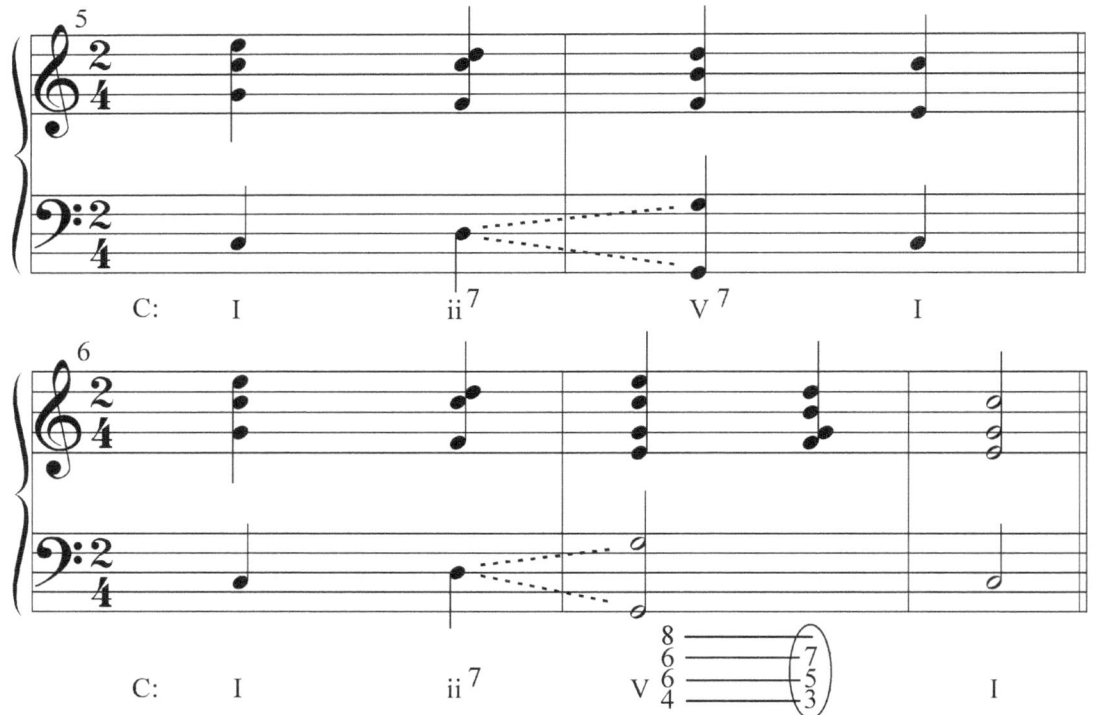

Exercise A–4: secondary harmonic progression, the X-chord with scale degree 2 in the bass

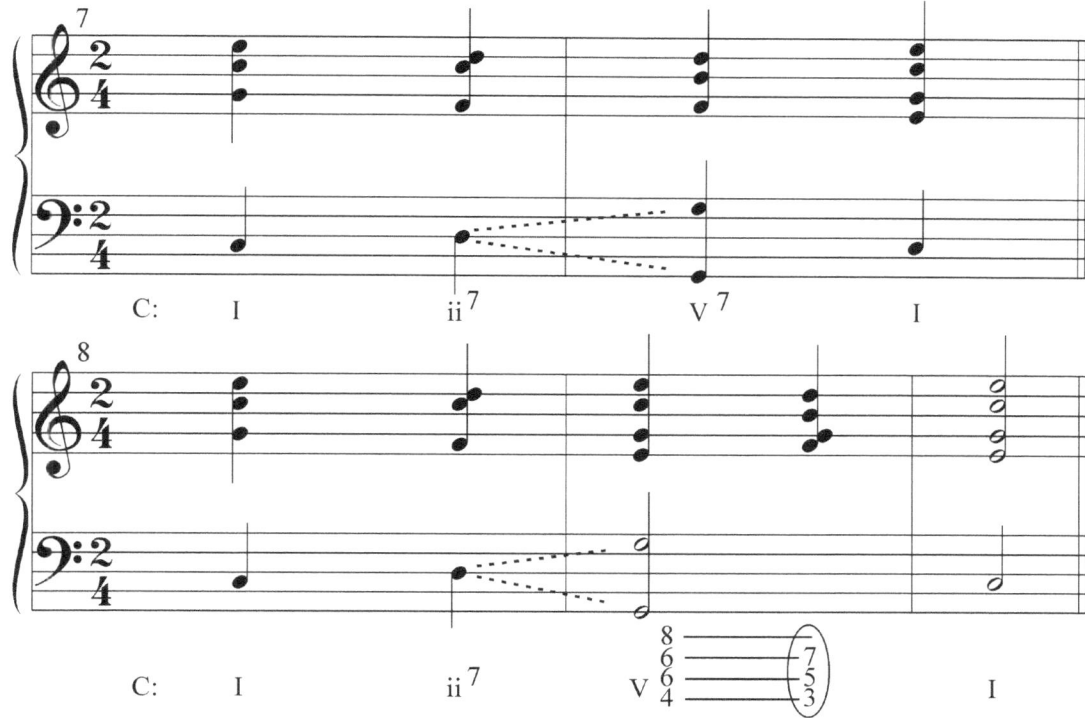

Exercise A–5: secondary harmonic progression, the X-chord with scale degree 4 in the bass

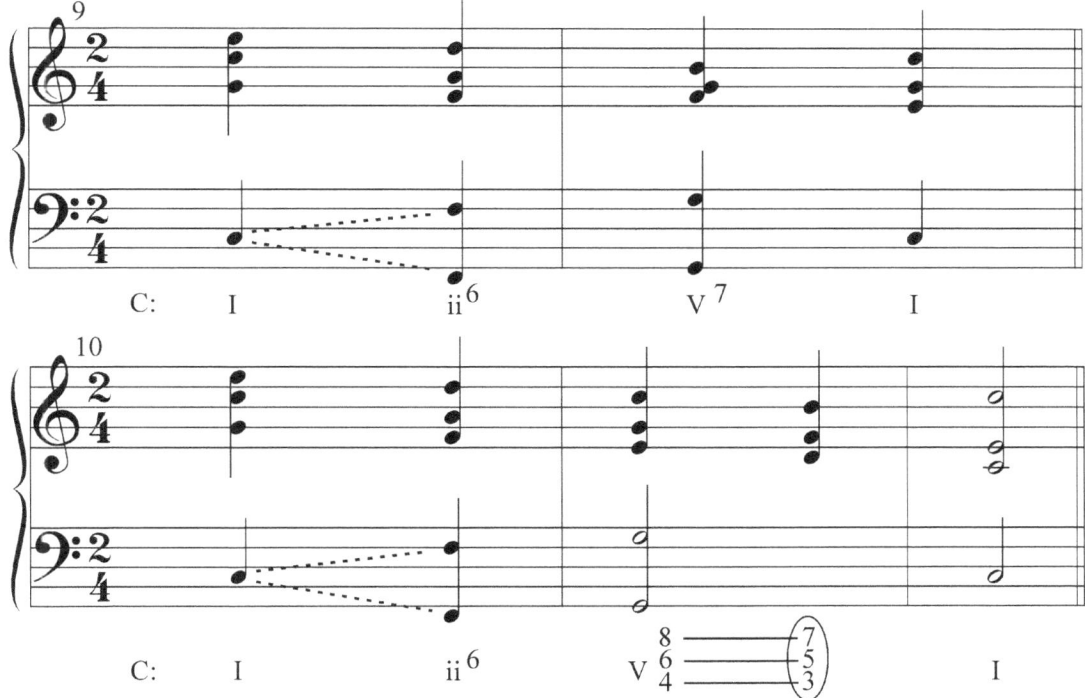

Exercise A–6: secondary harmonic progression, the X-chord with scale degree 4 in the bass

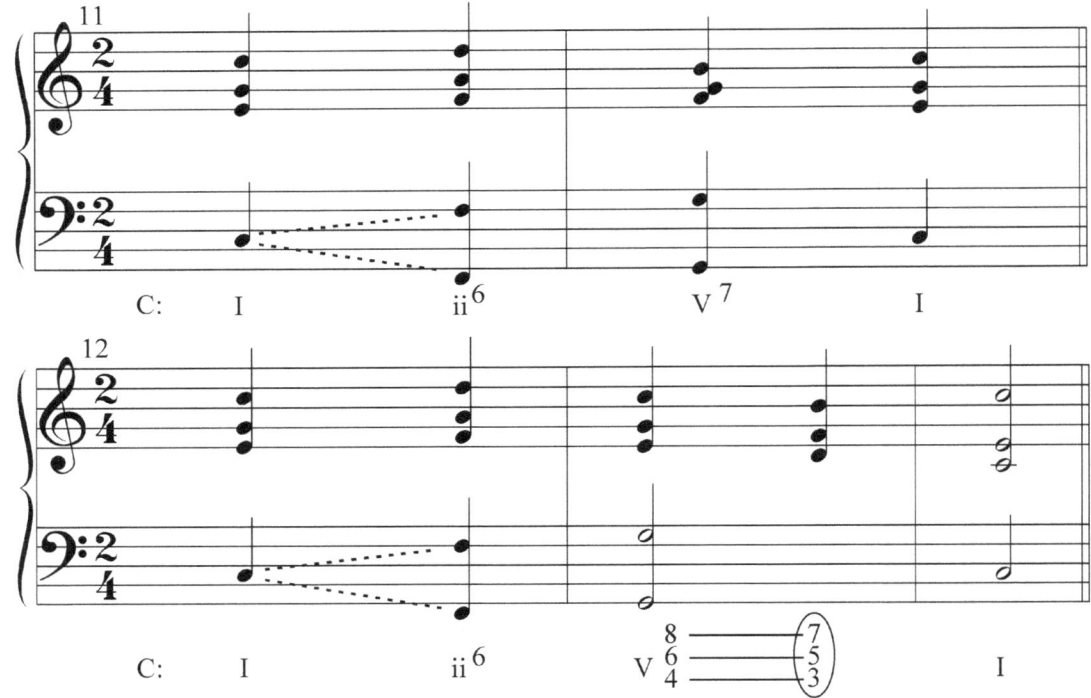

Exercise A–7: secondary harmonic progression, the X-chord with scale degree 4 in the bass

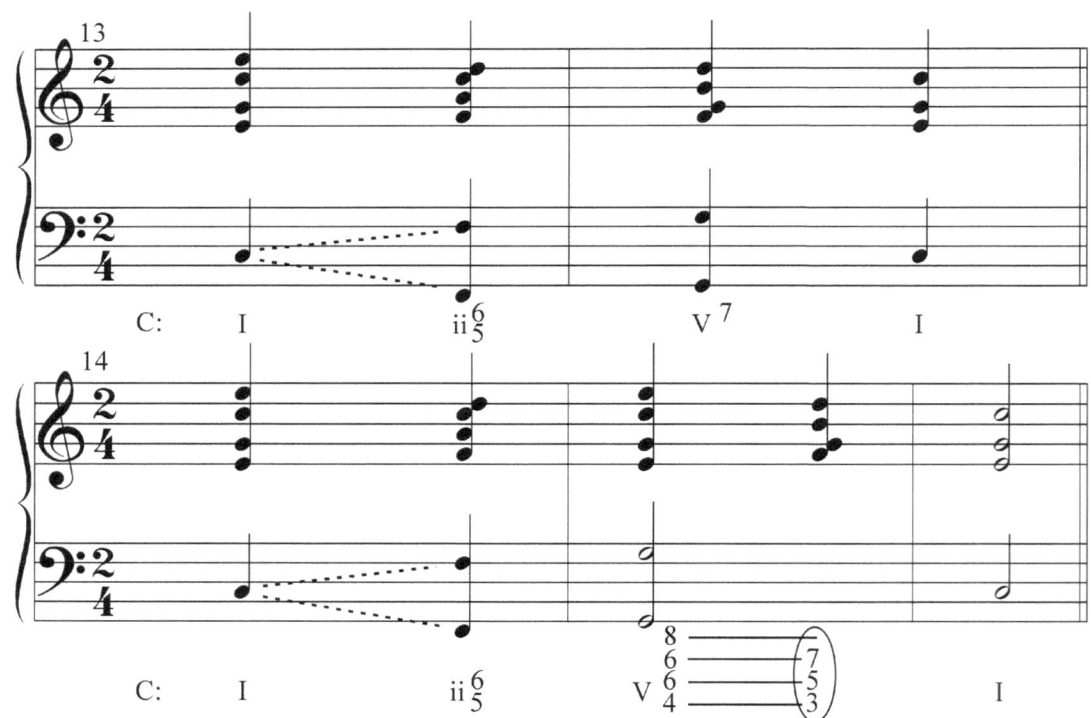

Exercise A–8: secondary harmonic progression, the X-chord with scale degree 4 in the bass

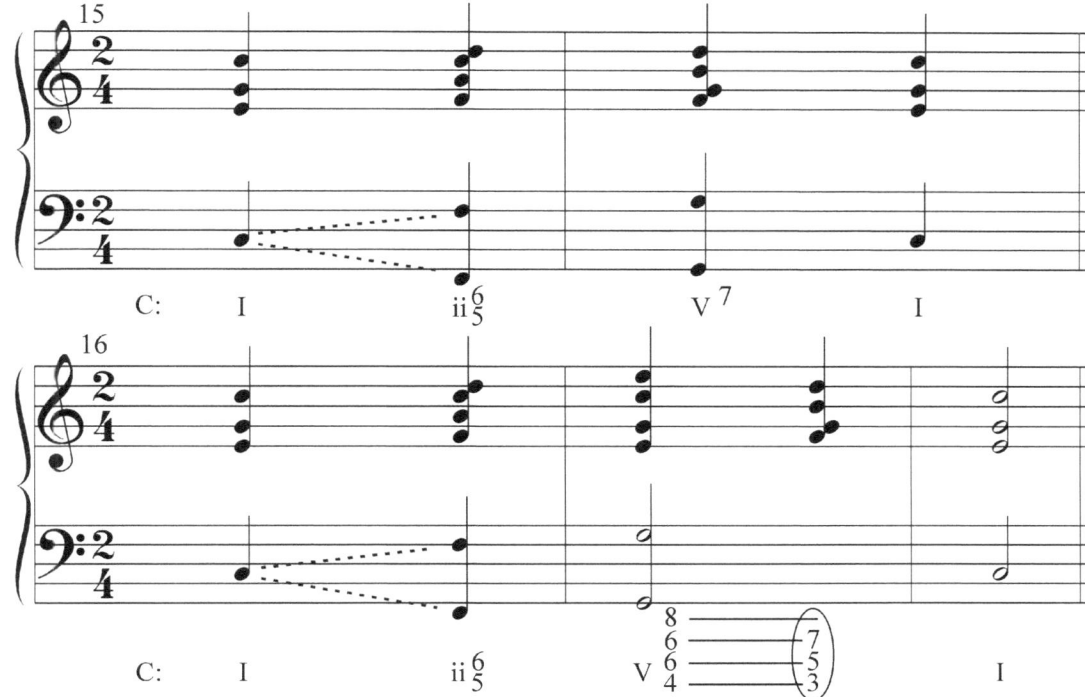

Exercise A–9: secondary harmonic progression, the X-chord with scale degree 4 in the bass

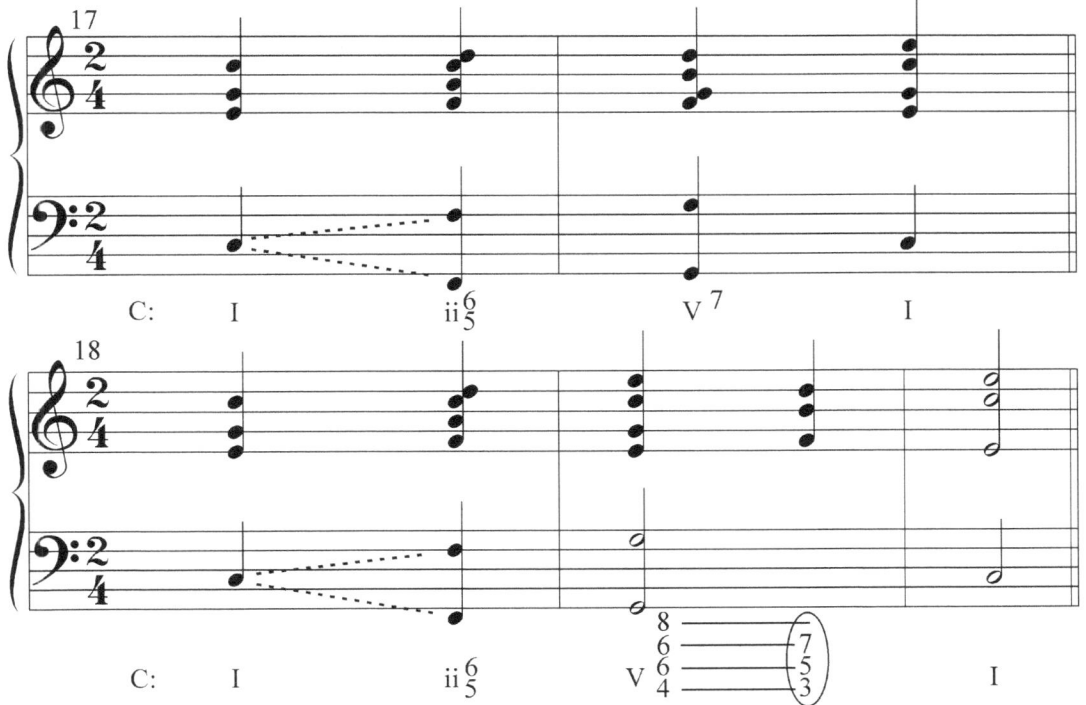

Exercise A–10: secondary harmonic progression, the X-chord with scale degree 4 in the bass

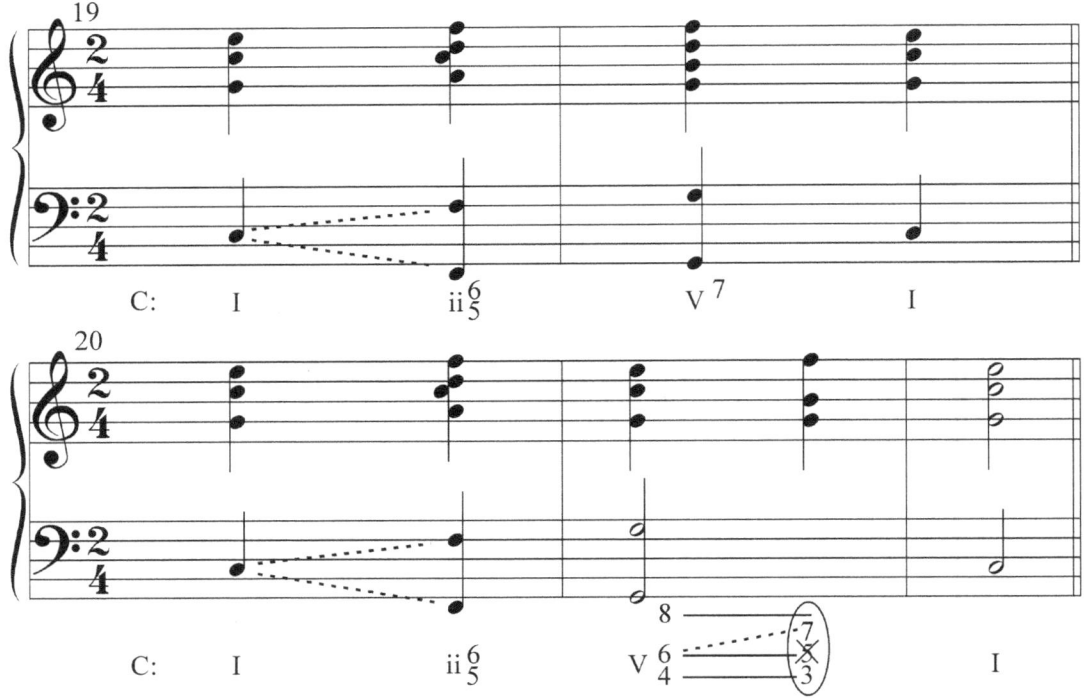

Exercise A–11: secondary harmonic progression, the X-chord with scale degree 4 in the bass

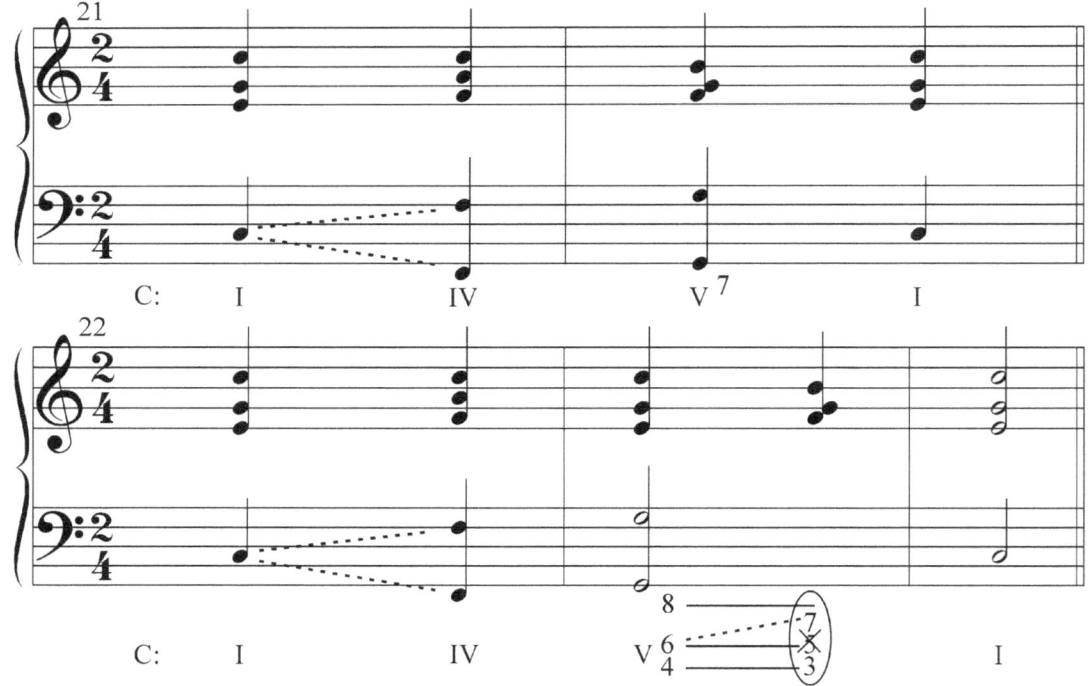

Exercise A–12: secondary harmonic progression, the X-chord with scale degree 4 in the bass

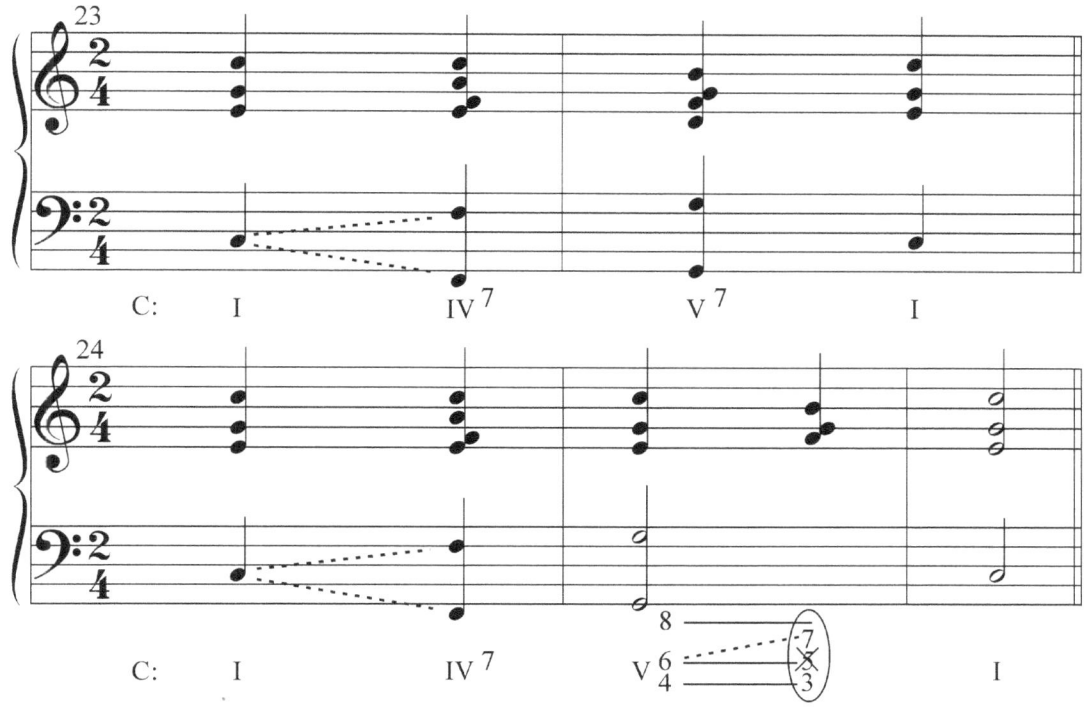

Exercise A–13: secondary harmonic progression, the X-chord with scale degree 4 in the bass

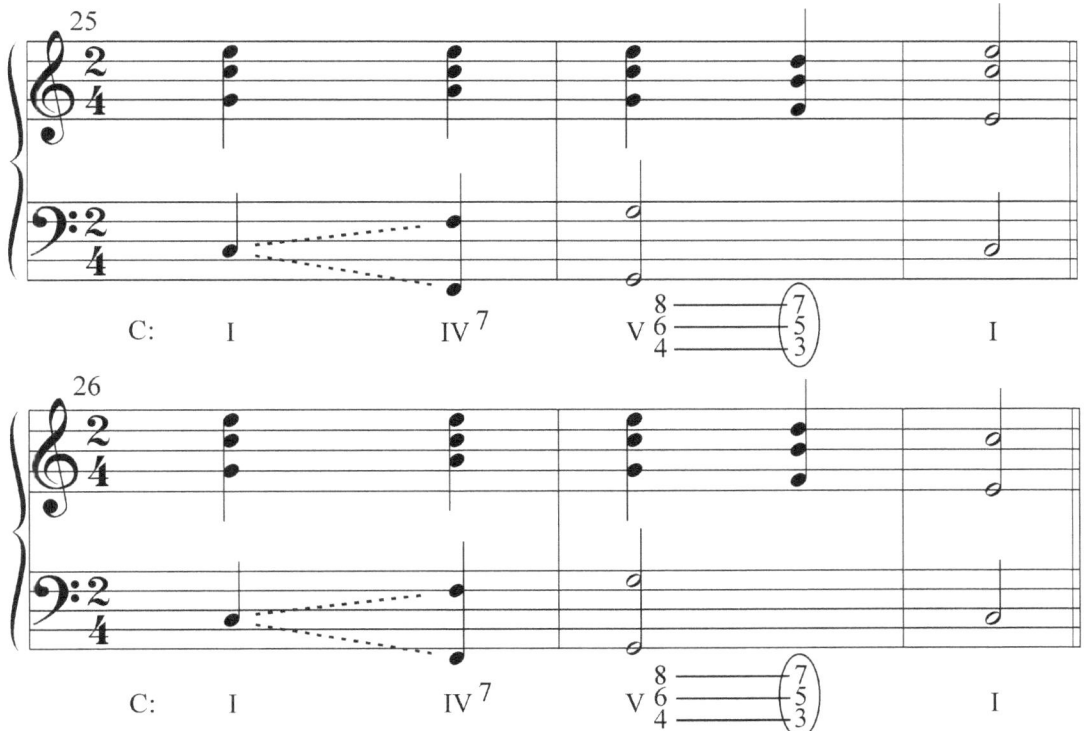

Exercise A–14: secondary harmonic progression, the X-chord with scale degree 4 in the bass

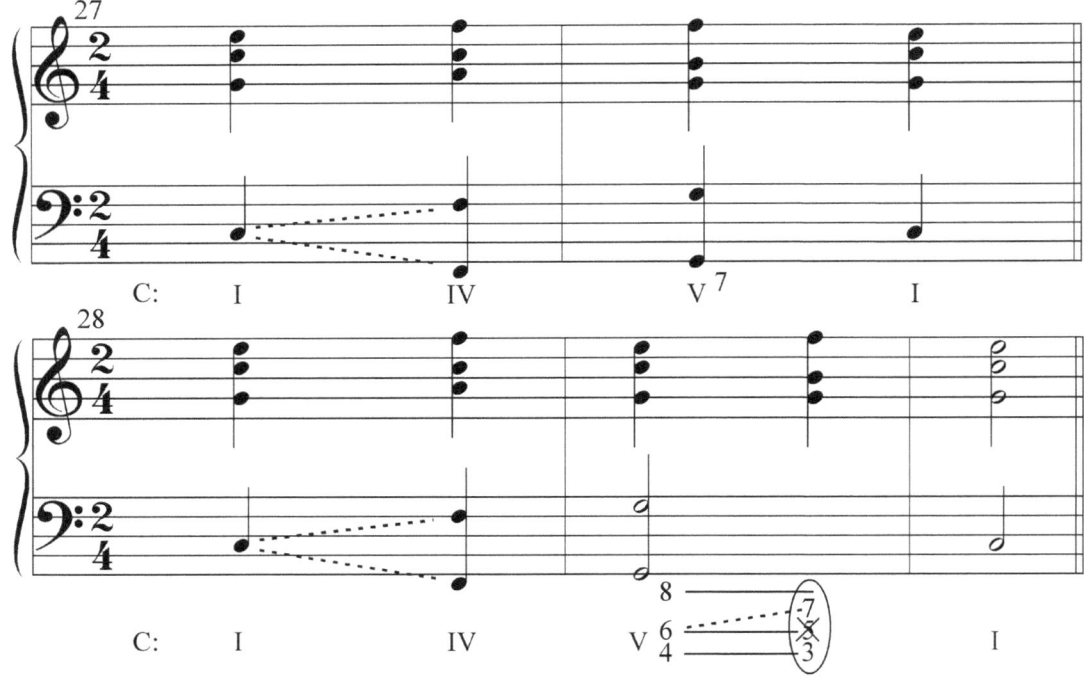

Exercise A–15: secondary harmonic progression, the X-chord with scale degree 4 in the bass

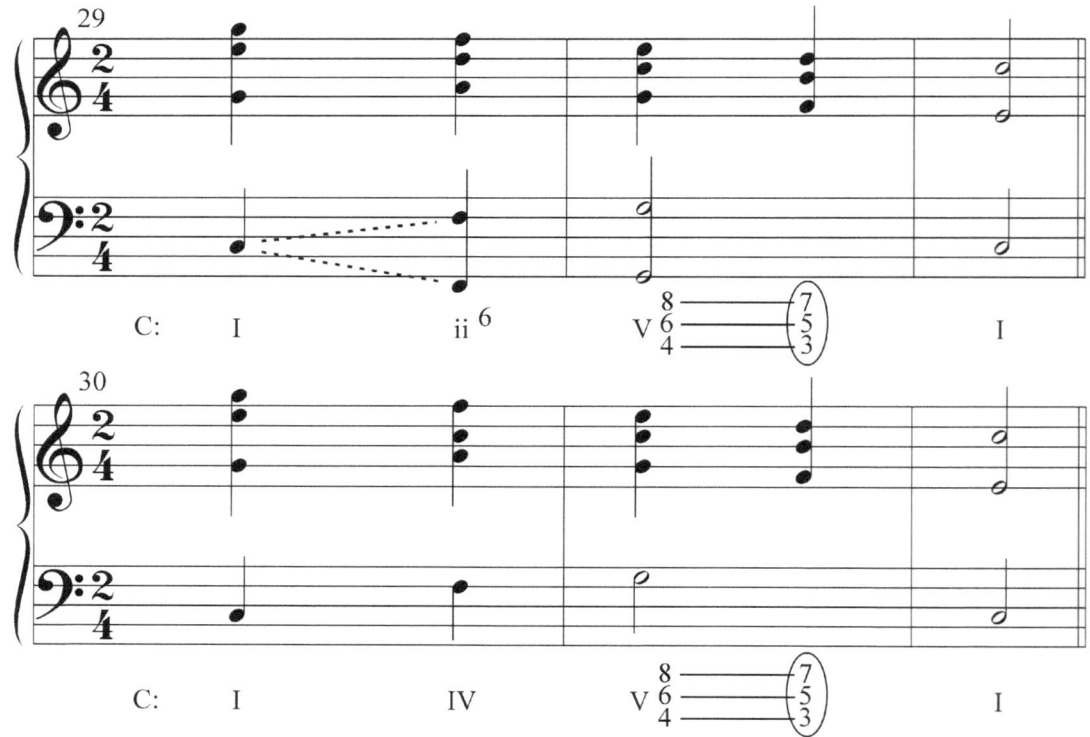

Exercise A–16: two-progression frameworks, BCP–SHP and SHP–SHP

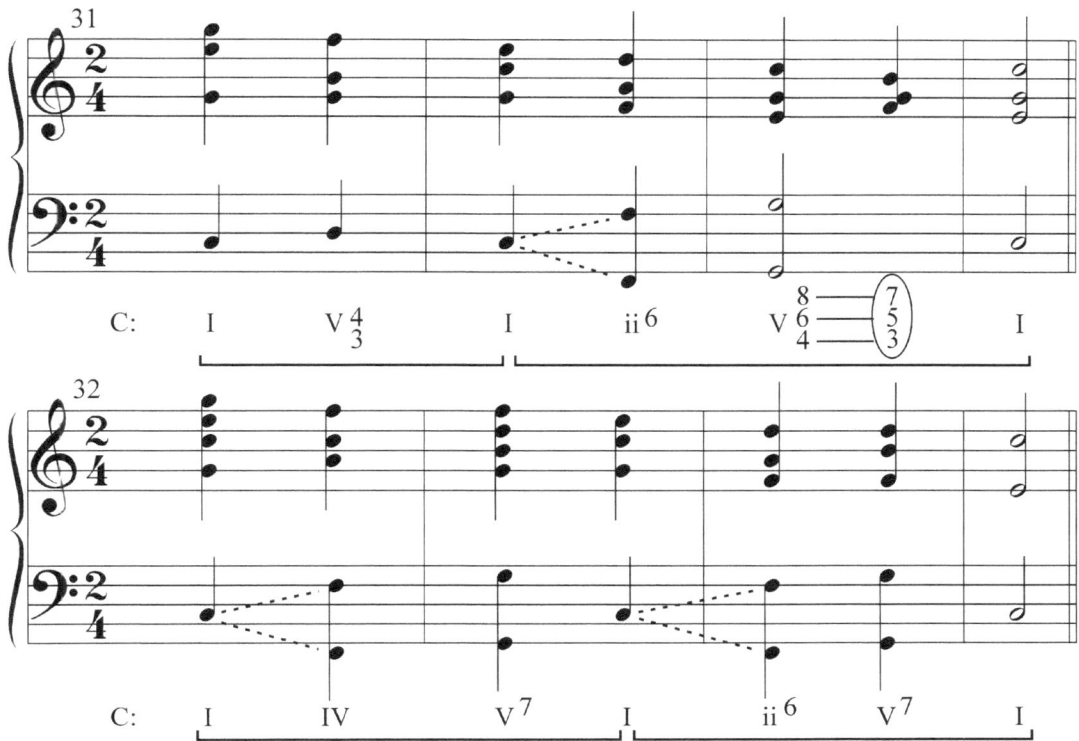

Exercise A–17: secondary harmonic progression, the X-chord with scale degree 3 in the bass

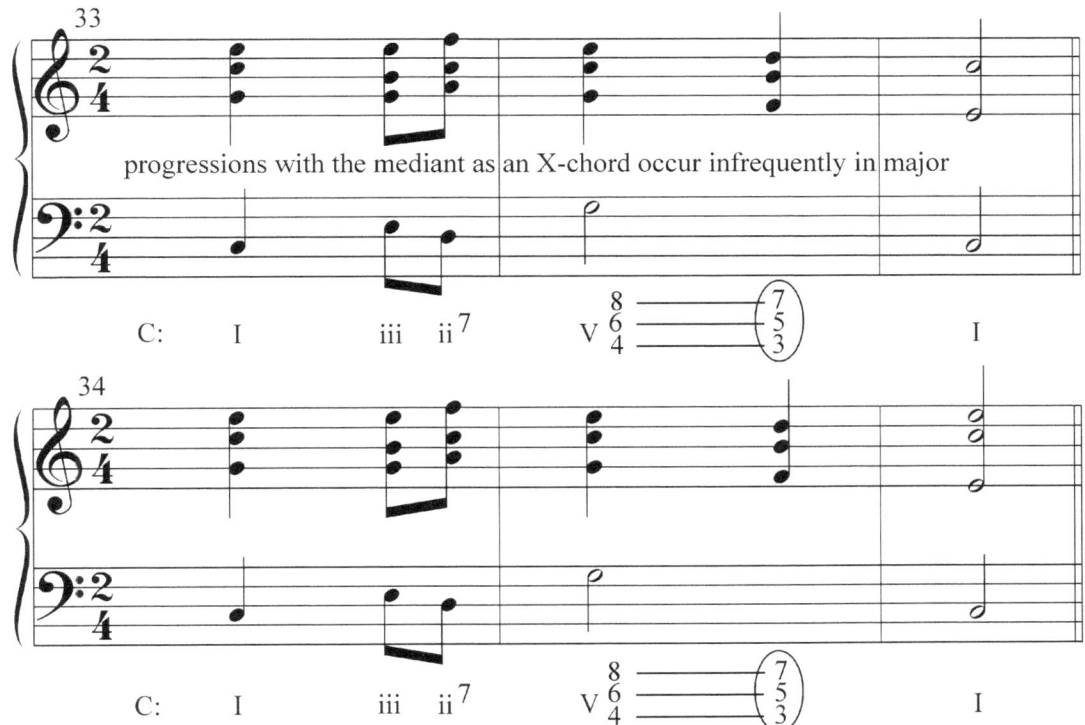

Exercise A–18: secondary harmonic progression, the X-chord with scale degree 3 in the bass

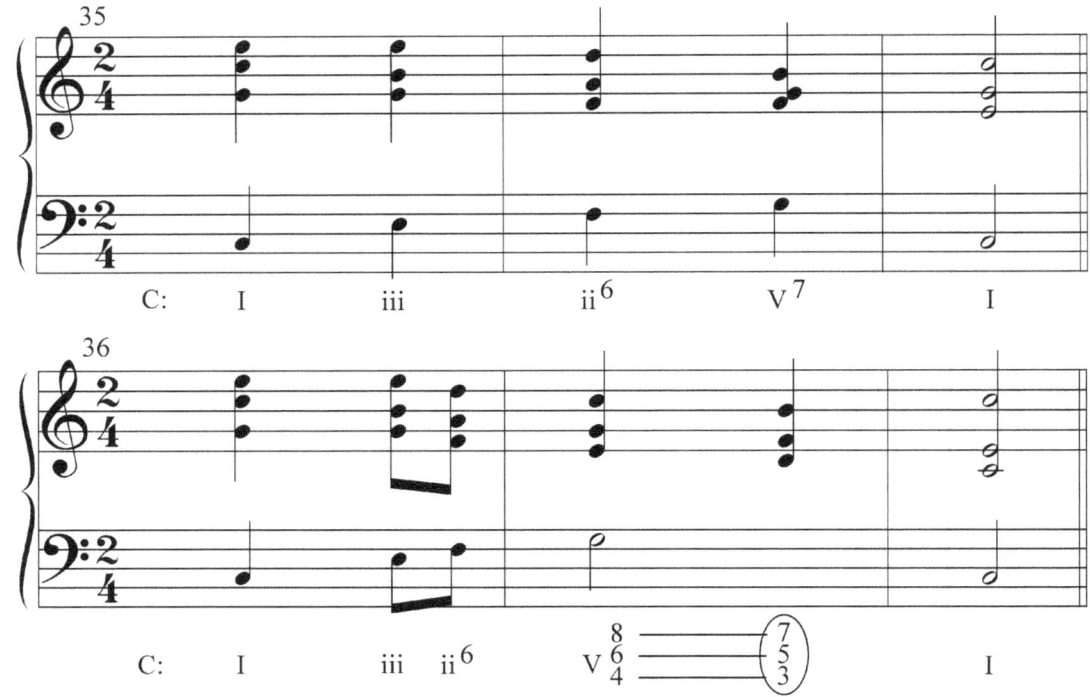

Exercise A–19: two-progression frameworks, SHP–SHP and SCP–SHP

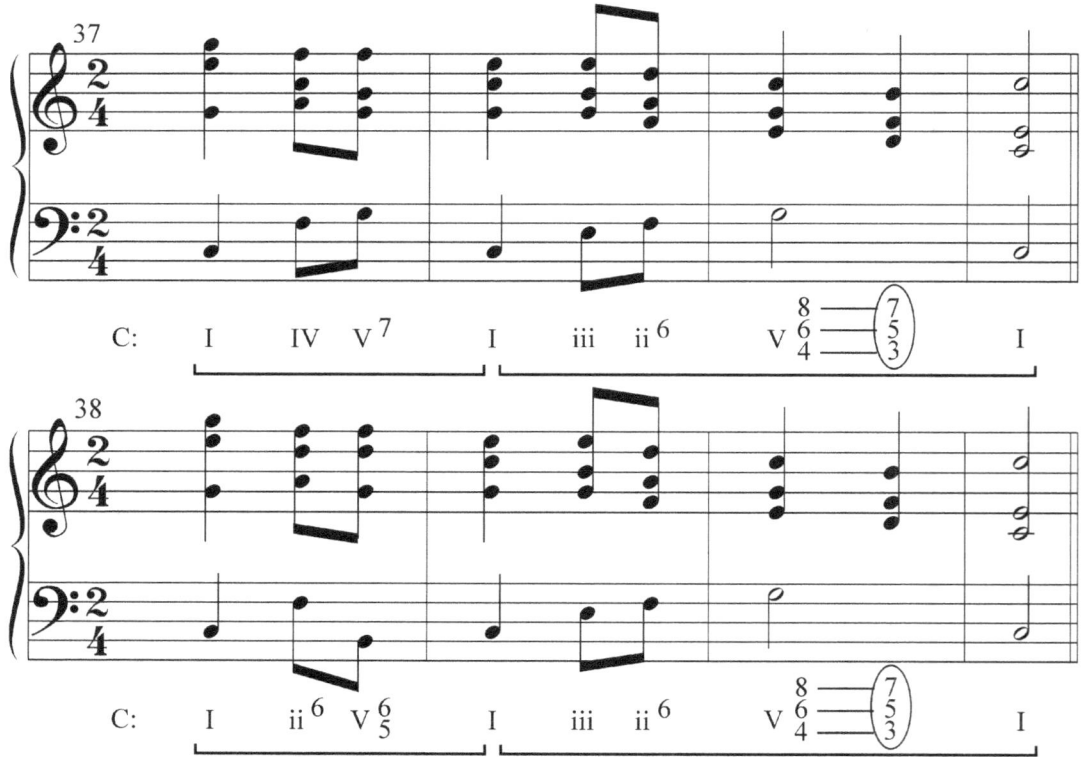

Exercise A–20: secondary harmonic progression, the X-chord with scale degree 6 in the bass

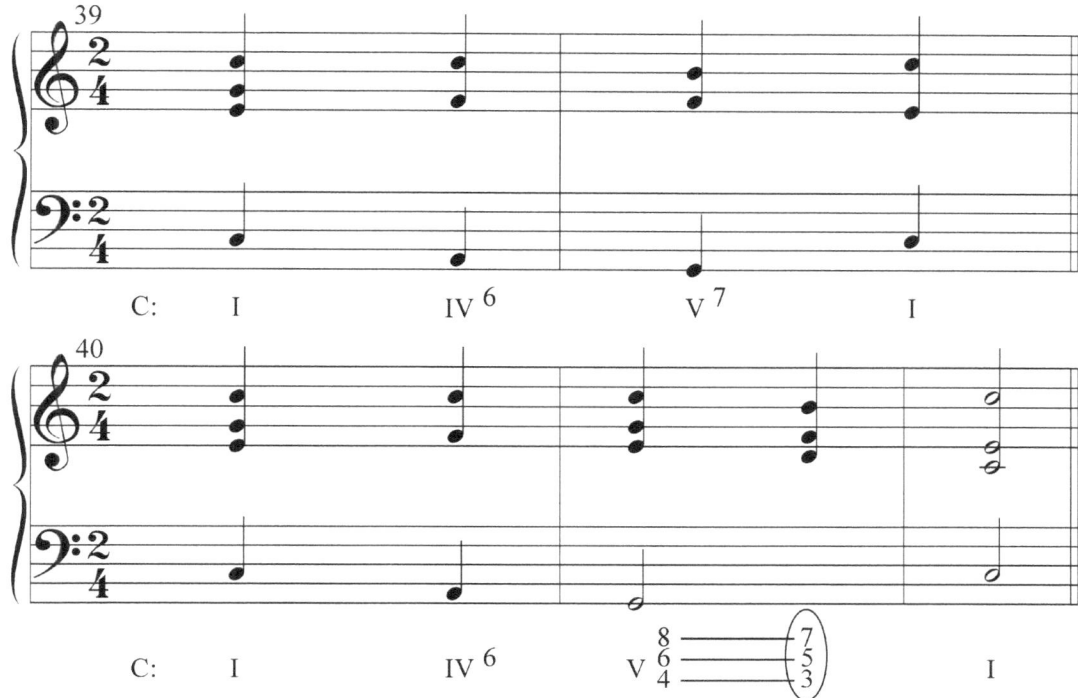

Exercise A–21: secondary harmonic progression, the X-chord with scale degree 6 in the bass

Exercise A–22: secondary harmonic progression, the X-chord with scale degree 6 in the bass

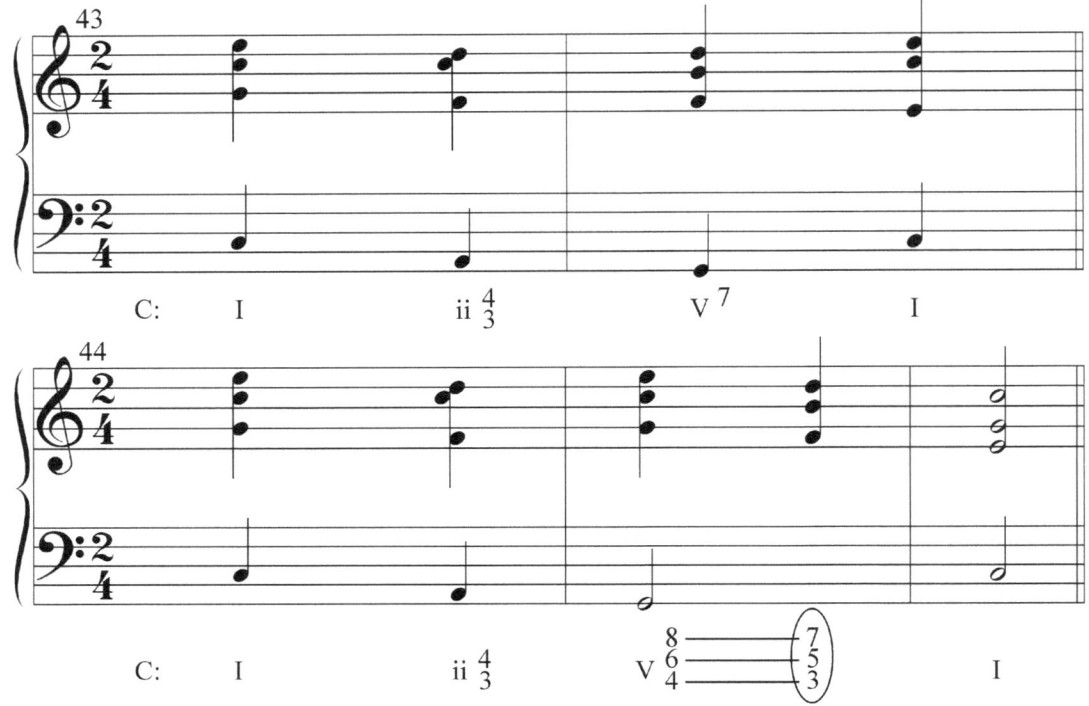

Exercise A–23: secondary harmonic progression, the X-chord with scale degree 6 in the bass

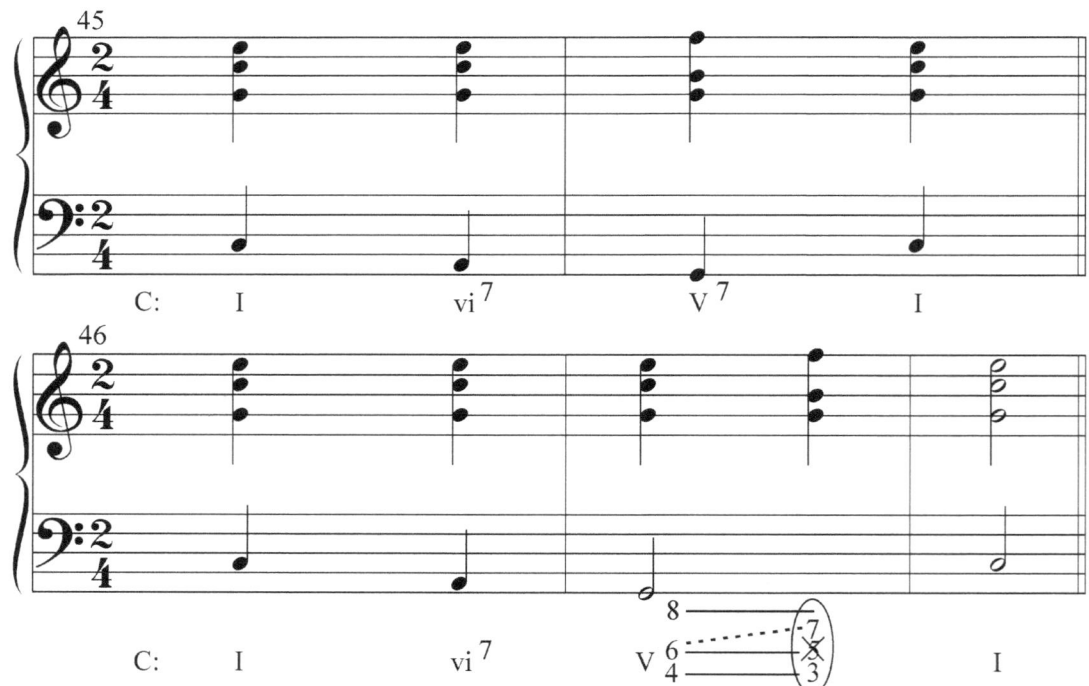

Exercise A–24: two-progression frameworks, SHP–SHP and SCP–SHP

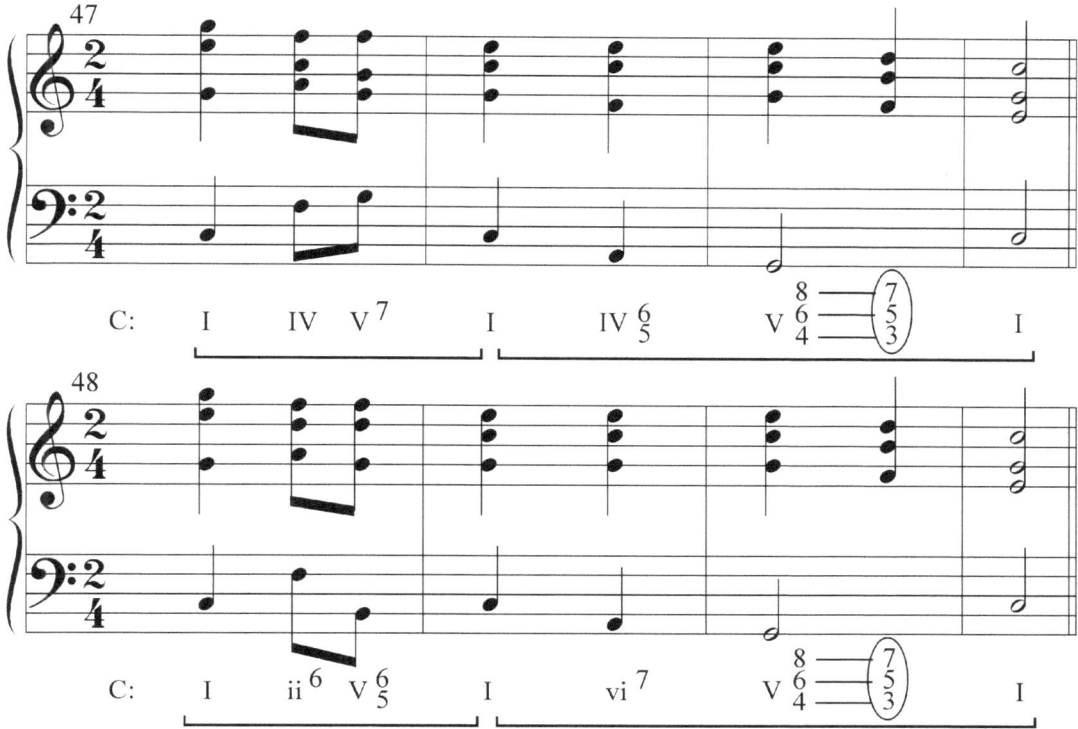

Exercise A–25: secondary harmonic progression, the X-chord with scale degree 2 in the bass

Exercise A–26: secondary harmonic progression, the X-chord with scale degree 2 in the bass

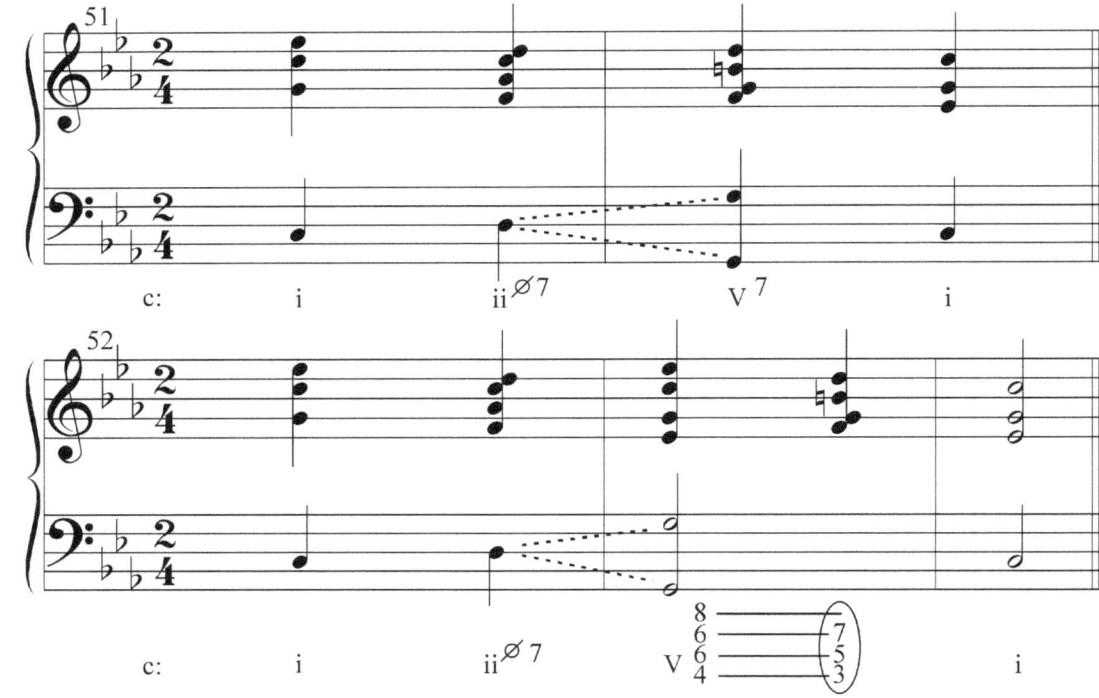

Exercise A–27: secondary harmonic progression, the X-chord with scale degree 2 in the bass

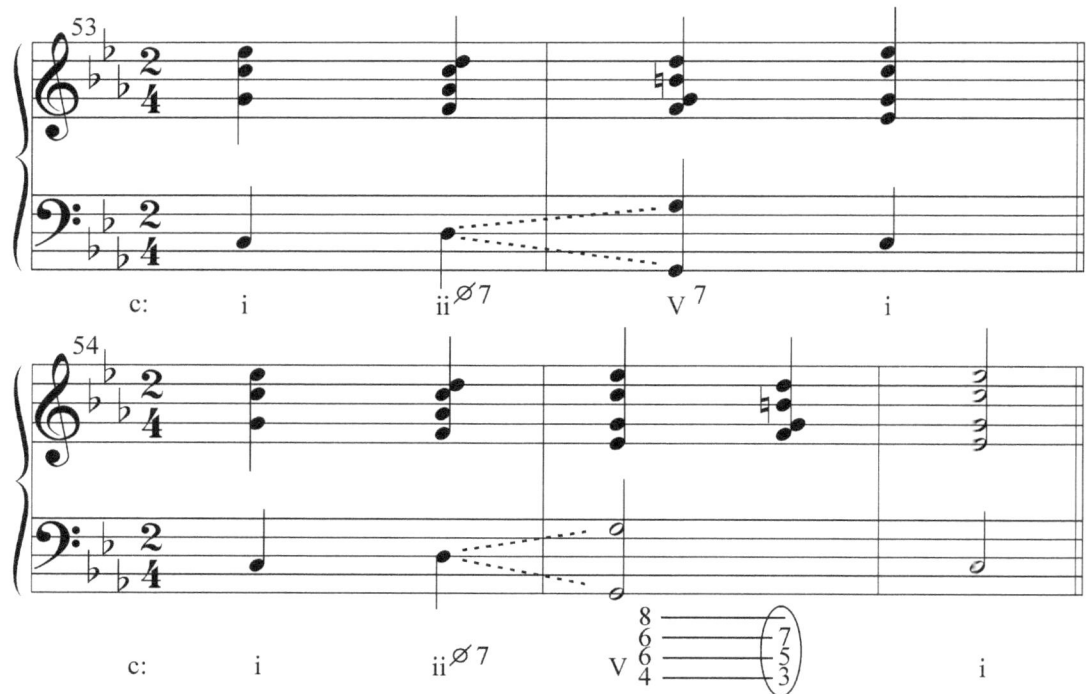

Exercise A–28: secondary harmonic progression, the X-chord with scale degree 4 in the bass

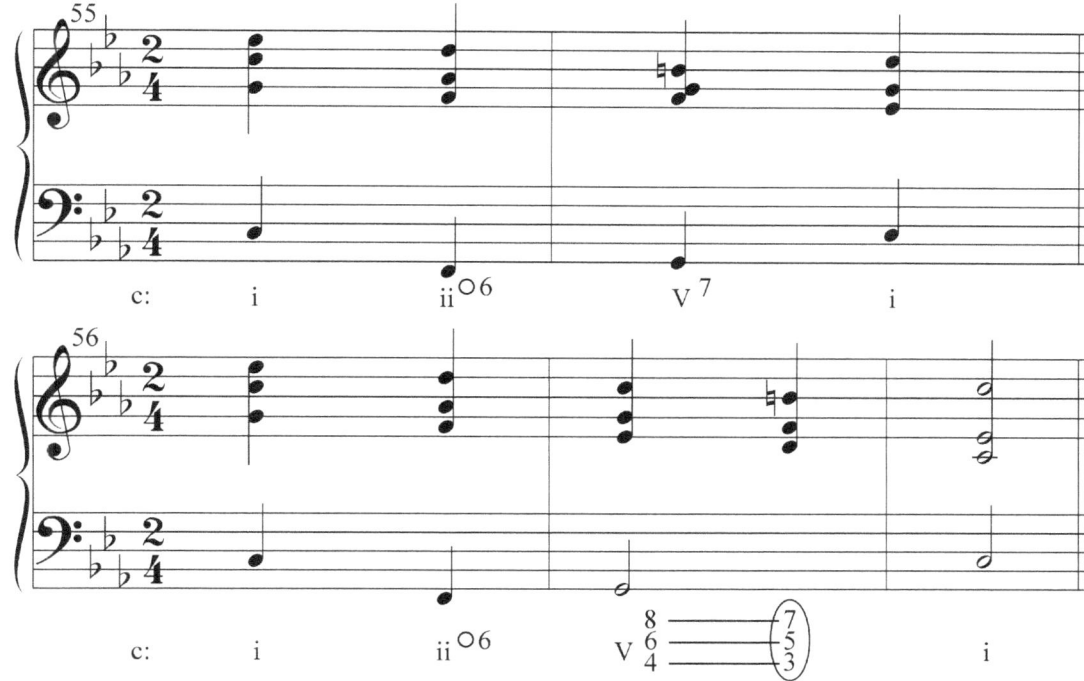

Exercise A–29: secondary harmonic progression, the X-chord with scale degree 4 in the bass

Exercise A–30: secondary harmonic progression, the X-chord with scale degree 4 in the bass

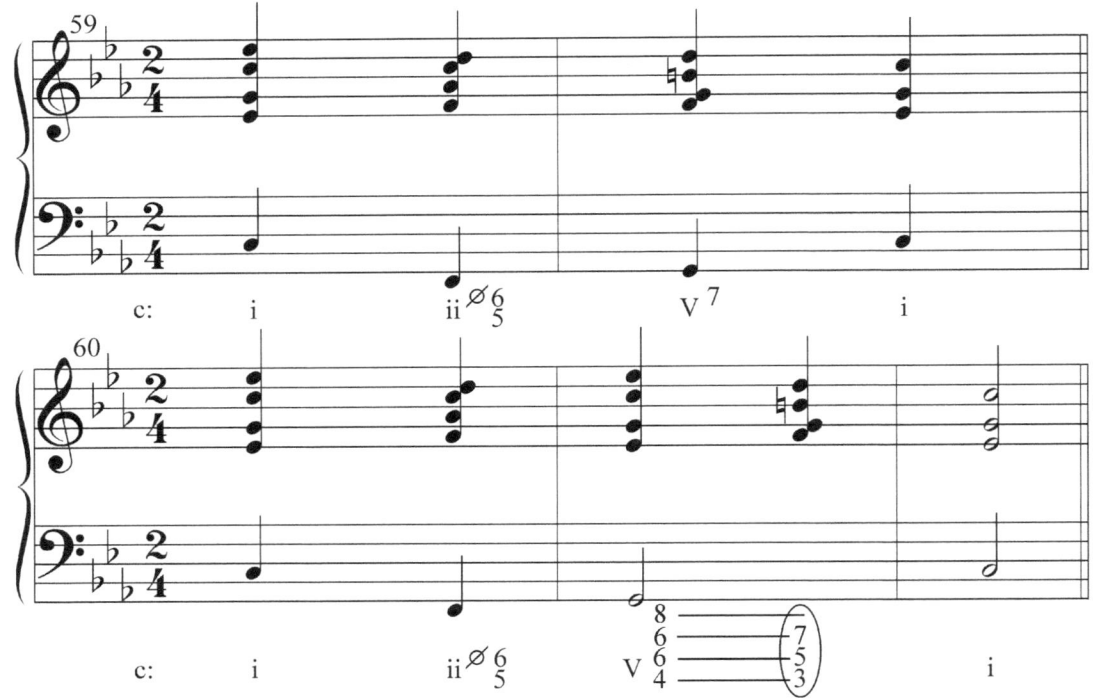

Exercise A–31: secondary harmonic progression, the X-chord with scale degree 4 in the bass

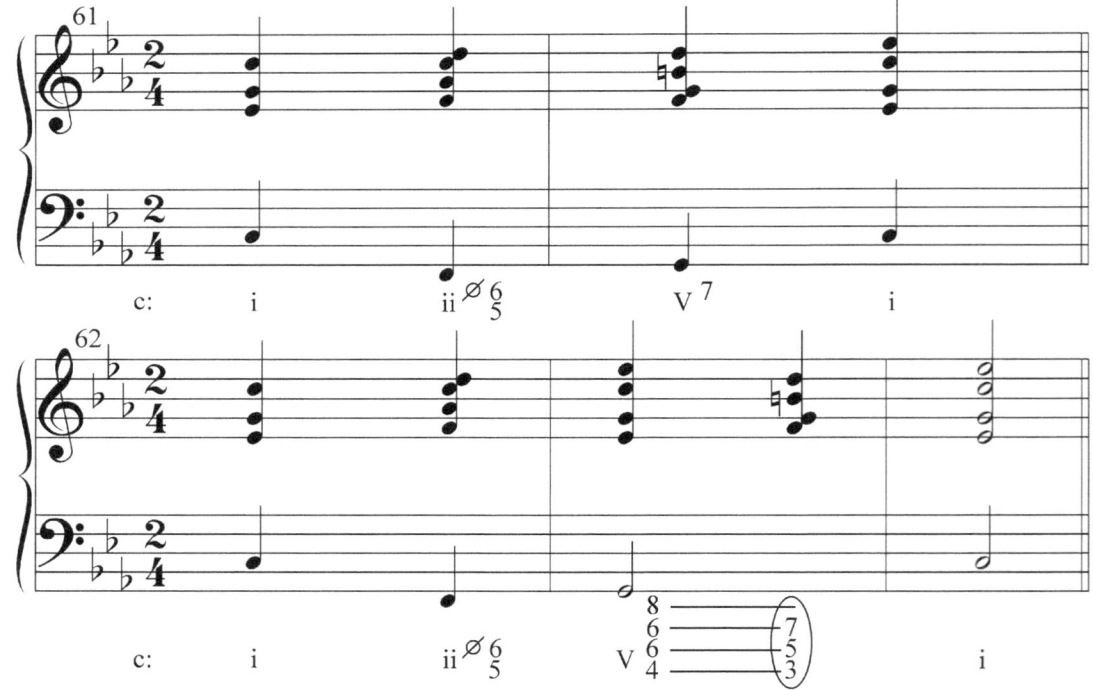

Exercise A–32: secondary harmonic progression, the X-chord with scale degree 4 in the bass

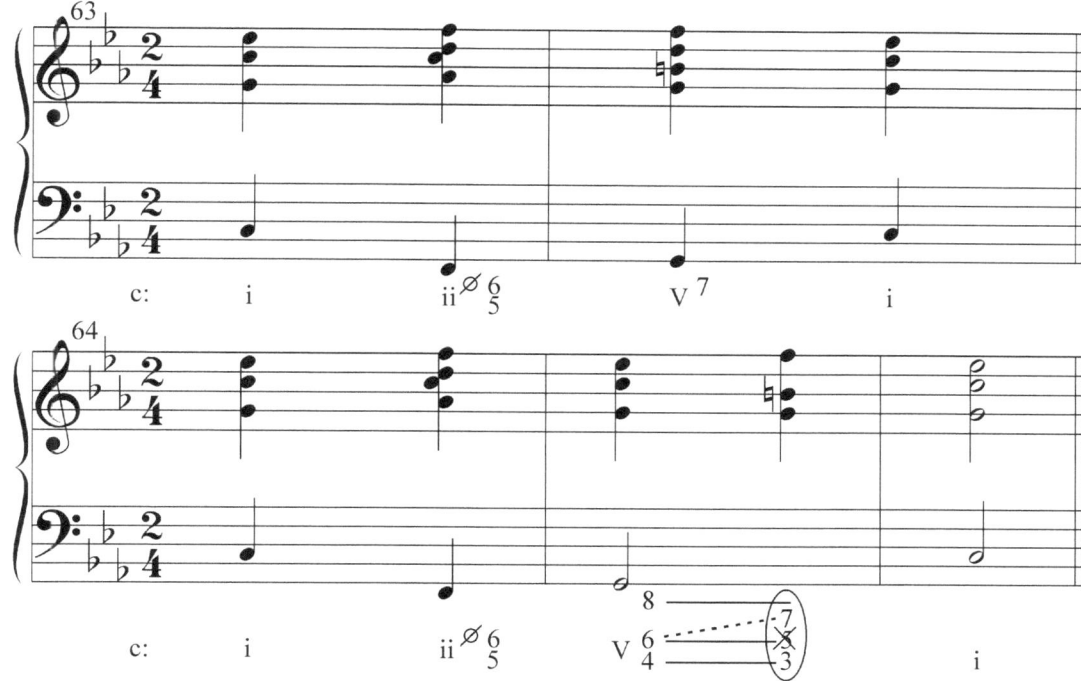

Exercise A–33: secondary harmonic progression, the X-chord with scale degree 4 in the bass

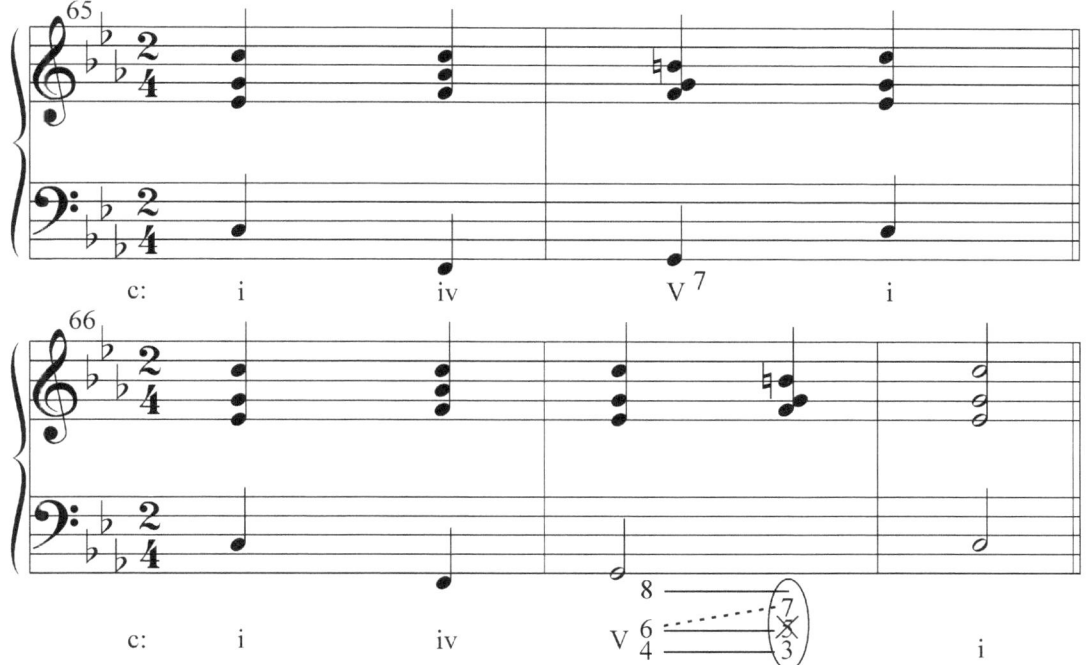

Exercise A–34: secondary harmonic progression, the X-chord with scale degree 4 in the bass

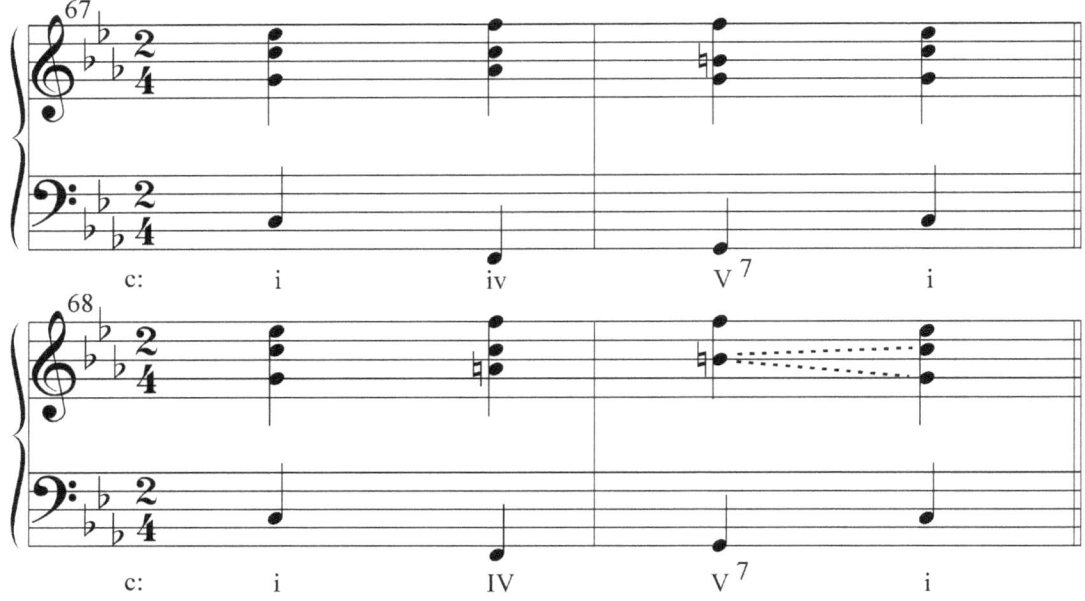

Exercise A–35: secondary harmonic progression, the X-chord with scale degree 4 in the bass

Exercise A–36: secondary harmonic progression, the X-chord with scale degree 4 in the bass

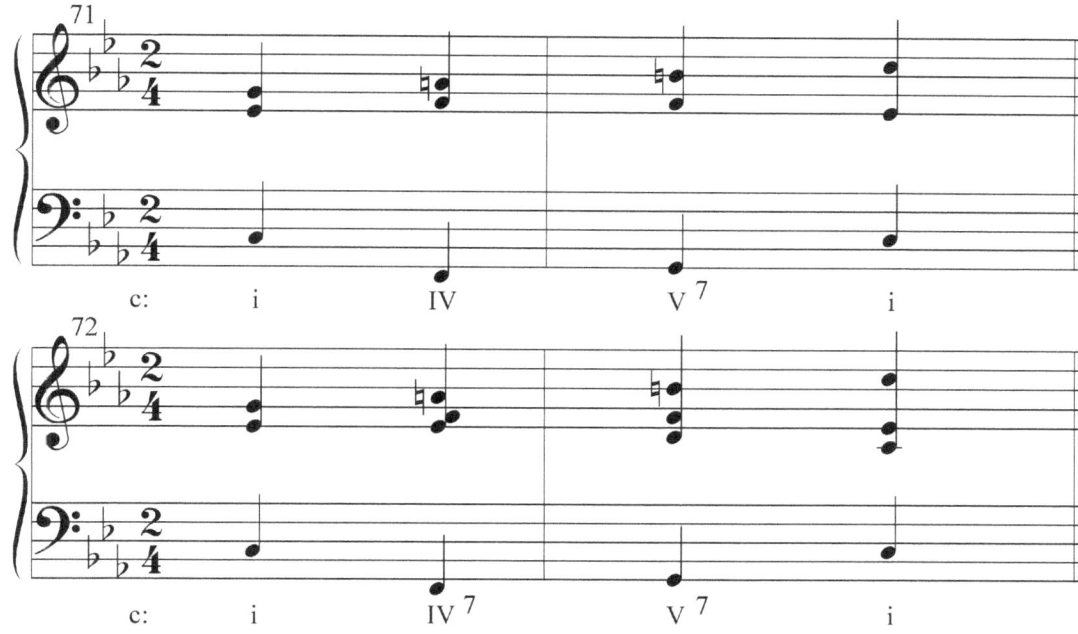

Exercise A–37: secondary harmonic progression, the X-chord with scale degree 4 in the bass

Exercise A–38: secondary harmonic progression, the X-chord with scale degree 4 in the bass

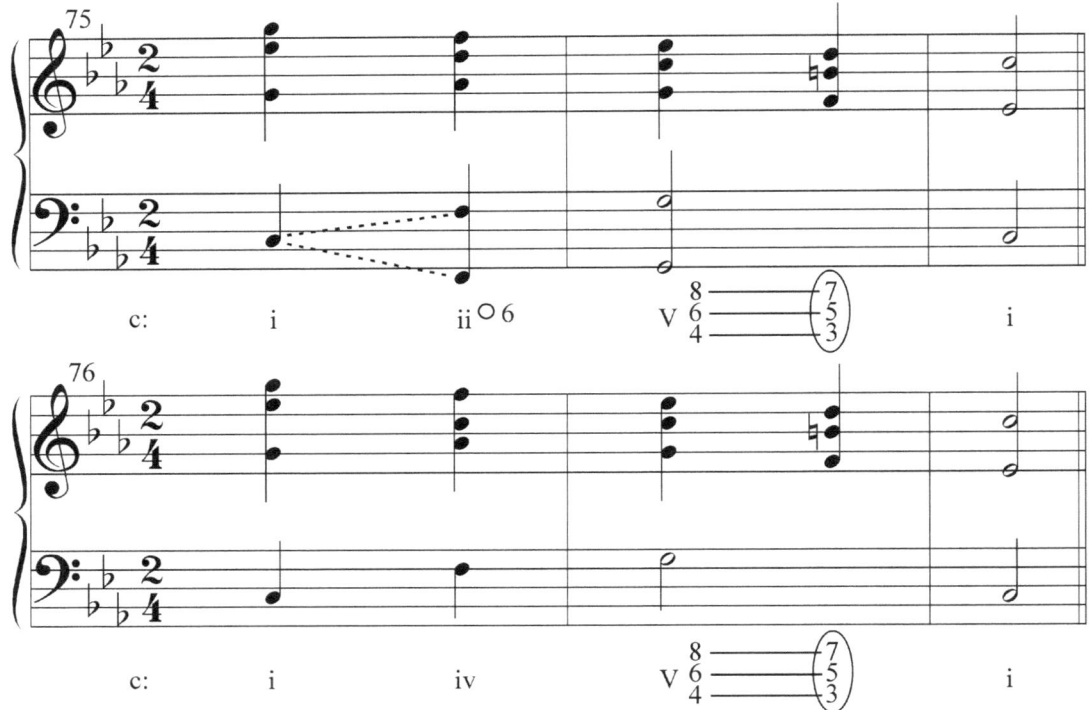

Exercise A–39: two-progression frameworks, BCP–SHP and SHP–SHP

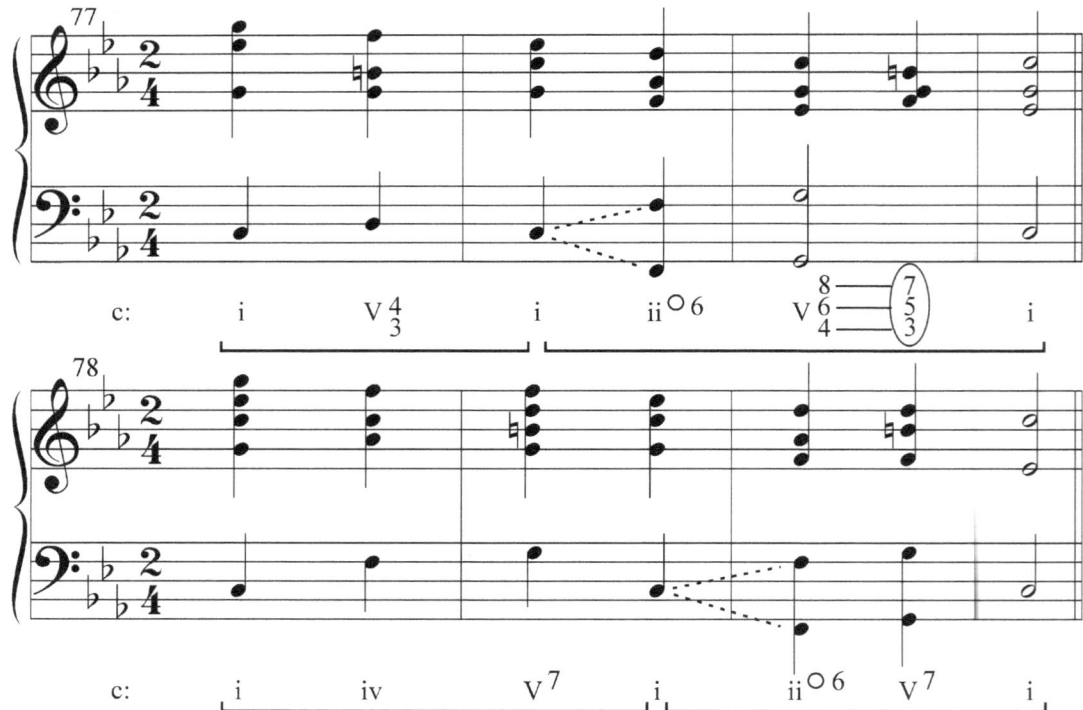

Exercise A–40: secondary harmonic progression, the X-chord with scale degree 3 in the bass

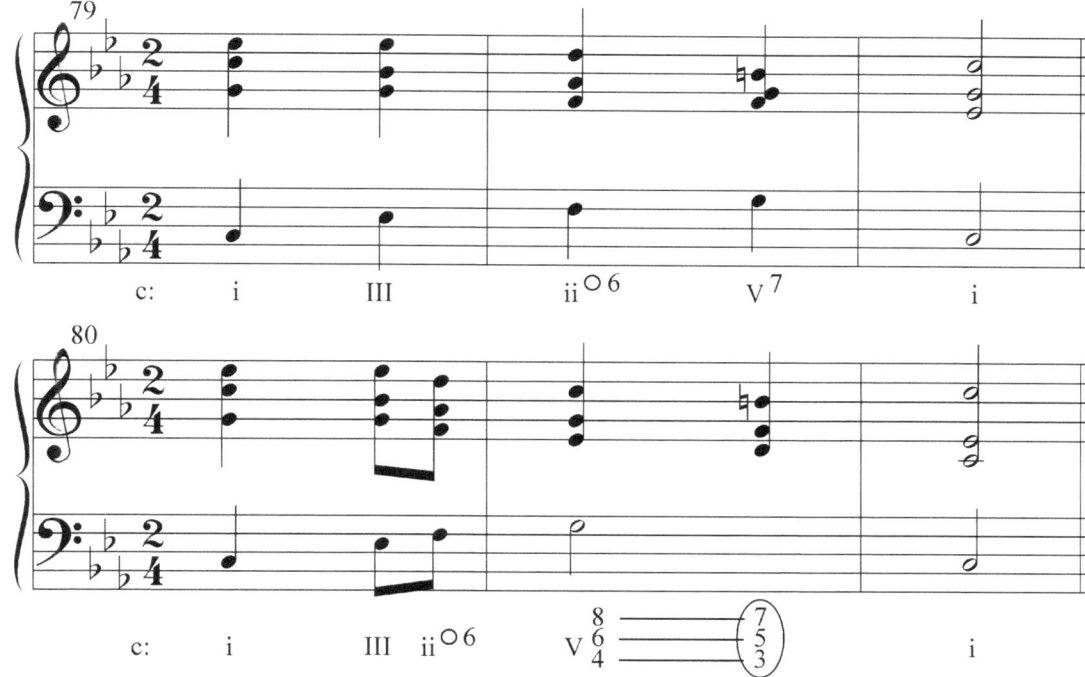

Exercise A–41: secondary harmonic progression, the X-chord with scale degree 3 in the bass

Exercise A–42: two-progression frameworks, SHP–SHP and SCP–SHP

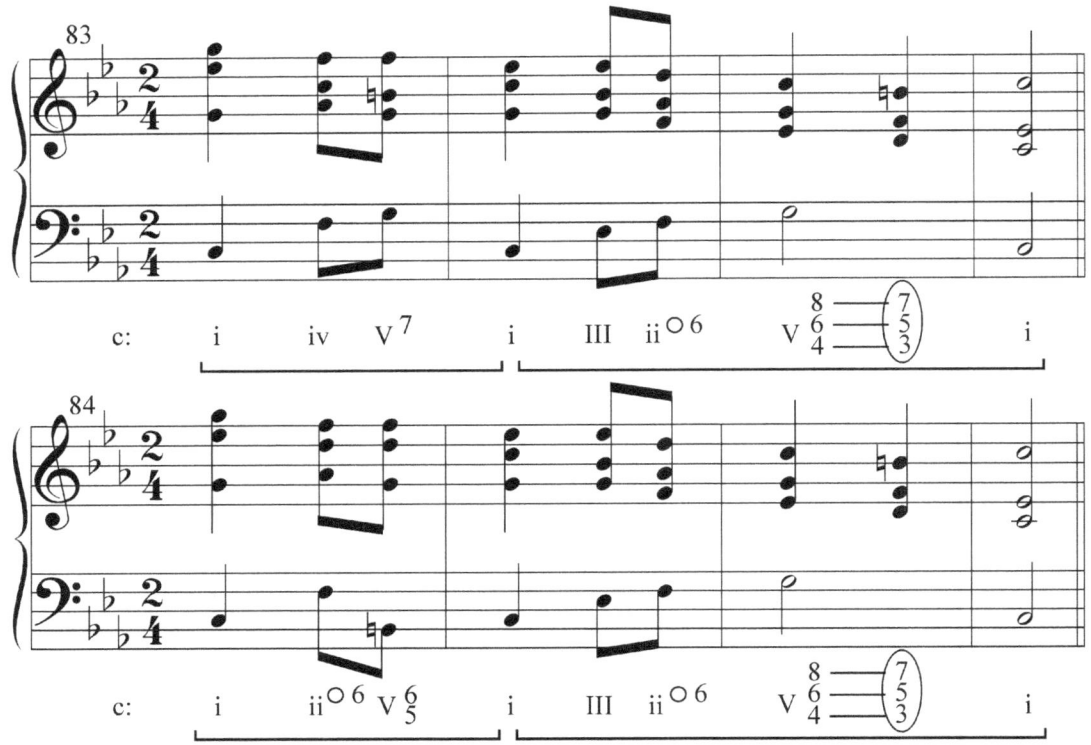

Exercise A–43: secondary harmonic progression, the X-chord with scale degree 6 in the bass

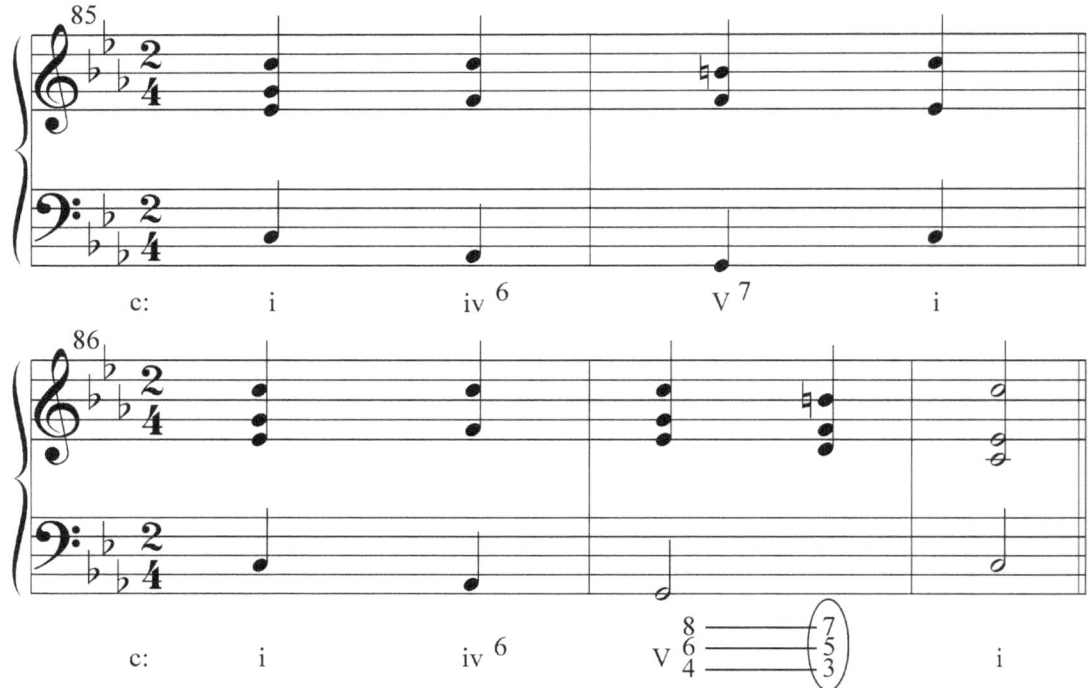

Exercise A–44: secondary harmonic progression, the X-chord with scale degree 6 in the bass

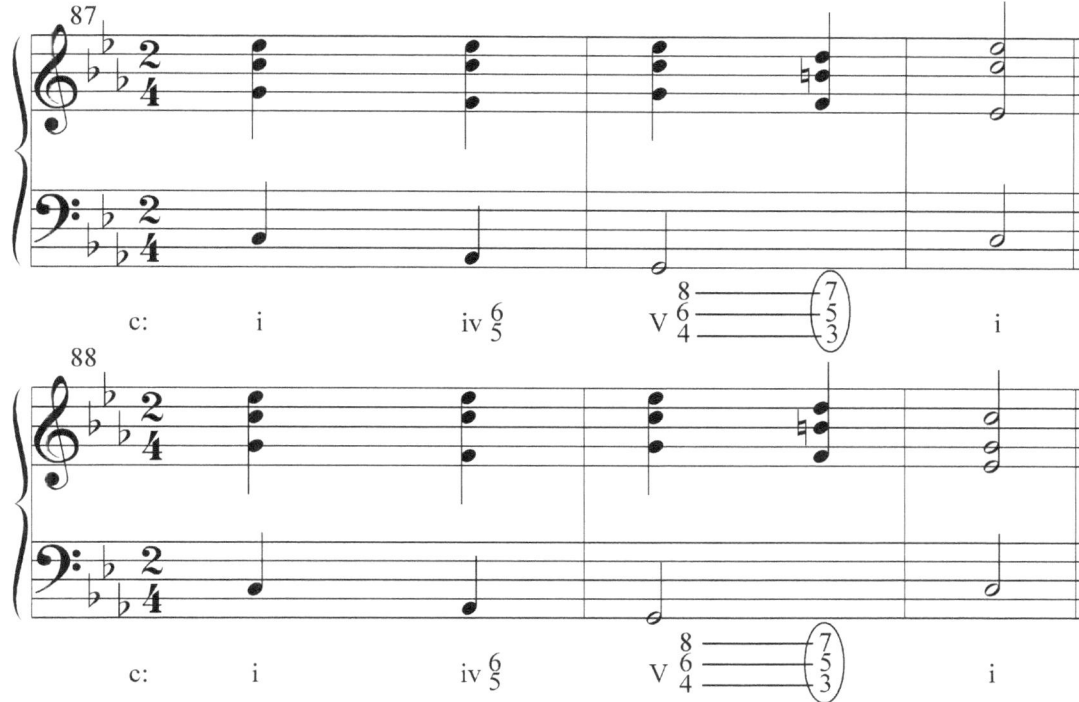

Exercise A–45: secondary harmonic progression, the X-chord with scale degree 6 in the bass

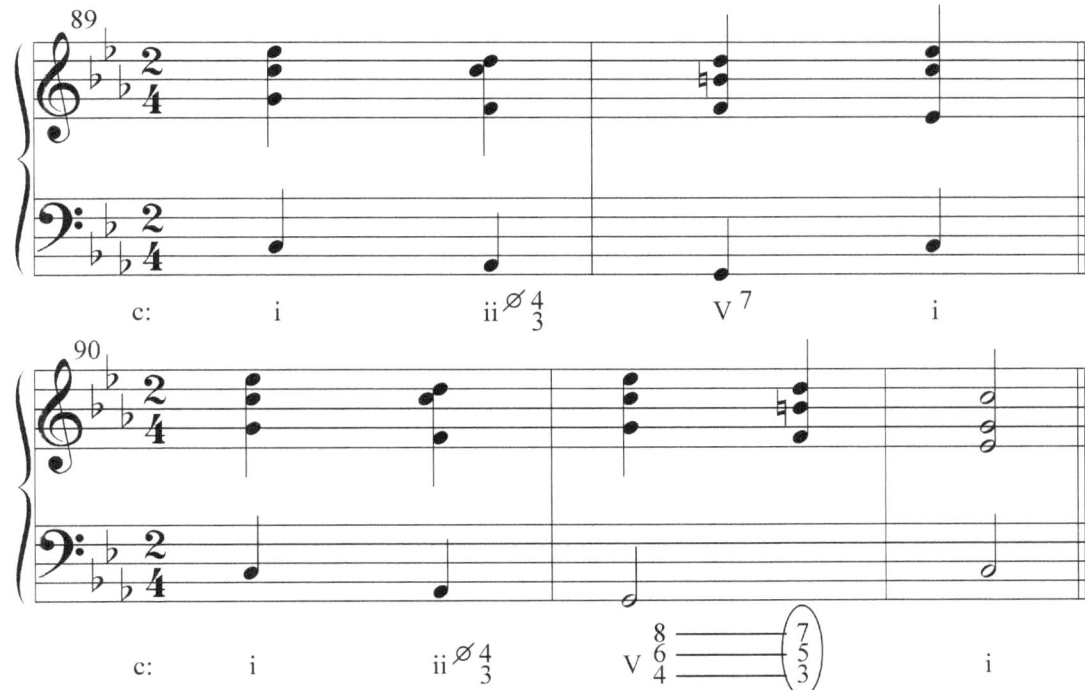

Exercise A–46: secondary harmonic progression, the X-chord with scale degree 6 in the bass

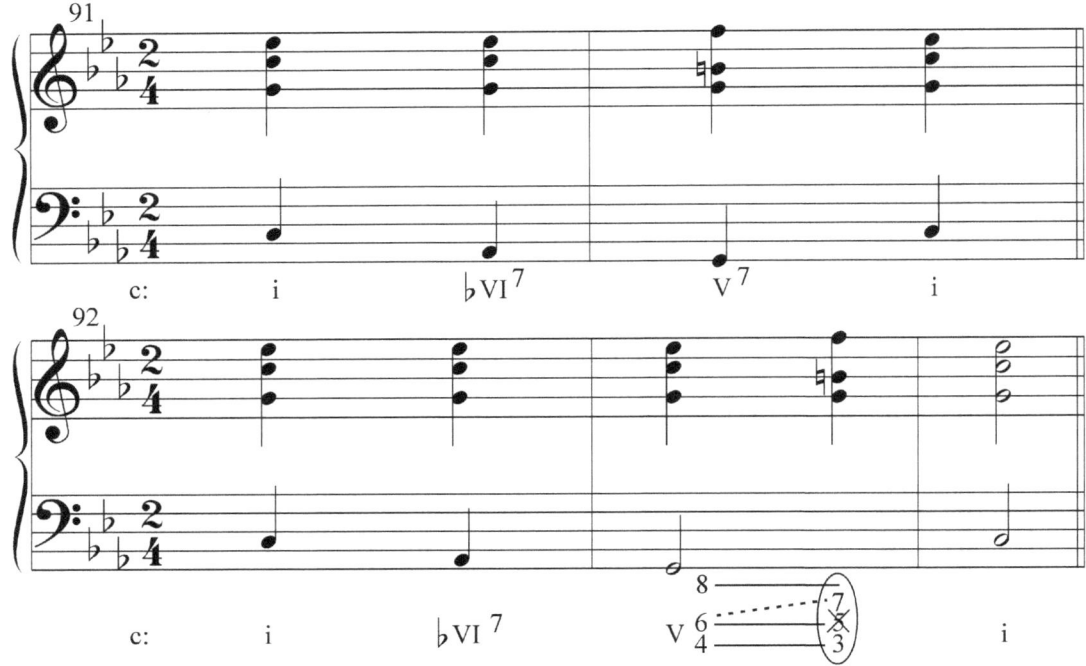

Exercise A–47: two-progression frameworks, SHP–SHP and SCP–SHP

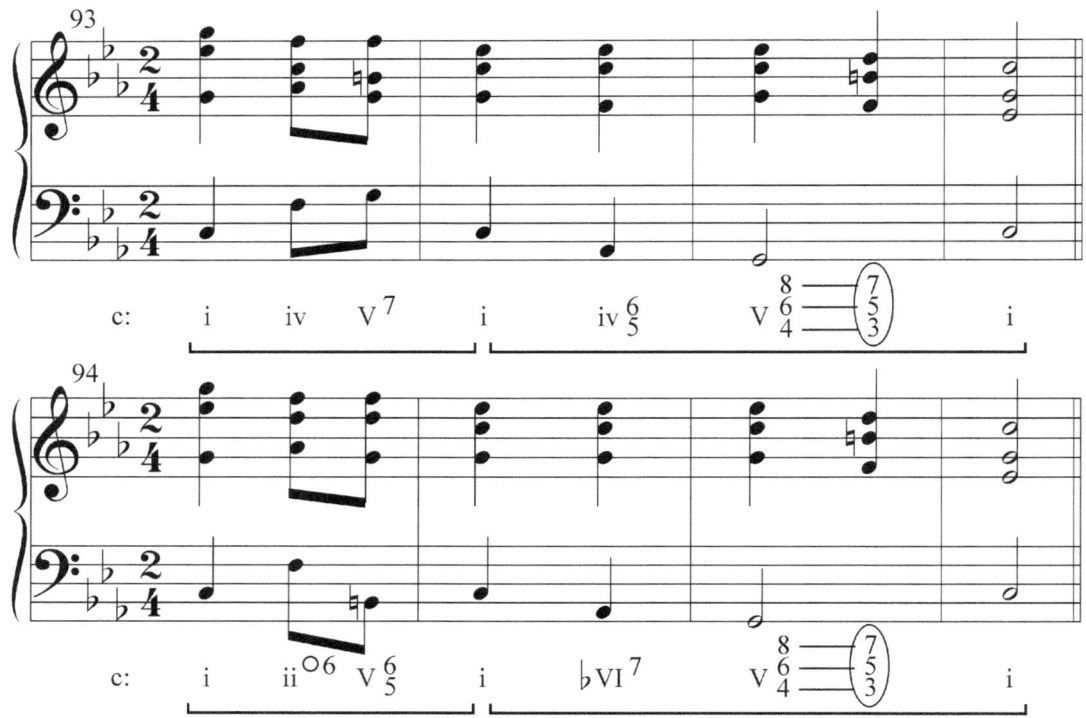

Exercise A–48: interlocking seventh chords in C major (harmonic and contrapuntal basses)

Notice the parallel octaves between the bass and the lowest part of the right hand in exercise 96 (and exercise 99 below). Since the exercise presents an instrumental style rather than a four-part vocal texture, the octaves should be interpreted not as an operation undermining the melodic independence of the upper parts but as a simple doubling of the bass line. Indeed, all of the parts in the right hand maintain optimal voice leading. Moreover, the descending chord sequence of interlocking sevenths weakens the effect of the octaves.

Exercise A–49: interlocking seventh chords in c minor (harmonic and contrapuntal basses)

Appendix B CLT Chords

In Chapter 6, we discussed the dominant family of chords, referring to the chord of the dominant as the tonal harmonic dominant and the chord of the leading tone as the tonal melodic dominant. We also borrowed and modified a term first used by Felix Salzer and Carl Schachter in *Counterpoint In Composition* (New York: McGraw-Hill, 1969), namely, the contrapuntal leading-tone chord. In this appendix, we shall abbreviate the contrapuntal leading-tone chord as the CLT chord, the V chord as the THD (tonal harmonic dominant), and the leading-tone triad or seventh as the TMD (the tonal melodic dominant).

CLT chords may function as either upward or downward passing chords or as complete or incomplete upper or lower neighbor chords. Moreover, the CLT chord is an essential component of either the complete or incomplete basic contrapuntal progression (an incomplete progression does not have an initial tonic).

Example B–1 illustrates the TMD triad in $^6_3$ position. Since the quality of the triad is diminished, it would be well to remember that the $^5_3$ and $^6_4$ positions of the chord are usually avoided because of the tritone interval between the lowest voice of the texture and one of the upper voices (see above, p. 54). (Notice the permissible succession of unequal 5ths in the alto and tenor voices, that is, B/F and C/G.)

Example B–1: the leading-tone triad (TMD) in $^6_3$ position

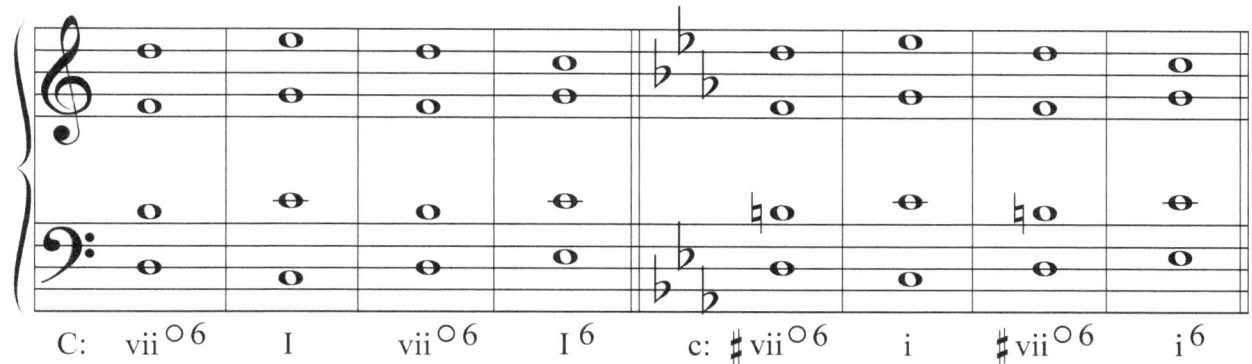

Once the TMD becomes a seventh chord, any position of the chord is acceptable, including the root position. In B–2b, the potential hazard of parallel 5ths prevents us from connecting the half-diminished TMD in first inversion to a root-position tonic (see the dotted lines showing the averted parallel 5ths). Thus, in order to avoid faulty motion, the chord of resolution has to be the I^6.

Example B–2

223

In example B–2e above, a conversion process involving two dominant-family chords takes place between a TMD in $^4_2$ position and either a root-position THD triad or THD seventh chord. Although not shown, this "conversion dominant" could also proceed in the reverse order, from the THD to the TMD.

In major, the chord of the leading tone is a half-diminished seventh; however, as we observed in Chapter 8, the leading tone cannot have the half-diminished seventh in minor, as the chord carries variable ♯6 as its seventh (pp. 150–151). The linear demands of ♯6 to move upwards to ♯7 and the harmonic tendency of the dissonant 7th to resolve downwards renders the chord useless. Therefore, in minor, the fully diminished seventh serves as the TMD; for its seventh component is variable ♭6, which always moves down to scale degree 5.

As demonstrated in example B–3c below, having the fully diminished seventh as the TMD enables us to connect to the tonic in *root position* because the 5th that occurs between its chord third and seventh is diminished, resulting in a succession of unequal 5ths, D/A♭ to C/G. If a half-diminished seventh were used instead of the fully diminished seventh, then the 5th between the chord third and seventh would be perfect, resulting in parallel 5ths from the TMD to the tonic (D/A to C/G).

Notice that in B–3f, we have a more powerful usage of the conversion dominant than that presented earlier in B–2e; for here, the difference between the fully diminished TMD and the THD is one half step, as the V chord is achieved when the seventh of the TMD moves down by half step to become the root of the V (A♭ to G), rather than by whole step (A to G).

Example B–3

Example B–4 illustrates the THD triad in $^6_3$ position.

Example B–4

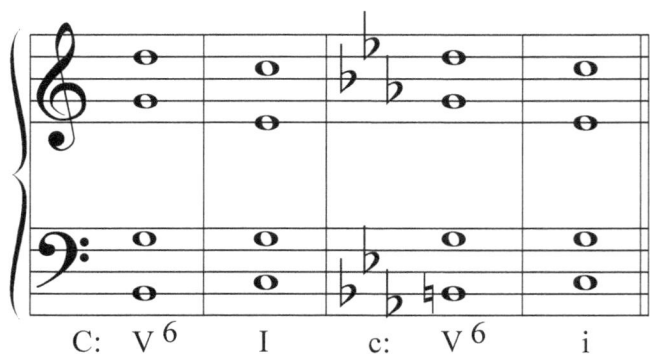

The $\frac{6}{4}$ position of the THD is limited by the restrictions imposed upon any $\frac{6}{4}$ chord. That is to say, the THD triad may occur as an upward or downward passing chord to a major or minor tonic (examples B–5a and 5d), as a complete upper neighbor to a major or minor tonic $\frac{5}{3}$ (examples B–2b and 2e), or as a complete lower neighbor chord to a major or minor tonic $\frac{6}{3}$ (examples B–2c and 2f).

Example B–5

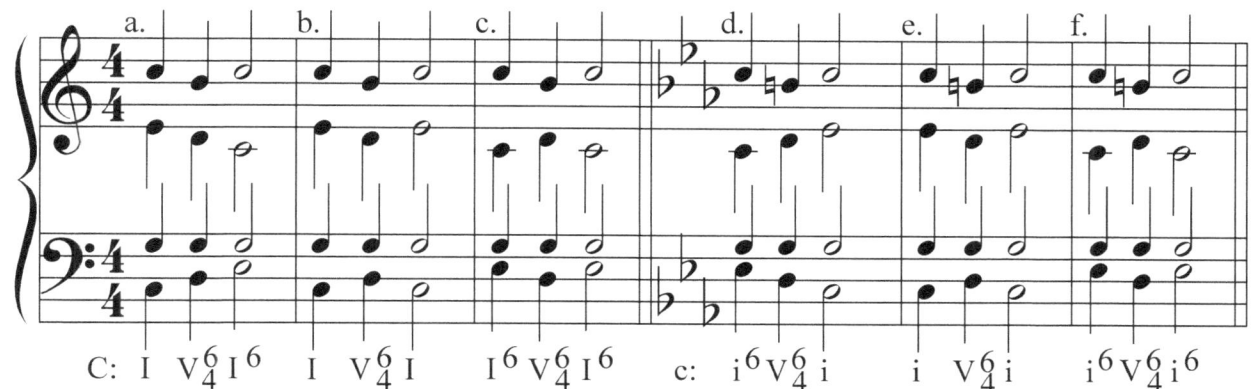

The THD chord of the seventh, shown in example B–6, occurs in any inverted position. As we shall see, the $\frac{4}{3}$ position of the THD, in which the consonant 3rd (D/F) formed above the bass "softens" the dissonant 4th from the chord fifth up to the root (D/G), may be used more freely than the $\frac{6}{4}$ position of its triadic counterpart.

Example B–6

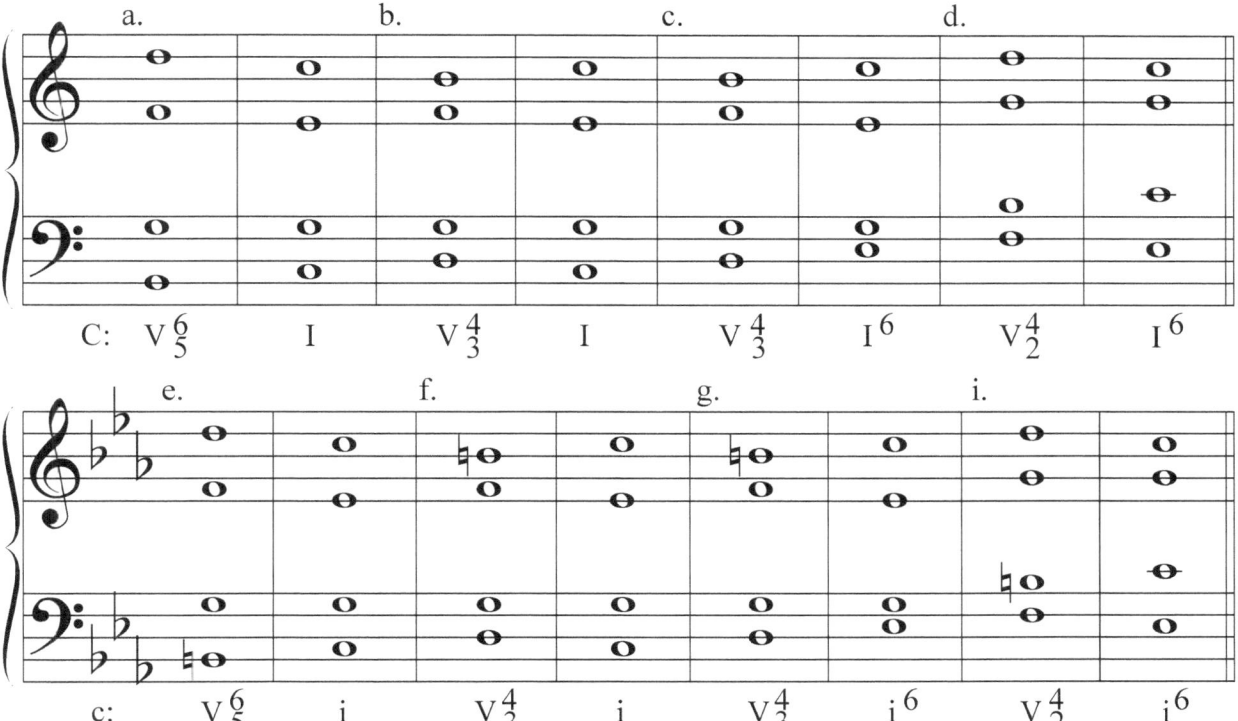

The second inversion of the seventh chord is the one position in which the dissonant 7th may resolve upwards by step under certain conditions. In example B–7, the V$^4_3$ chord is part of a contrapuntal progression that supports a motion in parallel 10ths between the bass and the soprano voices. The dissonant 7th continues upwards into either a 10th (examples B–7a and 7c) or a 12th (examples B–7b and 7d). The melodic activity between the bass and an upper voice overrides the traditional downward resolution.

Example B–7

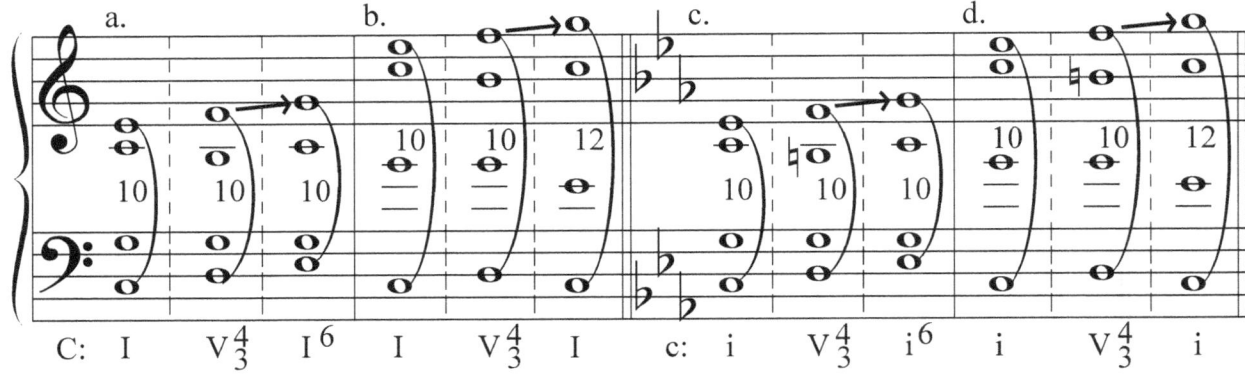

INDEX

A

accented complete neighbor tone, 186–187
   See also nonharmonic tones
accented passing tone, 105–106, 186, 192
   See also nonharmonic tones
accidentals, 12, 23, 26, 36
  double flats, 13
  double sharps, 13
  flat, 12–13, 17, 21–22, 23–26, 30, 34, 36–37, 39–40
  natural sign, 12
  sharp, 12–13, 17, 19, 20, 22–26, 30, 34–35 36–37, 39–40
acoustic interval, 47, 151, 177
active tones, 33, 38, 98–99
added 6th, 141, 178–179
Aeolian mode, 34, 59–61, 63, 66, 69–71, 74, 77, 78, 79, 81, 86, 88, 142, 144–145
alto clef, 14–15
Ambrose, Saint, 59
anticipation tone, 125–126, 139, 181–182, 185, 188, 194–195
anti-parallel motion, 97–98
apparent chord, 108–110, 112, 162, 172–173, 181
apparent seventh chord, 141, 156–157
appoggiatura, 181–182, 186, 190, 196
appoggiatura itself, 181, 186–187, 192, 195
appoggiatura six-four chord, 112
arpeggiated chord, 110–111
asymmetrical meter, 10
augmented 5th, 43, 46–47
augmented intervals, 28–32, 43, 151
augmented-major seventh chord, 153, 161–162, 174, 177, 179
augmented triad, 43–44, 46–47, 49, 56, 79, 116, 152–153, 161–162, 179
Augustine, Saint, 59
authentic cadence, 121–124, 133, 154, 156–158, 161, 165
auxiliary tone, 182

B

bar, 4
baritone clef, 15
bar line, 3–4
basic contrapuntal progression (BCP), xii, 133, 135–136, 169, 171–172, 197, 205, 216, 223
basic harmonic progression (BHP), xi–xii, 133–135, 169, 170–172
bass, 33, 44, 45, 51–54, 55–56, 92, 93, 96, 98, 100–104
bass clef, 14, 23, 25, 52
beams, 1
beat, 3–10
Boethius, Anicius Manlius Severinus, 59

C

cadence, 106, 112, 121–131, 133
  authentic cadence, 121–124, 133, 154, 156–158, 161, 165
  contrapuntal cadence, 121
  contrapuntal imperfect authentic cadence, 122, 124, 154, 161
  contrapuntal perfect authentic cadence, 122–123
  deceptive cadence, 122, 125–126
  half cadence, 122, 127–131
  harmonic cadence, 121
  harmonic imperfect authentic cadence, 122–123, 156
  harmonic perfect authentic cadence, 122, 154, 157, 165
  plagal cadence, 122, 126–127
  Phrygian cadence, 130–131
  semicadence, 127
cadential six-four chord, 105–108, 122, 128–130, 137–139, 147, 154, 156, 164, 172–173, 181, 188–189
cambiata tone, 184–185, 188, 192–195
   See also nonharmonic tones
C clef, 14–15
changing-note group, 183, 190
   See also nonharmonic tones

chord, 41–50, 52–57, 78–79, 91, 93, 98, 100–104
   eleventh, 113, 116, 133
   ninth, 42, 113, 116, 121, 133
   quartal harmony, 42
   secundal harmony, 42
   seventh, 42, 57, 113–119, 121, 123, 128, 133, 139–140, 141–179, 185–186, 189, 191–192, 193, 194, 221–222, 223–226
   tertian harmony, 42, 110, 113, 133, 156, 181
   thirteenth, 113, 116, 133
   triad, 41–50, 52–57
chordal skip, 102–104
chromatic half step, 17
chromaticism, 26–27, 99
chromatic scale, 17, 86–88
church modes, 59–89, 116, 141–145, 166
   Aeolian mode, 34, 59, 61, 63, 78–79, 88, 142, 144–145
   Dorian mode, 60–63, 78–79, 142, 144–145
   Ionian mode, 59–61, 63, 75, 78–79, 88, 141, 143
   Locrian mode, 60–61, 63, 78–79, 142–145, 166–167
   Lydian mode, 60–61, 63, 78–79, 142–143, 145, 167
   Mixolydian mode, 60–61, 63, 78–79, 142, 144
   Phrygian mode, 60–61, 63, 78–79, 130–131, 142–145, 167
circle of 5ths, 23–24, 36–37
clef, 14
   alto clef, 14–15
   baritone clef, 15
   bass clef, 14, 23, 25, 52
   C clef, 14–15
   F clef, 14–15, 23, 197
   G clef, 14–15, 23–25, 197
   mezzo-soprano clef, 15
   soprano clef, 15
   tenor clef, 15
   treble clef, 14, 23, 52
close position, 50, 52
close structure, 42, 50–52, 79
close voicing, 50, 52, 91
common practice period, 91
complete changing-note group, 183
   See also nonharmonic tones

complete neighbor tone, 109, 181–183, 186, 190
   See also nonharmonic tones
compound intervals, 27, 31, 98, 105, 114
compound meters, 5–7
conjunct motion, 28, 99, 133
consecutive motion, 97–98, 101,
consonance, 32, 92, 98, 105–107, 112, 114–115, 153, 159, 161, 187–188, 193
consonant 4th, 33, 105
contextual interval, 47, 151, 177
contrapuntal cadence, 121
contrapuntal imperfect authentic cadence, 122, 124, 154, 161
contrapuntal leading-tone chord (CLT chord), xii, 123–124, 133, 135, 159, 171, 223–226
contrapuntal perfect authentic cadence, 122–123
contra register, 15–16
   See also octave registers
contrary motion, 91, 96–98, 100–101, 119, 124, 127
conversion dominant, 224
cross relation, 101
cross-relation tritone, 168

D

deceptive cadence, 122, 125–126
diatonic half steps, 17
diatonicism, 26–27
diatonic scale, 17–18, 28–29, 30, 59, 148, 165
diminished intervals, 31–32, 43
diminished triad, 43–44, 46–49, 54, 56, 66, 76–78, 82, 116, 128, 139, 143–144, 150, 166, 179
direct motion, 94–96, 98, 101, 107
disjunct motion, 28, 133
dissonance, 32–33, 105–108, 111–112, 114, 119, 146, 151, 169, 173, 179, 187–188, 193
dissonant 4th, 33, 106–108, 130, 188, 225
dominant, 18, 34, 44, 47–48, 55–56, 66, 75–77, 79, 98, 100, 102–103, 105–110, 112, 121–128, 130–131, 133–134, 137–139, 141–148, 150, 152, 154, 156–164, 166–167, 169–173, 181, 188–189, 223–224
dominant seventh, 114–118, 141–147, 150, 153, 156, 158, 161–162, 165, 167, 171, 173–175, 179, 185–186, 189

Dorian mode, 60–63, 78–79, 142, 144–145
dots, 3, 5–7, 9–10
dotted rests, 3
double dot, 3
double flats, 12–13
double neighbor, 183, 190
    See also nonharmonic tones
double prime register, 15–16, 51
    See also octave registers
double sharps, 12–13
doubly augmented intervals, 28–29
doubly diminished intervals, 28–29
duple meter, 4–7, 9–10, 181
duplet, 9–10

E

ecclesiastical modes, 59
    See also church modes
échappée, 184–185, 188, 194–195
    See also nonharmonic tones
eighth note, 1–9, 139, 182
eighth rest, 1, 3
eleventh, 113, 116, 133
enharmonic equivalents, 12–13, 15, 113, 151
enharmonic keys, 24, 36–37
essential diatonic intervals, 28–29

F

F clef, 14–15, 23, 197
fifth, 42–50, 54, 56–57, 79, 82, 100–103, 106, 110, 113, 115, 117–119, 121–122, 125–126, 128–129, 131, 146–149, 152–156, 158–166, 169–174, 178–179, 185, 187, 189, 192–195, 225
figured bass, 44–45, 49, 79, 105, 107–109, 112, 114, 117–118, 149–150, 153, 155–156, 158, 162, 179, 189
first harmonic, 161–162, 269, 270
first inversion, 45–46, 56, 93, 105, 107–109, 111, 117–118, 124, 129, 131, 135–137, 140, 141, 146, 154, 156–158, 160–162, 170–172, 174, 177–179, 192, 194, 223
    six-five chord ($^6_5$ position), 118, 136, 154, 157, 172, 174–177, 179
    six-three chord ($^6_3$ position), 45, 49, 54, 56, 82, 100, 110, 112, 124, 126, 157, 223–224

first partial, 56–57
first principle of intervals, 29
five-three chord ($^5_3$ position or root position), 42, 44–46, 54, 56, 101, 107–110, 124, 137, 139, 223–224
flags, 1
flat, 12–13, 17, 21–26, 30, 34, 36–37, 38, 40, 47, 49, 109, 112, 148–149, 153, 155
four-part texture (four-voice texture), 50–51, 79, 103
  close position, 50, 52, 167
  close structure, 42, 50–53, 79
  close voicing, 50, 52, 91
  open position, 50
  open structure, 50–53, 79
  open voicing, 50, 91
  SATB, 51
four-three chord ($^4_3$ position), 118, 168, 171, 174–177, 226
four-two chord ($^4_2$ position), 118, 151, 155, 157, 174–177
frequency, 11, 56–57
fully diminished seventh, 145, 149–152, 174, 177–178, 224
fundamental frequency, 56–57

G

G clef, 14–15, 23–25, 197
grand staff, 14
great register, 15–16, 51, 197
    See also octave registers
great staff, 14–15, 50
Gregorian chant, 59
Gregory I, Saint (pope), 59

H

half cadence, 122, 127–131
half note, 1–3, 101, 106–108, 114–115, 125, 162, 181
half rest, 1
half step, 11–13, 17–19, 21, 23, 26–30, 33–34, 36, 38–41, 43, 45, 55, 59–63, 75, 78, 94–96, 117, 130, 142–143, 150, 163–164, 182, 183–184, 186
harmonic cadence, 121
harmonic embellishing chord, 134, 136, 140

harmonic imperfect authentic cadence, 122–123, 156
harmonic interval, 27, 41
harmonic minor, 34, 38–39, 47–49, 88, 116, 148
harmonic motion, 55, 98, 117, 121
harmonic perfect authentic cadence, 122, 154, 157, 165
harmonic series, 55–57, 100
  fundamental frequency, 56–57
  overtones, 56–57
  overtone series, 57
harmony, 28, 41–42, 59, 75, 99, 113, 115–116, 133, 151–152, 156, 186, 190, 197

I

imperfect authentic cadence, 121–124, 154, 156, 158, 161,
imperfect plagal cadence, 126–127
incomplete changing-note group, 183, 190
    See also nonharmonic tones
incomplete neighbor tone, 181, 184–185, 187
    See also nonharmonic tones
inflection, 30, 47, 87–88
interlocking seventh chords, 165, 221–222
intermediary chord (harmony), xi–xii, 137
    See also X-chord
interval inversion, 31, 44
intervals, 11–12, 23–24, 27–34, 38, 41–47, 52, 54–56, 59, 68, 82, 91–98, 101, 105–106, 108–109, 111–112, 113–114, 117–119, 121, 124–125, 131, 149–153, 155–156, 159–162, 166, 168, 173–174, 177, 179, 181–182, 189, 191–192, 194, 197, 223
Ionian mode, 59–61, 63, 75, 78–79, 88 141, 143

J

Jerome, Saint, 59

K

key, 18, 23–28, 31, 34–41, 43, 53–56, 59, 63–64, 67, 70, 73, 75, 79, 86, 108–109, 113, 121, 125–126, 131, 142, 152, 156, 165–168, 179, 181, 197

keynote, 18, 26, 63, 67
key signature, 23, 25–28, 30, 34–36, 38–39, 41, 59, 63, 65, 67, 73, 75, 79, 99, 108, 131, 142, 152, 178
  parallel major, 35–36, 38, 41, 61, 150
  parallel minor, 35–36
  relative major, 36
  relative minor, 34–36, 63, 66, 71

L

leading tone, 18, 26, 33–34, 38–39, 44, 47–48, 54–56, 75–76, 88, 93, 95, 98, 100, 102–103, 117, 119, 121–126, 130, 133, 135–139, 141–143, 147–151, 158–159, 161, 163, 166, 171, 173, 189, 223–224
ledger line, 14–15, 20, 23
like inflection, 30, 47
Locrian mode, 60–61, 63, 78–79, 142–145, 166–167
lower tetrachord, 19, 21–22
Lydian mode, 60–61, 63, 78–79, 142–143, 145, 167

M

major intervals, 31
major-minor tonal system, 33, 59, 91, 116, 141–142, 166
major scale, 17–23, 26, 29, 35, 61, 63, 75, 86–87
major 2nd, 31, 68, 174, 178–179, 182
major seventh chord, 116, 141–142, 153, 174
major triad, 43–49, 52, 56–57, 61, 76–77, 100, 103, 105, 107, 113–116, 121, 130, 147, 153, 158, 161, 163, 178–179, 182, 187, 192, 195–196
measure, 4–8, 10
mediant, 18, 34, 44, 47–48, 55–56, 61, 63, 75–77, 79, 100, 137, 141–144, 149, 153–154, 161–164, 171
melodic intervals, 28
melodic minor, 34, 38–41, 47–49, 88, 99, 116, 141–142, 148–150, 153, 155, 161, 164, 171
melodic motion, 28, 38, 40, 55, 117

meter, 3–10, 181
   asymmetrical meter, 10
   compound meters, 5–7
   duple meter, 4–7, 9–10, 181
   quadruple meter, 4–6, 10, 181
   simple meters, 5–6
   symmetrical meters, 4, 105, 277
   triple meter, 4–6, 10, 107
meter exchange, 9
   duplet, 9–10
   small triplet, 9
   triplet, 9
meter signature, 5
mezzo-soprano clef, 15
minor intervals, 31, 34
minor-major seventh chord, 155, 174, 176, 179
minor mode, 33–41, 44, 47, 49, 54, 63, 100, 116–117, 130, 139, 141, 145, 148, 150–151, 163, 166, 170
   Aeolian mode, 34, 59, 61, 63, 78–79, 88, 142, 144–145
   harmonic minor, 34, 38–39, 47–49, 88, 116, 148
   melodic minor, 34, 38–41, 47–49, 88, 99, 116, 141–142, 148–150, 153, 155, 161, 164, 171
   natural minor, 34, 36, 38, 40–41, 47–49, 59, 61–63, 66, 88, 130, 144, 148
minor 2nd, 38, 42, 121, 174, 182
minor triad, 43–49, 54, 56–57, 61, 76–78, 101, 109, 112, 116, 130, 139, 150, 155, 162, 164, 178–179
Mitchell, William J., xi
Mixolydian mode, 60–61, 63, 78–79, 142, 144
modal dominant, 166–167, 170
mode, 18–19, 23, 26–28, 30–31, 33–41, 43–44, 47–49, 53–56, 59–89, 99–100, 108–109, 113, 116–117, 130–131, 139, 141–148, 150–151, 156, 163, 165–168, 170, 179, 181
monophony, 59

N

natural minor, 34, 36, 38, 40–41, 47–49, 59, 61–63, 66, 88, 130, 144, 148

natural sign, 12
neighbor tone, 109–110, 158, 169, 171, 181–187, 190–196
   See also nonharmonic tones
ninth, 42, 113, 116, 133
non-appoggiaturas, 181–182, 184
   See also nonharmonic tones
nonchord tones (nonharmonic tones), 105
nonharmonic tones, 105–109, 112, 126, 130, 133, 137, 172–173, 181–182, 184, 186–192, 194–196
   anticipation tone, 125–126, 139, 181–182, 185, 188, 194–195
   appoggiatura, 181–182, 186, 190, 196
   appoggiatura itself (incomplete neighbor tone), 181, 186–187, 192, 195
   auxiliary tone, 182
   cambiata tone, 184–185, 188, 192–195
   changing-note group, 183, 190
   double neighbor, 183, 190
   échappée, 184–185, 188, 194–195
   neighbor tone, 109–110, 158, 169, 171, 81–187, 190–196
   non-appoggiaturas, 181–182, 184
   passing tone, 105–107, 114–115, 134, 156, 161, 181–182, 186, 188, 190–192, 194–195
   retardation, 189, 192
   suspension, 106–107, 113–115, 130, 146, 158, 160, 181, 186, 188–189, 191–192, 196
note head, 1, 30, 47, 49, 51–52, 95, 149, 155, 162

O

oblique motion, 91, 97–98, 101, 107, 126, 191
octave, 11–13, 15, 17–21, 23, 27–28, 31–32, 34, 36, 44–45, 50, 52, 61, 63, 75, 77, 86–87, 91–98, 101–102, 110, 114, 116, 119, 127, 135–136, 141, 144, 147, 154, 173, 189, 191–194, 197, 221
octave registers, 15, 21, 77, 116, 144
odd meter, 10
open position, 50
open structure, 50–53, 79
open voicing, 50, 91
outer voices, 93, 101, 122–124, 135–136, 197
overtones, 56–57
overtone series, 57

P

parallel major, 35–36, 38, 41, 61, 150
parallel duple meter, 9
parallel minor, 35–36
passing tone, 105–107, 114–115, 134, 156, 161, 181–182, 186, 188, 190–192, 194–195
perfect authentic cadence, 121–123, 156–157, 165
perfect 4th, 21, 31–33, 55, 68, 105, 117, 121, 139, 143
perfect 5th, 19, 21, 24, 31–32, 36–37, 43, 46, 55–57, 68, 91–94, 97–98, 117, 121, 124, 127, 142, 144, 146, 194
perfect intervals, 28, 31
perfect plagal cadence, 126
phrase, 105–107, 112, 121
Phrygian cadence, 130–131
Phrygian mode, 60–61, 63, 78–79, 130–131, 142–145, 167
piano staff, 14
picardy third, 130–131
pitch, 1, 11–15, 17–19, 21, 26–28, 30–31, 33–36, 38–42, 44–45, 47–49, 51, 55–57
plagal cadence, 122, 126–127
plainchant, 59
primary accents, 3–4, 8, 181
prime register, 15, 21, 51, 87
See also octave registers

Q

quadruple meter, 4–6, 10, 181
quadruple prime register, 15–16
See also octave registers
quartal harmony, 42
quarter note, 1–9, 181
quarter rest, 1, 4–5
quintuple prime register, 15–16
See also octave registers

R

real seventh chord, 115, 156–157, 160–161, 164, 179
relative major, 36
relative minor, 34–36, 63, 66, 71
re-sizing principle, 29–30
rest tones, 33, 38

retardation, 189, 192
See also nonharmonic tones
rhythm, 8, 105–108, 110–112, 121, 133, 181, 186, 192
rhythmic counting, 6–7, 9
rhythmic syllables, 6–8
Roman numeral chord symbols, 48–49, 78, 108, 117–118, 141, 145, 148, 150, 162, 167
root, 42–50, 52–57,
root position, 42, 44–46, 49, 52, 57, 79, 100, 102, 107–108, 111, 113, 116–117, 121, 128–129, 133–134, 138–139, 141, 151–152, 158, 161–162, 165–168, 170–172, 174, 177, 223–224

S

Salzer, Felix, xi–xii, 123, 223
SATB, 51
scale, 17–24, 26, 28–29, 36–38, 48, 59, 61–63, 73, 75, 86–88, 130, 133, 142, 168
scale degrees, 18
Schachter, Carl, xi–xii, 123, 223
Schenker, Heinrich, xi
secondary accents 3–5, 8, 181
secondary contrapuntal progression (SCP), xii, 133, 137, 139–140, 158–159, 169, 171–173, 197, 205, 216
secondary harmonic progression (SHP), xi–xii, 133, 137–139, 146, 157–158, 163–164, 169–173, 197–220
second inversion, 45–46, 49, 105, 117–118, 168
four-three chord ($^4_3$ position), 118, 168, 171, 174–177, 226
six-four chord ($^6_4$ position), 105–112, 118–119, 122–123, 128–130, 137–138, 147, 154, 156–157, 164, 172–173, 197–213, 216–222, 225
second principle of intervals (re-sizing principle), 29–30
secundal harmony, 42
semicadence, 127
seventh, 42, 57, 113–119, 121, 123, 128, 133, 139–140, 141–179, 185–186, 189, 191–194, 221–222, 223–226
sharp, 12–13, 17, 19, 20, 22–26, 30, 34–35, 36–37, 39–40

simple intervals, 27, 31, 33, 105, 114
simple meters, 4–7, 9–10, 181
six-five chord ($^6_5$ position), 118, 136, 154, 157, 172, 174–177, 179
six-four chord ($^6_4$ position), 105–112, 118–119, 122–123, 128–130, 137–138, 147, 154, 156–157, 164, 172–173, 197–213, 216–222, 225
sixteenth note, 1–8, 12–15, 88–89, 92–94, 96–106
sixteenth rest, 1–3
six-three chord ($^6_3$ position), 45, 49, 54, 56, 82, 100, 110, 112, 124, 126, 157, 223–224
sixty-fourth note, 1–2
sixty-fourth rest, 1
small register, 15–16, 21, 87, 197
 See also octave registers
small triplet, 9
solmization, 87–88
soprano clef, 15
staff, 1, 14–15, 23, 25, 42, 50, 53, 77, 108, 167
stem, 1, 30, 53, 79, 91, 197
sub-contra register, 15–16
 See also octave registers
subdominant, 18, 34, 43–44, 47–48, 55–56, 75–77, 79, 106, 108–110, 112, 125–126, 130–131, 134, 136–138, 140, 141–144, 146–147, 153, 156–160, 164, 166, 171
submediant, 18, 34, 44, 47–48, 55–56, 75–77, 79, 112, 125, 130, 137–138, 141–144
subtonic, 34, 38, 48, 55, 75–77, 79, 110, 131, 142–144, 148–149, 153–156
supertonic, 18, 34, 44, 47–48, 55–56, 75–77, 79, 107, 126, 128–130, 136–138, 140, 141–144, 146, 150, 166, 170–172
suspension, 106–107, 113–115, 130, 146, 158, 160, 181, 186, 188–189, 191–192, 196
 See also nonharmonic tones
syllable inflection, 87–88
symmetrical meters, 4, 10
syncopation, 8, 106, 181

T

tenor clef, 15
tertian harmony, 42, 110, 113, 133, 156, 181
tetrachords, 18–19, 21, 34, 39
third, 42–50, 54–57, 79, 82, 98, 100–103, 105–106, 110, 113, 117–118, 121, 125–127, 130–131, 145–147, 149, 150, 152–159, 161–162, 165, 169, 173–174, 178, 182, 185–186, 188–189, 224
third inversion, 117–118, 157, 174, 177
 four-two chord ($^4_2$ position), 118, 151, 155, 157, 174–177
thirty-second note, 1–2, 7
thirty-second rest, 1
ties, 3, 8
timbre, 56
time signatures, 5–7, 10
tonal center, 18, 33, 55, 66
tonal harmonic dominant (THD), 121–122, 133–134, 150, 157, 163, 167, 171, 223–225
tonality, 26–27, 53, 55–56, 117, 121, 148, 150
tonal melodic dominant (TMD), 121, 148, 150, 152, 223–224
tonic, 18, 27, 33–36, 38, 44, 47–49, 54–55, 59–61, 63–66, 75–78, 93, 95, 100, 107–110, 112, 117–119, 121–128, 130–131, 133–140, 141–150, 152, 154–159, 161–162, 165–167, 169–173, 188–189, 223–224
transposed modes, 61–86
treble clef, 14, 23, 25, 52
triad, 41–50, 52–57, 59–61, 63, 66, 75–79, 82, 91, 93, 98, 100–103, 105–107, 109–110, 112, 113–117, 121, 126, 128–131, 133, 135–136, 139–140, 141–150, 152–155, 157–159, 161–164, 166–167, 171, 174, 178–179, 182, 187, 189, 192, 195–196, 223–225
triple meter, 4–6, 10, 107
triple prime register, 15–16
 See also octave registers
triplet, 9
tritone, 32, 54–56, 66, 82, 98, 140, 158, 161, 166–168, 172, 223
two-progression framework, xi, 141, 169–173, 205–206, 209, 216, 218, 220

U

unaccented passing tone, 105, 186, 194
  See also nonharmonic tones
upper leading tone, 130, 143
upper tetrachord, 19–21, 39

V

variable scale degrees, 40–41, 47–49, 54, 98,
  148–149, 155, 197
voice, 50–54, 56–57, 73, 79, 82, 87, 91–103,
  105–107, 109–110, 112, 113–115,
  117, 119, 121–127, 130–131, 133–134,
  135–140, 145–148, 151, 154, 156–162,
  164–166, 168–173, 182, 185, 188–189,
  191–194, 196, 197, 221, 223, 226
voice exchange, 135–136
volume, 56

W

whole notes, 1–3, 79
whole rests, 1, 3
whole step, 12, 17–19, 26–28, 32–34, 38–39, 41,
  48, 55, 59, 64, 75, 94–96, 142, 182–184

X

X-chord, 137–140, 157–158, 162–164, 170–172,
  197–220
  See also intermediary chord (harmony)

Worksheets

Note: Since Chapter 1 constitutes a review of *Finding The Right Pitch: A Guide To The Study Of Music Fundamentals*, the worksheets begin with Chapter 2.

Basic Harmony Worksheet 2–1

Name _____

Worksheet 2–1 for Chapter 2: The Church Modes

Answer the following questions using the following terms: Ionian, Dorian, Phrygian, Lydian, Mixolydian, Aeolian, and Locrian.

1. What mode has half steps between scale degrees 2-3 and 5-6? _____

2. What mode has half steps between scale degrees 3-4 and 6-7? _____

3. What mode has half steps between scale degrees 1-2 and 5-6? _____

4. What mode has half steps between scale degrees 2-3 and 6-7? _____

5. What mode has half steps between scale degrees 1-2 and 4-5? _____

6. What mode has half steps between scale degrees 4-5 and 7-8? _____

7. What mode has half steps between scale degrees 3-4 and 7-8? _____

Basic Harmony Worksheet 2–2

Name _____

Worksheet 2–2 for Chapter 2: The Church Modes

Answer the following questions using the following terms: Ionian, Dorian, Phrygian, Lydian, Mixolydian, Aeolian, and Locrian.

1. What mode has half steps between scale degrees 3-4 and 6-7? _____

2. What mode has half steps between scale degrees 2-3 and 6-7? _____

3. What mode has half steps between scale degrees 1-2 and 4-5? _____

4. What mode has half steps between scale degrees 2-3 and 5-6? _____

5. What mode has half steps between scale degrees 1-2 and 5-6? _____

6. What mode has half steps between scale degrees 3-4 and 7-8? _____

7. What mode has half steps between scale degrees 4-5 and 7-8? _____

Basic Harmony Worksheet 2–3

Name _____

Worksheet 2–3 for Chapter 2: The Church Modes

Given the following octave ranges and clefs, create the indicated church modes by adding the appropriate accidentals; *do not change the first or last note of each octave*—that is the keynote.

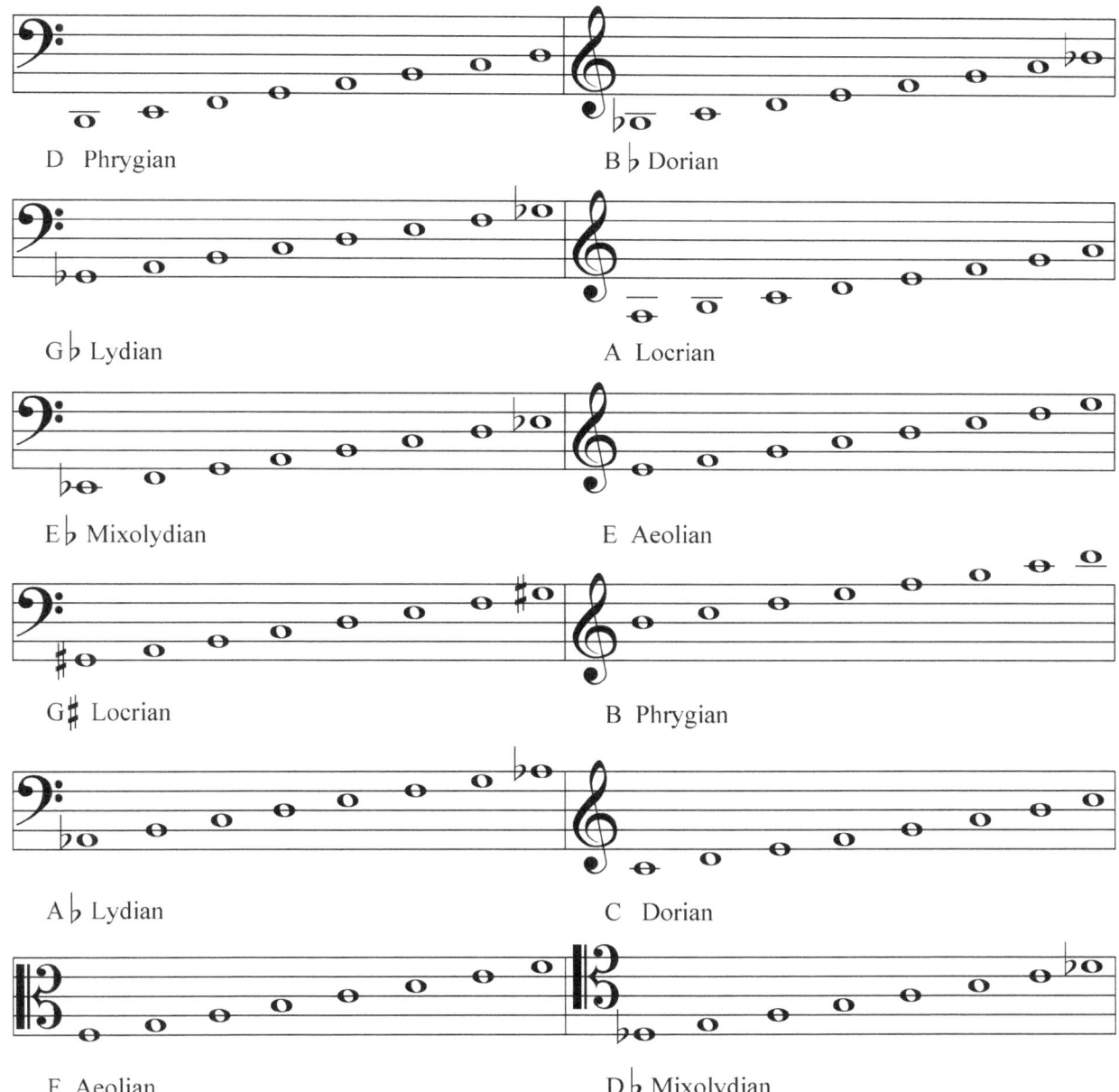

Basic Harmony Worksheet 2–4

Name _____

Worksheet 2–4 for Chapter 2: The Church Modes

Given the following octave ranges and clefs, create the indicated church modes by adding the appropriate accidentals; *do not change the first or last note of each octave*—that is the keynote.

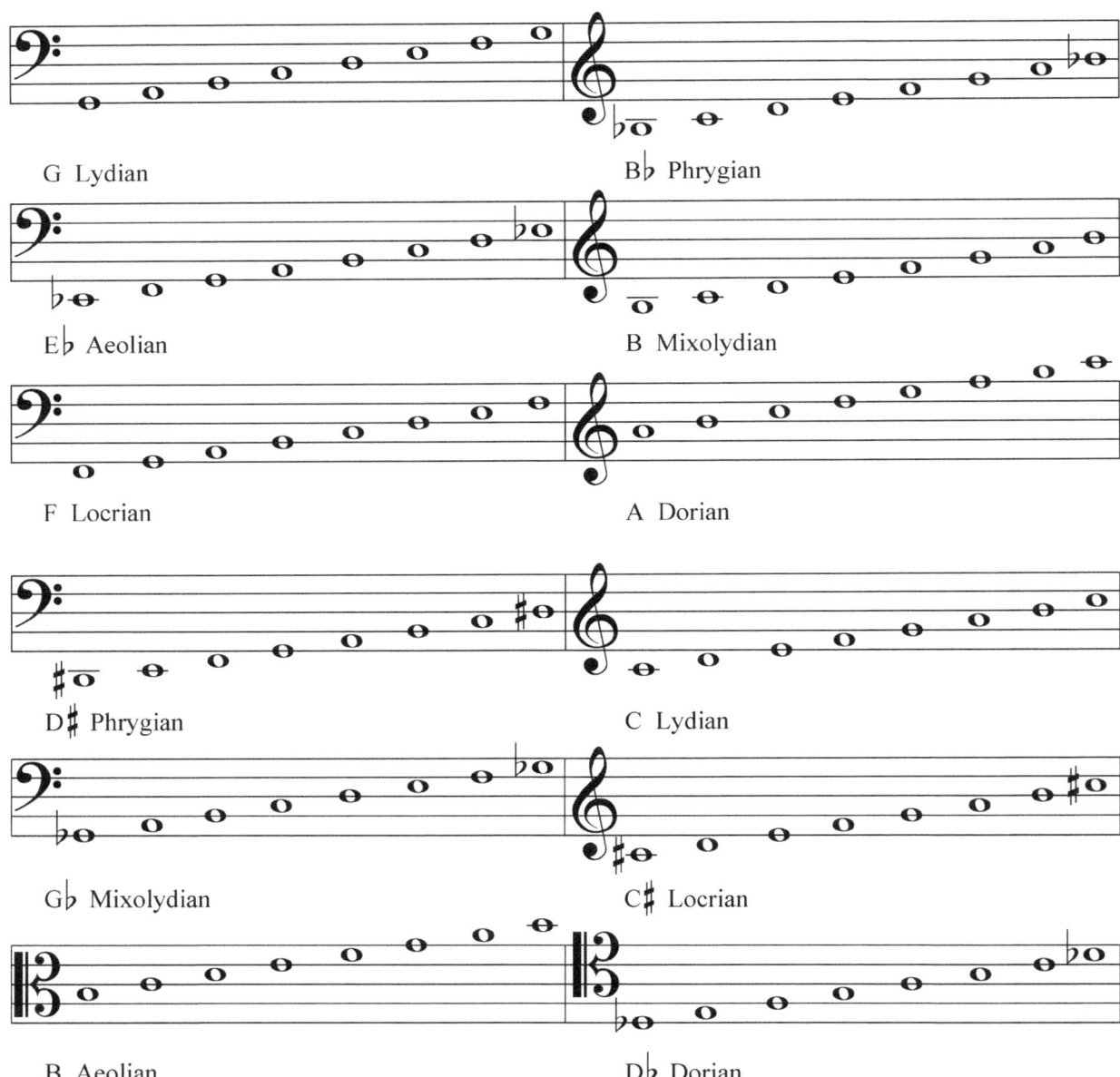

Basic Harmony Worksheet 2–5

Name _____

Worksheet 2–5 for Chapter 2: The Church Modes

Supply the correct key signature for the following transposed modes (that is, supply the correct number of sharps or flats):

Abbreviations

D = Dorian
P = Phrygian
Ly = Lydian
M = Mixolydian
A = Aeolian
L = Locrian

Example: G♯ L: __3♯__

Untransposed Major	Untransposed Mode	=	Transposed Major	Transposed Mode
C	B L (Locrian)	=	X (= A major)	G♯
1	7		1	7
Major 7th			Major 7th	

1. F♯ D : _____   6. F♯ A : _____

2. C   P : _____   7. E♭ P : _____

3. E♭ Ly : _____   8. A   Ly : _____

4. C♯ M : _____   9. E♭ M : _____

5. B♭ D : _____   10. A   L : _____

Basic Harmony Worksheet 2–6

Name _____

Worksheet 2–6 for Chapter 2: The Church Modes

Given the key (tonic note) and key signature (that is, the number of sharps or flats), name the mode using the following abbreviations:

D   =   Dorian
P   =   Phrygian
Ly =   Lydian
M   =   Mixolydian
A   =   Aeolian
L   =   Locrian

Example: E♭ 7♭ : __P__

Untransposed Major ↑ Untransposed Mode = Transposed Major   Transposed Mode
                        (E Phrygian)
         C   X   =   7♭ (= C♭ major)   E♭
         1_____3   1_____3
           Major 3rd   Major 3rd

1. C♯ 3♯ : ___P___   6. B♭ 6♭ : ___P___

2. B♭ 3♭ : ___M___   7. E 5♯ : ___Ly___

3. B 6♯ : ___Ly___   8. F 4♭ : ___A___

4. E♭ 5♭ : ___D___   9. B 3♯ : ___D___

5. C♯ 4♯ : ___A___   10. C♯ 2♯ : ___L___

Basic Harmony Worksheet 2–7

Name _____

Worksheet 2–7 for Chapter 2: The Church Modes

Supply the correct key signature for the following transposed modes (that is, supply the correct number of sharps or flats):

Abbreviations

D   =   Dorian

P   =   Phrygian

Ly =   Lydian

M   =   Mixolydian

A   =   Aeolian

L   =   Locrian

Example: G♯ L: __3♯__ ←

Untransposed Major	Untransposed Mode	=	Transposed Major	Transposed Mode
C	B L (Locrian)	=	X (= A major)	G♯
1 ———————— 7			1 ———————— 7	
Major 7th			Major 7th	

1. B   D: _____

2. E♭ A: _____

3. G♯ P: _____

4. F   M: _____

5. E   Ly: _____

6. A♭ M: _____

7. D♯ A: _____

8. A♭ Ly: _____

9. D   P: _____

10. G♯ M: _____

Basic Harmony Worksheet 2–8

Name _____

Worksheet 2–8 for Chapter 2: The Church Modes

Given the key (tonic note) and key signature (that is, the number of sharps or flats), name the mode using the following abbreviations:

D = Dorian
P = Phrygian
Ly = Lydian
M = Mixolydian
A = Aeolian
L = Locrian

Example: E♭ 7♭ : __P__

Untransposed Major → Untransposed Mode = Transposed Major   Transposed Mode
                         (E Phrygian)
        C   X   =   7♭ (= C♭ major)   E♭
        1_____3   1_____3
              Major 3rd   Major 3rd

1. B   6♯ : _____   6. D♭ 6♭ : _____

2. A   4♯ : _____   7. C♯ 5♯ : _____

3. F   3♭ : _____   8. F   5♭ : _____

4. C♯ 6♯ : _____   9. B   4♯ : _____

5. A   1♭ : _____   10. D   3♭ : _____

Basic Harmony Worksheet 2–9

Name _____

Worksheet 2–9 for Chapter 2: The Church Modes

Supply the correct key signature for the following transposed modes (that is, supply the correct number of sharps or flats):

Abbreviations

D = Dorian
P = Phrygian
Ly = Lydian
M = Mixolydian
A = Aeolian
L = Locrian

Example: G♯ L: __3♯__

Untransposed Major	Untransposed Mode	=	Transposed Major	Transposed Mode
C	B L (Locrian)	=	X (= A major)	G♯
1	7		1	7
Major 7th			Major 7th	

1. G   Ly :   __2♯__

2. F♯ M :   __5♯__

3. C   L :   __5♭__

4. E   A :   __1♯__

5. E♭ D :   __5♭__

6. F   L :   __6♭__

7. D♯ P :   __5♯__

8. D♭ Ly : __4♭__

9. C♯ A :   __4♯__

10. B♭ M :   __3♭__

Basic Harmony Worksheet 2–10

Name _____

Worksheet 2–10 for Chapter 2: The Church Modes

Given the key (tonic note) and key signature (that is, the number of sharps or flats), name the mode using the following abbreviations:

D = Dorian
P = Phrygian
Ly = Lydian
M = Mixolydian
A = Aeolian
L = Locrian

Example: E♭ 7♭ : __P__

Untransposed Major ↑ Untransposed Mode = Transposed Major   Transposed Mode
(E Phrygian)

   C   X   =   7♭ (= C♭ major)   E♭
   1_____3   1_____3
       Major 3rd   Major 3rd

1. G   3♭: __P__   6. G♯ 4♯: __P__

2. G♭ 7♭: __M__   7. F♯ 2♯: __P__

3. F♯ 4♯: __D__   8. A   2♯: __M__

4. B♭ 1♭: __Ly__   9. F♯ 7♯: __Ly__

5. E♭ 6♭: __A__   10. G   4♭: __L__

Basic Harmony Worksheet 2–11

Name _____

Worksheet 2–11 for Chapter 2: The Church Modes

Construct, in open structure with four voices using half notes only, the indicated triad in its correct position according to the context of the key and mode. The absence of figured bass in the circled chord symbol indicates root position. Remember that a circled Roman numeral constitutes a *generalized* type of chord symbol that, without describing the specific chord quality, nonetheless indicates the exact scale degree of the mode upon which a triad may be formed. Since this generalized type of chord symbol makes no distinction between triad qualities, the Roman numerals are all expressed in uppercase.

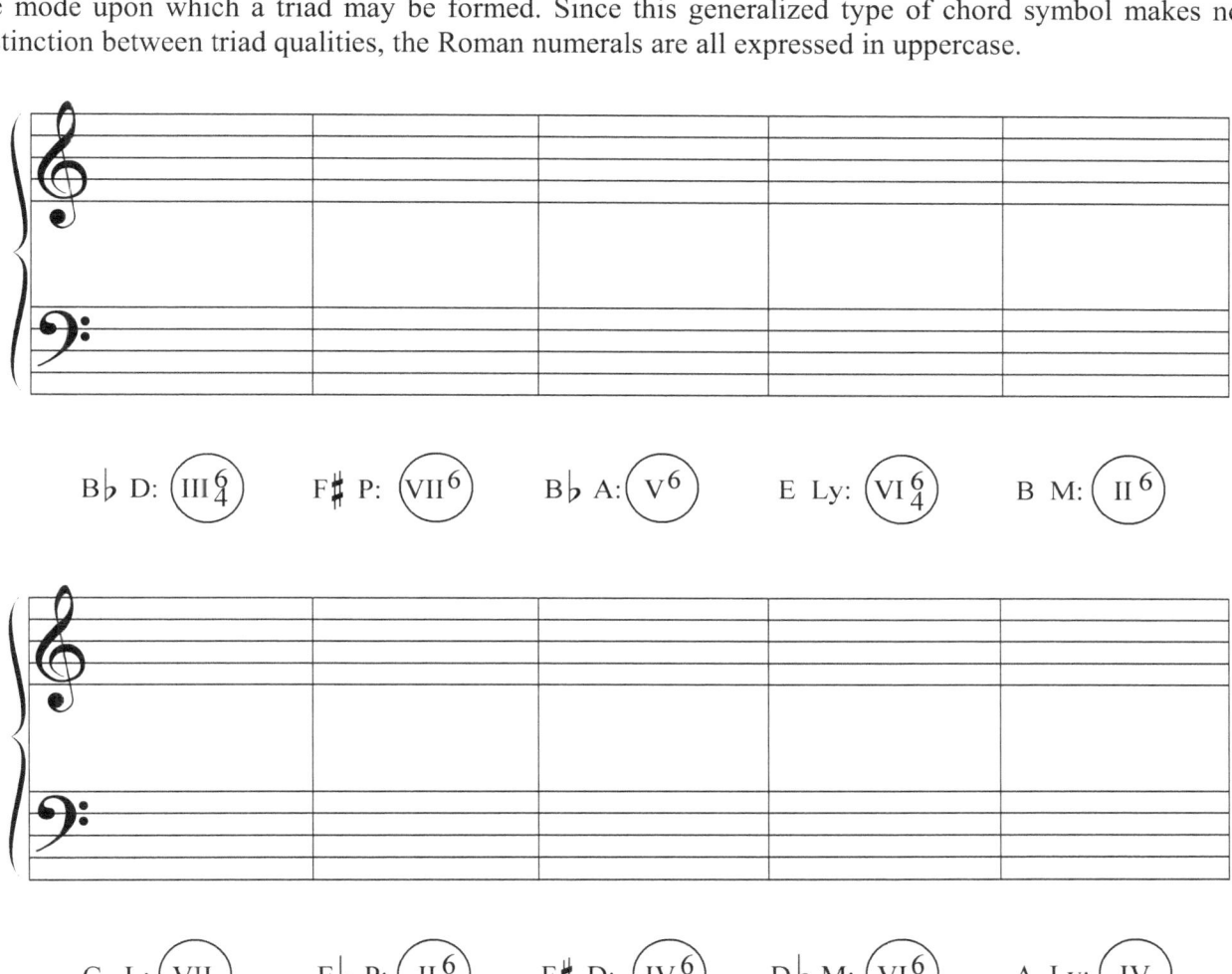

Abbreviations
D = Dorian
P = Phrygian
Ly = Lydian
M = Mixolydian
A = Aeolian
L = Locrian

Basic Harmony Worksheet 2–12

Name _____

Worksheet 2–12 for Chapter 2: The Church Modes

Construct, in open structure with four voices using half notes only, the indicated triad in its correct position according to the context of the key and mode. The absence of figured bass in the circled chord symbol indicates root position. Remember that a circled Roman numeral constitutes a *generalized* type of chord symbol that, without describing the specific chord quality, nonetheless indicates the exact scale degree of the mode upon which a triad may be formed. Since this generalized type of chord symbol makes no distinction between triad qualities, the Roman numerals are all expressed in uppercase.

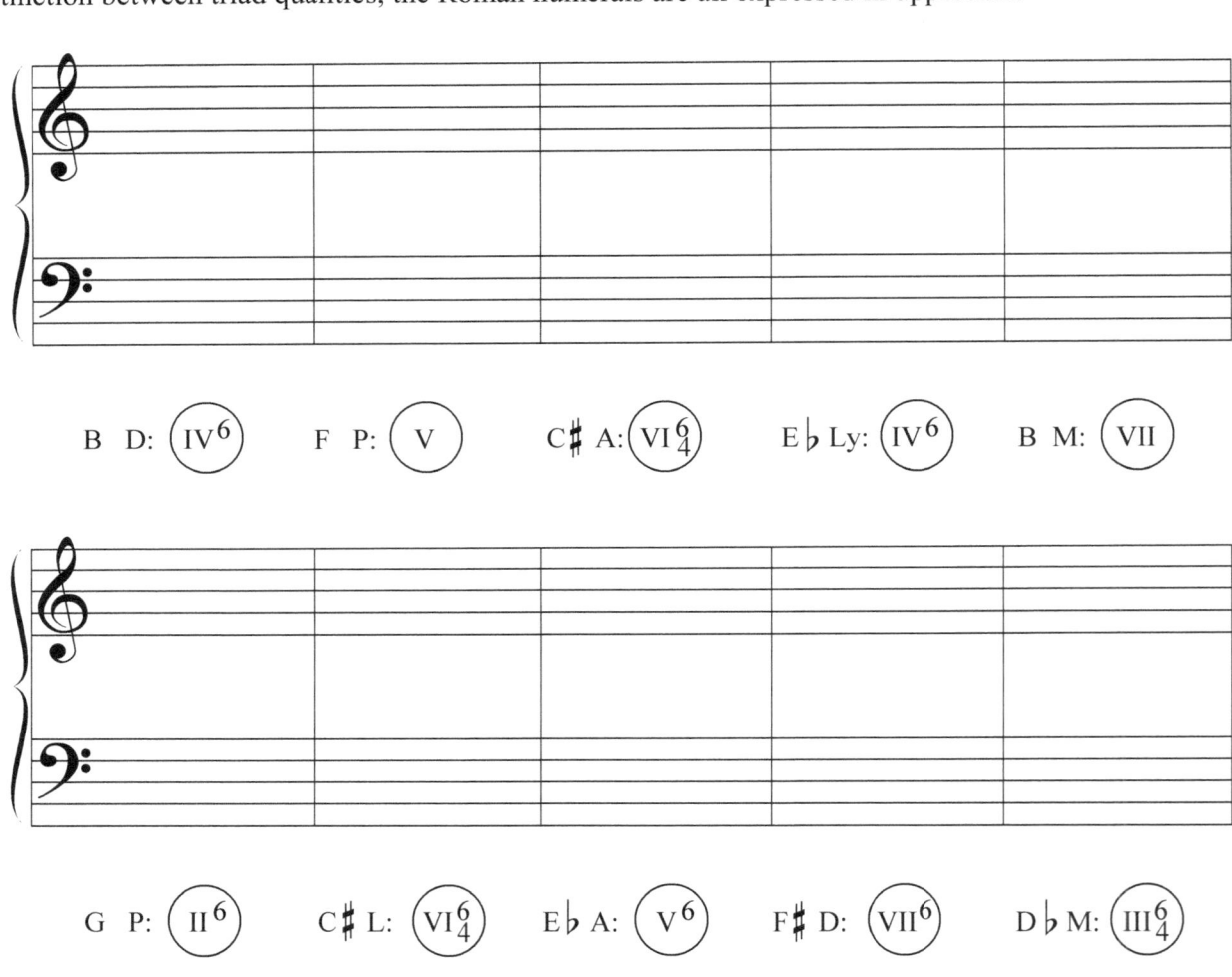

Abbreviations
D = Dorian
P = Phrygian
Ly = Lydian
M = Mixolydian
A = Aeolian
L = Locrian

Basic Harmony Worksheet 2–13

Name _____

Worksheet 2–13 for Chapter 2: The Church Modes

The Modal Matrix for Sharps: using ascending perfect 5ths, supply the appropriate keys from the left to the right side of the matrix. The completed matrix will provide you with the key signatures for all of the modes that take sharps. For example, a perfect 5th above G for the Ionian mode is D. The key signature for D Ionian (D major) is two sharps.

SHARPS	1♯	2♯	3♯	4♯	5♯	6♯	7♯	SHARPS
Ionian	G	D						Ionian
Dorian	A							Dorian
Phrygian	B							Phrygian
Lydian	C							Lydian
Mixolydian	D							Mixolydian
Aeolian	E							Aeolian
Locrian	F♯							Locrian

Basic Harmony Worksheet 2–14

Name _____

Worksheet 2–14 for Chapter 2: The Church Modes

The Modal Matrix for Flats: using ascending perfect 4ths, supply the appropriate keys from the left to the right side of the matrix. The completed matrix will provide you with the key signatures for all of the modes that take flats. For example, a perfect 4th above F for the Ionian mode is B♭. The key signature for B♭ Ionian (B♭ major) is two flats.

FLATS	1♭	2♭	3♭	4♭	5♭	6♭	7♭	FLATS
Ionian	F	B♭	E♭	A♭	D♭	G♭	C♭	Ionian
Dorian	G	C	F	B♭	E♭	A♭	D♭	Dorian
Phrygian	A	D	G	C	F	B♭	E♭	Phrygian
Lydian	B♭	E♭	A♭	D♭	G♭	C♭	F♭	Lydian
Mixolydian	C	F	B♭	E♭	A♭	D♭	G♭	Mixolydian
Aeolian	D	G	C	F	B♭	E♭	A♭	Aeolian
Locrian	E	A	D	G	C	F	B♭	Locrian

Basic Harmony Worksheet 2–15

Name _____

Worksheet 2–15 for Chapter 2: The Church Modes

Meter and Rhythm)

Given the following meter, write the counts directly under the appropriate note or rest and supply any missing bar lines.

    The challenge of this exercise is not in the counting but in the performance. You should be seated at a desk or table. To perform the exercise, tap both feet to the *half note* and execute the rhythms on a hard surface with both hands. You will find that if your feet remain constant with the half note, the beginnings of certain measures will not coincide with your feet—keeping your place is the real challenge. In the example, a dash under some of the counts indicates where your feet should tap. Do not try to play the exercise too quickly. A slow and steady pace is highly recommended.

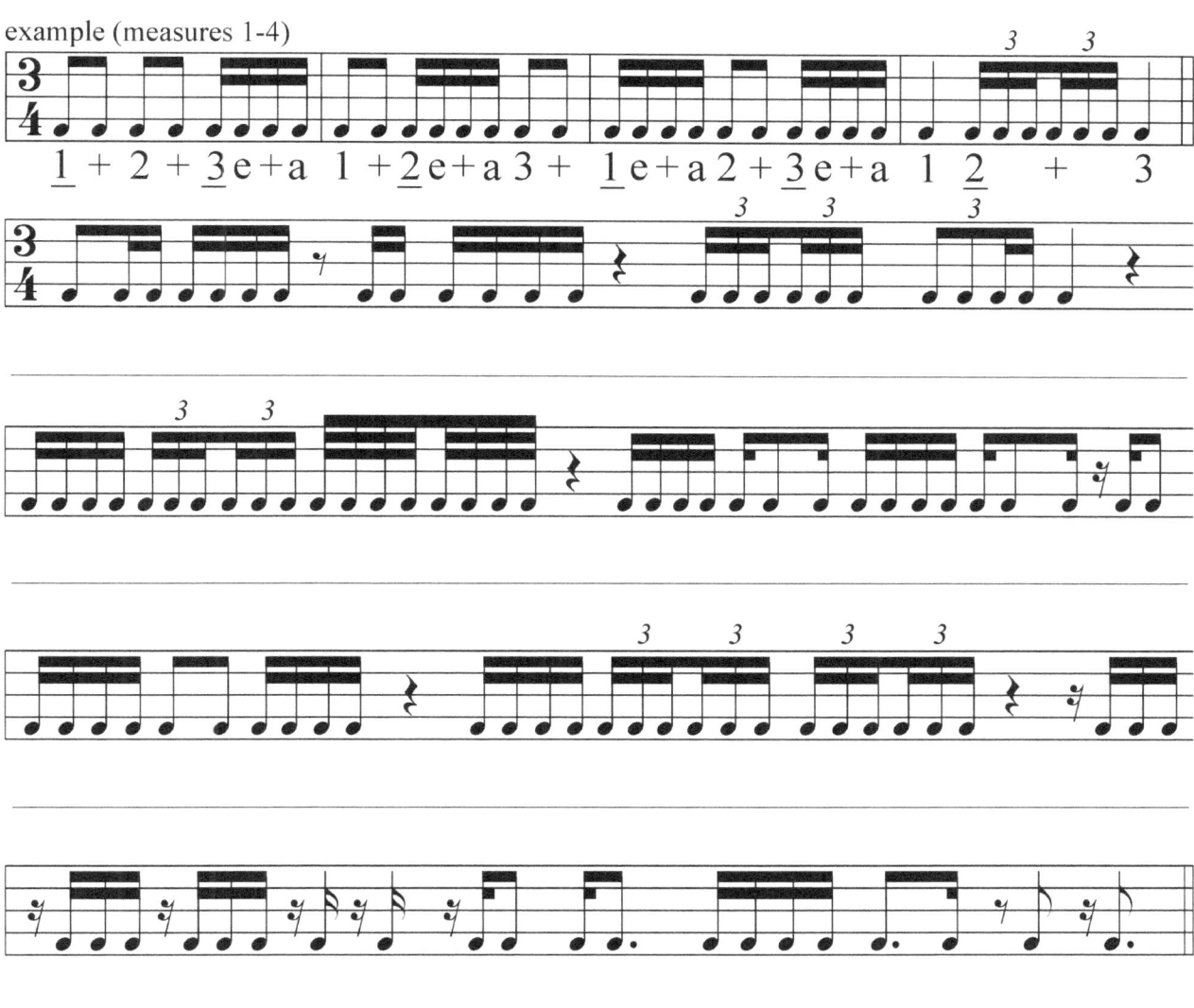

Basic Harmony Worksheet 3–1

Name _____

Worksheet 3–1 for Chapter 3: Voice Leading

Describe the motion between the two given voices (the voices are identifiable according to stem direction and clef). Correct motion takes a check mark (✓), incorrect motion an **x**. Use the following abbreviations for your descriptions. Include the interval of arrival in the description. (For example: Sim3 means similar motion to a 3rd. D5 is direct motion to a 5th. However, P3, which means parallel 3rds, indicates more than one interval.)

I. correct motion ✓
    Sim3, Sim6   =   Similar 3rd, 6th
    Sim5, Sim8   =   Similar 5th, 8ve
    O   =   Oblique Motion
    PP5–d5   =   Parallel Perfect 5th to Diminished 5th
    Pd5–P5   =   Parallel Diminished 5th to Perfect 5th
    P3, P6   =   Parallel 3rd, 6ths
    C3, C5, C6, C8 =   Contrary 3rd, 5th, 6th, 8ve

II. incorrect motion **x**
    D5, D8   =   Direct 5th, 8ve
    ConsP5, ConsP8 =   Consecutive Perfect 5ths, 8ves
    PP1, PP5, PP8 =   Parallel Perfect Unisons, 5ths, 8ves

motion: **Sim3**
✓ / x: **✓**

motion: _____ _____ _____ _____ _____

✓ / x : _____ _____ _____ _____ _____

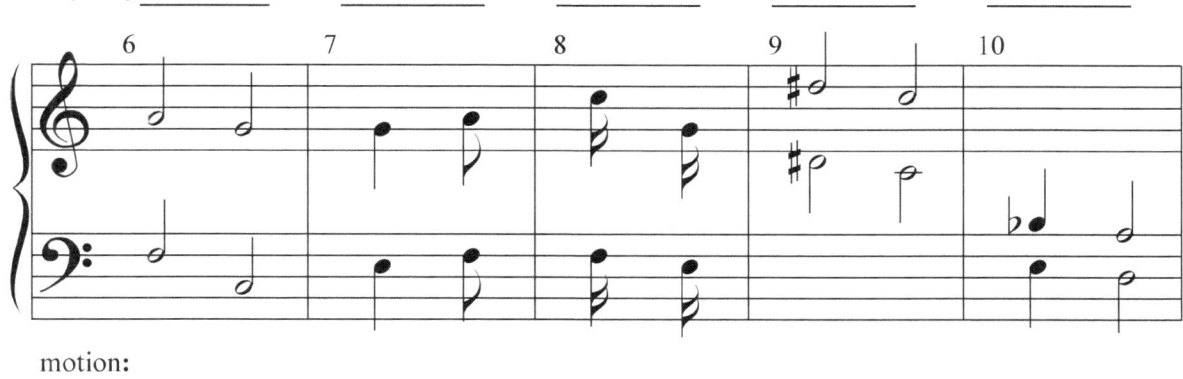

motion: _____ _____ _____ _____ _____

✓ / x : _____ _____ _____ _____ _____

Basic Harmony Worksheet 3–2

Name _____

Worksheet 3–2 for Chapter 3: Voice Leading

Describe the motion between the two given voices (the voices are identifiable according to stem direction and clef). Correct motion takes a check mark (✓), incorrect motion an ✗. Use the following abbreviations for your descriptions. Include the interval of arrival in the description. (For example: Sim3 means similar motion to a 3rd. D5 is direct motion to a 5th. However, P3, which means parallel 3rds, indicates more than one interval.)

I. correct motion ✓
- Sim3, Sim6 = Similar 3rd, 6th
- Sim5, Sim8 = Similar 5th, 8ve
- O = Oblique Motion
- PP5–d5 = Parallel Perfect 5th to Diminished 5th
- Pd5–P5 = Parallel Diminished 5th to Perfect 5th
- P3, P6 = Parallel 3rd, 6ths
- C3, C5, C6, C8 = Contrary 3rd, 5th, 6th, 8ve

II. incorrect motion ✗
- D5, D8 = Direct 5th, 8ve
- ConsP5, ConsP8 = Consecutive Perfect 5ths, 8ves
- PP1, PP5, PP8 = Parallel Perfect Unisons, 5ths, 8ves

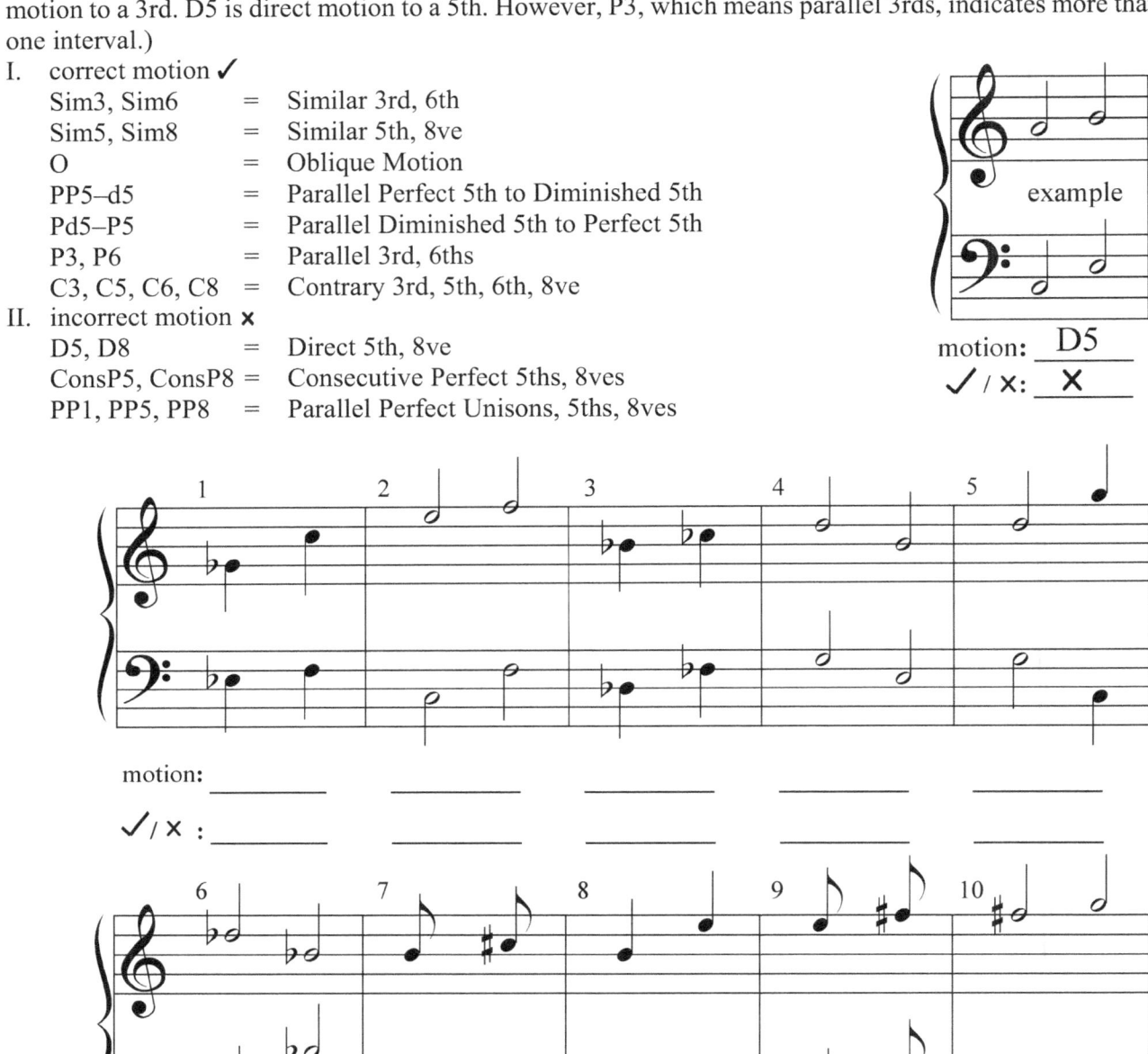

Basic Harmony Worksheet 3–3

Name _____

Worksheet 3–3 for Chapter 3: Voice Leading

Describe the motion between the two given voices (the voices are identifiable according to stem direction and clef). Correct motion takes a check mark (✓), incorrect motion an ✗. Use the following abbreviations for your descriptions. Include the interval of arrival in the description. (For example: Sim3 means similar motion to a 3rd. D5 is direct motion to a 5th. However, P3, which means parallel 3rds, indicates more than one interval.)

I. correct motion ✓
    Sim3, Sim6   =   Similar 3rd, 6th
    Sim5, Sim8   =   Similar 5th, 8ve
    O   =   Oblique Motion
    PP5–d5   =   Parallel Perfect 5th to Diminished 5th
    Pd5–P5   =   Parallel Diminished 5th to Perfect 5th
    P3, P6   =   Parallel 3rd, 6ths
    C3, C5, C6, C8 =   Contrary 3rd, 5th, 6th, 8ve

II. incorrect motion ✗
    D5, D8   =   Direct 5th, 8ve
    ConsP5, ConsP8 =   Consecutive Perfect 5ths, 8ves
    PP1, PP5, PP8 =   Parallel Perfect Unisons, 5ths, 8ves

motion: <u>consP5</u>
✓ / ✗: <u>✗</u>

Basic Harmony Worksheet 3–4

Name _____

Worksheet 3–4 for Chapter 3: Voice Leading

Describe the motion between the two given voices (the voices are identifiable according to stem direction and clef). Correct motion takes a check mark (✓), incorrect motion an ✗. Use the following abbreviations for your descriptions. Include the interval of arrival in the description. (For example: Sim3 means similar motion to a 3rd. D5 is direct motion to a 5th. However, P3, which means parallel 3rds, indicates more than one interval.)

I. correct motion ✓
   Sim3, Sim6   =   Similar 3rd, 6th
   Sim5, Sim8   =   Similar 5th, 8ve
   O   =   Oblique Motion
   PP5–d5   =   Parallel Perfect 5th to Diminished 5th
   Pd5–P5   =   Parallel Diminished 5th to Perfect 5th
   P3, P6   =   Parallel 3rd, 6ths
   C3, C5, C6, C8   =   Contrary 3rd, 5th, 6th, 8ve

II. incorrect motion ✗
   D5, D8   =   Direct 5th, 8ve
   ConsP5, ConsP8   =   Consecutive Perfect 5ths, 8ves
   PP1, PP5, PP8   =   Parallel Perfect Unisons, 5ths, 8ves

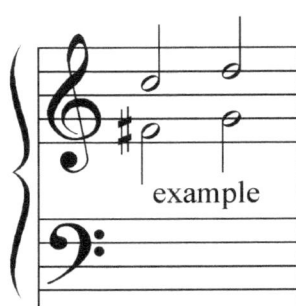

example

motion: Pd5–P5
✓ / ✗: ✓

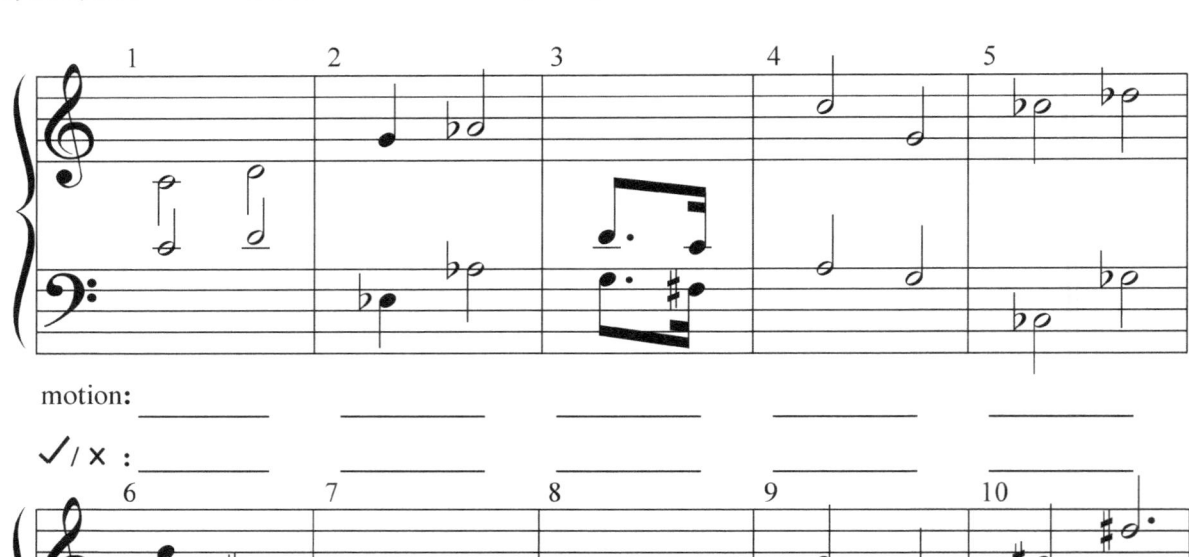

motion: _____ _____ _____ _____ _____
✓ / ✗: _____ _____ _____ _____ _____

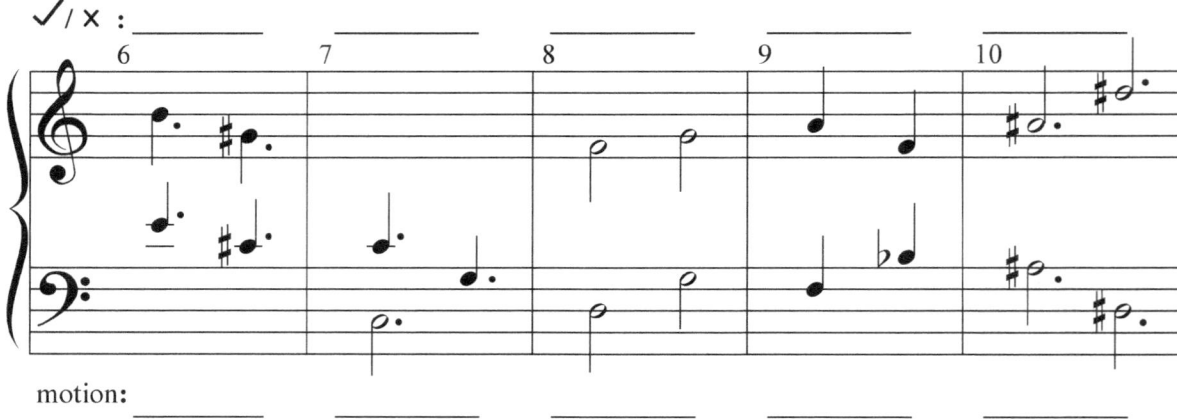

motion: _____ _____ _____ _____ _____
✓ / ✗: _____ _____ _____ _____ _____

Basic Harmony Worksheet 3–5

Name _____

Worksheet 3–5 for Chapter 3: Voice Leading

Describe the motion between the two given voices (the voices are identifiable according to stem direction and clef). Correct motion takes a check mark (✓), incorrect motion an **x**. Use the following abbreviations for your descriptions. Include the interval of arrival in the description. (For example: Sim3 means similar motion to a 3rd. D5 is direct motion to a 5th. However, P3, which means parallel 3rds, indicates more than one interval.)

I. correct motion ✓
    Sim3, Sim6   = Similar 3rd, 6th
    Sim5, Sim8   = Similar 5th, 8ve
    O   = Oblique Motion
    PP5–d5   = Parallel Perfect 5th to Diminished 5th
    Pd5–P5   = Parallel Diminished 5th to Perfect 5th
    P3, P6   = Parallel 3rd, 6ths
    C3, C5, C6, C8   = Contrary 3rd, 5th, 6th, 8ve

II. incorrect motion **x**
    D5, D8   = Direct 5th, 8ve
    ConsP5, ConsP8 = Consecutive Perfect 5ths, 8ves
    PP1, PP5, PP8   = Parallel Perfect Unisons, 5ths, 8ves

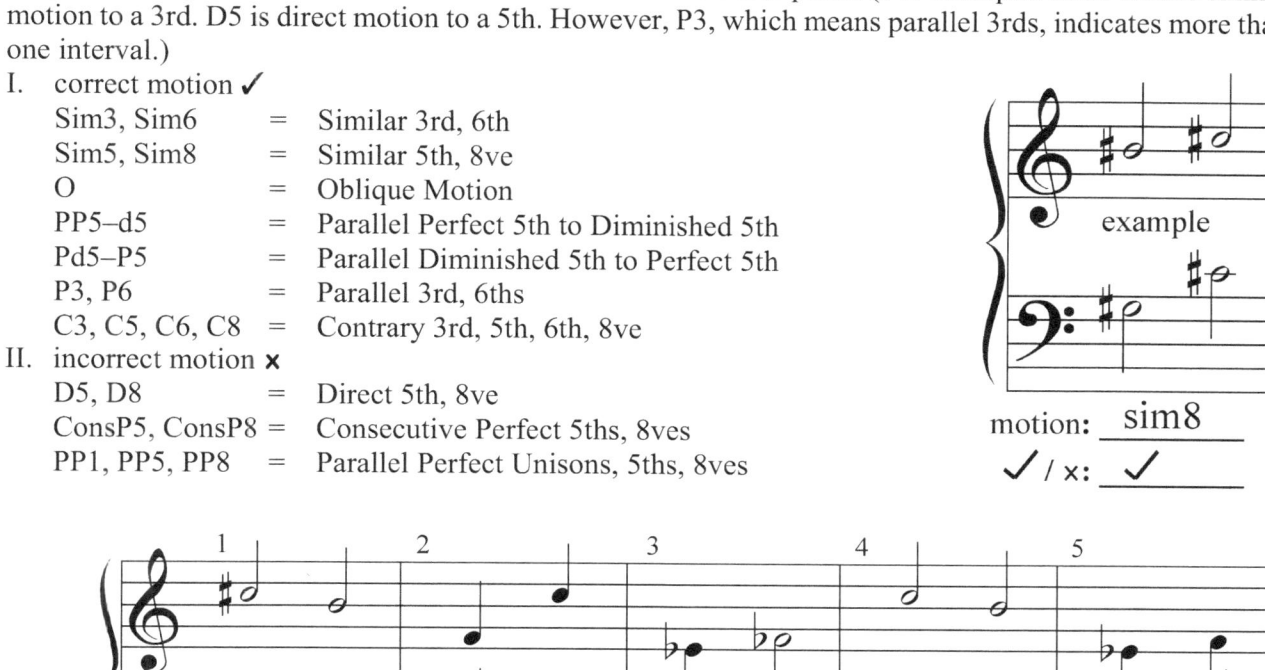

example

motion: __sim8__

✓ / **x**: __✓__

motion: _____ _____ _____ _____ _____

✓ / **x** : _____ _____ _____ _____ _____

motion: _____ _____ _____ _____ _____

✓ / **x** : _____ _____ _____ _____ _____

Basic Harmony Worksheet 3–6

Name _____

Worksheet 3–6 for Chapter 3: Voice Leading

Describe the motion between the two given voices (the voices are identifiable according to stem direction and clef). Correct motion takes a check mark (✓), incorrect motion an ✗. Use the following abbreviations for your descriptions. Include the interval of arrival in the description. (For example: Sim3 means similar motion to a 3rd. D5 is direct motion to a 5th. However, P3, which means parallel 3rds, indicates more than one interval.)

I. correct motion ✓
   Sim3, Sim6   = Similar 3rd, 6th
   Sim5, Sim8   = Similar 5th, 8ve
   O   = Oblique Motion
   PP5–d5   = Parallel Perfect 5th to Diminished 5th
   Pd5–P5   = Parallel Diminished 5th to Perfect 5th
   P3, P6   = Parallel 3rd, 6ths
   C3, C5, C6, C8   = Contrary 3rd, 5th, 6th, 8ve

II. incorrect motion ✗
   D5, D8   = Direct 5th, 8ve
   ConsP5, ConsP8   = Consecutive Perfect 5ths, 8ves
   PP1, PP5, PP8   = Parallel Perfect Unisons, 5ths, 8ves

Basic Harmony Worksheet 3–7

Name _____

Worksheet 3–7 for Chapter 3: Voice Leading

Meter and Rhythm

Given the following alternating meters, write the counts directly under the appropriate note or rest. Unlike previous exercises, the bar lines are not concealed here because the time signature changes in every measure. The courtesy time signatures at the end of three of staff systems indicate a change of meter in the next line of music. The challenge of this exercise is not in the counting but in the performance. You should be seated at a desk or table. To perform the exercise, tap both feet to the *half note* and execute the rhythms on a hard surface with both hands. You will find that if your feet remain constant with the half note, the beginnings of certain measures will not coincide with your feet—keeping your place is the real challenge. Every three measures, your feet should coincide with the beginning of the measure. In the example, a dash under some of the counts indicates where your feet should tap. Do not try to play the exercise too quickly.

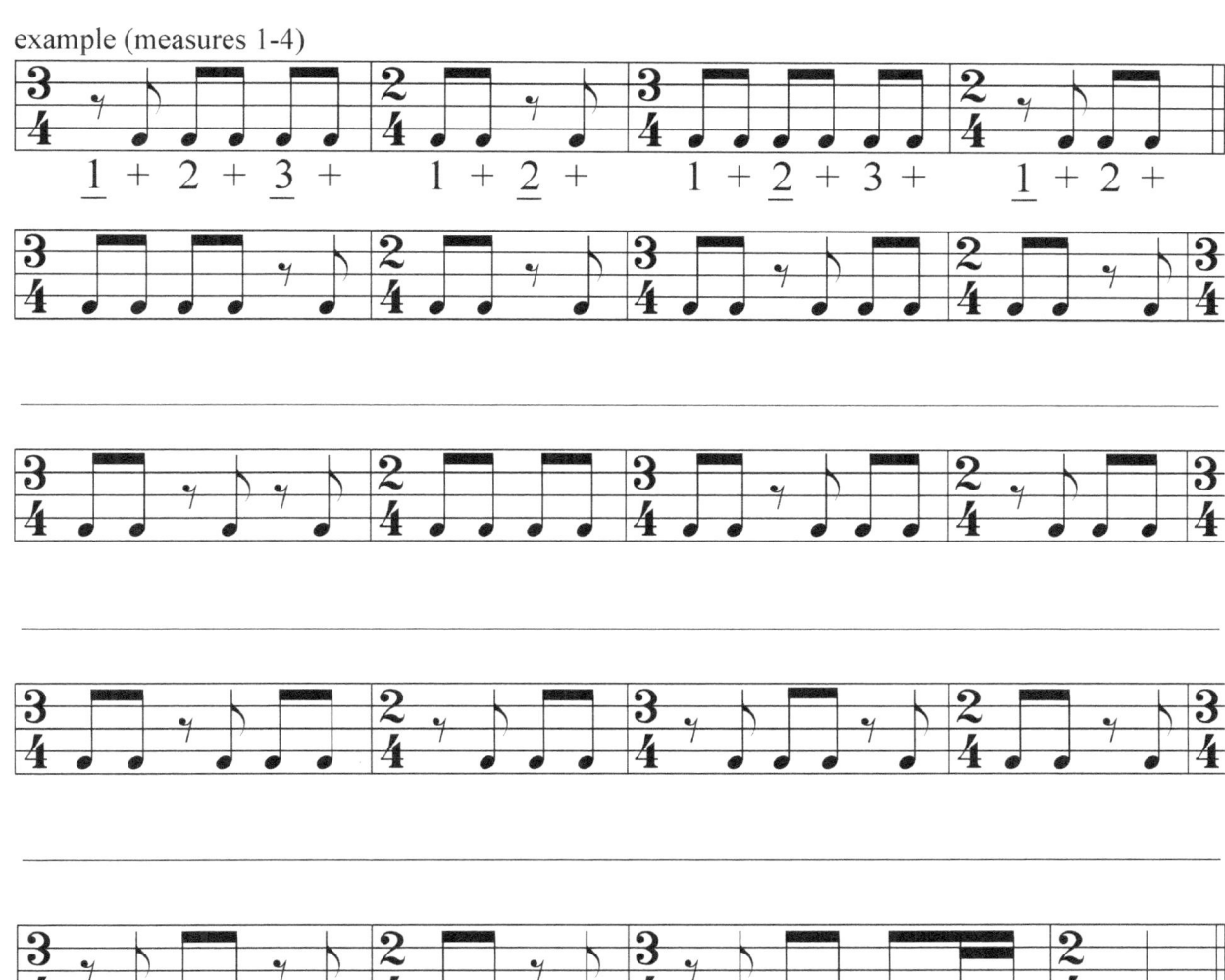

Basic Harmony Worksheet 4–1

Name _____

Worksheet 4–1 for Chapter 4: The Six-Four Chord

Given the clef, time signature, key, chord symbols, and various pitches to guide your, supply the missing voices in open structure. Then fill in the blank with the correct chord symbol for the indicated $^6_4$ chord. In those instances in which an apparent chord resolves into a real chord, such as the appoggiatura (noncadential) $^6_4$ and the cadential $^6_4$, *circle the figured bass of the real chord*. Within any single voice, move as conjunctly as possible, except when leaps are characteristic of the indicated $^6_4$ type, such as the appoggiatura (noncadential) $^6_4$ or the arpeggiated $^6_4$. Be careful to include any appropriate accidentals in exercises for the minor mode that conflict with the key signature.

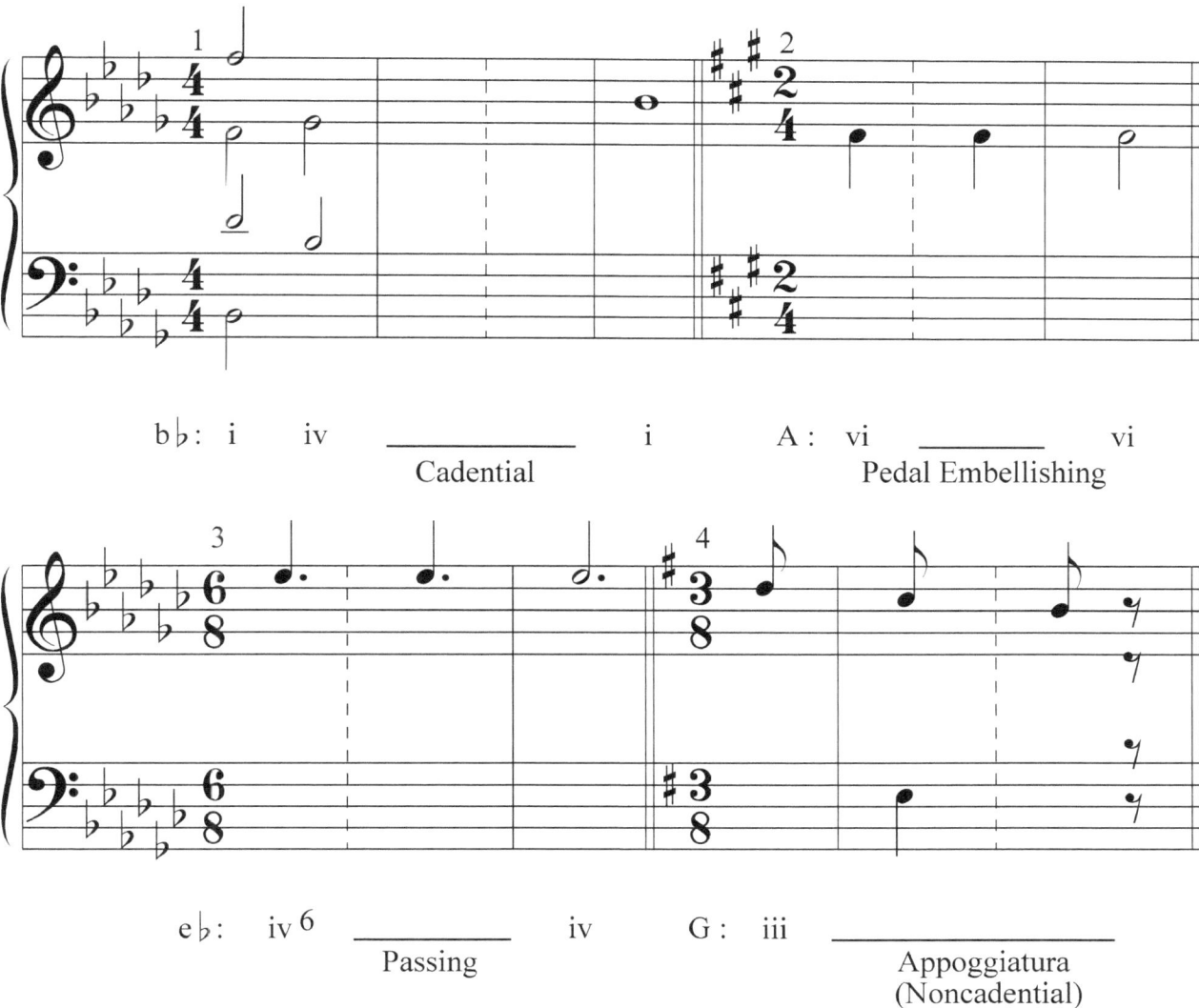

Basic Harmony Worksheet 4–2

Name _____

Worksheet 4–2 for Chapter 4: The Six-Four Chord

Given the clef, time signature, key, chord symbols, and various pitches to guide your, supply the missing voices in open structure. Then fill in the blank with the correct chord symbol for the indicated $^6_4$ chord. In those instances in which an apparent chord resolves into a real chord, such as the appoggiatura (noncadential) $^6_4$ and the cadential $^6_4$, *circle the figured bass of the real chord*. Within any single voice, move as conjunctly as possible, except when leaps are characteristic of the indicated $^6_4$ type, such as the appoggiatura (noncadential) $^6_4$ or the arpeggiated $^6_4$. Be careful to include any appropriate accidentals in exercises for the minor mode that conflict with the key signature.

Basic Harmony Worksheet 4–3

Name _____

Worksheet 4–3 for Chapter 4: The Six-Four Chord

Given the clef, time signature, key, chord symbols, and various pitches to guide your, supply the missing voices in open structure. Then fill in the blank with the correct chord symbol for the indicated $^6_4$ chord. In those instances in which an apparent chord resolves into a real chord, such as the appoggiatura (noncadential) $^6_4$ and the cadential $^6_4$, *circle the figured bass of the real chord*. Within any single voice, move as conjunctly as possible, except when leaps are characteristic of the indicated $^6_4$ type, such as the appoggiatura (noncadential) $^6_4$ or the arpeggiated $^6_4$. Be careful to include any appropriate accidentals in exercises for the minor mode that conflict with the key signature.

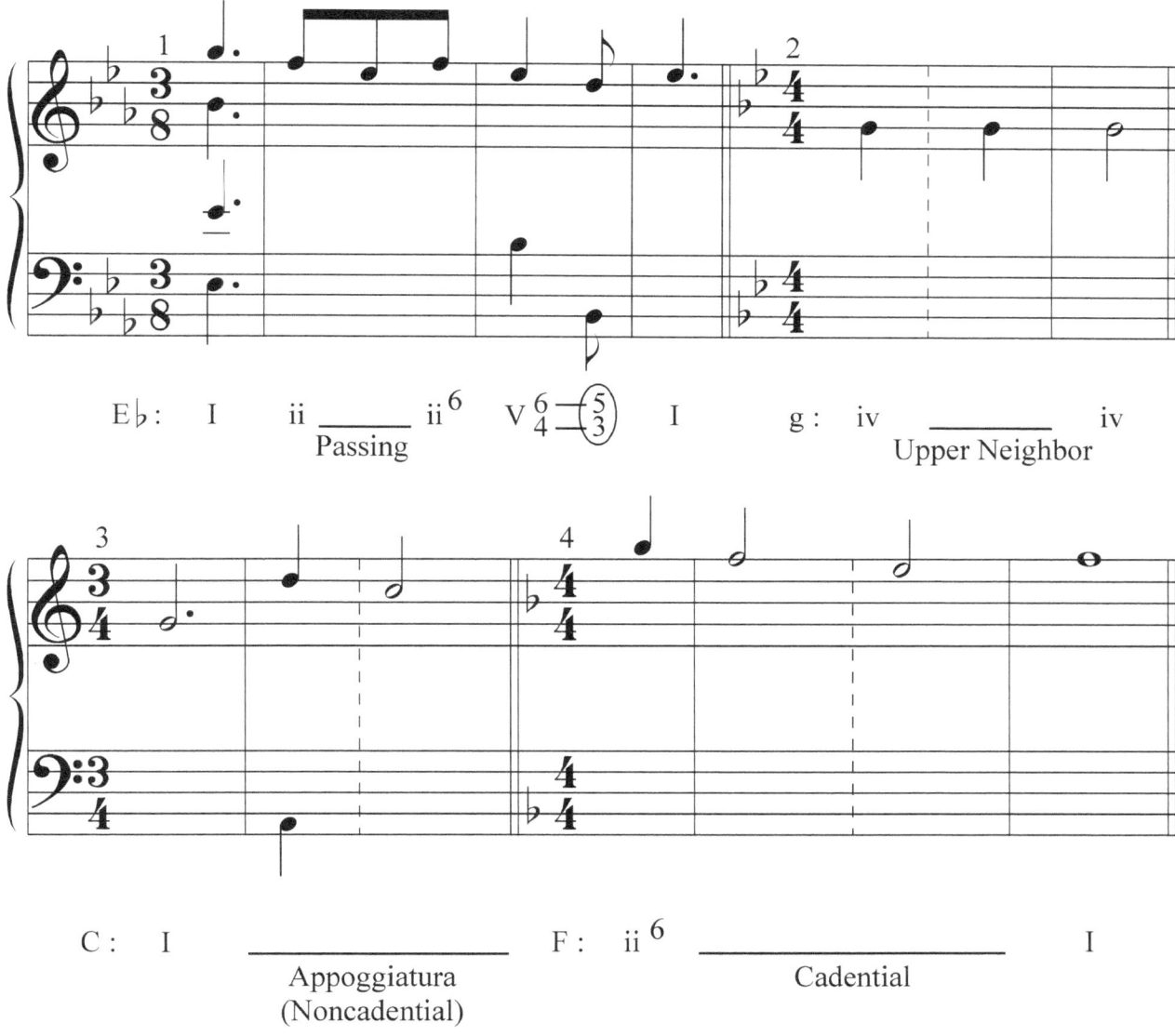

Basic Harmony Worksheet 4–4

Name _____

Worksheet 4–4 for Chapter 4: The Six-Four Chord

Given the clef, time signature, key, chord symbols, and various pitches to guide your, supply the missing voices in open structure. Then fill in the blank with the correct chord symbol for the indicated $^6_4$ chord. In those instances in which an apparent chord resolves into a real chord, such as the appoggiatura (noncadential) $^6_4$ and the cadential $^6_4$, *circle the figured bass of the real chord*. Within any single voice, move as conjunctly as possible, except when leaps are characteristic of the indicated $^6_4$ type, such as the appoggiatura (noncadential) $^6_4$ or the arpeggiated $^6_4$. Be careful to include any appropriate accidentals in exercises for the minor mode that conflict with the key signature.

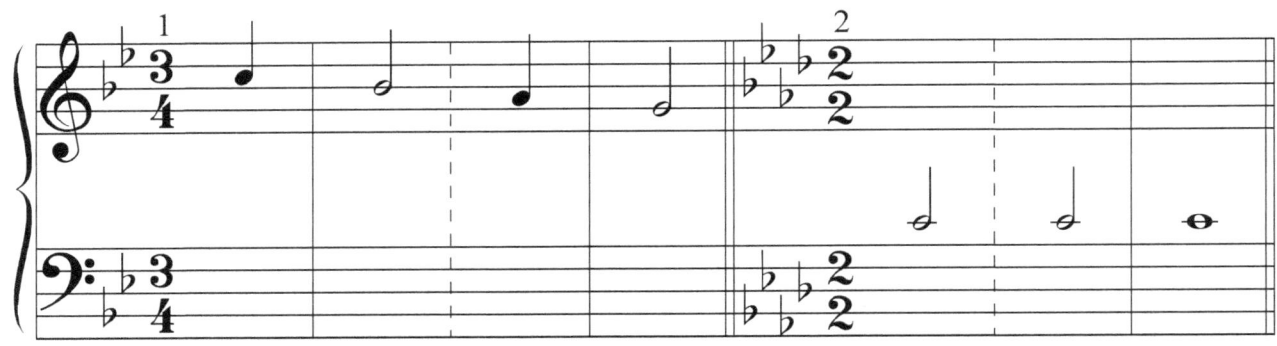

g :   ii°6 _____   i   f :   i⁶ _____   i⁶
            Cadential   Lower Neighbor

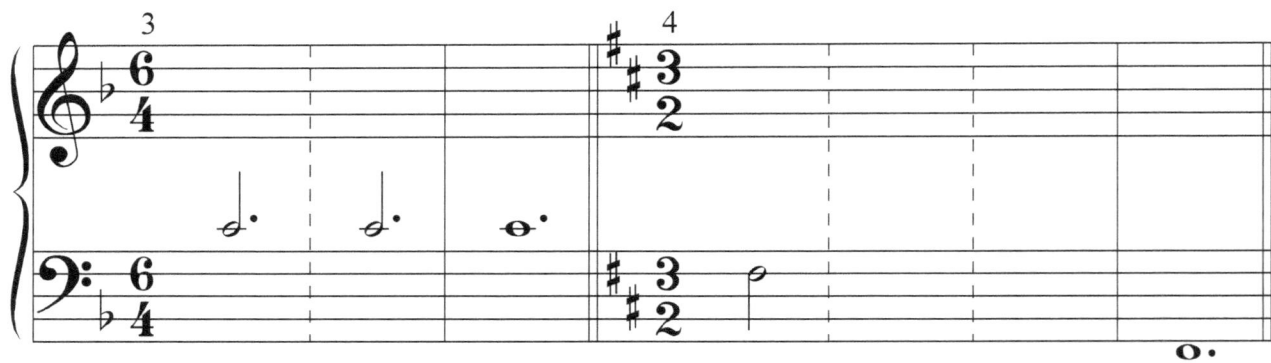

d :   ♭VII⁶ _____   ♭VII⁶   b :   V _____   V
             Pedal Embellishing   Arpeggiated: Complete

Basic Harmony Worksheet 4–5

Name _____

Worksheet 4–5 for Chapter 4: The Six-Four Chord

Meter and Rhythm

Given the following alternating meters, write the counts directly under the appropriate note or rest. Unlike previous exercises, the bar lines are not concealed here because the time signature changes in every measure. The courtesy time signatures at the end of three of staff systems indicate a change of meter in the next line of music.

    The challenge of this exercise is not in the counting but in the performance. You should be seated at a desk or table. To perform the exercise, tap both feet to the *dotted quarter note* and execute the rhythms on a hard surface with both hands. You will find that if your feet remain constant with the dotted quarter, the beginnings of certain measures will not coincide with your feet—keeping your place is the real challenge. Every six measures, your feet should coincide with the beginning of the measure. In the example, a dash under some of the counts indicates where your feet should tap. Do not try to play the exercise too quickly.

example (measures 1-6)

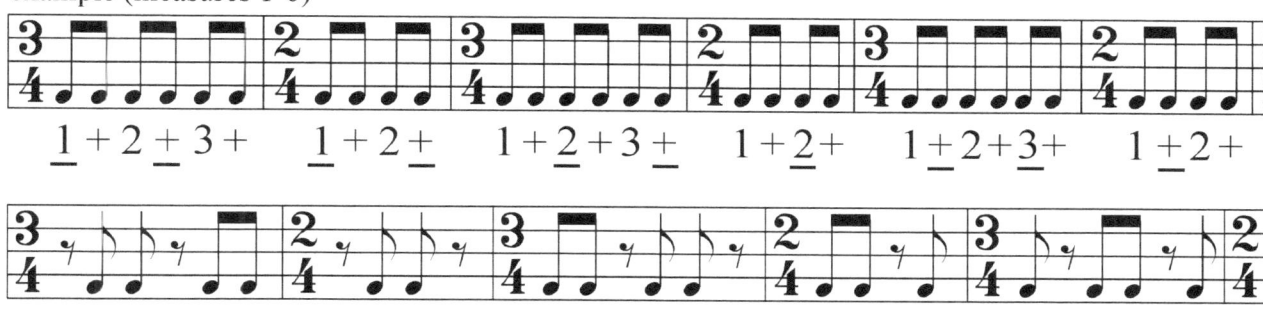

Basic Harmony Worksheet 5–1

Name _____

Worksheet 5–1 for Chapter 5: The Chord Seventh

Identify the quality of the root-position sevenths using one of the four possible answers given below (use the chord symbol for your answer not the number in parentheses):

(1) M7 = major seventh
(2) m7 = minor seventh
(3) D7 = dominant seventh
(4) ⌀7 = half-diminished seventh

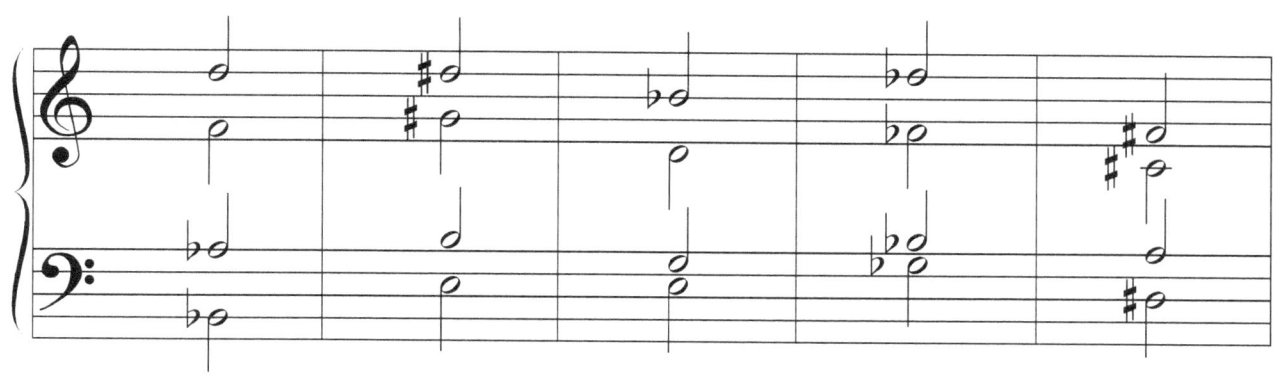

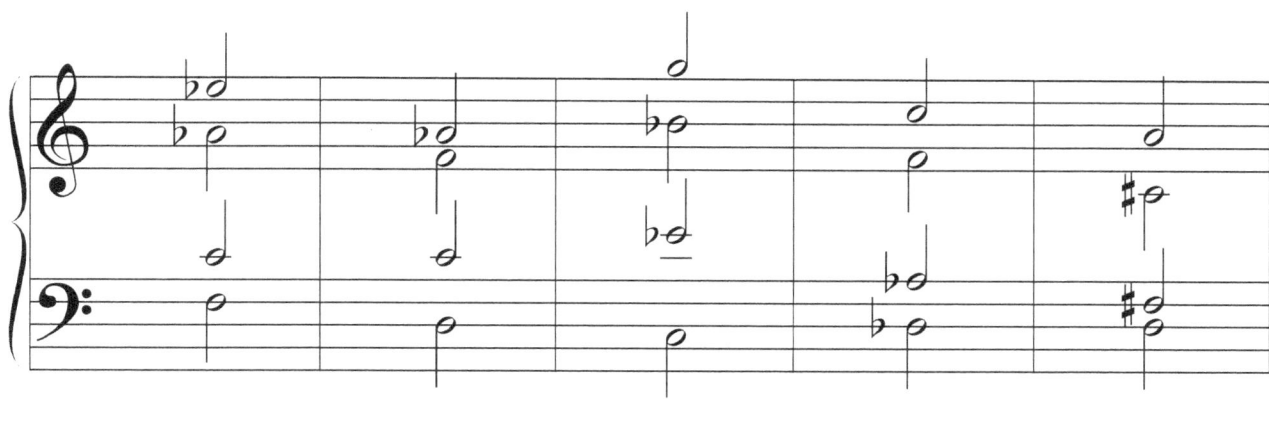

Basic Harmony Worksheet 5–2

Name _____

Worksheet 5–2 for Chapter 5: The Chord Seventh

Identify the quality of the root-position sevenths using one of the four possible answers given below (use the chord symbol for your answer not the number in parentheses):

(1) M7 = major seventh
(2) m7 = minor seventh
(3) D7 = dominant seventh
(4) ⌀7 = half-diminished seventh

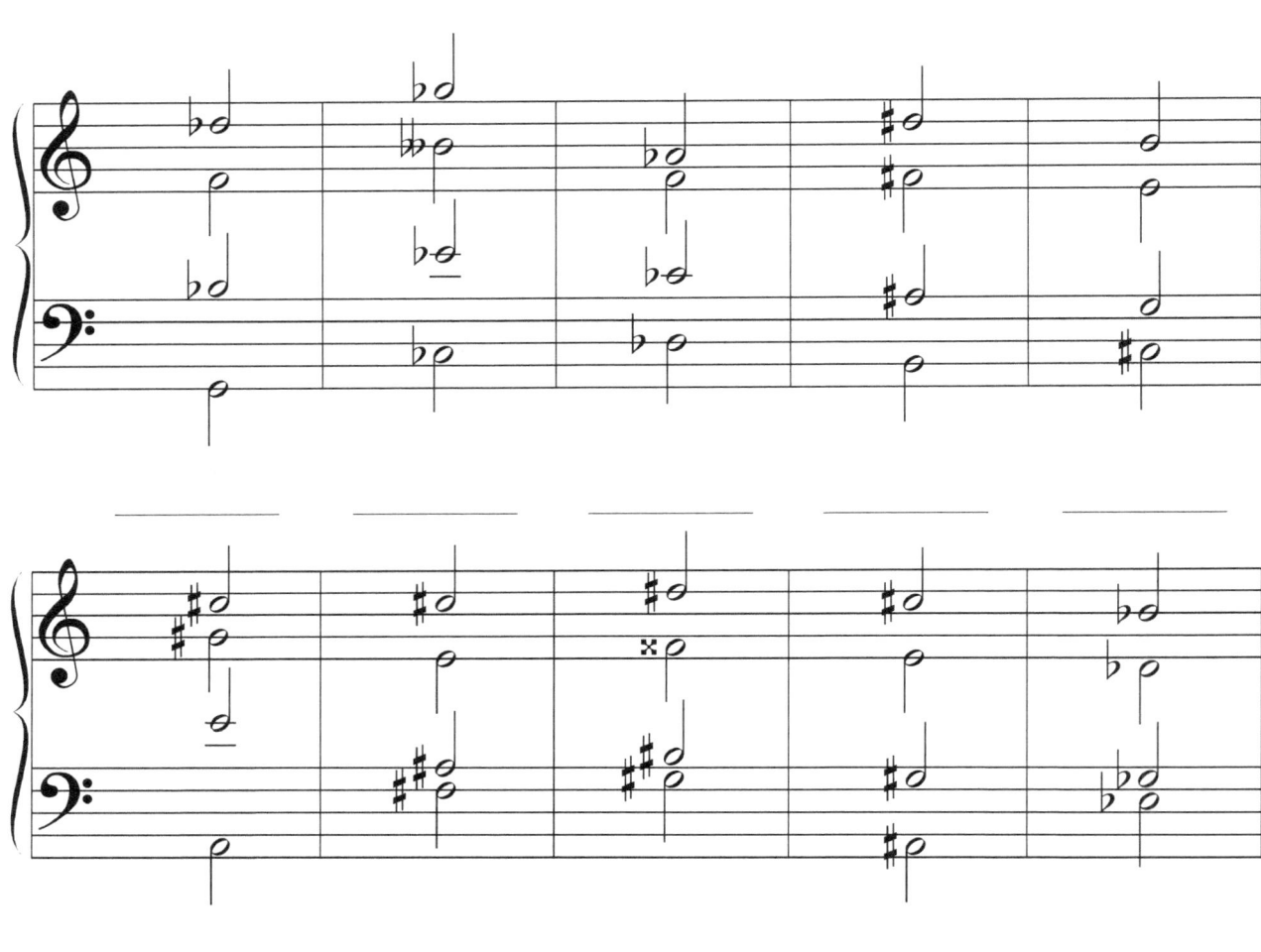

Basic Harmony Worksheet 5–3

Name _____

Worksheet 5–3 for Chapter 5: The Chord Seventh

Identify both the correct quality *and* position of the following seventh chords (use the chord symbol for your answer not the number in parentheses):

Chord Qualities:
    (1) M = major seventh
    (2) m = minor seventh
    (3) D = dominant seventh
    (4) ∅ = half-diminished seventh

Chord Positions: $\frac{7}{5}, \frac{6}{5}, \frac{4}{3},$ or $\frac{4}{2}$

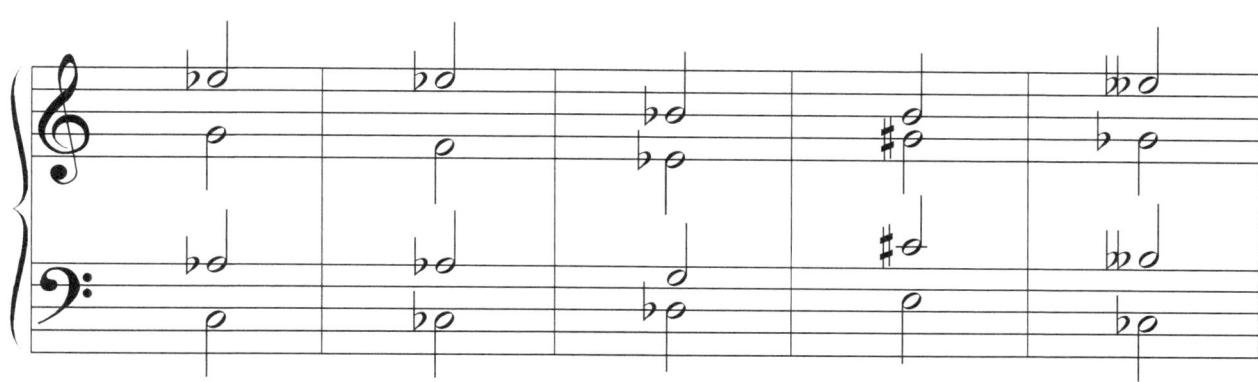

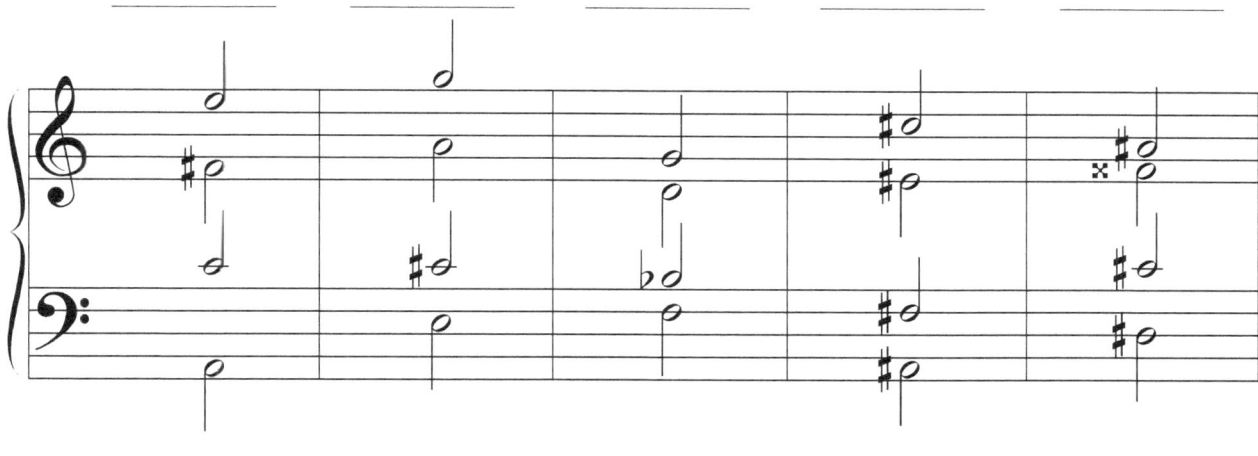

Basic Harmony Worksheet 5–4

Name _____

Worksheet 5–4 for Chapter 5: The Chord Seventh

Identify both the correct quality *and* position of the following seventh chords (use the chord symbol for your answer not the number in parentheses):

Chord Qualities: (1) M = major seventh
(2) m = minor seventh
(3) D = dominant seventh
(4) ø = half-diminished seventh

Chord Positions: $7, \begin{smallmatrix}6\\5\end{smallmatrix}, \begin{smallmatrix}4\\3\end{smallmatrix}, \text{ or } \begin{smallmatrix}4\\2\end{smallmatrix}$

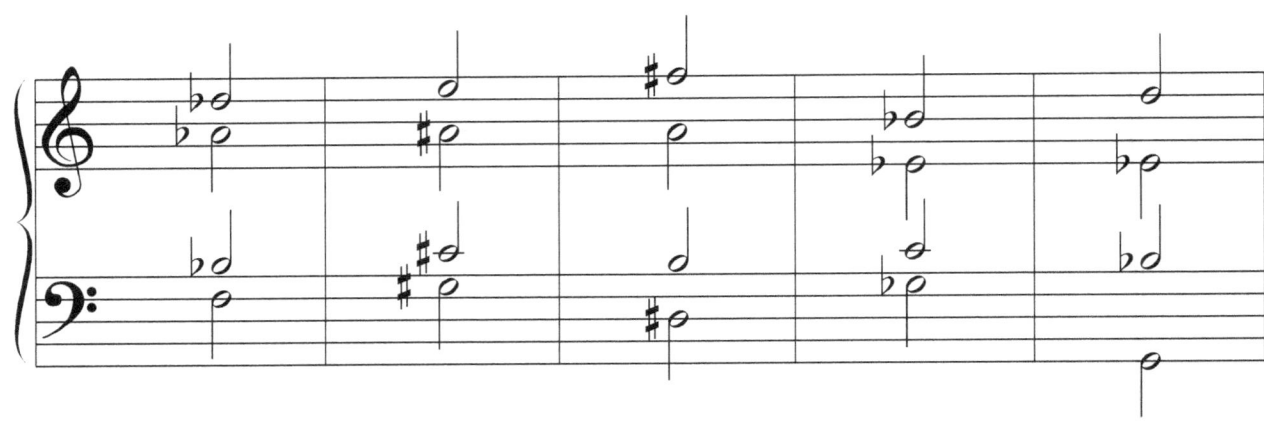

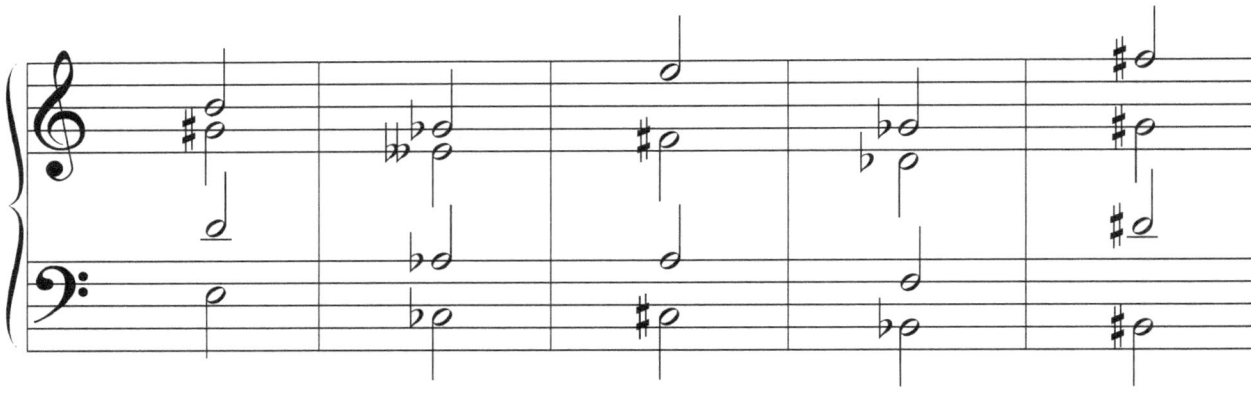

Basic Harmony Worksheet 5–5

Name _____

Worksheet 5–5 for Chapter 5: The Chord Seventh

Above the given bass and according to the indicated chord quality and position, construct the correct seventh chord in open structure for four voices using half notes only:

Chord Qualities:
(1) M = major seventh
(2) m = minor seventh
(3) D = dominant seventh
(4) ⦰ = half-diminished seventh

Chord Positions: $\begin{smallmatrix}7\\5\end{smallmatrix}, \begin{smallmatrix}6\\5\end{smallmatrix}, \begin{smallmatrix}4\\3\end{smallmatrix},$ or $\begin{smallmatrix}4\\2\end{smallmatrix}$

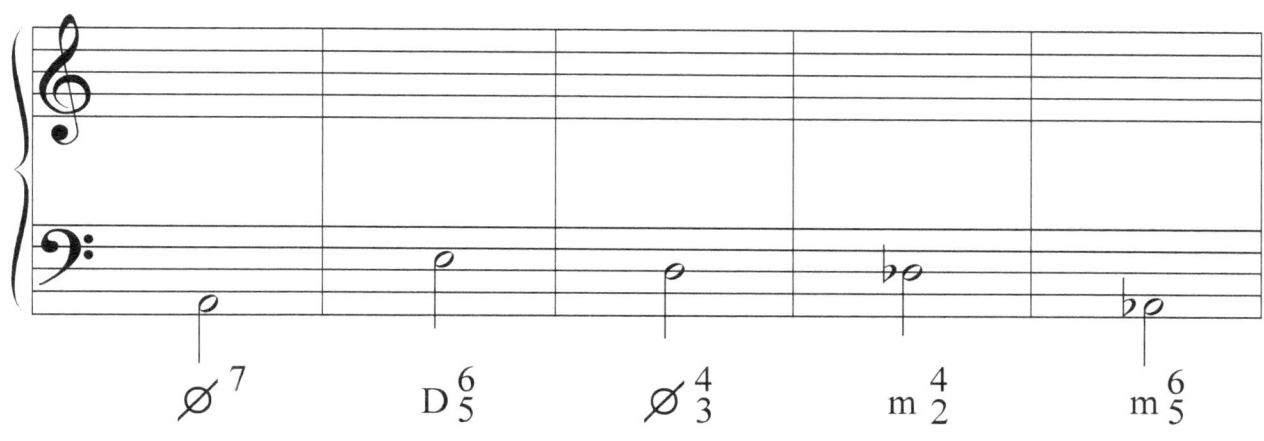

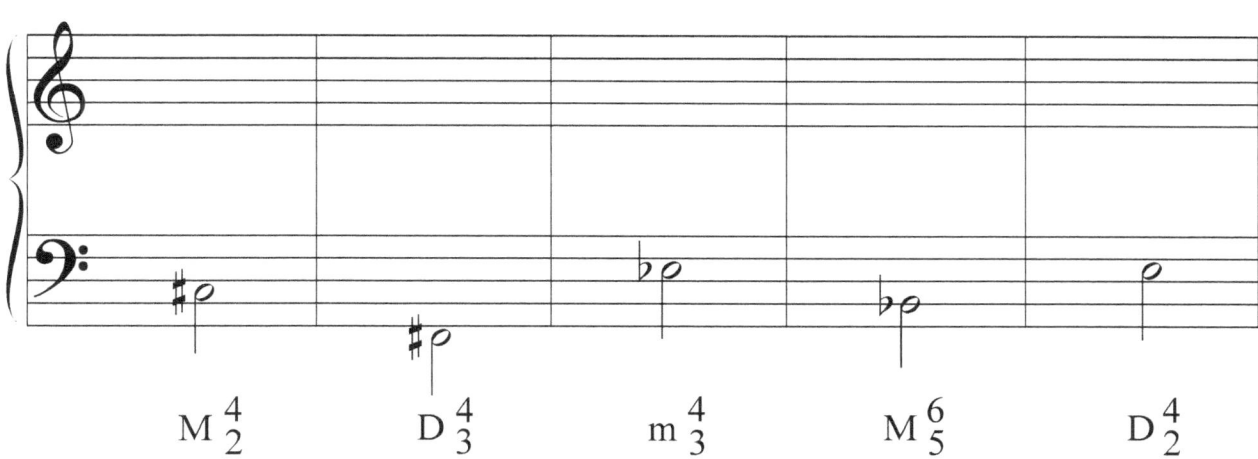

Basic Harmony Worksheet 5–6

Name _____

Worksheet 5–6 for Chapter 5: The Chord Seventh

Above the given bass and according to the indicated chord quality and position, construct the correct seventh chord in open structure for four voices using half notes only:

Chord Qualities:
    (1)   M = major seventh
    (2)   m = minor seventh
    (3)   D = dominant seventh
    (4) $\emptyset$ = half-diminished seventh

Chord Positions: $\frac{7}{}$, $\frac{6}{5}$, $\frac{4}{3}$, or $\frac{4}{2}$

Basic Harmony Worksheet 5–7

Name _____

Worksheet 5–7 for Chapter 5: The Chord Seventh

Meter and Rhythm

Given the following alternating meters, write the counts directly under the appropriate note or rest. Unlike previous exercises, the bar lines are not concealed here because the time signature changes in every measure. The courtesy time signatures at the end of three of staff systems indicate a change of meter in the next line of music.

    The challenge of this exercise is not in the counting but in the performance. You should be seated at a desk or table. To perform the exercise, tap both feet to the *half note* and execute the rhythms on a hard surface with both hands. You will find that if your feet remain constant with the half note, the beginnings of certain measures will not coincide with your feet—keeping your place is the real challenge. In the example, a dash under some of the counts indicates where your feet should tap. Do not try to play the exercise too quickly.

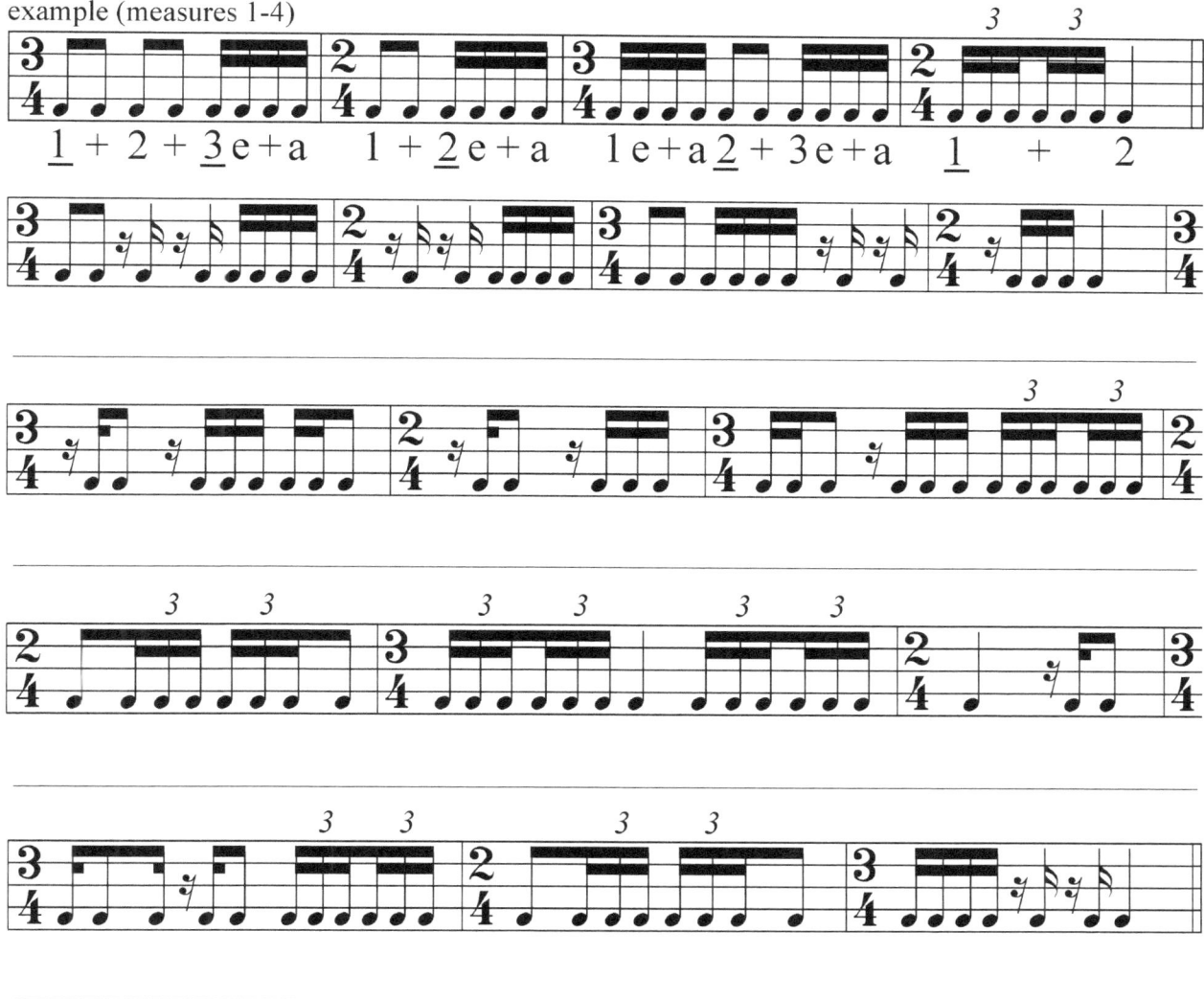

Basic Harmony Worksheet 6–1

Name _____

Worksheet 6–1 for Chapter 6: The Cadence

Using four voices (soprano, alto, tenor, and bass), construct the indicated cadence type and fill in the blanks with the correct chord symbols. Note carefully that the word cadential in the exercise refers to the second component of each cadence type and not to the cadential $^6_4$. In some of the cadences, however, you may want to use the cadential $^6_4$ as demonstrated in Chapter 6. All of the exercises are in $^4_4$ time.

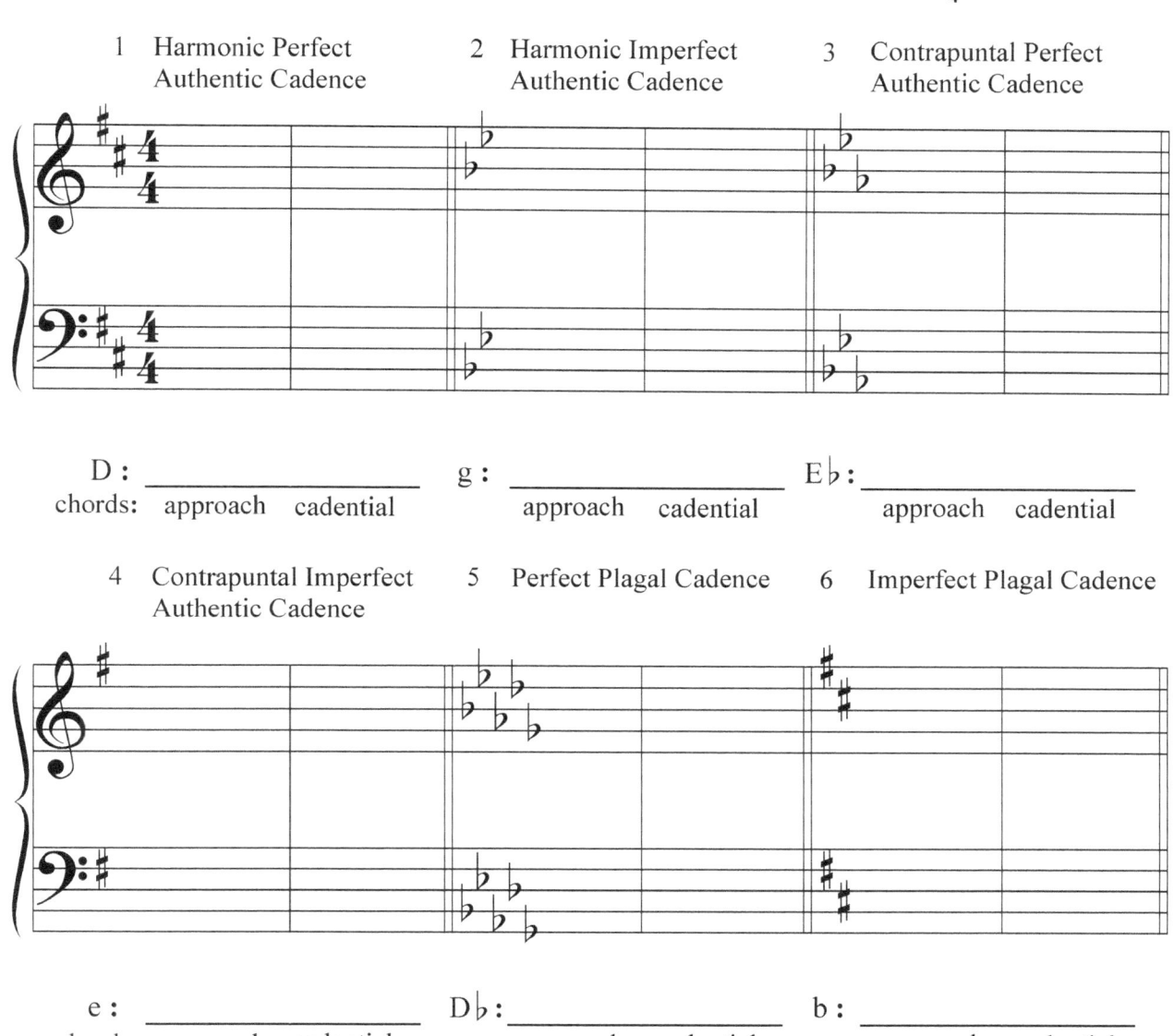

1 Harmonic Perfect Authentic Cadence
2 Harmonic Imperfect Authentic Cadence
3 Contrapuntal Perfect Authentic Cadence

D: _____   g: _____   E♭: _____
chords: approach cadential   approach cadential   approach cadential

4 Contrapuntal Imperfect Authentic Cadence
5 Perfect Plagal Cadence
6 Imperfect Plagal Cadence

e: _____   D♭: _____   b: _____
chords: approach cadential   approach cadential   approach cadential

Basic Harmony Worksheet 6–2

Name _____

Worksheet 6–2 for Chapter 6: The Cadence

Using four voices (soprano, alto, tenor, and bass), construct the indicated cadence type and fill in the blanks with the correct chord symbols. Note carefully that the word cadential in the exercise refers to the second component of each cadence type and not to the cadential $^6_4$. In some of the cadences, however, you may want to use the cadential $^6_4$ as demonstrated in Chapter 6. All of the exercises are in $^4_4$ time.

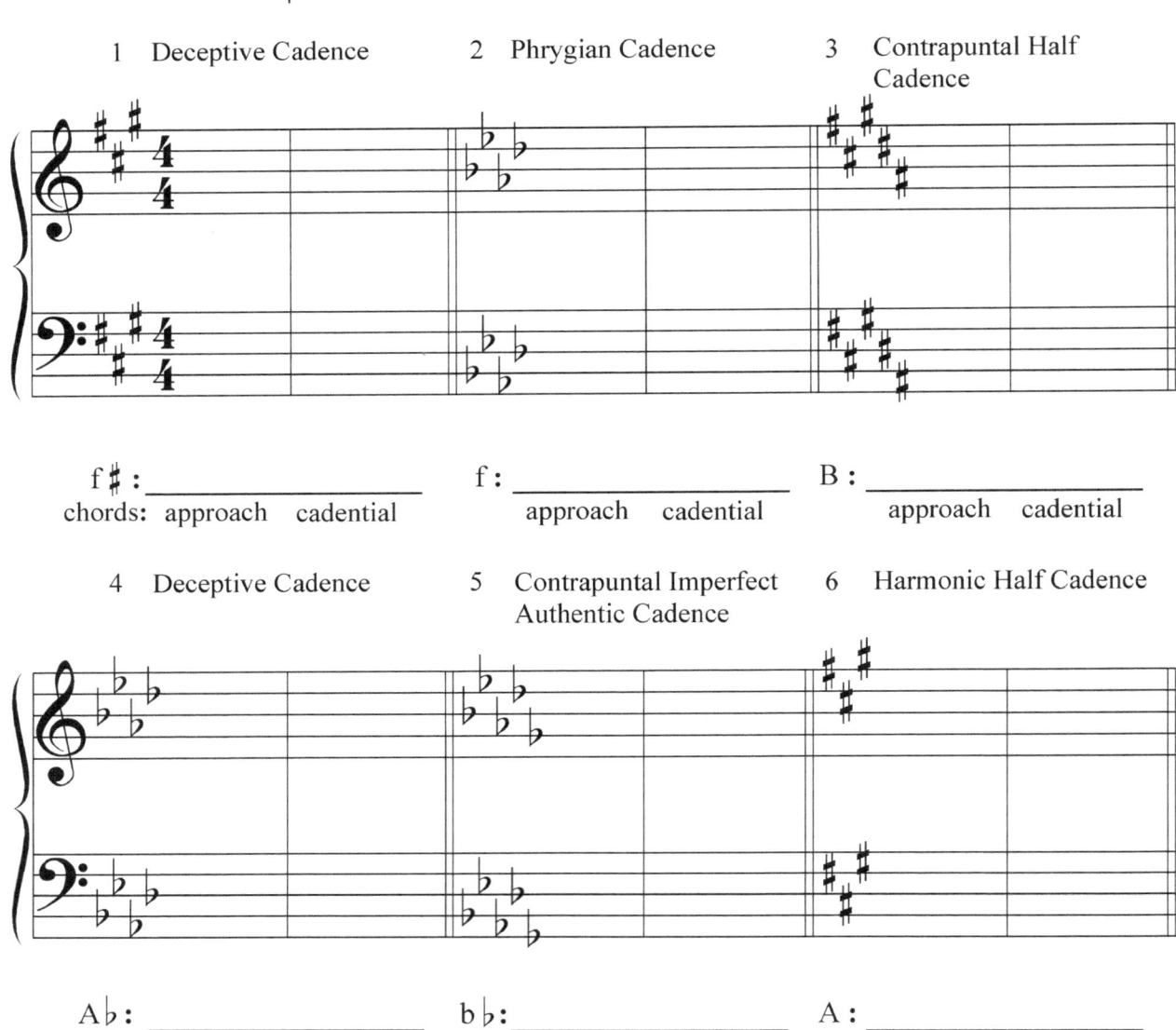

1 Deceptive Cadence 2 Phrygian Cadence 3 Contrapuntal Half Cadence

f♯: _____   f: _____   B: _____
chords: approach cadential   approach cadential   approach cadential

4 Deceptive Cadence 5 Contrapuntal Imperfect Authentic Cadence 6 Harmonic Half Cadence

A♭: _____   b♭: _____   A: _____
chords: approach cadential   approach cadential   approach cadential

Basic Harmony Worksheet 6–3

Name _____

Worksheet 6–3 for Chapter 6: The Cadence

Using four voices (soprano, alto, tenor, and bass), construct the indicated cadence type and fill in the blanks with the correct chord symbols. Note carefully that the word cadential in the exercise refers to the second component of each cadence type and not to the cadential $^6_4$. In some of the cadences, however, you may want to use the cadential $^6_4$ as demonstrated in Chapter 6. All of the exercises are in $^4_4$ time.

1. Harmonic Perfect Authentic Cadence
2. Harmonic Imperfect Authentic Cadence
3. Deceptive Cadence

a: _____ G♭: _____ d: _____
chords: approach cadential   approach cadential   approach cadential

4. Contrapuntal Imperfect Authentic Cadence
5. Perfect Plagal Cadence
6. Imperfect Plagal Cadence

F: _____ e♭: _____ E: _____
chords: approach cadential   approach cadential   approach cadential

Basic Harmony Worksheet 6–4

Name _____

Worksheet 6–4 for Chapter 6: The Cadence

Using four voices (soprano, alto, tenor, and bass), construct the indicated cadence type and fill in the blanks with the correct chord symbols. Note carefully that the word cadential in the exercise refers to the second component of each cadence type and not to the cadential $^6_4$. In some of the cadences, however, you may want to use the cadential $^6_4$ as demonstrated in Chapter 6. All of the exercises are in $^4_4$ time.

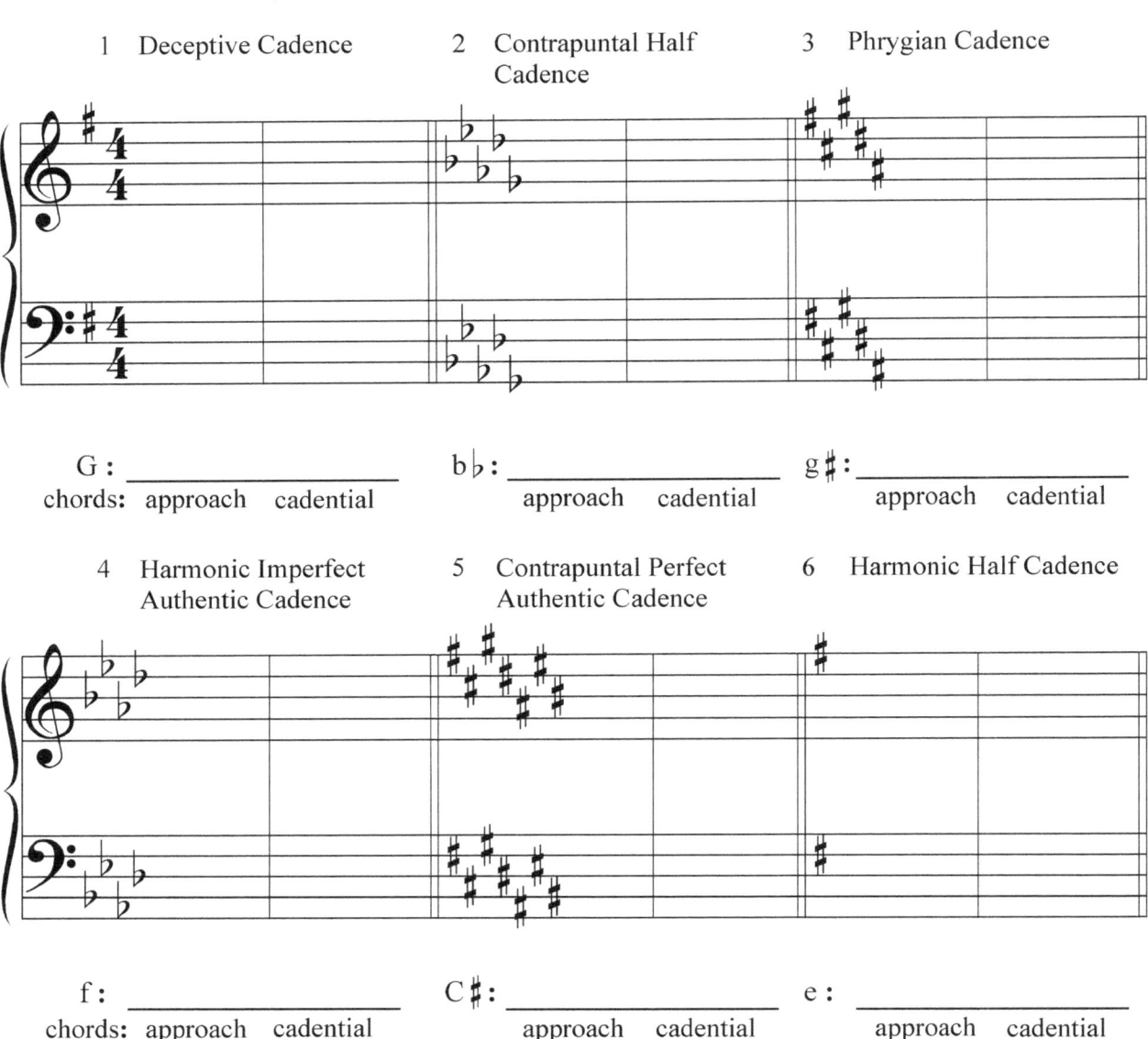

Basic Harmony Worksheet 6–5

Name _____

Worksheet 6–5 for Chapter 6: The Cadence

Using four voices (soprano, alto, tenor, and bass), construct the indicated cadence type and fill in the blanks with the correct chord symbols. Note carefully that the word cadential in the exercise refers to the second component of each cadence type and not to the cadential $^6_4$. In some of the cadences, however, you may want to use the cadential $^6_4$ as demonstrated in Chapter 6. All of the exercises are in $^4_4$ time.

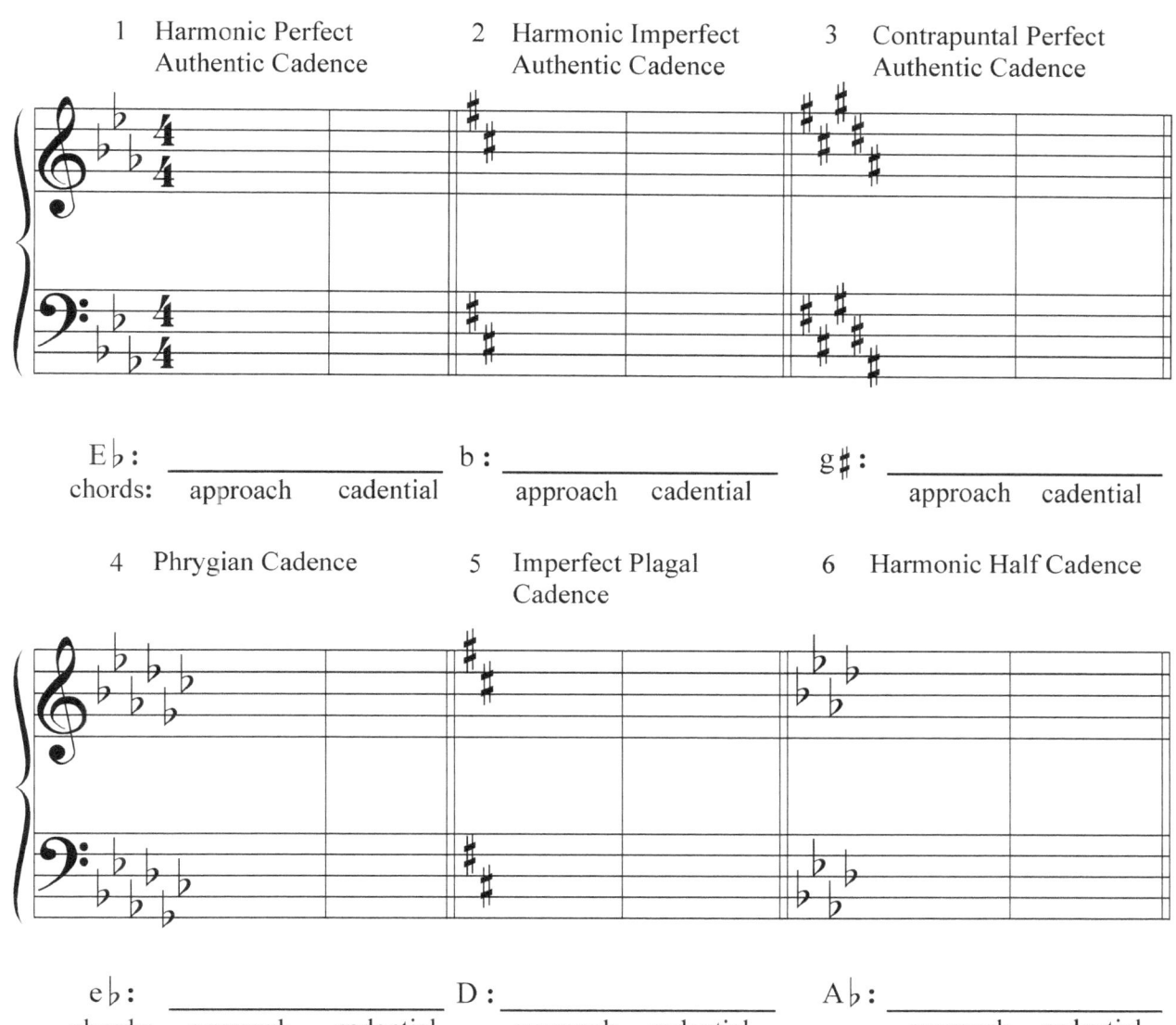

1. Harmonic Perfect Authentic Cadence
2. Harmonic Imperfect Authentic Cadence
3. Contrapuntal Perfect Authentic Cadence

E♭: _____ b: _____ g♯: _____
chords: approach cadential   approach cadential   approach cadential

4. Phrygian Cadence
5. Imperfect Plagal Cadence
6. Harmonic Half Cadence

e♭: _____ D: _____ A♭: _____
chords: approach cadential   approach cadential   approach cadential

Basic Harmony Worksheet 6–6

Name _____

Worksheet 6–6 for Chapter 6: The Cadence

Using four voices (soprano, alto, tenor, and bass), construct the indicated cadence type and fill in the blanks with the correct chord symbols. Note carefully that the word cadential in the exercise refers to the second component of each cadence type and not to the cadential $^6_4$. In some of the cadences, however, you may want to use the cadential $^6_4$ as demonstrated in Chapter 6. All of the exercises are in $^4_4$ time.

1. Contrapuntal Perfect Authentic Cadence
2. Perfect Plagal Cadence
3. Contrapuntal Imperfect Authentic Cadence

d: _____ F♯: _____ G: _____
chords: approach   cadential   approach   cadential   approach   cadential

4. Phrygian Cadence
5. Deceptive Cadence
6. Contrapuntal Half Cadence

c♯: _____ B♭: _____ f: _____
chords: approach   cadential   approach   cadential   approach   cadential

Basic Harmony Worksheet 6–7

Name _____

Worksheet 6–7 for Chapter 6: The Cadence

Using four voices (soprano, alto, tenor, and bass), construct the indicated cadence type and fill in the blanks with the correct chord symbols. Note carefully that the word cadential in the exercise refers to the second component of each cadence type and not to the cadential $^6_4$. In some of the cadences, however, you may want to use the cadential $^6_4$ as demonstrated in Chapter 6. All of the exercises are in $^4_4$ time.

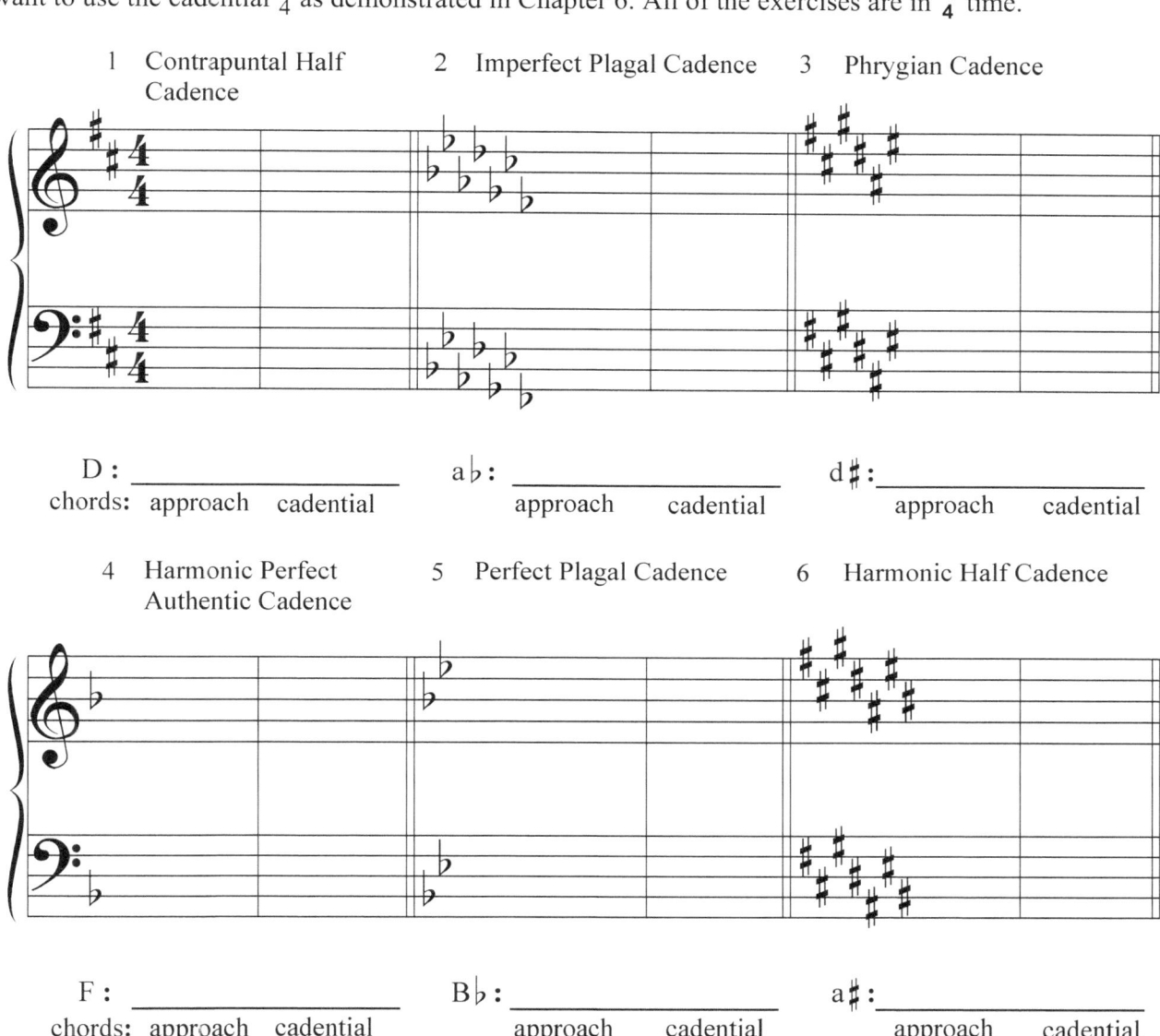

1. Contrapuntal Half Cadence

D: _____
chords: approach   cadential

2. Imperfect Plagal Cadence

a♭: _____
approach   cadential

3. Phrygian Cadence

d♯: _____
approach   cadential

4. Harmonic Perfect Authentic Cadence

F: _____
chords: approach   cadential

5. Perfect Plagal Cadence

B♭: _____
approach   cadential

6. Harmonic Half Cadence

a♯: _____
approach   cadential

Basic Harmony Worksheet 6–8

Name _____

Worksheet 6–8 for Chapter 6: The Cadence

Meter and Rhythm

Given the following alternating meters, write the counts directly under the appropriate note or rest and supply any missing bar lines. The symbol ♪=♪ indicates that sixteenth notes between different meters are equivalent and remain at a constant speed. This notation is particularly useful when the value of the beat between any two time signatures represents different note values (such as $\frac{5}{16}$ and $\frac{2}{4}$). The courtesy time signatures at the end of the staff systems indicate a change in meter in the next line of music. (Bar lines should *not* be placed after the courtesy signatures.)

    The challenge of this exercise is not in the counting but in the performance. You should be seated at a desk or table. To perform the exercise, tap both feet to the *quarter note* and execute the rhythms on a hard surface with both hands. You will find that if your feet remain constant with the quarter note, the beginnings of certain measures will not coincide with your feet—keeping your place is the real challenge. In the example, a dash under some of the counts indicates where your feet should tap.

Basic Harmony Worksheet 7–1

Name _____

Worksheet 7–1 for Chapter 7: The Chord Progression

Given the key and chord symbols, construct the following progressions. Use four voices (soprano, alto, tenor, and bass) in open structure (whenever possible). Based upon the given the meter, assign a rhythmic framework. The soprano voice, in particular, should adhere to the following guidelines when the progression moves between unlike chords:
  (1) either move upwards or downwards as conjunctly as possible, leaping no more than a single 3rd and then reversing direction by step (that is, moving in the opposite direction of the leap); or,
  (2) remain stationary (that is, maintain common tones between unlike chords), allowing the lower voices to move obliquely in relation to the soprano.

Any given tones in the soprano are guides for completing the progression. Chordal skips (re-voicing a chord) are permissible; however, chordal skips in the bass are limited to octave leaps only. Although the figured bass is limited to triads, you may want to use the chord seventh to facilitate the voice leading, particularly with the dominant immediately preceding the final tonic.

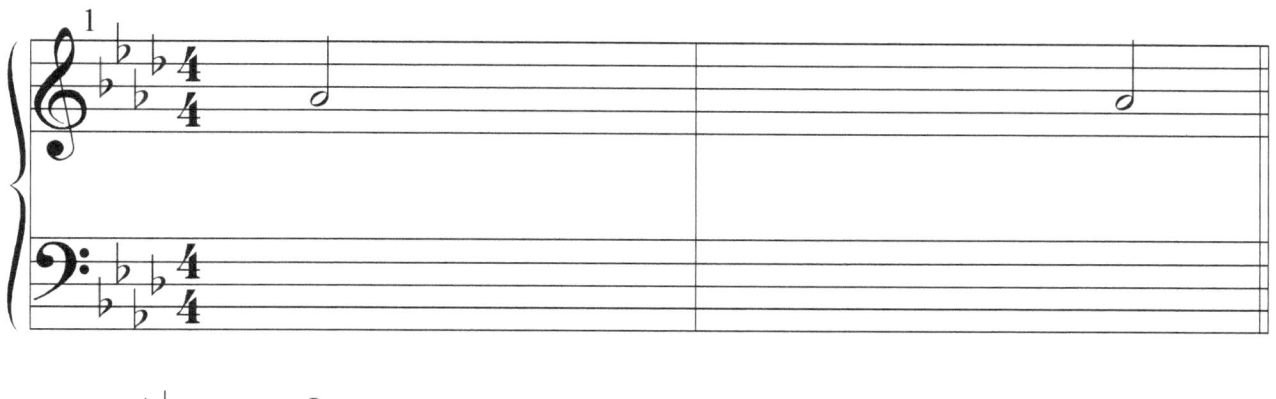

1. A♭:   I   IV   V   I

2. g: i   ii°6   V $^6_4$ — $\binom{5}{3}$ i

Basic Harmony Worksheet 7–2

Name _____

Worksheet 7–2 for Chapter 7: The Chord Progression

Given the key and chord symbols, construct the following progressions. Use four voices (soprano, alto, tenor, and bass) in open structure (whenever possible). Based upon the given the meter, assign a rhythmic framework. The soprano voice, in particular, should adhere to the following guidelines when the progression moves between unlike chords:
  (1) either move upwards or downwards as conjunctly as possible, leaping no more than a single 3rd and then reversing direction by step (that is, moving in the opposite direction of the leap); or,
  (2) remain stationary (that is, maintain common tones between unlike chords), allowing the lower voices to move obliquely in relation to the soprano.

Any given tones in the soprano are guides for completing the progression. Chordal skips (re-voicing a chord) are permissible; however, chordal skips in the bass are limited to octave leaps only. Although the figured bass is limited to triads, you may want to use the chord seventh to facilitate the voice leading, particularly with the dominant immediately preceding the final tonic.

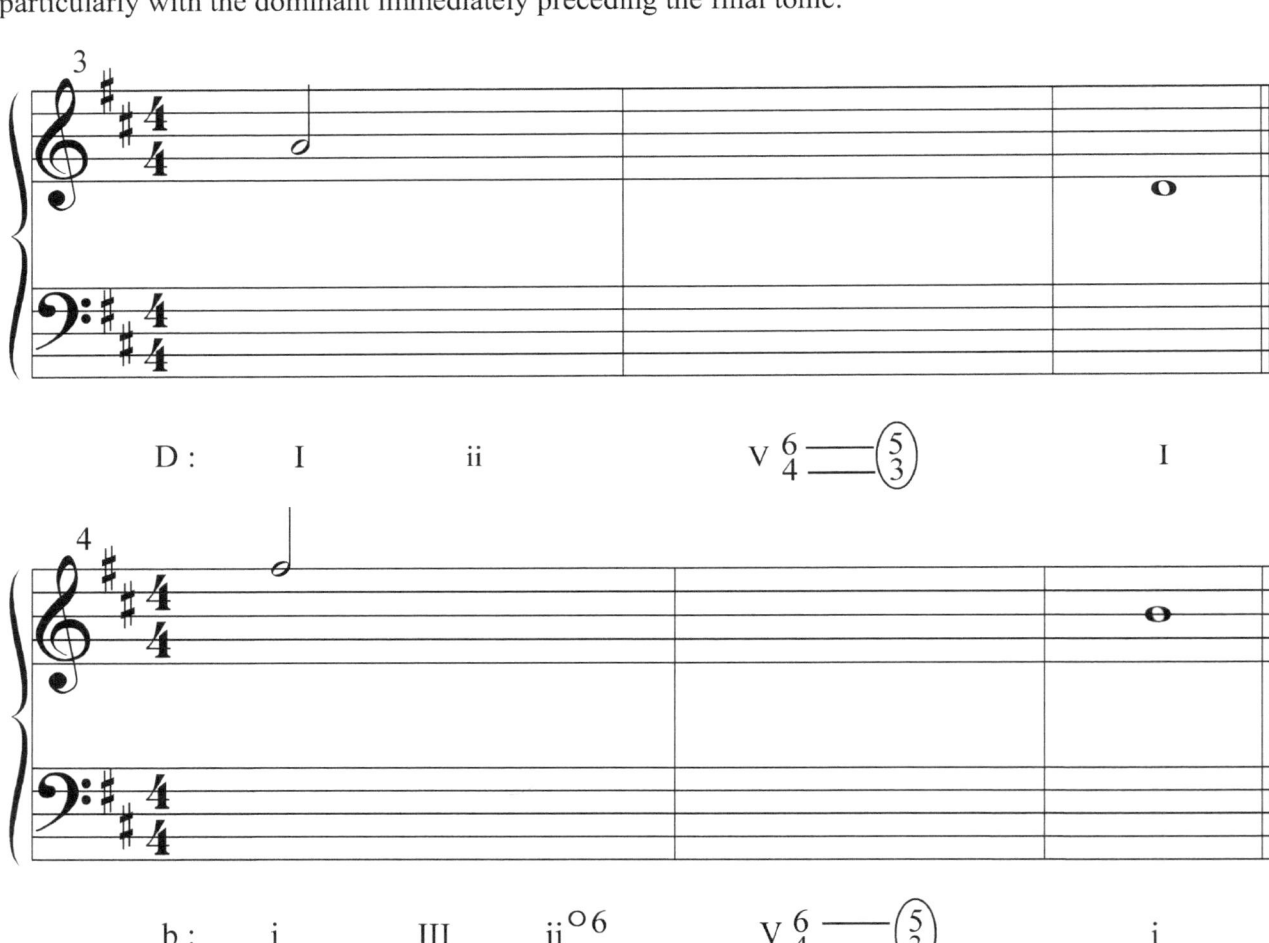

Basic Harmony Worksheet 7–3

Name _____

Worksheet 7–3 for Chapter 7: The Chord Progression

Given the key and chord symbols, construct the following progressions. Use four voices (soprano, alto, tenor, and bass) in open structure (whenever possible). Based upon the given the meter, assign a rhythmic framework. The soprano voice, in particular, should adhere to the following guidelines when the progression moves between unlike chords:
  (1) either move upwards or downwards as conjunctly as possible, leaping no more than a single 3rd and then reversing direction by step (that is, moving in the opposite direction of the leap); or,
  (2) remain stationary (that is, maintain common tones between unlike chords), allowing the lower voices to move obliquely in relation to the soprano.

Any given tones in the soprano are guides for completing the progression. Chordal skips (re-voicing a chord) are permissible; however, chordal skips in the bass are limited to octave leaps only. Although the figured bass is limited to triads, you may want to use the chord seventh to facilitate the voice leading, particularly with the dominant immediately preceding the final tonic.

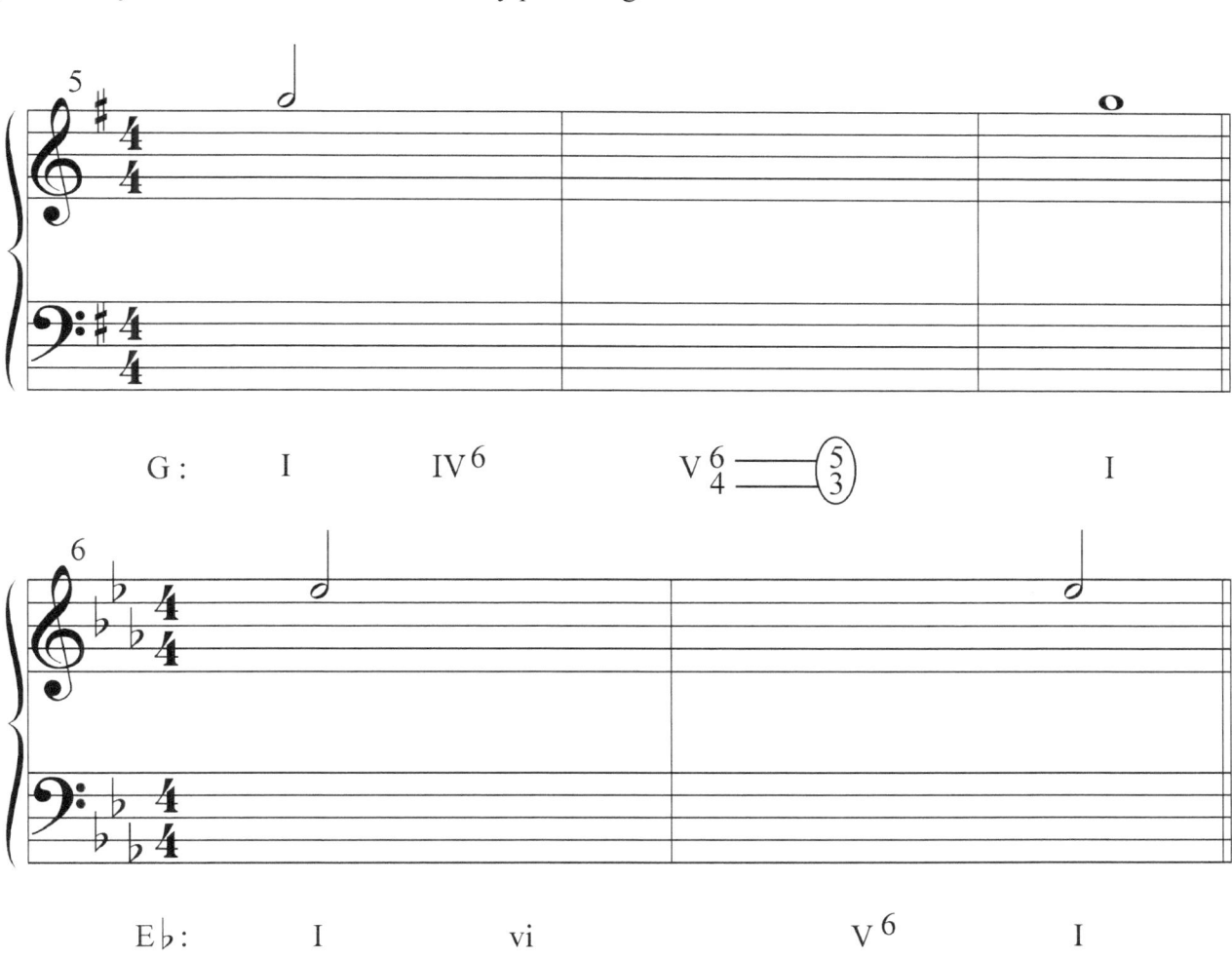

Basic Harmony Worksheet 7–4

Name _____

Worksheet 7–4 for Chapter 7: The Chord Progression

Given the key and chord symbols, construct the following progressions. Use four voices (soprano, alto, tenor, and bass) in open structure (whenever possible). Based upon the given the meter, assign a rhythmic framework. The soprano voice, in particular, should adhere to the following guidelines when the progression moves between unlike chords:
  (1) either move upwards or downwards as conjunctly as possible, leaping no more than a single 3rd and then reversing direction by step (that is, moving in the opposite direction of the leap); or,
  (2) remain stationary (that is, maintain common tones between unlike chords), allowing the lower voices to move obliquely in relation to the soprano.

Any given tones in the soprano are guides for completing the progression. Chordal skips (re-voicing a chord) are permissible; however, chordal skips in the bass are limited to octave leaps only. Although the figured bass is limited to triads, you may want to use the chord seventh to facilitate the voice leading, particularly with the dominant immediately preceding the final tonic.

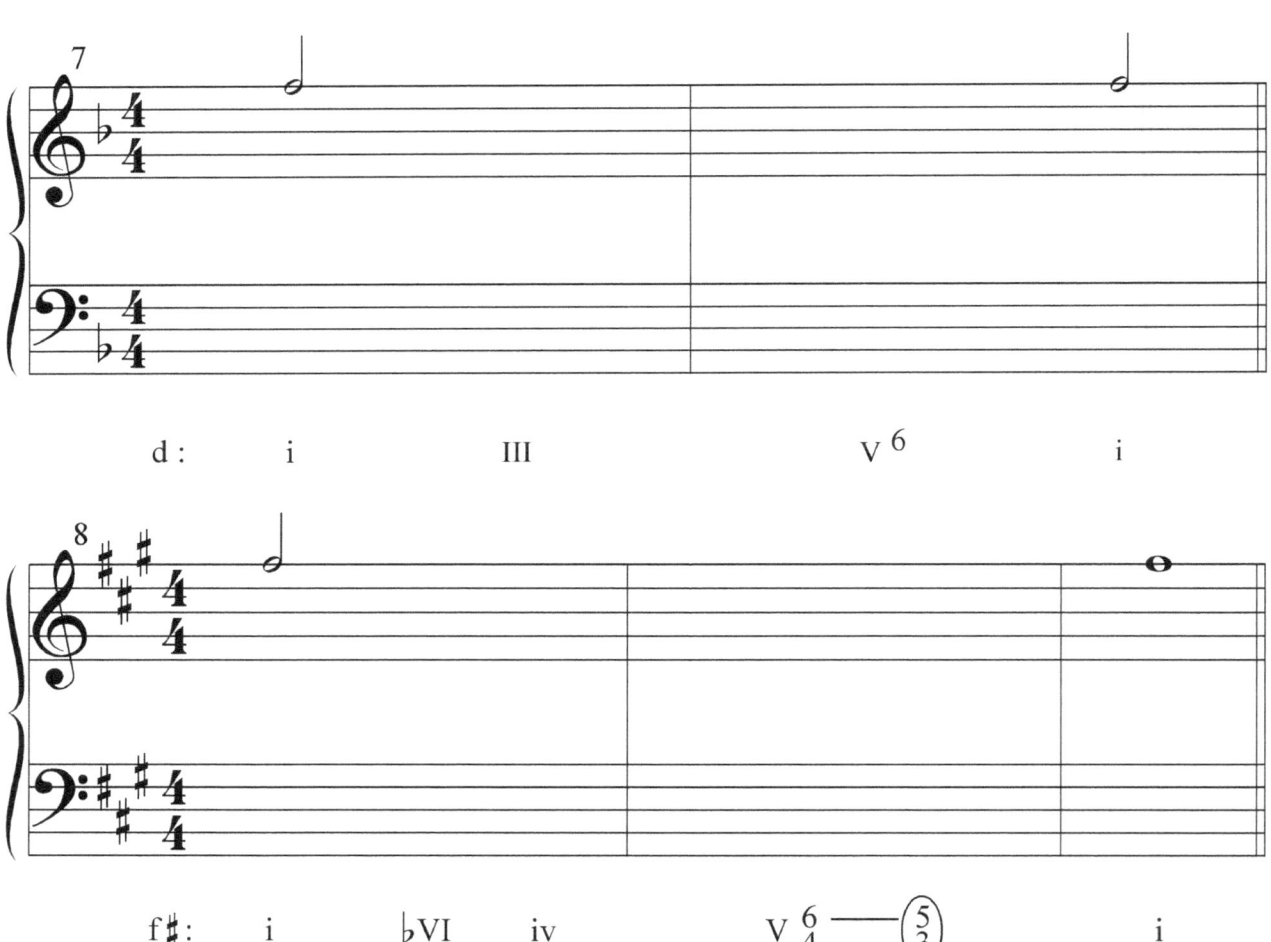

Basic Harmony Worksheet 7–5

Name _____

Worksheet 7–5 for Chapter 7: The Chord Progression

Given the key and chord symbols, construct the following progressions. Use four voices (soprano, alto, tenor, and bass) in open structure (whenever possible). Based upon the given the meter, assign a rhythmic framework. The soprano voice, in particular, should adhere to the following guidelines when the progression moves between unlike chords:
  (1) either move upwards or downwards as conjunctly as possible, leaping no more than a single 3rd and then reversing direction by step (that is, moving in the opposite direction of the leap); or,
  (2) remain stationary (that is, maintain common tones between unlike chords), allowing the lower voices to move obliquely in relation to the soprano.

Any given tones in the soprano are guides for completing the progression. Chordal skips (re-voicing a chord) are permissible; however, chordal skips in the bass are limited to octave leaps only. Although the figured bass is limited to triads, you may want to use the chord seventh to facilitate the voice leading, particularly with the dominant immediately preceding the final tonic.

Basic Harmony Worksheet 7–6

Name _____

Worksheet 7–6 for Chapter 7: The Chord Progression

Given the key and chord symbols, construct the following progressions. Use four voices (soprano, alto, tenor, and bass) in open structure (whenever possible). Based upon the given the meter, assign a rhythmic framework. The soprano voice, in particular, should adhere to the following guidelines when the progression moves between unlike chords:
(1) either move upwards or downwards as conjunctly as possible, leaping no more than a single 3rd and then reversing direction by step (that is, moving in the opposite direction of the leap); or,
(2) remain stationary (that is, maintain common tones between unlike chords), allowing the lower voices to move obliquely in relation to the soprano.

Any given tones in the soprano are guides for completing the progression. Chordal skips (re-voicing a chord) are permissible; however, chordal skips in the bass are limited to octave leaps only. Although the figured bass is limited to triads, you may want to use the chord seventh to facilitate the voice leading, particularly with the dominant immediately preceding the final tonic.

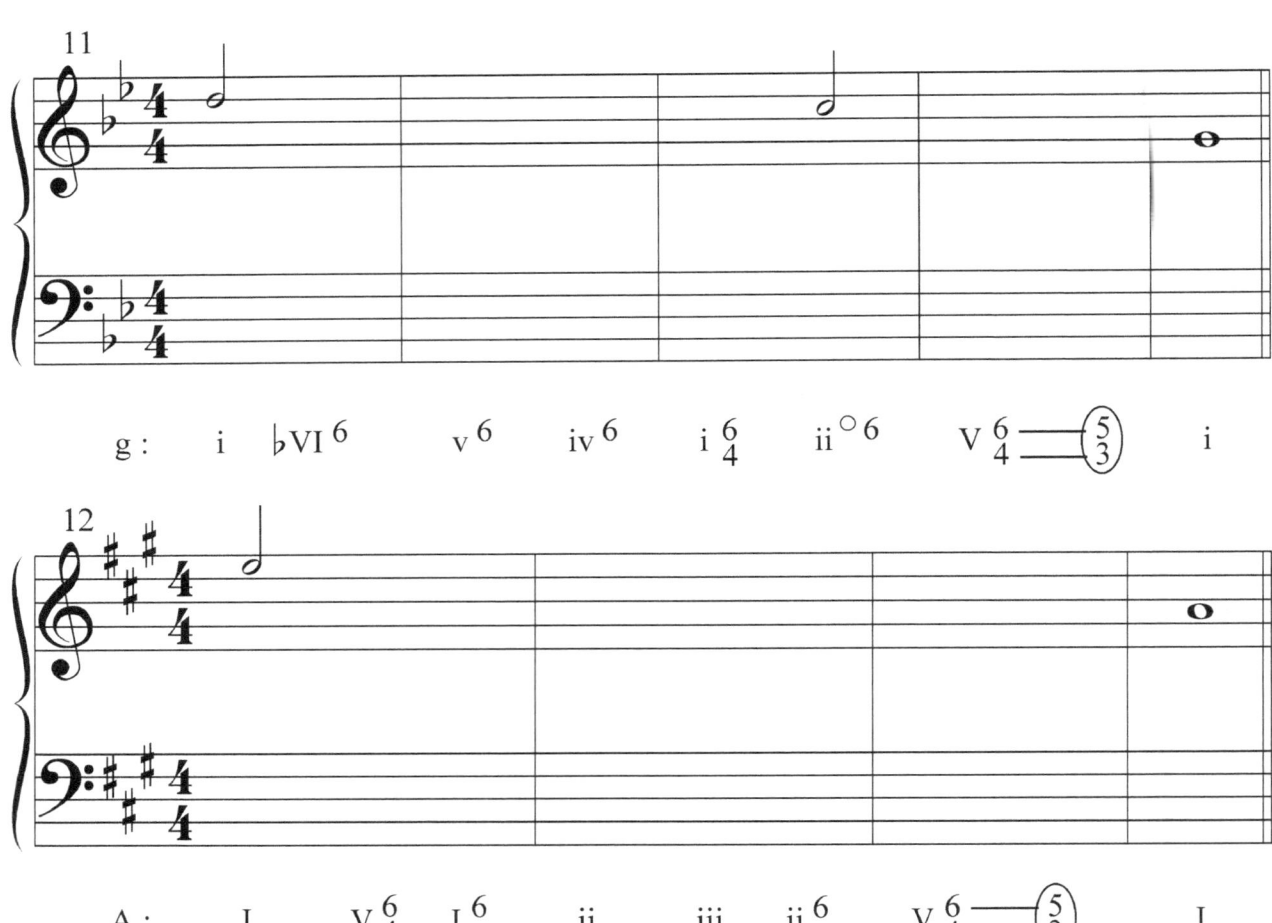

Basic Harmony Worksheet 7–7

Name _____

Worksheet 7–7 for Chapter 7: The Chord Progression

Given the key and chord symbols, construct the following progressions. Use four voices (soprano, alto, tenor, and bass) in open structure (whenever possible). Based upon the given the meter, assign a rhythmic framework. The soprano voice, in particular, should adhere to the following guidelines when the progression moves between unlike chords:
 (1) either move upwards or downwards as conjunctly as possible, leaping no more than a single 3rd and then reversing direction by step (that is, moving in the opposite direction of the leap); or,
 (2) remain stationary (that is, maintain common tones between unlike chords), allowing the lower voices to move obliquely in relation to the soprano.
Any given tones in the soprano are guides for completing the progression. Chordal skips (re-voicing a chord) are permissible; however, chordal skips in the bass are limited to octave leaps only. Although the figured bass is limited to triads, you may want to use the chord seventh to facilitate the voice leading, particularly with the dominant immediately preceding the final tonic. (The diminished triad of the supertonic in root position should be used only within the context of a sequence, such as the one in progression 14; however, it is rendered more acceptable by adding the seventh and omitting the fifth.)

Basic Harmony Worksheet 7–8

Name _____

Worksheet 7–8 for Chapter 7: The Chord Progression

Meter and Rhythm

Given the following alternating meters, write the counts directly under the appropriate note or rest and supply any missing bar lines. The symbol ♪ = ♪ indicates that eighth notes between different meters are equivalent and remain at a constant speed. This notation is particularly useful when the value of the beat between any two time signatures represents different note values (such as $\frac{5}{8}$ and $\frac{3}{4}$). The courtesy time signatures at the end of the staff systems indicate a change in meter in the next line of music. (Bar lines should not be placed after the courtesy signatures.)

    The challenge of this exercise is not in the counting but in the performance. You should be seated at a desk or table. To perform the exercise, tap both feet to the *quarter note* and execute the rhythms on a hard surface with both hands. You will find that if your feet remain constant with the quarter note, the beginnings of certain measures will not coincide with your feet—keeping your place is the real challenge. In the example, a dash under some of the counts indicates where your feet should tap.

Basic Harmony Worksheet 8–1

Name _____

Worksheet 8–1 for Chapter 8: The Chord Seventh Revisited

Using the example as a guide, supply two different names (or descriptions) for the seventh-chord qualities according to the indicated area of the given mode.

Mode Abbreviations
D   =   Dorian
P   =   Phrygian
Ly   =   Lydian
M   =   Mixolydian
A   =   Aeolian
L   =   Locrian

Chord and Interval Abbreviations
MT   =   major triad
mt   =   minor triad
d°t =   diminished triad
M⁷   =   major seventh (interval and chord quality)
m⁷   =   minor seventh (interval and chord quality)
D⁷   =   dominant seventh
ø⁷   =   half-diminished seventh

example (II⁷)   area of A: __ø⁷__   __d°t / m⁷__

1. (V⁷)   area of D: _____   _____

2. (III⁷)   area of M: _____   _____

3. (VI⁷)   area of Ly: _____   _____

4. (II⁷)   area of P: _____   _____

5. (VI⁷)   area of A: _____   _____

6. (VII⁷)   area of L: _____   _____

7. (VII⁷)   area of A: _____   _____

8. (IV⁷)   area of D: _____   _____

9. (V⁷)   area of Ly: _____   _____

10. (VII⁷) area of M: _____   _____

Basic Harmony Worksheet 8–2

Name _____

Worksheet 8–2 for Chapter 8: The Chord Seventh Revisited

Using the example as a guide, supply two different names (or descriptions) for the seventh-chord qualities according to the indicated area of the given mode.

Mode Abbreviations
D   =   Dorian
P   =   Phrygian
Ly =   Lydian
M   =   Mixolydian
A   =   Aeolian
L   =   Locrian

Chord and Interval Abbreviations
MT   =   major triad
mt   =   minor triad
d°t =   diminished triad
M⁷   =   major seventh (interval and chord quality)
m⁷   =   minor seventh (interval and chord quality)
D⁷   =   dominant seventh
ø⁷   =   half-diminished seventh

example (II⁷)   area of D: __m⁷__   __mt / m⁷__

1. (VII⁷)   area of D: __M⁷__   __MT / M⁷__

2. (V⁷)   area of A: __m⁷__   __mt / m⁷__

3. (IV⁷)   area of Ly: __ø⁷__   __d°t / m⁷__

4. (V⁷)   area of P: __ø⁷__   __d°t / m⁷__

5. (VII⁷) area of P: __m⁷__   __mt / m⁷__

6. (II⁷)   area of L: __M⁷__   __MT / M⁷__

7. (II⁷)   area of Ly: __D⁷__   __MT / m⁷__

8. (VI⁷)   area of D: __ø⁷__   __d°t / m⁷__

9. (III⁷) area of A: __M⁷__   __MT / M⁷__

10. (V⁷)   area of M: __m⁷__   __mt / m⁷__

Basic Harmony Worksheet 8–3

Name _____

Worksheet 8–3 for Chapter 8: The Chord Seventh Revisited

Using the example as a guide, supply two different names (or descriptions) for the seventh-chord qualities according to the indicated area of the given mode.

Mode Abbreviations
D   =   Dorian
P   =   Phrygian
Ly =   Lydian
M   =   Mixolydian
A   =   Aeolian
L   =   Locrian

Chord and Interval Abbreviations
MT =   major triad
mt =   minor triad
d°t =   diminished triad
M^7 =   major seventh (interval and chord quality)
m^7 =   minor seventh (interval and chord quality)
D^7 =   dominant seventh
$ø^7$ =   half-diminished seventh

example VI^7 area of L: D^7 MT / m^7

1. IV^7 area of L: m^7 mt / m^7

2. IV^7 area of P: m^7 mt / m^7

3. VI^7 area of M: m^7 mt / m^7

4. III^7 area of D: M^7 MT / M^7

5. III^7 area of P: D^7 MT / m^7

6. II^7 area of M: m^7 mt / m^7

7. V^7 area of L: M^7 MT / M^7

8. III^7 area of Ly: m^7 mt / m^7

9. IV^7 area of M: M^7 MT / M^7

10. VII^7 area of D: M^7 MT / M^7

Basic Harmony Worksheet 8–4

Name _____

Worksheet 8–4 for Chapter 8: The Chord Seventh Revisited

According to the specified key, mode, and chord position, construct the indicated seventh chord in four-voice open structure using half notes *only*.

Mode Abbreviations
D   =   Dorian
P   =   Phrygian
Ly   =   Lydian
M   =   Mixolydian
A   =   Aeolian
L   =   Locrian

F♯ D: (VII⁷)   D♭ M: (III⁷)   E♭ A: (V⁷)   G P: (II⁷)   B M: (VII⁷)

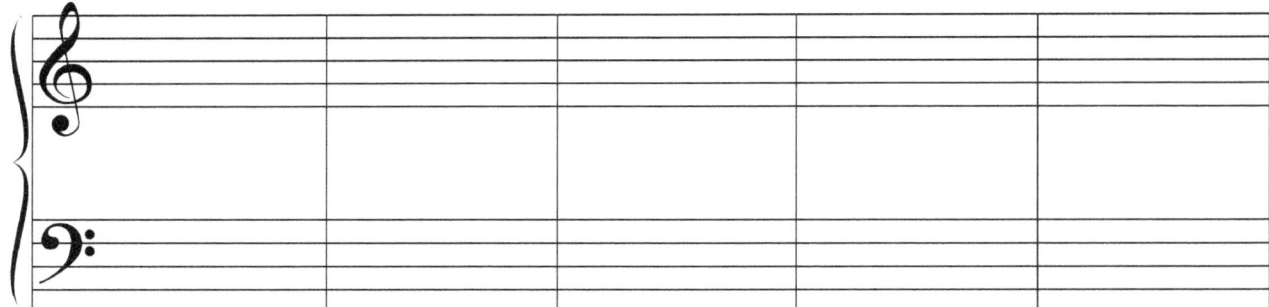

E♭ Ly: (IV⁷)   C♯ L: (VI⁷)   F♯ A: (VI⁷)   B D: (IV⁷)   F P: (V⁷)

Basic Harmony Worksheet 8–5

Name _____

Worksheet 8–5 for Chapter 8: The Chord Seventh Revisited

According to the specified key, mode, and chord position, construct the indicated seventh chord in four-voice open structure using half notes *only*.

Mode Abbreviations
D   =   Dorian
P   =   Phrygian
Ly =   Lydian
M   =   Mixolydian
A   =   Aeolian
L   =   Locrian

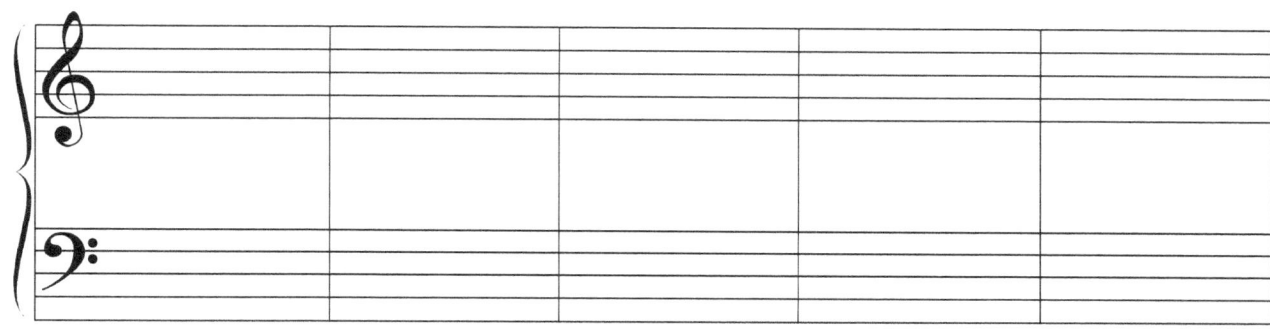

D♭ M: VI⁷   A Ly: IV⁷   F♯ D: IV⁷   C L: VII⁷   B M: II⁷

E♭ P: II⁷   E Ly: VI⁷   B♭ A: V⁷   B♭ D: IV⁷   F♯ P: VII⁷

Basic Harmony Worksheet 8–6

Name _____

Worksheet 8–6 for Chapter 8: The Chord Seventh Revisited

According to the specified key, mode, and chord position, construct the indicated seventh chord in four-voice open structure using half notes *only*.

Mode Abbreviations
D   =   Dorian
P   =   Phrygian
Ly   =   Lydian
M   =   Mixolydian
A   =   Aeolian
L   =   Locrian

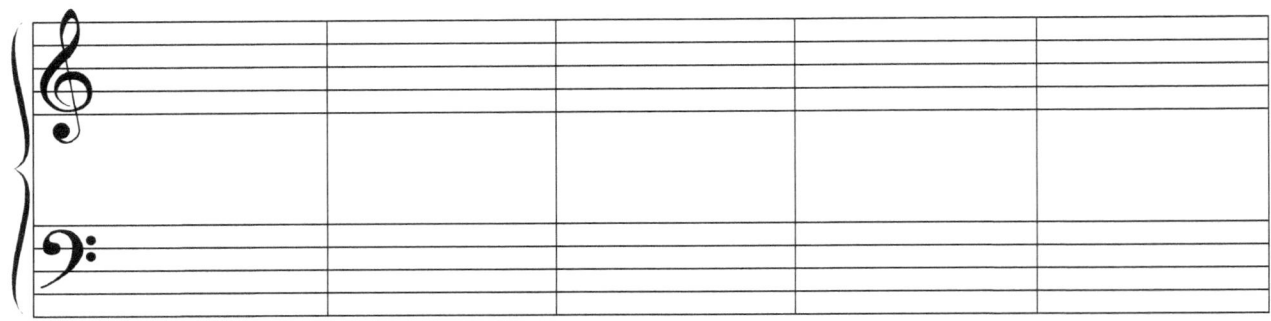

G♯ L: III $^6_5$ B A: II $^4_3$ D♭ Ly: V $^4_2$ C P: III $^4_3$ E D: VI $^6_5$

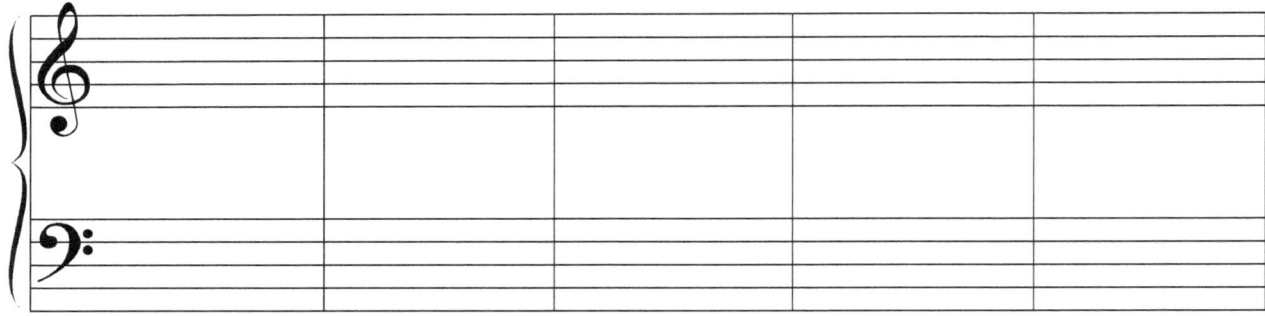

C♯ M: V $^6_5$ A L: II $^4_2$ B♭ Ly: VII $^4_3$ G♯ A: III $^4_2$ F M: IV $^6_5$

Basic Harmony Worksheet 8–7

Name _____

Worksheet 8–7 for Chapter 8: The Chord Seventh Revisited

According to the specified key, mode, and chord position, construct the indicated seventh chord in four-voice open structure using half notes *only*.

Mode Abbreviations
D = Dorian
P = Phrygian
Ly = Lydian
M = Mixolydian
A = Aeolian
L = Locrian

A D: II $^6_5$ G♭ Ly: III $^4_3$ A M: IV $^4_2$ D P: IV $^4_3$ C♯ A: VII $^6_5$

G L: V $^6_5$ C Ly: II $^4_2$ B♭ P: IV $^4_3$ D♯ A: IV $^4_2$ D L: I $^4_2$

Basic Harmony Worksheet 8–8

Name _____

Worksheet 8–8 for Chapter 8: The Chord Seventh Revisited

Identify the quality of the root-position sevenths using one of the three possible answers given below (use the chord symbol for your answer not the number in parentheses):

Possible Seventh Chords:
    (1) m-M7 = minor-major seventh (mt/M7)
    (2) A-M7 = augmented-major seventh (A+T/M7)
    (3) o^7 = fully diminished seventh

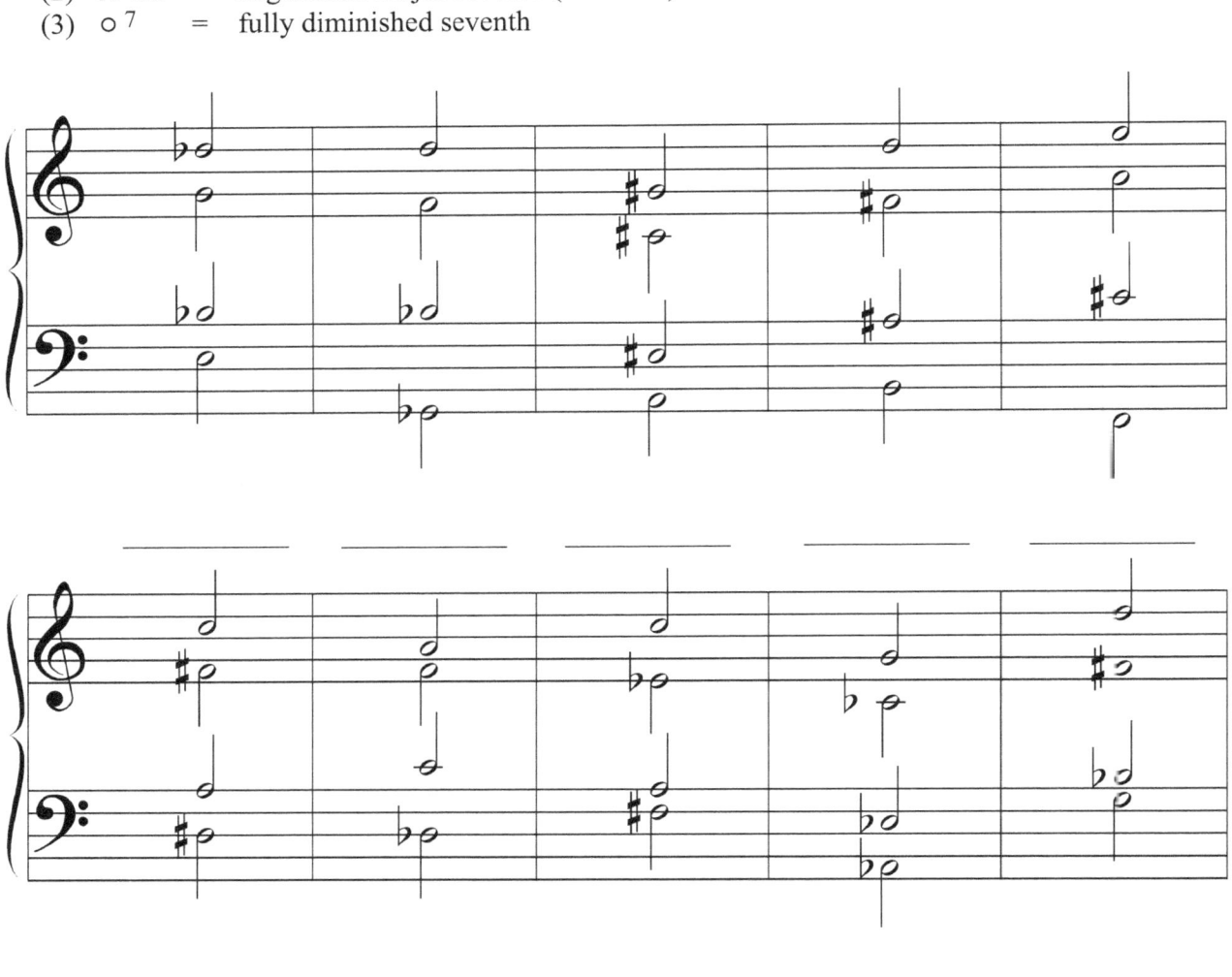

Basic Harmony Worksheet 8–9

Name _____

Worksheet 8–9 for Chapter 8: The Chord Seventh Revisited

Identify the quality of the root-position sevenths using one of the three possible answers given below (use the chord symbol for your answer not the number in parentheses):

Possible Seventh Chords:
    (1) m-M7 = minor-major seventh (mt/M7)
    (2) A-M7 = augmented-major seventh (A+T/M7)
    (3) o^7 = fully diminished seventh

Basic Harmony Worksheet 8–10

Name _____

Worksheet 8–10 for Chapter 8: The Chord Seventh Revisited

Identify both the correct quality *and* position of the following seventh chords (use the chord symbol for your answer not the number in parentheses):

Possible Seventh Chords:
    (1) m-M7 = minor-major seventh (mt/M7)
    (2) A-M7 = augmented-major seventh (A+T/M7)
    (3) o7 = fully diminished seventh

Chord Positions: $7, \; {}^6_5, \; {}^4_3, \; \text{or} \; {}^4_2$

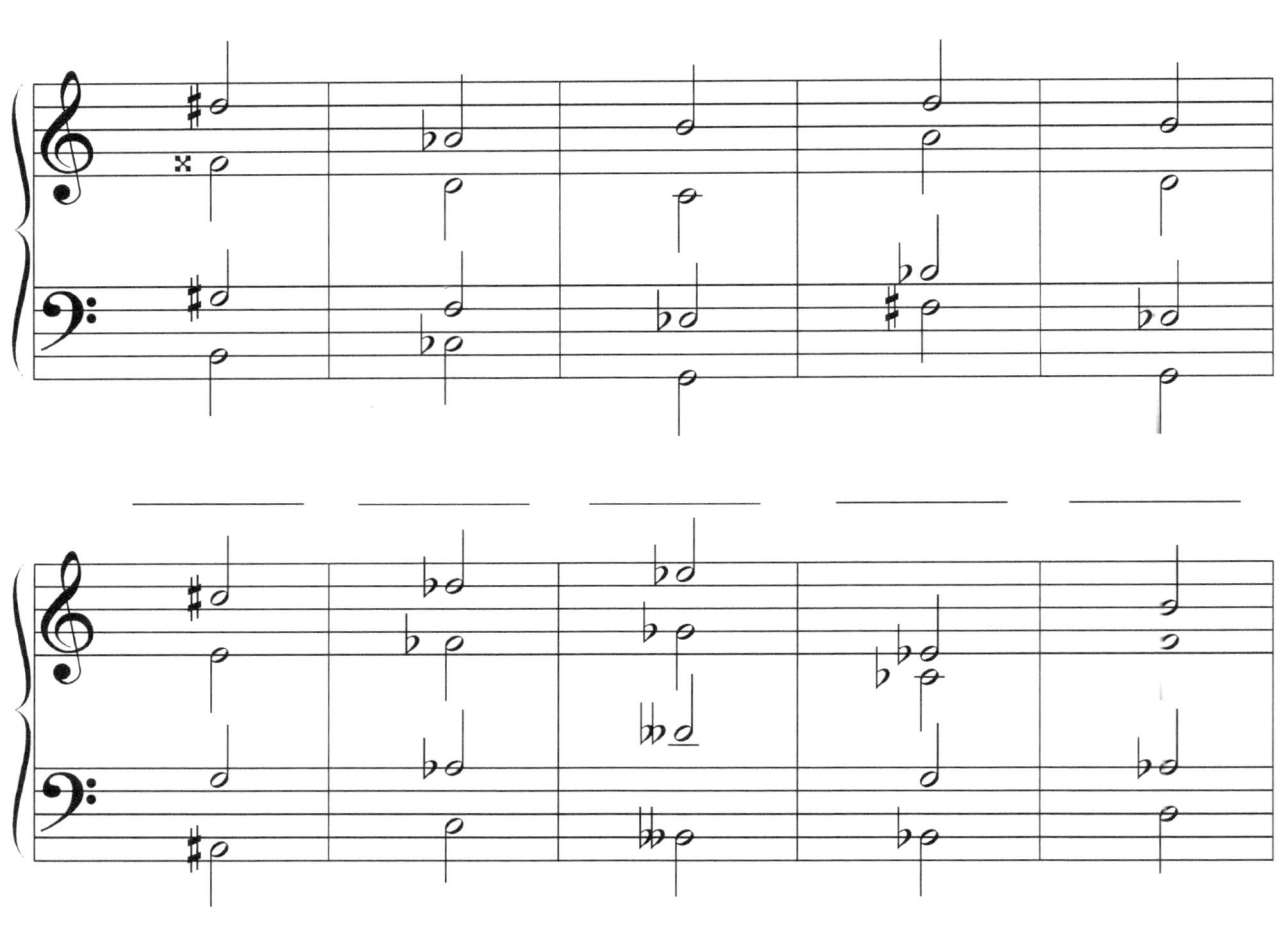

Basic Harmony Worksheet 8–11

Name _____

Worksheet 8–11 for Chapter 8: The Chord Seventh Revisited

Identify both the correct quality *and* position of the following seventh chords (use the chord symbol for your answer not the number in parentheses):

Possible Seventh Chords:
    (1) m-M7 = minor-major seventh (mt/M7)
    (2) A-M7 = augmented-major seventh (A+T/M7)
    (3) o7 = fully diminished seventh

Chord Positions: 7, $\frac{6}{5}$, $\frac{4}{3}$, or $\frac{4}{2}$

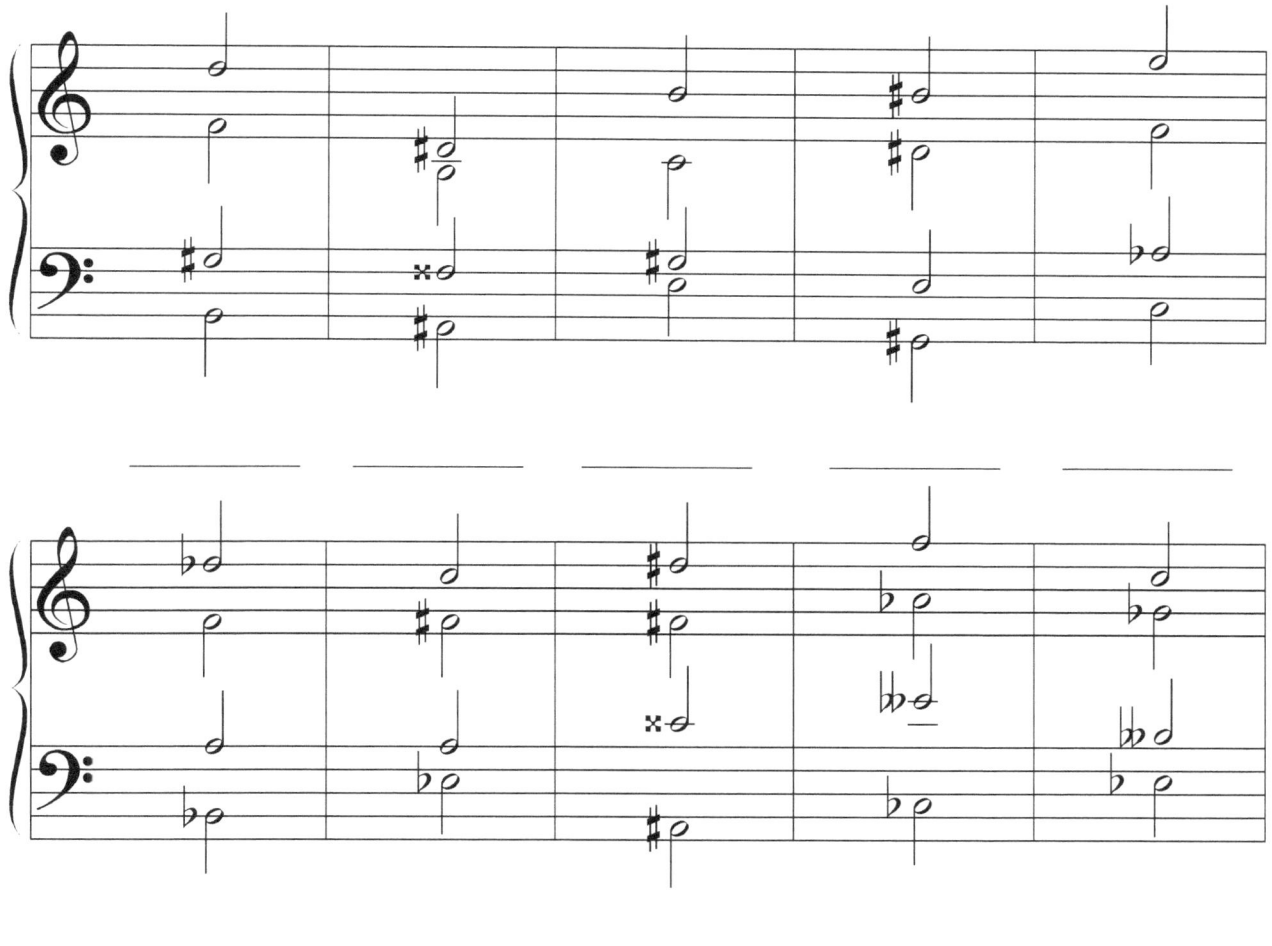

Basic Harmony Worksheet 8–12

Name _____

Worksheet 8–12 for Chapter 8: The Chord Seventh Revisited

Above the given bass and according to the indicated chord quality and position, construct the correct seventh chord in open structure for four voices using half notes only:

Possible Seventh Chords:
    (1) m-M7 = minor-major seventh (mt/M7)
    (2) A-M7 = augmented-major seventh (A+T/M7)
    (3) o7 = fully diminished seventh

Chord Positions: $7, \frac{6}{5}, \frac{4}{3},$ or $\frac{4}{2}$

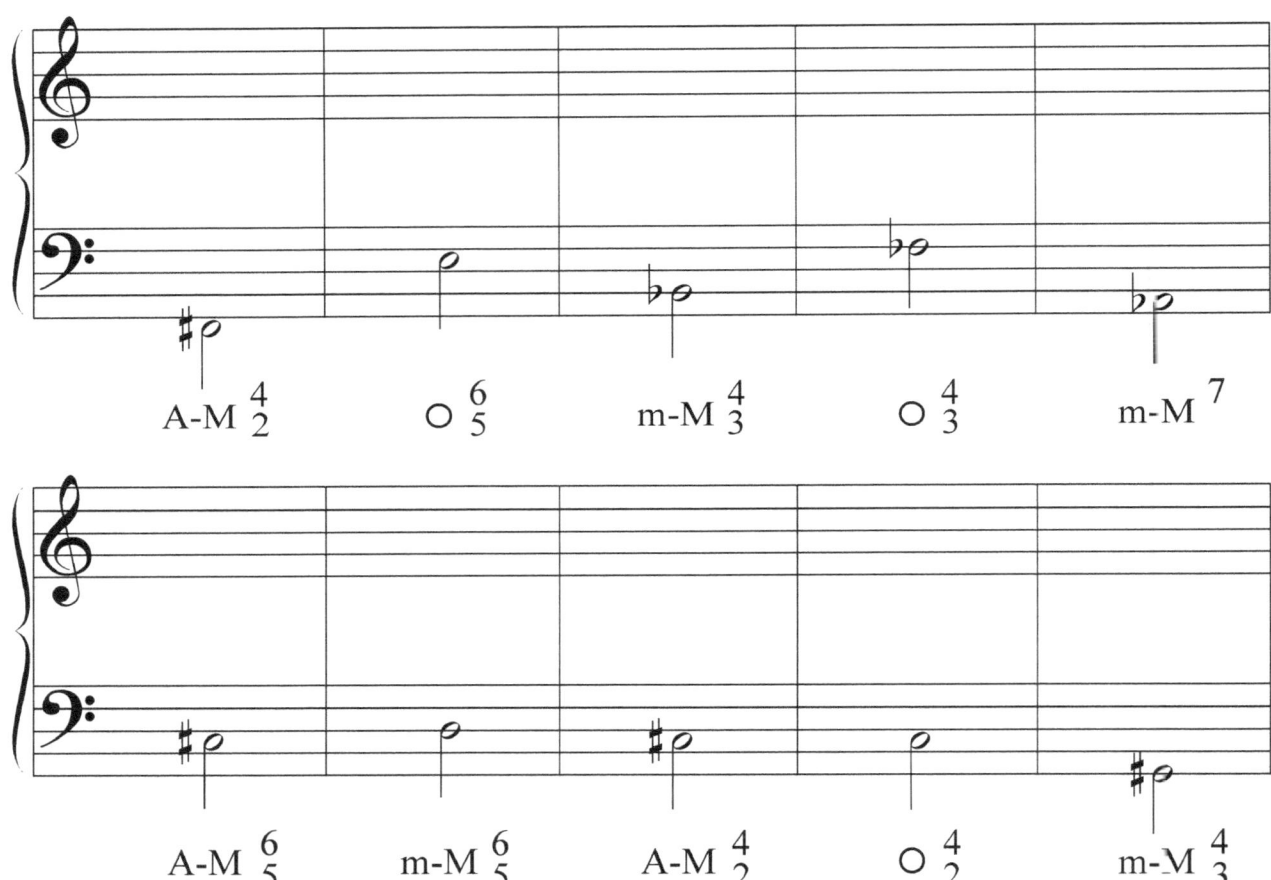

Basic Harmony Worksheet 8–13

Name _____

Worksheet 8–13 for Chapter 8: The Chord Seventh Revisited

Above the given bass and according to the indicated chord quality and position, construct the correct seventh chord in open structure for four voices using half notes only:

Possible Seventh Chords:
    (1) m-M7 = minor-major seventh (mt/M7)
    (2) A-M7 = augmented-major seventh (A+T/M7)
    (3) o7 = fully diminished seventh

Chord Positions: 7, $\frac{6}{5}$, $\frac{4}{3}$, or $\frac{4}{2}$

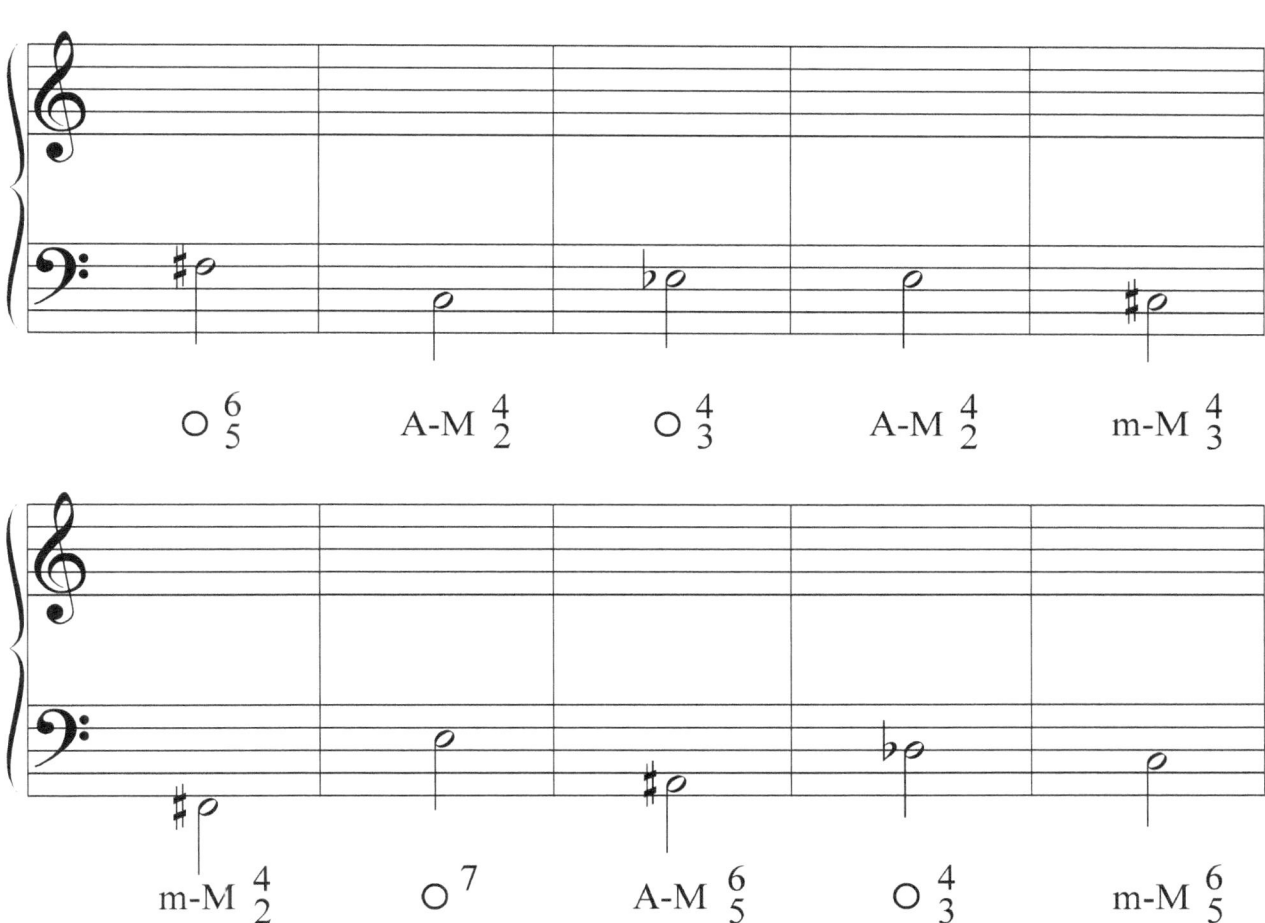

Basic Harmony Worksheet 8–14

Name _____

Worksheet 8–14 for Chapter 8: The Chord Seventh Revisited

Given the key, mode (uppercase is major and lowercase is minor), chord symbol, and figured bass, construct the appropriate seventh chord in four voices. Use half notes and open structure for your answers.

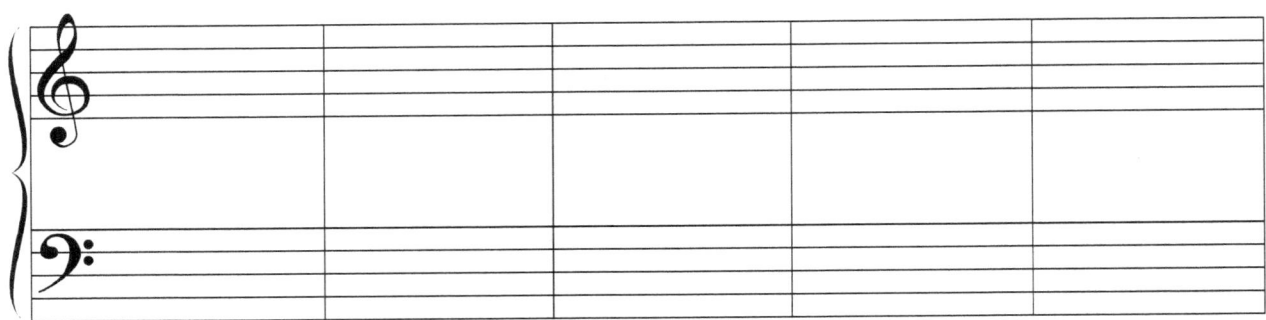

d: ii⌀$\frac{4}{3}$ A♭: IV$\frac{4}{3}$ f: ♯vii°$\frac{6}{5}$ E: IV$\frac{6}{5}$ b♭: ♭VI$\frac{4}{2}$

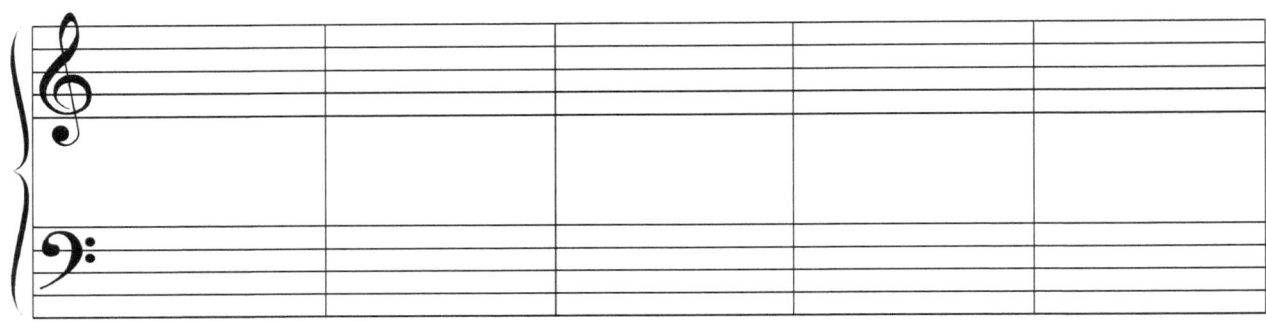

C♭: vii⌀$\frac{6}{5}$ e♭: i$\overset{(♭7)}{\frac{4}{3}}$ F♯: iii$\frac{4}{2}$ b: ♭VII$\overset{(♭7)}{\frac{6}{5}}$ D♭: vi$\frac{4}{2}$

Basic Harmony Worksheet 8–15

Name _____

Worksheet 8–15 for Chapter 8: The Chord Seventh Revisited

Given the key, mode (uppercase is major and lowercase is minor), chord symbol, and figured bass, construct the appropriate seventh chord in four voices. Use half notes and open structure for your answers.

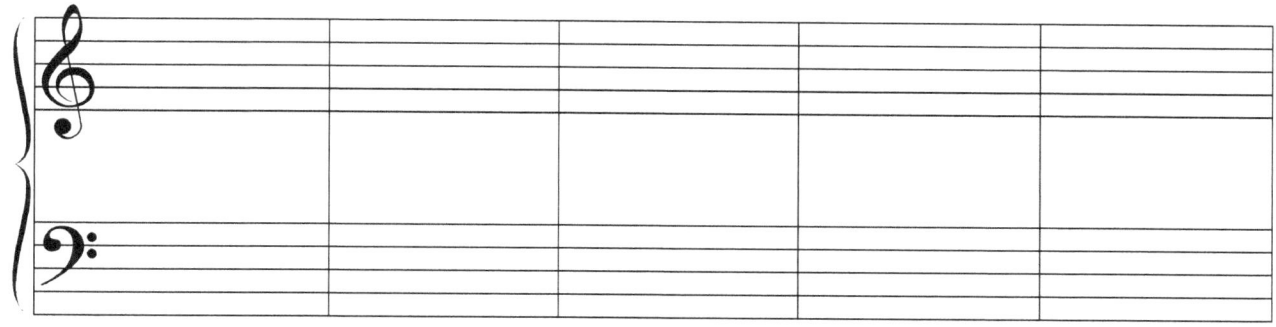

c♯: III $\frac{4}{2}$ E♭: V $\frac{4}{2}$ f♯: IV $\frac{6}{5}$ B: ii $\frac{4}{3}$ e: v $\frac{6}{5}$

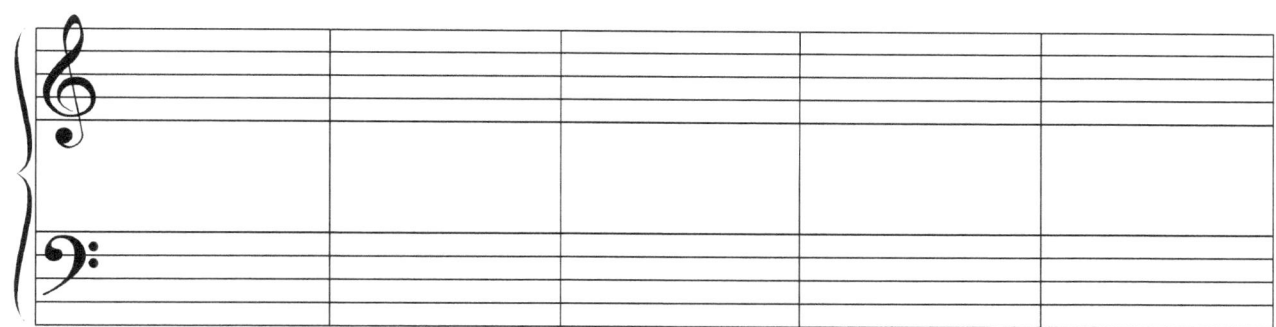

D: iii ^{7} g♯: V $\frac{4}{3}$ B♭: vi $\frac{4}{3}$ d♯: ♯vii° $\frac{6}{5}$ G♭: ii $\frac{4}{2}$

Basic Harmony Worksheet 8–16

Name _____

Worksheet 8–16 for Chapter 8: The Chord Seventh Revisited

Given the key, mode (uppercase is major and lowercase is minor), chord symbol, and figured bass, construct the appropriate seventh chord in four voices. Use half notes and open structure for your answers.

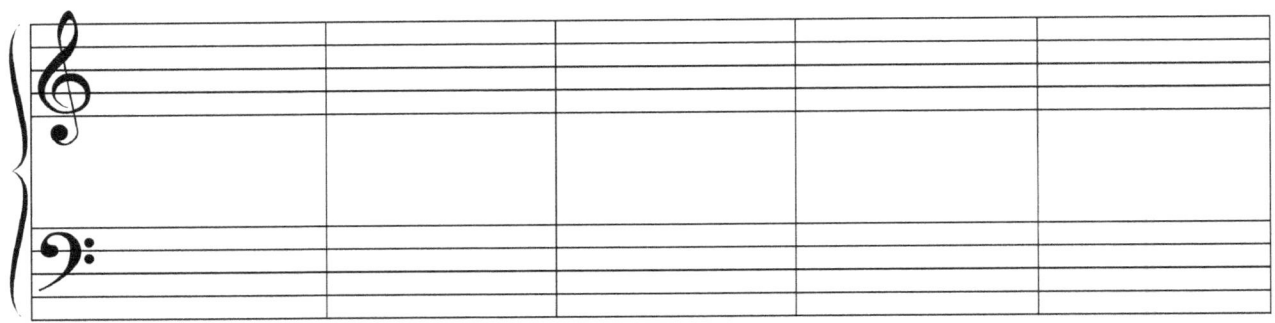

g: V$^6_5$ C♯: vii$\varnothing^4_3$ a♯: IV$^6_5$ D♭: iii$^4_2$ c: ♭VI$^4_2$

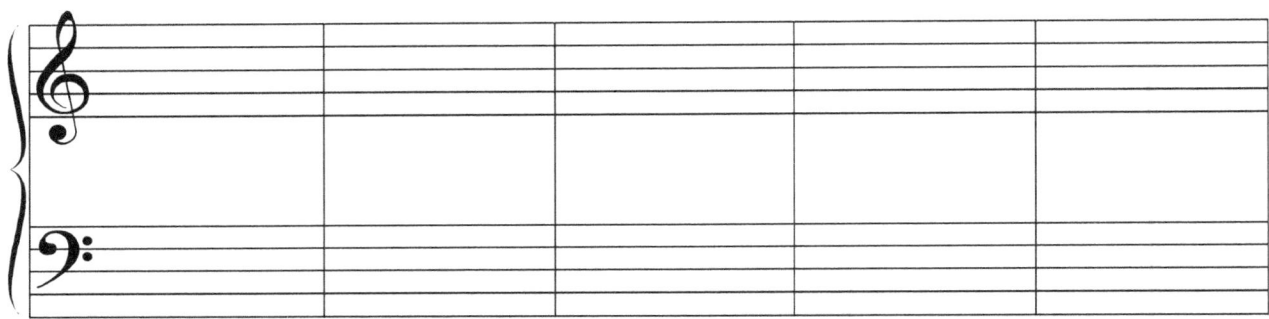

F: ii$^4_3$ a♭: ♯vi$\varnothing^7$ A: V$^6_5$ e♭: ♭VII$^{(♭7)}_{\;\;4\;3}$ F♯: vi$^6_5$

Basic Harmony Worksheet 8–17

Name _____

Worksheet 8–17 for Chapter 8: The Chord Seventh Revisited

Given the key, mode (uppercase is major and lowercase is minor), chord symbol, and figured bass, construct the appropriate seventh chord in four voices. Use half notes and open structure for your answers.

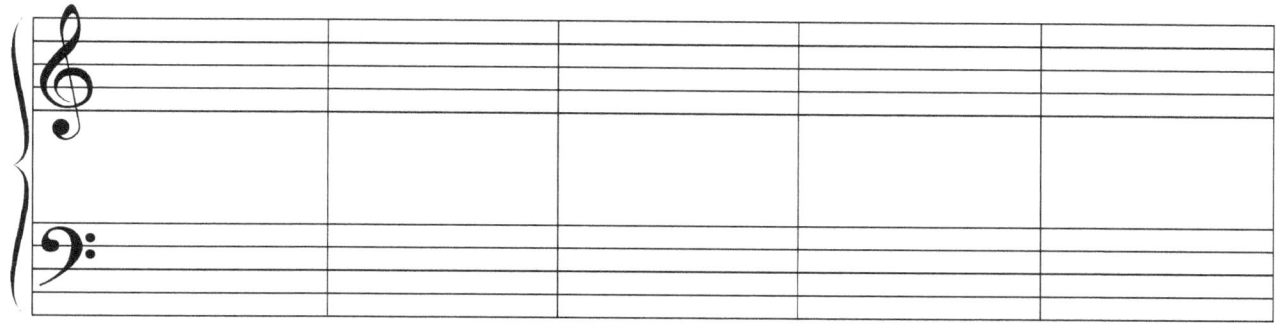

b♭: ♯vi⌀$^6_5$ F♯: vii⌀^{7} d♯: iv$^4_2$ G: vi$^4_3$ g♯: ♯vii°$^6_5$

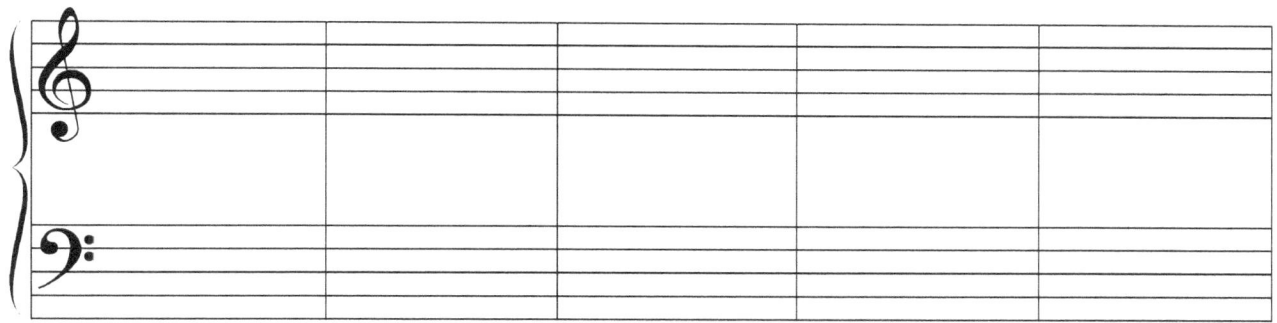

A♭: iii$^4_3$ c♯: ♭VI$^4_3$ B: IV$^6_5$ a♭: ♭VII$^{4}_{2}$ (♭7)   E: V$^4_2$

Basic Harmony Worksheet 8–18

Name _____

Worksheet 8–18 for Chapter 8: The Chord Seventh Revisited

Given the key and chord symbols, construct the following progressions (sevenths are optional except where indicated). Use four voices (soprano, alto, tenor, and bass) in open structure (whenever possible). Based upon the given the meter, assign a rhythmic framework. The soprano voice, in particular, should adhere to the following guidelines when the progression moves between unlike chords:
  (1) either move upwards or downwards as conjunctly as possible, leaping no more than a single 3rd and then reversing direction by step (that is, moving in the opposite direction of the leap); or,
  (2) remain stationary (that is, maintain common tones between unlike chords), allowing the lower voices to move obliquely in relation to the soprano.

Any given tones in the soprano are guides for completing the progression. Chordal skips (re-voicing a chord) are permissible; however, chordal skips in the bass are limited to octave leaps only.

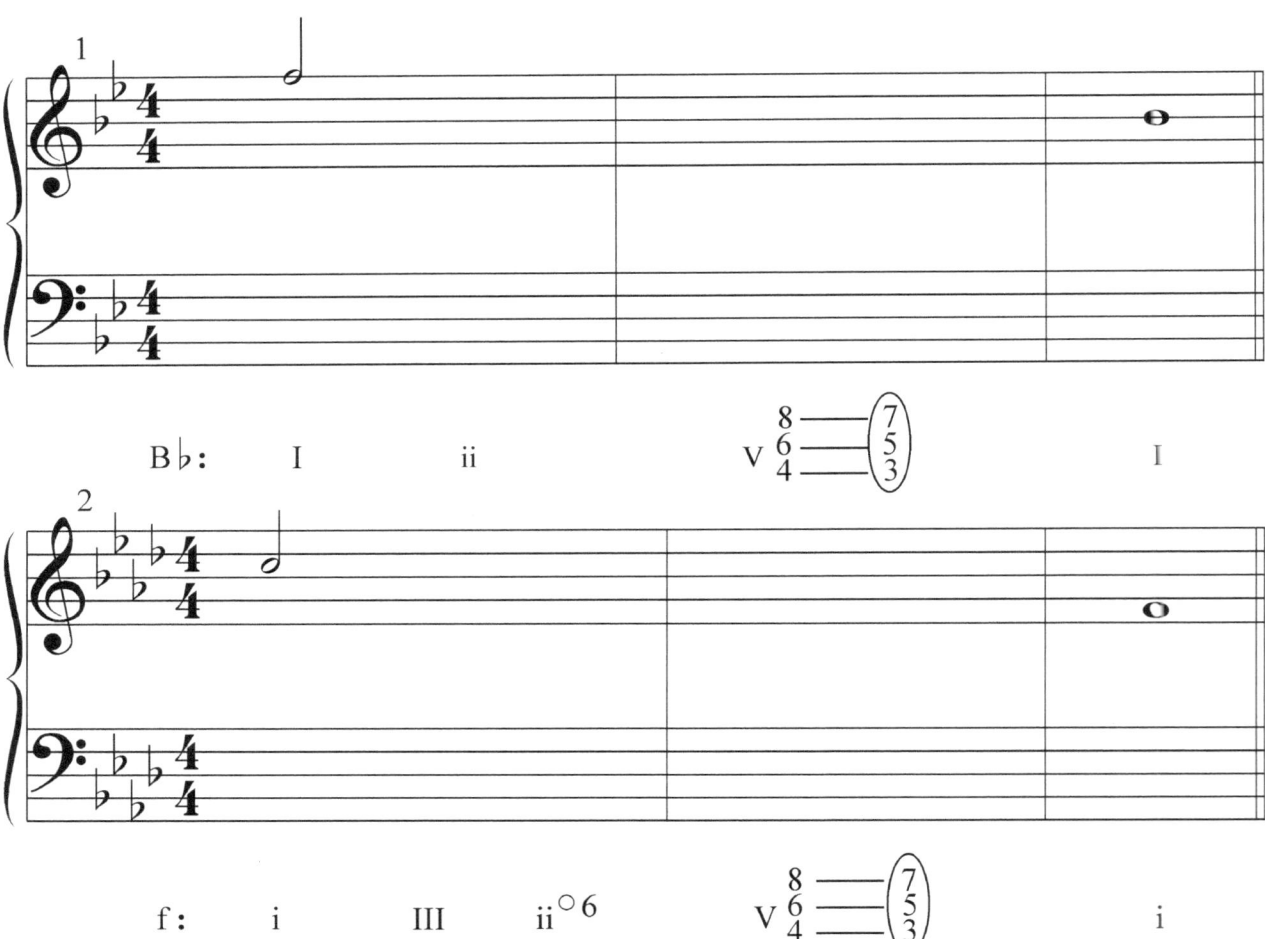

Basic Harmony Worksheet 8–19

Name _____

Worksheet 8–19 for Chapter 8: The Chord Seventh Revisited

Given the key and chord symbols, construct the following progressions (sevenths are optional except where indicated). Use four voices (soprano, alto, tenor, and bass) in open structure (whenever possible). Based upon the given the meter, assign a rhythmic framework. The soprano voice, in particular, should adhere to the following guidelines when the progression moves between unlike chords:
  (1) either move upwards or downwards as conjunctly as possible, leaping no more than a single 3rd and then reversing direction by step (that is, moving in the opposite direction of the leap); or,
  (2) remain stationary (that is, maintain common tones between unlike chords), allowing the lower voices to move obliquely in relation to the soprano.
Any given tones in the soprano are guides for completing the progression. Chordal skips (re-voicing a chord) are permissible; however, chordal skips in the bass are limited to octave leaps only.

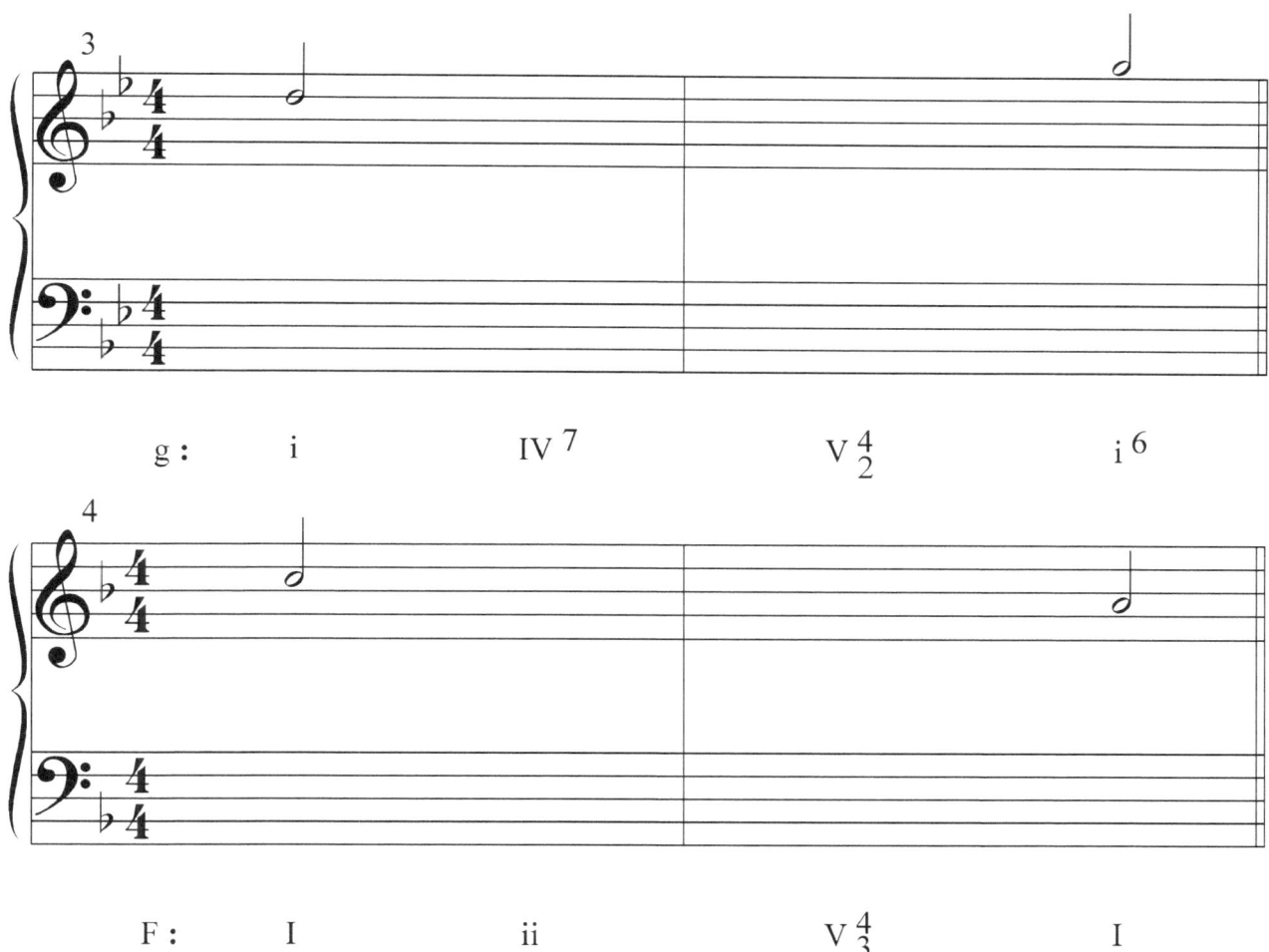

Basic Harmony Worksheet 8–20

Name _____

Worksheet 8–20 for Chapter 8: The Chord Seventh Revisited

Given the key and chord symbols, construct the following progressions (sevenths are optional except where indicated). Use four voices (soprano, alto, tenor, and bass) in open structure (whenever possible). Based upon the given the meter, assign a rhythmic framework. The soprano voice, in particular, should adhere to the following guidelines when the progression moves between unlike chords:
(1) either move upwards or downwards as conjunctly as possible, leaping no more than a single 3rd and then reversing direction by step (that is, moving in the opposite direction of the leap); or,
(2) remain stationary (that is, maintain common tones between unlike chords), allowing the lower voices to move obliquely in relation to the soprano.

Any given tones in the soprano are guides for completing the progression. Chordal skips (re-voicing a chord) are permissible; however, chordal skips in the bass are limited to octave leaps only.

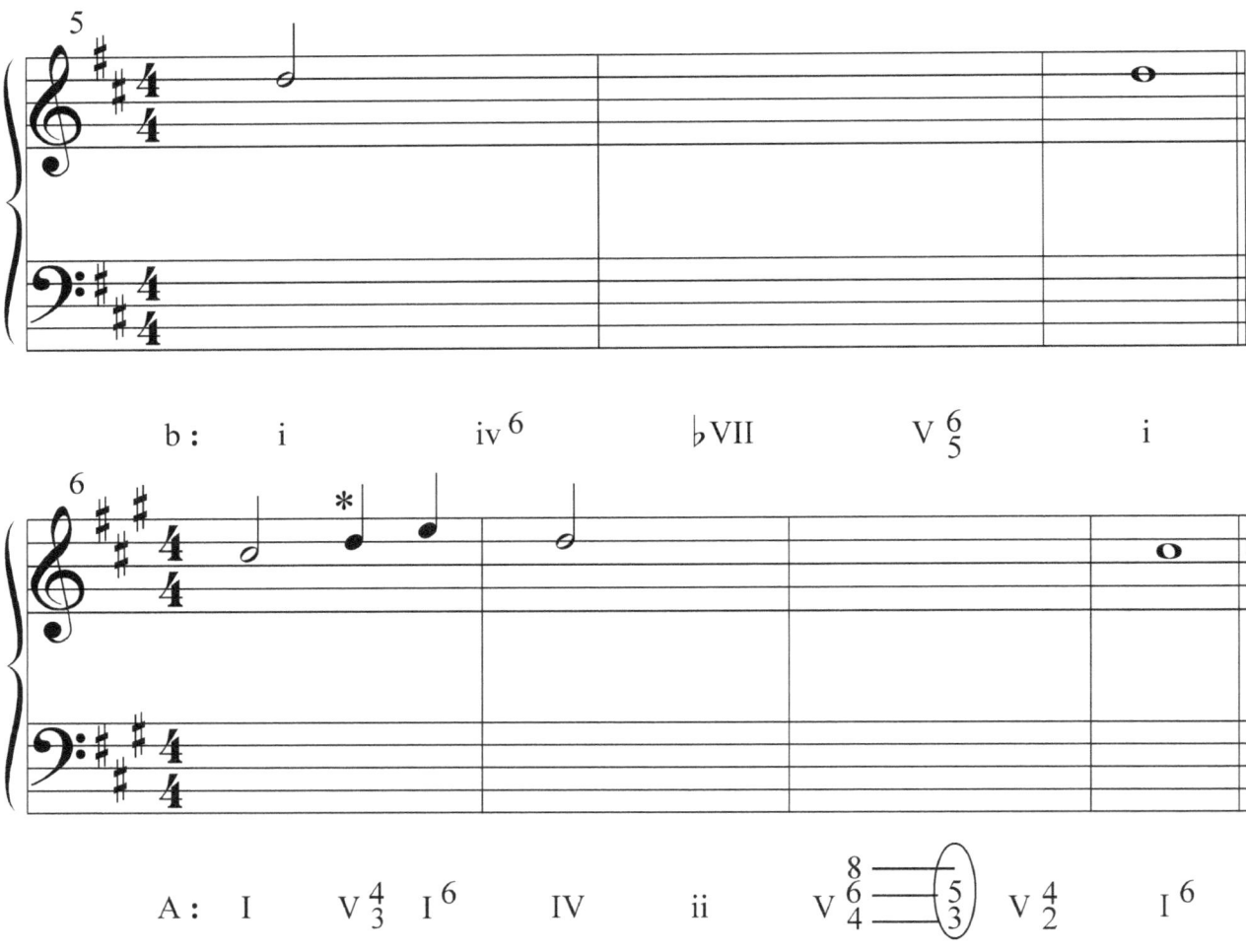

* In measure 1 of progression 6 (beat 3), notice that the chord seventh (D) of the dominant in second inversion does not move down as expected (see Appendix B, p. 226 above). You will also find parallel motion from a diminished 5th to a perfect 5th occurring between the soprano and one of the inner voices (measure 1, beats 3 and 4).

Basic Harmony Worksheet 8–21

Name _____

Worksheet 8–21 for Chapter 8: The Chord Seventh Revisited

Given the key and chord symbols, construct the following progressions (sevenths are optional except where indicated). Use four voices (soprano, alto, tenor, and bass) in open structure (whenever possible). Based upon the given the meter, assign a rhythmic framework. The soprano voice, in particular, should adhere to the following guidelines when the progression moves between unlike chords:
  (1) either move upwards or downwards as conjunctly as possible, leaping no more than a single 3rd and then reversing direction by step (that is, moving in the opposite direction of the leap); or,
  (2) remain stationary (that is, maintain common tones between unlike chords), allowing the lower voices to move obliquely in relation to the soprano.

Any given tones in the soprano are guides for completing the progression. Chordal skips (re-voicing a chord) are permissible; however, chordal skips in the bass are limited to octave leaps only.

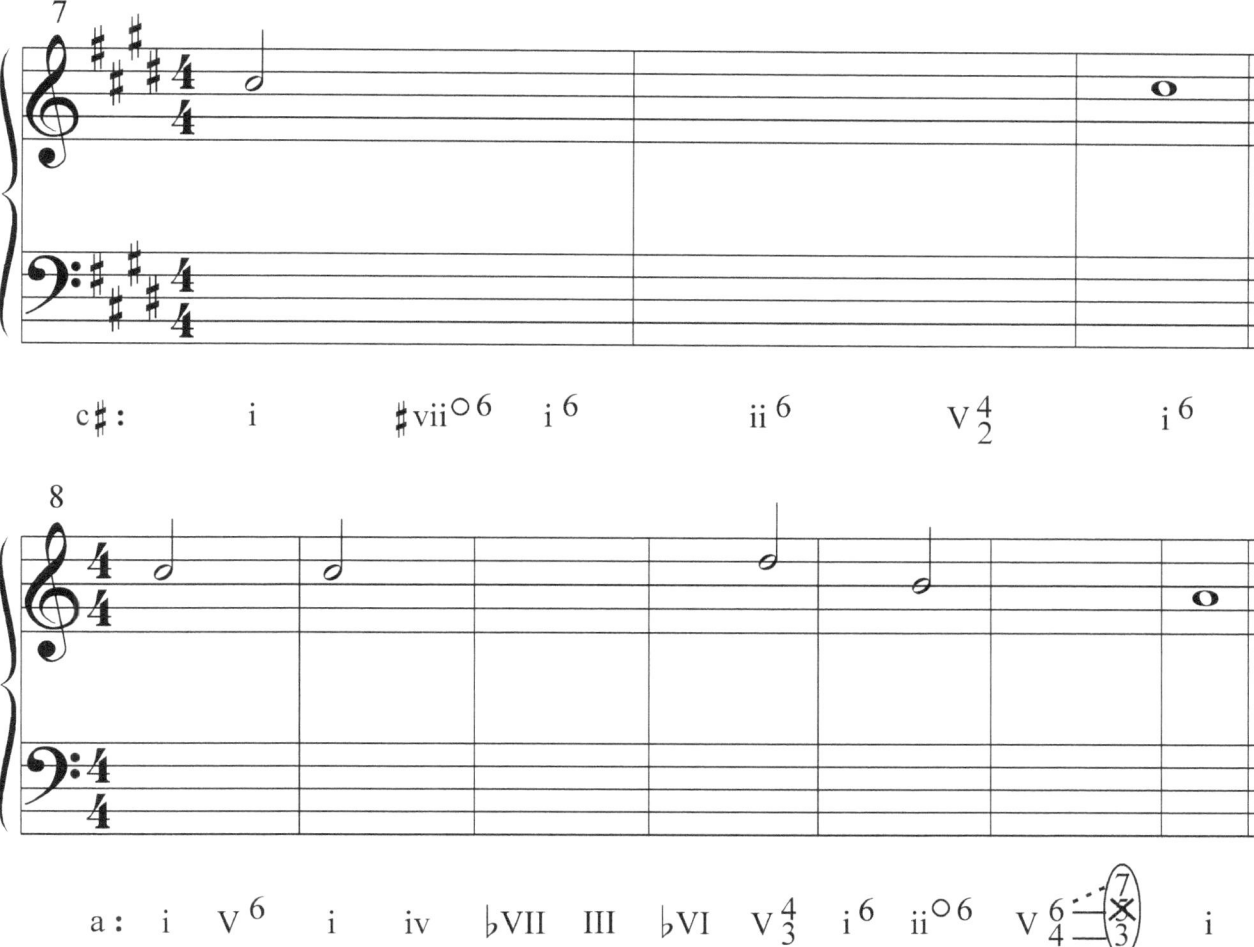

Basic Harmony Worksheet 8–22

Name _____

Worksheet 8–22 for Chapter 8: The Chord Seventh Revisited

Given the key and chord symbols, construct the following progressions (sevenths are optional except where indicated). Use four voices (soprano, alto, tenor, and bass) in open structure (whenever possible). Based upon the given the meter, assign a rhythmic framework. The soprano voice, in particular, should adhere to the following guidelines when the progression moves between unlike chords:
  (1) either move upwards or downwards as conjunctly as possible, leaping no more than a single 3rd and then reversing direction by step (that is, moving in the opposite direction of the leap); or,
  (2) remain stationary (that is, maintain common tones between unlike chords), allowing the lower voices to move obliquely in relation to the soprano.

Any given tones in the soprano are guides for completing the progression. Chordal skips (re-voicing a chord) are permissible; however, chordal skips in the bass are limited to octave leaps only.

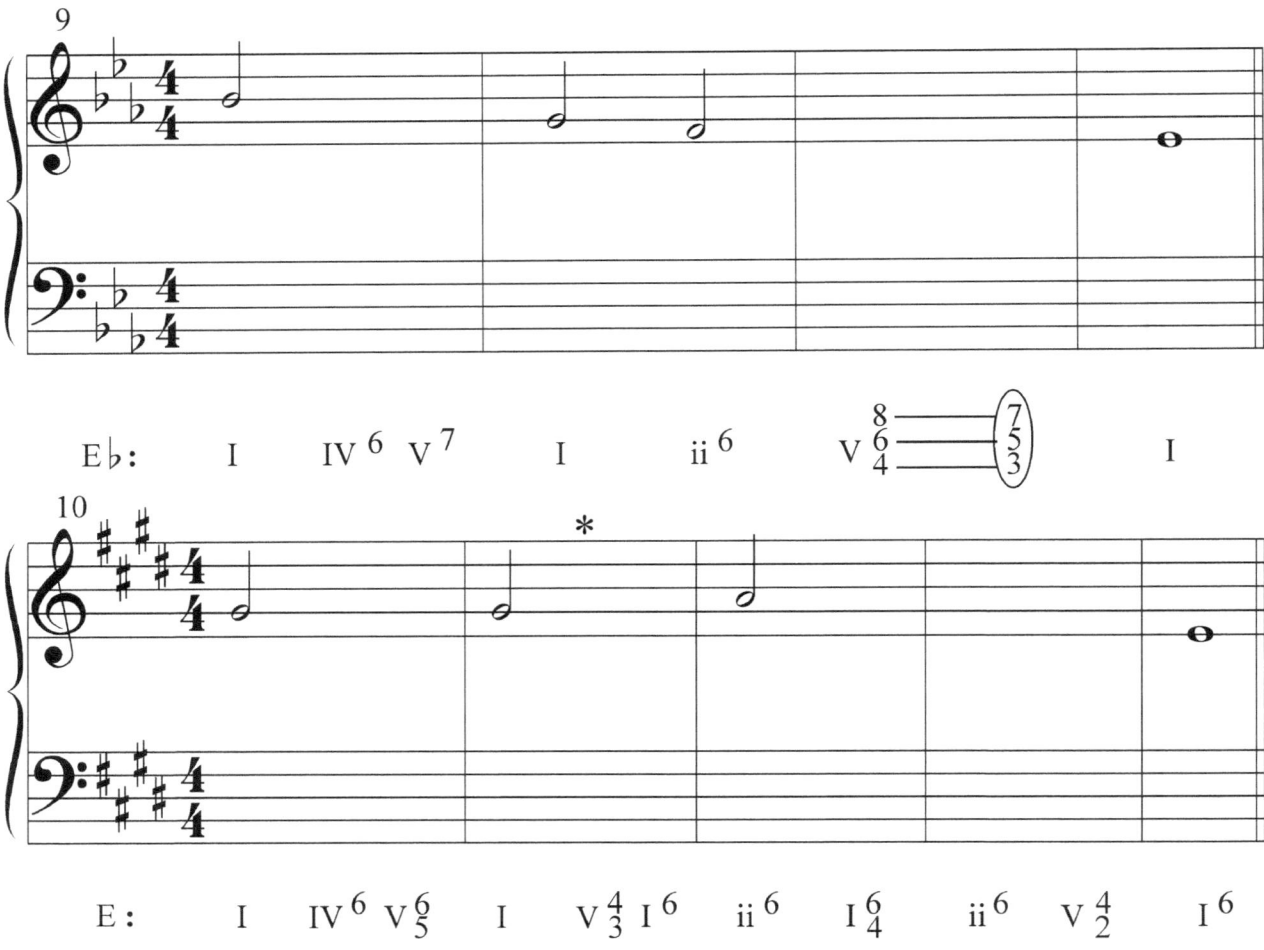

* In measure 2 of progression 10 (beat 3), notice that the chord seventh (A) of the dominant in second inversion does not move down as expected (see Appendix B, p. 226 above). You will also find parallel motion from a diminished 5th to a perfect 5th occurring between the soprano and one of the inner voices (measure 2, beats 3 and 4).

Basic Harmony Worksheet 8–23

Name _____

Worksheet 8–23 for Chapter 8: The Chord Seventh Revisited

Given the key, chord symbol, construct the following sequence. Use four voices in open structure (whenever possible). The chords at the beginning and end of the exercise are guides for completing the progression.

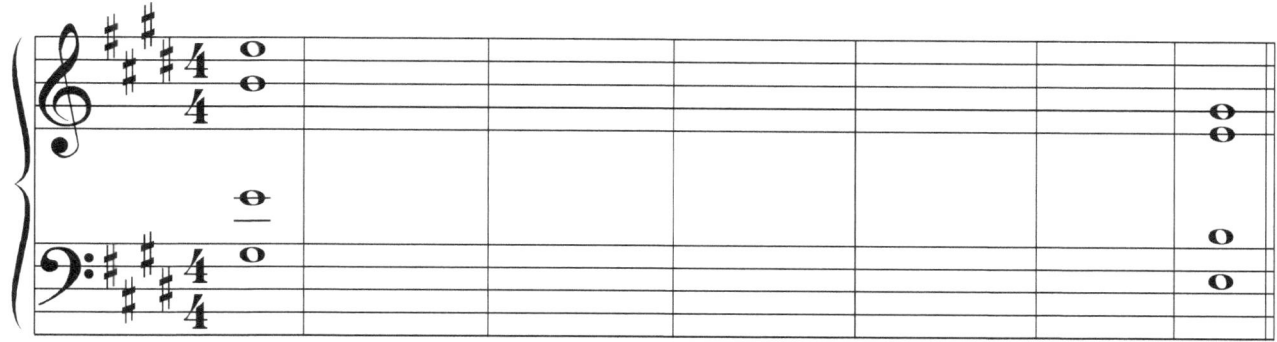

E: I^6 ii^7 V^7 I^7 IV^7 vii$\varnothing^7$ iii^7 vi^7 ii^7 V^7 I

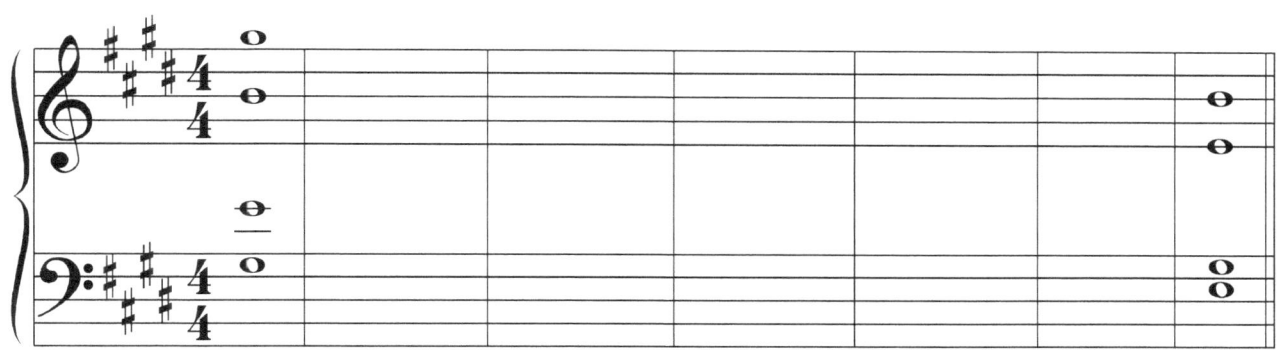

E: I^6 ii$^6_5$ V$^4_2$ I$^6_5$ IV$^4_2$ vii$\varnothing^6_5$ iii$^4_2$ vi$^6_5$ ii$^4_2$ V$^6_5$ I

Basic Harmony Worksheet 8–24

Name _____

Worksheet 8–24 for Chapter 8: The Chord Seventh Revisited

Given the key, chord symbol, construct the following sequence. Use four voices in open structure (whenever possible). The chords at the beginning and end of the exercise are guides for completing the progression.

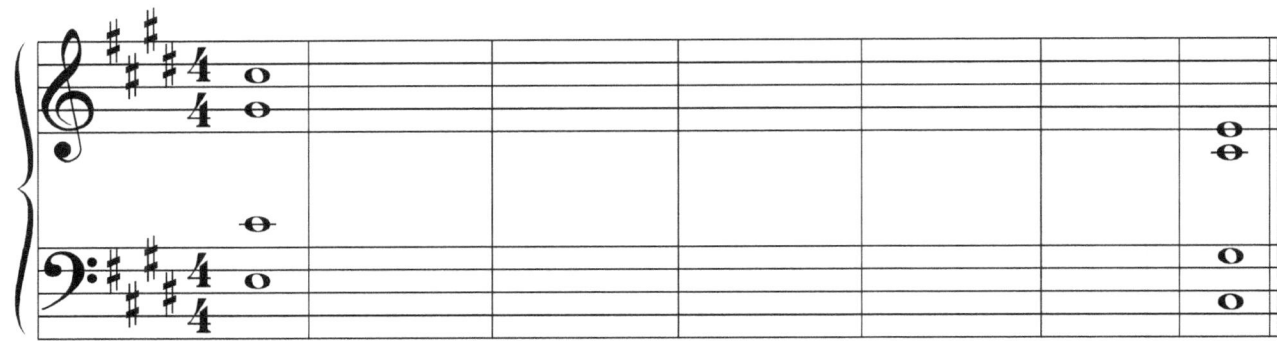

c♯:   i⁶   iiø⁷   v⁷   i♭⁷   iv⁷   ♭VII♭⁷   III⁷   ♭VI⁷   iiø⁷   V⁷   i

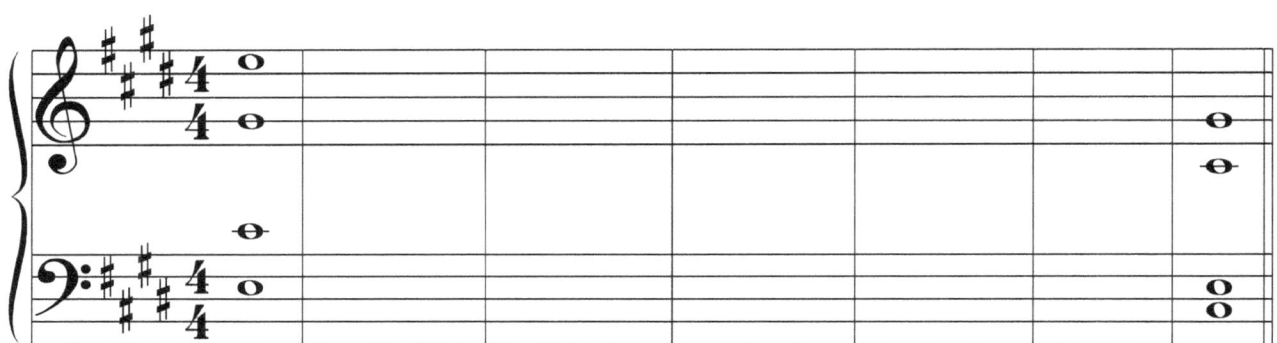

c♯:   i⁶   iiø⁶₅   v⁴₂   i⁶₅ (♭7)   iv⁴₂   ♭VII⁶₅ (♭7)   III⁴₂   ♭VI⁶₅   iiø⁴₂   V⁶₅   i

Basic Harmony Worksheet 8–25

Name _____

Worksheet 8–25 for Chapter 8: The Chord Seventh Revisited

Given the key, chord symbol, construct the following sequence. Use four voices in open structure (whenever possible). The chords at the beginning and end of the exercise are guides for completing the progression.

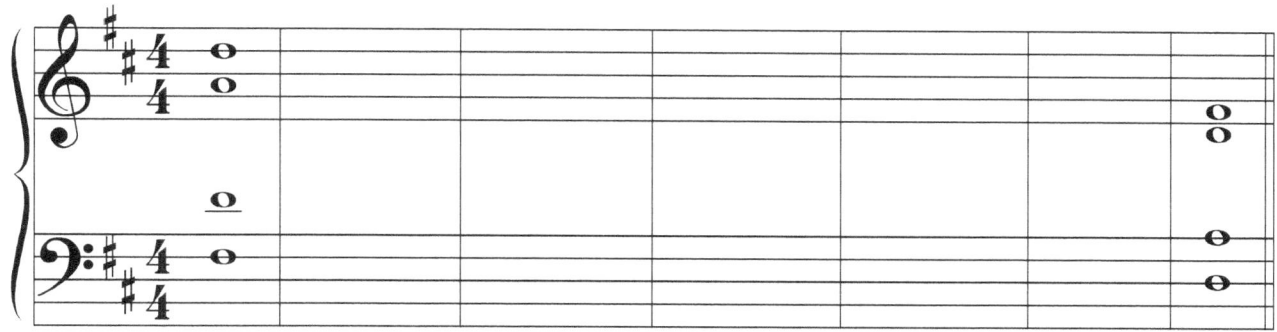

D: I^6 ii^7 V^7 I^7 IV^7 $vii^{\varnothing 7}$ iii^7 vi^7 ii^7 V^7 I

D: I^6 ii^6_5 V^4_2 I^6_5 IV^4_2 $vii^{\varnothing 6}_5$ iii^4_2 vi^6_5 ii^4_2 V^6_5 I

Basic Harmony Worksheet 8–26

Name _____

Worksheet 8–26 for Chapter 8: The Chord Seventh Revisited

Given the key, chord symbol, construct the following sequence. Use four voices in open structure (whenever possible). The chords at the beginning and end of the exercise are guides for completing the progression.

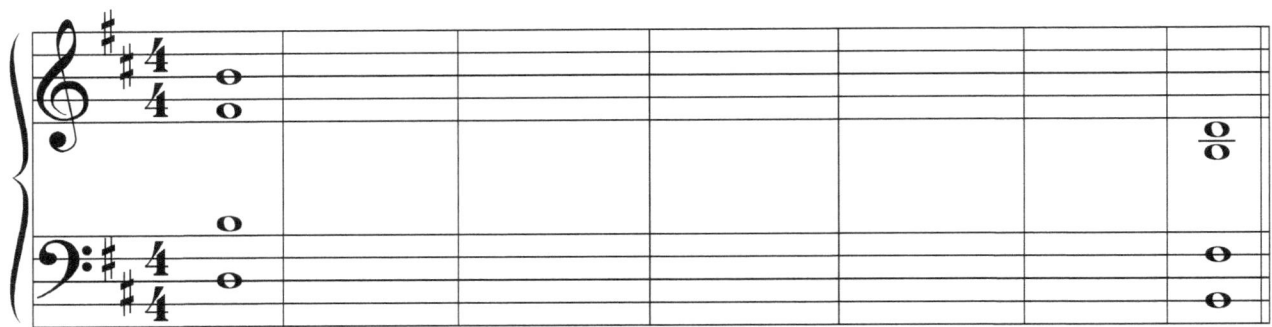

b: i⁶   iiø⁷   v⁷   i♭⁷   iv⁷   ♭VII♭⁷   III⁷   ♭VI⁷   iiø⁷   V⁷   i

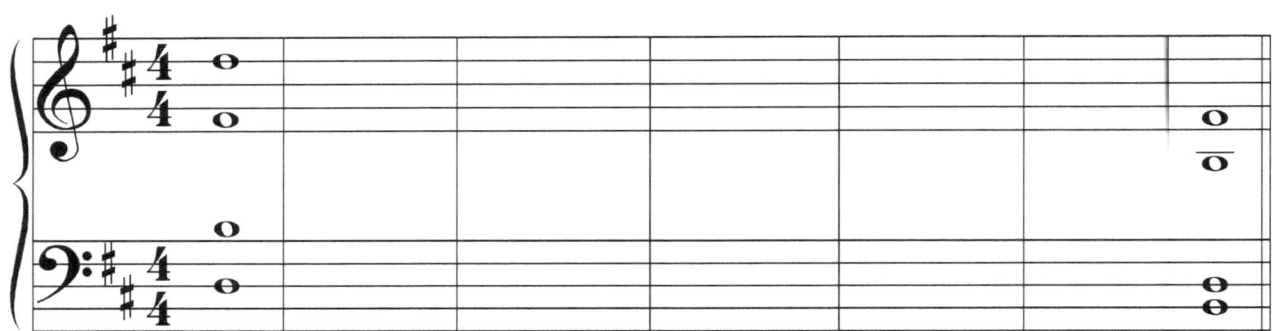

b: i⁶   iiø⁶₅   v⁴₂   i⁶₅(♭7)   iv⁴₂   ♭VII⁶₅   III⁴₂(♭7)   ♭VI⁶₅   iiø⁴₂   V⁶₅   i

Basic Harmony Worksheet 8–27

Name _____

Worksheet 8–27 for Chapter 8: The Chord Seventh Revisited

Meter and Rhythm

Given the following alternating meters, write the counts directly under the appropriate note or rest and supply any missing bar lines. Symbols such as ♪ = ♪ indicate that half notes between different meters are equivalent and remain at a constant speed. This notation is particularly useful when the value of the beat between any two time signatures represents different note values. The courtesy time signature at the end of a staff system tells the reader that a change in meter occurs in the next line of music.

    The challenge of this exercise is not in the counting but in the performance. It is possible to proceed directly to the exercise from the example without stopping. To perform the exercise, tap both feet to the *half note* and execute the rhythms on a hard surface with both hands (the last five measures work better tapping your feet to the *quarter note*). For all measures in $\frac{6}{8}$ time, count in 6 rather than 2.

Basic Harmony Worksheet 9–1

Name _____

Worksheet 9–1 for Chapter 9: Nonharmonic Tones

Before attempting the exercises in this section of worksheets, study examples 9–1a and 1b. Example 9–1a is not unlike the progressions in Chapters 7 and 8 and their accompanying worksheets. Example 9–1b, however, elaborates 1a with nonharmonic tones. Although the example is notated in quadruple meter with the quarter note as the value of the beat, a feeling of two beats per measure is evident, particularly if performed at either a moderate or fast tempo. Play both examples (or have a friend play them for you). Can you recognize the nonharmonic tones in 9–1b?

Example 9–1a: the secondary harmonic progression, from scale degree 3

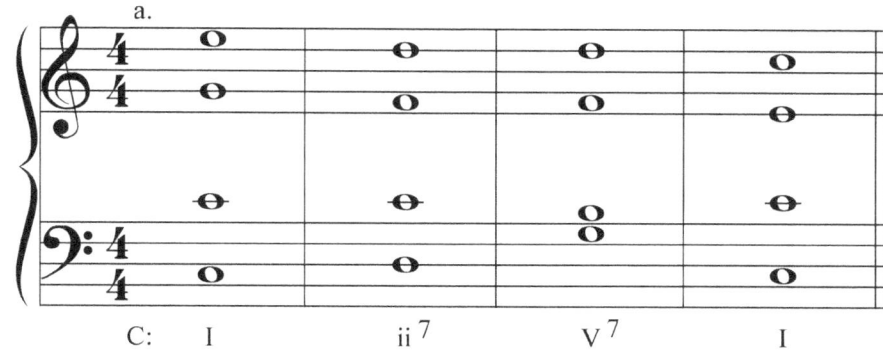

Example 9–1b: the secondary harmonic progression, from scale degree 3 with nonharmonic tones

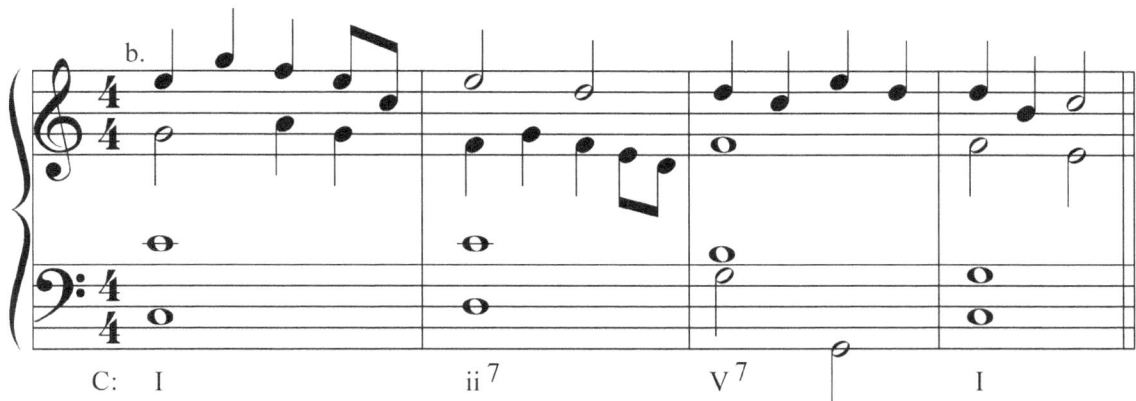

Basic Harmony Worksheet 9–2

Name _____

Worksheet 9–2 for Chapter 9: Nonharmonic Tones

Given the key and chord symbols, construct the following progressions adding both accented and unaccented nonharmonic tones. Use four voices (soprano, alto, tenor, and bass) in open structure (whenever possible). Based upon the given the meter, assign a rhythmic framework. As in the exercises for Chapters 7 and 8, you may use chordal skips (re-voicing a chord); however, chordal skips in the bass are limited to octave leaps only. Do not place nonharmonic tones in the bass voice.

Adding sevenths to some of the chords (except for the final tonic) is permissible, even with inversions as long as your seventh chord maintains the same chord position as the given triad. For example, you can transform a first-inversion triad into a first-inversion seventh chord. Note carefully, however, that the chord seventh is not to be counted as one of your nonharmonic tones. Unlike the worksheets for Chapters 7 and 8, the exercises for Chapter 9 do not include tones in the soprano to guide the completion of the progressions.

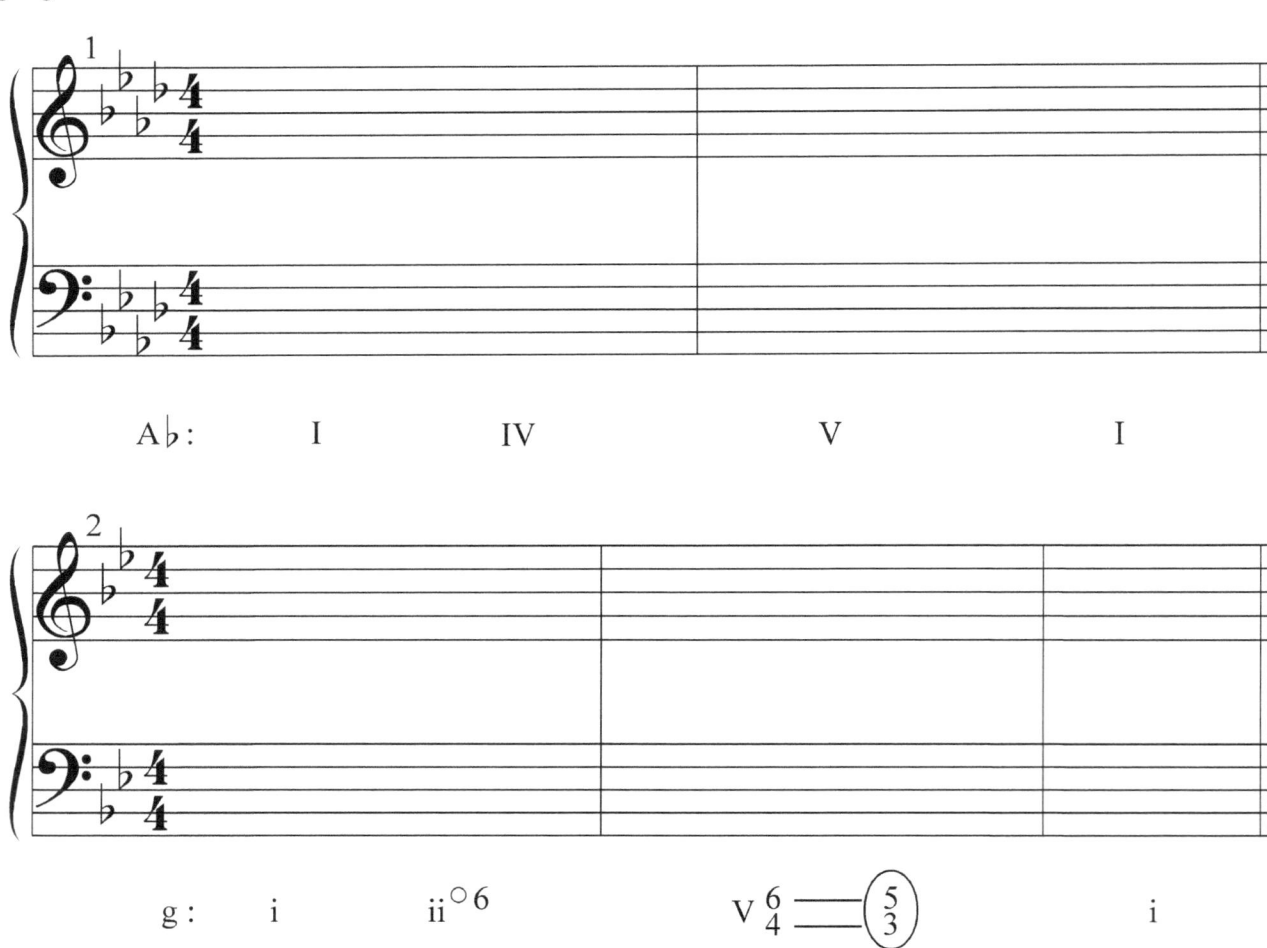

Basic Harmony Worksheet 9–3

Name _____

Worksheet 9–3 for Chapter 9: Nonharmonic Tones

Given the key and chord symbols, construct the following progressions adding both accented and unaccented nonharmonic tones. Use four voices (soprano, alto, tenor, and bass) in open structure (whenever possible). Based upon the given the meter, assign a rhythmic framework. As in the exercises for Chapters 7 and 8, you may use chordal skips (re-voicing a chord); however, chordal skips in the bass are limited to octave leaps only. Do not place nonharmonic tones in the bass voice.

Adding sevenths to some of the chords (except for the final tonic) is permissible, even with inversions as long as your seventh chord maintains the same chord position as the given triad. For example, you can transform a first-inversion triad into a first-inversion seventh chord. Note carefully, however, that the chord seventh is not to be counted as one of your nonharmonic tones. Unlike the worksheets for Chapters 7 and 8, the exercises for Chapter 9 do not include tones in the soprano to guide the completion of the progressions.

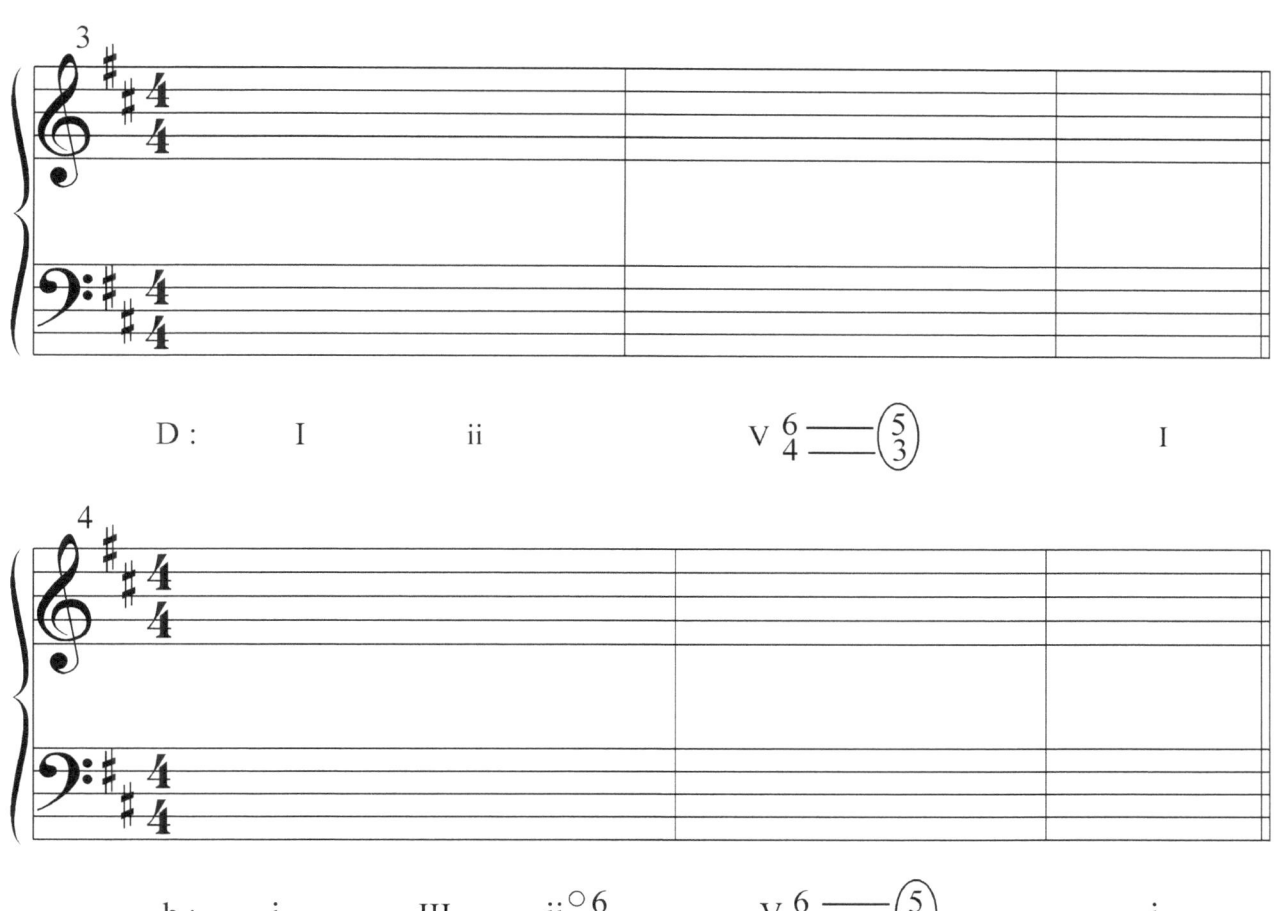

Basic Harmony Worksheet 9–4

Name _____

Worksheet 9–4 for Chapter 9: Nonharmonic Tones

Given the key and chord symbols, construct the following progressions adding both accented and unaccented nonharmonic tones. Use four voices (soprano, alto, tenor, and bass) in open structure (whenever possible). Based upon the given the meter, assign a rhythmic framework. As in the exercises for Chapters 7 and 8, you may use chordal skips (re-voicing a chord); however, chordal skips in the bass are limited to octave leaps only. Do not place nonharmonic tones in the bass voice.

  Adding sevenths to some of the chords (except for the final tonic) is permissible, even with inversions as long as your seventh chord maintains the same chord position as the given triad. For example, you can transform a first-inversion triad into a first-inversion seventh chord. Note carefully, however, that the chord seventh is not to be counted as one of your nonharmonic tones. Unlike the worksheets for Chapters 7 and 8, the exercises for Chapter 9 do not include tones in the soprano to guide the completion of the progressions.

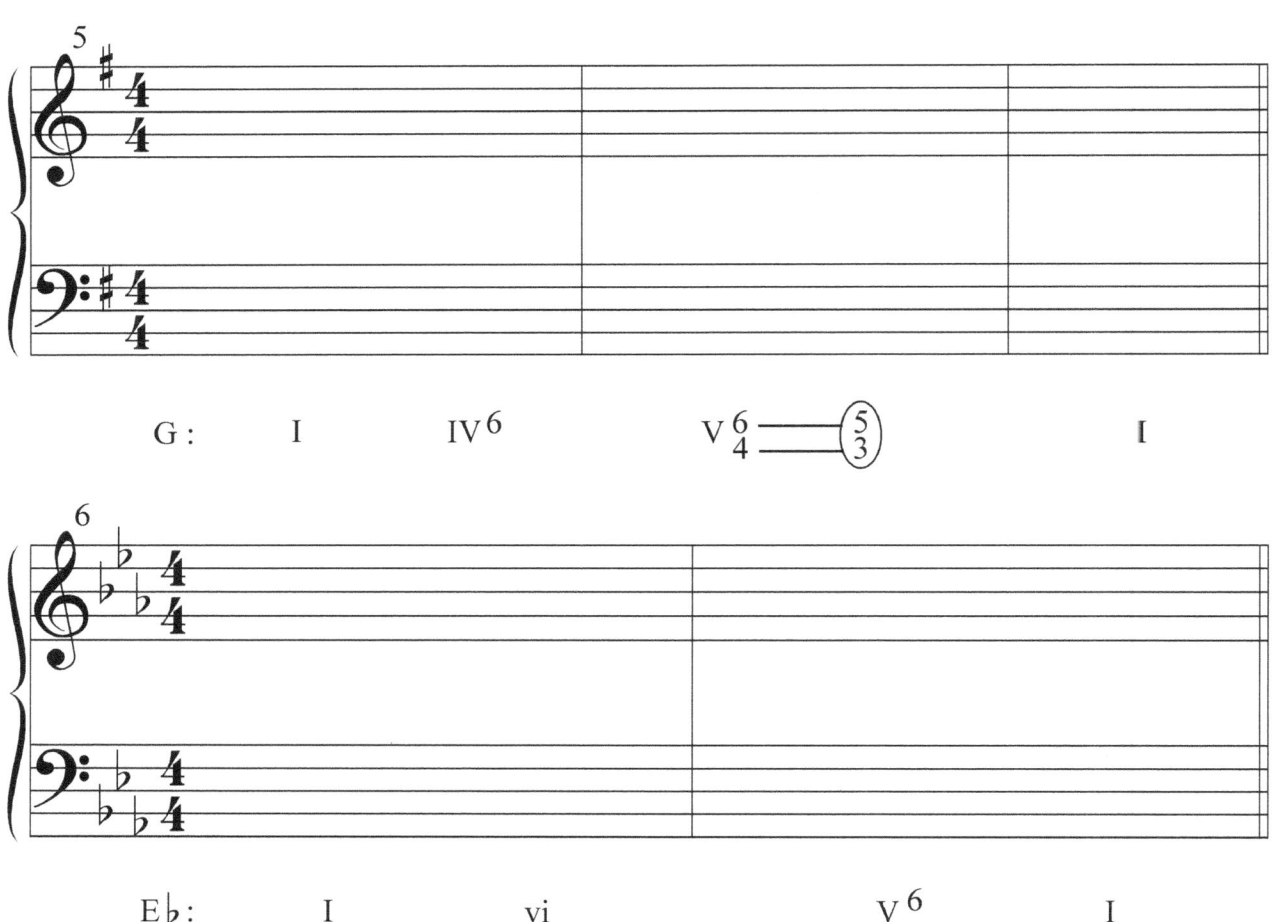

Basic Harmony Worksheet 9–5

Name _____

Worksheet 9–5 for Chapter 9: Nonharmonic Tones

Given the key and chord symbols, construct the following progressions adding both accented and unaccented nonharmonic tones. Use four voices (soprano, alto, tenor, and bass) in open structure (whenever possible). Based upon the given the meter, assign a rhythmic framework. As in the exercises for Chapters 7 and 8, you may use chordal skips (re-voicing a chord); however, chordal skips in the bass are limited to octave leaps only. Do not place nonharmonic tones in the bass voice.

Adding sevenths to some of the chords (except for the final tonic) is permissible, even with inversions as long as your seventh chord maintains the same chord position as the given triad. For example, you can transform a first-inversion triad into a first-inversion seventh chord. Note carefully, however, that the chord seventh is not to be counted as one of your nonharmonic tones. Unlike the worksheets for Chapters 7 and 8, the exercises for Chapter 9 do not include tones in the soprano to guide the completion of the progressions.

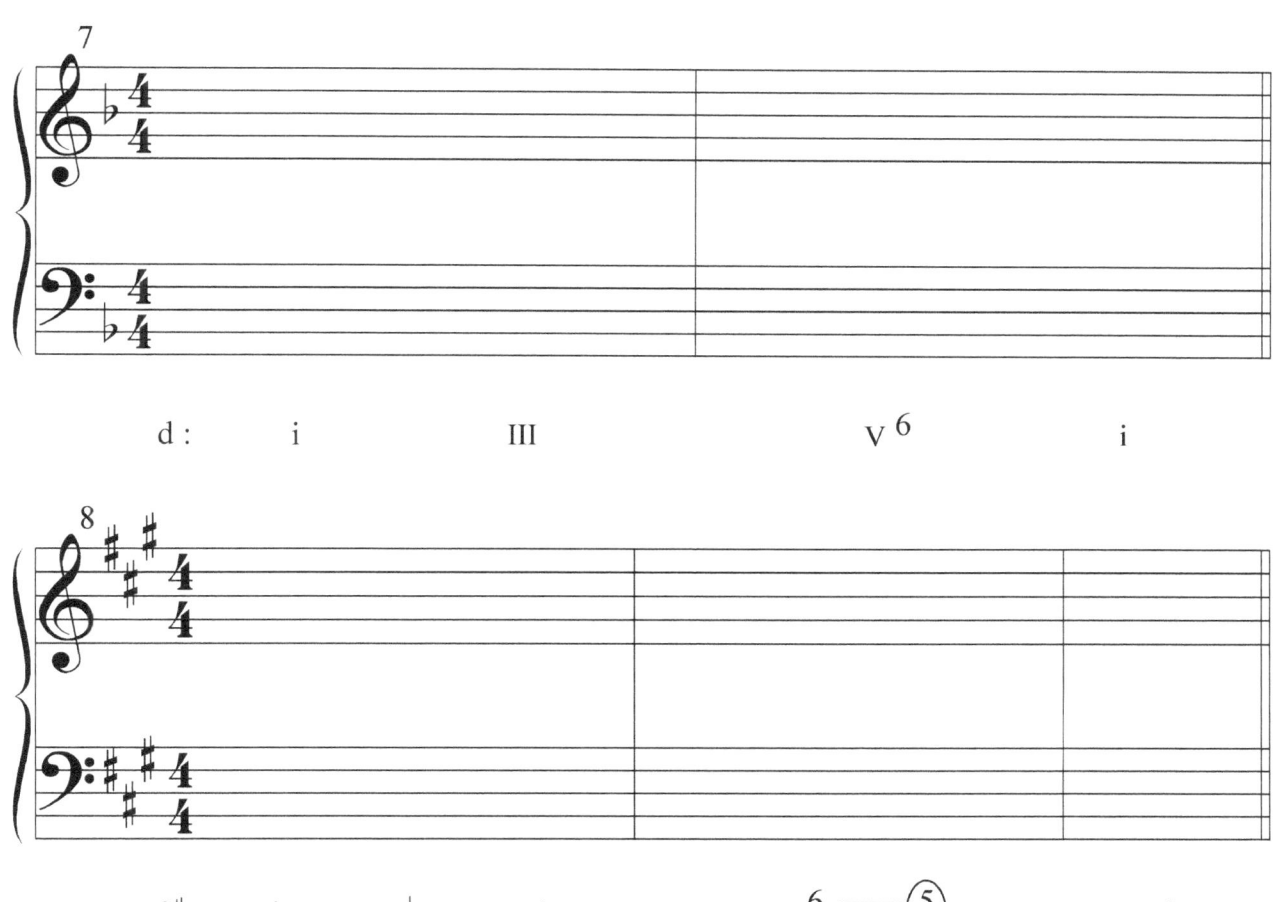

Basic Harmony Worksheet 9–6

Name _____

Worksheet 9–6 for Chapter 9: Nonharmonic Tones

Given the key and chord symbols, construct the following progressions adding both accented and unaccented nonharmonic tones. Use four voices (soprano, alto, tenor, and bass) in open structure (whenever possible). Based upon the given the meter, assign a rhythmic framework. As in the exercises for Chapters 7 and 8, you may use chordal skips (re-voicing a chord); however, chordal skips in the bass are limited to octave leaps only. Do not place nonharmonic tones in the bass voice.

Adding sevenths to some of the chords (except for the final tonic) is permissible, even with inversions as long as your seventh chord maintains the same chord position as the given triad. For example, you can transform a first-inversion triad into a first-inversion seventh chord. Note carefully, however, that the chord seventh is not to be counted as one of your nonharmonic tones. Unlike the worksheets for Chapters 7 and 8, the exercises for Chapter 9 do not include tones in the soprano to guide the completion of the progressions.

9

G: I   IV$^6_4$ I   ii^6 vi$^6_4$ ii^6 V   I$^6_4$ V   IV$^6_4$ I

10

f: i   V^6 i   ♭VII^6 III   ii°^{6} V$^6_4$ — ($^5_3$)   i

Basic Harmony Worksheet 9–7

Name _____

Worksheet 9–7 for Chapter 9: Nonharmonic Tones

Given the key and chord symbols, construct the following progressions adding both accented and unaccented nonharmonic tones. Use four voices (soprano, alto, tenor, and bass) in open structure (whenever possible). Based upon the given the meter, assign a rhythmic framework. As in the exercises for Chapters 7 and 8, you may use chordal skips (re-voicing a chord); however, chordal skips in the bass are limited to octave leaps only. Do not place nonharmonic tones in the bass voice.

Adding sevenths to some of the chords (except for the final tonic) is permissible, even with inversions as long as your seventh chord maintains the same chord position as the given triad. For example, you can transform a first-inversion triad into a first-inversion seventh chord. Note carefully, however, that the chord seventh is not to be counted as one of your nonharmonic tones. Unlike the worksheets for Chapters 7 and 8, the exercises for Chapter 9 do not include tones in the soprano to guide the completion of the progressions.

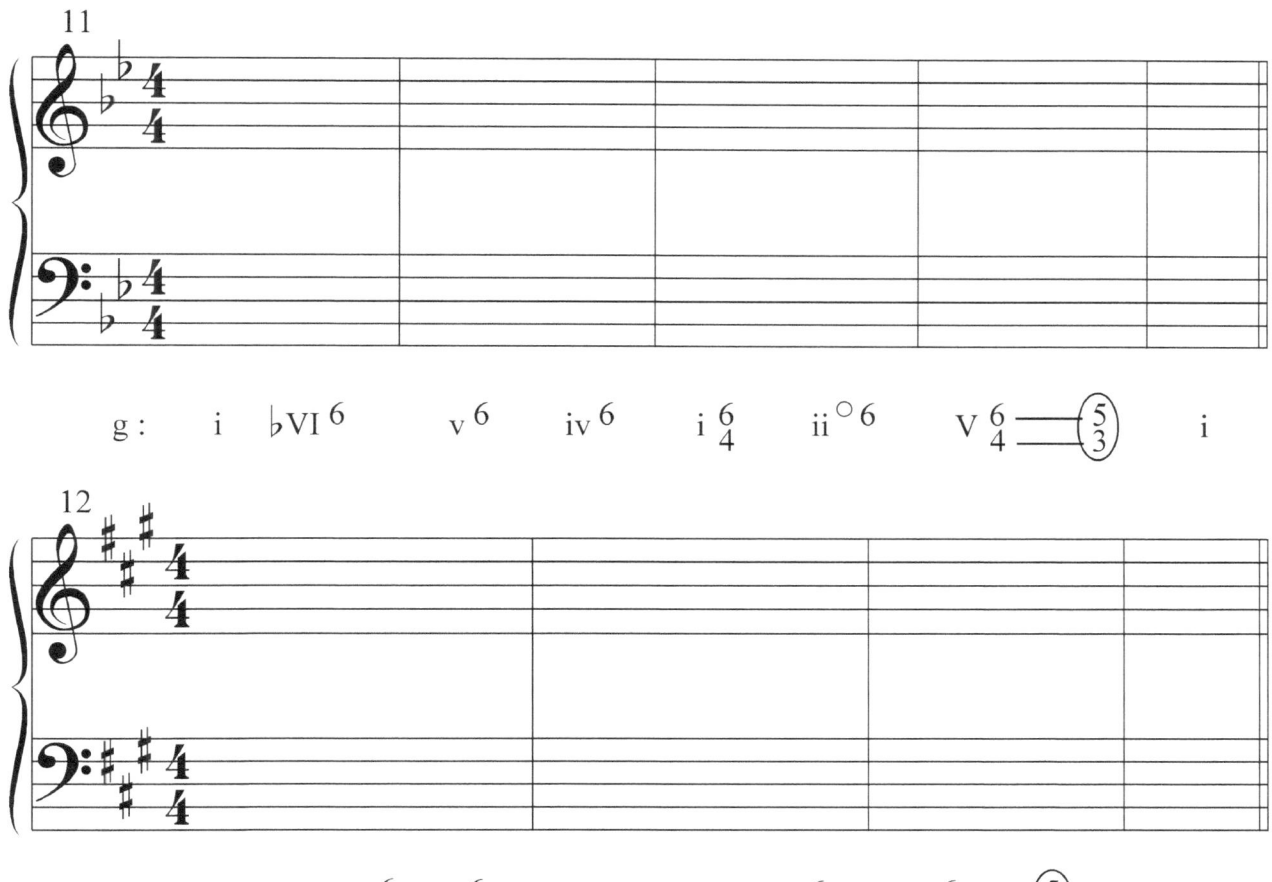

Basic Harmony Worksheet 9–8

Name _____

Worksheet 9–8 for Chapter 9: Nonharmonic Tones

Given the key and chord symbols, construct the following progressions adding both accented and unaccented nonharmonic tones. Use four voices (soprano, alto, tenor, and bass) in open structure (whenever possible). Based upon the given the meter, assign a rhythmic framework. As in the exercises for Chapters 7 and 8, you may use chordal skips (re-voicing a chord); however, chordal skips in the bass are limited to octave leaps only. Do not place nonharmonic tones in the bass voice.

    Adding sevenths to some of the chords (except for the final tonic) is permissible, even with inversions as long as your seventh chord maintains the same chord position as the given triad. For example, you can transform a first-inversion triad into a first-inversion seventh chord. Note carefully, however, that the chord seventh is not to be counted as one of your nonharmonic tones. Use seventh chords wherever indicated by the chord symbol. The specific voicing of the seventh within the cadential $^6_4$ is not indicated with figured bass. Unlike the worksheets for Chapters 7 and 8, the exercises for Chapter 9 do not include tones in the soprano to guide the completion of the progressions.

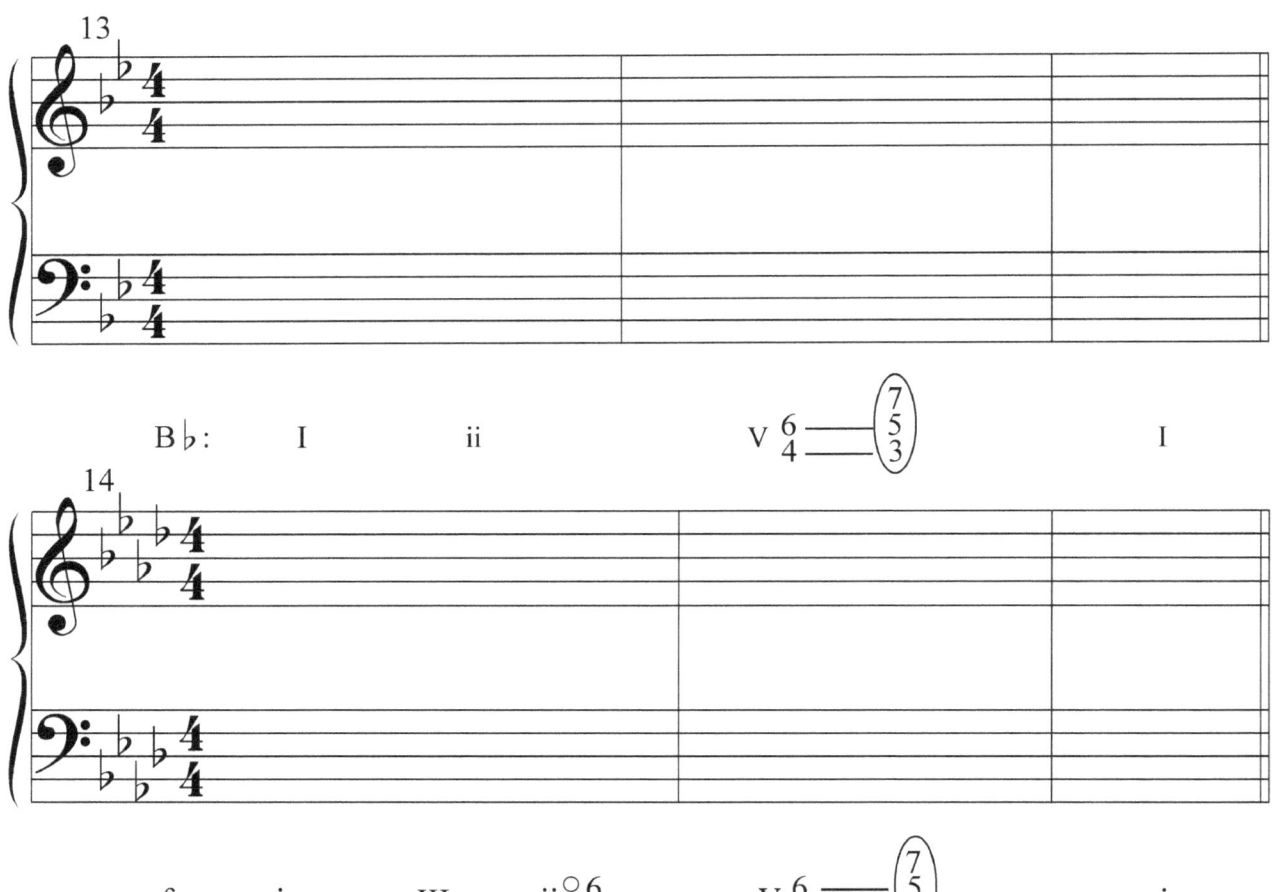

Basic Harmony Worksheet 9–9

Name _____

Worksheet 9–9 for Chapter 9: Nonharmonic Tones

Given the key and chord symbols, construct the following progressions adding both accented and unaccented nonharmonic tones. Use four voices (soprano, alto, tenor, and bass) in open structure (whenever possible). Based upon the given the meter, assign a rhythmic framework. As in the exercises for Chapters 7 and 8, you may use chordal skips (re-voicing a chord); however, chordal skips in the bass are limited to octave leaps only. Do not place nonharmonic tones in the bass voice.

    Adding sevenths to some of the chords (except for the final tonic) is permissible, even with inversions as long as your seventh chord maintains the same chord position as the given triad. For example, you can transform a first-inversion triad into a first-inversion seventh chord. Note carefully, however, that the chord seventh is not to be counted as one of your nonharmonic tones. Use seventh chords wherever indicated by the chord symbol. Unlike the worksheets for Chapters 7 and 8, the exercises for Chapter 9 do not include tones in the soprano to guide the completion of the progressions.

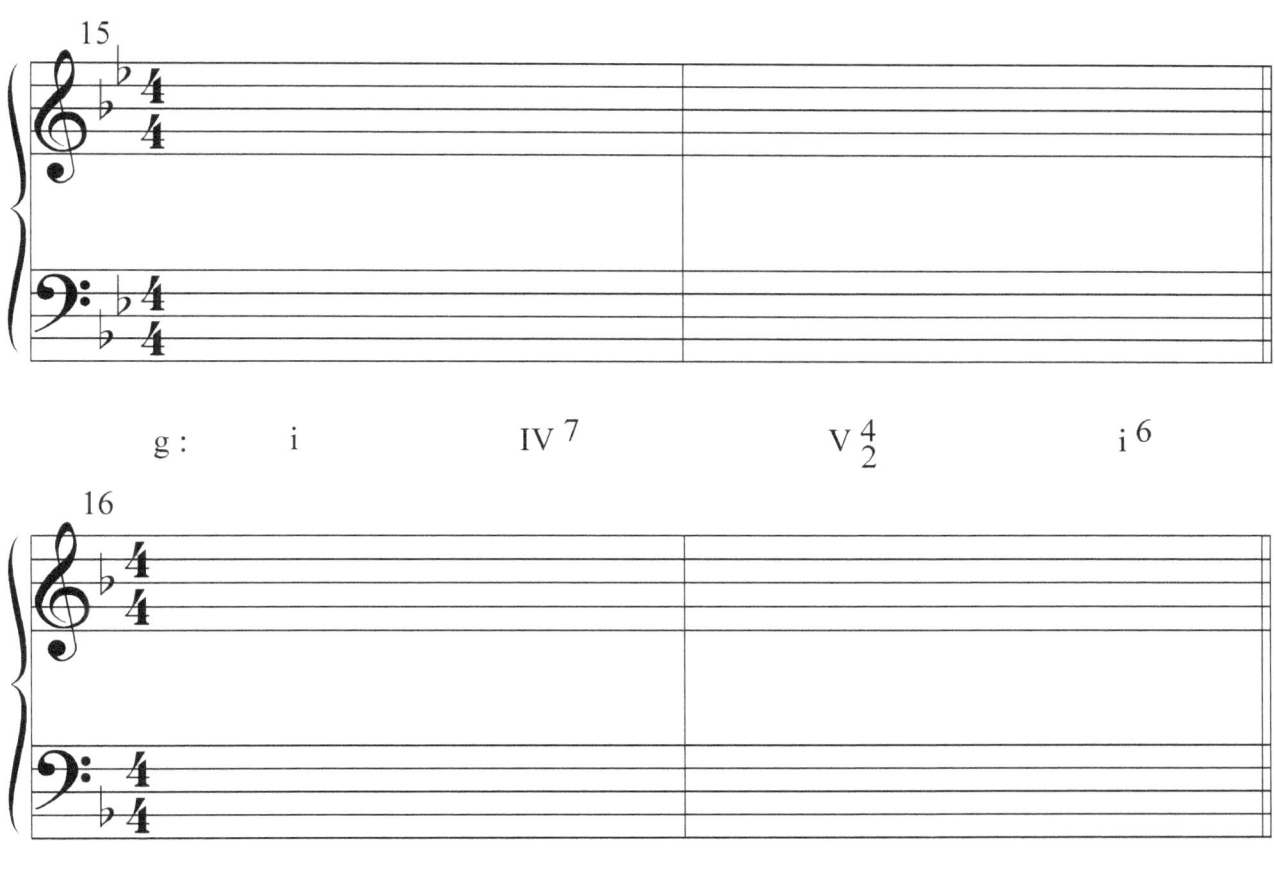

15

g: i   IV^7 V$^4_2$ i^6

16

F: I   ii   V$^4_3$ I

Basic Harmony Worksheet 9–10

Name _____

Worksheet 9–10 for Chapter 9: Nonharmonic Tones

Given the key and chord symbols, construct the following progressions adding both accented and unaccented nonharmonic tones. Use four voices (soprano, alto, tenor, and bass) in open structure (whenever possible). Based upon the given the meter, assign a rhythmic framework. As in the exercises for Chapters 7 and 8, you may use chordal skips (re-voicing a chord); however, chordal skips in the bass are limited to octave leaps only. Do not place nonharmonic tones in the bass voice.

    Adding sevenths to some of the chords (except for the final tonic) is permissible, even with inversions as long as your seventh chord maintains the same chord position as the given triad. For example, you can transform a first-inversion triad into a first-inversion seventh chord. Note carefully, however, that the chord seventh is not to be counted as one of your nonharmonic tones. Use seventh chords wherever indicated by the chord symbol. The specific voicing of the seventh within the cadential $^6_4$ is not indicated with figured bass. Unlike the worksheets for Chapters 7 and 8, the exercises for Chapter 9 do not include tones in the soprano to guide the completion of the progressions.

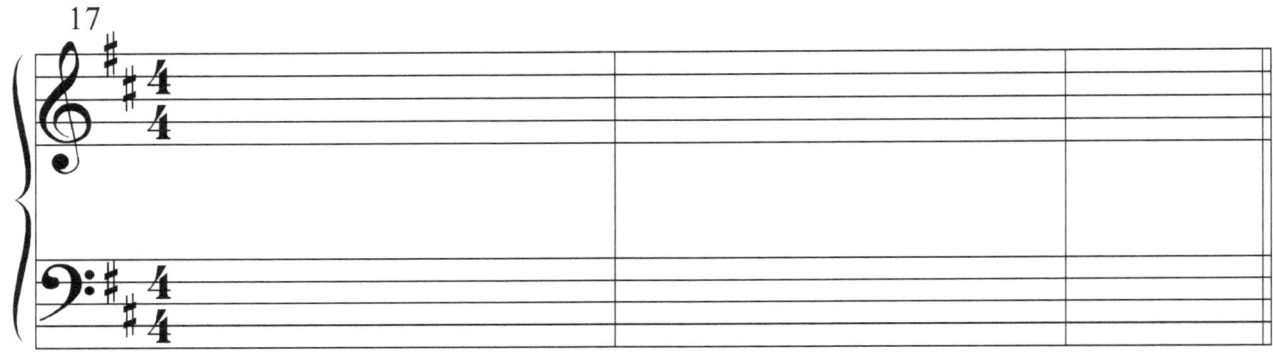

Basic Harmony Worksheet 9–11

Name _____

Worksheet 9–11 for Chapter 9: Nonharmonic Tones

Given the key and chord symbols, construct the following progressions adding both accented and unaccented nonharmonic tones. Use four voices (soprano, alto, tenor, and bass) in open structure (whenever possible). Based upon the given the meter, assign a rhythmic framework. As in the exercises for Chapters 7 and 8, you may use chordal skips (re-voicing a chord); however, chordal skips in the bass are limited to octave leaps only. Do not place nonharmonic tones in the bass voice.

    Adding sevenths to some of the chords (except for the final tonic) is permissible, even with inversions as long as your seventh chord maintains the same chord position as the given triad. For example, you can transform a first-inversion triad into a first-inversion seventh chord. Note carefully, however, that the chord seventh is not to be counted as one of your nonharmonic tones. Use seventh chords wherever indicated by the chord symbol. The specific voicing of the seventh within the cadential $^6_4$ is not indicated with figured bass. Unlike the worksheets for Chapters 7 and 8, the exercises for Chapter 9 do not include tones in the soprano to guide the completion of the progressions.

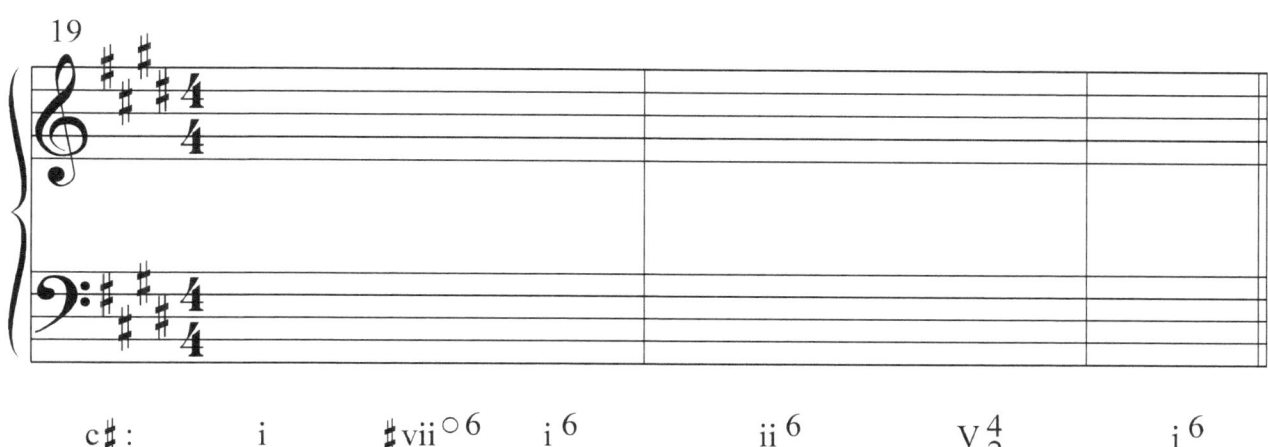

Basic Harmony Worksheet 9–12

Name _____

Worksheet 9–12 for Chapter 9: Nonharmonic Tones

Given the key and chord symbols, construct the following progressions adding both accented and unaccented nonharmonic tones. Use four voices (soprano, alto, tenor, and bass) in open structure (whenever possible). Based upon the given the meter, assign a rhythmic framework. As in the exercises for Chapters 7 and 8, you may use chordal skips (re-voicing a chord); however, chordal skips in the bass are limited to octave leaps only. Do not place nonharmonic tones in the bass voice.

    Adding sevenths to some of the chords (except for the final tonic) is permissible, even with inversions as long as your seventh chord maintains the same chord position as the given triad. For example, you can transform a first-inversion triad into a first-inversion seventh chord. Note carefully, however, that the chord seventh is not to be counted as one of your nonharmonic tones. Use seventh chords wherever indicated by the chord symbol. The specific voicing of the seventh within the cadential $^6_4$ is not indicated with figured bass. Unlike the worksheets for Chapters 7 and 8, the exercises for Chapter 9 do not include tones in the soprano to guide the completion of the progressions.

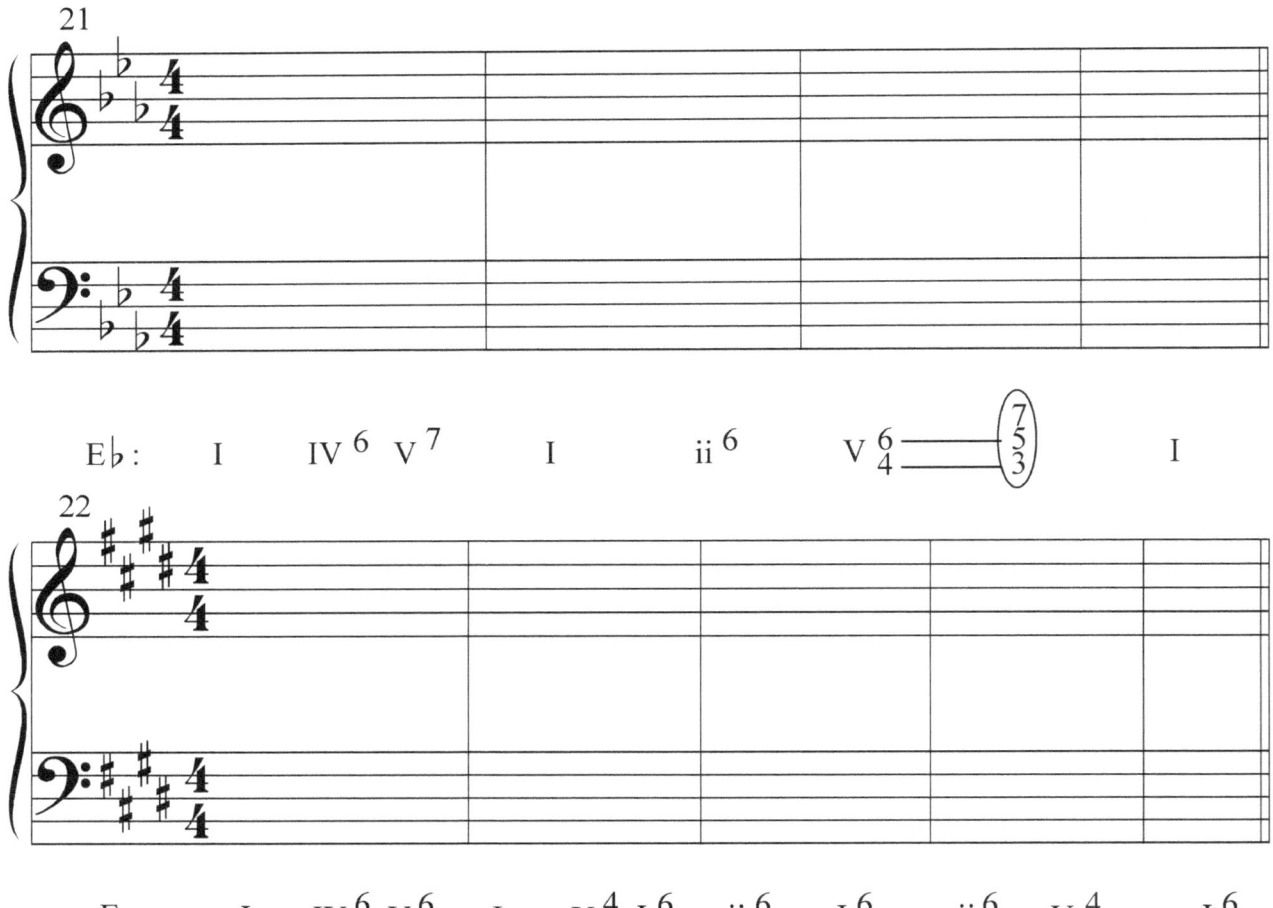

Basic Harmony Worksheet 9–13

Name _____

Worksheet 9–13 for Chapter 9: Nonharmonic Tones

Meter and Rhythm

Given the following alternating meters, write the counts directly under the appropriate note or rest and supply any missing bar lines. Symbols such as ♪ = ♪ indicate that eighth notes between different meters remain at a constant speed. This notation is particularly useful when the value of the beat between any two time signatures represents different note values. (such as $\frac{5}{8}$ and $\frac{3}{4}$). The courtesy time signatures at the end of the staff systems indicate a change in meter in the next line of music.

The challenge of this exercise is not in the counting but in the performance. To begin performing both the example and the exercise, tap both feet to the quarter note. Again, the eighth note in this exercise remains constant.

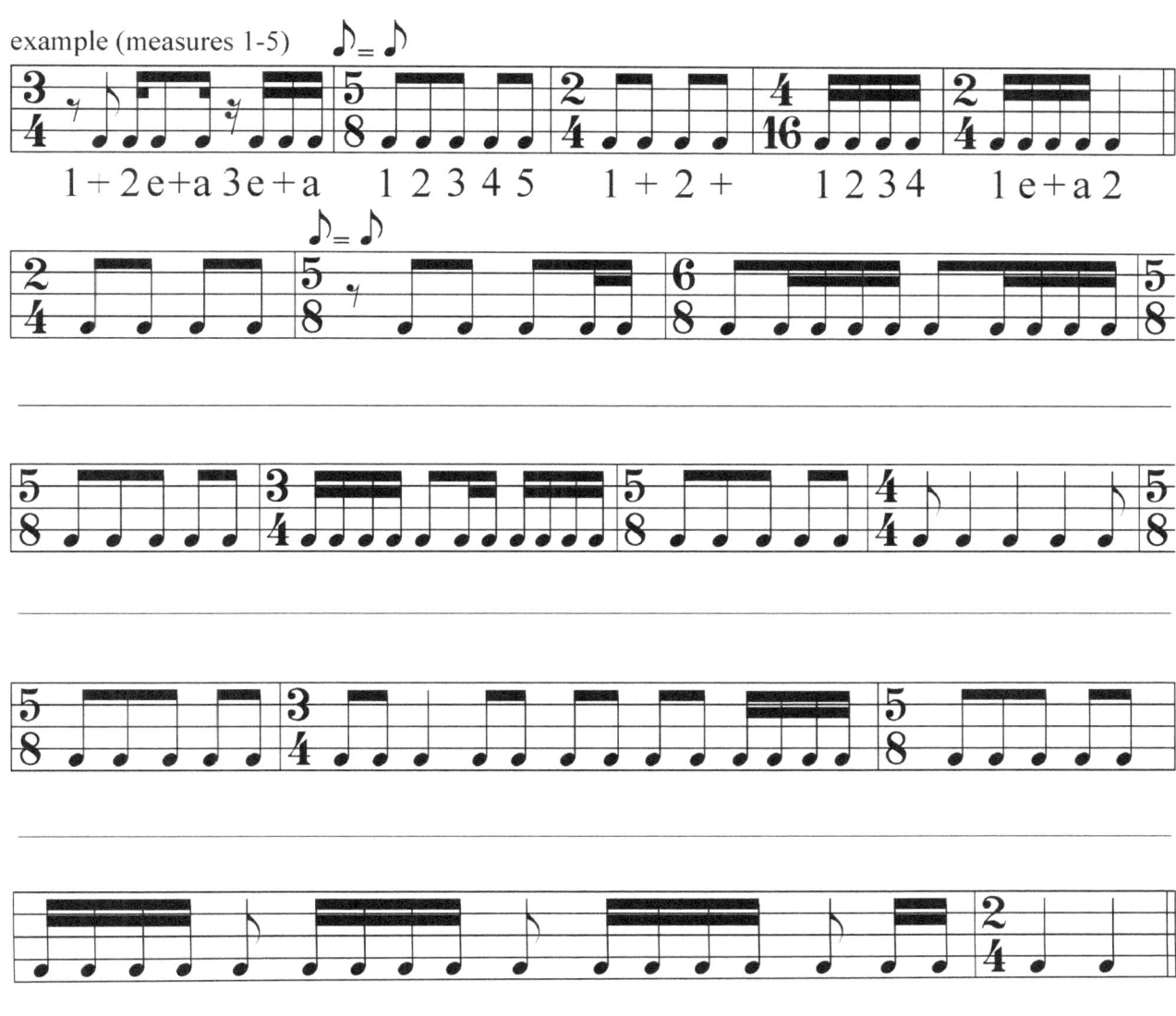

www.ingramcontent.com/pod-product-compliance
Lightning Source LLC
Chambersburg PA
CBHW082315230426
43667CB00034B/2735